RECORDS OF CIVILIZATION

SOURCES AND STUDIES

Edited under the auspices of the
Department of History, Columbia University

GENERAL EDITOR: W. T. H. Jackson, Professor of German and History

PAST EDITORS

1915-1926

James T. Shotwell, Bryce Professor Emeritus of the
History of International Relations

1926-1953
Austin P. Evans, Late Professor of History

1953-1962
Jacques Barzun, Seth Low Professor of History

Number XXIX
Medieval Handbooks of Penance

MEDIEVAL HAND-BOOKS OF PENANCE

A translation of the principal *libri poenitentiales* and selections from related documents ✛ ✛ ✛ by

JOHN T. McNEILL and HELENA M. GAMER

OCTAGON BOOKS

A DIVISION OF FARRAR, STRAUS AND GIROUX

New York   1979

Copyright 1938 Columbia University Press

Reprinted 1965
by special arrangement with Columbia University Press

Second Octagon printing 1979

OCTAGON BOOKS
A DIVISION OF FARRAR, STRAUS & GIROUX, INC.
19 Union Square West
New York, N.Y. 10003

LIBRARY OF CONGRESS CATALOG CARD NUMBER: 65-20970
ISBN 0-374-95548-4

Manufactured by Braun-Brumfield, Inc.
Ann Arbor, Michigan
Printed in the United States of America

Preface

I T IS doubtful whether any part of the source literature of medieval social history comparable in importance to the penitentials has been so generally neglected by translators. The difficulty of the texts and an unjust contempt on the part of some historians for the materials have probably contributed to this neglect. A number of recent studies have revealed the high historical importance of these booklets. A direct knowledge of their contents is here for the first time made possible to students who have not the time or the equipment to make use of the Latin documents.

The first two sections of the Introduction are designed to meet the needs of readers who are uninitiated in the field of the history of penance. These sections incorporate without indication a few sentences from my dissertation, *The Celtic Penitentials and Their Influence on Continental Christianity*, published in 1923. In order to avoid more extensive repetition numerous citations to that essay have been made in the notes. But the present statement represents an extensive reworking of the sources in the light of the more recent literature, and no pretense of total and detailed agreement with the earlier study is implied.

In order to give a true impression of these penitential books it seemed incumbent upon the translator to present the earlier and more influential documents of the series in their entirety, even though this involved some repetition of materials. Indeed, where repetition in substance occurs it often serves to clarify obscure provisions.

It is not implied that "earlier" penitentials were in all cases "more influential" than those of later date. But certainly the earliest Welsh and Irish examples, even those of a fragmentary sort, were influential in the highest degree. Most of their contents were poured into the larger and more formal books of the seventh century. The interest of these foundation documents is enhanced for us by the fact that they exhibit the primitive stage of the evolving type. Some of the subsequent documents were decisively influential both with respect

to their own circulation and use and for the contribution they made
to the still later literary development of the series. But in addition
to the recognition of their influence, such penitentials as those of
Cummean and Theodore and the Pseudo-Romanum seemed to call
for unabridged inclusion in this book, as revealing the character of
typical penitential handbooks of a time when the type had come to
full development.

The later and more dependent documents are represented by their
more original sections only. Some penitentials which have been
printed and discussed by editors have here been omitted entirely.
Appendix IV furnishes brief characterizations of the noteworthy
works of the series which have been excluded, and the information
there given will in each case indicate why the omission has seemed
justified. It is hoped that the separate introductions to the several
documents will help materially to make the work serviceable.

For a work of translation the volume contains an unusual amount
of technical data. The justification of this lies in the fact that the
published sources are in a state so defective that any translation
based solely upon them would be unsatisfactory and of doubtful
value. It was necessary, therefore, to go carefully into the manuscript
materials, to attempt many emendations, and to give reasons for
these and for the renderings derived from them. Because the paleographical problems were beyond my skill, the cooperation of an
expert paleographer was at once seen to be necessary, and that of
Dr. Gamer was fortunately secured.

Miss Gamer's part in the volume consists of: Section III of the
Introduction; Appendix V; the determination of doubtful readings
by detailed examination of the manuscripts, of which many were
studied directly in European libraries and others from photostats;
and a large share in the solution of the lexicographical problems presented by the numerous rare and obscure words and expressions.
Where the structure of the text was particularly baffling her advice
has often been sought with advantage to the translation. All defects
in the latter should, however, be laid to my charge.

With the exception of some choicely-phrased prayers, the originals
are nowhere marked by literary distinction. Indeed, many sentences
do violence to grammatical usage, and any attempt to render their
disjointed Latin into strictly formal English would be misleading.
The translation has been made with the primary aim of faithfulness

to the intention of the original and is in general literal, or nearly so. In many instances mere translation did not completely clarify a dark passage, and footnotes had to be employed. The notes serve chiefly to indicate the manuscript readings adopted and to shed light on other linguistic difficulties; some briefly explain historical matters, especially liturgical details and church usages no longer familiar, to which allusions are made in the text. The translations of scriptural passages, in so far as these are in agreement with the Vulgate, follow the Douay version.

For the obscure passages the procedure generally began with a fresh examination of the manuscript, or manuscripts, in order to secure readings accurate beyond doubt. Where reconstruction was unavoidable it was done in the light of the phraseology of the penitential literature in general, with consultation of other monastic and liturgical texts known to be similar in vocabulary and ideas and with the employment of any paleographical data that might serve to lead back from a disordered to a rational and probable construction.[1] By means either of parallels found or of philological considerations, or of both combined, many difficulties were resolved. Where certainty was not reached a conjectural rendering in harmony with the context was attempted. In such cases, and also wherever textual alterations have been adopted, the footnotes will enable the reader to check the method.

The greatest impediment to the student of the penitentials is the lack of a definitive text of most of the materials. The establishment of a text for the whole series would involve patient and prolonged labor. It will, I think, be acknowledged that Miss Gamer's researches have made a distinct contribution to this task, and that in the case of most of the documents selected the present translation utilizes many improved readings.

We are glad to acknowledge our indebtedness to numerous scholars. Professors C. H. Beeson and T. P. Cross, of the University of Chicago, have repeatedly responded to calls for help. Dr. W. W. Rockwell has placed at our disposal the resources of the Library of Union Theological Seminary and has suggested some books that might otherwise have been overlooked. I recall with gratitude conferences with Professor T. P. Oakley, now at Fordham University; with Professor Alexander Souter, of the University of Aberdeen;

---

[1] Cf. Introduction, Section III, pp. 55 ff., 68 ff., below.

with Professor David Duff, formerly of the University of Toronto; and with the late Professor S. B. Sniffen, of the University of Chicago. Assistance from some others is acknowledged in the footnotes on pages 119, 157, 428 f., below. Still others have lent their aid in ways more intangible through incidental conversations in which useful suggestions were made, of which they were perhaps scarcely conscious.

Miss Gamer desires to acknowledge the kindness and generosity of the librarians and administrators of the libraries in which she studied the manuscripts and from which she secured numerous photostats for this volume. These institutions are enumerated on pp. 56 ff. and 432 ff. She wishes also to thank Dr. Blanche B. Boyer for calling to her attention a number of manuscripts and placing at her disposal other materials on penitential documents.

Subventions generously provided by Columbia University and by the University of Chicago have covered the main expenses incurred in consulting manuscripts, in securing the needed photostatic copies, and in typing the manuscript for the press. The general editor, Professor Austin P. Evans, has earned the gratitude of the authors by his helpful advice on many points. A debt is likewise due to Miss I. M. Lynn, of the Columbia University Press, who prepared the manuscript for the press.

J. T. M.

Chicago
March 26, 1938

Contents

APPENDICES

———

Abbreviations

A.K.K.R.	Archiv für katholisches Kirchenrecht.
Cabrol, *Dictionnaire*	Cabrol, F., and H. Leclercq, Dictionnaire d'archéologie chrétienne et de liturgie.
C.S.E.L.	Corpus scriptorum ecclesiasticorum Latinorum.
Fournier and Le Bras	Fournier, P., and G. Le Bras, Histoire des collections canoniques en occident, depuis les fausses décrétales jusqu'au décret de Gratian.
Haddan and Stubbs	Haddan, A. W., and W. Stubbs, Councils and Ecclesiastical Documents relating to Great Britain and Ireland.
Hefele-Leclercq	Hefele, C. J., Histoire des conciles d'après les documents originaux.
Kenney	Kenney, J. F., The Sources for the Early History of Ireland. . . . I. Ecclesiastical.
McNeill	McNeill, J. T., The Celtic Penitentials and Their Influence on Continental Christianity.
Mansi	Mansi, J. D., Sacrorum conciliorum nova et amplissima collectio.
M.G.H.	Monumenta Germaniae historica.
Migne, *P.G.*	Migne, J. P., Patrologiae cursus completus. Series Graeca
Migne, *P.L.*	———— Patrologiae cursus completus. Series Latina.
Oakley	Oakley, T. P., English Penitential Discipline and Anglo-Saxon Law in Their Joint Influence.
Poschmann I	Poschmann, B., Die abendländische Kirchenbusse im Ausgang des christlichen Altertums.
Poschmann II	———— Die abendländische Kirchenbusse im frühen Mittelalter.
Schmitz I	Schmitz, H. J., Die Bussbücher und die Bussdisciplin der Kirche.
Schmitz II	———— Die Bussbücher und das kanonische Bussverfahren.

Wasserschleben, *Bussordnungen*	Wasserschleben, F. W. H., Die Bussordnungen der abendländischen Kirche nebst einer rechtsgeschichtlichen Einleitung.
Watkins	Watkins, O. D., A History of Penance.
Wilkins, *Concilia*	Wilkins, D., Concilia Magnae Britanniae et Hiberniae, A.D. 446–1718.
Z.K.G.	Zeitschrift für Kirchengeschichte.

Introduction

"... *ut Gregorius pastorali commemorat libro: Occultiora sunt vulnera mentium quam corporum, et ars est artium regimen animarum.*"—Council of Tribur, A.D. 895, can. 55. Based on Gregory the Great, *Cura Pastoralis*, c. 1.

Penance in the Ancient Church

THE DOCUMENTS translated in this book were employed in administering a religious discipline to our forefathers during their transition from paganism to Christianity and from barbarism to civilization. With peculiar intimacy they reveal the faults of men and of society in a far-off age, as well as the ideals of the monastic and ecclesiastical leaders on whom responsibility was laid for the guidance of souls. They form, therefore, a priceless record of one important stage of that perennial conflict of ideals with realities which marks the progress of man toward the attainment of a moral culture.

The ideal was founded in monastic asceticism; the reality in primitive brutality. It is doubtful whether the one or the other is more foreign to the prevailing modes of thought and life today. To comprehend and evaluate both is the task of history, whose concern is with man's experience. These antiquated manuals for confessors have a claim on the attention of all who seek an intimate knowledge of medieval life.

With few exceptions the texts have come to us in exceptionally forbidding Latin, and they have hitherto reposed in works known only to a few exploring scholars. It is difficult to appreciate the fact that a literature now so obscure had formerly an extensive circulation and exercised a function of the first importance. While the penitentials were primarily intended for the use of priests, it was sometimes found convenient to provide them in the vernacular in order, we may suppose, to make their contents comprehensible to the people. Of the surviving documents, some were probably compiled in Old Irish, and others in Old English. In some instances confessors were enjoined to read the penitential aloud to the sinner. A number of the booklets take the form of an elaborate series of questions to be recited to and answered by the confessant. Where, as is usual, these questionnaires are in Latin, they must ordinarily have been orally translated by the confessor. The *Penitential of Theodore* compiled by "Discipulus Umbrensium," is addressed "to all Catholics of the English, especially to the physicians of souls." A *Confessional* ascribed to Egbert was, according to its opening sentence, translated by the compiler into the English tongue "in order that the uneducated might be able the more easily to understand" its provisions. A "penitential (scrift boc) in English" was bequeathed, with other manuals, by Bishop Leofric (d.1072) to his cathedral of Exeter. While the authors sometimes caution against the use of their handbooks by persons not qualified to administer penance, they show no intention of restricting to those so qualified the knowledge of their contents. Nicholas I, following a principle earlier expressed in the "Order for Penance" prefixed to the *Tripartite St. Gall Penitential* and related documents, states that their possession by laymen is improper, but merely because laymen may not exercise a "ministry of judgment."[1] Alone among his contemporaries, Theodulf of Orleans, who wrote no penitential and was an advocate of the ancient canonical penance, for moral reasons advises against giving unguarded publicity to the unfamiliar sins listed in a penitential.[2] The lapse of centuries and the passing of an old discipline have robbed these medieval handbooks of their function and left them in obscurity. They can no longer be used, legitimately or perversely, in the confessional; but they can serve to illuminate the operation of a social process that profoundly affected innumerable lives in a bygone age.

In order to appreciate the place of the penitentials in the history of church discipline it is desirable to examine briefly the development of penance in the ancient Church. Only the most salient features of the subject can here be noticed. The special student will consult the histories and sources cited in the footnotes.

PUBLIC AND EXACTING CHARACTER OF THE ANCIENT CHURCH PENANCE

Christianity from the first applied austere standards of behavior, and in the course of its advance in the Graeco-Roman world developed a discipline for the correction of Christians who violated the code. In the first stage this took the form of public confession, made before the assembled congregation. In the graver offenses and in cases of impenitence or of public scandal, this discipline was accompanied by a period of exclusion from the fellowship. St. Paul's description of this exclusion, "to deliver unto Satan for the destruc-

---

[1] See below, pp. 284, 407.   [2] See below, pp. 395, 397.

tion of the flesh that the spirit may be saved,"[3] in all probability points to some severe remedial discipline. The passage was commonly explained at the beginning of the third century as indicating a practice equivalent to the penitential discipline of that time. Tertullian in his Montanist period attacked this prevailing interpretation, in a rigorist spirit denying that Paul could have authorized the restoration of the incestuous sinner.[4]

There was hesitation on the part of second- and third-century disciplinarians in permitting the restoration by penitence of those guilty of the major sins of idolatry, fornication, and the shedding of blood. The basis of this list was the Apostolic Decree of Acts 15:29.[5] Tertullian regarded these sins as "irremissible,"[6] and Origen condemned those ill-qualified priests who pretended by their prayers to secure remission for these offenses.[7] But the less rigorous point of view of Hermas, who permits the restoration of an apostate and of an adulteress,[8] and of Clement of Alexandria, who tells a story of the Apostle John's pardon of a baptized youth who had become a murderous bandit,[9] came in course of time to prevail, and no distinction for these sins was made in penitential procedure except in respect to the severity and duration of the penance.

The public character of the discipline is manifest throughout the patristic literature. Neither sins committed in secret nor those already given a scandalous publicity were exempt from the requirement of open confession and repudiation. M. J. O'Donnell, following Bellarmine, infers from certain statements of Irenaeus that in the late second century in both East and West, Christians guilty of mortal, even though secret, sin were obliged to undergo public penance: if they chose to decline it they could then only "cling to the slender hope that perhaps God's pardon could be gained without it."[10] More convincing than these passages, however, on the subject of open

[3] I Cor. 5:3–5.   [4] De pudicitia xiii. Cf. Watkins, I, 20, 88.
[5] "αἵματος" being understood in the sense of "bloodshed," and "πνικτῶν" omitted. See Watkins, I, 11 ff.
[6] De pudicitia ii.
[7] De oratione xxviii. Origen applies I John 5:16, "There is a sin unto death . . ." Cf. Watkins, I, 95, 134.
[8] Pastor of Hermas, Vis. ii. 2; Mand. iv. 1.
[9] Quis dives salvetur? (What Rich Man Shall Be Saved?), xiii. There is of course no certainty that the story has historical value.
[10] Penance in the Early Church, p. 57. For the passage see Watkins, I, 77 f., 101 f. Watkins doubts that the public confession involved a recital of the offenses, but he does so only on the basis of later usage. There is no indication of "sacramental absolution" in these passages.

confession for secret sin, are Tertullian's expressions enjoining it. "A grand reward of modesty, indeed, the concealment of a fault promises," says Tertullian; "if we conceal something from men's notice, shall we then conceal it from God?" "Is it better," he asks, "to be damned in secret than to be absolved in public?"[11] B. Poschmann, in his searching study of penance in the Western Church at the close of the ancient period, accepts the judgment of Morin that in Rome in the early fifth century secret and open offenses were alike subject to public penance.[12]

Not all offenses, however, were subject to penalty. A variety of the lighter everyday sins of Christians were dismissed by mere open acknowledgment in their assemblies. As attested by the *Teaching of the Twelve Apostles*, faults of this class formed the subject of mutual or public confession preceding the Eucharist each Sunday.[13] The Greek word "exomologesis" was used alike for this routine public confession of minor faults and for the humiliating procedure followed in the confession of offenses involving discipline and penance. Exomologesis involved so much self-abasement that the word itself came to embrace the idea of an act of penance and to be used with reference to works of satisfaction. Tertullian employs the same word in Latin, with an exposition which offers the earliest circumstantial description of penance itself. He calls it a "discipline for man's prostration and humiliation requiring a behavior conducive of mercy." It involves the wearing of sackcloth and ashes, engaging in fasts, and uttering groans, prayers, and outcries to God. The penitent is, moreover, enjoined "to bow before the feet of the presbyters and to kneel to those who are dear to God, to enjoin all the brethren to be his ambassadors to bear his deprecatory supplication" before God.[14]

This public procedure, in which the penitent in his humiliation implores the intercession of "all the brethren," was later to be replaced by a private and secret rite involving confession to and absolution by a priestly confessor and entailing acts of penance that were often mainly or wholly private. In this transformation of penance the penitential books were to play an important rôle.

---

[11] *De penitentia* x. The whole of this chapter is apropos.

[12] Poschmann I, pp. 6 ff. Such is also the view of E. Amann in his scholarly article "Pénitence-Sacrement," *Dictionnaire de théologie catholique*, XII, 783, 837.

[13] *Didache* IV, 14. Cf. Jas. 5:16, "Confess your sins one to another."

[14] *De penitentia* ix.

SYSTEMATIZATION OF PENANCE

Penance was a growingly prominent feature of church life in the third and fourth centuries, and was becoming more systematized. The crises in discipline created by persecution, and especially the Novatian schism, stimulated this development. Increasingly the authority of the clergy in penance is indicated. Cyprian is familiar with and enjoins confession of sins of thought to the "sacerdotes"— here probably the bishops—and urges the lapsed to seek from them "remission," and reconciliation with the imposition of hands.[15] Origen recommends seeking out "a skilled and merciful physician," "who knows the discipline of comfort and sympathy,"[16] who shall when consulted advise whether confession to the whole church is expedient for the soul's healing and the edification of others.[17] It is not here indicated that the physician of souls must be a cleric, but the presumption is that such will ordinarily be the case. Elsewhere Origen speaks of ejection from the Church "by the voice of a bishop," and points out that the victim of an act of expulsion "by the unjust judgment of those who are over the Church"[18] is still in reality within.[19] Such passages indicate a tendency to rest upon the official ministers responsibility and authority in confession, penitential satisfaction, and reconciliation. Nevertheless the typical penance of the Church long remained public, even for sins committed in secret.

The lapses due to persecution and to the temptations of the period after persecution ceased, the extension of the list of offenses for which penance was required or accepted, and the relaxation by which repeated acts of penance were permitted, all tended to increase the difficulties connected with the practice of penance, and to render necessary an increasingly systematic procedure. Despite urgent efforts on the part of leading bishops, penance was widely neglected. Where it was maintained, it shows a progressive systematization. In certain areas, during the third and fourth centuries, the so-called "stations" of penitents were in full vogue. By this arrangement penitents were divided into four classes, and to each was assigned a special position at the church meetings. The council of Nicaea[20]

[15] For an examination of the passages, see Watkins, I, 144 ff., 206 ff.
[16] "qui condolendi et compatiendi noverit disciplinam."
[17] Hom. ii, "On Psalm 37."
[18] "ut aliquis non recto iudicio eorum qui praesunt ecclesiae depellatur."
[19] Hom. xiv, "On Leviticus."   [20] Can. 11.

mentions three of these four classes. The one omitted is that of the συνκλαίοντες, or "weepers," who were in the first or lowest stage of penance, and whose station was outside the door of the church.[21] The other three stations were within the building. The ἀκροώμενοι, or "hearers," were placed in the vestibule; they were dismissed after the lesson and sermon and before the Eucharist.[22] The ὑποπίπτοντες, or "kneelers," were stationed further forward, yet in the rear of the congregation. When others stood during prayer these were required to kneel. They came to church clothed in sackcloth and with ashes on their heads.[23] Finally the συνιστάμενοι, or "co-standers," were mingled with the congregation although they were not yet permitted to communicate.[24]

The development of the penance system was no doubt considerably influenced by civil law. Morin notes that after Augustine's time penitential rules were extended to include "all crimes which the civil law punished with death, exile, or other grave corporal penalty."[25] But at an earlier date the codification of penance, in documents of only private authority and in decisions of church councils, was already beginning. In these canons specific periods of penitential satisfaction are indicated seriatim for a large number of offenses. A typical document of this class, and one which carried high authority in the Eastern Church, is the series of three canonical letters written by Basil of Caesarea to Amphilochius of Iconium.[26] This document approaches more closely than any non-Celtic work to the form of a penitential; yet the resemblance is superficial only. Basil's canons refer throughout to the system of graded penance, outlined above, and regularly subdivide the longer terms of penance into periods to be spent in each of the "stations." The word "exomologesis" is used to include both confession and penance which are parts of the same process of public humiliation. There is no suggestion that any other kind of penance is in existence. The penitentials, on the

---

[21] Gregory Thaumaturgus *Canonical Epistles*, can. 11. The 25th canon of the council of Ancyra calls this class the χειμαζόμενοι, or *hiemantes*, since they were exposed to the weather as they stood without to implore the prayers of the faithful.

[22] Gregory Thaumaturgus, *loc. cit.*　　[23] Jerome Ep. lxxvii, *C.S.E.L.*, LV, 40.

[24] Gregory Thaumaturgus, *loc. cit.*

[25] J. Morinus, *Commentarius historicus de disciplina in administratione sacramenti poenitentiae tredecim primis seculis* (2d ed., 1682), lib. v, c. 5, p. 264.

[26] These three letters are numbered cxcix, ccxvii, and clxxxviii in the epistles of Basil which may be found in Migne, *P.G.*, XXXII. They were written *ca.* 374–76. The canons contained in them are numbered continuously throughout the three letters.

other hand, know nothing of a public exomologesis, but assume that penance is determined by the confessor in private conference with the penitent; and the penalties they impose, while not uniformly ungraded, bear in general no relation to the classification of penitents presupposed by Basil.[27]

A further approach in the ancient Church to the system which was to develop under the influence of the penitentials is seen in the customs of early monastic discipline; but the parallel is not so close as some writers have claimed.[28] The correspondence consists in the fact of confession to, or consultation with, a trusted senior, as in the passage from Origen cited above. No doubt the habit of frequent confession cultivated in early monasticism passed into the monasteries of Wales and Ireland, from which the earliest penitentials emanate, and was a factor of importance in shaping some of the penitential procedures assumed or enjoined in them. But it has not been shown that such monastic confession was conceived of as sacramental or accompanied by private absolution. Poschmann regards it as spiritual direction rather than sacramental confession.[29]

WAS SECRET CONFESSION PRACTICED?

The view that private confession followed by public penance and reconciliation was the general practice in the ancient Church is favored or definitely asserted by numerous writers. In this connection reference is often made to the abolition by the Patriarch Nectarius, about 391, of the office of Presbyter of Penance at Constantinople. The incident is reported somewhat differently by two historians of the ancient Church.[30] This office had been instituted at the time of the Decian persecution, when a presbyter penitentiary was appointed by the bishop apparently to relieve the latter of the onerous duties of the administration of discipline. Dr. Watkins is convinced that the private confession was required.[31] Yet in both accounts the abolition

---

[27] Poschmann (II, p. 8) observes that the one entirely new aspect of the Celtic Penitentials is that they show no knowledge of the public church penance—"sie kennen nicht die Institution der öffentlichen Kirchenbusse."

[28] A. Hauck, *Kirchengeschichte Deutschlands*, I, 253; A. Lagarde, *The Latin Church*, pp. 55 f.; J. Ryan, *Irish Monasticism: Origins and Early Development*, pp. 353 ff.

[29] Poschmann I, pp. 230 f. Cf. McNeill, pp. 90 ff. (*Rev. celt.*, XL, 74 ff.).

[30] Socrates *Ecclesiastical History*, V, 19; Sozomen, *Ecclesiastical History*, vii, 16. The former is the earlier and the more reliable historian; the latter is inaccurate, and his text is suspected of interpolations.

[31] Watkins, I, 352 f. See also F. Frank, *Die Bussdisciplin der Kirche*, pp. 412 f.

of the office is stated to have been due to a scandal arising from an
unworthy deacon's attack upon a lady who had come to confession.
While some of Sozomen's phrases, such as his description of the
presbyter appointed as a "silent and prudent" person, suggest private
confession, this view does not explain the occasion of the offense or
the reason for the suppression of the office. The incident seems best
understood on the hypothesis that the offending deacon took advantage of knowledge gained while acting (with others) as an as-
sessor with the presbyter when the matron's confession was made.[32]

In discussing the public and private aspects of the penitential
discipline it is important to distinguish between confession and
penance. Private soul-guidance was, as we have seen, recommended
by Clement and by Origen, and there are indications of its practice
in pastoral work, as well as in monastic communities in the fourth
century.[33] Ambrose of Milan, according to his biographer, Paulinus,
heard the confessions of penitents and "told none but God" what
he learned from them.[34] This evidently refers to a confidential confession, and apparently it was not followed by a public acknowledgment
of sins in detail. Poschmann notes, however, that this passage has
nothing to do with the question of open or secret penance.[35] This
writer is strongly convinced that there was no secret church penance;
yet he thinks it "to say the least not unambiguously certain" that
open confession was required for secret sins, and regards with some
favor E. Vacandard's view that the only publicity required was in
the acts of penance rather than in the confession itself.[36] Similar is
the view of Watkins, who remarks on the difficulty of obtaining any

[32] Cf. McNeill, pp. 83 ff. (*Rev. celt.*, XL, 67 ff.). *Didascalia*, Chap. xi, shows that in
Syria bishops held courts of arbitration in which they were assisted by presbyters and
deacons. M. D. Gibson, *Didascalia apostolorum*, p. 60.

[33] Cf. Poschmann I, pp. 230 ff.

[34] *Paulini vita S. Ambrosii*, 39. Migne, *P.L.*, XIV, 43. Cf. A. Lagarde's discussion of
the doctrine and practice of penance in Ambrose: "La Pénitence dans les églises d'Italie
au cours des iv⁰ et v⁰ siècles," *Rev. de l'histoire des religions*, XCII (1925), 108–47. Lagarde
(pseudonym of J. Turmel) is convinced (p. 124) that the private consultation did not involve reconciliation.

[35] Poschmann I, p. 15.

[36] "Confession du 1ᵉʳ au xiiiᵉ siècle," Vacant et Mangenot, *Dictionnaire de théologie
catholique*, III, 838–99, especially pp. 857–59. Vacandard goes so far as to say (col. 859),
"La seule publicité que l'Église des premiers siècles ait exigée de ses enfants coupables de
péchés graves est celle de leur pénitence, appelée communément 'exomologèse.'" He recognizes the requirement of exomologesis, even for secret sins; but the exomologesis is penance
itself, not confession. Conversely, for the age of Ambrose, Lagarde states that the public
penance was itself a publication of sin, "un aveu de culpabilité fait à la face de l'Eglise,"
an implicit though not an explicit confession.—*Op. cit.*, pp. 115, 123.

"satisfying evidence that the public confession of sins by word of mouth ever . . . formed part of the formal discipline of penance."[37]

But it is incredible that exomologesis did not at the outset, in accordance with the primary meaning of the word, involve explicit and frank confession.[38] At every step in the evolution of discipline some official action to determine penance must have been necessary. It was natural that this should be largely controlled by the bishop or by presbyters appointed by him for the purpose. It was also natural that private consultation should precede the public exomologesis. The testimony of Tertullian about the year 200 and that of Maximus of Turin about 450 point definitely to open confession, even of secret sins, as customary in parts of Africa and Italy at these periods. Probably we should discern a gradual tendency, advancing unevenly in different areas, to make the private consultation the official confession, while the public exomologesis evolves into the series of public acts enjoined as penalties.

Augustine's references to penance and confession fail to show evidence for the medieval practices, but are in accord with what has just been said. The bishop takes the penitent into consultation, and advises him on the question of undergoing public penance. Augustine permits the avoidance of open confession for secret or nonscandalous sins. These are to be repented of in private with "conversion," prayer, alms giving, and fasting.[39]

Practice in fifth-century Italy shows considerable variation. Sozomen, in a passage cited above,[40] gives a description of penance at Rome about 450, features of which are the public appearance of the penitents in the church in the garb and with the demeanor of mourners and their privately undertaken austerities followed by

[37] Watkins, I, 422.

[38] Like μετάνοια and its Latin equivalent penitentia, which came to be used chiefly for outward acts of penance rather than in the primary sense of inward repentance, the word ἐξομολόγησις seems to have taken in the course of time the significance of the austerities commanded rather than the recital of sins.

[39] A. Lagarde, "Saint Augustine, a-t-il connu la confession?" Revue d'histoire et de littérature religieuses, IV (1913), 226–50. Poschmann has also opposed the view that the medieval practice of private penance was introduced by Augustine in: Hat Augustinus die Privatbusse eingeführt? (Braunsberg, 1920); Kirchenbusse und correptio secreta bei Augustinus (Braunsberg, 1923); and three articles on "Die kirchliche Vermittelung der Sündenvergebung nach Augustinus," Zeitschrift für Kathol. Theologie, XLV (1921). Poschmann's first study called forth a dissenting study by K. Adam, Die geheime Kirchenbusse bei dem hl. Augustinus (Munich, 1921), to which Poschmann replied. See especially his third article in the Zeitschrift, pp. 511 ff.

[40] Ecclesiastical History, vii, 16.

absolution and readmission to communion. Pope Leo the Great in 459 wrote a letter to the bishops of Campania, Samnium, and Picenum which contains a notable section on confession.[41] He here sternly condemns as "presumption" the practice of compelling penitents to read publicly a "libellus" containing a detailed confession of their sins. The practice has, he observes, no apostolic sanction, and it may needlessly inculpate Christians before their enemies and so subject them to legal punishment. Leo is here dealing with cases of secret offenses. He does not forbid public confession in such cases; he regards it indeed as "praiseworthy." What he does forbid is the compulsory reading of a written declaration of sins. This he regards as an innovation fraught with serious possibilities. In rejecting it, however, he goes so far as to pronounce unnecessary any public acknowledgment in detail of secret sins. He recommends as sufficient a "confession first offered to God and then to the bishop."[42] He fears that the continuance of the custom will cause many to avoid penance altogether.

Historians of penance have given much attention to this passage. H. C. Lea suggests that Leo here inaugurated the practice of "private penance for private sins."[43] B. Kurtschied states that the letter conveys the first clear and unambiguous authorization for secret confession and strict silence on the part of the confessor.[44] J. Tixeront uses the passage to support his contention that sacramental confession had always been secret.[45] Such is also the view of Vacandard in the article cited above. Poschmann finds in the utterance evidence of the fact that for secret offenses public penance was practiced with secret confession.[46] Watkins uses it to corroborate his opinion that detailed public confession of private sins was probably never obligatory.[47]

As negative evidence on open confession for secret sin, it is possible to take Leo's words too seriously. That which he definitely states to be contrary to "apostolic rule" (by which he can only mean tradi-

---

[41] Ep. clxviii, 2. Migne, *P.L.*, LIV, 1210.

[42] "Sufficit enim illa confessio, quae primum Deo offertur, tum etiam sacerdoti." "Sacerdos" is probably here to be read "bishop" as frequently in Leo's works. Cf. C. Gore, *Leo the Great*, p. 142.

[43] *History of Auricular Confession and Indulgences*, I, 183.

[44] *Das Beichtsiegel in seiner geschichtlichen Entwicklung* (1912), pp. 28–31. Revised English edition: *History of the Seal of Confession* (1927), p. 55.

[45] *Le Sacrement de pénitence dans l'antiquité chrétienne*, pp. 37, 62.

[46] Poschmann I, 11 ff.   [47] Watkins, I, 422 ff.

tional or general practice) is the public reading of the statement.[48] Certainly there is no evidence for the use of such a written catalogue of personal sins in public confession heretofore, and the introduction of such a procedure was in itself a startling departure from earlier practice.

But if Leo's indignation and surprise arise from the public confession itself rather than from the use of libelli, they must seem forced and exaggerated.[49] Not only were the bishops addressed accustomed to demand open confession of secret sin, but the procedure was recognized elsewhere in Italy. In the same period Maximus of Turin, as Poschmann indicates, clearly assumes that the confession of secret sins will be public when he reproves the sinner who like a fox conceals his sin, "blushing to confess the wickedness of his conduct in the midst of the church."[50]

It is a mistake, then, to regard Leo's statement as sufficient evidence for the prevalence of secret confession in his time. Nor can it be regarded as the legislation by which the practice was established in the West. Lea, indeed, notes that "centuries were to elapse" before the medieval secret penance system emerges, and indicates that libelli for public confession were in later times approved even by popes.[51]

Though private consultation was common and was probably coming to resemble the later secret confession, the fact remains that throughout the ancient period of the church the acts of satisfaction enjoined in penance were prevailingly public in character, and reconciliation was regularly a public rite.[52] That "mortal sins can be

[48] Lagarde, in the article cited in note 34 above, pp. 142 f., emphasizes Leo's determination that the public reading of what had been privately disclosed should cease, not that confession should take on a ritual character. Cf. Poschmann I, p. 14, and E. Göller "Papsttum und Bussgewalt in spätrömischer und frühmittelalterlicher Zeit," *Römische Quartalschrift*, XXXIX (1931), 130.

[49] One wonders indeed whether this imperious letter to the pope's neighboring bishops may not have been motivated by other considerations than those which appear in it.

[50] "in media ecclesia." Migne, *P.L.*, LVII, 523. Cf. Poschmann I, pp. 15 f.

[51] *History of Auricular Confession and Indulgences*, II, 73.

[52] See especially Poschmann I, pp. 204 ff., 229 f.; Amann, *op. cit.*, cols. 783, 837 ff. This view is tenaciously opposed by the learned Jesuit P. Galtier in his article "Pénitence, II. Confession" in D'Alès, *Dictionnaire de la foi catholique*, III, 1784–1865, and in his books *De penitentia, tractatus dogmatico-historicus* (1923) and *L'Église et la rémission des péchés* (1932). The last-named work has the interest of a running attack on the views of Poschmann, who in works cited above unfavorably notices Father Galtier's earlier studies. Galtier here objects to Poschmann's definitions, attempts to account for the silence on private penance of the Patristic literature, affirms sacramental private penance wherever "remission of sins without public penance" can be made to appear, and cites in evidence

absolved by secret satisfaction" is admitted by Gennadius of
Marseilles (d.496), but only in the case of those who enter the
monastic life and so come under "the yoke of perpetual lamentation."
This monastic substitute for public penance was in itself in a measure
public, since it meant withdrawal from secular life to a monastic
community and adoption of the monastic garb.

PENANCE NOT REPEATABLE

It is not to be supposed, however, that frequent penance for the
grave sins, the customary practice of later centuries, was yet permitted. But as the list of deadly sins was extended, whether because
they were looked upon with less repulsion and regarded as less grave
or because of an advance in the claims made for the Church's powers
of absolution, penance came to be a repeatable act. This relaxation
first appears in Antioch and Constantinople and is by Watkins
specially connected with Chrysostom,[53] whose mildness is shown not
only in this but also in the short terms of penance which he assigned.
In the West penance with reconciliation was not repeatable. "As one
baptism," says Ambrose, "so one penance."[54] Indeed the iteration of
penance is not permitted by the Western teachers before Caesarius,
bishop of Arles, 502–42, who admits those who have "sinned once or
twice," but not those who "add sins to sins."[55] This advanced position
was rejected in Spain, where the Third Council of Toledo in 589 invoked "the severity of the earlier canons" against the repetition of
penance and by requiring tonsure and penitential garb sought to
maintain its public character.[56] It is Watkins's judgment that the
rigor of Western practice helped to make it customary to postpone
penance until the approach of death and led to the decline of public
penance.[57] Advocates of public penance in the Middle Ages often
cited the patristic literature as evidence that the act of penance may
not be repeated.[58] In the penitentials, on the other hand, except

---

the procedure in cases of heresy and of minor sins. The treatise is more erudite than convincing.
   [53] Discussing the iteration of penance, Watkins (I, 346) remarks: "It is Chrysostom
who first throws limits to the winds."
   [54] "sicut unum baptisma ita una poenitentia," *De penitentia* II, x. Ambrose adds that
he is speaking of penance for the graver offenses, which is performed publicly.
   [55] Sermon, 258.
   [56] Cans. 11 and 12. Mansi, *Concilia*, IX, 995. Cf. Amann, *op. cit.*, col. 840.
   [57] Watkins, II, 557, 561.   [58] Poschmann (II, pp. 159 ff.) gives examples.

where life sentences are assigned, there is no impediment to the iteration of penance.

THE SACRAMENTAL ASPECT OF PENANCE

Penance had a sacramental as well as a disciplinary aspect. It was thought of not merely as a discipline for the restoration of sinners to the privileges of membership in the Church but as a means of supernatural grace annulling the consequences of sin and recovering the favor of God. The words attributed to Jesus: "Whosesoever sins ye remit they are remitted . . ."[59] and "Whatsoever thou shalt bind on on earth shall be bound in heaven,"[60] were held to convey the authority to "bind and loose" in such a way that the act was ratified in heaven. In the expanding Christian Church these passages were received as commissioning the Apostles with divine authority, and they lent powerful support to rising sacramentalism and sacerdotalism.

We have seen that in the earliest stage of the evolution of penance the whole body of the Christian community participated in the administration of discipline and in the act of receiving penitents. It is probable that even at this stage sacramental ideas should be recognized. To "deliver unto Satan"[61] was to exclude from sacramental grace, while it was also an act of the whole Church "gathered together." The view of Tertullian, referred to above, that certain sins are irremissible was a protest against the tendency to bring under the authority of the Church the function of remitting all offenses. Some sins, he believed, were so grave that they must be reserved to the judgment of God.[62] In this it was assumed, however, that in a wide range of offenses the Church exercised a power that was not only disciplinary but in a sense sacramental.[63] An early extension of the sacramental claims of the Church was involved in the admission to penance for the three capital sins listed from the Apostolic Decree —a relaxation opposed by rigorists like Tertullian, but authorized by the Roman bishop Callixtus (217-23)[64] and gradually thereafter generally adopted. Cyprian does not use the word "absolution," but

[59] John 20:23.   [60] Matt. 16:19.   [61] I Cor. 5:5.
[62] De pudicitia iii, xxi.   [63] De pudicitia xxi.
[64] For the literature on the difficult topic of the Edict of Callixtus, see E. Göller, "Papsttum und Bussgewalt," Römische Quartalschrift, XXXIX (1931), 77, n. 12. Cf. P. Galtier, L'Église et la remission . . . pp. 141-83.

A. d'Alès holds that he has sacerdotal absolution in mind when he speaks of remission made through the priests ("per sacerdotes"). Yet "to speak of an *opus operatum* in the sense of the later theology" says this writer, "would assuredly be to project forward the thought of Cyprian. But it is fair to say that he opened the road to that theology by the extreme energy with which he taught the connection between the ecclesiastical sentence and the divine pardon."[65]

The power to forgive sins was regarded as vested in the bishops who were thought of as heirs of the apostles or as representatives of Christ. In the *Didascalia*, a document of the Syrian Church of *ca.* 252–70, the rigorism that would withhold reconciliation from any is condemned, and bishops are urged to deal faithfully and mercifully with sinners since they are in the place of God and have received power to bind and loose. This power applies to all sins, even the worst. Expulsion from the Church by a bishop implies eternal damnation.[66]

The sacramental element in penance is suggested by the rite of the imposition of hands in reconciliation. The implications of this rite are not always clear, as it was employed in services not connected with penance, and at various times in the process of penance. In an ample study of the liturgical aspects of penance J. A. Jungmann strikingly remarks that the words of absolution of the later period expressed "what the earlier imposition of hands aimed to say."[67] Watkins finds "evidence for the laying on of hands as an outward sign of absolution" in various documents of the third, fourth, and fifth centuries but holds that "the use was by no means universal."[68] To employ the word "absolution," however, in connection with the reconciliation of penitents at this period would be misleading if it involved a recognition of the medieval application of the term. Absolution was granted not at the beginning of the penance but at its close, and it is not to be distinguished from reconciliation or re-admission to communion. No formularies of absolution of the period

---

[65] A. d'Alès, *La Théologie de Saint Cyprian,* p. 279; H. Koch, *Cyprianische Untersuchungen,* pp. 251–85, denies that Cyprian held a sacramental conception of penance. See especially pp. 281 ff.

[66] *Didascalia apostolorum* v–vii. Extracts from Mrs. M. D. Gibson's translation from the Syriac, with illuminating comment, are furnished by Watkins, I, 224 ff., 245 ff.

[67] *Die lateinischen Bussriten in ihrer geschichtlichen Entwicklung* (1932), p. 253.

[68] Watkins, I, 491 ff.

are preserved; and all information on the point indicates the use of a prayer, not of a declarative form.[69]

By the beginning of the fifth century the custom of an annual ceremony of reconciliation of penitents on Maundy Thursday was becoming established in the West. Innocent I refers to this fact in a letter to Decentius of Eugubium about 416, in which he states that it is "the custom of the Roman Church" to grant remission to penitents on the Thursday before Easter, "except in the case of illness." A penitent who is gravely ill may be received earlier, "lest he depart without communion."[70] The use of the word "remittendum" (remission is granted) seems to associate the sacramental element of the penance with the public act of reconciliation and to confute the argument of certain writers who contend for the recognition of a sacramental secret confession and absolution from the beginning.[71]

It is, in fact, impossible to determine how far Christians in general were led to think of the penitential discipline in terms of grace sacramentally imparted. There existed no clearly defined theology of the sacraments before Augustine, and he does not call penance a sacrament. His teaching on the efficacy of absolution is criticized for its vagueness by Father P. Pourrat. His view is expressed in an allegorizing reference (borrowed from Ambrose) to the "loosing" of Lazarus from his graveclothes.[72] Indeed the doctrine of absolution remained unorganized to the scholastic age.[73] The recognition of penance as a sacrament is only occasional before this period. The seven sacraments affirmed by the Council of Trent were first catalogued in an exclusive list in the twelfth century, apparently shortly before Peter Lombard accorded them systematic treatment.[74]

[69] "It probably took the form of a deprecatory prayer."—M. J. O'Donnell, *Penance in the Early Church*, rev. ed., p. 119. "No verbal absolution in any form but that of prayer is known to have been preserved . . . "—Watkins, I, 493. Galtier stresses the evidence that the prayer was held to be efficacious (*op. cit.*, pp. 70 ff., 100 ff., 128). Cf. the prayers given in the *Gelasian Sacramentary*, ed. by H. A. Wilson, pp. 64 ff.

[70] Ep. xxv: Migne, *P.L.*, XX, 559. Cf. Watkins, I, 310 f., 415; Jungmann, *op. cit.*, pp. 74 ff.

[71] This is the position of a number of conservative Roman Catholic theologians, including J. Tixeront, in *Le Sacrement de pénitence dans l'antiquité chrétienne* (1914), K. Adam, and P. Galtier in works cited above.   [72]Sermon ccclii, 8.

[73] "This (Augustine's) vague teaching on the efficacy of Absolution had its echo in the early part of the Middle Ages. It is adopted by Gregory the Great, and is still found, with few modifications, in Peter Lombard."—P. Pourrat, *Theology of the Sacraments*, authorized translation from the 3d French ed., p. 153. Cf. pp. 22 ff.

[74] Cf. Pourrat, *op. cit.*, pp. 258 ff.

While indubitably ideas rightly described as sacramental were associated with penance in the ancient Church, there was no authoritative teaching on the subject. The failure of the church fathers to present any specific formulation of the doctrine of penance and the absence of surviving liturgical forms render it impossible to judge with confidence what the prevailing ideas were in respect to a sacramental ministry of grace in the penitential discipline.

THE DEADLY SINS

One of the interests of moralists, and particularly of the early monastic disciplinarians, was the enumeration and classification of sins. The three principal or capital sins of the first stage of the Church were idolatry, or reversion to paganism; fornication, including incest, adultery, and other sexual sins; and bloodshed, or homicide.[75] These sins, not without protest, as we have seen, came to be regarded as remissible by the Church. But in the experience of life and the practice of soul guidance, attention was inevitably drawn to a variety of grave offenses of thought or action for which repentance was required. Thus Hermas personifies as temptresses the following twelve sins which, unless repented of, exclude from the kingdom of God: unbelief, incontinence, disobedience, deceit, sorrow, wickedness, wantonness, anger, falsehood, folly, backbiting, and hatred. Of these he regards the first four as stronger than the others.[76] Various other lists of grave or deadly sins appear in patristic literature. Thus Cyprian in his treatises *Of Jealousy and Envy* and *Of the Mortality*, shows an attempt to catalogue the principal sins in order.[77] But his aim is immediately practical in these works, and it is not clear that his list is intended as a fundamental formulation.

Augustine does not present a classified series of sins. He interprets the "crimen" (crime) which in I Tim. 3:10 disqualifies from church ministries, as consisting of such grave offenses as murder, adultery, impurity, theft, fraud, and sacrilege.[78] More characteristic of his psychology of sin is his reference to the vices which he finds

[75] Based on Acts 15:29. Other New Testament lists appear in Mark 7:21–22; Gal. 5:19–21; and Rev. 21:8.   [76] *Pastor Hermae*, Simil. ix. 15.

[77] *De zelo et invidia* 6, 17. *De mortalitate* 4. In exposition of the former passage see E. W. Benson, *Cyprian, His Life, His Times, His Work* (American ed. 1897), p. 453, and n. 1. Eight sins are listed in the latter work, viz.: avarice, lust, ambition, anger, pride, drunkenness, envy, and cursing. Migne, *P.L.*, IV, 603.

[78] *S. Joannis Evangel. Tract.* xli. 10; Migne, *P.L.*, XXXV, 1697.

allegorically figured in the beasts of the field, birds of the air, and fish of the sea, in Psalm 8:8–9. "These three kinds of vices," he remarks, "that is, carnal pleasure (voluptas carnis), pride (superbia), and curiosity (curiositas), comprehend all sins."[79]

In course of their experience in the monastic warfare upon sin and temptation, the responsible leaders of monasticism were concerned to describe and classify sins as physicians inform themselves of diseases and their symptoms. It was John Cassian, a profound student of Eastern monasticism and one of the foremost inspirers of the movement in the West, who first, about the time of Augustine's death, distinguished the "eight principal vices" and gave them a rational order. By Cassian the vices are named and arranged as follows: gluttony, fornication, avarice, anger, dejection (tristitia), languor (accedia), vainglory, and pride.[80] Cassian devotes books V–XII of his *Institutes* to the description and treatment of these sins, and accords them a similar though briefer treatment in his *Conferences*. The order is not, in his mind, the order of their gravity but more nearly the reverse of this. When he reaches the section on pride,[81] he holds this last-mentioned sin to be the first in importance and the germinal source of all the others.

Most of the penitentials were compiled by careful students of Cassian, and a number of them have been arranged on the plan of the eight vices first systematized in his writings.[82]

Gregory the Great radically revises Cassian's order of treatment of the deadly sins. He emphasizes pride (superbia) and lust (luxuria), of which the former is a revolt of the spirit against God and the latter a revolt of the flesh against the spirit.[83] In his schedule of sins, pride, "the captain of the devil's army" and "the beginning of all sin,"[84] is set apart as the chief, and from this principal sin seven other deadly sins extend in logical, or, according to his figure, in military order: vainglory, envy, anger, dejection, avarice, gluttony, and lust. Derived from or associated with each of these stands a troop of individual sins

---

[79] *Enarrationes in Psalmos* viii. 13; Migne, *P.L.*, XXXVI, 115.

[80] *De coenobiorum institutis* v, 1 (*ca.* 429). The same list occurs in his *Conlationes* v, 2; *C.S.E.L.*, XVII, 81; XIII, 121.

[81] *C.S.E.L.*, XVII, 206 ff. [82] See below pp. 99, 148, 156.

[83] *Moralia* xxvi. 28: Migne, *P.L.*, LXXVI, 364 f. Cf. T. H. Dudden, *Gregory the Great, His Place in History and Thought*, II, 384 ff., and P. Schulze, *Die Entwicklung der Hauptlaster- und Haupttugendlehre von Gregor dem Grossen bis Petrus Lombardus*, pp. 14 ff.

[84] Ecclus. 10:13.

of the same species.[85] Gregory's classification is followed by most medieval writers and makes its appearance in the penitential literature, notably in a ninth-century penitential formerly ascribed to Theodore and in Burchard's *Corrector*.[86]

THE DECLINE OF ANCIENT PENANCE

The widespread relaxation of moral discipline among the nominally Christian people of the late Western Empire is abundantly attested. "How changed is the Christian people now from its former character," writes Salvian of Marseilles about the middle of the fifth century. Over against Peter's punishment of Ananias and Paul's expulsion of a sinner from the Church, he cites the lamentable state of his times when almost all the members of the Church are guilty of revolting offenses.[87] The unrelieved picture of a depraved society drawn in detail by Salvian is scarcely paralleled in literature. Not even exile and want inflicted on them by the invading barbarians led the Gallo-Romans to abandon the shameless vices which they practiced even to old age. "Some of them, I suppose," says Salvian, "are relying on a foolish assurance of long life, or the intention of eventual penitence."[88] Penance, if practiced at all, was a death-bed repentance and reconciliation. "In the fifth century," says Watkins, summing up a mass of evidence, "penance in time of health was nearly lost in the West as in the East; and it would have to be regained."[89]

Our chief concern is with the West, where new methods of penance were to be introduced with the Celtic penitentials. The faithful if unskilled pen of Gregory of Tours portrays the rise of the Frankish power and the scene in Merovingian Gaul in the sixth century. His *History of the Franks*[90] consists mainly of a series of incidents marked by savage and unchecked brutality, treachery, intrigue, and corrup-

---

[85] *Moralia* xxxi. 87–88: Migne, *P.L.*, LXXVI, 620 f. Dudden, *op. cit.*, p. 388, has tabulated the whole scheme. Dudden has also pointed out the distinction in degrees of sin which runs through each category. Gregory distinguishes five degrees: "dilectum," "peccatum," "iniquitas," "scelus," and "crimen." While "peccatum" stains the soul, "scelus" destroys it.—*Op. cit.*, pp. 384 f.   [86] See below pp. 341 f.

[87] *On the Government of God*, VI, 1. Translation by Eva M. Sanford ("Records of Civilization"), p. 158.   [88] *Ibid.*, p. 195.   [89] Watkins, I, 465.

[90] This work may be consulted in the editions of W. Arndt and others, and of R. Poupardin, and also in the scholarly translation of O. M. Dalton, Oxford, 1927. Dalton's work is in two volumes, of which Vol. I is *Introduction*. For the passages referring to penance, see especially E. Göller's discussion in "Studien über das gallische Busswesen zur Zeit Cäsarius von Arles und Gregor von Tours," *A.K.K.R.*, CIX (1929), 117–26.

tion among princes, nobles, clergy, and common people.[91] There are a few sincere ascetics and a small minority of respectable clergy, but lay life is little affected by religion and quite untouched, it would appear, by any systematically practiced penitential discipline. In many cases the worst atrocities go unpunished. Frequently the perpetrators suffer vengeance in kind; occasionally they are forced to pay composition in accordance with Germanic law. Gregory looks to God, not usually to the Church or the State, to deal with the outrageous scoundrels who throng his pages; and he interprets their reverses as acts of God. His rare allusions to penitent sinners and to excommunication do not permit us to infer the existence of any functioning system of penance for persons in health in the Church of his time.

The probably late fifth-century *Statuta antiqua*[92] represents an attempt made in southern Gaul to restore the declining discipline. This document assigns to penitents the duty of bringing the dead to the church for burial and requires them to kneel even on days of remission.[93] In the same region Caesarius of Arles (d. 542 or 543), demands for the accumulated mass of daily, and in themselves minor, sins a "lowly and compunctious penance" (humilem et compunctam penitentiam)[94] which Poschmann identifies with the traditional public penance.[95] Caesarius describes the humiliating features of the public discipline; but permits young people to do penance by good works in private.

Watkins notes that "the private penance recognized by Caesarius was, so far as it appears, from beginning to end, a self-inflicted discipline," and that it "amounts to little more than the leading of a consistent life." The old public penance, according to Caesarius, could be performed twice; but a second admission to penance was the extreme of relaxation reached on this point; and the council of Toledo of 589, as already noted, reverted to the older rule. Watkins sees in the strictness by which public penance could be accorded only once or twice, a reason for the growing habit of postponing penance till the approach of death.[96] Probably we should also give much

---

[91] Modern historians of the period paint a picture almost equally dark. See, for example, Sir S. Dill, *Roman Society in Gaul in the Merovingian Age*.
[92] Cf. Poschmann I, p. 71.   [93] Canons 81 and 82: Mansi, III, 957.
[94] Migne, *P.L.*, XXXIX, 2220.   [95] Poschmann I, p. 85.
[96] Watkins, II, 556, 561.

weight to the disinclination of penitents, except under unusual emo-
tional stress, to undergo the humiliation attendant on penance. "I
have seen," says Ambrose, "penitents whose tears had hollowed a fur-
row on their faces, and who prostrated themselves on the ground to
be trampled upon by the feet of everyone; their pale faces, worn by
fasts, exhibited the image of death in a living body."[97] Such scenes
were apparently exceptionally rare by the fifth century, and still
more so in the sixth. The penance of the dying was, in the nature of
the case, devoid of the more humiliating features of penance in health.

The conquests of the Visigoths and Franks fundamentally transformed the West. This is manifested in the triumph of Germanic over
Roman law. To this fact, so far as Gaul is concerned, F. Lot attributes
much of the violence and disorder of the age. He notes that the system
of composition was totally ineffective as a guarantee against the
custom of revenge. The vendetta passed from the Germans to the
Roman population and stained with blood the society of medieval
Europe.[98]

The new barbarized society could not be subjected to the old discipline which had already proved too severe for the Roman Christians. After much ground had been lost and public penance had been
almost extinguished, a new system was to develop, more workable
in this turbulent state of society and more applicable to its needs.

[97] *De penitentia* II.i.5. Cf. P. de Labriolle, *Life and Times of St. Ambrose* (tr. by
H. Wilson), p. 286.
[98] *La Fin du monde antique et le début du moyen âge*, p. 462.

The Penitentials

THERE STILL exists no treatment on an adequate scale of the documentary history of the penitential books; and this is not the place to attempt such an inquiry. The separate introductions that accompany the documents given below will provide the reader with a brief summary of what is known about the date and origin of each. It is hoped that with the aid of sources and studies there cited some readers may be enabled to investigate for themselves special problems of authorship and date.[1] Our present interest is in the broader historical questions of the character, functions, and influence of the books.

RISE AND SPREAD OF THE PENITENTIALS

When all similarities between the penitentials and earlier writings on penance have been recognized, it is still evident that the emergence of the series marks a new departure. Not only do the penitentials indicate a new method of penitential discipline; they also constitute a means hitherto unemployed of guiding confessors in their task. From the inception of the use of these manuals arises a new era in the history of penance.

Some fifth-century materials connected with the name of St. Patrick have been included among our documents as bearing a definite relation to the series. They differ from the typical penitentials, yet certain of their canons are similarly framed. Insofar as they belong to the age of Patrick they may be regarded as anticipating in certain respects the principles of the penitentials.

The earliest of the extant documents definitely belonging to the class of penitentials are probably those ascribed to Welsh synods held under the influence of St. David. A possible historic link between Patrick and David is found in the fact that St. Cairnech, traditionally associated with Patrick in the compilation of the *Senchus Mór* (Irish code of laws), is to be identified with David's uncle, whose

---

[1] A useful short account of the penitentials is the article "Pénitentiels" by G. Le Bras in *Dict. de théologie catholique*, XII, 1160–79.

Welsh name was Carranog or Carantoc. Various accounts of the lives of saints represent the Irish monastic founder and leader, St. Finnian of Clonard, probably the author of the *Penitential of Finnian*, as associated with David, Gildas, and Codoc in Wales; and one of them records his presence at the synod of Brevi, from which one of the penitential documents is apparently derived. Finnian's Penitential is probably a little later than the documents associated with David but within the first half of the sixth century.[2] Without over-working the evidence or attempting to substantiate every detail of these alleged contacts, it seems justifiable to suppose that the Welsh and Irish saints just named were in fairly close relationship and that in the circle of these associations the documentary series had its beginnings. It may be that between the death of Patrick (461) and the work of David (*ca.* 500) the method of discipline which was to be formulated in the penitentials was being developed in the prac-tice of the Welsh and Irish monasteries, and it is not unlikely that schedules of penance of the sort were being written at a date earlier than that of the origin of any of the extant documents of the type. The title "Certain Extracts from a Book of David," found in the only existing manuscript of the document in question, suggests that the latter is only a fragment selected from a larger manual. As the texts stand Finnian's is the earliest of the books sufficiently comprehensive to serve the purpose of a general guide for confessors in their ministry.

In Wales and Ireland the social situation was far from ideal, but it was incomparably more stable than that in Gaul as described by Gregory of Tours. Moreover a definite religious revival was set on foot by these and other monastics, which came to exercise a profound and transforming influence on the whole population. The Rev. John Ryan, S. J., in his *Irish Monasticism: Origins and Early Development*,[3] following the views of many earlier writers has indicated the nature of this movement in both countries and stressed the influence of Gildas in Ireland.

In these countries we see, as nowhere else in the West at this period, the power of monastic religion to exert an influence upon the people as a whole. The penitentials took their rise in course of this effort and must have played an important part in its success. Before its invasion

---

[2] See W. J. Rees, *Lives of the Cambro-British Saints*, pp. 97 f.; A. W. Wade-Evans, *The Life of St. David*, p. 64; J. L. G. Meissner in *History of the Church of Ireland*, ed. W. A. Phillips (1933), I, 135; and below, pp. 86, 169 ff.   [3] Pages 148 ff.

by the Celtic monks, the continent saw no such religious movement. Similar books could probably have had no success had they
appeared at that time among the turbulent and intractable Franks;
and the English were still entirely pagan.

I have elsewhere presented evidence to show that a stream of pre-
Christian Celtic religious practices ran into the Christian expression
of religion, particularly in Ireland.[4] Dr. Ryan believes that I have
"stressed unduly" the survival of paganism, and in consequence
"exaggerated the differences between the Irish and the more ancient
form of penitential discipline."[5] He does not, however, examine in
detail the evidence in the matter, and he fails to indicate what would
be a just judgment, as distinct from an undue stress, on the subject
of pagan survivals. The question is not that of a possible "relapse"
into paganism after the first organization of Christianity, but rather
of the continuity of pagan elements caught up into the Christian
piety. It is impossible here to recite the numerous references in the
Christian literature that tend to substantiate this view. But, apart
from the question of pagan survivals as a whole, the penitentials themselves proclaim their accommodation to native custom in countless
details.[6] Their authors adopted the legal customs of the people with
respect to composition, or satisfaction to the injured party or his
relatives, and admitted the redemption of penance by money payments. The penalty of exile which they frequently enjoined is another
native element. And it is not impossible that some of the more definitely religious exercises, such as fasting and nocturnal singing prescribed in the penitentials, should be related to similar practices in
the pre-Christian Celtic custom. Examination of the Brahman codes
shows in another early Indo-European society the presence of di-
rectors of conscience. The resemblance of the functions of the
"acharya," or spiritual guide, in these documents, to those of the
"anmchara," soul friend or confessor, in Ireland,[7] is so close as to
point with reasonable probability to a racial institution of great
antiquity.[8] We may then feel confident that the rise and success of

[4] McNeill, pp. 99 ff. (*Rev. celt.*, XL, 83 ff.).   [5] Ryan, *op. cit.*, p. 355.
[6] McNeill, pp. 105 ff., 120 ff. (*Rev. celt.*, XL, 89 ff., 320 ff.). In his elaborate study of the
implications of the word "Busse," J. Weisweiler has adopted my main contentions. *Busse*
(Halle, 1930), pp. 253 ff.
[7] The word used in Wales was "beriglour" or "periglour." Neither the Irish nor the
Welsh term appears to be of Latin origin.
[8] McNeill, pp. 115 ff. (*Rev. celt.*, XL, 99 ff.). I note, however, that R. Pettazzoni holds
that the practice of confession of sins "did not belong originally to the Indo-European

the penitentials as a basis of discipline was aided by the accommodations they made to pre-Christian elements in the life of the Goidels, or Irish Scots, and of their close relatives, the Britons of Wales.[9]

The early books became the models for a series of imitators in Ireland, England, and the Continental lands. Investigators of the problems of date and authorship have not yet enabled us to speak with assurance of the origin of many of the documents. In fact, it must be confessed that it is still impossible to offer any more than a high degree of probability for the authorship of any of them prior to the work of Regino of Prüm, ca. 900; and his book on ecclesiastical discipline, while it contains penitential materials, is not a penitential. But while certainty in detail is not reached, in many cases the limits of possibility with respect to date, provenance, and authorship, can be narrowly drawn. As the documents arrange themselves in a series, we can discern with some degree of clarity the spread of the use of penitentials throughout Western Christendom. Data furnished in the introductions to the several documents below indicate that they were in use in Frankish lands by the late sixth century, in England in the late seventh century, in Italy apparently in the late eighth century, and among the Spanish Visigoths about the beginning of the ninth.[10]

In England the ancient public penance was never established, and Theodore of Tarsus, the chief organizer of the English Church, adopted the essentials of the Celtic discipline. On the Continent there was a memory of the ancient penance: it was often advocated but rarely performed. After the revival of penance in its new form, under the influence of Celtic missionaries, had well begun, ecclesiastical feeling was aroused against it. Various utterances of councils and persons show the attempt to suppress the penitentials, and, in combatting them, to revive the public system of penance on the basis of the canons of the ancient councils. By the opening of the ninth century, under the influence of the Carolingian revival, scholars and bishops were becoming more conscious of the Church's earlier traditions, usages and documents than they had been in the previous generation. The penitentials were now, however, coming into extensive use by priests who felt in their ministrations the need of some

element" even where Indo-Europeans are found practicing it in antiquity. "Confession of Sins in the Classics," *Harvard Theological Review*, XXX (1937), 1–14.

[9] There was also a strong Goidelic element in South Wales.

[10] See below, pp. 249 ff., 179 ff., 429 f., 285 ff.

convenient book of reference. Possession of a penitential rendered a priest comparatively independent of his bishop in the administration of penance. The books, however, carried no authority except such as might attach to the names of their authors or alleged authors. They were in disagreement in many details. The compositions and commutations which they sanctioned were already leading to grave abuses. For these reasons it is not surprising that episcopal opinion was marshaled against the penitentials. The synod of Chalon-sur-Saône in 813 wrathfully denounced the "libelli called penitentials, of which the errors are certain, the authors uncertain"; and that of Paris in 829 ordered the bishops to seek out these "booklets written against canonical authority" and give them to the flames, "that through them unskilled priests may no longer deceive men."[11]

The penitentials could not be thus summarily suppressed. Their use made possible the general spread of the discipline, while the bishops had nothing practicable to offer in their place. The demand for canonical penance was idle: as a working system the public discipline could hardly have been imposed on the Germanic peoples. It still existed in lifeless texts, but was rarely reverted to in practice.[12]

Raban Maur, abbot of Fulda and later archbishop of Mainz, in his *Poenitentium liber*[13] (*ca.* 842) and in other works, lent his learning to the episcopal cause; but his treatise is of too general a nature to compete with the penitentials as a handbook for the guidance of confessors. But already the solution of the conflict was at hand; it was to consist in the adoption by the bishops of the methods and materials of the penitentials, with such modifications as would bring them into superficial agreement with the older discipline. This is the significance of the *Pseudo-Roman Penitential* published by Halitgar of Cambrai and not improbably compiled by him, *ca.* 830.[14] To this document are attached certain liturgical elements, some of which are derived from the *Gelasian Sacramentary*, in which they were applied to the old public discipline. In point of fact, however, this

[11] Mansi, XIV, 102, 559.
[12] "It would be a mistake to suppose that because in a time of controversy this canonical penance was continually appealed to as the true remedy for the authorized practice, it was therefore in actual use to any large extent."—Watkins, II, 701.
[13] Migne, *P.L.*, CXII, 1397–1424. Cf. below, p. 179.
[14] See below, pp. 295 ff. It has been said that "what the bishops wanted was not the disappearance of these manuals, but their perfect orthodoxy."—Fournier and Le Bras, I, 112. In the view of these authors this end seemed now to have been attained, but the root of the disorder remained.

penitential put forth with the claim of Roman authority, gave fresh sanction to the quantity of insular materials which it contains.

DISTINCTIVE CHARACTER OF THE NEW PENANCE

According to the penitentials penance is to be administered privately at every stage; confession is to be made in secret to a qualified person, who is regularly, of course, a priest. Confession in the Eastern Church had often been made to monks whose asceticism commended them to penitents.[15] In Ireland this feature can also be detected in certain references. Even ascetic women apparently acted as confessors. Thus in the first life of St. Brendan this sixth century saint goes for confession to St. Ita of Cluain Credill, a virgin teacher who seems to have exercised the confessional.[16] Columban, too, in his youth obtained the spiritual advice of a saintly woman.[17] But the *Penitential of Columban* enjoins confession "to a priest"; and this is the usual language. The stress laid upon confession in the penitentials is shown by the detailed exactness required in making it. When once the hierarchy began to patronize and imitate the books, if not earlier, they were regarded as solely for the use of priests.

Confession was apparently made under seal of secrecy. B. Kurtschied finds no distinct evidence for the seal of confession either in the decisions of councils or in penitentials earlier than the ninth century.[18] But in medieval Ireland to disclose the information given in confession was one of four grave offenses for which there could be no penance.[19] We may probably assume that secrecy of confession was practiced under the system of the penitentials, and that its violation was regarded as, at least, irregular.

The acts of satisfaction according to the penitentials were ordinarily private, though not always necessarily secret. Finnian, it is

[15]This is stressed in A. Tetaert, *La Confession aux laïques dans l'église latine depuis de viii° jusqu'au xiv° siècle*, pp. vii ff., following K. Holl's *Enthusiasmus und Bussgewalt beim griechischen Mönchtum* (1898) and J. Hörmann's *Untersuchungen zur griechischen Laienbeichte* (1913). [16] C. Plummer, *Vitae sanctorum Hiberniae*, I, 137.

[17] Jonas, *Life of St. Columban*, 8. Cf. McNeill, p. 119 (*Rev. celt.*, XL, 103).

[18] *Das Beichtsiegel in seiner geschichtlichen Entwicklung*, p. 32; English edition, *History of the Seal of Confession* (1927), p. 57.

[19] W. Reeves, *The Culdees of the British Isles*, p. 91 (Rule of the Culdees, ninth (?) century); W. Stokes, ed., *Tripartite Life of St. Patrick*, I, clxiv. The *Leabhar Breac*, or *Speckled Book*, from which this rule is taken is a late compilation, but it is recognized as exhibiting ancient usages, and has been called by G. F. Stokes "the most valuable repertory now remaining of ancient Irish ecclesiastical affairs."—*Ireland and the Anglo-Norman Church*, p. 372.

true, clearly authorizes secret penance, and his language suggests the intention that it should normally be secret;[20] but the nature of many of the penalties precluded the possibility of complete secrecy in their performance. Penance was, however, now in general wholly private in the sense of being dissociated from the assembled church. There was no public exomologesis and no corporate knowledge of the matter on the part of the congregation; and if, as was sometimes the case, the penance involved excommunication, reconciliation was privately accorded during, or at the close of, the period of discipline.

Before the reactionary council of Toledo forbade the iteration of penance (589)—though probably the fact was unknown to the bishops present in that council—a number of penitential books had been written and put to use. They assert the principle, with scant courtesy to the Church fathers, that penance may take place whenever there are sins to be repented. The penance of the penitentials is available as often as it is sought. It is designed as the habitually repeated practice of all the faithful, not as the resort of penitents who had been exceptionally wicked. The saying: "Anyone without a soul-friend (anmchara) is like a body without a head" was attributed to St. Brigid and also to St. Comgall, Columban's teacher at Bangor.[21] Whatever its origin, this Old Irish proverb suggests the assumption that confession and penance were normal for all Christians. They became universally obligatory in the West in a decision of the Lateran council of 1215. The Lateran decree on penance requires confession to a priest followed by faithfully performed penance at least once a year and enjoins the priest, on pain of deposition and perpetual penance, not to reveal confession by word or sign. This decision means essentially that the Celtic penance had become, with modifications, the typical penance of medieval Europe.

It should, of course, be understood that the public performance of penance was never suppressed, and that it was occasionally practiced in the Middle Ages. The ecclesiastical opponents of the penitentials sought in vain to restore it as the dominant system, and liturgical documents conveying fragments of the early tradition, such as the *Gelasian Sacramentary*,[22] contained provision for public penance. The exercise of public penance was largely associated with

---

[20] *Penitential of Finnian*, 10. See below, p. 89.
[21] W. Stokes, *The Martyrology of Œngus*, pp. 65, 183; Plummer, *Vitae sanctorum Hiberniae*, I, cxvi.   [22] See below, p. 300, n. 27.

Lent, and the practice of excluding penitents from the church on Ash Wednesday and readmitting them on Maundy Thursday is widely attested.[23] This lenten penance is distinguished from the old public penance by Robert of Flamesbury (*ca.* 1207-12) who defines it as that penance which is performed at the beginning of the fast, called "solemn" because the penitents are cast out of the church "with solemnity, in ashes and sackcloth."[24] "Solemn penance" seems to have been increasingly prominent in the late Middle Ages. It could easily be associated with the Lateran requirement of annual penance. According to H. G. Feasy, it affected Reformation discipline, Anglican and Presbyterian. "The solemn ejection of penitents took place on Ash Wednesday, and is the 'godly discipline' of solemn and public penance which the compilers of the *Book of Common Prayer* were of opinion ought to be restored. It was vigorously enforced by the Presbyterians during their short term of ascendancy in the seventeenth century and is still in use in the ecclesiastical courts in the case of slander."[25] The Council of Trent enjoins "confession secretly to the priest alone," while it refers to public confession as not forbidden by Christ and yet "not commanded by a divine precept."[26]

CURIOUS AND EXTREME PENALTIES

The penalties imposed in the penitentials are numerous and varied. The prevalence of elements from the common monastic discipline is striking, and the extreme and fantastic forms sometimes assumed by early monastic asceticism are frequently observable. Prayers and outcries to God were encouraged in the earlier discipline: in the penitentials these expressions of repentance are accompanied and in a measure replaced by a series of ascetic acts.

When the penitentials were written, the Psalter was the chief liturgy of penitents; and psalmody is a very frequent element in the satisfactions they enjoin. Individual psalms or portions, psalm-se-

[23] Besides the principal historians of penance, see H. J. Feasy, *Ancient English Holy Week Ceremonial*, pp. 94 ff.   [24] See below, p. 353.

[25] *Ancient Holy Week Ceremonial*, p. 101. It is probable, however, that the Presbyterians were really seeking a return to the ancient public discipline: in point of fact they did not celebrate Ash Wednesday or Lent. In the Church of Scotland the *Form of Public Repentance*, 1567, enjoined a procedure modeled on that of the early Church, the deciding authority being the kirk-session. Cf. I. M. Clark, *A History of Church Discipline in Scotland*, pp. 150 f.

[26] Cf. H. L. Geddes and H. Thurston, *The Catholic Church and Confession*, p. 62, and below, p. 414.

quences based on the monastic "cursus," and more exacting exercises in psalmody, sometimes involving the repeated singing of the whole psalter, are commonplace requirements in these handbooks. The *Beati* (Ps. 118, in A.V. 119) is a favorite assignment, probably on account of its extraordinary length. There is a striking resemblance between this element in Irish penance and the penitential singing of sacred hymns in ancient India as prescribed in the Brahman codes,[27] and it is possible that monastic usage paralleled in this respect a pre-Christian Irish custom. So common was this exercise of psalmody in penance that it may go far to explain the "laus perennis," or perpetual praise, which was a notable feature of some continental Irish monasteries.[28]

Fasting is, of course, the most common of all ascetic practices, and most of the penalties here assigned include it in some form. As a penitential exercise it ranged from the reduction of the amount of food or the omission of a meal, to protracted and trying abstinence or the prohibition of all food except bread and water over long periods of time. Often, however, the restrictions of diet are complicated, stress being laid on abstinence from meat, butter, and other nutritive delicacies, and a measured ration of dry biscuit being prescribed. Wine, beer, and mead are often excluded or allowed only in small quantities. While water is as a rule the only liquid permitted to penitents, milk, buttermilk, and whey are occasionally prescribed.

An interesting but not quite unambiguous expression frequently met with in the earlier penitentials is *superpositio*,[29] here rendered "a special fast." It seems generally to refer to the extension of a fast, but its nature and duration are probably not the same in all contexts. In the strict and original sense it was apparently a Saturday fast, and L. Gougaud finds it continued or revived in a fast practiced in Ireland at the present time in preparation for the Sunday communion.[30] The explanation given in the ninth-century *Customs of Tallaght*, "half-ration and half-fast,"[31] may represent a late modification of what had once been a complete fast of a whole day.[32]

Penitential fasting among the Celts was sometimes severe; and we read of a "gathering of the saints of Ireland" to take counsel to-

[27] McNeill, p. 137 (*Rev. celt.*, XL, 337). [28] McNeill, p. 140 (*Rev. celt.*, XL, 340).
[29] See below, p. 120, n. 29.
[30] *Dévotions et pratiques ascétiques du moyen âge*, p. 146. [31] See below, p. 423.
[32] Gougaud, *loc. cit.*, thinks it derived from a fast which among the Greeks extended to two, three, or even four days.

gether because "they were grieved that penitents died on bread and water in the days of the elders who lived before them. Then they fasted against God for this"; whereupon an angel appeared to explain that on account of sin the fruits of the earth were no longer nourishing as in former days when water had been as sustaining to the body as milk was then, and that they should "mix meal with butter to make gruel," to save the lives of penitents. Three kinds of gruel were invented, and these were given to penitents of different degrees of sinfulness.[33]

There is, I believe, no other evidence that penitents died under the treatment; but no doubt some persons were physically unable to undergo the fasts prescribed, and this may partly account for the great variety of alternative penances by which protracted and oft-repeated fasts could be avoided. Short and severe austerities were substituted, in which parts of the offending body other than the stomach were made to share in the agonies of expiation. The more fantastic and exacting of the practices authorized in the penitentials are usually found in the "arrea," or substitute penalties, designed to shorten the period of discipline.

In this class may be mentioned various kinds of vigils accompanied by fatiguing postures and means of ensuring bodily discomfort or mental distress to prevent sleep. Thus in the Old Irish *Table of Commutations* we have reference to sleeping in water, on nettles, on nutshells, with a corpse in a grave, in a cold church, and in a secret chamber. Apparently "sleeping" means only lying down, as the penitent was to be engaged the while in "performing vigil and praying without ceasing."[34] Remaining all night in water was occasionally practiced as a voluntary austerity by monks,[35] and a variety of sleep-preventing devices were used among the early Eastern ascetics.

The cross-vigil was a practice requiring extraordinary concentration and in this respect resembling the methods of Hindu asceticism as it is still practiced. In the Old Irish document just cited we have frequent reference to it, and it appears in some of the other documents. The Irish penitent was required to stand with his arms extended, his body thus taking the form of a cross, while singing the

[33] See below p. 424; and on fasting against God, McNeill, pp. 130 ff. (*Rev. celt.*, XL, 330 ff.).
[34] See below, p. 144.
[35] Cf. Gougaud's chapter on ascetic immersion, *op. cit.*, pp. 155 ff.

Beati (176 verses in modern Bibles) not once only, but two, four, or even seven times.[36]

Other postures and gestures were frequently adopted. A vigil with psalmody or the recitation of the Lord's Prayer was sometimes performed by the penitent standing with the hands extended upward, a common attitude in prayer in antiquity. The body might be bent and the arms extended—a position one might suppose peculiarly difficult to retain. Numerous combinations of genuflexions and bowings with psalmody and prayers are indicated. A peculiar penance cited in the Bede materials and in Burchard's *Corrector* is the "palmatae," here translated "palm thumpings," as the word probably refers to the act of beating the open palms of the hands on the ground or pavement,[37] and not, as has been supposed by some, to strokes of the rod on the palms.

The word "disciplina" in the Middle Ages usually referred to the use of the rod or lash, and it was employed in that sense by Augustine.[38] Flagellation plays a prominent rôle in certain penitentials—chiefly in the Irish documents. One writer prescribes "one hundred lively blows." Another authorizes "one hundred blows with a thong," and elsewhere "seven hundred with a lash." In a commutation the penitent is offered "seven hundred honest blows seven times." Columban was a great advocate of flogging: he prescribes, for a monk who has conversed alone with a woman, two hundred strokes.[39]

Flagellation was sometimes self-inflicted. This may be inferred from the fact that at Tallaght washing the hands after applying the scourge was required of the penitent himself.[40] It does not appear, however, that lay penitents, or even in ordinary cases monks, were required by the penitentials to apply the scourge to their own backs. Flagellation became in later times a favorite method of subduing the flesh, and self-flagellation was practiced by leading ascetics from Peter Damian to Ignatius Loyola.

The monastic vow was sometimes required in satisfaction for a crime, though usually with an alternative. In our documents clerical

---

[36] "Seven Beati in honest cross-vigil," says the Old Irish *Table of Commutations*, 26. See below, p. 146. Among the German peoples maintaining the gesture of the cross was sometimes used as an ordeal to determine guilt. See F. Helbing and M. Bauer, *Die Tortur: Geschichte der Folter in Kriminalverfahren* (1926), p. 31.

[37] So Du Cange concludes, and cf. Poschmann II, p. 148. See below, pp. 231, 236, 344.

[38] Cf. Gougaud, *op. cit.*, pp. 175 ff.

[39] See below, pp. 145, 163, 260–65.   [40] See below, p. 423.

evildoers are often sentenced to be deprived of their rank. Either a cleric or a layman may be compelled to enter servitude to make amends to relatives of one whom he has slain. In one text it is ordered that upon repentance an unfaithful wife is to become "as a slave" to her husband. A not infrequent act of satisfaction is the redemption or the emancipation of a slave: as an alternative the value of a slave may be given to the poor. The giving of alms is often included with other satisfactions, and the *Penitential of Columban* joins with it the giving of a feast to the priest who has guided the penitent.[41]

For the greater offenses, especially for homicide, the sentence of exile is often prescribed. Sometimes this is referred to as "pilgrimage," and probably in many instances the Irish "peregrini," who often played a disturbing rôle in the Church on the continent, were penitents sent away on pilgrimage. Irish lives of saints and popular tales make numerous references to penitential pilgrimages. The penalty was probably rooted in the Celtic penal custom of exile noted by classical writers.[42] The *Penitential of Columban* in prescribing perpetual exile likens the penitent to Cain who became "a vagabond and a fugitive upon the earth"; while the *Synod of North Britain* consigns the penitent to "a monastery in another country," and Cummean places him "in the yoke of exile under another abbot."[43] Possibly these expressions indicate two forms which the penalty of exile might take. Certainly hagiographical literature supports the view that some monks and clerics sent on pilgrimage exercised much freedom of travel. Deprivation of weapons is sometimes specified in connection with exile.

A modified exile may be recognized in the practice of a temporary exclusion from the monastery or the church while the penitent remained under surveillance of the local authorities or of his confessor. The monastery of Iona was provided with a nearby penal colony to which recalcitrants were sent: Reeves has shown that this was on the neighboring island of Tiree.[44] Such provision for penitential separation under guidance may have been common. Isolation for considerable periods was sometimes required. An offender might be sentenced to "live secluded seven days" or to spend three days and nights alone "in a dark house." As a cure for dejection a monk is

---

[41] See below, p. 255.   [42] Cf. McNeill, pp. 134 ff. (*Rev. celt.*, XL, 334 ff.).
[43] See below, pp. 102, 170, 252.
[44] W. Reeves, *Life of St. Columba* (2d ed., 1874), pp. 303 ff.

to "do penance in another place on bread and water," until he can be joyful.[45]

Whereas crimes against the clergy are penalized in the penitentials with special severity, so also are offenses committed by them. Insofar as fear of penalty is a deterrent to crime the clergy were protected from the violence of others and at the same time induced to avoid wickedness themselves. Thus according to a Welsh document, while a layman apparently does two years penance for murder, the term for a monk is three years.[46] It is elsewhere stated that the penalty for a criminal bishop is to be left to the decision of the king. A cleric who committed murder might, according to another decision, be subject no less than a layman to life-long slavery to the slain man's relatives, following a term of exile, which for the cleric was ten years, whereas for a layman it was three.[47]

LEGAL CUSTOMS

The society, whether Celtic or Germanic, in which the penitentials were used, followed many primitive customs in the administration of justice which are reflected in the books. The customs referred to are survivals of primitivity and are common to Celts and Germans of the period of the penitentials, although absent from Roman law in its developed stage. Prominent among these usages is composition, or payment to relatives in satisfaction for murder or injury. In itself composition marks an advance on the still more primitive customs of retaliation and revenge, reversion to which was frequent in the early Middle Ages. The penitentials promoted the substitution of pecuniary satisfactions for revenge, thus coming to the aid of the progressive movement in customary law. The pattern of composition chiefly exhibited in them is Irish; even the documents prepared for use on Germanic soil sometimes employ the language of the earlier Irish works. But the Welsh and Germanic customs and codes were not widely dissimilar from the Irish in this respect, and the principle involved was everywhere understood.

To penitents who possessed property or could obtain pecuniary aid from relatives, the payment of a fine, even of a heavy one, was probably in most cases preferable to protracted courses of fasting

---

[45] See below, pp. 168.
[46] *Synod of the Grove of Victory*, canons 2 and 9. See below, pp. 171 f.
[47] See below, pp. 252, 254.

and psalmody. In the document known as the *Irish Canons*, as in the national codes, the penalty is sometimes stated purely in terms of composition;[48] but in the penitentials proper a frequent method is to indicate a combined penalty of payments and austerities. In practice this may have been somewhat elastically operated, on the principle stated in the *Old Irish Penitential:* "If the offender can pay fines his penance is less in proportion."[49] In other cases, the elements are not combined but offered to the penitent as alternatives.

The method of composition was ingeniously used to provide protection and insurance against violence, and for this purpose payments were graded according to the rank of the person slain or injured. So in our documents murder of or injury to a bishop is penalized in accordance with his rank, and the other clerical ranks are given proportional protection.[50] The scale of severer penalties for clerics than for laymen has already been indicated. Readers of the secular codes of the period will be particularly struck by the detail with which composition is indicated for all kinds of injuries to the body in its various parts, as well as for injuries to animals. We see numerous interesting reflections of these legal refinements in the penitentials; for instance, in case of injury Cummean requires payment not only of the doctor's bill but also of "the price" of a scar or blemish. In the *Irish Canons* the value of a female slave is demanded in compensation to a bishop, prince, or scholar for a scar which causes embarrassment in public for three years; and, apparently, for hairs plucked from a bishop's head hairs in the ratio of twelve to one are to be plucked from the head of his assailant. Crucifixion and maiming are penalties for which commutations are indicated;[51] such provisions mark a humanizing tendency.

The requirement of twofold or fourfold restitution for theft or damage appears in a number of the documents. It should perhaps be attributed to the influence of the Book of Exodus. It is not improbable that the acts of restitution prescribed in Exodus 21 and 22 reinforced the tendency of native law and aided in the establishment of the principle of composition in penitential practice.

Composition was also involved in the customs regarding marriage, and here again we observe a characteristic reinforcement of a prin-

---

[48] See below, pp. 124 f.   [49] See below, p. 166.
[50] For particulars see McNeill, pp. 124 ff. (*Rev. celt.*, XL, 324 ff.), and below, p. 405. Also cf. T. P. Oakley, "Commutations and Redemptions of Penance," *Catholic Historical Review*, XVIII (1932), 341–51.   [51] See below, pp. 124 f.

ciple of customary law. The bride price, called in Irish "tinol" or "tinscra," in Welsh "agueddy," and in our Latin documents "dos," was a payment made by the bridegroom to the bride's parents. The *Book of David* requires the payment of the "dos" in cases of seduction or rape in addition to a year's penance. Columban's *Penitential* makes the penance two years and states that the "pretium" (price) of the girl's humiliation is to be paid to the parents. On the other hand Finnian evades the legal custom and demands "alms" instead, while Theodore's work, shaped on English soil, drops even this substitute.[52]

In the period of the development of the penitentials the secular laws were being codified in the Celtic and Germanic lands. While the penitentials reaffirmed those elements in the legal inheritance of the people which particularly tended to security and justice, the secular codes on their part recognized the obligatory character of the penitential discipline and lent it substantial support. It is probably a matter of high historical importance that the secular and ecclesiastical disciplines effectively supplemented each other. This subject has been thoroughly explored by T. P. Oakley with reference to England.[53] Some illustrations of the legal recognition of penitential provisions with other relevant material from the laws of the Irish, Welsh, English, Franks, and Visigoths, are furnished in Chapter VIII below.

Closely related to composition is the commutation of penalties, especially when this took the form of the substitution of fines for austerities. In the Irish sources the principle, noted by H. d'Arbois de Jubainville,[54] of the equivalence of a year of penance and the value of a female slave, is traceable in several documents.[55] The customs of the age favored the acceptance of fines in lieu of penalties affecting the body; and modern society retains the alternative. If fines were payable to relatives the ecclesiastics might turn the method of commutation to the advantage of themselves or the Church; and a tendency to secure to the Church payments in composition is apparent.[56] The *Book of Llandaff* records that King Artmail of Gwent did pen-

---

[52] Cf. McNeill, p. 127 (*Rev. celt.*, XL, 327), and below, pp. 94, 184 f.

[53] *English Penitential Discipline and Anglo-Saxon Law in Their Joint Influence.* Chap. v, "The Anglo-Saxon Laws and Their Provisions on Penance," is of special value at this point. Dr. Oakley's article "The Coöperation of Medieval Penance and Secular Law," *Speculum*, VII (1932), 515–24, contains references to other areas.

[54] *Rev. celt.*, VIII (1887), 160.   [55] Cf. McNeill, p. 128 (*Rev. celt.*, XL, 328).

[56] J. W. Willis Bund concludes that "the Church accepted the old heathen penalty for murder and the proceeds went to form part of the endowment of the Church."—*Celtic Church in Wales*, p. 367.

ance for fratricide by deeding land to the Church."[57] Many of the Church's medieval possessions were acquired as gifts made expressly, in similar circumstances, for the good of the donor's soul.

The ordeal, or appeal to the tribunal of a deity, is a very ancient method of adjudging cases in which the evidence conflicts. It is rarely sanctioned in the penitentials, but the *Synod of North Britain* commands two who persistently accuse each other to be "put to the proof of fire and left to the judgment of God"; and the passage is copied in Cummean. The *Law of Adamnan* authorizes capital punishment by lot.[58] Scarcely less objectionable from the modern point of view is the method of compurgation, of which we have illustration in the *Welsh Canons.*[59] As generally practiced, compurgation was attestation on oath by a sufficient number of his relatives that the accused was innocent. The system encouraged perjury and amounted as evidence to no more than a demonstration of the good will of his own clan toward the accused. Perjury is an offense to which frequent reference is made in records of the period; possibly the severe penalties meted out for it in the penitentials had a deterrent effect on this evil.

FOLK-PAGANISM AND ITS REPRESSION[60]

We have seen that the authors of the penitentials made judicious adjustments to the traditional system of customary law and apparently incorporated in their works other elements of pre-Christian origin. But the attitude of Christianity to pagan supernaturalism had always been, generally speaking, one of hostility. In the early stages, its own supernaturalism, as compared with that of paganism everywhere, was marked by extraordinary simplification. It needed no magic but the miraculous power of Christ, no divination but the revealed teaching of the inspired writings or the promptings of the Holy Spirit. Christians recruited from paganism denounced the religion of their fathers for its confused variety of spiritual beings, and in Christian parlance the word "demon" ceased to have a neutral and came to have only a sinister meaning.

The cults which Christianity combatted in the Roman Empire constituted not one consolidated paganism but a diversified miscel-

---

[57] *Liber Landavensis,* ed. J. G. Evans, Oxford, 1893, pp. 237, 244 f.
[58] See below, pp. 136, 141.
[59] See below, pp. 374, 378, and Oakley, *op. cit.,* pp. 155 ff., 174 ff.
[60] For a fuller treatment of this subject see my article, "Folk-paganism in the Penitentials," *Journal of Religion,* XIII (1933), 450–66.

lany of religions at various stages of development and decay. Some of these were chiefly cultivated by lowly folk in obscure and rude worship by trees or springs or rustic sanctuaries. It was with reference to these that the word "paganism" was first used in its now historic sense. This "religion of rustics" ("paganorum") was condemned by Valentinian I in 368.

Christianity at that period launched, under the aegis of the Empire, a war of extermination on the old religions, as a result of which organized paganism was in course of time virtually crushed. It was, however, rather the superstructure than the foundation of paganism that was destroyed. Elemental paganism survived in the loyalties, rites, customs, and beliefs of the country folk, and it sturdily withstood the pressure of Church and State. Old fertility rites, associated with rural prosperity, were still honored; sacred wells, groves, and stones were still the scenes of strange worship; and such pagan practices as weather magic, healing magic, death-dealing magic, sex magic, divination in many forms, sorcery, necromancy, incantations at funerals, as well as the mirth and ceremonial of some of the old pagan festal seasons, were tenaciously maintained against all authority.

While Gallo-Roman paganism was proscribed and deteriorating the whole scene was changed by the Germanic invasions. In wide areas the people were uprooted and scattered, sadly deserting their resorts of worship. But at the same time the nominally Christian Germans contributed of their own ancestral religion; and the mingling of conquerors and conquered in Gaul brought a pooling of their resources of folk paganism. On the Eastern frontier of the Frankish Empire the old religion of the Saxons, Thuringians, and Bavarians was driven to cover, as was Roman paganism at an earlier stage, but it remained in household use.

Imperial laws, conciliar decisions, and the vigorous denunciations of ecclesiastical preachers, failed through long generations to extinguish the proscribed pagan practices. The writers of the penitential books took up the crusade for the suppression of these ancestral superstitions. Their anxious attention to the subject often led them to enlarge upon it in such a way as to supply historically priceless material on medieval pagan survivals. This is true of the documents written on Irish soil, and especially of some of those of continental origin. In particular Burchard's *Corrector* is a mine of primitive Ger-

manic folklore and pagan supernaturalism. Any adequate review of
the phenomena under this head would require many pages. All that
can be attempted here is to point to a small portion of the evidence
which the texts supply.

The documents contain certain references to pagans as "gentiles,"
but the word often obviously means merely "unbaptized persons";
and such persons may have postponed baptism for reasons other than
their belief in paganism. The *First Synod of St. Patrick* penalizes the
act of becoming surety for a "gentilis homo" and Bury takes this as
evidence that the document belongs to a period in which there were
still non-Christians in Ireland.[61] In general, however, the penitentials
are concerned with the paganism of nominally Christian people. Of
this the *Second Synod of Patrick* furnishes an admirable illustration,
when, in an enlightened spirit, it anathematizes those Christians who
believe in vampires and witches. The numerous references to wizards,
or "magi," in the Irish documents probably indicate the survival of
druid practices within the ranks of those amenable to the Christian
discipline. In these documents, too, such practices as the eating of
horse flesh and the drinking of the blood or urine of animals or men,
practices which in paganism had magical associations, are penalized.
The careful regulations with regard to clean and unclean foods combine scriptural prohibitions with taboos of local acceptance. The *Old
Irish Penitential* cites the making of a bogey as a magical means of
causing death. This and other Irish documents condemn the keening dirge, familiar in Ireland to the present day despite this early
ecclesiastical condemnation. So ineradicable was this custom among
the Irish that it was expedient to provide a penalty for a nun "who
becomes excited and shouts with utterances of this sort." The lamentation was of course ordinarily chanted by a woman.[62]

In a section on the worship of idols, the *Penitential of Theodore*
lists such offenses as: sacrificing to demons; placing a child on a roof
or in an oven to cure a fever; burning grains where a man has died,
for the health of the living and of the house; diabolical incantations;

[61] *Life of St. Patrick*, pp. 167, 245.
[62] See below, pp. 121, 154, 167. For the suggestion of a connection between the long-
protracted requiem in the Irish Church and the native custom of protracted and nocturnal
incantation over the dead, see McNeill, pp. 138 ff. (*Rev. celt.*, XL, 338 ff.). In the *Bigotian
Penitential*, keening ("bardicatio glandellae") is catalogued under the general heading
"de clamore," although in the catalogue of sins upon which this penitential is outlined
"clamor" is among the offspring of "ira" (anger). The author, however, adds the special
class of "clamor due to grief" ("clamor dolore excitatus").

auguries, divinations, and magical tricks. Numerous penitentials refer to "emissores tempestatum" (those who conjure up storms), the weather makers who are condemned in numerous church councils of the period.[63] The *Penitential of Bede* includes a section on auguries and divinations which condemns the use of the *Sortes sanctorum*, an oracular book including parts of Scripture used for supernatural guidance like the *Sortes Virgilianae;* taking a vow anywhere except in a church; placing a child on a roof or in an oven to cure fever; making a demonstration during the moon's eclipse in the belief that protection can be gained by shouting and magical arts; employing "curious jugglers and chanting diviners"; making amulets; celebrating Thursdays in honor of Thor (Jupiter), or masquerading in the skins of beasts on the Kalends of January according to pagan tradition. All these offenses occur in other penitentials written on Germanic soil, while some documents contain reference to many other superstitions of the same class.

Various classes of persons who comprise the despicable priesthood of the abhorred rites are mentioned. There is the "cariagus," or juggler; the "sortilegus," or fortune teller; the "hariolus,' or soothsayer; the "mathematicus," who takes away the minds of men by invocation of demons; and the "herbarius," or quack, who makes death-dealing concoctions of herbs. The *Pseudo-Roman Penitential* refers to those who attend festivals "in the abominable places of the pagans" and take food home from these to be eaten, and to the habit of lacerating the face with a sword or with the fingernails after the death of a relative. In Germany, as in Ireland, pagan rites survived in funeral customs, and Regino of Prüm inveighs against the diabolical songs, jests, and dances which take place at wakes. If one must sing on such occasions, says Regino, let him sing the Kyrie.[64]

The *Decretum* of Burchard of Worms, particularly the nineteenth book of this work, generally called Burchard's *Corrector*, has long been known as a rich mine for folk paganism.[65] Chapter V of the

---

[63] See below, pp. 227, 305. In Ireland the supernatural control of wind and weather was regarded as legitimate, at least for the saints, whose lives record numerous instances of the practice. [64] See below, pp. 305 f., 318 f.

[65] Jacob Grimm in his *Deutsche Mythologie*, first published in 1835, made numerous citations and included a series of extracts from Burchard in an appendix. E. Friedberg in a short semipopular essay, *Aus deutschen Bussbüchern* (1868), calls attention to the evidence on folklore in our documents and appends a selection of Burchard's canons. Some of the superstitions penalized in the *Corrector* are mentioned in the *Eighth century List of Superstitions*, appendix I, pp. 419 ff., below.

Corrector contains a series of one hundred and ninety-four paragraphs, about sixty of which have to do with superstitious beliefs
and practices. Here are condemned the practice of "sortes" (lots);
the worship of the sun, the moon, and the stars; shouting at the time
of the moon's eclipse; the employment of knots and bands made with
the use of magical formulae to save cattle from pestilence or to afflict
another's cattle with it; collecting medicinal herbs accompanied by
the chanting of formulae other than the Creed or the Lord's Prayer;
making offerings at stones or trees or crossroads.

Burchard was a rationalist, and he constantly condemns not only
the rites of paganism but also belief in their efficacy and all superstitious credulity. The widespread belief in night riding with the
queen of witches is described in a passage, borrowed by him from
Regino and ultimately derived from some other writer, in which this
alleged experience is attributed to delusions of the devil imparted in
dreams. "Who," it is reasonably asked, "does not see while sleeping
many things that he never saw while awake?"

Many curious burial customs are described in these pages. Certain
times and seasons were the occasions of pagan celebrations. German
and Romano-Gallic elements are mingled. Not only do we see the
village masquerade in the hides of cattle at the Kalends of January,
a custom denounced by Caesarius of Arles five centuries earlier, but
a number of good-luck household customs of the New Year. The
rustic who covets his neighbor's grain can bribe the goblins to trans-
port it to his own bins, by placing in his granary tiny bows and arrows for these industrious but playful sprites to amuse themselves
with. Various other supernatural beings inhabit the imagination and
command a ritual in their honor. Some misguided folk believe that
the three Fates determine the life of a child and may transform it
into a werewolf, or that there are wood nymphs who make ardent
but inconstant love to men. The attribution of supernatural functions
to birds and animals frequently occurs. Good or ill luck on a journey
is read in the flight of crows or owls. There are people who will not
stir out at night till the cock crows to banish the evil spirits.

Burchard gives the impression that women are specially prone to
belief in superstitions, and the section which he devotes to questions
for women is mainly concerned with these strange rites and beliefs.
The corpse of an unbaptized child is transfixed by a stake driven into
the earth to prevent its rising to harm the living; or more benignly,

⤨ the infant is buried with the sacred wafer in one hand and the sacred wine in the other. There are some extraordinary methods of sex magic. In case of marital incompatibility the husband may be done ⤨ to death by the use of bread made of wheat that had been caught in honey smeared on the wife's naked body. Burchard also describes a pretty and obviously primitive village ceremony for the relief of drought: the description is so perfect in detail that we suspect the stern bishop of a fine intellectual interest in the charming drama.

Clauses on superstition form a constituent part of most of the later penitentials of which selections are here given and frequently repeat the earlier material. Among other offenses in this class, however, the *Canons of Astesanus*, belonging apparently to the early fourteenth century, and Borromeo's *Penitential* in the sixteenth, condemn the use of the astrolabe for purposes of prognostication. This apparatus had been introduced in the West through the Spanish Moslems, possibly by Gerbert; it is described in various treatises of the eleventh century as an instrument of astrology.[66]

The penitentials add to the evidence supplied from other sources for the fact that in popular belief and custom medieval Christianity was intermingled with a large residuum of paganism. They also testify to the zeal of their authors to suppress these irrational and often debasing elements in the folk religion. In such regulations as those providing for the substitution of the Kyrie for funeral songs, or of the Creed or the Lord's Prayer for pagan formulae in magic, and in the requirement that vows be taken not in pagan shrines but in churches only, we may trace the Church's effort to get rid of alien and rival cults even at the cost of compromise with them. But in general the attitude on this question taken by the writers of penitentials is one of uncompromising puritanism and abhorrence of idolatry. How far their zeal was rewarded by success must not be judged alone by the prevalence in later ages of the practices they denounced. Probably the discipline induced many individuals to abandon finally their ancestral worship. But it is certain that folk paganism continued to flourish, and that magic, divination, necromancy, and astrology—sometimes illumined by foregleams of science—attracted increasing rather than diminishing attention in the later Middle Ages.

[66] See L. Thorndike, *A History of Magic and Experimental Science*, I (1923), chap. xxx, and below, p. 365.

Medicine for Sin[67]

The prevalence in the penitentials of the conception of penance as medicine for the soul will impress the reader.[68] The phraseology of this medical analogy also appears in the penance of the ancient Church; and a strain of medical thought runs through the larger aspects of patristic theology.[69]

But it is peculiarly in the penitentials that this view is developed, with special application of the medical principle advocated by the methodist school of physicians that "contraries are cured by their contraries." Themison of Laodicea who flourished at Rome *ca.* 50 B.C. is generally regarded as the founder of this school, although the doctrine of the contraries antedates him by centuries. The methodist school attained its zenith in Soranus of Ephesus, during the first quarter of the second century of our era. Soranus worked in Rome also and is favorably referred to by Tertullian and by Augustine. His principles are chiefly known through the work of Caelius Aurelianus of Numidia, a later methodist, possibly contemporary with Cassian. The methodist principle of the contraries dominated medical practice in the late classical period and at its close had so far become an axiom that Alexander of Tralles (525–605), the greatest medical authority of the period, assents to it in these words: "The duty of a physician is to cool what is hot, to warm what is cold, to dry what is moist, and to moisten what is dry."[70]

Although most of the early church fathers, including Clement, Origen, Tertullian, and Jerome, were familiar with medical thought, it was probably mainly through Cassian, a writer much used as an authority by the framers of the early penitentials, that the principle of the contraries came to be integrated with the idea of penitential medicine in these documents. The Eastern monks not infrequently served in hospitals, and Palladius in his contemporary description of the monks of Nitria informs us that they were provided with physicians.[71] Cassian paid extensive visits to the Egyptian and other East-

[67] For a fuller treatment of this subject, see my article "Medicine for Sin as Prescribed in the Penitentials," *Church History*, I (1932), 14–26.   [68] Cf. Poschmann II, pp. 21 ff.

[69] The subject has received careful investigation by A. von Harnack in "Medicinisches aus der ältesten Kirchengeschichte," *Texte und Untersuchungen zur Geschichte der altchristlichen Literatur*, VIII (1892). See especially pp. 137 ff. Cf. also M. Neuburger, *A History of Medicine* (tr. Playfair), I, 314 ff.

[70] J. J. Walsh, *Old Time Makers of Medicine*, p. 46. Cf. Neuburger, *op. cit.*, I, 107 ff., and H. Haeser, *Lehrbuch der Geschichte der Medizin*, 3d ed., I, 321 ff.

[71] E. A. W. Budge, *The Paradise of the Holy Fathers*, I, 100.

ern monastic colonies, and some years afterward (*ca.* 420–35) wrote his *Collationes*, in which he reports the discourses of distinguished abbots and saints of the desert. In *Coll.* xix. 14, 15 (Conference of Abbot John), it is explained that the cure for anger, dejection, and other sins lies in opposing to them their opposites; and the whole treatment of sins in the works of Cassian seems largely in accord with this precept.

A century after Cassian the Irish abbot Finnian in his penitential insists on the principle that in penance contraries are to be cured by their contraries. On this principle he says faults must be replaced by virtues; "and patience must arise for wrathfulness; kindliness . . . for envy; for detraction, restraint of heart and tongue; for dejection, spiritual joy; for greed, liberality."[72]

The *Penitential of Columban* shows the employment, though without the enunciation, of the same principle. "The talkative person is to be sentenced to silence; the disturber to gentleness; the gluttonous to fasting; the sleepy fellow to watchfulness." The *Penitential of Cummean* professes at the outset to prescribe "the health-giving medicine of souls." Having quoted a passage from Caesarius of Arles, based upon one which Cassian has enlarged from Origen, Cummean adds, "And so they [the fathers] determine that the eight principal vices contrary to human salvation shall be healed by these eight contrary remedies. For it is an old proverb: 'contraries are cured by their contraries' (contraria contrariis sanantur)." He applies his penitential medicine in detail: for example, "The idler shall be taxed with an extraordinary work, and the slothful with a lengthened vigil."[73] Similar materials will be found in many other documents.

The objective held in view with regard to this healing ministry of penance seems to have been in large degree the reconstruction of personality. The confessor was indeed taught to regard himself as a minister of supernatural grace; but not less prominent is the thought of the processes of penance as constituting a treatment in itself effective toward the recovery of the health that has been lost through sin. Lacking the sensitive humanitarianism generally professed and sometimes practiced today, the authors of these handbooks nevertheless had a sympathetic knowledge of human nature and a desire to deliver

---

[72] See below, pp. 92 f., 251 f. The principle, "contraria contrariis sanantur," is stated and illustrated by St. Pirmin in his *Scarapsus* (*ca.* 724), chap. xxvi. G. Jecker, *Die Heimat des hl. Pirmin des Apostels der Alamannen* (1927), p. 59. "Beiträge zur Geschichte des alten Mönchtums," XIII. [73] See below, pp. 100, 108.

men and women from the mental obsessions and social maladjust-
ments caused by their misdeeds. While in general the documents have
the appearance of exact schedules of equivalents between crime and
punishment, frequently the confessor is reminded that penalties are
to be not so much equated with offenses as adjusted to personalities.
"Not all are to be weighed in the same balance, although they be
associated in one fault" but there must be discrimination according
to cases.[74] The physician of souls must, like the modern psychiatrist,
identify himself as far as possible with the patient. "No physician,"
says the *Pseudo-Roman Penitential*, "can treat the wounds of the sick
unless he familiarizes himself with their foulness (nisi foetoribus
particeps fuerit)." The seemingly inhuman severity of some penalties
must be understood in the light of the social habits of an age in which
surgery and medicine were wholly unrefined and in which secular
penalties were still under the influence of primitive savagery. The
penitentials often reveal the considerateness of the experienced adviser of souls, wise in the lore of human nature and desiring to "minister to the mind diseased."

These handbooks offer a field of interest to the psychologist. Whatever may be found to praise or blame from the point of view of
psychotherapy, in the austerities prescribed, there can be no doubt
of the presence in them of the intention of a humane ministry. The
penitentials offer to the sinner the means of rehabilitation. He is
given guidance to the way of recovering harmonious relations with
the Church, society, and God. Freed in the process of penance from
social censure, he recovers the lost personal values of which his offenses have deprived him. He can once more function as a normal
person. Beyond the theological considerations, we see in the detailed
prescriptions the objective of an inward moral change, the setting up
of a process of character reconstruction which involves the correction
of special personal defects and the reintegration of personality.

THE INFLUENCE OF THE PENITENTIALS

That the penitentials exercised a wide influence upon church discipline and social morality can hardly be seriously denied. They furnished the basis for the practice of the confessional in the West.
Without their convenient help it is difficult to see how the local priest

[74] See below, p. 223. Gregory the Great, in his *Pastoral Care*, applies this principle in
detail to the methods of religious instruction, with no specific reference to penance.

could have carried on his task of personal guidance. Defective as they are when viewed from the standpoint of modern ideals, a sound historical judgment will ascribe to them a civilizing and humanizing rôle of no small importance.

They have been criticized severely by some writers as marked by a very unhealthy moral taint. In 1845, F. J. F. Bouvet drew from Burchard's *Corrector* shocking evidence of the evil influence of the confessional.[75] C. Plummer gives thanks, in his edition of Bede, that he is not compelled to believe that Bede had anything to do with such literature and takes occasion to say: "The penitential literature is in truth a deplorable feature of the medieval Church. Evil deeds, the imagination of which may perhaps have dimly floated through our minds in our darkest moments, are here tabulated and reduced to a system. It is hard to see how anyone could busy himself with such literature and not be the worse for it."[76] It is only fair to reply that but for these crude instruments of discipline it is very questionable whether we should have reached the stage of Victorian culture and restraint which makes it possible for Dr. Plummer to utter this verdict.

The men of that age wrote with a frankness foreign to polite letters in our time on matters connected with the functions of the body. The penitentials should be judged in this respect by the custom of the age. It should also be remembered that they are codes, comparable to the criminal codes of later times, and that such documents must perforce deal with unpleasing things. Nor is it probable that innocent souls were often injured by the suggestion to sin involved in the questionings applied as an aid to confession; for the modern habitual restraint of speech that would make such an experience injurious to many today was in all probability as lacking in ordinary conversation as it was in the penitentials.

Two criticisms of the books emerged in the period of their use. One of these has been noticed: their novelty, lack of authority, and divergence from the canonical penance of the previous age. By reason of their convenience and proved usefulness, they overcame this criticism, and it need only be mentioned here. More serious was the disapproval by moralists of the relaxing and corrupting effect of their commutations in money. Numerous illustrations both of the

[75] *De la confession et du célibat des prêtres*, pp. 195 ff.
[76] *Venerabilis Bedae opera historica*, I, cclvii f.

authorization of relaxing commutations and of protests against these are found within the present volume.[77] The extremes to which the authorization of money redemptions of penance went in some of the documents would be incredible if they were not clearly established. The vicarious penance of feudal servitors is also provided for in some penitentials and in documents of secular law. On the other hand the council of Cloveshoe (747) after prolonged discussion pronounced against the acceptance of psalm singing by substitutes in fulfillment of penitential requirements, when a certain rich man seeking reconciliation claimed that enough penance for three hundred years had been performed for him by others in singing, fasting, and alms.[78]

The problem of vicarious merit was an important one in the medieval church. The belief in the sharing of merit, arising as it did out of early and deeply-rooted ideas of the communion of saints and the solidarity of the whole fellowship, was one of the fundamental religious conceptions of the age. Secular custom likewise attested the solidarity of the tribe or clan, and the composition principle in primitive law involved a vicarious satisfaction by the relatives of the evildoer. That the same tendency would assert itself in the penitential discipline was perhaps inevitable; but it is remarkable that the writers of the books show no apprehension of moral danger and corruption in this direction. They were in fact, without realizing it, opening the door to a flood of abuses. Without violating the terms laid down by Pseudo-Cummean or by Regino the lax confessor could absolve rich and powerful penitents at no discomfort to them beyond an easy payment, and even this might be escaped if by their influence or power others could be induced to make satisfaction for them. It is no wonder that this led to grave corruption and that in later days John of Salisbury, in a vitriolic chapter on ecclesiastical abuses, protested against this dangerous trend in the administration of penance.[79]

At this point the penitentials are related to the rise of indulgences and to the abuses of the indulgence system. The word "indulgentia" in Roman law and in Christian thought meant anciently the merciful mitigation of a penalty due. In connection with the ancient penance, as Leclercq points out, "indulgence" consisted in the anticipation of

---

[77] See below, pp. 142 ff., 268 f., 319 ff.   [78] See below, pp. 394, 405, 410.
[79] *Policraticus*, VII, 21. See the edition of C. C. J. Webb, II, 194 f., or Migne, *P.L.*, CXCIX, 693.

reconciliation or restoration to communion before the completion of penance. Under the influence of the penitentials there was usually no excommunication and no reconciliation. Indulgence is now seen in the remission of penitential exercises and involves an element of compensation and commutation. "Commutations and redemptions played a considerable rôle in the Middle Ages, as the most effective causes of the debasement of tariff-penance (la pénitence tarifée); at the same time these practices greatly favored the introduction of indulgences properly so-called."[80]

"Corruptio optimi pessima." The penitentials were the work of earnest reformers of discipline, and they helped to lead our forefathers from a low and primitive to a higher stage of moral culture.[81] But they contained certain humanely-designed provisions permitting the substitution of payments for penitential austerities, which lent themselves too readily to gross abuses and sowed the seed of an evil harvest.

Penitentials continued to appear occasionally in various parts of Europe until the sixteenth century. With the exception of a some-

[80] H. Leclercq, art. "Indulgence," in Cabrol, *Dictionnaire*, VII, i, 539 f. The view that indulgences owed their origin in part to the commutation and redemption provisions of the penitentials is not affected by the discussion offered by T. P. Oakley in the article cited in n. 50. It is quite obvious, as Dr. Oakley shows in detail, that not all the penitentials contain tariffs of commutations and that in the Irish and Welsh series it is the later rather than the earlier documents that specifically authorize the practice. I should not care to say with Dr. Oakley that the authors of those documents which omit such provisions "steadfastly withstood the commuting and redeeming of penance." But even if we regard them as definitely unfavorable to the tendency, it remains true, as Dr. Oakley recognizes, that "the substitute good works of the lenient group prepared the way for indulgences."

Added in proof: In "Alleviations of Penance in the Continental Penitentials," *Speculum*, XII (1937), 488–502, Dr. Oakley endeavors to show that under the penitentials composition was rare and the discipline ordinarily "severe." He states that if a map could be drawn to illustrate the use of severe, intermediate, and lenient penitentials it would show a great preponderance of the areas colored as "severe." He admits, however, the impossibility of making such a map, qualifying this admission by the words, "in any exact sense." But since there was nothing to prevent the circulation of any type of penitential in any diocese, the very conception of such a map seems to me illusory. Even the (ineffective) condemnations of the offending booklets by the councils of 813 made no distinction between the more rigorous and the laxer documents. We have good reason to think that some of the latter (e.g., the *Pseudo-Cummean*) were among the most widely circulated of the entire series. Various penitentials of various degrees of severity and lenience may often have competed in the same diocese. It is to be fully recognized that many of the books contain no authorization of money commutations, but alleviations of penance were common enough to justify the statement just quoted from Leclercq and that of Morinus (*Commentarius*, X, 16): "Prima relaxatae poenitentiae occasio est poenitentiae canonicae redemptio."

[81] On their civilizing rôle see especially Oakley, *English Penitential Discipline*, pp. 193 ff., and Fournier and Le Bras, I, 56 ff.

what more original work by St. Charles Borromeo the later books are largely imitative of the earlier ones. The Reformation churches abandoned most of the presuppositions of the penitentials and devised their own forms of discipline.[82] In the Reformed churches penance was for a time in a considerable degree revived, with a strong element of the humiliating public discipline of antiquity. In Roman Catholicism the function of the penitentials has been assumed by other agencies, especially by the extensive literature on casuistry and the cure of souls and by the instruction in penance provided for priests in training.

[82] For the views of leading Protestant authorities on penitential discipline see J. T. McNeill, "Historical Types of Method in the Cure of Souls," *Crozer Quarterly*, XI (1934), 323–34.

The Condition of the Texts

IN THE PAST the chief interest of the students of penitentials has centered about the subject matter as a source material for the development of canon law and for religious and social conditions of the times. Certain sections were frequently quoted in the Latin; few were ever translated. The chief handicap of a translator lies in the complete lack of a well-established text. The earliest editions of many documents were printed from one manuscript only. When more than one manuscript was known and referred to, no attempt was made at careful evaluation. The text was published from whatever manuscript looked most promising; very few variants were included in the notes. Little, if any, attention was given to age, origin, or script of the codex. In fact, in old and learned works such as d'Achéry's *Spicilegium*, Mabillon's *Museum Italicum*, the *Thesaurus novus anecdotorum* of Martène and Durand, Mansi's *Sacrorum conciliorum nova collectio*, Fleming's *Collectanea sacra*, and in the early volumes of the *Monumenta Germaniae historica*, in most cases even the early numbers of manuscripts were omitted. As a consequence of this neglect a great many codices from which early printed editions have been drawn have never been identified. What is more serious, the text of the *St. Hubert Penitential* (in its complete form), the *Fleury Penitential*, and certain sections of the *Frankish Law* must depend entirely on the respective first editions, since Martène and Durand, Baluze, and Fleming failed to indicate the signature of the manuscripts they used, and neither the original nor any other codex containing these penitentials has ever been found.

The two most important published collections of penitentials are by Wasserschleben and Schmitz.[1] Wasserschleben was the first to

---

[1] F. W. H. Wasserschleben, *Die Bussordnungen der abendländischen Kirche*, Halle, 1851; H. J. Schmitz, *Die Bussbücher und die Bussdisciplin der Kirche*, Mainz, 1883, and *Die Bussbücher und das kanonische Bussverfahren*, Düsseldorf, 1898. For a discussion of editions cf. also T. P. Oakley, *English Penitential Discipline*, New York, 1923.

attempt a critical edition, in his collection of 1851. He felt keenly
the futility of reëditing without the aid of new manuscripts to illumine
"the prevailing darkness and confusion in this part of the history of
sources."[2] His search brought to light a large amount of penitential
material, and thanks to great learning and astoundingly good judgment his work is indispensable even today. His method consisted in
comparing the known manuscripts of a given penitential, in selecting
the one he thought best, in copying it carefully, and finally, with it as
a basis supplemented by the other manuscripts, in constructing a
fairly coherent and orderly text. He was fully aware of the inevitable
imperfections of a text of this type. And yet, in spite of the relatively
small number of manuscripts at his disposal and in spite of the errors
that crept into the transcriptions and the inadequacy of the critical
apparatus his choice of manuscripts and readings together with his
emendations and interpretations, based on a rare knowledge of legal
Latin, were highly felicitous, as subsequent studies and newly-found
manuscripts have proved.

Schmitz, on the other hand, though he speaks critically in his two
volumes of penitentials of errors in the transcriptions of his predecessor, was not nearly so careful a scholar as Wasserschleben. He was
a collector rather than a scholar. Possessed of vast industry, he
traveled from library to library in Europe discovering many new
manuscripts. Herein lay his chief merit. Although he realized the
value of a fuller critical apparatus and diligently copied text after
text, he lacked Wasserschleben's acumen in organizing and coördinat-
ing his material. In place of an orderly whole we have spread out before us many parts partially, but not consistently, worked out in
minute detail. Frequently Schmitz shapes the material to fit his
theory instead of formulating his theory from the evidence before
him. His dates for the manuscripts are wholly unreliable; his knowledge of paleographical and philological matters is slight and inaccurate; his transcriptions have many and grave errors; even when he
reprints Wasserschleben's text he is by no means faultless.

Oddly enough Schmitz failed to utilize the superior work on British
and Irish documents by Haddan and Stubbs.[3] These editors had
furnished a much better edition of some of the documents found in

---

[2] Wasserschleben, *Bussordnungen*, p. iii.
[3] *Councils and Ecclesiastical Documents relating to Great Britain and Ireland*, Oxford,
1869-78.

Schmitz. They had ferreted out fresh material, especially from British libraries, and then included a fairly workable list of variants. Furthermore, they succeeded in sifting hitherto confused versions of a number of penitentials and, as in the case of Theodore, in picking out the authentic older version. For the prologue of Theodore they linked several parts that had been scattered in widely-separated localities. Still, in their edition likewise there remained errors.[4]

There are other regional collections, notably Kunstmann's *Die lateinischen Poenitentialbücher der Angelsachsen* (1844) and Hildenbrand's *Untersuchungen über die germanischen Pönitentialbücher* (1851) for which the reader may be referred to Wasserschleben's critical remarks in the Preface to his *Bussordnungen*.[5] Kunstmann added little to the work of earlier editors, whereas Wasserschleben approves highly of Hildenbrand's critical study of the sources.

In 1677 Petit published a meager monograph on Theodore. Wasserschleben's monographs on Regino's *Ecclesiastical Discipline* (1840) and especially his valuable and thorough edition of *Die irische Kanonensammlung* (1874 and 1885) were epochal for their time.[6] Within the last few decades a number of such studies have been made. Albers[7] claims to have published the genuine *Bede* from a Vatican manuscript (Barberini Lat. 477, formerly XI. 120) which he supplements with some readings from another Vatican codex (Pal. Lat. 294). Zettinger[8] discovered the genuine *Cummean* in Vatican Pal. Lat. 485.

There are two codices at Turin which contain the *Penitential of Columban*. Only one is complete, and from this one Seebass published his penitential. Seebass, furthermore, made a study of the *Regula coenobialis* of Columban. He distinguished two recensions and edited them from one main manuscript each, supplemented by readings from a number of others. For the most part, therefore, these editions

---

[4] Finsterwalder's "restlos genau" notwithstanding (*Die Canones Theodori Cantuariensis und ihre Ueberlieferungsformen*, Weimar, 1929, p. 6); I have tested their transcriptions of the Cambridge codex, Corpus Christi College 320, for *Theodore*, and the Vatican codex, Pal. Lat. 485, for *Egbert*.

[5] It would take us too far afield to attempt to discuss the editions of the Anglo-Saxon laws, the ancient Irish laws, and the Frankish codes from which selections have been made in chaps. viii and ix of this volume, inasmuch as they do not contain penitentials proper.

[6] But cf. the note by Kenney, *Sources for the Early History of Ireland* (New York, 1929), I, 247: "an excellent edition in its time, but a new treatment is needed." Wasserschleben edited his text from only one of two recensions. An edition based on both is needed.

[7] See the introduction to the translation in chap. iii, below.

[8] J. Zettinger, "Das Poenitentiale Cummeani," *A.K.K.R.*, LXXXII (1902), 501-40. See the introduction to the translation in chap. i, below.

are based on a single manuscript, always a precarious method, and especially so when the editor's transcription is not faultless.[9]

As far as is known to us, no extant manuscripts of penitentials date back much further than the eighth century, so that the distance in time between our oldest manuscripts and the original documents amounts to nearly half a century in a few cases, and in most cases to several centuries.[10] In view of this, it is doubtful if any single extant codex is "genuine," that is, if it represents the original so closely that one may safely dispense with a critical study and comparison of all the other manuscripts.

We are fortunate in possessing two careful transcriptions by the paleographer E. A. Lowe, which he made in connection with a study of two of the famous missals. The first, the *Bobbio Penitential*, a part of the *Bobbio Missal*, is taken from a single extant codex, Paris, Bibl. Nat. Lat. 13246, saec. VIII.[11] The other, the *Paris Penitential*, is also from a unique manuscript, Paris, Bibl. Nat. Lat. 7193, saec. VIII, which, as Lowe discovered, belonged originally to a Vatican manuscript of the *Gelasian Sacramentary*.[12] These transcriptions reproduce abbreviations and symbols as they occur. Suggestive interpretations and parallels add to the value of his work, leaving the reader, to be sure, to construe his own text.

The most ambitious attempt so far in editing the text of a penitential was made in 1929 by P. W. Finsterwalder in *Die Canones Theodori Cantuariensis und ihre Ueberlieferungsformen*. He studied and evaluated all the known manuscripts, discovered several very important new ones, grouped his material according to traditions of

---

[9] I have tested Zettinger's copy of codex Vat. Pal. Lat. 485 and found many inaccuracies and a few bad errors. For example, in the troublesome passage (p. 102 of this translation) where Cummean speaks of allowances in food, Zettinger prints "paxmatiui I XII pol." whereas the manuscript has "paxmatiui .i." at the end of one line, continuing with "XII pol." on the next. Elsewhere in this manuscript ".i." occurs with the meaning *id est*. Here the position also makes it quite plausible |that ".i. XII pol." was on the margin of the codex from which Vat. Pal. Lat. 485 was copied, to explain the quantity of the bread which was to be used ("paxmatiui"). Zettinger's failure to see this is all the more surprising since he suggested such a solution for other, apparently superfluous, numbers in the text.

[10] The only nearly contemporary manuscripts of the penitentials in chaps. i–v, below, appear to be those of the related Burgundian and Bobbio penitentials, possibly also several MSS of the *Pseudo-Cummean* (see below, p. 63), the *Paris Penitential*, and two manuscripts of the *Tripartite St. Gall Penitential*. Probably, however, not all manuscripts have been dated accurately.   [11] See p. 278, n. 4, below.

[12] Cf. "The Vatican MS of the Gelasian Sacramentary and Its Supplement at Paris," by E. A. Lowe, in the *Journal of Theological Studies*, XXVII (July, 1926), 357–73.

Theodore documents, worked out family relationships, and printed a text for each separate group. I have examined closely only the *"U"* group. Unfortunately, Finsterwalder's slight command of philological and paleographical material marred his method. His remarks on manuscripts are in part wrong or misleading,[13] his transcriptions and collations are very faulty,[14] his critical apparatus is wholly unreliable and, in fine, he does not establish a text. He prints a text which is almost as obscure and untranslatable in spots as were the previous texts.

Obscurities in a text may be accounted for in two ways. Some readings have been correctly transmitted but are obscure due to medieval Latinity. In this case a problem of interpretation arises. Other readings do not reproduce the original but have been corrupted by successive scribes in transmission. They require textual reconstruction. It may be safely said that many difficulties in our texts of the penitentials are due to corruptions in transmission. Not until critical editions with a workable text and ample apparatus have been made can the translator hope to give a reliable rendering of these important sources.

THE MANUSCRIPTS

Early in the progress of the translation it became apparent that most of the editions were inadequate for a clear understanding of the texts, and an examination of some of the major manuscripts, especially of the earlier and more difficult documents, seemed desirable. Opportunely, I could avail myself of part of a year's residence abroad, in 1930–31, to carry out such an investigation. Since then, other manuscripts also have been studied from photostats.[15]

The immediate purpose was twofold: to obtain some light on difficult words and phrases at certain crucial points in the text, and to test generally the accuracy of the editions. The results of the latter task have been incorporated in the discussion of the editions; the footnotes throughout the volume indicate, at least in part, what help the manuscripts gave on obscure points.

[13] See footnotes 21, 26, and 36, below.

[14] Even the new readings from Vat. Pal. Lat. 554, in which he had discovered a valuable version of the difficult epilogue, are neither complete nor correct. E.g., for "illa esse iudicia" this manuscript reads "eius esse iudicia"; for "omnibus qui horum causa," "omnibus uos qui horum causa"; for "contra inminentes ictus," "contra iminentes ictus" (not "contra imminenter," as Finsterwalder asserts in footnote e, p. 334).

[15] For a list of manuscripts, see Appendix V and a discussion of the Appendix, below, p. 68.

The method used for testing the editions consisted of collating with the printed texts a number of the penitentials, whole or in part. The selection of passages to be collated was determined somewhat by the difficulties encountered in translating. Thus the collations served to clarify obscurities in the Latin as well. The following list of manuscripts will indicate the extent of the collations. Of these codices some have been employed by editors of texts, many others have been merely mentioned,[16] and still others have been discovered after the texts were published.[17]

Collations of Manuscripts

With Wasserschleben

London, British Museum

Cotton Otho E XIII, for the *Canons of Adamnan*, from photostats of the MS.

Oxford, Bodleian Library

Hatton 42, for the *Canons of Adamnan* and the *Welsh Canons*, from photostats.

Paris, Bibliothèque Nationale, fonds Latin

3182, for the *Preface of Gildas*, the *Synod of the Grove of Victory*, the *Synod of North Britain*, and the *Penitential of Finnian*, from the MS; for the *Welsh Canons*, the *Irish Canons* and the *Canons of Adamnan*, from photostats.

3846, for part of the *Penitential of Theodore*, from the MS.

12021, for the *Penitential of Finnian*, from the MS; for the *Welsh Canons*, the *Irish Canons*, and the *Canons of Adamnan*, from photostats.

Rome, Biblioteca Vaticana

Pal. Lat. 294, for the *Penitential of Egbert*, from the MS.

St. Gall, Stiftsbibliothek

150, for the *Penitential of Finnian*, from photostats.

Vienna, Nationalbibliothek

2195, for the *Penitential of Theodore*, from the MS.

2223, for the *Penitential of Theodore*, from the MS.

2233, for the *Penitential of Finnian*, from the MS.

Würzburg, Universitätsbibliothek

Mp th q 32, for the *Penitential of Theodore*, from the MS.

With Schmitz

Paris, Bibliothèque Nationale, fonds Latin

8508, for the *So-called Roman Penitential*, from the MS.

12315, for the *So-called Roman Penitential*, from the MS.

---

[16] For example, British Museum, Codex Cotton Otho E XIII for *Adamnan*.
[17] For example, Oxford, Bodl. Hatton 42; see below, p. 131.

Rome, Biblioteca Vaticana
  Pal. Lat. 294, for the *Penitential of Egbert*, from the MS.
  Pal. Lat. 554, for the *Penitential of Egbert*, from the MS.

With Haddan and Stubbs

Cambridge, Corpus Christi College
  320, for the *Penitential of Theodore*, from the MS.
London, British Museum
  Cotton Otho E XIII, for the *Canons of Adamnan*, from photostats.
Oxford, Bodleian Library
  Hatton 42, for the *Canons of Adamnan* and the *Welsh Canons*, from
  photostats.
Rome, Biblioteca Vaticana
  Pal. Lat. 485, for the *Penitential of Egbert*, from the MS.

With Finsterwalder

Berlin, Staatsbibliothek
  Hamilton 132, for the *Penitential of Theodore* (part of Book Two),
  from the MS.
Cambridge, Corpus Christi College
  320, for the *Penitential of Theodore*, from photostats.
Rome, Biblioteca Vaticana
  Pal. Lat. 485, for the *Penitential of Theodore*, from the MS.
  Pal. Lat. 554, for the *Penitential of Theodore*, from the MS.
Vienna, Nationalbibliothek
  2195, for the *Penitential of Theodore*, from photostats.
  2223, for the *Penitential of Theodore*, from photostats.
Würzburg, Universitätsbibliothek
  Mp th q 32, for the *Penitential of Theodore*, from photostats.

With Zettinger

Rome, Biblioteca Vaticana
  Pal. lat. 485, for the *Penitential of Cummean*, from the MS.

Dr. McNeill used photostats of a codex of the British Museum
(Additional 30853) together with the text of de Berganza for the
translation of the *Penitential of Silos*. On some of the obscure spots in
the *Penitential of Cummean*, we consulted photostats of an uncial
MS in the Royal Library at Copenhagen (Ny kgl. S.58, s. VII/VIII.)[18]
For the MSS of *Alain de Lille*, see Appendix V.

In a few cases it was deemed advisable to study a group of manuscripts to determine their relationship and to establish a tentative
text. The Latin text of the *Penitential of Finnian* was quite prob-

[18] For details on the use of these two MSS see the introduction to the documents in
chaps. v and i respectively, of this volume, and n. 53, below.

lematical. Wasserschleben's version seems to rest on the St. Gall codex, Stiftsbibliothek 150. An examination of the manuscripts shows that the St. Gall codex presents a good version, but that Vienna, Nationalbibliothek 2233 is, on the whole, the better manuscript. These two are clearly related and represent one branch of the family. The other two, Paris 3182 and 12021, are no less clearly related and represent another tradition. They are not so complete as the first branch, but they have been used to confirm the readings of the Vienna manuscript where it differs from the St. Gall. The notes in the translation will indicate the changes that have been made on the basis of this examination.

Another important penitential which offered a great many problems of translation is that of Theodore, especially the prologue and the obscure epilogue. In view of the imperfections in Finsterwalder's text and in order to obtain an independent estimate of the relative worth of the few manuscripts that contain the prologue and the epilogue, I have made a collation and a stemma of the prologue and of a major portion of the first book from Vienna 2195 (V),[19] Vienna 2223 (W), Würzburg Mp th q 32 (H), Vat. Pal. Lat. 485 (Pal), and Cambridge CCC 320 (C). The reason for choosing these manuscripts is that they alone contain parts or all of the prologue or the epilogue. My results show that H and W are closely related, as Finsterwalder postulated; more than that, it is not unlikely that they have been copied from the same manuscript. Furthermore, I agree with Finsterwalder that V, Pal, and C are related in some fashion; but I find from a tabulation of all readings as well as a select list of test readings that V, not Pal, stands apart from the rest within the group of three and that it most resembles C, whereas Pal often shows resemblance to W and H. For instance, in I. iii. 4, V on the one hand reads "et qui furat(a) de⸀tertiam" (the "a" of furata has been erased), and C similarly, "et cui furata det tertiam"; on the other hand, W and H both read "et qui furata monet det tertiam," and Pal similarly, "et qui furat ammonet det tertiam." In I. vii. 6 C and V read "famis non nocet quam (V quia) aliud est legitimum aliud quod necessitas cogit"; W reads "famis nihil est," Pal, "nihil est," and H omits the entire phrase. V (I. ii. 22), reads "a deo id est de amore et amicitia si dixerit sed non," and C reads the same except for "ab eo" in place of "a deo"

---

[19] The letters are those of Finsterwalder.

and "si non" in place of "sed non" (due to a confusion of the "s" symbol for "sed"); but W and H read "a deo si aut (W uses the "h" symbol) dix̄ id est de amore et amicitia sed non," and Pal reads "a deo si autem (the "h" symbol) dixerit de amore et amicitia sed non."[20]

The separate position of V can be illustrated by the following examples:[21] In I. iii. 3, V reads "manet in penitentia per omnia," C, W, and H read "peniteat per omnia," Pal, "penitere per omnia"; I.vii.11, V reads "sabbo^la" (possibly "sabbo^lo"); the others either "saliuo" or "saliua"; in I.vi.4, V reads "autem," the other manuscripts all read "uero"; I.viii.6, V, "monachus uero," the others, "monachus"; I.ix.10, V, "biduanam," corrected by another hand to "bigamam," the others, "uiduam." In all these examples Finsterwalder has not accepted the readings of V for his text. The context, however, and the meaning of the passages favor the readings of V in not a few cases. Equally striking examples do not occur in Pal to set it apart. It is also noteworthy that a great number of careful corrections are to be found in V which change incorrect readings to correct readings. There does not seem to be sufficient similiarity with the other manuscripts to prove that the scribe had access to one of them. It is not improbable, however, that a corrector of V used a manuscript from which C was copied or the branch of C descended.

[20] It is not clear why Finsterwalder prints "haec" for "autem" in his text, inasmuch as "autem" makes good sense, unless perhaps he mistook the "autem" symbol for "haec"—a common error.

[21] In proof of this a difference in readings is valuable only when the other readings are uniform or related. When Finsterwalder, p. 133, n. 1, tries to show the separation of the V group from the W group, he uses many examples that are not pertinent; e.g., in quoting the readings of W and H against V Pal C he says (I.vii.5) "degnis>egris, egressis." Actually the MSS read: W and H "degnis," V "de egris," Pal "egris," C "de egressis." The first form, "degnis," arose from a confusion of r and n, which is common in Insular script, and a contraction of "de egris," probably found in the common prototype of both. Thus W and H show a closer relation to V than V shows to Pal and C. "De egris" is the correct form (see also below). Again, Finsterwalder says "sanctorum (scōrum)>scottorum," whereas "scōrum" is to be found only in W; H C V have "scottorum"; Pal has "Sgottorum." There are other such cases among his examples; e.g., p. 134, n. 1, he tries to prove the independent character of the variants of Pal compared with those of the other MSS. In this connection he misuses the "egris" readings mentioned above, adding besides with regard to Pal "egris," "gegenüber allen andern HSS die richtigste Lesart," but in his text (p. 298) he prints "de aegris." Furthermore, p. 134, footnote 2: I.ii.1, "marita> maritata" gives a wrong impression: "marita" is not in Pal alone and "maritata" in all others; on the contrary, V alone has "maritata" and all others have "marita." Again, I.vii.6, "statt famis . . . cogit: nihil est," as has been discussed above, cannot serve to indicate the separate position of Pal "gegen die eigne Gruppe." Likewise in footnote 3 of the same page, "nur in V 'id est de amore et amicitia' " is incorrect, inasmuch as the same phrase occurs also in C (see above in text). Other similar examples could be cited.

In any case V would seem to be a most important and reliable manuscript. It is valuable to note that only Pal and V contain the entire prologue, and, of the two, V has fewer omissions.

To reconstruct the archetype of the *Penitential of Theodore* seems a hopeless task. From the prologue, the epilogue, and certain remarks in the text[22] we learn that there were many versions and interpretations of Theodore's teachings and that "Discipulus Umbrensium," the author of the compilation before us, tried to distinguish between the good and the bad. It is difficult, however, to tell whether the text as we have it is that of the compiler or whether it has been revised again since his time. Two passages are of special significance in this connection. (a) I.xii.5: W and C read, "in iudicio episcopi est illius" (W omits "illius"); W, C, and Pal (not all in the same order; Pal and C are alike except that "in . . . illius" is lacking in Pal) continue "locis hoc in quibusdam non additur esse in iudicio episcopi"; V omits both phrases; H is fragmentary and does not extend as far as this, at least not in its legible part.[23] (b) I.xii.7: all MSS except H read "et [Pal, ut] hoc necessarium in quibusdam codicibus non est." Apparently in both canons we have what was originally a marginal gloss on the restricting phrase of a provision, which some copyists included in the text.

To study thoroughly the *Penitential of Bartholomew of Exeter* is beyond the scope of this work. It is a lengthy, late document from which only paragraphs could be presented in this volume. Dr. McNeill found a few paragraphs of the document in *Reliquiae antiquae* by Wright[24] printed from a London manuscript, British Museum, Cotton Faustina A VIII. Accordingly, it was thought best to secure photostats of the entire penitential from this manuscript, supplemented by a few others listed in the Catalogue of the King's Collection, British Museum, namely, 5 E VII art. 3, 7 E I, and 8 D III art. 2 of the Royal MSS, and Cotton Vitell. A XII, of which we procured small sections common to all. From a comparison of these I found that 5 E VII art. 3 and 7 E I of the Royal MSS and Cotton Vitell. A XII apparently belong in one group and differ considerably from that of Cotton Faustina A VIII. The third Royal MS, 8 D III

[22] For a detailed discussion of this see Finsterwalder, chap. iii D.

[23] Minor variants are here omitted. See also, p. 195, n. 88.

[24] For details, see p. 346 below. Added in proof: An edition by A. Morey has recently appeared. It was made from one MS only (Cotton Vitell. A XII), but the following and some other MSS are listed.

art. 2, is incomplete and was either influenced from another source or written by a poor scribe. The four other MSS listed in the catalogue, Paris, Bibl. Nat. Lat. 2600, Oxford, St. Johns College 3 A 3 and 10 (163 and 165), and a fragment in the British Museum, King's collection 8 C XIV, art. 1, have not been examined.

In addition to the unprinted material from *Bartholomew*, two shorter, unprinted sections have been translated directly from the MSS and included in this volume, one in the *Silos Penitential* from the British Museum manuscript and the other from Paris 3182 in the *Irish Canons*.

Limited as the investigation of the manuscripts has been, it has produced a few important incidental results.

In view of the inadequate documentary history of the penitentials, it is of vital importance to gain accurate knowledge of the date and origin of the codices by which the documents have come down to us. Very few manuscripts are definitely dated. Most of the library catalogues are either incomplete or unreliable. It is not surprising to find errors in dating in the older editions of penitentials.[25] Within recent years, however, especially since the time of the great medievalist Ludwig Traube, real progress has been made in paleography through scholarly studies of scripts, abbreviations, symbols, and other determinants, so that now the majority of codices can be dated with a fair degree of accuracy. It is to be regretted that not all modern writers on penitentials have kept pace with this progress.[26] I have attempted to date the manuscripts consulted, independently, on the basis of script, abbreviations, and other characteristics. In many in-

---

[25] Wasserschleben, Haddan and Stubbs, and others, are more nearly correct than Schmitz whose dating is almost invariably wrong, very often several centuries too late. Cf. note 26 below.

[26] The result is often a confusing variety of dates for a single codex; e.g., Paris Bibl. Nat. Lat. 12021 is one of the most important manuscripts of penitentials. It can be definitely assigned to saec. IX (especially because of the abbreviation for "tur"). Lindsay dates it thus (*Notae Latinae*, p. 475). Esposito (*Hermathena* XX, 236) in speaking of Finnian calls it X/XI. Finsterwalder (*Die Canones Theodori*, 1929) lists the codex on p. 5 with the date X/XI; on p. 11 he repeats the date, but in enigmatic fashion: "s.X/XI (nach Maassen), s.VIII (nach Knust)"; then he discusses the manuscript, and closes with this sentence: "Die HS. wird damit wohl ins 9./10 Jahrhundert gesetzt werden können." Lindsay is not quoted in this connection, although Finsterwalder knew his date for the codex (see p. 12 n. 4, where he quotes Lindsay for the place of origin). The amazed reader is left to wonder not only which date is correct, but what is Finsterwalder's real opinion on the subject. Nor is this merely a slip; the situation for Paris Bibl. Nat. Lat. 3182 and St. Gall Stiftsbibl. 150 and other manuscripts is similar. It is curious that Finsterwalder did not recognize Lindsay, the expert, as his superior in the field of paleography (see his remarks on codex 320 of Corpus Christi College, *op. cit.*, pp. 98 f., and note 36 below).

stances we are fortunate in having the support of such experts in
paleography as W. M. Lindsay,[27] C. H. Beeson,[28] and E. A. Lowe,[29]
for our manuscripts. Occasionally we find a manuscript that is
peculiarly noncommittal as to its age. For example, it is difficult to
date the large, two-column codex Paris. Bibl. Nat. Lat. 3182. This
contains valuable Insular, chiefly Irish, material for some of which
it is the only source.[30] The script is large, resembling the type that
was used in the twelfth century in imitation of the ninth century
Carolingian minuscule and yet not unlike the large script of the
tenth or eleventh century. The abbreviations are few in number, but
they reveal the Insular character of the original from which it was
copied.[31] Bradshaw claims a Breton origin for the manuscript because
of "Breton glosses." Wasserschleben thinks it was written in Fécamp,
Normandy, and that the glosses may be Welsh. Mommsen concurs
with Wasserschleben and dates the manuscript saec. X/XI; Knust,
whose notes Wasserschleben and others used, dates it saec. XI/XII,[32]
Kenney records saec. XI. I am inclined to believe that the manuscript was not written later than saec. XI and not earlier than saec.
X/XI, accepting Mommsen's date as the most probable one. In this
I am supported by the opinion of Professor Beeson who saw the
manuscript in Paris.[33]

The age of a codex may be of vital importance in determining the
date when the document was written. This is especially the case when
our knowledge of a given piece of writing rests solely on the evidence
we find in the manuscripts. Obviously the latest possible date for
such a document is fixed by the date of the earliest manuscript. Two
examples will illustrate the point. The *Bobbio Penitential* has come
down to us in a single manuscript, Paris Bibl. Nat. Lat. 13246.

[27] *Notae Latinae*, Cambridge, 1915; *Palaeographia Latina*, 1922-29.

[28] *Isidor-Studien*, München, 1913. Cf. also *Penit. Silense*, p. 285, below.

[29] On the Paris and Burgundian penitentials, cf. "The Vatican MS of the Gelasian
Sacramentary and Its Supplement at Paris," by E. A. Lowe, in *The Journal of Theological
Studies*, XXVII (July, 1926), 357 ff. On the *Bobbio Penitential*, see note 11, above.

[30] For example, the *Book of David*, the *Synod of North Britain*, the *Synod of the Grove
of Victory*, the *Preface of Gildas*, and others. But see App. V, p. 434, n. 1.

[31] I have noticed the Insular symbol for "autem" several times in the MS, also the
same symbol corrected to "haec," and again added above the line; $\overline{qn}$ for "quando," tñ
for "tamen," *et al.*

[32] Finsterwalder, *op. cit.*, p. 14 f. and Mommsen, *M. G. H.*, *Auct. ant.* XIII (*Chron. Min.*
III), (1898), 11.

[33] In *A Supplement to Notae Latinae*, recently published by D. Bains at the request of
W. M. Lindsay (Cambridge, 1936), the MS is dated "saec. XI" and the glosses are called
Breton.

MS Paris, Bibl. Nat. Lat. 3182, p. 281 (the end of the *Preface of Gildas* and the beginning of the *Synod of North Britain*) See p. 62 (cf. also pp. 56 and 174)

Wasserschleben assigned both manuscript and penitential to saec. VII or VIII. Schmitz subsequently changed this to the middle of the eighth century. Lowe, in his illuminating study of the *Bobbio Missal*, gave reasons to believe that the manuscript was written somewhat nearer A.D. 700 and thereby added approximately half a century to the age of the penitential as well. Another case in point is that of the *Penitential formerly thought to be Cummean's*. After Zettinger discovered the genuine *Cummean* in a Vatican manuscript, the *Pseudo-Cummean* was explained as a compilation drawn from the true *Cummean* and other penitentials, originating in the ninth century. On examining the manuscripts, however, I find that some of them belong to the eighth century, one possibly to the late seventh.[34] This forces us to advance the commonly-accepted date of the document to saec. VII ex. or saec. VIII in.

The character of a script[35] and its "symptoms"[36] are not only indices to age and scriptorium but to less obvious fields of inquiry as well. Not infrequently a manuscript written several centuries after the archetype will reveal to us the ultimate origin of the docu-

[34] For example, Paris, Bibl. Nat. Lat. 1603 (cf. Lindsay, *Not. Lat.*, p. 471: " 'saec. VIII ex.' "); Cologne, Dombibl. 91 (Lindsay, p. 453: " 'saec. VIII' "); St. Gall, Stiftsbibl. 150 appears to belong at least to the early part of saec. IX, probably VIII/IX; Copenhagen, Ny kgl. S.58 is dated "s.VII/VIII" in the catalogue, but it seems hardly older than the beginning of saec. VIII. Munich, Staatsbibl. Lat. 6243 is certainly saec. VIII ex., possibly earlier.

[35] Early editors, especially Schmitz, often erred in naming scripts; for example, Paris Bibl. Nat. Lat. 7193 is written in eighth-century uncials (as Wasserschleben stated correctly, *Bussordnungen*, p. 412; cf. Lowe, *op. cit.* in *Journal of Theological Studies*, XXVII [July, 1926], 357 ff.). Schmitz (II, p. 326) calls it Visigothic.

[36] The editors say very little about the "symptoms" of a manuscript, that is, the abbreviations, symbols, and the like. Finsterwalder is a notable exception. He goes to the other extreme, devoting much space to minute and nonessential descriptions of the form of a codex, its binding, and the like (cf. also Levison's review in *Savigny Stiftung für Rechtsgeschichte, kan. Abt.*, XIX [1930], 706 f.) but often failing to mention essentials. For instance, he says of Codex 320 Corpus Christi College, Cambridge, that the abbreviations in the Theodore section are in the main Continental, and he continues: "neben l steht 'vel,' 'est' ist meist ausgeschrieben oder mit ē abgekürzt, niemals aber finden wir das insulare ÷; 'pro' ist stets ausgeschrieben, 'tantum' in tantū gekürzt. Neben insularem p̄ kommt auch ebenso 'per' ausgeschrieben vor, ebenso die kontinentale Abkürzung p; für 'id est' findet sich .i." (p. 97). The list is misleading; if ÷ is Insular, so is .i.; p̄ for "per" is normally found also in Insular codices (Lindsay, *Not. Lat.*, p. 496); and above all he fails to note the important Insular abbreviations, the "h" symbol for "autem," c̄ for "cum," s̄r for "super," tñ for "tamen," the "q" symbols for "quia" and "quod" (see Lindsay, *op. cit.*, pp. 495 ff.), all of which point definitely to an Insular original from which this manuscript was copied. A similar criticism can be made of Finsterwalder's discussion of Paris, Bibl. Nat. Lat. 3182 (on p. 14) and other codices. Among misleading details, on p. 16 the abbreviations .i. for "id est" and q for "quia" should not be called "rein irisch." See Lindsay, *op. cit.*, pp. 499, 500.

ment through a few symbols peculiar to the foreign script of the original, copied by an ignorant but faithful scribe who did not understand them. Beyond all other scripts the Insular is characterized by numerous abbreviations. The Irish monasteries where it originated were poor, and parchment was dear. Therefore the scribes worked out an intricate system of abbreviations and symbols, deriving it from Tironian notes and ancient *notae iuris*. In the seventh century the script and symbols spread to England. Soon this national hand, named Insular by Traube, was carried to the Continent by English and Irish missionaries who founded many monasteries in various lands. These institutions housed scriptoria in which the Insular style flourished. Not for long did the Insular hand continue on the Continent; but the influence of the abbreviations lasted, and the Continental scribes continued to copy them into their manuscripts. Through these symptoms we can trace Insular origin and contact.[37]

More than eighty years ago Wasserschleben suggested a Celtic origin for the penitentials, but Schmitz later argued persistently and stubbornly for an ultimate Roman origin. He based his arguments chiefly on two phrases, "ex poenitentiali Romano" and "ex scrinio Romanae ecclesiae," which recur on the margins of the manuscripts and in the texts of penitentials. The original *Roman Penitential* has been lost, according to Schmitz, but large portions of it survived in a few documents, the penitential in Halitgar's collection, the *Tripartite St. Gall*, the *Valicellanum* I and II, the *Casinense*, and the *Arundel*.[38] Other scholars, most effectively Fournier, have contradicted the view of Schmitz; they studied the individual canons of these penitentials and demonstrated that they contained chiefly Celtic material brought to the Continent by Irish and Anglo-Saxon missionaries. In reviewing the intricate controversy[39] Kenney finds himself obliged to refrain from judgment.

If we consider the manuscripts of which we have some detailed knowledge from the point of view of paleography, one fact soon becomes apparent: the majority of the documents have come down to us in manuscripts which are written in Insular script or else in Continental hands that show contact with Insular writing. Furthermore, a list of libraries where these manuscripts were written or to which

---

[37] For a discussion of some Insular symptoms in penitential MSS see nn. 31 and 36 above.

[38] Schmitz I, pp. 468 ff.; II, pp. 177, 179.   [39] Kenney, p. 239.

they formerly belonged is for the most part identical with a list of the main monasteries founded by the English and especially the Irish.[40] It is natural to find abundant Insular evidence in the documents of Chapters I–IV; they are all written by, or attributed to, Insular authors. Of the penitentials in Chapters V and VI, none can definitely be connected with Insular authors.[41] But even here some Insular influence can be observed. Let us consider briefly one important group in each of the two chapters.

The first group, in Chapter V (Anonymous and Pseudonymous Frankish and Visigothic Penitentials), consists of three related documents: the Burgundian, the Bobbio, and the Paris penitentials. The *Burgundian Penitential*, in turn, is closely related to the Fleury and the St. Hubert penitentials, for of the sixty-two canons of the *St. Hubert*, forty-three are substantially identical with those of the *Burgundian*, and the *Fleury Penitential* bears close resemblance to the *St. Hubert*.[42] As has been stated elsewhere,[43] the manuscripts of the Fleury and St. Hubert penitentials are not known today. For each of the other three we possess one codex. The eighth-century uncial codex of the *Paris Penitential*, Paris, Bibl. Nat. Lat. 7193, is characterized by a great many Insular abbreviations.[44] The Brussels manuscript of the *Burgundian Penitential*, Bibl. Roy. 8780–93, now Brussels 2493, in pre-Carolingian minuscule, contains very few abbreviations; but Lowe points out[45] that it has a curious error in common with the manuscript of the *Paris Penitential* which links the two together. The manuscript of the *Bobbio Penitential*, Paris, Bibl. Nat. Lat. 13246, is written in a mixed script, partly uncial, partly half-uncial, and partly large minuscule. It shows strong Irish influence and may have been written at Luxeuil, an Irish center.[46] At all events, as Lowe concludes, both the Paris and the Bobbio penitentials belong to the Burgundian class and all are of French origin, from some great school of writing not unfamiliar with Irish and Anglo-Saxon manuscripts.

[40] For example, Fulda, Lorsch, Mainz, Corbie, Würzburg, Cologne, Reichenau, St. Gall, Bobbio.

[41] Unless, perchance, Kunstmann's identification of Clement be correct; see p. 271, below.

[42] Cf. the introductory remarks preceding the translations of these documents in Chap. V, below.   [43] See p. 51, above.

[44] See Lowe's transcription in *op. cit., Journal of Theological Studies*, XXVII (July, 1926), 357 ff.   [45] *Op. cit.*, p. 360.

[46] See Lindsay, *Not. Lat.*, p. 476, and the edition of the *Bobbio Missal* cited in note 4, p. 278, below.

The second group, in Chaps. V and VI, comprises the *Tripartite St. Gall* and the *So-called Roman Penitential*, chief among the documents on which Schmitz based his theory of Roman origin.[47] I have not seen many of the manuscripts that Schmitz lists in this group, and those I did see I could examine but briefly.[48] A more extensive examination of the remainder of the manuscripts would probably reveal Insular evidence. At least, I have found several codices of the other books of Halitgar which show definite contact with Insular script in the abbreviations and decorative initials. They appear to be of saec. X and saec. X/XI.[49] The evidence for the Insular origin of the *Tripartite St. Gall* is very much stronger. The oldest of the three manuscripts is a Vienna codex of saec. VIII/IX, Nationalbibl. 2223, written entirely in Anglo-Saxon script.[50] The same codex is a valuable source for the *Penitential of Theodore*. Another early codex of the *Tripartite* is in the Stiftsbibliothek St. Gall, No. 150, of saec. IX or VIII/IX. A heading reads "Prefatio Cummeani Abbatis in Scothia ortus," but the text is that of the *Tripartite*. The Insular abbreviations which I noted in my cursory examination are not plentiful, and yet contact with Insular influence is brought out further by the fact that the same manuscript contains an excellent version of *Finnian*.

Despite the belief expressed in Haddan and Stubbs[51] there is every reason to suppose that the libraries of England, as well as those of the Continent, contain fresh material for penitentials. Among the more important finds since Haddan and Stubbs may be listed such recent discoveries as the new readings for *Theodore*, Book I, in Vat. Pal. Lat.

---

[47] The others, mentioned above, p. 64, are discussed in the section on documents omitted, in Appendix IV. According to Schmitz the *Arundel*, the *Casinense*, and *Valicellanum* II are largely identical with *Valicellanum* I, which in turn was related to the *Merseburg Penitential*. They are all supposed to contain only a "Roman" kernel, like the two discussed above in the text. Incidentally, the manuscript of the *Valicellanum* I (Vall. E 15) is no longer lost (as Schmitz [I, p. 229] states). It had been removed to the private library of the last ecclesiastical librarian "so as not to be lost," when the Italian government took over the library as Biblioteca Vallicelliana. At his death it passed into the hands of an antiquarian and was thus "rediscovered" together with eight other codices.

[48] Schmitz lists approximately twenty MSS of Halitgar, of which I have examined six. The *Tripartite St. Gall* is extant in three codices, of which I have seen two.

[49] Rome, Vat. Lat. Regin. 263; Vat. Lat. 1339 (containing the *Pseudo-Cummean*); Vat. Lat. 1347 and Vat. Lat. 1352 (said by Haddan and Stubbs, III, 414, to have been copied from Oxford, Bodleian 718, with reference to *Egbert*); Vat. Lat. 5751 (containing the *Pseudo-Cummean* and formerly belonging to Bobbio, according to a note in a late hand).

[50] A reference to "uuolafrido episcopus" leads Lindsay (*Not. Lat.*, p. 492) to suggest that it belonged to Walafridus Strabo of Reichenau. Finsterwalder (*op. cit.*, p. 110) thinks it was written in the Insular scriptorium of Mainz or Fulda.

[51] *Councils*, I, Introduction, p. 9.

485, the hitherto missing part of the epilogue of Theodore in Vat. Pal. Lat. 554, both by Finsterwalder, the genuine *Cummean* in Vat. Pal. Lat. 485 by Zettinger, and British Museum Add. 30853 as the only known manuscript of the *Penitential of Silos* by Romero-Otazo. It is a significant fact that three of these four discoveries were made in codices that have long been known for other penitentials contained therein. Doubtless, a reëxamination of some of the other well-known codices will prove quite fruitful.

And there is other promise of future finds. While examining manuscripts of the earlier documents and looking through catalogues in the Vatican and in less explored centers, I noticed a number of codices with penitential material which had not been listed by editors of penitential texts. The time at my disposal was very brief and, unfortunately, my finds consisted only of material which was not to be included in this volume, as for instance the first five books of *Halitgar*, parts of *Egbert* and *Bede*, and unidentified documents. But Dr. McNeill and I did observe and make use of a few new manuscripts in other connections. The *Bartholomew* situation has been discussed elsewhere, likewise that of Alain de Lille's *Penitential Book*. The word "Poenitentiale" after MS Copenhagen Ny kgl. S. 58 8° in Traube's list of uncial manuscripts (edited by P. Lehmann)[52] directed my attention to a valuable early manuscript of the *Penitential formerly thought to be Cummean's*.[53] Incipits and explicits led to two discoveries. While studying the photostats of codex Oxford, Bodl. Hatton 42, for the text of the *Canons of Adamnan*, I noticed that the last lines of the *Welsh Canons* preceded the beginning of the *Canons of Adamnan*. On further investigation it was found that this manuscript contains the entire text of the *Welsh Canons*. A similar experience occurred very recently, when I looked up Wasserschleben's reference[54] to *Serapaeum* III, p. 120. The passages there quoted from the *Welsh Canons* in Lyon 203 suggested to Wasserschleben the similarity of the text of this manuscript to that of Paris, Bibl. Nat. Lat. 3182, which also contains the *Welsh Canons*. The explicit given in the *Serapceum* ends with the incipit of the *Canons of Adamnan*. Although I was not able to follow up the thread, it is reasonable to

---

[52] L. Traube, *Vorlesungen und Abhandlungen*, I (München, 1909), 191.

[53] Miss Ellen Jórgensen, keeper of the MSS, kindly furnished information on this Copenhagen codex and sent photostats of it. A table of contents is given in her catalogue (*Catalogus codicum Latinorum medii aevi bibliothecae Regiae Hafniensis*, 1926). Cf. also above, n. 34, p. 63. [54] *Bussordnungen*, p. 124.

suppose that Lyon 203 contains both the *Welsh Canons* and the *Canons of Adamnan* and is related to Oxford, Bodl. Hatton 42.

The lists of manuscripts and their editors in Appendix V indicate what codices of the penitentials proper, as they are represented in Chapters I–VII of this volume, are extant. The *Welsh Canons* of Chapter VIII have been added to this list, partly due to their importance and early date, partly because they have been translated in their entirety. For the remainder of the documents, of which only small portions have been included, one or two editions are mentioned at the beginning of each translation. These lists represent an attempt to bring together scattered material in a fairly complete and workable form and, it is hoped, will prove useful as a starting point for future study of the original documents. For several penitentials I could not list any manuscripts; they are known from a single old transcription.[55]

THE LATINITY

With very few exceptions, the medieval handbooks of penance that have come down to us were written in Latin. Of the non-Latin documents, the Anglo-Saxon, Old Irish, and Icelandic have received considerable attention in the past and have been rendered into English, Latin, or German by modern translators whose work was of service for the present volume. Of the quality of these translations or of the language of their originals I am not able to judge. But they form only a small part of the penitential literature. Inasmuch as the bulk of the material is not only in Latin but also, in many places, in exceptionally intricate Latin, it seems pertinent to comment briefly on the Latinity of the penitentials.

We are not concerned here with the troublesome obscurities that grew up as a result of corruption in the transmission of the texts.[56] The problem before us arises from peculiarities of this type of medieval Latin and from idiosyncrasies of the authors. Like most medieval Latin texts the penitentials contain a great number of difficult words and constructions for which the dictionaries offer no aid. The translator of a medieval text is not so fortunate as he whose task it is to translate a classical document. The existing dictionaries of medieval Latin do not even begin to cover the field.

The penitentials were written in more or less formal church Latin

---

[55] Cf. p. 51, above.   [56] That point has been discussed above, pp. 55 f.

egregias illa depravata incorrect... eiusd... iudicia meritis a...
e quibus non pauca cum passim a pluribus mixta simq; tenentur par...
posuimus ut xpo dno iuuante sequentibus libris ex eis praecipua iuxta
modulum nostrum corrigamus. Sed adhuc de illo dubitantes opere aliqui
inquibusda ...s necessaria opusculis adnectimus & maximae libello paeni
tentiae quae a prudente posse facile sciri aduersa ... postea igitur sup his
ad defensionem patris nostri theodori dilectionis uestri tum quantum possumus
satisfacere Quorum in aliorum catholicorum dictis plenam non inuenerat
expositionem eu ideo frequentas ... De quib; non inmerito omnibus uos
qui horum carissimi causa ea iudicantes difficilia extasse ut me illorum
agone xpo puobis anathe dia cer ... crucem meritus uestris contra imminentes
ictus dextra hentam dextra leuaq; defensatis obsecro quib; facilius est
laborantib; detrahere quam studio laboris desudare & quia do nostri
quidam sapientissimos suggillare ecclesiae dei linguae suae uolubilitate
dedicerunt. Semi loquor hieronimum quem mali loquum hominibus
inquiunt. Augustinum multi locum esidorum glosarum conpositum ...
taceo dereliquis cumsem aiunt gregorium apostolium nostrum ea dixisse facile
quae ceteri prius exposuerunt cristis aliorum callibus ingrediens.
Indenouite audiui quod horreo dicere quendam uentri cosum gerulum
fabularum sectatorem legis di latorem & operis coqus mundi scrip
rem sugilla quid inquiens ipse moyses marius uel scire uel eis dicere
mea igitur defensio apud tales quae esse potest qui in conparatione eo
quos praeposui nihil sum grati agit sum id quod sum quaeutina in meum ...
non fiat peum qui ex nihilo cuncta creando potens est & de minimis
magna efficere per quo habeat auctor quicuque catholicus licentiam a nob
siquid uspiam inuenerit de his quod possit emendare id ratione pa...
quasi nisi uincantur quae sequenda non sunt cum aequalitate tenen...
con tentionem illis moueat In modicam quibus dictum est non in con
tentione & emulatione sed induimini dnm ihm xpm.

MS Rome, Vat. Pal. Lat. 554, f. 1 (the epilogue of the
Penitential of Theodore)
See p. 67 (cf. also p. 55, n. 14)

with a strong admixture of legal and canonical terms. They abound in local and technical expressions for which we lack the proper aids. Of this nature, for example, are the names and quantities of food of which a penitent cleric may partake in the beginning of the *Preface of Gildas* and elsewhere. Again, as in other ecclesiastical documents there are many Greek words, some of which are disguised, due to the ignorance of the scribes. For example, the form "ebibatus" in the *Book of David* X is a misspelling for "epibatus" (layman) from the Greek ἐπιβάτης, apparently due to the scribe's associating it with "ebibo" (drain). In the *Egbert-Bede* material there appears a strange word which Wasserschleben[57] prints as "caraios" (accusative plural), Schmitz in his first volume as "ceraios," in his second as "caraios" but with a note saying the MS reads "karajoc."[58] A glance at the manuscript (Rome, Vat. Lat. 294), explains the dubious "karajoc" as actually καραγος, thus misrepresenting the gamma and the "s" lunatum. The words "caragus," "caragius," and "carajius" are easily located in Du Cange, and in less conspicuous places also "carajus" and a reference to "καράγιοι = inter magos." The *Thesaurus* has "caragius" and says that it is probably of Greek origin. The word means "juggler" and occurs in the Albers's *Bede* in this volume.[59]

There are also words of other languages that have been corrupted in popular use. The meaning of "suturalia"[60] remained a mystery until by chance Mr. McNeill met the words "sotulares," "subtalares" in descriptions of clerical dress.[61] These pointed the way to "sotilares," "subtalaria," glossed by Du Cange "calcei" (shoes). Occasionally some rare words are explained on the margins by subsequent scribes, and now and then there are explanations or glosses even in the text, as in the *Poenitentiale Valicellanum* I. A gloss on "delator" in connection with "dilatus" in paragraph 74 of that penitential[62] removes whatever doubt there may have been about the meaning of "dilator" and "dilatus" in other places. On the other hand, glosses

---

[57] *Bussordnungen*, p. 239.

[58] See Schmitz I, p. 581; II, p. 668. He prints these forms in his text without further explanation and in spite of the fact that he uses the words "caraji," "caragus," "caragius" in discussing the *Poenitentiale Valicellanum* I and the *Penitential of Egbert* elsewhere; cf. I, pp. 234, 568. [59] See below, p. 229.

[60] *Corrector of Burchard*, 103. Wasserschleben reads (chap. xci) "situlalia" with variants "scutularia," "suturalia."

[61] J. W. Clark, *The Observances of the Augustinian Priory of S. Giles and S. Andrew at Barnwell, Cambridgeshire* (Cambridge, 1897), pp. lxxx, lxxxi.

[62] For details see *Synod of North Britain*, p. 171, n. 14.

may prove a hindrance. The *Irish Canons*, among other documents, are especially rich in perplexing glosses in the vernacular. In the *Penitential of Cummean*,[63] marginal glosses have become part of the text and are not easily distinguished from it.

It would be a great help to have indices or glossaries for the penitentials. A comparison of parallel passages has illumined many a hidden meaning and cleared away many a doubt. To mention a striking example, the parallel passages in the *Irish Collection of Canons* were of great value in interpreting the *Irish Canons*. Such a comparison would often prevent an overhasty emendation. In the *Irish Canons*, I, 4, the text speaks of wizards, cohabiters, heretics, and the like, and among them mentions "praeco" (literally, a crier). Kuno Meyer emended the reading to "praedo" (robber), since it seemed to him that a crier had no pertinence in that connection. But in the *Irish Canons*, XLIV, 8, the same word "praeco" occurs in a similar context. A slightly different interpretation, namely, that of hawker, mountebank, is not out of keeping with the passage.

In addition to rare, obscure, and corrupt words, the translator of the penitentials often has to struggle with unusual syntactical problems. It is a well-known fact that the medieval writers were not bound by rigid rules of syntax. They wrote as the spirit moved, not as grammar dictated. We may forego an enumeration of the common examples and comment instead on two or three peculiarities of syntax in the penitentials, caused for the most part by the nature of the material.

The penitentials were written primarily for clerics who were fairly familiar with the subject matter contained therein but who needed a book of ready reference for the variety and quantity of penance to be administered. The directions are given in a terse, matter-of-fact style. As in ritualistic literature, there are many elliptical expressions. If some of these expressions have not been transmitted in incorrect form, we must assume that they were easily filled in with familiar phrases by the priest. Some ellipses can be readily filled in even today. For others we lack the familiarity with the subject which the priests of that age possessed. For instance, we should like to be certain of the meaning of the last sentence in *Finnian*, 9: "clericus autem pecuniam dare non debet aut illi aut ille" (there is something like a

[63] Zettinger's *Cummean* II, 2; see pp. 102 f., below.

cedilla on the final "e" in the Vienna manuscript, standing for the double letter "ae"). Again, in the *Preface of Gildas,* paragraph 4, we find: "Si autem peccatum voluerit monachus facere, anno et dimedio." If a variation on the passage in *Cummean* is pertinent, we have here an ellipsis of considerable extent. For *Cummean* reads: "Si autem post peccatum voluerit monachus fieri, in districto praeposito ex alii (sc. exilii) anno et dimedio."[64]

Another peculiarity is due to the incapacity of the writer to express his thoughts correctly. The prologue and epilogue of *Theodore* would seem to suffer from such illiteracy. Likewise, the following sentences suggest difficulties of the same nature: "dubitet facere aut victor aut victus fuerit" (*Finnian,* 2); "quis caballum alterius inpastoriaverit et suum pastoriaverit, si pastoriam agnoverit, sine dubio cum caballo non dubitet invadere et suum proprium eum esse praecipimus" (*Welsh Canons,* 63).

Other difficulties, especially in the earlier documents, may have been caused by ambitious attempts on the part of a scribe to correct what he considered an obscurity in the text. Thus a bad matter was made worse.

It is hard to distinguish in all cases between the various causes of obscurities, whether they are due to elliptical expressions, illiteracy, or unhappy corrections. No doubt many of the existing obscurities will be clarified when workable texts of the penitentials have been made.

[64] See *Penitential of Cummean,* II, 5. Cf. also *Theodore,* II, iv, 1, p. 202, n. 117, below.

Documents

CHAPTER I

Early Irish Penitential Documents

1. CANONS ATTRIBUTED TO ST. PATRICK

[FOR DISCUSSION of the origin and date of these canons see J. H. Todd, *Life of St. Patrick*, pp. 486 ff.; Haddan and Stubbs, *Councils and Ecclesiastical Documents relating to Great Britain and Ireland*, II, 328 ff.; and J. B. Bury, *Life of St. Patrick*, pp. 233 ff. In opposition to the other historians mentioned, Bury contends for the genuineness, in substance, of the first set of canons. He thinks their later dating by Todd is based on arguments which apply only to canons 25, 30, 33, 34, and a clause of canon 6—passages which may be explained as interpolations. Apparently later, and less authoritative, are the canons of the second series. Bury notes that the *Collectio canonum Hibernensis* (*ca.* 700) ascribes to Patrick the canons which it quotes from "Synodus I" but does not ascribe to him those which it quotes from "Synodus II." Haddan and Stubbs, while holding an early date for the second series of canons, have pointed out[1] that one of them (27) is in direct contradiction to a passage in the *Confession* of St. Patrick. Bury shows reasons for believing that this document is derived from the acts of an Irish synod of the seventh century.[2]

The inclusion of these canons in a collection of penitential documents may not seem entirely justifiable. They are not strictly within the class of penitential materials, since they do not consist of lists of offenses with periods of penance. Yet they have to do with church discipline and excommunication, and in some of the canons the duration of the penance is determined. Their authors seem, however, to have approached the whole question of discipline in a somewhat different way from that of the authors of the great penitential documents. Hence, even if Patrick's authority is to be claimed for some of them, he can hardly be regarded as the founder of the typical Irish penance. Instead, the principle of the ancient public discipline seems to be reflected in many of the canons, although there is no evidence of public reconciliation. Whatever their date and source, they represent a type of discipline which gave place in Ireland to that represented by the foundation documents of our series.

[1] *Op. cit.*, II, 333.
[2] *Life of St. Patrick*, p. 239. See also, Hefele-Leclercq, II (2). 888 ff.

Their inclusion here will serve the purpose of comparison, and enable the reader to visualize the transformation wrought by the founders of the type of penance exhibited in the penitentials of Finnian and Columban.

Both documents are here translated from the edition by Haddan and Stubbs,[3] who used a manuscript of Corpus Christi College, Cambridge,[4] and the previous editions of Spelman[5] and Wilkins.[6] Haddan and Stubbs have noted the parallels with the *Collectio canonum Hibernensis;* but their citations of this collection are numerically not consonant with the subsequently published definitive edition of this latter document by H. Wasserschleben: *Die irische Kanonensammlung*, Leipzig, 1885. The citations of the *Collectio* here given follow the numerical scheme adopted by Wasserschleben. A photostatic copy of the codex CCCC 279 at the disposal of the authors has also been consulted. For further reference to sources and literature Kenney (p. 169) should be consulted.]

Canons of a Synod of Patrick, Auxilius, and Iserninus

Here begins the Synod of the Bishops, that is, of Patrick, Auxilius, and Iserninus.[7] We give thanks to God, the Father, the Son, and the Holy Spirit. To the presbyters, the deacons, and the whole clergy, Patrick, Auxilius, Iserninus, bishops, send greeting: It behoves us rather to admonish those who are negligent than to condemn the things that have been done, as Solomon says: "It is better to reprove than to be angry."[8] Copies of our decision are written below, and begin thus:

1. If anyone for the redemption of a captive collects[9] in the parish[10] on his own authority, without permission, he deserves to be excommunicated.

---

[3] *Op. cit.*, II, 328–38.

[4] Codex CCCC 279, ninth-tenth century. There exists a fifteenth-century Corpus Christi College manuscript, No. 298, which is imperfect. Kenney, p. 169.

[5] Henry Spelman, *Concilia, decreta, leges, constitutiones, in re ecclesiarum orbis Britannici*, I (1639), 52 ff.

[6] David Wilkins, *Concilia Magnae Britanniae et Hiberniae*, I (1737), 2 f.

[7] Auxilius and Iserninus were associated with Patrick in establishing Christianity in southern Ireland. The previous history of Auxilius is unknown. Iserninus was an Irishman whose original name was Fith. Bury (*op. cit.*, p. 49) thinks both were ordained deacons at Auxerre with Patrick. They are said in the *Annals of Ulster* to have begun their work in Ireland in 439, seven years after the inauguration of Patrick's mission. In connection with their labors both are regularly referred to as bishops. Bury regards the document as an episcopal circular letter rather than the findings of a synod.

[8] Ecclus. 20:2. Cf. *Coll. can. Hib.*, lxvi, 18.

[9] The text in Haddan and Stubbs is "si quis in questionem captivis quaesierit." The *Coll. can. Hib.*, xlii, 25, has "si quis redemptionem captivi inquisierit."

[10] "in plebe," as in canons 3, 24, 27, and 33, below, and often in Welsh documents. See A. W. Wade-Evans, *Y-Cymmrodor*, XXII (1910), 33 n. 4.

2. Every reader[11] shall become acquainted with the church in which he sings.

3. There shall be no wandering cleric in a parish.

4. If anyone receives permission, and the money[12] has been collected, he shall not demand more than that which necessity requires.

5. If anything is left over, he shall place it on the altar of the priest that it may be given to some needy person.[13]

6. If any cleric, from sexton[14] to priest, is seen without a tunic, and does not cover the shame and nakedness of his body;[15] and if his hair is not shaven according to the Roman custom,[16] and if his wife goes about with her head unveiled, he shall be alike despised by laymen and separated from the Church.

7. Any cleric, who, having been commanded, on account of negligence does not come to the assemblies of matins or vespers, shall be deemed a stranger, unless perchance he was detained in the yoke of servitude.

8. If a cleric becomes surety for a pagan in any amount, and it turns out (which is not strange), that through some craftiness that pagan fails the cleric, the cleric shall pay the debt with his own property; for if he fights with him in arms, he shall be justly reckoned to be outside the Church.[17]

9. A monk and a virgin, the one from one place, the other from another, shall not dwell together in the same inn, nor travel in the same carriage from village to village, nor continually hold conversation with each other.

10. If anyone has shown the beginning of a good work in psalm singing and has now ceased, and lets his hair grow, he is to be excluded from the Church unless he restores himself to his former condition.

[11] The word "denique" (lastly) appears after "lectores," and seems to suggest that this provision is quoted from a series of which it is the final member.

[12] "pretium." Evidently money to ransom a captive. *Coll. can. Hib.*, xlii, 26 a, has "pretium captivi."

[13] *Coll. can. Hib.*, xlii, 26 a, has "to needy persons and captives."

[14] "hostiario." The *Coll. can. Hib.* devotes a "book" of three capitula to the duties of this official: lib. vii, *De ostiario.* Cf. *Ancient Laws of England*, ed. B. Thorpe, II, 347 (Canons of Aelfric, 10): "Ostiarius is the church doorkeeper whose duty it is to announce the hours with bells, and unlock the church to believing men, and to shut the unbelieving without."   [15] "turpitudinem ventris et nuditatem."

[16] See Bury, *op. cit.*, p. 240, for the view that the foreign tonsure was introduced in Patrick's time. This provision is contained in *Coll. can. Hib.*, lii, 7, in slightly variant language and is there ascribed to St. Patrick.   [17] Cf. *Coll. can. Hib.*, xxxiv, 2.

11. If any cleric has been excommunicated by someone, and another receives him, both shall alike exercise penance.

12. Alms shall not be accepted from any Christian[18] who has been excommunicated.

13. It is not permitted to the Church to accept alms from pagans.

14. A Christian who slays, or commits fornication, or in the manner of the pagans consults[19] a diviner, for each single offense shall do penance for a year. At the completion of a year of penance he shall come with witnesses and afterwards be absolved[20] by the priest.

15. He who commits theft shall do penance for half a year, twenty days on bread [and water], and if it can be done, he shall restore the stolen goods; so shall he be denied [admission] into the Church.

16. A Christian who believes that there is a vampire in the world,[21] that is to say, a witch, is to be anathematized; whoever lays that reputation upon a living being,[22] shall not be received into the Church until he revokes with his own voice the crime that he has committed and accordingly does penance with all diligence.

17. A virgin who has taken the vow to God to remain chaste and afterwards marries a husband in the flesh shall be excommunicate until she is converted: if she has been converted and desists from her adultery she shall do penance, and thereafter they shall not dwell in the same house or in the same village.

18. If anyone is excommunicate he shall not enter a church, not even on the eve of Easter, until he accepts[23] a penance.

19. A Christian woman who takes a man in honorable marriage and afterwards forsakes her first husband and is joined to an adulterer —she who does this shall be excommunicate.

20. A Christian who defrauds anyone with respect to a debt in the manner of the pagans, shall be excommunicated until he pays the debt.[24]

21. A Christian to whom someone has defaulted and who brings

---

[18] *Coll. can. Hib.*, xl, 8, has "any cleric."
[19] Reading "aruspicem interrogaverit" from *Coll. can. Hib.*, xxviii, 10, for "ad aruspicem juraverit."   [20] "resolvetur."
[21] Spelman suggests "speculo" (mirror) for "saeculo."
[22] "quicumque super animam famam istam imposuerit."
[23] "recipiet." When the penance is imposed and assumed the prohibition to enter a church is removed, but it is not indicated that the penitent is admitted to communion before the penance is performed.
[24] Substantially quoted in *Coll. can. Hib.*, xxxiii, 1, ed. Wasserschleben, p. 118, but there ascribed to "sinodus Romana."

him to judgment, not to the church so that the case may there be investigated—whoever does this shall be an alien.

22. If anyone gives his daughter in honorable marriage, and she loves another, and he yields to his daughter and receives the marriage payment,[25] both shall be shut out of the Church.

23. If anyone of the presbyters builds a church, he shall not offer [the sacrifice in it] before he brings his bishop that he may consecrate it; for this is proper.

24. If a new incumbent[26] enters the parish he shall not baptize, nor offer, nor consecrate, nor build a church until he receives permission from the bishop; but whoever seeks permission from the tribesmen[27] shall be an alien.

25. If any things have been given by religious men on those days in which the bishop sojourns in the several churches, the disposition of the pontifical gifts, as is the ancient custom, shall appertain to the bishop, whether for necessary use or for distribution to the poor, as the bishop himself may determine.

26. But if any cleric contravenes this and is caught seizing the gifts, he shall be separated from the Church as one greedy of filthy lucre.[28]

27. Any cleric who has recently entered the parish of a bishop is not permitted to baptize and offer, nor to do anything: if he does not act accordingly he shall be excommunicate.

28. If one of the clerics is excommunicate, he shall make his prayer alone, not in the same house with his brethren, and he may not offer or consecrate until he has corrected himself.[29] If he does not act accordingly he shall be doubly punished.

29. If anyone of the brothers[30] wishes to receive the grace of God,[31]

---

[25] "dotem." The bride-price, or marriage payment, given by the bridegroom to the father of the bride. In Irish it was called "tinscra" or "tinol," in Welsh "agueddy." The father's portion strictly formed part of the larger gift of the bridegroom to the bride, called in Irish "coibche," in Welsh "cowyll." See *Ancient Laws of Ireland*, ed. by W. N. Hancock and others, I, 155; II, 383; IV, 61; V, 293; *Ancient Laws and Institutes of Wales*, ed. by A. Owen, I, 81ff; W. K. Sullivan, in Introduction to E. O'Curry, *On the Manners and Customs of the Ancient Irish*, I, cxlii ff.   [26] "advena."

[27] Cf. *Coll. can. Hib.*, xliii, 4, which has for "gentibus," "infidelibus et laicis" (unbelievers and laymen).

[28] I Tim. 3:8; Titus 1:7, 11; I Peter 5:2.

[29] To this point the canon resembles *Coll. can. Hib.*, xl, 9, which has, however, "baptize" for "consecrate."

[30] "fratrum." But the reference is to pagan or unbaptized members of the community.

[31] That is, baptism. Leclercq interprets this part of the sentence: "Tous ceux qui demanderont le baptême," *op. cit.*, p. 894.

he shall not be baptized until he has done [penance for] a period of forty days.

30. Any bishop who passes from his own into another parish shall not presume to ordain, unless he receives permission from him who has authority there;[32] however, on Sunday he may offer according to arrangement,[33] and he shall be satisfied with compliance in this matter.

31. If one of two clerics who, as it happens, are in conflict over some disagreement hires an enemy who has offered himself to one of them to slay [the other], it is fitting that he be called a murderer. Such a cleric is to be held an alien to all righteous men.[34]

32. If one of the clerics wishes to aid a captive he shall succour him with his own money; for if he delivers him by stealth many clerics are railed against on account of one thief. He who so acts shall be excommunicate.

33. A cleric who comes to us from the Britons without a certificate,[35] even if he dwells in the parish, is not permitted to minister.

34. With us, likewise, a deacon who departs into another parish, not having consulted his abbot and without letters, ought not to distribute food, and he ought to be punished with penance by his own presbyter whom he has despised. And a monk who goes wandering without consulting his abbot ought to be punished.

Here end the determinations of the Synod.

CANONS OF THE ALLEGED SECOND SYNOD OF PATRICK

1. *Of dwelling with sinful brethren.*—Concerning what you have commanded with respect to dwelling among sinful brethren, hearken unto the Apostle who says: "With such an one not so much as to eat."[36] Thou shalt not partake of his food with him. Likewise if thou art an ox and treadest out the corn, that is, if thou art a teacher and teachest: "Thou shalt not muzzle the ox,"[37] and: "Thou art worthy

---

[32] Literally, "from him who is in his own principate" ("qui in suo principatu est").

[33] "susceptione."

[34] The text is probably corrupt. *Coll. can. Hib.,* x, *x,* is parallel, but has marked differences of language and construction. Ed. by Wasserschleben, p. 29.

[35] "sine epistola." See Leclercq's note, *op. cit.,* p. 896, and Bury, *op. cit.,* p. 244. Perhaps the regulation is consciously based on the council of Antioch (341), canons 7 and 8; Mansi, II, 1311. The council of Laodicea (*ca.* 380) prohibited (can. 42) the clergy from traveling without letters canonical. Hefele-Leclercq, *op. cit.,* I(2), 1020; Mansi, II, 572.

[36] I Cor. 5:11.   [37] Deut. 25:4; I Cor. 9:9.

of thy reward";[38] but "Let not the oil of the sinner fatten thy head."[39] But thus far rebuke and chastise.[40]

2. *Of their offerings.*[41]—Be content with thy clothing and food; reject other things that are the gifts of the wicked since the lamp takes nothing but that by which it is fed.

3. *Of penance after fall.*[42]—It is determined that the abbot give attention to the matter of those to whom he assigns the power of binding and loosing; but more fitting is pardon, according to the examples of the Scripture. If with weeping and lamentation and a garment of grief, under control, a short penance [is more desirable][43] than a long one, and a penance relaxed with moderation.

4. *Of the rejection of the excommunicated.*[44]—Hearken unto the Lord when he saith: "If he will not hear thee let him be [to thee] as the heathen and the publican."[45] Thou shalt not curse, but thou shalt reject an excommunicated person from communion and from the table and from the Mass and from the Pax;[46] and if he is a heretic, after one admonition avoid him.[47]

5. *Of suspected cases.*—Hearken unto the Lord when he saith: "Suffer both to grow until the harvest,"[48] that is, "until he cometh who will make manifest the counsels of the hearts,"[49] that thou make not judgment before the Day of Judgment. Behold Judas at the table of the Lord, and the thief in paradise.

6. *Of the punishments of the Church.*—Hearken again unto the Lord when he saith, "Whosoever shall shed innocent blood, his blood shall be shed:"[50] but [it is to be shed] by him who carries the sword; moreover, the chief magistrate is held innocent in punishment. Of others, however, [the matter is determined] by the evangelical law, from that place in which it says: "And of him that taketh

---

[38] I Tim. 5:18.   [39] Ps. 140:5.   [40] Cf. Ps. 93:10.

[41] "oblationibus." So Wilkins. Haddan and Stubbs read "observationibus." A "book" of sixteen capitula devoted to offerings is contained in the *Coll. can. Hib.* (Lib. xvii). Cap.13 cites the gifts of Nebuchadnezzar to Daniel as a precedent for receiving the gifts of sinners.

[42] "ruinas." Cf. p. 89, n. 10, below.

[43] *Coll. can. Hib.*, xvii, d, has "melior est penitentia brevis reddenda."

[44] Heading supplied by Spelman.

[45] Based on Matt. 18:17; but for "hear thee" the Vulgate has "hear the church."

[46] "After he had thus given his benediction the bishop, at the words *Pax Domini sit semper vobiscum*—The peace of the Lord be with you evermore—sent forth the kiss of peace." D. Rock, *The Church of Our Fathers*, ed. by G. W. Hart and W. H. Frere, IV, 46.

[47] Titus 3:10.   [48] Matt. 13:30.

[49] I Cor. 4:5.   [50] Gen. 9:6.

away thy goods, ask them not again."[51] But, if he restores anything, gladly receive it in humility.

7. *Of questions concerning baptism.*[52]—They determine that those who have received the tradition of the symbol be not rebaptized, from whomsoever they have received it, since the seed is not defiled by the wickedness of the sower. But if they have not received it, it is not rebaptism, but baptism. We believe that those who have lapsed from the faith are not to be absolved unless they are received with imposition of hands.

8. *Of accused persons taken from a church.*—A church is not made for the defense of accused persons; but judges ought to be persuaded that they would slay with spiritual death[53] those who flee to the bosom of mother Church.

9. *Of those who have fallen after attaining to clerical rank.*—Hearken to the canonical institutes. Whoever falls when he has clerical rank[54] shall arise without rank. Content with the name [of cleric] alone, he shall lose his ministry; except that when he sins in the sight of God alone, he does not withdraw [from his ministry].

[No. 10 is lacking.]

11. *Of the separation of the sexes after fall.*—Each one shall consider in his conscience whether the love and desire of sin have ceased, since a dead body does not harm another dead body; if this is not the case they shall be separated.

12. *Of offering for the dead.*—Hearken unto the Apostle when he saith: "There is a sin unto death, for that I say not that any man ask."[55] And [to] the Lord: "Give not that which is holy to dogs."[56] For he who did not in his life deserve to receive the sacrifice, how shall it be able to help him after death?

13. *Of the sacrifice.*—On the eve of Easter, [even] if it is permissible to carry it outside, it is not to be carried outside, but brought down to the faithful. What else signifies it that the Lamb is taken in one house,[57] but that Christ is believed and communicated under one roof of faith?

[51] Luke 6:30.   [52] "De baptismatis incertis."

[53] That is, by removing the offenders. Leclercq paraphrases "ut spirituale morte eos occiderent" by the words "de faire mourir par l'épée de la pénitence," which is neither the equivalent of the Latin nor any more comprehensible. Probably the idea is that the soul's safety rather than that of the body alone was sought by flight to the Church, and was thought of as forfeited with his removal. This canon is contained in *Coll. can. Hib.* xxviii, 14, d, with slight variants from the present text; it is there ascribed to "a synod of the Romans."   [54] "cum gradu."   [55] I John. 5:16.   [56] Matt. 7:6.

[57] Probably an allegorical reference to Exod. 12:3–4.

14. *Of votive or legal abstinence from food.*—It is established that after the coming of Christ the Bridegroom, he shall set forth no fixed laws of fasting. But the difference between the Novationists and the Christians is that whereas a Novationist abstains continually, a Christian does so for a time only, that place, time, and person should in all things be regarded.[58]

15. *Of leaving or of teaching one's own country.*—One's country is first to be taught, after the example of Christ; and afterwards if it does not make progress, it is to be abandoned, according to the example of the Apostle. But he who is able to do it may take the risk, teach and show himself everywhere; he who is not able, let him be silent and depart. One, you recall, is sent by Jesus to his own house; another is commanded to follow Him.[59]

16. *Of false bishops.*—He who is not chosen by another bishop, according to the Apostle, is to be condemned; thereafter he is to be deposed and degraded to [the status of] the rest of the people.

17. *Of the provost of the monks.*—There are monks who dwell as solitaries without worldly resources, under the power of a bishop or an abbot. But they are not [really] monks, only pretenders to philosophy, that is, despisers of the world.[60] Each one ought to be drawn to the perfect life in mature[61] age, that is, from twenty years, not in witnessing to, but in fulfilling, his vow: as saith this [passage], "Let each do as he hath purposed in his heart,"[62] and, "That I shall render my vows in the sight of the Lord,"[63] and so forth. With whatever vow he is bound, the location of places limits it, if excess is to be avoided in all things in life; for they are called in cold and nakedness, in hunger and thirst, in vigils and fasts.[64]

---

[58] *Coll. can. Hib.*, xii, 15, c., introduced by "Statuunt Romani" instead of "Statutum" as in our text.   [59] Luke 8:39; Matt. 9:9.

[60] Reading "saeculi" for "sollicite"; "pretenders to philosophy" is inexact but conveys a suggestion of the sense intended. The expression used is "vactro-periti." On this canon Haddan and Stubbs (II, 335) make the following note: " 'Bactro-peratae" from βάκτρον and πήρα, is a contemptuous name for 'philosophi,' applied by S. Jerom (*in Matt.* xix) to corrupt monks: who as he proceeds to say were 'contemptores sæculi.' For 'sollicit' in the text should probably be read 'sæculi.' But even so amended, some words seem to have dropped out of this text." βάκτρον means a staff; πήρα a pouch or wallet, to carry victuals. (The expression βακτρο-προσαίτης was applied to a class of peripatetic mendicant philosophers who carried a staff.)

[61] "perfecta."   [62] Based on II Cor. 9:7.

[63] "Domini" for "populi" (of the people) in the Vulgate, Ps. 115:18.

[64] The sense of this vague language seems to be that the ascetic regulations applicable to those who are called "in cold and nakedness," and so forth, should vary with locality and climate.

18. *Of the three seeds of the Gospels.*[65]—The "hundredfold" are the bishops and teachers, who are all things to all men. The "sixtyfold" are the clergy and widows who are continent. The "thirtyfold" the lay folk who are faithful, who perfectly believe in the Trinity. Beyond these there is nought in the harvest of the Lord. Monks and virgins we combine with the "hundredfold."[66]

19. *Of the proper age for baptism.*—On the eighth day they are catechumens; thereafter they are baptized in the solemn feast days[67] of the Lord, that is at Easter, Pentecost, and Epiphany.

20. *Of parishes.*—We are not to speak with the monks whose wickedness is unusual, we who not improperly maintain the unity of the parish.

21. *Of monks to be retained or dismissed.*—Let every one enjoy his fruit in the church in which he has been instructed, unless the cause of greater success requires that he bear to another's [church] the permit of his abbot (?).[68] If, indeed, there appears a weightier[69] cause, it shall be said with blessing: "Behold the Lamb of God,"[70] each one seeking not the things that are his own but those which are Jesus Christ's.[71] But they do not permit their subjects to run about on the claim of a vocation.

22. *Of taking the Eucharist after a fall.*—After a proving of the flesh it is to be taken, but especially on the eve of Easter;[72] for he who does not communicate at that time is not a believer. Therefore short and limited are the seasons for such persons, lest the faithful soul perish, famished by so long a time of correction,[73] for the Lord saith: "Except you eat the flesh of the Son of Man, you shall not have life in you."[74]

23. *Of taking an oath.*—"Swear not at all."[75] Following from this, the series of the lection teaches that no other creature is to be sworn

---

[65] Cf. Matt. 13:8.

[66] This interpretation of the Parable of the Sower is based upon the exposition of St. Jerome, who teaches that "the hundredfold signifies the crown of virginity, the sixtyfold, the labor of widows, while the thirtyfold . . . denotes the bond of marriage." Hieronymus *Epistolae* cxxxiii. 8. Cf. *Epp.* xxii. 15; xlvii. 2; lxvi. 1, where similar language is used. See also the reference in the *Penitential of Finnian*, can. 46, p. 96, below.

[67] "solemnitatibus."

[68] "nisi causa maioris profectus ad alternis ferre permissa [Wilkins: permisso] abbatis cogat."   [69] "utilior."   [70] John 1:36.   [71] Based on Phil. 2:21.

[72] On the offices of Holy Saturday in the Anglo-Saxon Church see Rock, *Church of Our Fathers*, IV, 106 ff.

[73] "ne anima fidelis intereat tanto tempore ieiuna medicinae."

[74] John 6:54.   [75] Matt. 5:34.

by, none but the Creator, as is the custom of the prophet: "The Lord liveth,"[76] and "My soul liveth," and "The Lord liveth in whose sight I stand."[77] But there is "an end of controversy"[78] unless [the oath is] by the Lord. For by all that a man loves, by this does he make oath.[79]

24. *Of the contention of two without witnesses.*—They determine that before he takes communion he who is being approved shall testify by the four holy gospels, and then he shall be left to the judgment of fire.[80]

25. *Of the bed of a dead brother.*—Hear the decree of the synod: "A surviving brother shall not enter the bed of a dead brother." For the Lord saith: "and they shall be two in one flesh":[81] therefore the wife of thy brother is thy sister.[82]

26. *Of a prostitute wife.*—Hearken unto the Lord when he saith: "He who is joined to a harlot is made one body."[83] Also, "An adulteress shall be stoned;[84] that is, she shall die for this fault, that she may cease to increase who does not cease to commit adultery. Further, if a woman has become corrupted, does she return to her former husband?[85] Moreover, it is not permitted to a man to put away his wife, except because of fornication[86]—and if he says it is for that reason: hence, if he marries another, as if after death of the former, [authorities] do not forbid it.

27. *Of the will of the maiden or of the father in marriage.*—What the father wishes, the maiden shall do, since the head of the woman is the man.[87] But the will of the maiden is to be inquired after by the father, since "God left man in the hand of his own counsel."[88]

28. *Of the first or the second vows.*—First vows[89] and first marriages are to be observed in the same way, that the first be not made void for the second, unless they have been stained with adultery.

29. *Of consanguinity in marriage.*—Understand what the Law saith, not less nor more: but what is observed among us, that they be

---

[76] I Kings (I Samuel in A.V.) 25:26.

[77] III Kings (I Kings in A. V.) 17:1.   [78] Heb. 6:16.

[79] This canon, with variations, is ascribed to St. Jerome in *Coll. can. Hib.*, xxxv, 3.

[80] Reading: "qui adprobatur" for "quid probatur" and "flamma" for "fama" in accordance with *Coll. can. Hib.*, xvi, 14.   [81] Gen. 2:24.

[82] This canon is also found in *Coll. can. Hib.*, xlvi, 35, b. Numerous synods prohibited marriage to a deceased brother's wife.

[83] I Cor. 6:16.   [84] Lev. 20:10; Deut. 22:22.

[85] Based apparently on Jer. 3:1.   [86] Based on Matt. 19:9.

[87] Eph. 5:23. The Douay version renders "vir" and "mulier," "husband" and "wife," respectively; in our text the Scripture words are construed as applying to father and daughter. Cf. I Cor. 11:3.   [88] Ecclus. 15:14.   [89] Apparently vows of betrothal.

separated by four degrees, they say they have neither seen nor read.[90]

30. *Of the assertion of customs.*—What is never forbidden is permitted. Truly the laws of the Jubilee are to be observed, that is, the fifty years, that a doubtful method be not established in the change of time.[91] And therefore every business transaction[92] is confirmed by subscription.[93]

31. *Of the pagans who believe before baptism: how they receive penance.*—The sins of all are indeed remitted in baptism; but he who with a believing conscience lives for a time as an unbeliever[94] is to be judged as a believing sinner.

Here ends the Synod of Patrick.

2. THE PENITENTIAL OF FINNIAN (*ca.* 525–50)

[THE BEST indications of the authorship of the *Poenitentiale Vinniai* point to Finnian of Clonard, a distinguished Irish monastic founder and teacher who died in or about A.D. 550. This Finnian was early reputed to have studied and associated with the British saints, Gildas, David, and Cadoc.[1] The Latin *Life of Cadoc* by Lifris narrates that Finnian, with other young Irish scholars, accompanied Cadoc on the latter's return from Ireland to Britain.[2] He appears also in the *Life of St. David* by Rhygyvarch participating in a British synod.[3] There is a high probability that the Vinniaus of the penitential is the "Vennianus auctor" referred to in the letter of Columban to Gregory the Great. Columban states that this Vennianus asked advice from Gildas on unstable monks.[4] Columban, in his own penitential, made extensive use of the *Penitential of Finnian*. The suggestion is irresistible that this Finnian is the "Vennianus an

---

[90] The "Law" is apparently the Old Testament Law. It is here declared authoritative in matters of consanguinity in marriage. The subject of "say" (dicunt) is perhaps the uninstructed, whether clerics or laymen.

[91] This canon is incoherent and the text is apparently confused. The reference is of course to the Jubilee Year of Lev. 25:9–13. *Coll. can. Hib.*, xxxvi, 8, has "ut non affirmentur incerta tempore veterato" (that doubtful matters be not established by antiquity) for "ut non adfirmetur incerta vice ratio temporis" in the present text.

[92] "negotiatio." Perhaps the idea of confirmation by subscription is connected with the requirement in Lev. 25:10, 13: "Ye shall return every man unto his possession."

[93] Omitting "Romanorum" (of the Romans). It is omitted in *Coll. can. Hib.*, xxxvi, 8.

[94] "infidelis," that is, apparently, without baptism.

[1] W. Stokes, *Lives of Saints from the Book of Lismore*, p. 223; De Smedt and De Backer, *Acta sanctorum Hiberniae*, col. 191 f.

[2] Chap. viii: "Finian videlicet Macmoil." W. J. Rees, *Cambro-British Saints*, p. 36; but cf. Chap. ix, where two youths, "Finnian videlicet, et Macmoil," are referred to (*ibid.*, p. 38). In Chap. xl (*ibid.*, p. 79), Finnian is referred to as the pupil (discipulus) of Cadoc.

[3] A. W. Wade-Evans, *Life of St. David*, p. 40.

[4] "Vennianus auctor Gildam de his interrogavit et ellegantissime ille rescripsit," *Epistolae Columbani*, ed. by W. Gundlach, *M.G. H.*, *Ep. Merov. et Karol. Aevi*, I, 159.

author" of Columban's letter, and at the same time the Finian, Findian, or Finnian of the lives cited, namely, Finnian of Clonard.[5] This view is rendered the more probable by the fact that Columban was the pupil in turn of two of the pupils of Finnian of Clonard, Sinell, and Comgall. It is indeed probable that through these distinguished disciples of Finnian of Clonard, Columban fell heir to the work of their master and was inspired to contribute in later life a fresh booklet to the series of penitentials.

This important penitential is more ample than any of the sixth-century Welsh documents. It not only exhibits the methodical treatment of sins and their appropriate penalties for clergy (canons 1-34) and laity (canons 35-53) but also provides some element of theoretic explanation of the uses of penance. Finnian closes his booklet with the claim that it is in accordance with Scripture and the opinions of very learned men. He shows no consciousness of originating a tradition, and it may be inferred that his work does little more than codify what he thought best in the practice of penance among his associates. His "doctissimi" doubtless included some of his notable Welsh and Irish contemporaries. Materials from Jerome and Cassian have also been directly or indirectly used.

The *Penitential of Finnian* is extant in three ninth-century manuscripts, St. Gall, Stiftsbibl. 150, Vindob. 2233, and Paris, Bibl. Nat. Lat. 12021—of which the last mentioned is of Breton origin but copied from an Insular original—and in the tenth or eleventh century Paris, Bibl. Nat. Lat. 3182, which contains numerous other penitential elements. It has been edited by Wasserschleben[6] and by Schmitz.[7]]

In the name of the Father and of the Son and of the Holy Ghost.

1. If anyone has sinned in the thoughts of his heart and immediately repents, he shall beat his breast and seek pardon from God and make satisfaction, that he may be whole.

2. But if he has frequently entertained [evil] thoughts and hesitated to act on them, whether he has mastered them or been mastered

---

[5] Schmitz regards Finnian of Moville as the author of the penitential; but his argument is highly unconvincing (I, p. 498 f.). See McNeill, pp. 32-38 (*Rev. celt.*, XXXIX, 266-72), and Kenney, p. 240. On other grounds O. Seebass also finally favored Finnian of Moville as the writer (*Z.K.G.*, XIV [1894], 430 ff.), supposing that the *Prefatio Gildae* (see below p. 174), which Finnian apparently consulted, was written by Gildas about 565 and therefore after the death of Finnian of Clonard. Although this view is adopted by M. Esposito ("Latin Learning in Medieval Ireland," *Hermathena*, XX [1930], 238 f.) and by L. Gougaud (*Christianity in Celtic Lands*, p. 285), it still seems to me unsatisfactory in the light of the probabilities and possibilities in regard to the dates of Gildas, and of his relations, just indicated, with Finnian of Clonard.   [6] *Bussordnungen*, pp. 108-19.

[7] Schmitz I, pp. 497-509. Kenney's citation of alleged editions by D'Achéry and Martène is apparently due to applying to this document a note in Wasserschleben's Introduction, p. 10, which there applies to the *Coll. can. Hib.* See Kenney, p. 240. For a discussion of the text of Finnian, see above, pp. 57 f.

by them, he shall seek pardon from God by prayer and fasting day and night until the evil thought departs and he is whole.

3. If anyone has thought evil and intended to do it, but opportunity has failed him, it is the same sin but not the same penalty; for example, if he intended fornication or murder, since the deed did not complete the intention he has, to be sure, sinned in his heart, but if he quickly does penance, he can be helped. This penance of his is half a year on an allowance, and he shall abstain from wine and meats for a whole year.

4. If anyone has sinned in word by an inadvertence and immediately repented, and has not said any such thing of set purpose, he ought to submit to penance, but he shall keep a special fast; moreover, thereafter let him be on his guard throughout his life, lest he commit further sin.

5. If one of the clerics or ministers of God makes strife, he shall do penance for a week with bread and water and seek pardon from God and his neighbor, with full confession and humility; and thus can he be reconciled to God and his neighbor.

6. If anyone has started a quarrel and plotted in his heart to strike or kill his neighbor, if [the offender] is a cleric, he shall do penance for half a year with an allowance of bread and water and for a whole year abstain from wine and meats, and thus he will be reconciled to the altar.

7. But if he is a layman, he shall do penance for a week, since he is a man of this world and his guilt is lighter in this world and his reward less in the world to come.

8. But if he is a cleric and strikes his brother or his neighbor or sheds blood, it is the same as if he had killed him, but the penance is not the same. He shall do penance with bread and water and be deprived of his clerical office for an entire year, and he must pray for himself with weeping and tears, that he may obtain mercy of God, since the Scripture says: "Whosoever hateth his brother is a murderer,"[8] how much more he who strikes him.

9. But if he is a layman, he shall do penance forty days and give some money to him whom he struck, according as some priest or judge determines. A cleric, however, ought not to give money, either to the one or to the other (?).[9]

[8] I John 3:15.
[9] "pecuniam dare non debet . . . aut illi aut illę." Cf. also Introduction pp. 70 f, above. "Illę" may stand for a feminine form of "illi" = "illae."

10. But if one who is a cleric falls miserably through fornication[10] he shall lose his place of honor,[11] and if it happens once [only] and it is concealed from men but known before God, he shall do penance for an entire year with an allowance of bread and water and for two years abstain from wine and meats, but he shall not lose his clerical office. For, we say, sins are to be absolved in secret by penance and by very diligent devotion of heart and body.

11. If, however, he has long been in the habit of sin and it has not come to the notice[12] of men, he shall do penance for three years with bread and water and lose his clerical office, and for three years more he shall abstain from wine and meats, since it is not a smaller thing to sin before God than before men.

12. But if one of the clerical order falls to the depths of ruin[13] and begets a son and kills him, great is the crime of fornication with homicide, but it can be expiated through penance and mercy. He shall do penance three years with an allowance of bread and water, in weeping and tears, and prayers by day and night, and shall implore the mercy of the Lord, if he may perchance have remission of sins; and he shall abstain for three years from wine and meats, deprived of the services of the clergy, and for a forty-day period in the last three years he shall fast with bread and water; and [he shall] be an exile in his own country, until a period of seven years is completed. And so by the judgment of a bishop or a priest he shall be restored to his office.

13. If, however, he has not killed the child, the sin is less, but the penance is the same.

14. But if one of the clerical order is on familiar terms with any woman and he has himself done no evil with her, neither by cohabiting with her nor by lascivious embraces, this is his penance: For such time as he has done this he shall withdraw from the communion of the altar and do penance for forty days and nights with bread and water and cast out of his heart his fellowship with the woman, and so be restored to the altar.

15. If however he is on familiar terms with many women and has given himself to association with them and to their lascivious em-

[10] "ruina fornicationis." Cf. canons 12, 15, 27.
[11] "coronam suam," his crown, or honor; here perhaps with a reference to his public functions. Cf. can. 21.
[12] Reading with the Vienna manuscript "notitiam" for "nocentiam."
[13] "ruina maxima." Literally, "by the greatest calamity."

braces, but has, as he says, preserved himself from ruin,[14] he shall do penance for half a year with an allowance of bread and water, and for another half year he shall abstain from wine and meats and he shall not surrender his clerical office; and after an entire year of penance, he shall join himself[15] to the altar.

16. If any cleric lusts after a virgin or any woman in his heart but does not utter [his wish] with the lips, if he sins thus but once he ought to do penance for seven days with an allowance of bread and water.

17. But if he continually lusts and is unable to indulge his desire, since the woman does not permit him or since he is ashamed to speak, still he has committed adultery with her in his heart. It is the same sin though it be in the heart and not in the body; yet the penance is not the same. This is his penance: let him do penance for forty days with bread and water.

18. If any cleric or woman who practices magic misleads anyone by the magic, it is a monstrous sin, but [a sin that] can be expiated by penance. Such an offender shall do penance for six years, three years on an allowance of bread and water, and during the remaining years he shall abstain from wine and meats.

19. If, however, such a person does not mislead anyone but gives [a potion] for the sake of wanton love to some one, he shall do penance for an entire year on an allowance of bread and water.

20. If some woman by her magic misleads[16] any woman with respect to the birth of a child, she shall do penance for half a year with an allowance of bread and water and abstain for two years from wine and meats and fast for six forty-day periods with bread and water.

21. But if, as we have said, she bears a child and her sin is manifest, she shall do penance for six years with bread and water (as is the judgment in the case of a cleric) and in the seventh year she shall be joined to the altar; and then we say her honor[17] can be restored and she should don a white robe and be pronounced a virgin. So a cleric who has fallen ought likewise to receive the clerical office in the seventh year after the labor of penance, as saith the Scripture:

---

[14] "ruina."

[15] Reading with the Vienna manuscript "ita iungat se" for "iungantur" (Wasserschleben erroneously reads "jungatur").

[16] "partum alicuius femine deciperit." For "deciperit" three manuscripts have "perdiderit" with the meaning: "destroys a woman's child."

[17] "coronam." Cf. can. 10.

"Seven times a just man falleth and ariseth,"[18] that is, after seven years of penance he who fell can be called "just," and in the eighth year evil shall not lay hold on him. But for the remainder [of his life] let him preserve himself carefully lest[19] he fall; since, as Solomon saith, as a dog returning to his vomit[20] becomes odious, so is he who through his own negligence reverts to his sin.

22. But if one has sworn a false oath, great is the crime, and it can hardly, if at all, be expiated; but none the less it is better to do penance and not to despair: great is the mercy of God. This is his penance: first, he must never in his life take an oath, since a man who swears much will not be justified and "the scourge shall not depart from his house."[21] But the medicine of immediate penance in the present time is needful to prevent perpetual pains in the future; and [it is needful] to do penance for seven years and for the rest of one's life to do right, not to take oaths, and to set free one's maidservant or manservant or to give the value of one [servant] to the poor or needy.

23. If any cleric commits murder and kills his neighbor and he is dead, he must become an exile for ten years and do penance seven years in another region. He shall do penance for three years of this time on an allowance of bread and water, and he shall fast three forty-day periods on an allowance of bread and water and for four years abstain from wine and meats; and having thus completed the ten years, if he has done well and is approved by testimonial of the abbot or priest to whom he was committed, he shall be received into his own country and make satisfaction to the friends of him whom he slew, and he shall render to his father or mother, if they are still in the flesh, compensation for the filial piety and obedience [of the murdered man] and say: "Lo, I will do for you whatever you ask, in the place of your son." But if he has not done enough he shall not be received back forever.

24. But if he killed him suddenly and not from hatred—the two having formerly been friends—but by the prompting of the devil, through an inadvertence, he shall do penance for three years on an allowance of bread and water, and for three more years he shall abstain from wine and meats; but he shall not remain in his own country.

---

[18] Prov. 24:16. [19] Reading, with the Vienna manuscript, "ne" for "nec."
[20] Prov. 26:11. [21] Ecclus. 23:12.

25. If a cleric commits theft once or twice, that is, steals his neighbor's sheep or hog or any animal, he shall do penance an entire year on an allowance of bread and water and shall restore fourfold to his neighbor.

26. If, however, he does it, not once or twice, but of long habit, he shall do penance for three years.

27. If anyone who formerly was a layman, has become a cleric, a deacon, or one of any rank, and if he lives with his sons and daughters and with his own concubine,[22] and if he returns to carnal desire and begets a son with his concubine, or says he has, let him know that he has fallen to the depths of ruin;[23] his sin is not less than it would be if he had been a cleric from his youth and sinned with a strange girl, since they have sinned after his vow and after they were consecrated to God, and then they have made the vow void. He shall do penance for three years on an allowance of bread and water and shall abstain for three years more from wine and meats, not together, but separately, and then in the seventh year [such clerical offenders] shall be joined [to the altar] and shall receive their rank.

28. But if a cleric is covetous, this is a great offense; covetousness is pronounced idolatry,[24] but it can be corrected by liberality and alms. This is the penance for his offense, that he cure and correct contraries by contraries.[25]

29. If a cleric is wrathful or envious or backbiting, gloomy or greedy, great and capital sins are these; and they slay the soul and cast it down to the depth of hell. But there is this penance for them, until they are plucked forth and eradicated from our hearts: through the help of the Lord and through our own zeal and activity let us seek[26] the mercy of the Lord and victory in these things; and we shall continue in weeping and tears day and night so long as these things are turned over in our heart. But by contraries, as we said, let us make haste to cure contraries and to cleanse away the faults from our hearts and introduce virtues in their places. Patience must arise for wrathfulness; kindliness, or the love of God and of one's neighbor, for envy; for detraction, restraint of heart and tongue; for

[22] Reading "clientela" for "cleventella." The Vienna manuscript has "clentella."
[23] "ruina maxima."
[24] Based on Col. 3:5.
[25] The principle here affirmed, and elaborated in the following canon, is probably derived by Finnian from Cassian. C.S.E.L., XIII(2), 548 ff. Cf. Introduction, pp. 44 f.
[26] Reading with the Vienna manuscript "petamus" for "petimus."

dejection,[27] spiritual joy; for greed, liberality; as saith the Scripture: "The anger of man worketh not the justice of God";[28] and envy is judged as leprosy by the law. Detraction is anathematized in the Scriptures; "He that detracteth his brother"[29] shall be cast out of the land of the living. Gloom devours or consumes the soul. Covetousness is "the root of all evil,"[30] as saith the Apostle.

30. If any cleric under the false pretense of the redemption of captives is found out and proved to be despoiling churches and monasteries, until he is confounded, if he has been a "conversus," he shall do penance for an entirè year on an allowance of bread and water and all the goods which were found with him of those things which he had gathered shall be paid out and lent to the poor: for two years he shall abstain from wine and meat.

31. We require and encourage contributing for the redemption of captives; by the teaching of the Church, money is to be lent to the poor and needy.

32. But if he has been a "conversus" he is to be excommunicated and be anathema to all Christians and be driven from the bounds of his country and beaten with rods until he is converted,—if he has compunction.[31]

33. We are obliged to serve the churches of the saints as we have ability and to suffer with all who are placed in necessity. Pilgrims are to be received into our houses, as the Lord has written; the infirm are to be visited; those who are cast into chains are to be ministered to; and all things commanded of Christ are to be performed, from the greatest unto the least.[32]

34. If any man or woman is nigh unto death, although he (or she) has been a sinner and pleads for the communion of Christ we say that it is not to be denied to him if he promise to take the vow, and

[27] "tristitia," gloom, depression, sadness, sorrow. Cf. II Cor. 7:10, a passage sometimes cited by monastic writers on the subject: "The sorrow of the world worketh death."
[28] James 1:20.   [29] James 4:11.   [30] I Tim. 6:10.
[31] The "conversus" in Irish monasticism was a convert "who had spent a large portion of his life in worldly pursuits."—J. Ryan, *Irish Monasticism*, London, 1931, p. 216. Cassian has numerous references to compunction as a penitent state of mind. He reports discussions of "the diverse causes of compunction" and "the various characteristics of compunction." The most striking evidence of compunction consisted in tears, but sometimes it was attended by shouts of joy, sometimes by silence. Apparently the word "compunctio" was used to cover a variety of phenomena not dissimilar to those which often attended conversion in the Evangelical Revival; but in the penitential discipline the element of mass suggestion was relatively slight. See especially *Collationes*, viiii, 26 and 27, *C.S.E.L.*, XIII(2), 273.
[32] This passage is evidently based on Matt. 25:35-36, 42-43.

let him do well and he shall be received by Him. If he becomes a novice let him fulfill in this world that which he has vowed to God. But if he does not fulfill the vow which he has vowed[33] to God, [the consequences] will be on his own head. As for us, we will not refuse what we owe to him: we are not to cease to snatch prey from the mouth of the lion or the dragon, that is of the devil,[34] who ceases not to snatch at the prey of our souls; we may follow up and strive [for his soul] at the very end of a man's life.

35. If one of the laity is converted from his evil-doing unto the Lord, and if he has previously wrought every evil deed, that is, the committing of fornication and the shedding of blood, he shall do penance for three years and go unarmed except for a staff in his hand, and shall not live with his wife. But in the first year he shall do penance on an allowance of bread and water and not live with his wife. After a penance of three years he shall give money for the redemption of his soul and the fruit of repentance into the hand of the priest and make a feast for the servants of God, and in the feast [his penance] shall be ended; and he shall be received to communion and shall resume relations with his wife after an entire and complete penance, and if it is satisfactory he shall be joined to the altar.

36. If any layman defiles his neighbor's wife or virgin daughter,[35] he shall do penance for an entire year on an allowance of bread and water, and he shall not have intercourse with his own wife; after a year of penance he shall be received to communion, and shall give alms for his soul. So long as he is in the body, he shall not go in to commit fornication again with a strange woman; or if [he defiles] a virgin two years shall be his penance, the first with bread and water. In the other [year] he shall fast for forty days, abstain from wine and meat, and give alms to the poor and the fruit of his penitence into the hands of his priest.[36]

37. If anyone has defiled a vowed virgin and lost his honor and begotten a child by her, let such an one, being a layman, do penance for three years; but in the first year he shall go on an allowance of bread and water and unarmed and shall not have intercourse with his own wife, and for two years more he shall abstain from wine and meats and shall not have intercourse with his wife.

[33] Following the Vienna manuscript: "non impleat votum quod voverit."
[34] Manuscripts "diaboli." Wasserschleben has "diabolum," erroneously.
[35] "virginem." Cf. I Cor. 7:36–38.
[36] The words "or if . . . priest" are found only in the Vienna manuscript.

38. If, however, he does not beget a child, but nevertheless[37] defiles the virgin, [he shall do penance for] an entire year on an allowance of bread and water, and for half a year he shall abstain from wine and meats, and he shall not have intercourse with his wife until his penance is completed.

39. If any layman with a wife of his own has intercourse with his female slave, the procedure is this: the female slave is to be sold, and he himself shall not have intercourse with his own wife for an entire year.

40. But if he begets by this female slave one, two, or three children, he is to set her free, and if he wishes to sell her it shall not be permitted to him, but they shall be separated from each other, and he shall do penance an entire year on an allowance of bread and water and shall have no further intercourse with his concubine but be joined to his own wife.

41. If anyone has a barren wife, he shall not put away his wife because of her barrenness, but they shall both dwell in continence and be blessed if they persevere in chastity of body until God pronounces a true and just judgment upon them. For I believe that if they shall be as Abraham and Sarah were, or Isaac and Rebecca, or Anna the mother of Samuel, or Elizabeth the mother of John, it will come out well for them at the last. For the Apostle saith: "And let those that have wives be as if they had none, for the fashion of this world passeth away."[38] But if we remain faithful we shall receive what God hath given whether unto prosperity or unto adversity, always with joy.

42. We declare against separating a wife from her husband; but if she has left him, [we declare] that she remain unmarried or be reconciled to her husband according to the Apostle.[39]

43. If a man's wife commits fornication and cohabits with another man, he ought not to take another wife while his wife is alive.

44. If perchance she is converted to penance,[40] it is becoming to receive her, if she has fully and freely sought this, but he shall not give her a dowry,[41] and she shall go into service to her former hus-

---

[37] Wasserschleben reads: "tantum" but the manuscripts have "tamen."
[38] I Cor. 7:29, 31.
[39] I Cor. 7:11.
[40] An unnecessary "et" occurs after "penance."
[41] "sed dotem ei non dabit." This "dos" here referred to is apparently the "coibche" or gift of the bridegroom to the bride. See above, pp. 36 f., 79, and below, pp. 254, 383.

band; as long as he is in the body she shall make amends in the place of a male or a female slave, in all piety and subjection.

45. So also a woman, if she has been sent away by her husband, must not mate with another man so long as her former husband is in the body; but she should wait for him, unmarried, in all patient chastity, in the hope that God may perchance put patience in the heart of her husband. But the penance of these persons is this—that is, of a man or woman who has committed fornication: they shall do penance for an entire year on an allowance of bread and water separately and shall not sleep in the same bed.

46. We advise and exhort that there be continence in marriage, since marriage without continence is not lawful, but sin, and [marriage] is permitted by the authority of God not for lust but for the sake of children, as it is written, "And the two shall be in one flesh,"[42] that is, in unity of the flesh for the generation of children, not for the lustful concupiscence of the flesh. Married people, then, must mutually abstain during three forty-day periods in each single year, by consent for a time,[43] that they may be able to have time for prayer for the salvation of their souls; and on Sunday night or Saturday night they shall mutually abstain, and after the wife has conceived he shall not have intercourse with her until she has borne her child, and they shall come together again for this purpose, as saith the Apostle.[44] But if they shall fulfill this instruction, then they are worthy of the body of Christ, as by good works they fulfill matrimony, that is, with alms and by fulfilling the commands of God and expelling their faults, and in the life to come they shall reign with Christ, with holy Abraham, Isaac, Jacob, Job, Noah, all the saints; and there they shall receive the thirtyfold fruit which as the Savior relates in the Gospel, he has also plucked for married people.[45]

47. If the child of anyone departs without baptism and perishes through negligence, great is the crime of occasioning the loss of a soul; but its expiation through penance is possible, since there is no crime which cannot be expiated through penance so long as we are in this body. The parents shall do penance for an entire year with bread and water and not sleep in the same bed.

[42] Matt. 19:5; Mark 10:8.
[43] I Cor. 7:5.   [44] I Cor. 7:5.
[45] Matt. 13:8. See above, p. 84, note 66. For "they shall reign" the text reads "thou shalt reign."

48. But if a cleric does not receive a child [to baptism], if it is a child of the same parish[46] he shall do penance for a year on bread and water.

49. He is not to be called a cleric or a deacon who is not able to baptize and to receive the dignity of a cleric or a deacon in the Church.

50. Monks, however, are not to baptize, nor to receive alms; if, then, they do receive alms, why shall they not baptize?

51. If there is anyone whose wife commits fornication with another man, he ought not to hold intercourse with her until she does penance according to the penalty which we laid down above, that is, after an entire year of penance.[47] So also a woman is not to hold intercourse with her husband, if he has committed fornication with another woman, until he performs a corresponding penance.

52. If anyone loses a consecrated object[48] or a blessing of God, he shall do penance for seven days.

53. He shall not go to the altar until his penance has been completed. Here endeth: thanks be to God.

Dearly beloved brethren, according to the determination of Scripture or the opinion of some very learned men I have tried to write these few things concerning the remedies of penance, impelled by love of you, beyond my ability and authority. There are still other authoritative materials,[49] concerning either the remedies or the variety of those who are to be treated, which now by reason of brevity, or the situation of a place, or from poverty of talent, I am not permitted to set down. But if anyone who has searched out the divine Scripture should himself make larger discoveries, or if he will produce or write better things, we will both agree with him and follow him.

Here endeth this little work which Finnian adapted to the sons of his bowels, by occasion of affection or of religion, overflowing with the graces of Scripture, that by all means all the evil deeds of men might be destroyed.

[46] "ex una plebe."
[47] Can. 45.
[48] "creaturam." Cf. p. 112, n. 76, below. The Albers text of the *Penitential of Bede* explains "creatura" as "incense, thuribles, tablets, or a sheet for writing, or holy salt, bread newly consecrated, or anything of that sort." See below, p. 230.
[49] "testimonia."

3 . THE PENITENTIAL OF CUMMEAN (*ca.* 650)

[A SERIES of "iudicia," or decisions, on matters of penance, attributed to an Irish abbot named Cummean or Cominianus, were in circulation in the Frankish Empire in the early ninth century. The belief that Cummean was the author of a penitential book is attested by the appearance of his name in connection with the so-called *Excarpsus Cummeani*.[1]

J. Zettinger has given reasons for identifying the work here translated as the original *Penitential of Cummean*. The manuscript, Codex Vat. Pal. Lat. 485, was written in the monastery of Lorsch (a center of Irish influence) in the ninth century. From internal evidence and detailed comparison with other penitentials, Zettinger concludes that the book was compiled about the middle of the seventh century in either Scotland or Ireland. In another manuscript, Codex Vat. 1349, the prologue of this document is given with an ascription to "Cumianus Longus" (Cummean the Long). This leads Zettinger further to suggest the author's identification with this Cummean, whom he, however (following A. Theiner, *Disquisitiones criticae*, 1836, p. 280), mistakenly supposes to have become abbot of Iona. Cummean or Cummine the Long ("Fota" or "Foda"), who lived about 592–662 A.D., was a son of King Fiachna of West Munster, founded the monastery of Kilcummin, King's County, and may be the distinguished Cummean of St. Brendan's foundation of Clonfert. By some he has been identified with the bishop Cummean who, leaving Ireland at the age of seventy-five, spent his later life, a period of more than twenty years, in the monastery of Columban at Bobbio, and died there in the reign of Liutprand (711–44).[2] The publication, since Zettinger's study, of the *Old Irish Penitential* edited by Dr. Gwynn,[3] which has references to "Cummine Fota" some of which harmonize with passages in the present document, lends support to the view of his authorship of this penitential. Even if we suppose that the author went to the Continent, it still seems rather probable that the document originated in Ireland. There is no reason to connect it with Iona. That it was known in Ireland in the seventh century seems probable from parallels in the *Irish Canons*. W. Finsterwalder has indicated also a high probability for its use by Theodore or by Eoda, the first compiler of the *Penitential of Theodore*, 665–90.[4] Penitential texts of later origin ascribed to Cummean show the influence of Continental councils, of which Zettinger finds here

[1] See below, pp. 266 ff.

[2] Wasserschleben, *Bussordnungen*, pp. 61 ff.; W. Stokes, *The Martyrology of Oengus*, p. 243; Kenney, pp. 420, 428, 516; J. O'Hanlon, *Lives of the Irish Saints*, VIII, 288 ff. (cf. VI, 605 ff.). It was Cummean the White (Ailbe or Fionn, d. 669), son, or more probably grandson, of another Fiachna, who was Abbot of Iona. W. Reeves, *Life of St. Columba*, 1st ed., pp. 119, 342, 373 ff.; R. I. Best and H. J. Lawlor, *The Martyrology of Tallaght*, p. 19. The inscription on the tomb erected by Liutprand to the Bobbio Cummean is translated by M. Stokes, *Six Months in the Apennines*, pp. 171 ff. See also my "Note on Cummean the Long," *Rev. celt.*, L (1933), 289 ff.; and T. P. Oakley's detailed comparison with Gwynn's *Old Irish Penitential* in "A Great Penitential and Its Authorship," *Romanic Review*, XXV (1934), 25–33.   [3] See below, pp. 155 ff.   [4] See below, pp. 180 f.

no trace. In these texts Cummean is several times described as an abbot of Irish birth—"abbas in Scotia ortus." Possibly the fame of the aged Cummean of Bobbio led his Continental admirers to regard him as the author of the penitential. The genuine penitential was evidently used as a basis for later formulations to which Cummean's name was attached.

The work is greatly indebted to the writings of Cassian, and depends for its plan on his scheme of the eight principal sins. The translation is made from Zettinger's edition, which is given with a valuable intro-duction under the title "Das Poenitentiale Cummeani," *A.K.K.R.*, LXXXII (1902), 501–40. The manuscript has also been consulted. In addition a few corrections have been made from the seventh or eighth century uncial manuscript Copenhagen Ny Kgl. S. 58 of the *Excarpsus Cummeani*. Cf. p. 67, above.]

Here begins the Prologue of the health-giving medicine of souls.

As we are about to tell of the remedies of wounds according to the determinations of the earlier fathers, of sacred utterance to thee, my most faithful brother, first we shall indicate the treatments by the method of an abridgment.

The first[5] remission then is that by which we are baptized in water, according to this [passage]: "Unless a man be born again of water and of the Holy Spirit, he cannot see the Kingdom of God."[6] The second is the emotion of charity, as this [text] has it: "Many sins are remitted unto her for she hath loved much."[7] The third is the fruit of alms, according to this: "As water quencheth fire so doth alms extinguish sin."[8] The fourth is the shedding of tears, as saith the Lord: "Since Ahab wept in my sight and walked sad in my presence I will not bring evil things in his days."[9] The fifth is the confession

---

[5] This passage, ending with "in Paradise," is substantially a quotation from Caesarius of Arles (*ca.* 470–542), *Homilies* XII (Migne, *P.L.*, LXVII, 1075). The dependence extends to most of the peculiarities of the scriptural quotations, which differ considerably from the approved text of the Vulgate. This little homily in Caesarius is entitled "Of the Twelve Remissions of Sins." Cummean uses "remissio" only in the first of the series, but the word is understood with the numeral adjective in each subsequent instance. Caesarius himself has done little more than compress a more amply phrased passage in Cassian. The latter's *Conference of Abbot Pinufius*, chap. viii (*Collationes*, XX, viii, *C.S.E.L.*, XIII, 561 ff.), contains a list of penitential works, described by Cassian as "fruits of penitence by which we attain to the expiation of our sins." Cassian's list is identical with that of Caesarius, except for the latter's insertion of the numerals, and his transfer of the second remission to the twelfth place in his list. Cassian in a rather lax spirit presents these remissions as alternative ways of obtaining pardon. The principle is similar to that of the commutations in the penitentials. His table of remissions is in turn largely dependent on Origen's *Second Homily on Leviticus*, which offers a numbered list of seven remissions. These are: baptism, martyrdom, almsgiving, forgiveness of others, conversion of sinners, fulness of love, and penance with tears. Migne, *P.L.*, XI, 418.   [6] John 3:5.   [7] Luke 7:47.

[8] Ecclus. 3:33.   [9] III Kings (=I Kings in A.V.) 21:29.

of offenses, as the Psalmist testifies: "I said, I will confess my in-
justices to the Lord, and thou hast forgiven the iniquity of my sin."[10]
The sixth is affliction of heart and body, as the Apostle comforts us:
"I have given such a man to Satan unto the destruction of the flesh,
that his spirit may be saved in the day of our Lord Jesus Christ."[11]
The seventh is the amendment of morals, that is, the renunciation
of vices, as the Gospel testifies: "Now thou art whole, sin no more,
lest some worse thing happen to thee."[12] The eighth is the intercession of the saints, as this text states: If any be sick, "let him bring
the priests of the church and let them pray for him, lay their hands
upon him, and anoint him with oil in the name of the Lord, and the
prayer of faith shall save[13] the sick man and the Lord shall raise him
up, and if he be in sins they shall be forgiven him," and so forth; and
"the continual prayer of a just man availeth much before the Lord."[14]
The ninth is the merit of mercy and faith, as this says: "Blessed are
the merciful for they shall obtain mercy."[15] The tenth is the conversion and salvation of others,[16] as James assures us: "He who
causeth a sinner to be converted from the error of his way shall save[17]
his soul from death and shall cover a multitude of sins";[18] but it is
better for thee if thou art sick, to lead a solitary life than to perish
with many. The eleventh is our pardon and remission, as He that is
the Truth has promised, saying: "Forgive and ye shall be forgiven."[19]
The twelfth is the passion of martyrdom, as the one hope of our
salvation pardoned even the cruel robber, God replying to him:
"Amen I say to thee this day thou shalt be with me in paradise."[20]

Therefore, since these things are cited on the authority of the
canon, it is fit that thou shouldst search out, also, the determinations
of the fathers who were chosen by the mouth of the Lord, according
to this passage: "Ask thy father and he will declare[21] unto thee, thy
elders[22] and they will tell thee";[23] moreover, let the matter be referred to them.[24] And so they determine that the eight principal vices

---

[10] Ps. 31:5.   [11] I Cor. 5:5.   [12] John 5:14.
[13] Reading with Vulgate "salvabit" for "salvavit."
[14] Jas. 5:14–16.   [15] Matt. 5:7.
[16] "aliorum," as in Caesarius. *Pseudo-Cummean* has "alienorum" (strangers), a variation perhaps suggested by Eph. 2:12, "alienati a conversatione Israel."
[17] "salvabit" for "salvavit" as in note 13.
[18] Jas. 5:20.   [19] Luke 6:37.   [20] Luke 23:43.
[21] Reading "adnuntiabit" for "adnuntiavit."
[22] "seniores." Vulgate, "maiores."   [23] Deut. 32:7.
[24] "causa deferatur ad eos." Perhaps a reflection of "ad deos utriusque causa perveniet"
(the cause of both parties shall come to the gods). Exod. 22:9.

contrary to human salvation shall be healed by these eight contrary remedies. For it is an old proverb: Contraries are cured by contraries;[25] for he who freely commits what is forbidden ought freely to restrain himself from what is otherwise permissible.[26]

I. Of Gluttony[27]

1. Those who are drunk with wine or beer, contrary to the Savior's prohibition (as it is said, "Take heed that your hearts be not overcharged with surfeiting and drunkenness or with the cares of this life lest perchance that day come upon you suddenly, for as a snare shall it come upon all that dwell upon the face of the whole earth,"[28]) and [that] of the Apostle; ("Be not drunk with wine wherein is luxury")[29]—if they have taken the vow of sanctity, they shall expiate the fault for forty days with bread and water; laymen, however, for seven days.

2. He who compels anyone, for the sake of good fellowship,[30] to become drunk shall do penance in the same manner as one who is drunk.

3. If he does this on account of hatred, he shall be judged as a homicide.

4. He who is not able to sing psalms, being benumbed in his organs of speech,[31] shall perform a special fast.

5. He who anticipates the canonical hour,[32] or only on account of appetite takes something more delicate than the others have, shall go without supper or live for two days on bread and water.

6. He who suffers excessive distention of the stomach and the pain of satiety [shall do penance] for one day.

7. If he suffers to the point of vomiting, though he is not in a state of infirmity, for seven days.

[25] See Introduction (p. 44 f.) and the *Penitential of Finnian*, 28, 29, p. 92 above.

[26] "qui enim inlicita licenter commisit, a licitis licet cohercere se debuit." For the translation "licenter" is substituted for "licet," assuming that there were originally abbreviation strokes over the "e" and the "t" to make it read "licenter." In order to indicate the play upon the form "licet" in the original the sentence might be rendered: "He who freely commits that which may not be freely committed ought freely to restrain himself from committing [even] that which may be freely committed."

[27] "gula." For the use in *Pseudo-Cummean* and other penitentials of Cassian's scheme of the Deadly Sins see P. Schulze, *Die Entwicklung der Hauptlaster- und Haupttugendlehre von Gregor dem Grossen bis Petrus Lombardus*, pp. 68 ff.

[28] Luke 21:34-35.   [29] Eph. 5:18.   [30] "humanitatis gratia."

[31] Reading with *Pseudo-Cummean*, I, 9, "stupens in linguis" for "stupens se linguis." *Preface of Gildas*, 10, has "e" for "in."   [32] That is, the proper time to take food.

8. If, however, he vomits the host, for forty days.

9. But if [he does this] by reason of infirmity, for seven days.

10. If he ejects it into the fire, he shall sing one hundred psalms.

11. If dogs lap up this vomit, he who has vomited shall do penance for one hundred days.

12. [One who] steals food [shall do penance] for forty days; if [he does it] again, for three forty-day periods; if a third time, for a year; if, indeed, [he does it] a fourth time, he shall do penance in the yoke of exile under another abbot.

13. A boy of ten years who steals anything shall do penance for seven days.

14. If, indeed, afterward [at the age] of twenty years he adds to this any considerable theft, for twenty or forty days.

II. Of Fornication

1. A bishop who commits fornication shall be degraded and shall do penance for twelve years.

2. A presbyter or a deacon who commits natural fornication, having previously taken the vow of a monk [?], shall do penance for seven years. He shall ask pardon every hour; he shall perform a special fast during every week except in the days between Easter and Pentecost. After the special fast he shall use bread without limitation and a dish spread with some butter, that is to say, a farthing's worth,[33] and he shall live in this way on Sunday. On other days his allowance of bread shall be a loaf of dry bread[34] [made from] a twelve-"polentae" vessel full of flour and a refection cooked with a little fat, garden vegetables, a few eggs, British cheese, a Roman half-pint (the quantity of six hen's eggs) of milk[35] on account of the weakness of

---

[33] "hoc est quadrante." Zettinger thinks marginal glosses have crept into the text: possibly this is one. The translation is conjectural. Perhaps there is some connection between the word "quadrante" here and the "quarter-ration" (O Ir "cethramthu") of the *Old Irish Penitential*, p. 160, below.

[34] Reading "paximati" for "paxmativi," as in Codex Copenhagen Ny Kgl. S. 58 fo. 8. Cf. also p. 54 and 175. "Paximatium" or "paxamatium" is the παξαμάδιον, a small hard loaf or biscuit baked on ashes. Cassian reports a decision of some of the Egyptian desert fathers making two of these the regular daily allowance for ascetics. He also indicates that two cost about three denarii, and that they weighed scarcely a pound. Cassian, *Inst.* IV, xiv; *Coll.* II, xi, xix, xxiv, xxvi; XIX, iv. Cf. H. E. G. White, *History of the Monasteries of Nitria and of Scetis*, p. 202. "Polenta," here a measure, is, according to Du Cange equivalent to "Pognadina" (Cf. French "poignet," wristband) perhaps a handful.

[35] "cimina plenitudo, VI. ovorum, gall. Romana lactis." Reading "himina" for "cimina," as in the Copenhagen manuscript, and punctuating after "himina" and "gall." The words placed in parenthesis in the translation were probably originally a marginal

bodies in this age; a Roman pint of whey or buttermilk[36] for his thirst, and enough water, if he is a worker; and he shall have his bed provided with a small amount of hay. Through three forty-day periods yearly he shall add something, as far as his strength permits. He shall at all times deplore his guilt from his inmost heart. Above all things he shall adopt an attitude of the readiest obedience. After a year and a half he shall take the Eucharist and come to peace and sing the psalms with his brethren, lest his soul within him perish through so long a time of the celestial medicine.[37]

3. If [the culprit] is a monk of inferior status, he shall do penance for three years, but his allowance of bread shall not be increased. If he is a worker let him take a pint of Roman milk and another of whey and as much water as the intensity of his thirst requires.

4. If a presbyter or a deacon without monastic vow has sinned thus, he shall do the same penance as a monk not in holy orders.

5. But if after the offense he wants to become a monk, he shall do penance in this way in a designated place of exile[38] for a year and one-half. However, the abbot has authority to modify this, if his obedience is satisfactory to God and to his own abbot.

6. He who sins with a beast shall do penance for a year; if by himself, for three forty-day periods, [or] if he has [clerical] rank, a year; a boy of fifteen years, forty days.

7. He who defiles his mother shall do penance for three years, with perpetual pilgrimage.

8. Those who befoul their lips shall do penance for four years; if they are accustomed to the habit they shall do penance for seven years.

9. So shall those who commit sodomy do penance for seven years.

10. For femoral masturbation, two years.

gloss; as their omission in *Pref. Gild.* and their unnatural position in the present text would indicate. In ancient Ireland liquid measures were based upon a given number of hen's eggs. Cf. below p. 160, n. 4. Zettinger suggests the Anglo-Saxon measure "galleta," "galo," but with "ovorum" we should probably read "gallinarum" and translate as above.

[36] The words "XII plenitudo VI gall.," are inserted here, evidently a gloss which has been thrown into disorder. If the "himina" is equivalent to six eggs, the "sextarius" (Roman pint) would be equivalent to twelve, as the glossator was apparently trying to say.

[37] "ieiunia" (fasts), omitted from translation. It is not in *Pref. Gildae* and is probably an explanatory gloss on "celestial medicine." Or perhaps we should read the gloss in the sense of "fasting from the celestial medicine" (of the Eucharist). Cf. the *Old Irish Penitential*, II, 4, p. 160, below.

[38] Reading "exsili" for "ex alii," as in *Pseudo-Cummean*, II, 26; Schmitz II, p. 611.

11. He who merely desires in his mind to commit fornication, but is not able, shall do penance for one year, especially in the three forty-day periods.

12. He who is polluted by an evil word or glance, yet did not wish to commit bodily fornication, shall do penance for twenty or forty days according to the degree of his sin.

13. But if he is polluted by a violent assault of the imagination he shall do penance for seven days.

14. He who for a long time is lured by imagination to commit fornication, and repels the thought too gently, shall do penance for one or two or more days, according to the duration of the imagination.

15. He who is willingly polluted during sleep, shall arise and sing nine psalms in order, kneeling. On the following day he shall live on bread and water; or he shall sing thirty psalms, kneeling at the end of each.

16. He who desires to sin during sleep, or is unintentionally polluted, fifteen[39] psalms, he who sins and is not polluted, twenty-four.

17. A cleric who commits fornication once shall do penance for one year on bread and water; if he begets a son he shall do penance for seven years as an exile; so also a virgin.

18. He who loves any woman, [but is] unaware of any evil beyond a few conversations, shall do penance for forty days.

19. But he who kisses and embraces, one year, especially in the three forty-day periods.

20. He who loves in mind only, seven days.

21. If, however, he has spoken but has not been accepted by her, forty [days].

22. A layman who turns to fornication and the shedding of blood shall do penance for three years; in the first, and in three forty-day periods of the others, with bread and water, and in all [three years] without wine, without flesh, without arms, without his wife.

23. A layman who defiles his neighbor's wife or virgin [daughter][40] shall do penance for one year with bread and water, without his own wife.

24. But if he defiles a vowed virgin and begets a son, [he shall do

[39] Text has "XII, XV." *Excerpts from the Book of David*, 9, has "XV psalmos." A glossator has apparently corrected XII to XV, and the numeral has been drawn into the text.
[40] Cf. p. 94, n. 35, above.

penance] for three years without arms; in the first, with bread and water, in the others without wine and flesh.

25. If he does not beget, but defiles, he shall do penance for one year and one-half without delicacies and without his wife.

26. But if he enters in unto his woman-slave, he shall sell her and shall do penance for one year.

27. If he begets a son by her, he shall liberate her.

28. In the case of one whose wife is barren, both he and she shall live in continence.

29. If any man's wife deserts him and returns again, he shall receive her without payment,[41] and she shall do penance for one year with bread and water. The man shall do likewise if he has taken another to wife.

30. He who is in a state of matrimony ought to be continent during the three forty-day periods and on Saturday and on Sunday, night and day, and in the two appointed week days,[42] and after conception, and during the entire menstrual period.

31. After a birth he shall abstain, if it is a son, for thirty-three [days]; if a daughter, for sixty-six [days].[43]

32. A man whose child dies on account of neglect without baptism [shall do penance] for three years; in the first with bread and water, in the other two without delicacies and without the married relationship.

33. If a cleric from the same parish does not accept him,[44] he shall do penance for one year; if [he is] not of the same parish, for half a year.

III. Of Avarice

1. He who commits theft once shall do penance for one year; if [he does it] a second time, for two years.

2. If he is a boy, forty or thirty days, according to his age or state of knowledge.

3. He who hoards what is left over until the morrow through ignorance shall give these things to the poor. But if [he does this] through contempt of those who censure him, he shall be cured by

[41] "sine dote," without marriage dowry. See above, p. 79.
[42] That is, Wednesday and Friday.   [43] Lev. 12:4–5.
[44] Apparently the child, "filius," in 32.

alms and fasting according to the judgment of a priest. If, indeed, he persists in his avarice he shall be sent away.

4. He who recovers from one who is carrying them off[45] things that are his own, against the contrary command of the Lord[46] and of the Apostle, shall give to the poor those things which he has recovered.

5. He who plunders another's goods by any means, shall restore fourfold to him whom he has injured.

6. If he has not the means of making restitution, he shall do penance as we have stated above.

7. He who steals consecrated things shall do penance as we have said above, but in confinement.

8. He who makes a false oath shall do penance for four years.

9. But he who leads another in ignorance to commit perjury shall do penance for seven years.

10. He who is led in ignorance to commit perjury and afterwards finds it out, one year.

11. He who suspects that he is being led into perjury and nevertheless swears, shall do penance for two years, on account of his consent.

12. He who bears false witness shall first satisfy his neighbor, and in so far as he has wronged his brother, with such judgment shall he be condemned, a priest being the judge.

13. He who fails to fulfill any of those things for which the Lord said, "Come ye blessed of my father," etc.,[47] for whatever time he has continued thus, for that time he shall do penance, and he shall live liberally[48] to the end of his life [?];[49] but if he does otherwise, he shall be sent away.

14. A cleric who has an excess of goods shall give these to the poor; but if he does not, he shall be excommunicated.

15. If he afterwards does penance, he shall live secluded in penance for the same [length of] time as that in which he was recalcitrant.

16. One who lies because of cupidity shall make satisfaction in liberality to him whom he has cheated.

[45] Reading "auferenti" for "auferentem," as in a manuscript of the *Capit. Iud.* cited in Schmitz II, p. 238, and in *Pseudo-Cummean*, VIII, 4, Schmitz II, p. 628.

[46] Probably a reference to Matt. 5:39-42 and similar passages counseling nonresistance.

[47] Matt. 25:34.

[48] Evidently in the sense of giving alms liberally.

[49] "tenileto."

17. One who lies through ignorance, however, and does not know it, shall confess to him to whom he has lied and to a priest and shall be condemned to an hour of silence or fifteen psalms.[50]

18. If [he] verily [did it] by intention, he shall do penance by three days of silence, or three[51] psalms if he can [sing].

IV. Of Anger

1. He who, justly or unjustly, makes his brother sad shall mollify by a satisfaction the rancor he has conceived, and so he shall be able to pray.

2. But if it is impossible to be reconciled with him,[52] then at least he shall do penance, his priest being judge.

3. He who refuses to be reconciled[53] shall live on bread and water for as long a time as he has been implacable.[54]

4. He who hates his brother shall go on bread and water as long as he has not overcome his hatred; and he shall be joined to him whom he hates in sincere charity.

5. He who commits murder through nursing hatred in his mind,[55] shall give up his arms until his death, and dead unto the world, shall live unto God.

6. But if it is after vows of perfection, he shall die unto the world with perpetual pilgrimage.

7. But he who does this through anger, not from premeditation, shall do penance for three years with bread and water and with alms and prayers.

8. But if he kills his neighbor unintentionally, by accident, he shall do penance for one year.

9. He who by a blow in a quarrel renders a man incapacitated or maimed shall take care of [the injured man's] medical expenses and shall make good the damages for the injury[56] and shall do his work until he is healed and do penance for half a year.

---

[50] The penitential known as *Capitula iudiciorum Cummeani*, XV, 6, has "five" for "fifteen" here. Schmitz II, p. 235.   [51] *Capit. Iud.* has "thirty." Schmitz II, *loc. cit.*

[52] Literally, "received by him."   [53] Literally, "does not receive him."

[54] The words "homicida illa" (*sic*) are omitted. In the *Capit. Iud.* these words instead occur after the passage rendered above: "Qui odit fratrem suum homicida est," "He that hateth his brother is a murderer" (I John 3:15), Schmitz II, p. 246. The word "homicida" has probably strayed into canon 3 from canon 4 which no longer contains it.

[55] "odii meditatione"; malice aforethought.

[56] "macule pretium" (the price of the blemish). Cf. pp. 124, 225, n. 49.

10. If he has not the wherewithal to make restitution for these things, he shall do penance for one year.

11. He who gives a blow to his neighbor without doing him harm,[57] shall do penance on bread and water one or two or three forty-day periods.

12. One who curses his brother in anger shall both make satisfaction to him whom he has cursed and live secluded for seven days on bread and water.

13. He who utters in anger harsh but not injurious words shall make satisfaction to his brother and keep a special fast.

14. But if [he expresses his anger] with pallor or flush or tremor, yet remains silent, he shall go for a day on bread and water.

15. He who [does not betray it but] nevertheless feels incensed in his mind[58] shall make satisfaction to him who has incensed him.

16. He who will not confess to him who has incensed him, that pestilential person shall be sent away from the company of the saints; if he repents, he shall do penance for as long as he was recalcitrant.

V. Of Dejection[59]

1. He who long harbors bitterness in his heart shall be healed by a joyful countenance and a glad heart.

2. But if he does not quickly lay this aside, he shall correct himself by fasting according to the decision of a priest.

3. But if he returns to it, he shall be sent away until, on bread and water, he willingly and gladly acknowledges his fault.

VI. Of Languor[60]

1. The idler shall be taxed with an extraordinary work, and the slothful with a lengthened[61] [?] vigil; that is, he shall be occupied with three or[62] [six?] psalms.

2. Any wandering and unstable man shall be healed by permanent residence in one place and by application to work.

[57] Reading with Zettinger (*op. cit.*, p. 514) "et non nocuit" for "et non novit" (without knowing it).
[58] *Capit. Iud.*, XXIX, 2 (Schmitz II, p. 246) has "si quis mentis tantum sentit commotionem" (if anyone feels only a perturbation of mind) for "Qui mente tamen sentit commotionem," here.   [59] "tristitia."   [60] "accidia."   [61] "propensiori."
[62] Evidently a numeral is omitted, probably "six" as in the *Bigotian Penitential*, VI, ii, 2. In a parallel passage *Pseudo-Cummean*, X, 2, "tribus vel septem" (three or seven), Schmitz II, p. 631, and *Capit. Iud.*, XXXI, has: "id est iv vel vii psalm. occupetur." Schmitz II, p. 247.

VII. Of Vainglory[63]

1. The contentious also shall subject himself to the decision of another; otherwise he shall be anathematized, since he is among the strangers to the Kingdom of God.

2. One who boasts of his own good deeds shall humble himself; otherwise any good he has done he shall lose on account of human glory.

VIII. Of Pride

1. He who takes up any novelty outside the Scriptures, such as might lead to heresy, shall be sent away.

2. But if he repents, he shall publicly condemn his own[64] opinion and convert to the faith those whom he has deceived, and he shall fast at the decision of his priest.

3. He who proudly[65] censures others for any kind of[66] contempt shall first make satisfaction to them and then fast according to the judgment of his priest.

4. The disobedient shall remain outside the assembly, without food, and shall humbly knock until he is received; and for as long a time as he has been disobedient he shall go on bread and water.

5. The blasphemer, too, shall be healed by a similar seclusion.

6. He who murmurs shall be put apart and his work shall be rejected; he shall remain with the due half loaf of bread[67] and water.

7. The envious shall make satisfaction to him whom he has envied; but if he has done him harm, he shall satisfy him with gifts and shall do penance.

8. He who for envy's sake defames [another] or willingly listens to a defamer shall be put apart and shall fast for four days on bread and water.

9. If the offense is against a superior, he shall do penance thus for seven days and shall serve him willingly thereafter.

10. But, as someone says, to speak true things is not to defame; but, according to the Gospel, first rebuke him between thee and him

[63] "iactantia."
[64] Reading "suam" for "sua."
[65] Reading "superbia" for "superbos," as in the Copenhagen manuscript, fol. 31.
[66] Reading "qualibet" for quaslibet," with *Pseudo-Cummean*, XI, 1, and Schmitz II, p. 631.
[67] "cum semipane debito." Reading with Zettinger, "debito" for "debeo," as in *Capit. Iud.*, XXX, 2, Schmitz II, p. 247.

alone; afterwards, if he will not hear thee, call another; and if he will not hear you [both], tell the Church.[68]

11. He who is informed on and he who lays the information are persons of the same status. If he who is informed on denies [his guilt] they shall do penance together for one year, two days in each week on bread and water, and two days at the end of each month, while all the brethren hold them in subjection and call upon God as their judge.[69]

12. But if they persist in obstinacy after the lapse of a year, they shall be joined to the communion of the altar, under the proof of fire, and left to the judgment of God.

13. If at any time one of them confesses, to the extent to which he has inflicted hardship on the other his own [hardship] shall be increased.

14. If anyone, diligently garrulous, injures his brother's good name, he shall do penance in silence for one[70] or two days.

15. But if he did it in conversation, he shall sing twelve psalms.

16. One who retells evil [tales] not for the sake of the welfare of the hearers,[71] [but] lest others should consent to them, or for the sake of blaming the evil or confirming the good, or out of pity for the sorrowful,[72] is held to be a physician [of souls]; [but] if these three [motives] are lacking [he is considered] a detractor, and he shall sing thirty psalms in order.

17. He who offers an excuse to the abbot or the stewards, if he is ignorant of the rule, he shall do penance for one day; if he knows the rule, he shall keep a special fast.

18. He who intentionally disdains to bow to any senior shall go without supper.

19. He who is silent about his brother's sin which is unto death, shall rebuke him with confidence, and for so long a time as he was silent he shall live on bread and water.

20. If it was a slight sin that he kept silent about, he shall indeed rebuke him, but he shall do penance with psalms or fasting according to the judgment of his priest.

[68] Matt. 18:15–17.

[69] Canons 11–13 are evidently taken from the *Synod of North Britain*, pp. 5–7. For an explanation of the phraseology, see below, p. 171, n. 14.

[70] Reading "I die" for "ei die."   [71] "recipientium."

[72] That is, probably, to encourage those cast down by remorse for their own similar faults.

21. He who rebukes others boldly shall first conciliate them and then sing thirty psalms.

22. He who imputes a shameful sin to his brother, especially before he rebukes him, shall make satisfaction to him and do penance for three days.

23. He who speaks with a woman alone, or remains under the same roof [with her] at night, shall go without supper.

24. If [he does this] after being forbidden, he shall do penance on bread and water.

25. Some [authorities] give the ruling that twelve three-day periods are the equivalent of a year,[73] which I neither praise nor blame.

26. Others, one hundred days with half a loaf and an allowance of dry bread and water and salt, and [the penitent] shall sing fifty psalms during each night.

27. Others, fifty special fasts, with one night intervening.

28. Others determine that the penance of the sick shall consist in the giving of alms, that is, the price of a man[servant] or a maidservant; but it is fitting if anyone gives the half of all the things that he possesses, and if he have wronged anyone, that he restore him fourfold.[74]

IX. Of Petty Cases

1. If by some accident anyone negligently lose the host, leaving it for beasts and birds to devour, if it is excusable he shall do penance for three forty-day periods; if not, for a year.

2. He who not without knowing it gives the communion to one who is excommunicate, shall do penance for forty [days].

3. So [shall] he [do penance] who eats of a dead thing unaware; but if not [unaware], he shall do penance for a year.

4. Now let it be noted that for whatever time anyone remains in his sins, for so long shall he do penance.

5. If any work is imposed on anyone and he does it not, on account of contempt, he shall go without supper.

6. He who does not arrive at the end of the second psalm shall sing eight psalms in order.

[73] "pro anno repensanda." This paragraph introduces a series of four commutations in penance of which 26 and 27 seem to be unique. The others have parallels in the *Irish Canons*, II, 6, and the *Penitential of Theodore*, I, vii, 5. The latter is apparently dependent on Cummean.

[74] Luke 19:8.

7. If he is aroused after the mass, he shall repeat whatever his brethren have sung and shall beg for pardon.

8. If moreover a second time he does not come, he shall go without supper.

9. If anyone in error changes any of the words of the sacraments, where the [word] "danger"[75] is noted, he shall keep three special fasts.

10. If one by neglect lets fall the host to the ground, a special fast shall be assigned.

11. We ought to offer the sacraments on behalf of good kings, never on behalf of evil kings.

12. Presbyters are not forbidden to offer on behalf of their bishops.

13. Those who furnish guidance to the barbarians shall do penance for fourteen years, even if it does not result in the slaughter of the Christians; but if [it turns out] otherwise they shall give up their arms and until death, being dead to the world, shall live unto God.

14. He who despoils monasteries, falsely saying that he is redeeming captives, [shall] go for one year on bread and water, and everything that he has taken he shall give to the poor, and he shall do penance for two years without wine and flesh.

15. He who loses a consecrated object[76] shall do penance for seven days.

16. He who eats of the flesh of a dead animal,[77] of whose [manner of] death he is unaware, shall live the third part of a year on bread and water and the rest [of it] without wine and flesh.

X. *Let Us Now Set Forth the Determinations of Our Fathers before Us on the Misdemeanors*[78] *of Boys*

1. Boys talking alone and transgressing the regulations of the elders, shall be corrected by three special fasts.

2. Those who kiss simply shall be corrected with six special fasts; those who kiss licentiously without pollution, with eight special fasts; if with pollution or embrace, with ten special fasts.

3. But after the twentieth year (that is, adults) they shall live at

---

[75] "periculum." On the "periculosa oratio," see W. Stokes, *Thesaurus Palaeohibernicus*, II, 252, and the *Stowe Missal*, II, 40, in "Henry Bradshaw Society [Publications]," Vol. XXXII. After the elevation of the chalice the priest chants the miserere, "and the people kneel, and here no voice cometh lest it disturb the priest . . . that his mind separate not from God while he chants this lesson. Hence its 'nomen' is 'periculosa oratio.'" From a paragraph contained in an Old Irish treatise on the Mass appended to the *Stowe Missal* (ca. 792–812). Cf. below, p. 177, n. 29.   [76] "creaturam." Cf. p. 97, n. 48, above.

[77] Literally, "of a dead body of animal flesh."   [78] "ludis."

a separate table (that is, in continence)[79] and excluded from the church, on bread and water.

4. Children who imitate acts of fornication,[80] twenty days; if frequently, forty.

5. A boy who takes communion in the sacrament although he sins with a beast, one hundred days.

6. But boys of twenty years who practice masturbation together and confess [shall do penance] twenty or forty days before they take communion.

7. If they repeat it after penance, one hundred days; if frequently, they shall be separated and shall do penance for a year.

8. [One of] the above-mentioned age who practices femoral masturbation, one hundred days; if he does it again, a year.

9. A small boy misused by an older one, if he is ten years of age, shall fast for a week; if he consented, for twenty days.

10. A small boy, if he eats anything that has been stolen, shall do penance for seven days.

11. If after his twentieth year he adds to this any considerable theft, he shall do penance for twenty days.

12. If in the age of manhood he adds anything similar, forty days; if it is repeated, one hundred days; if it becomes a habit, a year.

13. A man who practices masturbation by himself, for the first offense, one hundred days; if he repeats it, a year.

14. Men guilty of homosexual practices, for the first offense, a year; if they repeat it, two years.

15. If they are boys, two years, if men, three or four years; but if it has become a habit, seven years, and a method of penance shall be added according to the judgment of this priest.

16. [Substantially repeats II, 8, page 103, above.]

17. A boy coming from the world who has recently sought to commit fornication with some girl but who was not polluted, shall do penance for twenty days; but if he was polluted, one hundred days; if indeed, as is the usual thing, he fulfills his intention, for a year.

18. He who eats the skin of his own body, that is, a scab, or the vermin which are called lice, or his own excreta—with imposition of

---

[79] The words "id est adulti, id est continentes" occur after "twentieth year"; but they appear to be two glosses not originally connected.

[80] "Minime [sic!] vero fornicationem imitantes et irritantes se invicem, sed coinquinati non sunt propter immaturitatem aetati."

hands of his bishop he shall do penance for an entire year on bread and water.

19. One who instead of baptism blesses a little infant shall do penance for a year apart from the number[81] or fulfill it with bread and water.

20. If the infant dies having had such blessing only, that homicide shall do penance according to the judgment of a council.[82]

21. Small boys who strike one another shall do penance for seven days; but if [they are] older, for twenty days; if [they are] adolescents, they shall do penance for forty days.

XI. Of Questions concerning the Host

1. He who fails to guard the host carefully, so that a mouse eats it, shall do penance for forty days.

2. But he who loses it in the church, that is, so that a part falls and is not found, twenty days.

3. But he who loses his chrismal[83] or only the host in what place soever, if it cannot be found, three forty-day periods or a year.

4. One who pours anything from the chalice upon the altar when the linen is being removed shall do penance for seven days; or if he has spilled it rather freely, he shall do penance with special fasts for seven days.

5. If by accident[84] the host falls from [the officiant's] hand into the straw, he shall do penance for seven days from the time of the accident.

6. He who pours out the chalice at the end of the solemn Mass, shall do penance for forty days.

7. One who vomits the host because his stomach is overloaded with food, if he casts it into the fire, twenty days, but if not, forty.

8. If moreover dogs consume this vomit, one hundred.

---

[81] "extra numerum." Perhaps "fratrum" (of his brethren), or "fidelium" (of the faithful), or some equivalent, has been dropped after "numerum."   [82] "senatus."

[83] Not as suggested in Migne, P.L., CV, 701, note d, the palla corporalis or linen cloth to cover the chalice, but what would now be called the pyx. "The vessel which we now call a pix, employed for thus keeping the Eucharist, was then known under the name of Chrismal, and was often made of gold and richly jewelled. A particular form of prayer was used at the blessing of the chrismal; by many it was often carried about the person, and to lose it was a negligence to be atoned for by going through many weeks of penance." D. Rock, The Church of Our Fathers, I, 108–9. In footnotes to this passage Rock supplies illuminating quotations. Parallels appear in the Penitential of Bede, XIV, 6, the Pseudo-Roman, 68, and the Regula of Columban, pp. 309, 230. 260, below.

[84] Reading "accidenti" for "cadentis," from Capit. Iud., XXXIV, 1, in Schmitz II, p. 249.

9. But if it is with pain, and he casts it into the fire, he shall sing one hundred psalms.

10. If anyone neglects to receive the host and does not ask for it, and if no reason exists to excuse him, he shall keep a special fast; and he who, having been polluted in sleep during the night, accepts the host, shall do penance likewise.

11. A deacon who forgets to bring the oblation until the linen is removed when the names of the departed[85] are recited, shall do penance likewise.

12. He who gives to anyone a liquor in which a mouse or a weasel is found dead, shall do penance with three special fasts.

13. He who afterwards knows that he tasted such a drink, shall keep a special fast.

14. But if those little beasts are found in the flour or in any dry food or in porridge or in curdled milk, whatever is around their bodies shall be cast out, and all the rest shall be taken in good faith.

15. He who with unfit hand touches liquid food shall be corrected with one hundred lively[86] [?] blows.

16. But if there is any discoloration of the liquor, the distributor shall be corrected by a fast of seven days.

17. He who takes this unaware and afterwards recognizes it, for fifteen days shall torture his empty stomach with fasting.

18. Whoever eats or drinks what has been tainted by a household beast, namely, the cat, shall be healed with three special fasts.

19. He who acts with negligence toward the host, so that it dries up and is consumed by worms until it comes to nothing, shall do penance for three forty-day periods on bread and water.

20. If it is entire but if a worm is found in it, it shall be burned and the ashes shall be concealed beneath the altar, and he who neglected it shall make good[87] his negligence with fourteen days [of penance].

21. If the host loses its taste and is discolored, his fast shall be completed in twenty days; if it is stuck together, seven days.

22. He who wets the host shall forthwith drink the water that was in the chrismal; and he shall take the host and shall amend his fault for ten days.

23. If the host fall from the hands of the celebrant to the ground and is not found, everything that is found in the place in which it

---

[85] "pausantium."   [86] "animalibus."
[87] Reading "solvat" for "salvat," with *Capit. Iud.*, XXXIV, 1, in Schmitz II, p. 250.

fell shall be burned and the ashes concealed as above, and then the priest shall be sentenced to half a year [of penance].

24. If the host is found, the place shall be cleaned up with a broom, and the straw, as we have said above, burned with fire, and the priest shall do penance for twenty days.

25. If it only slipped to the altar, he shall keep a special fast.

26. If he spills anything from the chalice to the ground through negligence, it shall be licked up with the tongue; the board shall be scraped; [what is scraped off] shall be consumed with fire [and] concealed as we have said above; he shall do penance for fifty[88] days.

27. If the chalice drips upon the altar the minister shall suck up the drop and do penance for three days, and the linens which the drop touched shall be washed three times, the chalice being placed beneath to receive the water used in washing.[89]

28. If the chalice drips when it is washed inside,[90] the first time twelve psalms shall be sung by the minister; if it happens a second time . . . if a third time, three. . . . [91]

29. If the priest stammers over the Sunday prayer which is called "the perilous,"[92] if once, he shall be cleansed with fifty strokes; if a second time, one hundred; if a third time, he shall keep a special fast.

But this is to be carefully observed in all penance: the length of time anyone remains in his faults; with what learning he is instructed; with what passion he is assailed; with what courage he stands; with what tearfulness he seems to be afflicted; and with what oppression he is driven to sin. For Almighty God who knows the hearts of all and has bestowed diverse natures will not estimate [various] weights of sins as [worthy] of equal penance,[93] as this prophecy saith, "For the gith[94] shall not be threshed with saws, neither shall the cart wheel

---

[88] The manuscript has the abbreviation "l" with a stroke through it, i.e., "vel," as rendered by Zettinger. Disregarding the stroke as an inadvertence, we have the numeral "fifty." *Capit. Iud.*, XXIV, 1 (Schmitz II, p. 249) prescribes forty days for this offense.

[89] Evidently the spot was to be sponged without the removal of the linen from the altar. *Capit. Iud.* has an interesting provision of a penance of three days if only the first linen was affected, seven days if the second was tinged, if the third, nine days, if the fourth, fifteen days (Schmitz II, p. 249). This indicates the use of four linen cloths. "Three cloths of white linen" are required in Roman Catholic churches today, and optionally the "antependium" (frontal) may be used.—John F. Sullivan, *The Visible Church*, p. 112.

[90] Perhaps when it is lifted and allowed to turn over in preparation for the application of a washcloth.   [91] Text incomplete.   [92] "periculosa." See note 75, p. 112, above.

[93] "non aequali paenitudinis pondera peccatorum pensabit." *Excarp. Cumm.* has "non aequali lancea paenitudinis."   [94] A. V. "fitches," i.e., vetches.

turn about upon the cummin, but the gith shall be beaten with a rod and the cummin with a staff, but bread corn shall be broken small";[95] as saith this passage, "The mighty shall be mightily tormented."[96] Whence a certain wise man saith: "To whom more is intrusted, from him shall more be exacted."[97] Thus the priests of the Lord learn, who preside over the churches; for a part is given to them together with those for whose faults they make satisfaction.[98] What[99] is it then to make satisfaction for a fault unless when thou receive the sinner to penance, [and] by warning, exhortation, teaching, lead him to penance,[100] correct him of his error, amend him of his faults, and make him such that God is rendered favorable to him after conversion, thou art said to make satisfaction for his fault? When, therefore, thou art such a priest, and such is thy teaching and thy word, there is given to thee a part of those whom thou correctest, that their merit may be thy reward and their salvation thy glory.

This book written by Comminianus has been finished.

4 . THE IRISH CANONS (*Canones Hibernenses, ca. 675*)

[BESIDES the two series of canons traditionally connected with the name of St. Patrick, which have been given above, there exist two important early Irish collections[1] of which the earlier is translated below. This is the series known as the *Canones Hibernenses*—the *Irish Canons*. It was printed by Martène and Durand[2] from the later of the two codices in which it is preserved—the important Codex Paris. Bibl. Nat. Lat. 3182, in which this document begins with Section II. Wasserschleben has edited the work[3] from a ninth-century St. Germain codex[4] and from this Paris manuscript. The text is rendered difficult by numerous corruptions and by the insertion of Old Irish glosses. The document apparently belongs to the seventh century. It is quoted in the *Penitential of Theodore* (*ca.* 668–90)[5] and in the *Collectio canonum Hibernensis* (*ca.* 700).[6]

---

[95] Is. 28:27–28.   [96] Wisd. 6:7.   [97] Probably based on Luke 12:48.

[98] This sentence is grammatically simple but the meaning is not clear. Evidently, as in the concluding sentence of the passage, the reference is to the good priest's spiritual participation in the penance and its rewards.

[99] Reading with the manuscript "quid" for Zettinger's "qui."

[100] "to penance" redundant, and omitted in *Pseudo-Cummean*, I.

[1] For the second of these, see below, pp. 139 ff.

[2] *Thesaurus novus anecdotorum* (1717), IV, 13 ff.   [3] *Bussordnungen*, pp. 136–44.

[4] Now Paris 12021. This codex, however, contains only Sections I and II. It forms the basis of the text followed for these sections. Both manuscripts contain Section II, and here show some widely divergent readings. Codex Paris. 3182 forms the sole text for Sections III to VI.   [5] See, however, pp. 179 ff, below, for the date of this work.

[6] See footnotes 46, 63, 84, pp. 123, 125, 128, below.

The work is divided into six sections, each a unit in itself and clearly marked off from the others with respect to its contents. Interesting features are the minute schedule of penances for the use of polluted water (Section i); the remarkable scale of commutations by which penances are shortened (Section ii); and the fines imposed for injuries to ecclesiastics (Section iii). Section iv is a unique code of penalties for inhospitality. Section v, on the law of dogs, has no ecclesiastical significance. Section vi deals with tithes and first fruits on the basis of the Book of Exodus and closes in what is probably an appended passage with an adroit scriptural argument for the liberal principle of accepting the good judgments of the heathen.

In the titles of three of the six sections the authority of a synod is claimed for the canons of the particular section. It is impossible to connect the book or its parts with any particular synod or series of synods. We know that in Ireland synods were frequently held.[7] The character of this series of canons lends the impression of a laborious, coöperative task on the part of persons favorable to the Church and familiar with Irish national customary law. Secular and ecclesiastical authorities may have coöperated in the preparation of the canons, as they are known to have united in the work of certain Irish conventions. It may seem fanciful to suggest that the parts of the document were severally prepared by half a dozen subcommittees of a synod and adopted by the synod as a whole; but its structure and claims of synodical authority seem to accord with this conjecture.]

I. Of the Teaching[8] of an Irish Synod and the Discourse of Gregory Nazianzen concerning Unnumbered Sins[9]

1. The penance of a parricide is fourteen years, or half as long if [he commits the deed] on account of ignorance, on bread and water and with satisfaction.[10]

2. This is the penance of a homicide: seven years shall be served, on bread and water.

3. The penance of a homicide [is] seven years on bread and water, or as Monochoma says,[11] ten.

---

[7] See J. Ryan, *Irish Monasticism*, pp. 188 f. Ryan thinks they were held in conjunction with the triennial national assemblies.   [8] "disputatione."

[9] The second member of this double title is obviously erroneous. Its presence may indicate that some early manuscript of the document contained a work so entitled and attributed to Gregory.

[10] "satisfactione." Apparently a reference to the "éric" paid to surviving relatives, corresponding to the "wergeld" of the Anglo-Saxons. The "éric" included the "coirp-díre" or body-fine, which for all classes was reckoned at seven "cumhals" (ancillae, female slaves), and the "enech-lann" or honor-price, which was graded according to the rank of the person slain or injured. Cf. *Ancient Laws of Ireland*, ed. W. H. Hancock and others, I, 15, 68 f.; III, 70, 99.

[11] Wasserschleben has mistakenly read "Monochema." This phrase ("ut dicit Mono-

4. This is the penance of a wizard,[12] or of one who is given over to evil,[13] if he believes in it,[14] or of a hawker,[15] or of a cohabiter,[16] or of a heretic, or of an adulterer: seven years on bread and water.

5. The penance of one who has intercourse with a woman, seven years on bread and water. The penance of one who has intercourse with a neighbor woman, fourteen years or nine.

6. The penance for the destruction of the embryo of a child[17] in the mother's womb, three and a half years.

7. The penance for the destruction of flesh and spirit, seven and a half years on bread and water, in continence.

8. The life price[18] for the destruction of the embryo and the mother, twelve female slaves.[19]

---

choma") reads like an interpolation; unless we are to think of it as a curious record of a minority view advocated by a rigorist named Monochoma in a synod in which, as the title suggests, these canons were formulated. The name Monochoma does not occur in lists of Celtic saints. P. F. Moran has suggested the identification of "Monochema" with Mainchin the Wise (d. 652), *Essays on the Early Irish Church*, p. 271. A closer resemblance appears in the name of Mochumma, Bishop of St. Machay, whose date is indefinitely placed by O'Hanlon as "probably in the fifth, sixth or seventh century." J. O'Hanlon, *Lives of the Irish Saints*, I, 580. Cf. McNeill, p. 27 (*Rev. celt.*, XXXIX, 261), n. 3. The identification is rendered the more probable by the correction of the reading.

[12] "magi." "magus" frequently occurs in Hiberno-Latin documents as the equivalent of "drui," a druid. This fact probably accounts for the charge, launched by the Romanizers of the seventh century, that the Irish tonsure was derived from Simon Magus. See P. W Joyce, *Social History of Ancient Ireland*, I, 233; J. Rhys, *Lectures on the Origin and Growth of Religion as Illustrated by Celtic Heathendom*, p. 213; L. Gougaud, *Les Chrétientés celtiques*, p. 198; E. O'Curry, *Lectures on the Manuscript Materials of Ancient Irish History*, 2d ed., p. 271; McNeill, p. 102 (*Rev. celt.*, XL, 86). A reversion to druidic magic is probably to be understood here.

[13] "votivi mali."

[14] "si credulus." A glossator has added words which have been altered to read "id dem ergach." Probably the original gloss was "id [est] díbergach" (that is, a marauder), as suggested by W. Stokes, *Thesaurus Palaeohibernicus*, II, 38, n. g. For this and other Old Irish glosses in this document Professors T. P. Cross, R. I. Best, and O. Bergin have kindly lent their expert advice. Dr. Bergin remarks, "If 'demergach'='díbergach,' it looks as if the glossator mistook 'credulus' for 'crudelis.'" Since the list of offenders in the passage is already somewhat miscellaneous, it is not impossible that "crudelis" (a cruel man) is the original word. This would perhaps lend color to Meyer's suggestion mentioned, but not adopted, in the following note.

[15] For "praeconis" (of a mountebank or hawker) K. Meyer would read "praedonis" (of a robber). *Rev. celt.*, XV (1894), 493, n. 2. But "precones" appears in *Coll. can. Hib.*, xliv, 8. Cf. also p. 70, above.

[16] "cohabitatoris." Cf. below, I, 23.

[17] "liquoris materiæ filii."   [18] "pretium animae."

[19] "ancillae," Old Irish "cumhal." The cumhal was a measure of value, and was equivalent to three cows or twelve fatted fowls. The "coirp-díre" or body-price of a man in ancient Ireland was seven cumhals or twenty-one cows. Cf. p. 118, n. 10, above. The parallel passage in the *Bigotian Penitential* IV, ii, 2, has fourteen instead of twelve "ancillae." Perhaps this is arrived at by estimating two lives at seven cumhals each.

9. Twelve fowls or thirteen[20] shekels[21] are the value of each female slave.

10. The life-price for the destruction of the child and the mother, twelve female slaves.

11. The penance for a mother's destruction of her own child, twelve years on bread and water.

12. The penance for drinking blood or urine,[22] seven and a half years on bread and water, followed by the imposition of the hand of the bishop.

13. The penance for eating horseflesh,[23] four years on bread and water.

14. The penance for eating flesh which dogs have been eating is forty days on bread and water.

15. The penance for eating the flesh of a dead beast, forty days[24] on bread and water.

16. The penance for the illicit drinking of [what has been contaminated[25] by] a dog, one year.

17. The penance for the drinking of what has been contaminated by an eagle or a crow[26] or a blackbird[27] or a cock or a hen, fifty days on bread and water.

18. The penance for the illicit drinking of what has been contaminated by a cat,[28] five days on bread and water and special fast.[29]

---

[20] F. Seebohm, *Anglo-Saxon Law*, p. 105, discussing the value of a "cumhal," thinks this should read "XII" instead of "XIII."

[21] "sicli." Among the Anglo-Saxons the "siclus" was, according to Du Cange, equal to two silver "denarii."

[22] Probably used for medicinal purposes; but medicine and magic were confused. Cf. L. Thorndike, *History of Magic and Experimental Science*, I, 766 ff.; II, 360, 813, 860.

[23] Reading "equi" for "aequi." See McNeill, p. 27 (*Rev. celt.*, XXXIX, 261) and cf. W. Reeves, *Life of St. Columba* (1st ed.), p. 51, and n. *d*. The *Penitential of Theodore*, II, xi, 4, and the *Pseudo-Cummean*, I, 23, permit the eating of horseflesh, but state that "it is not the custom." See below, pp. 208, 248.

[24] Reading "XL dies" for "XLII."

[25] The *Bigotian Penitential*, I, 5, 5, supplies the equivalent of the phrase in brackets. These words are inserted without brackets in canons 17 to 23, below.

[26] Reading "corvi" for "curbi."

[27] Reading "graculi" for "graule." The parallel passage in *Poenit. Bigot.* I, 5, 6, has "ingarola" for "ingarrula" (magpie: literally, chatterer).

[28] "muricipis," a mouse catcher. Cf. the *Merseburg Penitential*, 86 (Wasserschleben, *Bussordnungen*, p. 400), "the household beast which is 'muriceps.'" Du Cange, however, cites the use of "muriceps" as a bird that catches mice, "avis quae mures capit," which may refer to an owl or a hawk. The sense of a mousetrap, as in the old theological metaphor, "muriceps diaboli," seems inadmissible here.

[29] "superpossitio." Du Cange cites numerous instances of the use of "superpositio" in in the sense of "superpositio ieiunii," an extra or stricter fast, "ieiunium strictius." The

19. The penance for the illicit drinking of what has been contaminated by the carcass of a beast, forty days and nights on bread and water.

20. The penance for the illicit drinking of what has been contaminated by the dead body of a mouse, seven days on bread and water.

21. The penance for the illicit drinking of what has been contaminated by a layman or a laywoman, forty days on bread and water.

22. The penance for eating or sleeping in the same house or in the same bed with a layman or a laywoman, forty days on bread and water.

23. The penance for the illicit drinking of what has been contaminated by a pregnant servant woman[30] or one who cohabits with her, forty days on bread and water.

24. The penance for eating in the same house or on the same table-rug [?][31] with them, forty days on bread and water.

25. The penance for sleeping in the same house with them, twenty days on bread and water.

26. The penance for the wailing of a woman[32] after [the death of] a layman or a laywoman, fifty days on bread and water.

---

synod of Elvira (305) in its canons 23 and 26 refers to the "superpositio" as a special fast of a whole day kept on Saturday. Cf. A. J. Binterim, *Denkwürdigkeiten der christ-katholischen Kirche*, V, 2, 63; L. Duchesne, *Les Origines du culte chrétien*, 2d ed., pp. 212–14; H. Williams, *Gildae de excidio Britanniae, Fragmenta . . . Cymmrodorion Record Series*, III, 276, n. 3; Leclercq in Hefele-Leclercq, I, 1, 234, n. 4. Watkins (II, 604) describes "superpositio" as "a rigid fast for a whole day." A gloss on the *First Vallicellian Penitential* is interpreted by Schmitz to mean that a "superpositio" (superimpositio) was the extension of a fast from about 3 p.m. to evening or midnight. Schmitz I, p. 314 ff. See also above, pp. 31, 88, 102, 110 ff, and below, p. 176, n. 21.

[30] "glantelle prignantis" (*sic!*). *Poenit. Bigot.* I, vi, 2, has "quod intinxerat glancella, i.e., ancella in utero habens filium," and so forth. See also Du Cange, *s.vv.*, "glancella," "glandella."

[31] "singa." This word is not given in any available glossary. The word 'sging" appears in two Irish lives of Coemgen, I, 31; II, 16. Plummer, *Lives of Irish Saints*, I, 129, 150. In his glossary, Plummer gives the form "scing." He translates the word "glove"; but his note on it (II, 343) shows various guesses by Irish scholars, one of which is "rugs." He thinks it is probably an Irish form of the Old Norse "skinn" or of the English "skin." The contexts in which it is found would be better satisfied by "rug" than by "glove"; in both lives the reference is to the saint's proposal to make a "sging" out of an otter's skin. Why should he wish to make a glove instead of a pair of gloves? In ancient Ireland the custom obtained of covering tables, such as were used for dining, with rugs made of hides. P. W. Joyce, *A Social History of Ancient Ireland*, II, 113. Possibly we have here a variant of the same word, and if so the sense of "table rug" or "tablecloth" seems justified.

[32] Reading "bardicationis glandellae," from *Poenit. Bigot.* IV, vi, 2, for "bardigi

27. If [the dirge is sung] after [the death of] a servant woman with [a babe] in her womb, or after [the death of] one who cohabits with her, forty days on bread and water.

28. If after [the death of] a cleric of the parish, twenty days on bread and water.

29. If after [the death of] an anchorite or a bishop or a scribe[33] or a great prince[34] or a righteous king, fifteen days on bread and water.

II. Of Equivalents[35]

1. The equivalent of a special fast, one hundred psalms and one hundred genuflections, or the three fifties[36] and seven canticles.[37]

2. The equivalent of a three-day period [of penance], a night and a day in a station[38] without sleep except a little, or the three [times] fifty psalms with canticles,[39] and the office[40] of the twelve hours, and

capalbiae" of the text. The first of these words is connected with "bardus," a bard. The canon penalizes the Irish pagan custom of "keening," or wailing a dirge over a corpse. Cf. E. J. Gwynn, "An Irish Penitential," *Eriu*, VII (1914), 171, and p. 167, below. The dirge, which often contained a recital of the virtues and achievements of the dead, was frequently sung by a woman. Joyce refers to the custom as "mentioned in the most ancient writings and continued to the present day." *Social History of Ancient Ireland*, II, 540. Mr. Synge has made keening a feature of his play, *Riders to the Sea*. On the question of the influence of this practice on monastic psalm singing, especially in connection with the requiem for the dead, see McNeill, pp. 138 ff. (*Rev. celt.*, XL, 338 ff.).

[33] "scribam." Not merely a skilled writer. The word carried the respect indicated by the classification with an anchorite, bishop, or prince. Abbots were often honored with the appellation "scriba." In general the word corresponds to the office of the "fir legind," man of reading or learning, the principal teacher of the monastery. See W. Reeves, *Adamnan's Life of St. Columba*, p. 365; E. Windisch, *Irische Texte*, I, *Wörterbuch, s.vv.*, "fer" and "legim," and below, p. 371, n. 8.

[34] "principem magnum." Cf. III, 1, p. 124, below "excelsi principis." Probably the ruler of a "túath" or small province. H. d'Arbois de Jubainville, "Études sur le Senchus Mór," *Rev. historique de droit français et étranger*, V (1881), 6.

[35] "De arreis incipit." "Arreum" is Latin for the Old Irish "arra," which K. Meyer renders "equivalent, substitute, commutation." *Rev. celt.*, XV (1894), 486. This section is of historic importance as a remarkable early series of commutations. See above, p. 35 ff., and below, p. 142 ff.   [36] That is, the one hundred and fifty psalms in the Psalter.

[37] "cantica." From "cantica spiritualia," or "spiritual songs," Eph. 5:9. The canticles were portions of scriptures or sacred hymns sung in various parts of the liturgy. For the nine principal canticles see art. "Cantiques," in Cabrol, *Dictionnaire d'archéologie chrétienne et de liturgie*. In the *Antiphonary of Bangor* six canticles appear. These include the "Te Deum" and the "Gloria." See F. E. Warren, *The Antiphonary of Bangor*, Pt. I (Henry Bradshaw Society, IV, 1892), p. xv.

[38] On the use of this word in early church penance and fasting see the article "Station Days" in the *Catholic Encyclopedia*, and cf. p. 7 ff., above. The word is used here in a sense different from that of the fourth century, as the act of penance was private. The station may be supposed to have been kept in a church, as in canon 4, below, when it is not otherwise provided.

[39] "With ten canticles, standing and praying" is the provision in the Codex Paris. 3182.   [40] "missa."

twelve genuflections in each hour, with the hands extended[41] for prayer.

3. The equivalent of a year, three days with a dead saint in a tomb without food or drink and without sleep, but with a garment about him and with the chanting of psalms[42] and with the prayer of the hours, after confession of sins to the priest and after the [monastic] vow.

4. The equivalent of a year, a three-day period in a church without food, drink, sleep, or a garment, and without a seat; and the chanting of psalms with the canticles and the prayer of the hours; and in these twelve genuflexions[43] after confession of sins in the presence of priest and people, after the monastic vow.

5. The equivalent of a year, twelve days and nights on twelve biscuits[44] amounting to the size of three loaves.[45]

6. The equivalent of a year, twelve three-day periods.[46]

7. The equivalent of a year, a month in great sorrow, so that he is in doubt[47] of his life.

8. The equivalent of a year, forty days on bread and water and a special fast in each week and forty psalms and sixty genuflexions and the praying of the hours.

9. The equivalent of a year, fifty days in a long special fast[48] and sixty psalms and genuflexions [and] the praying of the hours.

10. The equivalent of a year, forty days on water and corn[49] and two special fasts each week [and] forty psalms and genuflexions and prayer every hour.

11. The equivalent of a year, a hundred days on bread and water and prayer every hour.

---

[41] "manus sopinatae" (the hands reaching backwards). The Codex Paris. 3182 has "palme supernae" (the palms upraised).

[42] Perhaps "of the psalms," meaning the whole psalter.   [43] "genuculationes."

[44] "bucillas" (mouthfuls). Codex Paris. 3182 has "bucellas." An early gloss on "bucella" is "morsella panis" (a morsel of bread). For "bucellae" Du Cange gives "panes parvuli rotundi" (little round cakes).

[45] Reading with Codex Paris. 3182 "mensurae de tribus panibus." Codex Paris. 12021 has: "de tribus panibus qui efficiuntur de tertia parte coaird siir throscho" (Wasserschleben erroneously reads "troscho"), literally, "of three loaves which are made from the third part of the food of long fasting." For the Old Irish words see Stokes, *Thesaurus Palaeo-hibernicus*, II, 38, n. *h*.

[46] Cf. the *Penitential of Theodore*, I, vii, 5, p. 190, below.

[47] Reading "dubius" for "dubibus."

[48] Codex Paris. 3182 has "fifty days and nights on an allowance of bread and water."

[49] Reading "fordobor 7 ith" for "fordo borfiit." Stokes, *Thesaurus Palaeohibernicus*, II, 38, n. *i*.

12. All these fasts [are] without flesh and wine (except a little beer),[50] in another's church[51] during the time.[52]

III. Canons of an Irish Synod[53]

1. The blood of a bishop, a superior prince, or a scribe which is poured out upon the ground, if the wound requires a dressing,[54] wise men judge that he who shed the blood be crucified or pay [the value of] seven female slaves.

2. If [he pays] in specie, he shall pay the third part of silver and an amount of gold equal to the size of a crown,[55] and also a like amount in a precious jewel the size of an eye.

3. For the embarrassment[56] of his scar or wound in a meeting or in any crowd to the third year or longer, if he does not waive his claim,[57] he who committed [the deed] shall pay the value of a female slave.

4. If, however, the blood of the bishop does not fall to the ground, and if he does not require a dressing, the hand of his assailant shall be cut off or he shall pay half [the value of] seven female slaves, if he did it on purpose. But if he did not do it on purpose, he shall pay the price of a female slave.

5. One who strikes or molests a bishop without shedding blood shall pay half the price of seven female slaves.

6. But if any of his hairs are plucked out, satisfaction shall be made for every hair, that is, twelve hairs[58] for each up to twenty. For even if more were plucked out, it is not stated that satisfaction is due for this.[59]

[50] Reading "cervisia" for "herbisa."
[51] "cella," a common word for a church building in Hiberno-Latin documents.
[52] The Codex Paris. 3182 adds here: "The penance of those years of which the equivalent is indicated at length in the above statements shall be performed without flesh, wine, butter and sweet milk."
[53] "Sinodus Hibernensis decrevit."
[54] "colirio," Greek κολλύριον, a salve. Collyrium, colerium, colirium, are the chief Latin forms.
[55] "comparem verticis de auro latitudinem." See J. Loth, "Compensations pour crimes et offenses chez les Celtes insulaires," Rev. celt., XLVIII (1931), 332–51. Loth argues that the honor-price may have been paid with a gold plaque the size of the face.
[56] "admiratione" (the public gaze).
[57] "si non indulgeat."
[58] Reading "de capillis" for "discipuli." To translate literally "pupils" seems hardly justified.
[59] "Licet enim maius evulsum fuerit, quasi proprium reddi non dicitur." Cf. Ancient Laws of Ireland, III, 353, where fines for cutting off the hair are indicated; and especially IV, 363, 365. Among penalties for injury to a "virgin-bishop" it is stated (p. 365) that:

7. The blood of a presbyter which is poured out on the ground until the dressing checks it: the hand of the assailant[60] shall be cut off, or he shall pay half the value of seven female slaves, if he did it on purpose. But if not on purpose, he shall make restitution[61] with the value of a female slave.

8. If it does not go to the ground, the striker shall pay the value of a female slave; if [he pays] in specie, he shall pay the third part of it in silver; he shall make restitution for his blow with the value of a female slave, for his molestation he shall atone[62] as we said above. Patrick said: everyone who has dared to steal or seize those things that belong to a king, a bishop, or a scribe, or to commit any [other crime] against them, or to esteem them lightly and despise them, shall pay the value of seven female slaves or do penance for seven years with a bishop or a scribe.[63]

IV. Of the Refusal of Hospitality to the Clergy[64]

Let the wise man observe what benefits Abraham and Lot received for their kindness in receiving strangers, but let him likewise

---

"if any of his hair is pulled out there is a 'sed' for every hair of it to twenty hairs." The word "sed" or "set" is exceedingly common in the Old Irish laws and usually has the sense of cows or other valuables given in compensation. Cf. *Ancient Laws of Ireland*, VI, 688.

[60] Literally, "murderer."

[61] Literally, "he shall be healed," or absolved from his sin.

[62] "motatio ejus . . . sanetur," his disturbance [of the presbyter] shall be healed (or absolved).

[63] This canon is contained in the *Coll. can. Hib.*, xlviii, 5, where it is attributed to "sinodus Hibernensis."

[64] "De iectione ecclesie graduum ab ospicio," (literally, of the casting out from hospitality of the ranks of the Church). The word "iectio" is obscure except as it is defined in this passage. Martène and Durand, and Wasserschleben, have without explanation omitted the whole introductory portion of this section, from "ecclesie" in the heading to "excommunicationis causa" (reason for excommunication) below. Before securing a photostat of the manuscript I had held that "iectio" referred to "inhospitality and the refusal to succor the helpless," *Celtic Penitentials*, p. 30 (*Rev. celt.*, XXXIX, 264). This view seemed obvious from the language of canon 5, and it is now fully corroborated by the evidence of the hitherto suppressed paragraphs. Others have suggested that the word refers to "evictions." Cf. Oakley, p. 29. Dr. Gamer's transcript of the passage omitted by the editors is here inserted for the benefit of students of the Latin text. The punctuation has been altered in a few places.

Codex Paris. 3182, f. 306 (*Canones Hibernenses*): De iectione ecclesie graduum ab ospicio.

Abraham et Loth de sua benignitate in acceptione hospitum sapiens enim aduertat quae bona acceperunt, Sodoma uero quam paenam meruerat de iectione eorum, et opere nefando similiter sciat.

De iectione item a̅g̅ [Augustinus?].

Duo quoque episcopi in parte heremi erant, quorum nomina in scriptura memorantur, id est Iustinus et Pauconius. Iustinus igitur Pauconium adit, sed eum non suscepit, non

be aware what punishment Sodom[65] brought upon itself by rejecting them and for a wicked deed. Further, on the refusal of hospitality, Augustine [?][66] [says]:

Moreover there were two bishops in a desert place whose names are recorded in a written work, namely, Justinus and Pauconius. Justinus, then, came to Pauconius, but he declined to receive him, not, however, by reason of unkindness, but from custom. Since he would not receive the man to hospitality, he that was cast out complained of him that cast him out to a certain holy man,[67] saying, "What penance shall this man have for the deed just recited?" That aged and wise man of God answered and said: "He ought to fast seven days on bread and water." If he had cast him out because of unkindness, a year would have been assigned[68] for [each] day [required] in this instance, when because of custom or inexperience he failed to admit him.

Thus it is as the simple story shows. The Apostles said in the Gospel, "Let us send fire upon the city which does not receive us";[69] yet, as an example of grace, Christ forbade them to send fire. There is a certain man in the East who received into hospitality Christ with the Twelve Apostles, and from that time until this day he is no older, and his young wife does not age, and he lacks no good thing, and does not toil; but as Christ left him, so he is, with his house,[70] as Gregory attests. And Christ says in the Gospel: "if they will not receive you, shake off the dust from your feet,[71]—that is, in[72] excommunication."

1. One who casts out a poor man slays him, since the sixth or seventh or eighth or ninth part of his death is his rejection.[73] Who-

---

causa tamen inclementiae sed consuetudine. Quia hominem in hospicium non recipiat, iectus autem iectorem ad quendam sanem ["sanē" for "senem" or "sanctum"?] accusavit dicens: quam paenitentiam hic homo habet de opere prius memorato? Ipse uir dei, senex et sapiens, respondens ait: VII diebus debet penitere in pane et aqua; si pro inclementia hunc iecisset annus pro die hic acciperetur, dum pro consuetudine et imperitia illum non accipit. Ita est sicut in simplici historia ostenditur.
Item in Euangelio apostoli dixerunt:
Mittamus ignem super civitatem quae non nos suscipit, tamen exemplo indulgentiae Christus eos ignem mittere prohibuit. Est quidam uir in oriente qui Christum accepit in hospicio cum XII apostolis, et ab illo tempore usque in hunc diem nec senior cum sua muliere iuuencula non senescenti [apparently so corrected from "senescente"] cui non deest aliquid boni et non laborat. Sed quomodo relinquit eum Christus sic est cum sua domu, quem Gregorius testatur, et Christus dicit in euangelio: si non uos recipiant iecite puluerem de pedibus uestris, id est excommunicationis causa. Item qui eicit. . . .

[65] Based on the story in Gen. 19:1–29.   [66] "ag."
[67] Reading "sanctum" for "sanem." Possibly the correction should be "senem" (old man).   [68] Literally, "received."   [69] Based on Luke 9:54.
[70] For a variation of this story see W. Stokes, *Tripartite Life of St. Patrick*, I, 28 ff. It is manifestly a Christian appropriation of Ovid, *Metamorphoses*, VIII, 626–724.
[71] Matt. 10:14; Mark 6:11; Luke 9:5.   [72] "causa."   [73] "iectio."

ever is able to succor[74] one who is about to perish and does not succor him, slays him . . . [75] the throat of a hungry stranger when food is denied him, as he cannot live more than eight days hungry, without food and drink. Therefore the eighth part of his death is required for his rejection, and sometimes the fifth part is received on account of the dignity of him who has been rejected.

2. If anyone rejects a bishop and if the latter has died, the price of his blood shall be received from him;[76] he shall pay the value of fifty female slaves, that is, seven female slaves for each rank, or he shall do penance for fifty years; and of these, seven female slaves shall be taken for his rejection.[77]

3. So also for the other [ranks], to [that] of sexton, whatever the judges judge to be the blood price of each rank of those seven ranks, the seventh part of the death of each shall be paid for his rejection.

4. If a bishop of bishops has been rejected, the fifth part of his death is his rejection; that is, the value of eight female slaves and two-thirds[78] of one female slave.

5. If one of the little ones[79] who go about in the name of God without the rank of ecclesiastical orders is not received into hospitality, the ninth part of his death is his rejection.

6. Whoever does not receive a superior prince or a scribe or an anchorite or a judge, whatever[80] the judges who shall judge at that time judge to be due of his death price,[81] that is, the seventh part, shall be taken for his rejection.

V. A Synod of Wise Men: concerning Dogs[82]

1. Now a chained dog, whatever mischief[83] he does in the night shall not be paid for.[84] And whatever mischief a dog of the flocks

---

[74] Reading "qui succurrere" for "quis occurrere."

[75] There seems to be an omission here.   [76] That is, from the offender.

[77] In this and the following canon the payment for the death of a bishop is arrived at by multiplying the body-price of an ordinary man, seven cumhals or female slaves, by the number of the bishop's rank above a layman—seven times seven, stated in round numbers as "fifty." Note the relation of this to the provision in III, I, p. 124, above, and the dictum of Patrick, following III, 8, p. 125, above; and on the legal protection of ecclesiastics, see p. 36, above.   [78] "duae partes."

[79] "de minimis." Possibly children attached to monasteries and engaged in errands for the monks. See below, p. 129, n. 102.

[80] Reading "quantum" as above in paragraph 3. The MS has qndū. Wasserschleben has "quandiu" (as long as).   [81] "debitum occisionis eius."

[82] The law of dogs was carefully worked out in ancient Ireland, where dogs were bred for various purposes. Three distinct uses to which dogs were put are indicated in canons 1 and 4 below. See also *Ancient Laws of Ireland*, I, 127, 145; II, 119. These canons are

does in the byre[85] or in the pastures of his flocks shall not be paid for; but if he goes beyond bounds, what mischief he does shall be paid for.

2. Whatever a dog eats, nothing is paid for his first offense unless he is alone. If he repeats the offense a second or a third time what he does or eats shall be paid for.[86]

3. Concerning those who kill a dog that guards the flocks or stays in the house, wise men say: He who kills a dog that guards the flocks shall pay five cows for the dog and supply a dog of the same breed and restore whatever wild animals eat from the flock, by the end of the year.[87]

4. The constitutions of the wise: He who kills a dog of the four doors—namely, of the house where his master dwells, and of the fold of sheep, and of the byres of the calves and of the oxen—shall pay ten cows and substitute a dog of the same breed that will do the dead one's services.[88]

VI. *The Synod Thus Wisely Teaches concerning Tithes*[89]

1. The authors say that the tithes of the flock ought to be offered once, and therefore "it shall be most holy";[90] that is, a tithe ought not to be offered out of these a second time. But others in sound faith affirm that we are to give to God tithes, every year, of animals and humans,[91] since we have the benefits of the same every year.

2. With respect to all [produce] except the fruits of the ground, of which a tithe is once offered to the Lord, [we should do] as it is said: "Whatsoever is once consecrated to God shall be holy of holies to the Lord."[92] The tithe ought not again to be offered for these, as saith

---

purely secular: the "wise men" who are credited with framing them may not have been ecclesiastics; but it seems possible that the same "sinodus" is referred to in Section VI, which is distinctly ecclesiastical. The section illustrates the principle of restitution which elsewhere enters largely into the penitential literature.   [83] "mali."

[84] *Coll. can. Hib.* liii, 5, adds: "by his master; however, if he commits any violence in the day his master shall pay."

[85] "bovello," glossed "buorch" in Codex Paris. 3182.

[86] Codex Paris. 3182 has: "But if he has offended" ("peccaverit," "sinned") a second time the master of the dog that ate shall pay." The application of "peccaverit" to a dog shows an interesting extension of the use of the ecclesiastical vocabulary; but the expression is apparently a copyist's alteration.

[87] "usque ad caput anni" (literally, until the beginning of the year).

[88] Literally, "doing the works of the same."

[89] "Item synodus sapientia sic de decimis disputant (*sic!*)."

[90] "sanctum sanctorum erit." Cf. Exod. 30:10; Lev. 27:28.

[91] Cf. can. 5, n. 102.   [92] Lev. 27:28.

Colman,[93] the teacher. The tenth part of the fruits of the ground ought to be offered each year, since they spring up each year.

3. Tithes are not only for animal creatures, they apply to humans [also].[94] And so the "first fruits,"[95] that is, the first fruits of everything, and the animal which is first born in the year, which is similar to the first fruits;[96] moreover, the first-born of animals likewise, not those of men only but those of animals which may be sacrificed.[97]

4. Tithes are in the flocks and in the fruits of the ground; or, tithes are in the flocks, first fruits in the fruits (of the ground); first fruits are whatever is born of the flocks before others are born in that year.

5. To know what is the amount of the first fruits: it is an omer;[98] as others [say], it is nine loaves or twelve loaves; then "loaves of proposition,"[99] the material of nine loaves or of twelve loaves. Of vegetables, as much as the hand[100] can hold. These things ought to be presented at the beginning of harvest,[101] and they were offered once in the year to the priests at Jerusalem. Nowadays, however, each person to the monastery of which he is a monk;[102] and besides charity abounds among these, and the first-born are in males only, never in females.

6. As others say: if he has no[103] property for the tithe he does not pay tithes.

7. As others [say]: How is it proper for anyone to offer tithes to the Lord? If he has nought but one cow or ox, he shall divide the value of the cow in ten and give the tenth part to the Lord. So also in other cases.

8. The Lord commands a willing victim. Therefore he saith, "No

[93] Not improbably Colman of Lann Elo (Lynally) is meant. Cf. C. Plummer, *Vitae sanctorum Hiberniae*, I, lvci, 258–73; *Lives of Irish Saints*, II, 162–76, 347; J. Ryan, *Irish Monasticism*, pp. 129 f. He was a nephew of St. Columba and died in 610 or 611. See J. O'Hanlon, *Lives of the Irish Saints*, IX, 593 ff. Another prominent Colman (d. 674 or 676) was the abbot of Lindisfarne, later of Innisboffin. O'Hanlon, *op. cit.*, VIII, 110 ff. The name was exceedingly common: 113 Colmans appear in the *Martyrology of Donegal*.

[94] "per mortalia fiunt."

[95] "primitiae," translated "firstfruits" in the Douay version.

[96] "primitiva."   [97] Cf. Exod. 13:2; 34:19–26.

[98] "gomer." The "omer" (homer in A.V.) was the tenth part of an "ephah" (Exod. 16:36) and was the amount required for one person's food for one day (Exod. 16:16).

[99] Exod. 25:30; 35:13; 39:35; 40:21. A.V. has "shewbread."

[100] "pugnus" (the fist).   [101] "estatis" (of summer).

[102] Perhaps we should understand this to apply to children presented to monasteries, as were the oblates of medieval monasticism. In Ireland the monastery had a legal claim on the first-born son, and on one in every seven sons of a father. Weaklings were excluded from designation to the clerical life, "that the worst may not fall to the church."—*Ancient Laws of Ireland*, III, 39.   [103] "minus" perhaps "rather little" or "too little."

man taketh[104] my life away from me," and so forth. Of such, what
God does not punish neither ought men to punish;[105] and in the case
of those who quickly turn from guilt to penance, it is read in Exodus
in the instance of[106] the adoration of the calf: "And standing in the
gate of the camp, Moses said: If any man be for God, let him join
with me; and all the sons of Levi gathered themselves together unto
him. And he said unto them: Thus saith the Lord God of Israel: Put
[every] man his sword upon his thigh," and so forth, till he saith:
"Let every man kill his neighbor and his brother and his friend."
And a little farther on Moses said: "You have consecrated your hands
this day to the Lord; every man in his son and in his brother, that a
blessing may be given unto you."[107] Here endeth, Amen.[108] The
people of Israel ought to have been ruled by the Ten Commandments
of the law, since for the sake of these God smote the Egyptians with
the ten plagues; therefore are there ten commandments; while[109]
there are precepts in the law which God did not command, but [for
example] Jethro the kinsman of Moses told Moses to choose seventy
leading men[110] who would judge the people with Moses; and this is
the judgment, that if we find judgments of the heathen good, which
good Nature[111] teaches them, and it is not displeasing to God, let us
keep them.

5 . PENITENTIAL WRITINGS OF ADAMNAN

The Canons of Adamnan (679–704)

[THE CIRCUMSTANCES of the origin of the following canons are quite unknown. The sole reason for attributing them to Adamnan is the mention
of his name as author in all the manuscripts. Adamnan was a very distinguished leader of the Iro-Scottish Church. He was born about A.D.
621–26, probably in southwestern Donegal, Ireland, became abbot of
Iona in 679 and died in 704. He wrote the principal life of his distinguished predecessor, St. Columba. He was influential in Ireland, to
which he made protracted visits during his later years. It is the con-

---

[104] Reading "tollit" as in Vulgate, John 10:18, for "tollat."

[105] Reading "vindicare" for "vindicari."   [106] "pro."

[107] The quoted passages are from Exod. 32:26–29, with slight variations from the
Vulgate.

[108] Probably "finit amen" here originally marked the end of the document.

[109] "ubi."

[110] "principes." In Exod. 18:21, Vulgate has "viros potentes et timentes Deum"
(Douay version: "able men, such as fear God").

[111] "natura bona." The capitalization of "Nature" seems justified, as "docet" which
follows indicates a philosophical personification.

jecture of Haddan and Stubbs that these canons were "probably passed by some Irish council under Adamnan's influence." These editors have given us the best edition of the document,[1] making some improvements on the edition of Wasserschleben.[2] The only other complete printing is by Luc d'Achéry, who makes them conclude (Nos. cxlix–clxviii) a set of canons ascribed to Theodore.[3] The manuscripts used by the editors are the ninth-century St. Germain codex, now Paris. 12021; the tenth or eleventh century Paris. 3182; and a damaged manuscript of about the same date in the British Museum, Cotton, Otho E XIII. In addition, the ninth-century Bodleian Codex Hatton 42 has here been consulted. Kenney lists also the Orléans Codex 221, Bibl. de la ville, written by Jonubrus, a Breton, about 800. These canons are also found in the Lyons Codex 203, where they follow the *Welsh Canons* given below, pp. 372–82.

The most accurate study of Adamnan's life is by William Reeves, whose "Memoir of St. Adamnan" constitutes an appendix to the Preface of his first edition of *Adamnan's Life of St. Columba*.[4] J. O'Hanlon, *Lives of the Irish Saints*, IX, 476 ff., has an extended account.

The canons are in the main a set of careful regulations regarding clean and unclean meats and the contamination caused by contact with dead bodies of animals or men. They attempt to apply the regulations of Exodus and Leviticus to the conditions of seventh century Ireland. Most of the prohibitions commend themselves on sanitary grounds as providing a necessary minimum of protection to health. Similar provisions are found in some of the greater penitentials, *e.g.*, the *Penitential of Theodore*, I, vii, 6–12; II, xi, 1–9; the *Pseudo-Roman Penitential*, canons 98 ff.]

1. Marine animals cast upon the shores, the nature of whose death we do not know, are to be taken for food in good faith, unless they are decomposed.

2. Cattle that fall from a rock, if their blood has been shed, are to be taken; if not, but if their bones are broken and their blood has not come out, they are to be rejected as if they were carrion.[5]

3. [Animals] that have died in water are carrion, since their blood[6] remains within them.

---

[1] *Councils*, II, 111 ff.   [2] *Bussordnungen*, pp. 120 ff.

[3] *Spicilegium, sive collectio veterum aliquot scriptorum* . . . Paris, 1723, I, 490 f. Mansi XII, 154 f. has eight canons. Partial editions by Martène, Migne, and Robertson are cited by Kenney, p. 245.

[4] This work appeared in 1857; in the second edition, 1874, this section is replaced by an Introduction based on notes from the first edition.

[5] "morticina." The Douay Version renders "morticinum" "carcass." But the modern use of "carcass" is less restricted. The reference here is to an animal that has died of itself and is offensive. The word is often applied to a human corpse. Where in this document it refers to animals the sense seems usually best conveyed by "carrion."

Literally, "whose blood."

4. [Animals] seized by beasts and half alive are to be taken by bestial men.

5. A half alive animal seized by sudden death is carrion if an ear or other part is cut off.

6. Swine's flesh that has become thick or fat on carrion is to be rejected like the carrion by which it grows fat. When, however, [the swine] has grown smaller and returned to its original thinness, it is to be taken. But if it has eaten carrion once or twice,[7] after this has been ejected from its[8] intestines it is to be taken in good faith.[9]

7. Swine that taste the flesh or blood of men are always forbidden. For in the Law an animal that pushes with the horn, if it kills a man, is forbidden;[10] how much more those that eat a man. Nevertheless their young[11] are to be preserved. What the uncleanness of the mothers[12] does not pollute is permitted.[13]

8. Hens that taste the flesh of a man or his blood are in a high degree unclean, and their eggs are unclean; but their chicks are to be preserved.[14]

9. A cistern in which is found either the corpse of a man or [the carcass] of a dog or of any animal is first to be emptied, and the slime (because the water of the cistern moistened it) is to be thrown out, and it is clean.[15]

10. That which is contaminated by a cow is to be taken with a clear conscience, for why should we exclude[16] the contamination of a cow and not reject the milk tasted by a sucking calf? But nevertheless, on account of the weak conscience of the brethren, not[17] on account of uncleanness, it is to be cooked, and then it is to be accepted by men.[18]

11. That which is contaminated by swine is to be cooked, and distributed to unclean men.[19] For swine eat things clean and unclean; but cows feed only on grass and the leaves of trees.

[7] Codex Cotton, Otho E XIII, reads "once, twice or thrice."
[8] Literally, "their."   [9] This sentence is omitted in Codex Paris. 3182.
[10] Based on Exod. 21:29; 21:36.   [11] "foetus."
[12] Reading "matrum" with the Hatton and Cotton manuscripts, instead of "mogitum" in the published editions from Codex Paris. 12021.
[13] D'Achéry suggested "licite" for "linquite." The Hatton manuscript has "licidae."
[14] The last sentence of canon 7 occurs here in the Hatton manuscript.
[15] Cf. Lev. 11:36.   [16] Literally, "excommunicate."
[17] Haddan and Stubbs would omit "non."
[18] Reading with the Hatton and Cotton manuscripts "ab hominibus," for "ab omnibus" (by all).
[19] Cf. Lev. 11:24–32.

12. That which is contaminated by a crow can be cleansed by no cooking,[20] on account of our doubtful[21] conscience; for who knows what forbidden flesh he had eaten before he contaminated our liquid.[22]

13. That which is contaminated by a leech[23] is by no means to be taken, either without cooking or after cooking.

14. Things drowned in water are not to be eaten, since[24] the Lord hath prohibited the eating of flesh that contains blood.[25] For in the flesh of an animal drowned in water the blood remains coagulated. This the Lord prohibits, not because in those days men ate raw flesh, since it would be none too sweet,[26] but because they had been eating drowned and carrion flesh. And the Law written in metrical fashion says, "Thou shalt not eat carrion flesh."[27]

15. Stolen cattle[28] are not to be taken by Christians whether in trade or as gifts: for what Christ[29] rejects, how shall the soldier of Christ receive? For the weeping of the robber's victim[30] makes void his alms.

16. Of a wife who is a harlot, thus the same man explained, "That she will be a harlot, who has cast off the yoke of her own husband, and is joined to a second or a third husband; and her[31] husband shall not take another [wife] while she lives; for we do not know whether that verdict which we read in questions of the Romans was attested by acceptable or false witnesses."[32]

[20] Or possibly "by no [amount of] effort," if we read with the Hatton and Cotton manuscripts "contentione" for "coctione."

[21] "dubiam" is omitted in the Hatton and Cotton manuscripts.

[22] Haddan and Stubbs read "nostrum . . . intinxerit." The Cotton manuscript reads "nostrum inlicitum intinxerit"; the Hatton has "nostrum inliquitum intinxerit." Editors have suggested "nostrum lac intinxerit" (contaminated our milk), but there is no previous mention of milk.

[23] Reading "abdella" for the manuscript reading "aduella," in place of "mustella" (weasel).   [24] "unde" (whence).

[25] Lev. 17:10–14; Deut. 12:16; 12:23. This sentence is omitted in the Hatton and Cotton manuscripts.

[26] "quia non esset dulcior"; perhaps: "would not be sweeter" [than cooked flesh].

[27] Based on Lev. 5:2; 17:15; and other passages.

[28] The Cotton manuscript is illegible here. The other manuscripts read: "Praedarum pecora." Editors have suggested "pecunia" (the fruits of plunder) for "pecora."

[29] "Christus" in the Hatton and Cotton manuscripts, omitted in the others.

[30] Reading with the Hatton manuscript: "invassi" for "invasit."

[31] Literally, "whose."

[32] "quia nescimus illam auctoritatem quam legimus in quaestionibus Romanorum, utrum idoneis an falsis testibus ornatam fuisse." Possibly we should render this difficult passage: "for we do not know that authority to have been distinguished which we read in questions of the Romans: whether by acceptable or by false witnesses." The Hatton manu-

17. The same man confirms [the statement] that flesh of which some is eaten by beasts is unclean, not carrion only, since the blood of that forbidden flesh has been shed by beasts.

18. A beast that has only been seized with a deadly bite and not quite killed is to be eaten by sinners and by bestial men—the ear or any part[33] which the beast contaminated with its teeth having been cut off and given to the dogs. For it seems to him fitting that human beasts should eat the flesh that has been served to beasts.

19. In like manner he forbids the eating of the marrow of the bones of stags of which wolves have eaten.

20. Likewise he forbids the eating of stags, although we observe that, because the legs have been broken, a little of their blood has flowed about the feet; affirming that they are carrion, from the fact that the higher blood had not flowed, which is the guardian and seat of life,[34] but was clotted within the flesh. Although the extremity of the blood has been shed through some extreme member, nevertheless the thicker and denser blood in which the life has its seat remains clotted within the flesh. But if then he has not disturbed the seat of life by reason of a wound that is not inflicted,[35] it is not shedding of blood but only an injury to an extreme part. Therefore, also, he who eats this flesh shall know that he has eaten the flesh with the blood; since the Lord has forbidden this,[36] it is not the cooking of the flesh but the shedding of the blood that is lacking.[37] And this that is said above ought to be understood of beasts which have died after the cutting off of an ear[38] [when they were] in extreme weakness. Nevertheless,[39] the fat and the hides we shall have for diverse uses.[40]

---

script, however, reads: "unde nescimus illam auctoritatem quam legimus in quaestionibus Romanorum utrum idoneis an testibus falsis ornatum fuisse." The Cotton follows this except that two or three words after "Romanorum" are illegible and they are followed by: "idoneis testibus an falsis orta co. ēe. fuisse."

[33] Reading with Hatton and Cotton "aure vel qualibet parte."

[34] Lev. 17:14; Deut. 12:16, 23.

[35] Reading with the Hatton and Cotton manuscripts "causa vulneris inlisi."

[36] The Hatton and Cotton manuscripts read "since the Lord has forbidden to eat the flesh with the blood."

[37] Reading with the Hatton and Cotton manuscripts "deerat" for "dederat."

[38] Haddan and Stubbs add "vel tantum scissam" (or only the cutting); the Hatton and Cotton manuscripts originally omitted this. The Hatton text was corrected to read "vel(?) tantum abscisa aure"; this with the context may be rendered "which, although only an ear had been cut off, being in extreme weakness, afterwards died."

[39] Reading with the Hatton and Cotton manuscripts "tamen" (t̄m) for "tantum."

[40] Lev. 7:24.

SELECTIONS FROM THE LAW OF ADAMNAN (*ca. 697, with later embellishments*)

[THE *Cáin Adamnáin* is another document in Old Irish connected with the name of Adamnan, abbot of Iona. It was edited with a translation by the late Kuno Meyer in *Anecdota Oxoniensia*, "Medieval and Modern Series," 1905. From its contents it was called in the Annals of Ulster, "The Law of Innocents." But the word "cain" is properly translated "tribute," and is appropriate because of the fact that the document sets down payments to be made to "the communities of Adamnan" for violations of the law which it embodies. Because of its revolutionary assertion of the rights of women and children it is a very remarkable document in social history. It opens with a somewhat extended professedly historical section showing how, through the influence of his mother, Adamnan came to be the liberator of the women of Ireland. Meyer was prevented by illness from writing an adequate introduction to the work. He believed that the two manuscripts which he used go back to the lost *Book of Raphoe*, and that "our text was originally composed during the Old-Irish period, probably in the ninth century" (Preface, p. viii). There is fairly conclusive evidence, however, that the essential terms of the Law were set forth by a synod held at Tara under Adamnan's influence in A.D. 697.[1]

The selections given comprise practically all the material in the document which bears on penance and restitution. They offer an excellent series of illustrations of the practices of composition and commutation of penance in Ireland. Notes here inserted from Meyer's edition are followed by his initials in square brackets. I am indebted to the Clarendon Press for permission to reproduce these selections. Except in canon 33 I have followed Meyer's text without change.]

33.[2] Here begins the speech of the angel to Adamnan:

After fourteen years Adamnan obtained this Law of God, and this is the cause. On Pentecost eve a holy angel of the Lord came to him, and again at Pentecost after a year, and he seized a staff, struck his side, and said to him, "Go forth into Ireland, and make a law in it that women be not in any manner killed by men, by stabbing[3] or any other form of death, either by poison, or in water, or in fire, or by any beast, or in a pit, or by dogs, but that they shall die in their lawful bed. Thou shalt establish a law in Ireland and Britain for the sake of the mother of each

---

[1] W. Reeves, *Life of St. Columba*, 1st ed., pp. l, 179; J. O'Hanlon, *Lives of the Irish Saints*, IX, 507 ff. On the other literature of the subject, the reader may consult Kenney, pp. 245 f.   [2] Meyer, p. 23.

[3] This paragraph is peculiar in being given in Latin. In it I have followed Meyer's translation mainly, but I have altered a few words and expressions. For "iugulatione" here Meyer has "slaughter," which seems too general in the context. While the regulation may be Adamnan's, the legendary element is probably much later than his time.

one, because a mother has borne each one, and for the sake of Mary mother of Jesus Christ, through whom all are. Mary besought her Son on behalf of Adamnan about this Law. For whoever slays a woman shall be condemned to a twofold punishment, that is, his right hand and his left foot shall be cut off before death, and then he shall die, and his kindred shall pay in full seven female slaves, and one-seventh part of the penance. If, instead of life and amputation, a fine has been imposed, the penance is fourteen years, and fourteen female slaves shall be paid. But if a host has done it, every fifth man up to three hundred shall be condemned to that punishment; if few, they shall be divided into three parts. The first part of them shall be put to death by lot, hand and foot having first been cut off; the second part shall pay in full fourteen female slaves; the third shall be cast into exile beyond the sea, under the rule of hard regimen; for the sin is great when any one slays the mother and the sister of Christ's mother and the mother of Christ, and her who carries the spindle and who clothes every one. But he who from this day forward puts a woman to death and does not do penance according to the Law, shall not only perish in eternity, and be cursed for God and Adamnan, but all shall be cursed that have heard it and do not curse him, and do not chastise him according to the judgment of this Law."

This is the speech of the angel to Adamnan.

35. Whoever wounds or slays a young clerical student or an innocent child under the ordinance of Adamnan's Law, eight *cumals* for it for every hand (engaged) with eight years of penance, up to three hundred *cumals;* and one year of penance for it for each one from three hundred to one thousand or an indefinite number; and it is the same fine for him who commits the deed and for him who sees it and does not save to the best of his ability. If there is neglect or ignorance, half the fine for it, and . . . that it is neglect and that it is ignorance.

41. A further enactment of the Law, that payment in full fines is to be made to Adamnan for every woman that has been slain, whether a man has a share in it, or cattle or a hound or fire or a ditch or a building,—for everything that is made is liable in the Law, both ditch and pit and bridge and fireplace and [door]step and pools and kilns, and every other danger, except the woman deserves it. But one-third is left to be kept. If it is a witless person, the other two-thirds shall die. The one-third is his who has the right to it.

43. There shall be no cross-case or balancing of guilt in Adamnan's Law, but each one pays for his crimes for his own hand. Every trespass which is committed in Adamnan's Law, the communities of

Adamnan are entitled to a . . . of it, apart from women, whether it be innocents, or clerics, or any one to whom they commit it, viz., a *cumal forbaich* to the community of Hi[4] where seven *cumals* are paid, and half a *cumal* from seven half-*cumals*. Six *séts* on thirty *séts*, three *séts* on five *séts*.

44. One-eighth of everything small and great to the community of Adamnan from the slaying of clerics or innocent children. If it be a life-wound any one inflicts on a woman or a cleric or an innocent, seven half-*cumals* are due from him, fifteen *séts* upon the nearest and remoter kindred as being accomplices. Three *séts* for every white blow,[5] five *séts* for every drawing of blood, seven *séts* for every wound requiring a tent, a *cumal* for every confinement to bed, and payment of the physician besides. If it be more than that, it goes upon half-dues for killing a person. If it is a blow with the palm of the hand or with the fist, an ounce of silver (is the fine) for it. If there be a green or red mark, or a swelling, an ounce and six scruples for it. For seizing women by the hair, five wethers. If there is a fight among women with outrage (?), three wethers.

45. Men and women are equally liable for large and small dues from this on to (any) fights of women, except outright death. For a woman deserves death for killing a man or a woman, or for giving poison whereof death ensues, or for burning, or for digging under a church,[6] that is to say, she is to be put into a boat of one paddle as a sea-waif (?) upon the ocean to go with the wind from land. A vessel of meal and water to be given with her. Judgment upon her as God deems fit.

46. If it be charms from which death ensues that any one give to another, the fines of murder followed by concealment of the corpse (are to be paid) for it. Secret plunderings and . . . which are traced (?) to (one of) the four nearest lands, unless these four nearest lands can lay them on any one particularly, they swear by the . . . of their soul that they do not know to lay it upon any one and pay it themselves. If they suspect any one and prove it, it is he who shall be liable. If the probability lie between two or a greater number, let their names be written upon leaves; each leaf is arranged around a lot, and the lots are put into a chalice upon the altar. He on whom the lot falls is liable.

[4] Iona.   [5] I.e., a blow that neither draws blood nor causes discolouring. [K.M.]
[6] viz. to look for treasure. [K.M.]

47. If offenders who violate the Law do not pay, their kindred pay full fines according to the greatness of his crime, and after that (the offender) becomes forfeited, and is banished until the end of the law. One-half of seven *cumals* for accompliceship upon every direct and indirect kindred afterwards. If there be assistance and shelter and connivance, it is death for it; but such as the fine (of the principals) was such shall be that of the accomplices.

48. A further enactment of the Law: they shall feed the stewards of Adamnan's Law, whatever their number, with the good food of their people, viz. five men as guarantors, and the feeding of every one who shall levy the dues of the Law shall be according to the wealth of every one, both chieftain and church and people. A *cumal* for leaving any one of them fasting, while fines are being levied, and offenders with regard to feeding, and they sustain a joint contract of debts unless they feed them. Two *cumals* to them from offenders.

49. This is the exemption of every guarantor who comes to levy this tribute, viz. the guilt of their family does not come upon them so long as they support guarantors and while they are in possession and do not escape; but their own guilt (comes upon them) or the guilt of their offspring and of their children and of their retainers.

50. If it be rape of a maiden, seven half-*cumals* (is the fine) for it. If a hand (is put) upon her or in her girdle, ten ounces for it. If a hand (is put) under her dress to defile her, three ounces and seven *cumals* for it. If there be a blemish of her head or her eyes or in the face or in the ear or nose or tooth or tongue or foot or hand, seven *cumals* are (to be paid) for it. If it be a blemish of any other part of her body, seven half-*cumals* for it. If it be tearing of her dress, seven ounces and one *cumal* for it.

51. If it be making a gentlewoman blush by imputing unchastity to her or by denying her offspring, there are seven *cumals* (to be paid) for it until it comes to (the wife of) an *aire désa*.[7] Seven half-*cumals* if it be the wife of an *aire désa*. From her onwards to a *muiri*,[8] seven ounces.

52. If women be employed in an assault or in a host or fight, seven *cumals* for every hand as far as seven, and beyond that it is to be accounted as the crime of one man. If a woman has been got with child by stealth, without contract, without full rights, without dowry,

[7] "Chief of land." See Meyer's note, p. 46.
[8] "lord." See Meyer's note, p. 46.

without betrothal, a full fine for it. Whatever . . . which is of hand-produce, great or small, whatever of dye-stuff, or wood or beans. If it be red dye of a cloak . . . of a cloak for it.

6. FROM AN IRISH COLLECTION OF CANONS

(Collectio canonum Hibernensis, ca. 700–725)

[THE SECOND of the two canonical works referred to in the introduction to the last document is the *Collectio canonum Hibernensis*, or *Irish Collection of Canons*. This document differs widely in its characteristics from the *Irish Canons* given above. It is an elaborate compilation from scriptural texts, conciliar decisions, and extracts from the Church Fathers. A considerable amount of its material is of Irish origin. Many of its canons are attributed to wrong authors or sources. While it was almost certainly begun in the Irish Church, textual evidence seems to point to its preservation in Brittany.[1] E. W. B. Nicholson has contended with some cogency that it originated at Iona and that its compiler may have been Adamnan himself.[2] There is impressive evidence, however, that it was compiled by two monks, Rubin of Dair Inis (d. 725) and Cuchuimne of Iona (d. 741).[3] The definitive edition is that of Wasserschleben, *Die irische Kanonensammlung* (2d ed., 1885). Most investigators favor for the compilation a date near the end of the seventh century. While the *Collectio canonum Hibernensis* sometimes sheds light on textual problems in the penitential literature and is helpful on some questions of date and origin, it contains in fact little of penitential nature. Under the title "De penitentia" (Liber xlvii) are twenty capitula consisting of extracts of a general character from other sources than Irish. None of these have the characteristics of the typical materials of the penitential books. Scattered through the work are numerous capitula the contents of which belong properly to the medieval penitential literature, but most of these are derived from sources elsewhere translated in this book. The few that are included below either vary widely from the earlier parallels or are found in their earliest known form in the *Collectio*.]

---

[1] H. Bradshaw, *The Early Collection of Canons Known as the Hibernensis, Two Unfinished Papers*, 1893. Bradshaw had previously (1885) published the first of these papers as "A Letter to Wasserschleben"; the letter is given, with many misprints, in the second edition of Wasserschleben's *Die irische Kanonensammlung*, pp. lxiii ff.

[2] "The Origin of the Hibernian Collection of Canons," *Zeitschrift für celtische Philologie*, III (1901), 99 ff. W. Finsterwalder has recently revived A. Nürnberger's suggestion ("Ueber die Würzburger Hs. der irischen Canonensammlung," *A.K.K.R.*, LX[1888], 3–84) that the compiler was St. Boniface. *Die Canones Theodori Cantuariensis und ihre Ueberlieferungsformen*, p. 180. The argument for this is highly conjectural. The evidence provided by Nürnberger (pp. 34 ff.) may be taken to point to the use of the *Irish Collection* by Boniface, rather than to his compilation of it.

[3] See Kenney, pp. 248–49, and L. Gougaud, *Christianity in Celtic Lands*, p. 280. Gougaud confidently adopts this view.

Lib. II, cap. 25. Of the Time in Which the Priests Ought to Be Absent from a Church, and of Their Penance If They Are Absent beyond the Time

a. An Irish synod has decreed that a priest shall be absent from his church only one day; if he is absent two days, he shall do penance for seven days with bread and water; moreover, if a dead man is brought to the church and [the priest] is absent, he ought to do penance, since he is answerable for the man's penalty.[4]

b. If he is absent from the church one Sunday, he shall do a penance of twenty days on bread and water; but if for two or three days, he is to be deposed from the honor of his rank.[5]

XXVIII, 5. Of the Penance for Homicide Committed Unintentionally

A Roman treatise declares:[6] "First definition: he who shedding blood takes flight, forfeits all;[7] chiefly he shall be absolved by reconciliation with the next of kin[8] of the slain man. Second definition: he shall be condemned to a pilgrimage of seven years or else remain in the bosom of the protecting church unto the end of his life."

XXVIII, 10. Of Diverse Penances of Murderers Who Slay Intentionally

b. An Irish synod says, All murderers, if they are converted with all their heart, shall perform a penance of seven years strictly under the rule of a monastery.

XXIX, 6. Of Theft Committed in a Church

An Irish synod has decreed: A first theft committed in a church is, however, to be compensated for, and penance is to be done according to the judgment of a priest; and he makes this [judgment] in accordance with the clemency of the church. But if it is done a second time, double or quadruple restitution is to be made. But if the goods of a man of the world[9] are carried off, and the church is catholic and free from all obligation,[10] the damage shall be made good to the owner, and the interest of it shall go to the church. If indeed the

---

[4] "poenae reus illius."

[5] Section i, 9, quotes the canons of councils for the exile and degradation of a bishop in case of repeated or habitual absence, but without assigning terms of penance.

[6] "Disputatio Romana disputat."

[7] "perfectioni mancipetur": literally, "shall be completely sold(?)."

[8] "promimi."   [9] "mundialis hominis."   [10] "censu."

church is under obligation to the king,[11] the same damage shall be made good to the owner, and the interest shall go to the king and the church.

XXIX, 7. Of the Penance of One Who Steals in a Church

Patrick says: He who has stolen treasure either from a holy church or within the city where martyrs and the bodies of the saints sleep—the lot shall be cast on three things: either his hand or his foot shall be cut off; or he shall be committed to prison, to fast for such time as the seniors shall determine and restore entire what he carried off; or he shall be sent forth on pilgrimage and restore double, and shall swear that he will not return until he has completed the penance and [that] after the penance he will be a monk.

XXXVII, 27. Of the Penance of One Who Rails against a Good Prince

Patrick says: He who murmurs words of railing against a good prince through hatred or envy, shall do penance for seven days on bread and water, as did Mary for murmuring against Moses.[12]

XLII, 22. Of What Punishment They Deserve Who Desert Infants in a Church of God

The Irish synod: Persons who unknown to the abbot desert infants in a church of God, if there are bishops buried in it or if [bishops] are present, shall do penance for three years and a half. If they commit murder in it, they shall do penance for seven years. This is because the bishop has seven grades[13] and the church is septiform.[14] If they have no bishops and the church is small, they shall do penance for a year and a half.

XLIV, *8. Of a Decree of Irishmen on the Violation of Relics*

Whoever violates the relics of bishops or martyrs by murder, shall do penance for seven years as a pilgrim. If by theft, for three

---

[11] "sub censu regali."   [12] Num. 12:14–15 (For "Mary" A.V. has "Miriam").

[13] That is, "is in the seventh rank of ecclesiastics." See above, p. 127, n. 77.

[14] On the basis of passages such as Rev. 1:4, 11, 13; Ps. 118, 164; and Job 1:2 various groups of seven were employed allegorically to refer to the whole body of the Church (ecclesiae universitas) or to the fulness of operation of the Spirit in the Church. See Garnerus (twelfth century) *Gregorianum* XV, vi, Migne, *P.L.*, CXCIII, 448; P. E. Kretzmann, "Der Spiritus septiformis," *Concordia Theological Monthly*, III (1932), 245–51. On the custom of building seven churches together in Ireland, see J. H. Todd, *Life of St. Patrick*, pp. 32–35.

years. But if he slays on the bounds of a holy place in which laymen are given hospitality, one year. Let us concede to later times [by saying] fifty days, since that is not to be called a holy place into which murderers with their despoilings, thieves with their thefts, adulterers, perjurers, hawkers,[15] and wizards have entrance. Not only ought every holy place to be cleansed within, but also its bounds, which have been consecrated, ought to be clean.

7. AN OLD IRISH TABLE OF COMMUTATIONS

(8th century)

[CLOSELY RELATED to Section II of the *Canones Hibernenses* is a remarkable document in Old Irish, apparently of somewhat later date. It consists of an extended schedule of equivalents or commutations to be applied in penitential cases. It has been published with a translation by Kuno Meyer under the title "An Old Irish Treatise *De arreis*," in *Revue celtique*, XV (1894), 485-98. Variant readings from a Dublin manuscript are given by E. J. Gwynn, "De Arreis," *Ériu*, V (1911), 45 f. In a short philological introduction Meyer expresses doubt about the date of the document, but is confident that "it cannot have been later than the eighth century." Meyer uses in his title and throughout the translation the Latin form "arreum" of the Irish word "arra," which he explains as "equivalent, substitute, commutation."[1] The translation is reproduced from Meyer's text without change. Most of his footnotes are omitted as of no special value in the present context, and some of my own are added. I have ventured to omit the subheadings translated by Meyer. In most cases they are somewhat inappropriate. Meyer's notes are indicated by the bracketed initials [K.M.]. The few Latin words which he has left in the text will probably be readily understood. The document is of special interest for the variety of harsh penalties which it sanctions, and for its repeated reference to "saving a soul out of hell."]

1. The *arreum* for saving a soul out of hell, viz. 365 paternosters and 365 genuflexions and 365 blows with a scourge on every day to the end of a year, and fasting every month saves a soul out of hell. For this *arreum* for redeeming the soul that deserves torments in the body has been made according to the number of joints and sinews that are in a man's body.

2. Another *arreum*, viz. the three fifties[2] every day, with their

---

[15] "precones." In classical Latin "praeco" was sometimes used in the sense of "auctioneer." Cf. *Can. Hib.* I, 4, p. 119, above.

[1] Meyer, *op. cit.*, p. 486.

[2] The one hundred and fifty psalms. Cf. canons 14, 20.

conclusion of the Beati[3] to the end of seven years, saves a soul out of hell.

3. Another *arreum* which is no longer, viz. a Lauda and the Beati and a pater noster after each psalm to the end of three years.

4. Each of these *arrea* saves a soul out of hell, if it can be interceded for at all.[4]

5. Now, every penance, both for severity and length of time in which one is at it, depends on the greatness of the sin and on the space of time which one perseveres in it, and on the reason for which it is done, and on the zeal with which one departs from it afterwards. For there are certain sins which do not deserve any remission of penance, however long the time that shall be asked for them, unless God Himself shortens it through death or a message of sickness; or the greatness of the work which a person lays on himself; such as are parricides and manslaughters and man-stealings, and such as brigandage and druidism and satirising,[5] and such as adultery and lewdness and lying and heresy and transgression of order. For there are certain sins for which half-penances with half-*arrea* atone. There are others which an *arreum* with one third of penance atones for. There are others for which an *arreum* only atones.

6. For these are the four things which the wise man has recounted for which the *arrea* are made, viz. for a speedy parting from the sin after its commission, for fear of increasing the sins, for (fear of) life being shortened before the end of the penance which the confessor adjudges be attained, for (fear of) chastising the body of Christ and His blood through the chastisement of penance.

7. Now, as there is a difference between laybrothers and clerics, between nuns and laysisters,[6] so there is a difference between their

[3] i.e. the 118th psalm (*Beati immaculati*). [K.M.]

[4] lit. if its *ecnairc* (intercession, prayer for the dead) can be sung at all. [K.M.]

[5] Probably the making of defamatory verses—an offense frequently referred to in early Irish literature.

[6] In canons 7 and 8 the words translated by Meyer "lay-sister," "lay-brother" mean literally "laywoman" and "layman," respectively. In appropriate contexts the Latin equivalent "laica," "laicus" may be interpreted in the technical monastic sense suggested by Meyer's rendering; but it is doubtful if such a use is intended here. The words "athlaech," "ath-laeches," employed in their plural forms in canon 8, are literally equivalent to "former layman," "former laywoman." C. Plummer renders "athlaech" "ex-warrior," and makes it equivalent to "conversus," a novice who has been converted late in life. See the glossaries at the end of his *Vitae sanctorum Hiberniae, s.vv.* "conversus," "relaicus," "athlaech," and the passages there referred to. However, "ath-laech" here may be Finnian's "laicus ante" (*Poenit. Vinn.* 27), i.e., a cleric or monk who has not been brought up in a monastery but spent his early life in lay society.

work and penance. There is also between the *arrea* which it is right for them to perform.

8. First, the *arrea* of former lay-brothers and lay-sisters: sleeping in waters, sleeping on nettles, sleeping on nut-shells, sleeping with a dead body in a grave; for there is hardly a laybrother or laysister that has not had a share in manslaughter. These now are the *arrea* that are right for clerics and nuns, except those of them that have slain a man, unless (something) be done to increase the reward, viz. they to sleep in cold churches or in secret chambers, performing vigil and praying without ceasing, viz. without sitting, without lying, without sleeping, as though they were at the mouth of hell, save that a little weariness may take place in a sitting posture only between two prayers.

9. These now are the *arrea* which the holy man judges (an equivalent) for "black fasting"[7] after a great crime, viz. one hundred blows with a scourge, or the three fifties with their hymns and with their canticles.

10. Another *arreum*, viz. one hundred paternosters in cross-vigil[8] and "Deus in adiutorium" usque "festina" (ps. 69, 1) three times at the end of every pater noster, and genuflexion at every "Deus," and meditating intently on God. It is an *arreum* for a black fast of three days[9] to any one who does this three times.

11. An *arreum* for fasting for any one that can read: the three fifties with their canticles while standing up, and celebrating every canonical hour, and twelve genuflexions and the arms stretched out towards God at the hours of the day, with earnest thought towards heaven.

12. An *arreum* for a black fast on account of a great crime for any one who does not read, viz. 300 genuflexions and 300 honest blows with a scourge; crossvigil at the end of every hundred until the arms are tired; "Oh God I beseech an end, may mercy come to me," "I believe the Trinity," this is what he shall sing without ceasing until the *arreum* shall have come to an end, and strike his breast frequently at it with earnest repentance to God. It is an *arreum* for a three days' fast for him to do this three times.

---

[7] *dub-throscud*, now *trosgadh dubh*, a fast during which no whitemeats (banbiad), such as milk, cheese, eggs, etc. are taken. [K.M.]

[8] See Introduction, p. 32, above.

[9] *tredain*, now *trosgadh treidhin*, from Lat. *triduanum*, a fast of three days, during which only one collation is taken; still practised privately by many people. [K.M.]

13. An *arreum* for fasting on account of small common sins, viz. "Alleluia, Alleluia, in manus" usque "veritatis," a paternoster to the end. Let this be sung thirty times in cross-vigil and thirty genuflexions and thirty blows with a scourge after it.

14. An *arreum* of pure prayers for seven years of hard penance to save a soul from the tortures of hell, viz. one hundred offerings, hundred and fifty psalms, one hundred Beati, one hundred genuflexions at every beatitude, one hundred paternosters, one hundred soul-hymns.

15. Another *arreum:* a year of three days' black fasts without drink, without food, without sleep. A night in water, a night on nettles without a garment, another on nutshells.

16. Another *arreum:* twelve three days' fasts one after another. A meal to satiety between every two fasts.

17. Another *arreum:* to sing two Beati in crossvigil without lowering of arms (while) at it.

18. Again, another *arreum:* "Miserere mei Deus" to be sung forty times in cross-vigil or while standing up, and a paternoster with every psalm, and "Deus in adiutorium" usque "festina" three times at the end of each psalm.

19. Another *arreum:* seven months in a prison on water and bread from none to none upon the soil or floor, with fervent prayer, with celebration of every hour with constant determination.

20. This is an *arreum* for the 150 psalms, viz. a paternoster twelve times and "Deus in adiutorium" usque "festina" after every paternoster. A paternoster fifteen times and "Deus in adiutorium" usque in finem after every paternoster atones for every sin, with earnest repentance from the heart.

21. An *arreum* for a three days' fast for any one that does not read, viz. a day with a night without sleeping, without sitting down, except when he lets himself down for genuflexion. "Of God I beseech an end," "may mercy come to me," "I believe the Trinity," this he shall sing without ceasing. A paternoster and a credo twelve times in crossvigil, and three genuflexions with either, and "Deus in adiutorium" usque "festina" three times with every prayer is an *arreum* for a three days' fast. Thirty three days' fasts in this manner are an *arreum* for a year of penance for a cleric, ut Gregorius constituit.

22. An *arreum* for impositions of scourging, viz. 700 honest blows seven times.

23. Another *arreum* of genuflexions, viz. 200 honest genuflexions with bending of the body without negligence.

24. Another *arreum:* to be standing without a staff, without rest, until the three fifties with the canticles have been sung.

25. Another *arreum* of crossvigil until fifty psalms have been sung, or the Beati four times, and the arms must not touch the sides until the singing is finished, though there be nothing else to support thee by.[10]

26. An *arreum* for a week of hard penance on water and bread, viz. seven Beati in honest crossvigil and a credo and paternoster and "Hymnum dicat" with every beatitude.

27. Again, an *arreum* for a week for any one that has not read, viz. 700 honest genuflexions, and seven honest blows, crossvigil at the end of every hundred until the arms are tired.

28. An *arreum* for a fortnight, to do this twice.

29. An *arreum* for twenty nights, to do this three times.

30. An *arreum* for forty nights on water and bread, to do it in one day, if at the need of death.

31. This is an *arreum* for a year for sudden repentance, viz. to sing 365 paters while standing up, the arms unwearied towards heaven. The elbows must not touch the sides at all, with intent meditation on God, and let not voice enter the speech, and to sing a Beati in a stooping posture, thy face towards the earth and thy arms stretched out by thy sides. Or, it is the body that is stretched out on the earth on its face, and the arms stretched out by the side. It is Patrick who ordains this vigil, and Colum Cille[11] and Maedoc of Ferns[12] and Molacca Menn[13] and Brennain,[14] the great-grandson of Alta, and Colum son of Crimthan[15] and Mocholmóc of Inisceltra.[16]

With Enda in Aran[17] this law was left. Four chief sages of Ireland

---

[10] The construction of the Irish here is obscure to me, but the sense must be as I have translated. [K.M.]

[11] St. Columba of Iona, d. 597.

[12] St. Maedoc, or Aedhan, of Ferns, d. *ca.* 625.

[13] St. Malaga, *ca.* 600. See Kenney, p. 406; O'Hanlon, I, 336; VIII, 189.

[14] One of the numerous Brendans.

[15] This Colum (d. 549) was the founder, after the legendary MacCreiche, of the monastic establishment of Inisceltra. Kenney, pp. 384–85.

[16] A number of Colmans were commonly styled Mocholmóc. The name is not found in R. A. Macalister; "The History and Antiquities of Inis Cealtra," *Proc. of Roy. Ir. Acad.*, XXXIII, C (1916), 93–174.

[17] Enda of Aran, d. *ca.* 540. See O'Hanlon, III, 911 ff.

ordained its practice to every son of life who desires Heaven, viz. Ua Mianadan and Cummin Fota[18] and Murdebur[19] and Mocholmóc mac Cumain from Aran.[20]

32. An *arreum* for a year of hard penance, which Ciaran mac int sáir[21] adjudged to Oennu macu Laigse grandson of Comsola grandson of Dibrech: to be three days and three nights at it in a dark house or in some other place where no hindrance comes. And there must be no collation of a three days' fast save three sips of water every day. This, however, is the *arreum*, viz. to sing 150 psalms every day while standing up without a staff, and genuflexion at the end of every psalm, and a Beati after every fifty, genuflexion between every two chapters(?) and "Hymnum dicat" after every Beati in crossvigil, and he must not let himself down into a lying posture . . . but in a sitting posture, and celebration of every hour besides . . . and intent meditation of the passion of Christ with contrition of heart and earnest repentance to God with remembrance of the sins, every one of them that he remembers.

33. An *arreum* for fifty nights of hard penance to be done in one day, which Colum Cille and Mobí Clárenech[22] adjudged by the counsel of the archangel Michael, viz. Dominus regnavit (?ps. 96 or 98), Exaudi Domine iustitiam meam (ps. 16), Domini est terra (ps. 23), Beatus que intellegit (ps. 40), Deus noster refugium (ps. 45), Exaudi Deus deprecationem (ps. 60), Nonne Deo (ps. 61) Exaudi Deus orationem meam cum (ps. 63), Te decet (ps. 64), Domine refugium (ps. 89), Domine exaudi (ps. 101), Domine probasti (ps. 138), Eripe me Domine (ps. 139), Domine clamavi (ps. 140). Voce (ps. 141), Domine exaudi (ps. 142). "Gloria et honor Patri et Filio et Spiritui Sancto" at the end of every psalm, and seven genuflexions, and "Deus in adiutorium" usque "festina" three times, and a paternoster once while standing up between every two psalms until the whole *arreum* shall have ended.

---

[18] Cummean the Long, d. *ca.* 662, apparently the author of the *Penitential of Cummean.* See above, p. 98.

[19] Commemorated in the *Martyrology of Gorman*, Nov. 2, as "great Murdebair whom I praise." Edition of W. Stokes, p. 211.

[20] No doubt identical with "Colman, son of Comman from eastern Aran," *Martyrology of Gorman*, Nov. 21. Stokes, *op. cit.*, p. 223.

[21] That is, "Ciaran the carpenter's son." Stokes, *op. cit.*, p. 173 (Sept. 9).

[22] A pupil, with Columba, of Finnian of Clonard. See W. Reeves, *Adamnan's Life of St. Columba*, 1st ed., p. lxxii.

8. SELECTIONS FROM THE BIGOTIAN PENITENTIAL

(ca. 700–725)

[THE *Penitential of Cummean,* the *Old Irish Penitential* published by Gwynn, and the present document are obviously closely related. Kenney, citing Gwynn's notes on the subject, is inclined to place the *Poenitentiale Bigotianum* between the other two of the series, and therefore "about the end of the seventh or in the eighth century." He then remarks: "It has usually been classed as a continental penitential of Irish derivation, but there seems no good reason for not classifying it as an original Irish production, which its character and manuscript connections suggest."[1] This conjecture is supported by manuscript evidence. The only manuscript in which the penitential is preserved (Paris. 3182, formerly Bigotianus 89) is a codex written in Brittany or in the monastery of Fécamp in Normandy in the tenth or eleventh century. The script is continental, but the abbreviations, and other features, give evidence that the document descended from an Insular original. It is noteworthy that the codex in which it occurs is mainly a collection of Insular materials. It is impossible to say whether *Bigotianum* is earlier or later than the *Old Irish Penitential,* but Gwynn and Kenney regard it as the earlier document. Both these works follow the scheme of the eight principal sins given by Cassian in his *Institutes,* V, i, and *Collationes,* V, ii, as also do Cummean and Pseudo-Cummean.[2]

The penitential opens with an extended introductory section in exposition of the theory of penance. This section is translated below in its entirety. The main body of the document is entitled: "Eight Chapters on the Remedies of the Vices." For this section the parallels with the earlier literature are indicated by Wasserschleben who gives the full text.[3] Schmitz has indicated the parallels without giving the text.[4] Celtic and Anglo-Saxon penitentials are virtually the only sources used in these canons. Only a few of the provisions show sufficient originality to make their inclusion here desirable.]

Jerome,[5] a man of blessed memory, carefully admonished the pastors and teachers of the Church that they should take note of the qualities of the faults of sinners, saying: Let the power of the physician become greater in the degree in which the fever of the sick man increases. Hence those who take care to heal the wounds of others

---

[1] *Op. cit.,* p. 241.

[2] See pp. 98 ff., 266 f. Cf. Schulze, *Die Entwicklung der Hauptlaster- und Haupttugendlehre* . . . , p. 72.

[3] *Bussordnungen,* pp. 441–60.

[4] Schmitz I, pp. 707–11. Cf. Schmitz's discussion of the document, *ibid.,* pp. 705–7.

[5] The passage here attributed to Jerome bears resemblance to a passage cited by Wasserschleben, *Bussordnungen,* pp. 441 f., from the *Collectio* of Anselm of Lucca. Cf. *Pseudo-Cummean,* p. 267, below.

are to observe carefully what is the age and sex of the sinner, with what learning he is instructed, with what courage he is distinguished, with how great force he has been driven to sin, with what kind of passion he is assailed, how long he remained in sinful delight, with what sorrow[6] and labor he is afflicted, and how he is separated from worldly things. For God despiseth not the contrite and humbled heart,[7] and wise men are to look carefully to this in regulating penance, lest they punish with the rod a crime worthy of the sword and smite with the sword a sin worthy of the rod; and according to Gregory, great care is to be taken by pastors lest they carelessly bind what ought not to be bound and loose what ought not to be loosed.[8]

Now having composed these canons on penance, I confess that if in this apportionment of penance more or less should be approved before the eyes of the Creator, it is not our audacity that is responsible, for we have expounded the decrees of greater men,[9] not our own. The equivalent of a year: to fast seven days and nights. As another says: fast three continuous weeks and thou shalt be saved. We have arranged, piece by piece, compendious selections on the various remedies of wounds, according to what is approved by the ancient authors. Every irreligious person is unrighteous and a sinner, but it does not follow conversely that we can say that every sinner and unrighteous person is also irreligious. For irreligion properly appertains to those who have not the knowledge of God or have changed a known transgression; but sin and unrighteousness receive healing according to the nature of the faults[10] after the wounds of sin and unrighteousness. Hence it is written: "many are the scourges of sinners,"[11] and not everlasting destruction, according to this [word] of the Lord: "For what doth it profit a man if he gain the whole world and suffer the loss of his soul,"[12] or cause its loss[?][13] Whence it seems to be indicated that some sins have to do with loss,[14] but not with destruction; although he has suffered loss "yet he himself is to be

---

[6] "quali lacrimabilitate" (what kind of tearfulness).

[7] Ps. 50:19.

[8] Gregory the Great, *Hom. in Evangelium*, II, xxvi, 5–6; Migne, *P.L.*, LXXVI, 1200 f.

[9] "Maiorum," possibly "of the elders".

[10] "pro qualitate vitiorum." "Vitia" appear to be here character defects left by acts of sin; but the whole passage is clumsy and may be corrupt.

[11] Ps. 31:10. The writer is clumsily stressing the point that the Scriptures encourage the penitent and do not in all cases threaten the sinner with damnation.

[12] Matt. 16:26.

[13] "detrimentum," derived apparently from I Cor. 3:15.   [14] "dampnum."

saved, yet so as by fire.''[15] Hence I believe, and John in his Epistle says, that there are some sins unto death, some not unto death,[16] but unto loss. I do not think it easy for any man to be able to distinguish; for it is written: "Who can understand sins.''[17] Therefore he who "shall be saved by fire," shall be saved. As if one melts and dissolves by fire gold mixed with base lead that all may be made good gold, since the gold of that land which the saints are to inhabit is said to be good gold;[18] and as a furnace tries gold, so temptation tries righteous men. Therefore all must come to the fire—must come to the proving; but truly it both melts and cleanses the sons of Juda. But if one comes thither, many good works result,[19] and if he brings any little unrighteousness, that little is dissolved and cleansed at last as lead by fire, and he remains all gold; and if anyone bears more of lead thither, he is the more burned, so that he may be the more melted away and yet that some little purified gold may remain. But if anyone who is all lead comes thither, it happens to him as it is written, he is plunged into the deep as lead in a mighty sea. In this sacrament also in Leviticus a woman is said to become unclean who has conceived seed and borne a child; not only will she be unclean but doubly[20] unclean, for it is written that she remains in uncleanness for twice seven days. However, if she bears a male child, on the eighth day the child shall be circumcized and she shall be clean, for in the seventh day can be seen the time of the present life. For on the seventh day the world was finished,[21] in which while we are placed in the flesh we cannot be pure to perfection, unless the eighth day come, that is, unless the time of the holy future arrive; in which day, however, he who is masculine and plays the man, immediately on the coming of that holy future, is cleansed, and immediately the mother who bore him is made clean,[22] for he shall receive in the Resurrection his flesh purified from its vices. But if he had in him nothing manly with which to resist sin, if he was remiss and effeminate in his actions, his sin is such that it is not forgiven either in the present age or in that which is to come. He passes through both the first and the second

---

[15] I Cor. 3:15.   [16] Based on I John 5:16.   [17] Ps. 18:13.

[18] Based on Gen. 2:11–12.

[19] "sequi multa opera bona." Perhaps we should read "sequuntur opera bona" (good works result); or else we should insert "dicitur" (many good works are said to result).

[20] "dupliciter," here, "in two degrees," as the following sentences show. The author proceeds to allegorize Lev. 12:2–5.

[21] Gen. 2:2–3.

[22] Reading with Wasserschleben "munda" for "multa."

week of her uncleanness, and finally, entering the third week[23] he is cleansed from the uncleanness which the woman incurred by child-bearing. Perhaps it is of this that Isaiah says: "And it shall come to pass," saith he, "that in that day the Lord shall visit upon the host of heaven, on high, and upon the kings of the earth, on the earth. And they shall be gathered together as in the gathering of one bundle into the pit. And they shall be shut up[24] there in prison: and after many days they shall be visited."[25] Therefore also the Lord [saith] that both the devil and all his satellites and all wicked men and liars shall perish forever, and the Christians, if they have been overtaken in sin, shall be saved after punishments. The nature and extent of these punishments shall, we doubt not, be weighed, as I have said, not only according to the diversity of the faults but also according to the difference in strength of each of the sinners, whether with respect to training or to age—justly, indeed, as by the Lord, the righteous judge, but diversely, as by the Creator who knoweth all in the bounty of his nature.[26]

And, indeed, as the Creator by fixed laws gratifies the nature of the corn, so also he shall be gracious to all, in discernment of their virtues or qualities, according to this word of the prophet: "For the gith shall not be threshed with saws, neither shall the cart wheel turn about upon cummin, but gith shall be beaten out with a rod and cum-min with a staff. But bread corn shall be broken small,"[27] as this passage says: "The mighty shall be mightily tormented";[28] "according to the measure of the sin shall the measure also of the stripes be."[29]

Taught therefore by these examples, while for thee also the care of taking revenge on sin, that is, of healing souls, is truly manifold, both because sins are diverse, and because of a distinction, as I have said, in the virtues and qualities of sinners, I have rightly collected into brief space the deeds of the holy fathers, the physicians of those who were returning to the Lord from their sins, together with the forgotten tenor of their words,[30] that thou, forsooth, punish

---

[23] Emending "aborrire septimana" to "adorsus septimanam."
[24] Reading "claudentur," as in Vulgate, for "conlaudenter." [25] Isa. 24:21–22.
[26] Emending "libertate" to "liberalitate."
[27] Isa. 28:27–28. For "gith" the A.V. has "fitches" (modern "vetches"). For the parallel passage in Anselm of Lucca see Wasserschleben, *Bussordnungen*, p. 441, and p. 267 n. 10, below. [28] Wisd. 6:7. [29] Deut. 25:2.
[30] Emending "obmissa verborum . . . vias" to "obmissas verborum . . . vias."

not with the rod an offense worthy of the sword, nor with the sword
one worthy of the rod.

Moreover, remember how great merit it is to thee to "convert a
sinner from the error of his way."[31] There are, of course, other remissions of sins of which the Scriptures are replete with examples. Of
these the first is that in which we are baptized unto the remission
of sins;[32] the second consists in the passion of the martyrs; the third
is that which is given through alms; the fourth lies in the fact that
we forgive the sins of our brethren; the fifth in the abundance of
charity; the sixth in penance. Nevertheless this seventh remission,
[which occurs], as I said, when anyone converts a sinner from the
error of his way, is not the least[33] of these. For thus saith the divine
scripture: "For he that converteth a sinner from the error of his way
shall save his soul from death and shall cover a multitude of his
sins.[34] This also is written in Leviticus: The priest who offers this
and makes satisfaction, it shall be for his own sin.[35] The priests of
the Lord, who preside over the churches, learn that part has been
given to them[36] together with those for whose misdeeds they make
satisfaction. But what is it to make satisfaction for a misdeed? If
thou take the sinner, and by warning, exhortation, teaching, instruction, lead him to penance, restraining him[37] from his error, amend
him of his faults, and render him such that God may be satisfied
by his conversion to Him, thou shalt be said to make satisfaction
for a misdeed. When, therefore, thou art such a priest and such is
thy teaching and thy word, there is given to thee a part of those
whom thou hast corrected, that their merit may be thy reward[38]
and their salvation thy glory. Ezekiel saith, "The wickedness of
the wicked shall be upon him":[39] and from this saying the judgment
follows, that the righteous ought not to be with sinners and likewise
that if they have dwelt[40] with them and have been slain no settlement with any bishop or church shall be made. Also it is said: "There
are three ways in which the just are separated from the unjust—
by the Mass, the table, and the Pax";[41] it is differently stated in
Ezekiel.

---

[31] Jas. 5:20.   [32] Mark 1:4; Luke 3:3.   [33] "extrema."
[34] Based on Jas. 5:20.   [35] Cf. Lev. 7:7–8; 19:22.
[36] Reading "eis" for "ejus," as in *Pseudo-Cummean*.
[37] *Pseudo-Cummean* reads "correxeris" (correct him) for "coercens."
[38] Reading with *Pseudo-Cummean* "illorum meritum tua sit merces" for "illorum inter-
itus marcescit."   [39] Ezek. 18:20.
[40] Reading "habitaverint" for "habitaverit."   [41] See above, p. 81, n. 46.

Of the troop of vices which sever the human race from the Kingdom of God, the Apostle says: "The works of the flesh are manifest:
which are adultery, fornication, uncleanness, luxury, idolatry,
murders, witchcrafts, enmities, contentions, emulations, heresies,
animosity, wraths, quarrels, dissensions, sects, envies, hatreds,
drunkenness, revelings, and such like. And they who do such things
shall not obtain the Kingdom of God.[42] Likewise the Apostle: "Do
not err, for neither fornicators nor idolaters nor adulterers nor liers
with mankind nor thieves nor covetous nor drunkards shall possess
the Kingdom of God."[43]

So far the Apostle. Now Isidore: "There are eight chief vices—from
which arise a copious multitude of faults—gluttony,[44] fornication,
avarice, languor,[45] wrath, dejection, vainglory, and lastly the very
leader and queen of these, pride." Thus far Isidore.[46] Further Cassian
says: "Of gluttony[47] are born drunkenness, foolish delight in many
words, dulness of sense, and uncleanness; of fornication, filthiness in
speech, scurrility, stupid talk, blindness of mind, inconstancy, love of
the present world, and horror of the future; of avarice,[48] lying, fraud,
thefts, perjury, greed of filthy lucre, false testimonies, acts of
violence, inhumanity, rapacity, and enmities; of wrath, murders,
clamor, indignation, strifes, pride of mind,[49] insults, and reproaches;
of dejection, rancor, smallness of mind, bitterness, despair, malice,
indifference about things that are commanded; of languor, idleness,
drowsiness, unseasonableness, wandering about, instability of mind
and body, verbosity, curiosity; of vainglory,[50] contentions, heresies,
boasting, taking up with novelties, hypocrisy, obstinacy, discords
and hatred; of pride, contempt, envy, disobedience, blasphemy,
murmuring, detraction, and witchcrafts."

EIGHT CHAPTERS ON THE REMEDIES OF FAULTS

I. Of Gluttony

i. If any bishop or any ordained man has the vice of habitual

---

[42] Gal. 5:19-21. The order varies slightly from that of the Vulgate text, while "adultery," "idolatry," "heresies," and "animosity" are inserted, and "immodesty" is omitted in
this document.　　[43] I Cor. 6:9-10.　　[44] "Gula."　　[45] "accedia."

[46] In his *Quaestiones in Deuteronomium,* Chap. xvi, Isidore of Seville speaks of the seven
principal vices, but lists the eight noted by Cassian, with some change in the words employed and in the order followed. Migne, *P.L.,* LXXXIII, 366. Cf. E. Göller, "Das span-
isch-westgotische Busswesen," *Römische Quartalschrift,* XXXVII (1929), 259, 302.

[47] "gastrimargia."　　[48] "filargiria."

[49] "tumor mentis." Cf. "tumor animi," Deut. 18:22.

[50] "cenodoctia," properly "cenodoxia" (ξενοδοξία). Cf. Cassian, *Coll.* V, ii: "cenodoxia id
est jactantia seu vana gloria."

drunkenness, he shall retire or be deposed. On the penance of drunkenness we have said enough above in the interrogatory.[51]

iii. 1. He who vomits the host by reason of greediness shall do penance for forty days; but if with the excuse of unusual and too rich food and from the fault not of excess but of the stomach, thirty; if by reason of infirmity, twenty.

III. Of Avarice

v. *Of lying.*—1. Solomon saith: "The mouth that belieth killeth the soul."[52]

2. He who lies from cupidity shall satisfy with liberality him of whom he has taken advantage.

vi. *Of inhumanity.*—1. He who does not perform any of these things concerning which the Lord saith, "Come ye blessed of my Father,"[53] and so forth, shall do penance for as long a time as he remains in this state and shall live liberally thereafter; but if he does not, he shall be cut off.[54]

2. A cleric who has goods in excess of what he needs shall give them to the poor; but if he does not he shall be excommunicated. But if [he continues in this] after a time of penance, he shall live in penance apart for a period equal to that in which he was recalcitrant.

IV. Of Anger

vi. *Of clamor.*—6. If any nun becomes excited and shouts with sounds of this sort,[55] she shall be corrected with double the penance prescribed above.

7. Concerning the making of lamentation and its being deservedly reckoned for good, it is said in the Law: "Jacob the son of Isaac, was lamented for forty days in Egypt and a whole week in the Land of Canaan."[56] And [it is said of] Christ in the New [Testament] that the women wept for him;[57] and it is found written in the canon with almost innumerable examples from the Scriptures. And [weeping] for

---

[51] "quaestiuncula." The document referred to is not extant. It may have been a set of questions and penalties for the use of the confessor, like the series of questions in the *Pseudo-Bede* (Wasserschleben, *Bussordnungen*, pp. 253 f.) and that in the *Corrector et medicus* of Burchard, below, pp. 325 ff.   [52] Wisd. 1:11.   [53] Matt. 25:34.

[54] That is, excommunicated.

[55] The reference is to the "bardicatio" or "keening" of mourners over a corpse referred to in paragraphs 2–5, which are here omitted because substantially identical with the *Irish Canons*, I, 26–29, pp. 121 f., above. Cf. also the *Old Irish Penitential*, v, 17–18, p. 167, below.   [56] Based on Gen. 50:3–10.   [57] Cf. Luke 23:27.

him who ought not to be wept for,[58] is deservedly imputed for evil.

vii. *Of the fact that no one ought to receive the sacrifice unless he is clean and perfect*[59] *and nothing mortal is found in him.*—Christ, moreover, when he had raised up the damsel, commanded her to eat:[60] that is, after she was perfect, whole, and free from infirmity, that is, [made] whole by Christ. Peter and James and John and her father and her mother being present—that [is?] everybody after he has confessed his faults and cast them away and after the grace of God has come and the heavenly Father and the Church are present with him, then, whole in good works, he shall receive the sacrifice.

VI. Of Languor

ii. *Of sloth.*—1. A wise man saith: "If thou loathest death why dost thou love sleep?" For sleep is the continual imitation of death.

2. The slothful shall be cured with vigils and prayers, that is, he shall be occupied with three or six psalms.

3. In the examples of the saints a certain brother says: "If it happens that I am laden with sleep and the hour of my service has passed, my soul for shame then does not desire to fulfill its task"; and an elder has said: "If it happens [that thou] sleep till dawn, when thou awakest, arise, close thy door and windows and do thy work. For it is written: 'Thine is the day and Thine is the night,'[61] and God shall be at all times glorified."

VIII. Of Pride

vi. We ought to avoid this fault, which is never increased by manly deeds, that is, by fasting and vigils and abstinence; indeed through obscure and lowly service it vanishes, and especially through humility and pure prayer as from the inmost heart. Let us say, as saith the psalmist, "From my secret sins cleanse me, O Lord."[62]

9. SELECTIONS FROM AN OLD IRISH PENITENTIAL

(ca. 800)

[THE *Old Irish Penitential* from which the following selections are taken survives in a fifteenth century manuscript in the collection of the Royal

---

[58] "pro quo non ploratur" (for whom it is not wept).

[59] Emending "mundum et perfectum," agreeing with sacrifice, to "mundus et perfectus."   [60] Mark 5:43.   [61] Ps. 73:16.   [62] Ps. 18:13.

Irish Academy, and fragments of it are found in four other manuscripts. The principal manuscript is described by E. J. Gwynn and W. J. Purton in the *Proceedings of the Royal Irish Academy*, XXIX, Section C (1911), 115 ff. Dr. Gwynn has edited the penitential with a translation in *Ériu*, VII (1914), 121–95 ("An Irish Penitential"). It follows an arrangement corresponding to the eight principal sins enumerated by Cassian. It is closely related to the *Bigotian Penitential* (see above, pp. 148 ff.), and shows the influence of Cummean and of Theodore. From these and other relationships, Gwynn holds that the book "cannot have been put together much before 800."

Like the *Bigotian*, the *Old Irish Penitential* is an exposition of penance as much as it is a code. But in this respect both are dependent on Cassian's treatment of the sins and of monastic penance. Cassian's material, including the principle that "contraries are cured by their contraries," was utilized by earlier Irish writers, particularly, as we have seen, by Finnian (see *Poenitentiale Vinniai*, 28, 29, and n. 20, p. 92, above) and by Cummean (cf. *Poenitentiale Cummeani*, introductory paragraph, p. 101). In both the *Bigotian Penitential* and the present document this theme is elaborated, apparently on the basis of a fresh reading of Cassian —although the actual citations of Cassian cannot all be verified. While neither is a translation of the other, they are close parallels. It may possibly be explained on the supposition that both used a common source not now extant. If there was direct borrowing, the Bigotian is probably the parent document.

The text shows evidence of a confusion of the leaves of the source manuscript used by the scribe and of the loss of the original closing section on pride. Possibly, too, part of the opening section on gluttony has been lost, though a considerable portion of it has been incorporated in the section on luxury. The original structure of the document has been ingeniously elucidated by Dr. Gwynn.

The citations of "Cummine Fota" (Cummean the Long) are of interest. It would be satisfying to be able to show that the author of the penitential here used Zettinger's *Cummean* alone. Unfortunately the evidence is too vague to sustain, although it does tend to support, this conclusion. The citation in ii, 21 (here omitted), and the alleged quotation in iii, 15, do not exactly tally with the contents of any extant work ascribed to Cummean; but the latter may be a free interpretation of our *Poenitentiale Cummeani*, iii, 9. The other two quotations (iii, 2, and iii, 12) agree with the statements in *Poenitentiale Cummeani*, while one of them (iii, 12) is out of agreement with the *Excarpsus Cummeani*. Thus far the document favors a use of Zettinger's *Cummean*. A complete analysis of the parallels is provided by T. P. Oakley, "A Great Irish Penitential and Its Authorship," *Romanic Review*, XXV (1934), 25–33. Dr. Gwynn has not used Zettinger's study and text and cites the *Excarpsus* as the genuine *Penitential of Cummean*. Because of differences he is led to suggest that the name *Poenitentiale Cummeani* was applied to a "collection which differed somewhat from the Latin penitential that bears his name, especially in containing some rules which are excluded from the latter but have been included in the *Capit. Iud.*" (p. 129). Zettinger's *Cummean* answers in general Dr. Gwynn's description of this to him hypothetical work. Dr. Gwynn's notes are mainly on the Old Irish text, but they contain some material on the related Latin penitentials and should be consulted by the special student.

The opening paragraphs of the penitential are from a document previously published by K. Meyer, *Zeitschrift. für celtische Philologie*, III (1901), 24 ff. It ascribes the compilation of the penitential to "the venerable of Ireland"—a vague expression which at least appears to claim group authorship if not to suggest the authority of an ecclesiastical synod.

The major part of the extant portion of the penitential is here given from Dr. Gwynn's text, and with his generous consent. The sections omitted consist of (1) the homiletic paragraphs with which each chapter is introduced (this includes the whole of the extant fragment of Chapter VII), (2) paragraphs 8 to 11 inclusive of Chapter IV, which are similarly hortatory, and (3) a part of Chapter II dealing with fornication, most of which Dr. Gwynn has thought best to render into Latin rather than English, and none of which is significant for any originality.]

Chapter I. Of Gluttony

2.[1] Anyone who eats the flesh of a horse, or drinks the blood or urine of an animal, does penance for three years and a half.

3. Anyone who eats flesh which dogs or beasts have been eating, or who eats carrion, or who drinks the liquid in which the carrion is, or who drinks the leavings of fox or raven or magpie (?) or cock or hen, or who drinks the leavings of a layman or laywoman or of a pregnant woman, or who eats a meal in the same house with them, without separation of seat or couch, does penance for forty nights on bread and water.

4. Anyone who drinks liquid in which there is a dead mouse does seven days' penance therefor.

Anyone who drinks the leavings of a cat does five days' penance.

Anyone who drinks or eats the leavings of a mouse does penance for a day and a night. Theodore says that although food be touched by the hand of one polluted or by dog, cat, mouse, or unclean animal that drinks blood, that does the food no harm.

5. Anyone who breaks a fast that is proclaimed in church keeps a double fast thereafter as penance.

[1] Gwynn, p. 147.

6. Anyone who is sick is allowed to eat meals at any hour of the day or night.

7. Anyone who drinks beer till he is tipsy in spite of the prohibition of Christ and the Apostles, if he be in orders, does forty days' penance. If he be in lawful wedlock, seven days. If anyone out of hospitality constrains his fellow to get tipsy, he who causes his tipsiness does the like penance. If it is through enmity that he does it, he who causes the tipsiness does penance as if he were a homicide. If his tipsiness does not hinder him [from his duties] except that he is unable to chant the Psalms, or say Mass, or such-like, he keeps a fast therefor.

8. Anyone who commits a theft of meat or drink from his brother while tipsy keeps a fast therefor, as well as the punishment for tipsiness. If he commit the theft without the brethren's [knowledge], it is three fasts or a fortnight's strict penance.

9. Anyone who steals food gets forty days the first time, and forty more the second time, a year the third time, and exile under the yoke of a strange abbot the fourth time. If it be boys of ten years old, they get seven days: if over twenty years, twenty days' penance.

10. Anyone who eats till he makes himself ill, or till his skin gets tight, keeps a fast or two days on bread and water. If he vomits, it is seven days.

11. Anyone who [touches] food with unclean hands, a hundred lashes are laid on his hand. If the color of the liquor be at all troubled with some unclean thing, the cook does forty days' penance. The man who drinks it unwittingly, and afterwards learns what he has done, does five days' penance.

12. Anyone who gives another anything in which there has been a dead mouse or dead weasel, three fasts are laid on him who gives it, and he who thereafter learns what has been done, a fast on him. If it is in any other dry food, in porridge or in thickened milk, the part round it is thrown away, the rest is consumed.

13. Anyone who resolves to keep a fast [for one day] or three days or forty nights or a year, and breaks it of himself without being compelled by anyone else, does double penance.

14. Anyone who takes a vow that he will not eat flesh or bacon or butter, or will not drink beer or milk, is bound to take three morsels or three sips of each of them at Easter and Christmas against the occurrence of disease and suffering; or against distress through famine or scarcity falling upon the people, so that all the victuals they have

perish, except the particular thing which he has vowed [not] to partake of; or in case of a repast provided by a confessor, who has no other sort of victuals which the man may eat who has taken that vow of abstinence for God's sake; so that it is for God's sake that the relaxation is granted, when it so happens, and so that he gets a reward for what he does.

15. Anyone who eats food and drinks beer until he vomits, if he be a regular monk, does thirty days' penance. If this is caused by disease, or if it happens after a long fast, or in rejoicings at the eight festivals of the year, or if it be a confessor's repast, or if it be on holy feast days, if they do not drink beyond the measure which the confessor prescribes,—in all such cases there is no harm.

16. Anyone who fasts on a Sunday through carelessness or austerity does a week's penance on bread and water.

17. Anyone who drinks the leavings of a dog, or of one red with [the blood of] men, or a robber, or one that slays his mother or father or brother, or who lies with his mother or sister or daughter, or a contumacious [?] bishop or priest after he has violated his orders without repenting, does a year's penance on bread and water.

18. Anyone that is sickly is allowed a meal at any hour of day or night.

19. Anyone who eats before the rest, or eats food that is daintier than the brethren's food, unless it be disease or natural infirmity that causes him to do so, or unless he is (un)able to eat anything else, habitually, must keep a fast or[2] two days on bread and water therefor.

20. Anyone who is suddenly seized by an attack of disease, a fast for him the first night: if it comes of a demon, he is the lighter thereby; if of God, let the cause of it be seen.

21. Anyone who drinks the blood of a cat, three fasts therefor. Anyone who eats his vermin or the scab of his body, a hundred nights on bread and water.

Chapter II. Of Luxury

2.[3] Anyone holding the rank of a bishop, who transgresses in respect of a woman, is degraded and does penance twelve years on water diet, or seven years on bread and water.

---

[2] Neither here, nor in art. 10, above, a typographical error, as might be supposed, but apparently to be read in the sense of "that is."   [3] Gwynn, p. 141.

3. If he be a priest, or a deacon who has taken a vow of perpetual celibacy, he spends three and a half years on bread and water, with a fast in every week of the time, except between the two Christmases and between the two Easters and at Pentecost, and such persons have relaxation on the high festivals of the year, and on Sundays and on the fifty nights between Easter and Pentecost: that is to say, they get porridge made with good milk, or a fair quarter of a *selann*[4] if there be no milk, and they are allowed dry relishes of all sorts of fruit at all seasons, and they are also allowed an extra portion of bread in the Saturday night's fast, and a quarter ration of gruel and whey-water (on which there is no cream of curds or buttermilk) every day: a jug of good milk, if the nature of a man's constitution be sickly, and a scrape of gruel on bread. If, however, he be not sickly, the allowance is bread and water or . . . or the whey water we have mentioned if it be within reach. He may not lie on feathers nor on a cushion, nor on a good bed. He may not take off his shirt except it be to stitch or wash or cleanse it.

4. Additional labor is laid on penitents in the three Lents of the year, as their strength can bear it. Obedience and humility are required of them, besides going to Communion at the end of three and a half years for the higher orders, at the end of a year and a half for the lower orders generally, that their souls may not perish for want of Christ's body by reason of the long period of penitence; and thereafter they receive the salutation of good brethren, and they sing the Psalms in their place among the rest of the brethren.

5. There is required of them also remorse and lamentation for their sins, and that they should desire their brethren to pray God for them that their sins may be remitted by means of penance and penitence.

6. If it be a man of a lower rank than a priest or deacon who transgresses in this point through lust, he does penance three years, but the measure of his bread and whey-water is increased, that it may suffice him for vigils and labor: that is, he gets a prime *bochtan*[5] of good milk, besides whey-water as much as he needs.

7. For the rations of those in orders who are doing penance have been appointed, if they do not do labor, as follows: they are to get

---

[4]See *Ancient Laws of Ireland*, VI. Glossary, *s.v.* "selaind." The word had been understood as a measure of about the quantity of four eggs.

[5] A measure containing "The full of 12 eggshells." K. Meyer, *Irish Lexicography*, *s.v.*

six ounces' weight of bread, with a little gruel spread on it, and kitchen herbs, and a few dry eggs, a jug of good milk, if a man is sickly, and a *bochtan* of buttermilk or curds.

Chapter III. Of Avarice

2.[6] Anyone who makes a habit of thieving and stealing and robbing through covetousness, Theodore says, seven years' penance therefor. According to Cummine Fota it is a year the first time, two the second time. If boys do such things, it is forty nights (or twenty nights) of penance, or else their penance is according to their age. If the culprit can pay the érics[7] which God has appointed in law and rule, his penance is consequently less.

3. If anyone steals a sheep, he must restore four sheep in its place; if a cow, five cows; if a horse, two horses in its place; if a pig, two pigs in its place. If each of these animals be found in the thief's possession alive, he pays double, that is, a beast in addition to the other. He pays double also for inanimate chattels, that is, the price together with the original price.

4. If there is nothing that he can pay for it, he gives service in place of it. If he offers it to God and does penance as his confessor prescribes, and does not possess anything that he can pay (as fine), he pays nothing to man, save only penance with a token of good will.

5. The apostle Paul says: Let him who has lived by robbery and theft cease therefrom, and let him labor with his hands, so that he may have what he can give . . . in alms to the poor and needy. For as water quenches fire, so almsgiving quenches sins. Christ says: Anyone who has much wealth or substance should distribute half of it to the poor and needy.

6. As for him who desires to reach the pitch of perfectness, he distributes all he has to the poor and needy and goes on a pilgrimage or lives in destitution in a communal church till he goes to Heaven.

7. Anyone who plunders an altar or shrine, or steals a Gospel-book, seven years' penance. If it be a bell, or crozier or service-set, it is forty years on bread and water.

[6] Gwynn, p. 155.
[7] Compensations.

8. Anyone who breaks into an oratory, four years' penance therefor. If a refectory, four years on bread and water.

9. Anyone who takes a reward to kill a man or to bear false witness or to bring a false suit or to give false judgment, does three and a half years' penance.

10. Anyone who persists in avarice to the end of his life must go on a pilgrimage or must distribute the value of seven cumals to the poor and needy for his soul's good.

A cleric (or nun) who lives in a communal church and has somewhat more than suffices him, whatever it be, let him give it to the poor and needy of the church where he lives. If he does not, let him be excommunicated from the church where he lives. If he repents, he is to do penance apart, for as long as the sin has been on his conscience, without express command of the elders: for it is worse for a communal church in which there is the worth of a *dirna*[8] of private property or stolen goods than if a fire were burning it, by reason of the quantity of murmuring and envy and ill-feeling that is caused by the man that owns it, as John Cassian accounts it.

11. Anyone who does not pay what he owes does penance therefor as for theft, as if what he owes were a theft he had committed.

12. Anyone who takes a false oath in church on a book of the four Gospels, does ten years' penance (fourteen years according to Colum Cille, seven (or four) according to Cummine).

13. Anyone who leads his fellow into perjury, let him do seven years' penance. He who commits perjury in ignorance, a year's penance.

14. If he knows that it is a perjury, but commits it under promise or to shield another, a year's penance. If for a bribe, seven years' penance. If under compulsion laid upon him, a year's penance. If under the hand of a bishop or priest or deacon, or at an altar or consecrated [cross], three years' penance.

15. Cummine Fota says: Whatever be the emblem on which a downright perjury is sworn, the man who swears it is bound to seven years' penance, unless it be through his folly or imbecility.

If little boys [commit perjury] through fear or to shield another, a year of strict penance on bread and water, or its equivalent, is laid upon him who takes the oath. If it be light women or girls, three years or the equivalent.

---

[8] This word is used to mean a stone, and also a large weight.

16. Anyone who gives false testimony or false witness or false judgment against his neighbor, must ask his pardon in his presence, and pay a price for anything he may testify against him, or else do penance according to the sin he swears to against his fellow.

17. If the falsehood is uttered in ignorance, and does no harm to the person about whom it is uttered, full penitence is required thereupon, and a silent fast is kept as well, or twelve psalms, or a hundred blows with a thong on the hand of him who utters the falsehood in ignorance.

If anyone utters such a falsehood deliberately, without doing harm, he spends three days in silence except for the appointed prayers or readings; or else he receives 700 blows of a lash on his hands and keeps a half-fast or recites the hundred and fifty psalms.

18. Anyone who utters a falsehood in words whereof good results, by giving a false description to a man's enemies, or by carrying pacific messages between disputants, or by anything that rescues a man from death, there is no heavy penance, provided it is done for God's sake.

19. Anyone who is himself conscious of any falsehood or unlawful gains let him confess privately to a confessor or to an elder who may be set over him. If there be none such, let him make his own confession to God, in whose presence the evil was done, so that He shall be his confessor; and let him perform a vigil and a fast and prayers to God diligently.

20. Anyone who hides from his confessor the sins he should confess until someone else discovers them, double penance upon him. If no one does so (?), he is to be expelled from the community of the brethren.

21. Anyone who conceals a capital sin for his fellow's sake, let him do penance on bread and water for as long a time as he hid it; for the guilt is the same in God's eyes, whether a man does the evil or conceals it for his sake who does it, if he do not proclaim and correct it. If the sin that is concealed be trivial, both do penance for that sin, according to the penance assigned to it.

22. When two persons of equal rank and equal standing have a dispute without witnesses, and one of them asserts a falsehood, both do penance for the space of a year, or until one of them admits the lie, and they are put on bread and water for two days in every week, and keep a two days' fast every month, and they pray to

God diligently that He may pass just judgments upon them, and they fast a whole year in their dispute, and receive the body of Christ who shall be their judge at the Doom, and it is left to God's award. If it comes to pass that one of them makes full confession, his penance is increased according to the amount of labor he has brought upon his neighbor, and he earnestly begs forgiveness of him and of the brethren generally.

23. Anyone who disputes violently about anything, and says: "I did not do this or that":—or anyone who imagines something which he does not see, or know, except in the heat of contention, and does not say "unless perchance" or "under correction":—does penance therefor with three fasts.

Chapter IV. Of Envy

2.[9] Anyone who is envious, or malicious, or offensive to his brethren, let him ask pardon penitently and earnestly of him whom he has offended in envy and malice, and let him do penance on bread and water for as long a time as there had been hatred in his heart. If evil has resulted from his envy, let him pay as much as was lost by his fault, if it was in the form of property: if not, let him ask pardon tearfully and penitently.

3. Anyone who reviles his mother or father or sister or brother or his prince or prior or an elder who is above him in age or instruction, let him make confession and do penance seven days on bread and water, or the equivalent, which cancels it. If he reviles anyone else, three days and a half. If it becomes a fixed habit with him so that he does not remember to restrain himself, he is to be expelled from the church to a place of penance until he can give up that vice.

If the words are spoken not in carping nor in envy, but out of compassion to the body and soul of him for whom they are intended, no penance is imposed in respect of any man, but it is reckoned as meritorious, if no other profit results . . . in labor and prayer.

4. Anyone who is guilty of envious fault-finding, or anyone who loves to hear it, let him do penance for four days on bread and water, and let him make amends to him against whom he makes mischief. If it is against one who is set over him that the mischief-making is directed, seven days' penance is imposed thereupon. But some say that telling the truth is not mischief-making, if it be done ac-

[9] Gwynn. p. 161.

cording to the Gospel rule, that is: Speak your mind first between you twain: if he does not amend, then call in some one else to support you; if this does not mend matters, let the thing be spoken before all the people.

5. Anyone who makes mischief against his brother through [love of] talk or drunkenness, let him spend a day in a silent fast. If it be through gossiping that he finds fault, he recites twelve psalms, or receives a hundred blows on his hands.

There are, however, four cases in which it is right to find fault with the evil that is in a man who will not accept his cure by means of entreaty and kindness: either to prevent someone else from abetting him to this evil; or to correct the evil itself; or to confirm the good; or out of compassion for him who does the evil. But anyone who does not do it for one of these four reasons, is a fault-finder, and does penance four days, or recites the hundred and fifty psalms naked.

6. Anyone who rails at his fellow through envy and malice, let him ask his pardon with gentleness and recite thirty psalms or do penance for a day and a night on bread and water.

7. Anyone who murmurs without just cause and one who prompts another to do so, and one who likes to listen to murmuring, and does not examine into it—all such persons do three days' penance on bread and water, and he who actually commits the offense is separated, and his work [is rejected], and he is put on a half-ration of bread, or half the brethren's allowance of bread only, and a little water therewith, until he be cured of murmuring; since everyone is allowed (?) to make a request to his senior in regard to anything he may need, whether clothing or food.

Chapter V. Of Anger

2.[10] Anyone who kills his son or daughter does penance twenty-one years. Anyone who kills his mother or father does penance fourteen years. Anyone who kills his brother or sister or the sister of his mother or father, or the brother of his father or mother, does penance ten years: and this rule is followed to seven degrees both of the mother's and father's kin—to the grandson and great-grandson and great-great-grandson, and the sons of the great-great-grandson, as far as the finger-nails. . . . Seven years of penance are assigned for

[10] Gwynn, p. 167.

all other homicides; excepting persons in orders, such as a bishop or a priest, for the power to fix their penance rests with the king who is over the laity, and with the bishop, whether it be exile for life, or penance for life. If the offender can pay fines, his penance is less in proportion.

3. Anyone who kills a man in revenge for his father or mother or brother or sister does four years' or forty nights' penance therefor.

4. Anyone who kills a man in battle or in a brawl or . . . a year and a half or forty nights, provided he does not pursue the slaughter after the fight is won.

5. Anyone who kills himself while insane, prayers are said for him, and alms are given for his soul, if he was previously pious. If he has killed himself in despair or for any other cause, he must be left to the judgment of God, for men dare not offer prayers for him—that is, a Mass:—unless it be some other prayer, and alms-giving to the poor and miserable.

6. A woman who causes miscarriage of that which she has conceived after it has become established in the womb, three years and a half of penance. If the flesh has formed, it is seven years. If the soul has entered it, fourteen years' penance. If the woman die of the miscarriage, that is, the death of body and soul, fourteen cumals [are offered] to God as the price of her soul, or fourteen years' penance.

7. Anyone who gives drugs or makes a bogey or gives a poisonous drink so that someone dies of it, seven years' penance, as for a homicide. If no one dies of it, three years' penance.

8. Anyone who hurts his fellow in a quarrel so as to leave a blemish on him, has to pay the leech's fee, and to do his work until he is well, and does half a year's penance and pays a price for the blemish, according to what the leech judges fair. If he has not the price to pay, he does a further year's penance.

9. Anyone who strikes his fellow, but not deliberately, forty or sixty [days'] penance. If it be a cleric who thus strikes another, it is thrice forty nights or a year of penance.

10. Anyone who kills his brother without premeditation, without quarrel, without wrath, yet it happens by his deed, that is a year of penance. If he does it in anger, without premeditation, three years' penance.

11. Anyone who kills his fellow in anger and with premeditation, and intent, after taking a vow of renunciation, the penance for him

is a life of exile in destitution, unless pious anchorites grant him remission.

12. Anyone who vexes his fellow about any matter, reasonable or unreasonable, the remedy is to beg his pardon that he may be healed in spirit: for God hearkens to prayer on this condition, that our neighbor's spirit be healed. If he will not accept his excuses, let [the offender] himself do penance in proportion to the vexation he causes to his fellow, or according as an elder adjudges: and let him who will not accept his excuses do penance on bread and water until he does accept them, and as long as there is hatred in his heart.

13. Anyone who curses his neighbor, let him beg his pardon, and let him undergo a week's strict penance.

Anyone who speaks bitter words to his fellow (while it is not from his heart), let him ask his pardon and keep a fast. If his brother turns red or pale before him, or if he is taken with a trembling, yet keeps silence and does not contradict him, his penance is a day on bread and water.

14. Anyone who feels in his mind no more than a stirring of anger, let his mind make peace with [his brother].

Anyone who does not make confession to him who has stirred his anger cannot remain in the community of the brethren of the church lest a plague come thereof. The nature of concealed anger is likened to fire in wood.

15. Anyone who cannot attain to forgiving his brother in his heart for that which caused his anger, let him repent earnestly before God.

16. If anyone raises his voice in speaking to someone at a distance or to a deaf man, there is [no] penance. If the raising of his voice is attended with anger, whether at a distance or near by, penance is done according to the sin and the transgression. If it be illness that provokes any outcry, it is not to be passed over for the moment.

17. A married woman or a penitent nun who makes lamentation over a layman or laywoman, fifty nights' penance. If it be over a married woman or a penitent nun who dies in childbed, or a member of the household, forty nights' penance. If over a cleric of the laity, twenty nights' penance. If over a bishop or king or confessor or ruler of a chief town, fifteen nights' penance.

18. If it be a novice who happens to commit one of the offenses here mentioned, he has double penance, compared with a married woman.

Chapter VI. Of Dejection

2.[11] Anyone therefore whom the Devil has mocked by means of grief and sorrows, such as the loss of friends or relatives or of anything else, so that it allows him to do nothing good, but [only] to despair, let him first keep a three days' fast without food or drink; if he relapses into the same state afterwards, it is forty nights on bread and water.

3. If he should be in grief and sadness so that he cannot be roused, the monk does penance in another place on bread and water, and returns no more into the community of the brethren, until he be joyful in body and soul.

[11] Gwynn, p. 173.

CHAPTER II

Early Welsh Penitential Documents

---

1. CANONS OF SIXTH-CENTURY WELSH SYNODS

(*ca.* 500–525)

[THE CIRCUMSTANCES of the Welsh synods in which the following penitential canons were promulgated are obscure. In his *Life of St. David*[1] Rhygyvarch of Menevia (1057–99) tells in florid style of David's leadership in two synods held at places which he calls Brevi and Victoria, respectively. According to Rhygyvarch the purpose of both synods was to expel Pelagianism and secure adherence to Rome. He has not, however, seen the decrees of the synods, which, he says, "owing to the frequent and cruel attacks of enemies, have become void, and being almost forgotten, have ceased to be."[2] Haddan and Stubbs regard the description of the synods by Rhygyvarch as "purely fabulous";[3] and their connection with Pelagianism is discarded by practically all modern authorities. There is, however, a strong probability that the canons here given are in reality those shaped by the synods of David's time. They have been preserved, apparently, in Brittany[4] and are contained in a tenth or eleventh century codex, Paris. Bibl. Nat. Lat. 3182, which includes other notable penitential fragments. E. Martène and U. Durand[5] first published the text. It has been edited by Wasserschleben,[6] by Schmitz,[7] and by Haddan and Stubbs.[8] Schmitz follows the dates supplied by the Bollandists for these synods, *viz.*, 519 and 529. Haddan and Stubbs fix the date of the later synod at the year 569. Rhygyvarch allows an indefinite period of time between the two synods.[9] While specific dates cannot be assigned, fairly solid evidence can be shown for a date con-

---

[1] Text edited with a translation by A. W. Wade-Evans in *Y-Cymmrodor*, XXIV, 4 ff. An English edition with more extensive notes is *The Life of St. David*, London, 1923, by the same editor.   [2] Wade-Evans, *Life of St. David*, p. 27.

[3] Haddan and Stubbs, I, 116.

[4] H. Bradshaw, *The Early Collection of Canons Known as the Hibernensis*, 1893. Cf. above, p. 139.—For another MS see App. V, n. 1, below.

[5] *Thesaurus novus anecdotorum* (Paris, 1717), IV, 7 ff.

[6] *Bussordnungen*, pp. 103 f.

[7] Schmitz I, pp. 490 ff.

[8] *Councils*, I, 116 ff.

[9] *Y-Cymmrodor*, XXIV, 24.

siderably earlier than 569 for the death of David.[10] We should probably assign the synods to a period roughly half a century earlier than that favored by Haddan and Stubbs, or about the beginning of the sixth century.

The penalties in these canons are mild in comparison with those prescribed in most of the penitential literature. However, a tendency to greater severity may be seen in the later of the two synods. The last canon of this synod provides for an automatic grading downward of penalties for the laity from those assigned for the clergy.]

THE SYNOD OF NORTH BRITAIN[11]

1. Anyone who sins with a woman or with a man shall be sent away to live in a monastery of another country and shall do penance, after he has confessed, for three years in confinement; and afterwards, as a brother subject to that altar he shall do penance at the discretion of his teacher;[12] if he is a deacon, for one year; if a presbyter, for three years; if a bishop or abbot, for four years; each being deprived of his order.

2. Whoever is guilty of masturbation shall do penance in confinement for a year; a boy of twelve years, for forty [days], or three forty-day periods. A deacon shall do penance for a year in confinement, and for half a year with his brethren; a priest, for a year in confinement and for another year with his brethren.

3. A monk who has stolen consecrated things shall do penance for a year in exile[13] and another year with his brethren. But if he repeats the offense he shall suffer exile.

4. He who steals food shall do penance for forty days. If the offense is repeated, for three forty-day periods. For a third offense he shall do penance for a year; for a fourth he shall do penance in the yoke of exile under another abbot.

---

[10] See especially E. M. B. Nicholson's argument in "The *Annales Cambriae* and their so-called Exordium," *Zeitschrift für celtische Philologie*, VIII (1910), 121 ff.; and A. W. Wade-Evans, "Note on St. David," *Y-Cymmrodor*, XXII (1910), 144 ff. Nicholson strongly contends that David died in 547; Wade-Evans arrives at the date 505, and believes that David was then in his forty-fourth year, having been born in 462. Cf. Wade-Evans, *Welsh Christian Origins* (Oxford, 1934), p. 146.

[11] Or northern Wales. Wade-Evans points out that while Brevi is not strictly in North Wales, it would be convenient to northern delegates and is "north relative to most of South Wales."—*Life of St. David*, p. 112.

[12] "doctoris." The use of this word may be accounted for by the fact that the offices of teacher and confessor were often combined in Celtic Christianity. See McNeill, pp. 118 f. (*Rev. celt.*, XL, 102 f.).

[13] The manuscript has "id est exilio" (that is, in exile) above the line, by a corrector.

5. He who is informed on and he who lays the information shall be adjudged as persons of the same status.[14] If he who is informed on[15] denies [his guilt] he shall do penance for a year, two days a week on bread and water, and two days at the end of each month, all the brethren subjecting him to them and calling upon God as their judge.

6. But if they persist in their obstinacy, after the lapse of a year they shall be joined to the communion of the altar,[16] under the proof of fire, and left to the judgment of God.

7. If at any time one of them confesses, to the extent to which he has inflicted hardship on the other his own [hardship] shall be increased.

The Synod of the Grove of Victory

1. He who commits theft once shall do penance for one year; more than once, for two years.

2. He who slays his brother not with malice aforethought, if from sudden anger, shall do penance for three years.

3. Likewise shall an adulterer do penance for three years.

4. They who afford guidance to the barbarians,[17] fourteen[18] years, even though there befall no slaughter of the Christians or effusion of blood or dire captivity. If, however, such things do take place the offenders shall perform penance, deprived of arms, for the rest of life. But if one planned to conduct the barbarians to the Christians, and they did not act according to his will,[19] he shall do penance for the remainder of his life.

---

[14] The passage is of somewhat doubtful meaning. Cf. above, p. 69. This sentence reads: "Dilatus et dilator consimili persona judicentur" (One who is informed on and the informer are to be judged in like character). Cf. *Pref. Gild.* 27, p. 178, below. Doubtless to the scribe "dilatus" and "dilator" were interchangeable respectively with "delatus" and "delator." Cf. *Poenit. Valicellanum* I, 74, where the manuscript reads "dilatus (Schmitz I, p. 300, misreads "dilatus") et delator." In the early church councils "delator" signifies one who lays information against Christians before the secular judges. So Mansi: "qui ad iudices saeculares christianos deferebat," in a note on canon 73 of the synod of Elvira, A.D. 305, Mansi, *Concilia*, II, 17, 53. Cf. II, 473 (Arles, 314, can. 14); VII, 881 (Arles, 442(?), can. 24).

[15] "dilatus." But *Poenit. Valicell.*, I, 74, has "Si quis dilatus et delator negaverit" (if one has been informed on and the informer denies it) and perhaps we should read "delator" here: "If the informer denies that he has laid the information." Cf. *Cummean*, VIII, 11, p. 110, above, where both are to do penance.

[16] Emending "alterius" to "altaris." Cf. *Cummean*, VIII, 12, p. 110, above.

[17] Apparently a reference to the Anglo-Saxons, who were, of course, still pagans.

[18] Manuscript "XIIII," misread "XIII" by Wasserschleben.

[19] "et non ad vota sibi." The text may be corrupt.

5. He who swears a false oath, four years. He who leads another unknowingly to perjure himself, seven years. He who is led into [perjury] unknowingly and later knows of it, one year. He who suspects that he is being led into perjury and yet swears, on account of his agreement to do so, two years.

6. He who defiles his mother, three years with perpetual pilgrimage.

7. He who sins with a dog or with an animal, two and a half years.

8. [In substance:] He who is guilty of sodomy in its various forms shall do penance for four, three, or two years according to the nature of the offense.[20]

9. All that we have said applies if a man has made the vow of perfection. But if the offense occurs before the vow is taken, a year is deducted from each [of the three above]; as to the rest, a reduction is made as it ought to be so long as he has not taken the vow.

2. CERTAIN EXCERPTS FROM A BOOK OF DAVID

(ca. 500–525)

[THE VALUABLE Codex Paris. 3182 is the source for this group of canons. The *Excerpta quaedam de libro Davidis* has been printed by Martène and Durand;[1] by Wasserschleben;[2] by Schmitz;[3] and by Haddan and Stubbs.[4] Noteworthy features of these canons are the stress laid on the motives of offenders, the accommodation to the customary law of the people in respect to the payment made to the parents in case of seduction, and the provision for commutation where the payment cannot be made. The ascription of the document to David is based only on the meager evidence of the title.]

1. Priests who are about to minister in the temple of God, who through greediness drink wine or strong drink[5] negligently, not ignorantly, shall do penance for four days; but if they do so out of contempt of those who censure them forty days.

2. Those who become drunk from ignorance, fifteen days; from negligence, forty days; from contempt, three forty-day periods.

3. One who constrains another to get drunk for the sake of good fellowship[6] shall do the same penance as the drunken man.

---

[20] "Qui facit scelus virile, ut sodomite, IV annis. Qui vero in femoribus, III annis, manu autem, sive alterius sive sua, II annis."   [1] *Op. cit.*, IV, 10. *See also* App. V, n. 1.
[2] *Bussordnungen*, pp. 101 f.   [3] Schmitz I, 492 f.   [4] *Op. cit.*, I, 118 ff.
[5] Reading "siceram" for "ciceram." Cf. Luke 1:15.   [6] "humanitatis gratia."

4. One who under the influence of hatred or of wantonness[7] constrains others to drunkenness that he may basely put them to confusion or ridicule, if he has not done adequate penance, shall do penance as a slayer of souls.

5. Those who commit fornication with a woman who has become vowed to Christ or to a husband, or with a beast, or with a male, for the remainder [of their lives] dead to the world shall live unto God.

6. But one who sins with a virgin or a widow not yet under vows, shall pay the bride-price[8] to her parents and do penance for a year. If he has not the bride-price, he shall do penance for three years.

7. A bishop who willfully commits murder or any kind of fornication or fraud, shall do penance for thirteen years; but a presbyter seven years on bread and water, and a repast on Sunday or Saturday; a deacon, six years; a monk not in holy orders, four years— unless they are hindered by infirmity.

8. He who intentionally becomes polluted in sleep shall get up and sing seven psalms and live on bread and water for that day; but if he does not do this he shall sing thirty psalms.

9. But if he desired to sin in sleep but could not, fifteen psalms; if, however, he sinned but was not polluted, twenty-four; if he was unintentionally polluted, fifteen.

10. The saints of old decreed that a bishop should do penance for twenty-four years for capital sins; a presbyter, twelve; a deacon, seven; and a virgin, a reader, and a monk, the same; but a layman,[9] four years.

11. Now, however, the penance of a presbyter, a deacon, a subdeacon or a virgin who falls, as well as of anyone who puts a man to death, who commits fornication with beasts or with his sister or with another's wife, or who plans to slay a man with poisons, is three years. During the first year he shall lie upon the ground; during the second his head is to be laid upon a stone; during the third, upon a board; and he shall eat only bread and water and salt and some pease porridge. Others prefer thirty periods of three days, or [pen-

---

[7] "luxuriae."

[8] "dos." The "dos" was a payment to the parents made by the husband of their daughter at her marriage. See above, p. 37, n. 52, and p. 95, n. 41. Columbanus refers to it as "humiliationis pretio" (the price of her defilement). See the *Penitential of Columban*, B. 16, below, p. 254. In the same document, can. 14, he refers to the "pretium pudicitae" (the price of her shame) paid to a husband whose wife has been violated.

[9] "ebibatus." See Du Cange, *s.v.* "epibata," and above, p. 69.

ances] with special fasts, with food and bed as aforesaid, with food at nones,[10] until the second year. Another penance is for three years, but with a half-pint of beer or milk with bread and salt every second night with the ration of dinner; and they ought to supplicate God regularly in the twelve hours of the nights and of the days.

12. But thenceforth it is not permitted to a priest to offer the sacrifice or for a deacon to hold the cup or to rise to higher rank.

13. He who receives usury shall give up those things that he has received.

14. He who enjoys the fruits of robbery or fraud, half a year.

15. He who kisses a virgin in secret shall do penance for three days.

16. He who takes a false oath in the church shall restore four times that for which he made the oath.

3. THE PREFACE OF GILDAS ON PENANCE

[THE *Prefatio Gildae de penitentia* is probably to be ascribed to St. Gildas, the contemporary and associate of St. David and author of an important work on the *Fall of Britain*. Gildas lived, apparently, about 493–570.[1] He was a devout and austere monk, and the *Preface on Penance* concerns only the penances of monks and clergy. As in other early British canons the penances are milder than those assigned in later usage. The *Preface* has been preserved in one manuscript only, the Codex Paris. 3182. Editions of the document are in Martène and Durand,[2] Wasserschleben,[3] Schmitz,[4] Haddan and Stubbs,[5] and Williams.[6] Williams has supplied valuable footnotes and a translation. The present translation has been made independently, though in some details it has profited from a subsequent comparison with that of Williams.]

1. A presbyter or a deacon committing natural fornication or sodomy who has previously taken the monastic vow shall do penance for three years. He shall seek pardon every hour and keep a special

---

[10] "nona hora" (the ninth hour), about three in the afternoon.

[1] The date of Gildas's birth has been the subject of much discussion. His own statements, his relations with Finnian of Clonard, and an ingenious note by M. Arthur de la Borderie on a statement of Bede ("La Date de la naissance de Gildas," *Rev. celt.*, VI (1885), 1 ff.) point to the conclusion that he was born in 493. See McNeill, pp. 35 ff. (*Rev. celt.*, XXXIX, 269 ff.). H. Williams distrusts Borderie's suggestion, but also thinks the traditional date of 516 for Gildas's birth to be erroneous. *Cymmrodorion Record Series*, III, 62 f. For an unusual view of the work, *The Fall of Britain*, attributed to Gildas, see A. W. Wade-Evans, *Welsh Christian Origins*, pp. 289 ff.   [2] *Thes. Nov. Anecd.*, IV, 7 f.

[3] *Bussordnungen*, pp. 105–08. See App. V. n. 1.

[4] Schmitz I, pp. 494–97.

[5] *Op. cit.*, I, 113–15.

[6] H. Williams, *Gildas*, in *Cymmrodorion Record Series*, III (1899), 272–85.

fast[7] once every week except during the fifty days following the Passion.[8] He shall have bread without limitation and a refection with some butter spread over it[9] on Sunday. On the other days his allowance of bread shall be a loaf of dry bread[10] and a dish[11] enriched with a little fat,[12] garden vegetables, a few eggs, British cheese, a Roman half-pint of milk in consideration of the weakness of the body in this age,[13] also a Roman pint of whey or buttermilk for his thirst, and enough water if he is a worker.[14] Let him have his bed meagerly supplied with hay. For the three forty-day periods[15] let him add something as far as his strength permits. Let him deplore his guilt from his inmost heart. Above all things let him show the readiest obedience. After a year and a half he may take the eucharist and come to peace and sing the psalms with his brethren, lest his soul perish utterly from so long a time[16] of the celestial medicine.

2. If any monk of lower rank[17] does this, he shall do penance for three years, but the allowance of bread shall be increased.[18] If he is a worker,[19] let him take a Roman pint of milk and another of whey and as much water as the intensity of his thirst requires.

3. If it is a presbyter or a deacon without monastic vow who has sinned, he shall do the same penance as a monk not in holy orders.

[7] See above, pp. 31, 120 f.

[8] See below, p. 308. The period of rejoicing really began with Easter day.

[9] "ferculo aliquatenus butiro impingato" (a refection somewhat fattened with butter). "Ferculo" is literally a tray or platter, but is here apparently used by metonymy for a course or meal.

[10] "panis paxmati." Cf. above, p. 102, n. 34.

[11] Reading with Martène "misoclo" for "miso." In the manuscript "a clo" or "a do" is suprascript between "miso" and "parvum."

[12] "parvum impinguato," literally, "fattened a little."

[13] "istius evi."

[14] "operarius." In Celtic monasteries "operarii fratres" were those of the monks who were fit to labor. Cf. W. Reeves, *Life of St. Columba* (1874), pp. cvii, 210. It may be assumed that the "operarius" here is a monk, in view of canons 2 and 3.

[15] "quadragesimas." For the three forty-day periods or "the three lents," see *Penit. Theod.*, II, xiv, 1, p. 212, below.

[16] Haddan and Stubbs suggest the addition of "inopia," to make the meaning: "through lack of the celestial medicine for so long a time." This gains some support from the *Old Irish Penitential*, II, 4, p. 160, above, "that their souls may not perish for want of Christ's body." But penance itself is frequently referred to as medicine in the penitentials, and the insertion seems unnecessary. On the interpretation adopted above the wise author recognizes the possibility of injurious severity. The passage in the *Penitential of Cummean*, II, 2, p. 103, above, bears the same interpretation.

[17] That is, in lower clerical orders than those mentioned in can. 1.

[18] A parallel passage in the *Pseudo-Cummean*, II, 24, has "non gravetur" (shall not be increased). Schmitz I, p. 621.

[19] "operarius." Cf. above, n. 14.

4. But if a monk intends to commit such a sin, he shall do penance for a year and a half.[20] However, the abbot has authority to modify this if his obedience is pleasing to God and the abbot.

5. The ancient fathers commanded a penance of twelve years for a presbyter and seven for a deacon.

6. A monk who has stolen a garment or any [other] thing shall do penance for two years as stated above, if he is a junior; if a senior, one entire year. One who is not a monk, likewise a year, and especially the three periods of forty days.

7. If a monk after loading his stomach vomits the host during the day, he shall not venture to take supper, and if it is not on account of infirmity he shall expunge his offense with seven special fasts.[21] If it is from infirmity, not from gluttony, with four special fasts.

8. But if it is not the host, he is to be punished with a special fast of one day and with much reproach.

9. If one by a mishap through carelessness loses some of the host, he shall do penance for three forty-day periods, leaving that for beasts and birds to devour.

10. But if on account of drunkenness one is unable to sing the psalms, being benumbed in his organs of speech,[22] he shall be deprived of his supper.

11. One who sins with a beast shall expiate his guilt for a year; if by himself alone, for three forty-day periods.

12. One who holds communion with one who has been excommunicated by his abbot, forty days.

13. One who unwittingly eats carrion,[23] forty days.

14. It is to be understood, however, that for whatever time one remains in sin, by so much is his penance to be increased.

---

[20] Variations of this canon are found in *Pseudo-Bede*, III, 9, and *Egbert*, V, 5, and in *Cummean*, II, 5 and *Pseudo-Cummean*, II, 25, on the basis of which the words may be amended to read "If a presbyter or a deacon after such a sin wants to become a monk." See also p. 103, above.

[21] In the *Regula coenobialis* of Columban, 5, we find "superpositio silentii," there rendered "a special penalty of silence"; and it may be that "superpositio" in the same document elsewhere (6) should have "silentii" supplied to complete the sense. See below, p. 261. Such an interpretation would again seem applicable to can. 8 of the present document, where the penitent has to submit to "much reproach." We might think of his being reproached by his brethren for his sins during the "superposition" without permission to reply. But it seems best here to follow the common meaning of "superpositio." See above, pp. 31, 120 f.

[22] "stupens e linguis." Cf. *Cummean*, I, 4, p. 101, above, and n. 31.

[23] Cf. above, p. 131, n. 5.

15. If a certain task has been enjoined on one and through contempt he leaves it undone, he shall go without supper; but if through an oversight, he shall go without half his daily portion.

16. But if he undertakes another's task, he shall modestly make this known to the abbot, none else hearing it, and he shall perform it if he is commanded to do so.

17. Now, he that for a long time holds anger in his heart is in [a state of] death. But if he confesses his sin, he shall fast for forty days; and if he still persists in his sin, two forty-day periods. And if he [then] does the same thing, he shall be cut off from the body as a rotten member, since wrath breeds murder.

18. One who is offended by anyone ought to inform the abbot of the matter, not indeed in the spirit of an accuser, but of a physician; and the abbot shall decide.

19. One who has not arrived by the end of the second psalm[24] shall sing eight psalms in order; if when he has been aroused he comes after Mass,[25] he shall repeat in sequence whatever the brethren have sung; but if he comes at the second [reading(?)][26] he shall go without supper.

20. If through inattention[27] anyone has confusedly uttered[28] any of the sacred words where "danger"[29] is noted, [he shall do penance] for three days or perform three special fasts.

21. If by neglect the host[30] has fallen to the ground, [the offenders] shall go without supper.

22. He who willingly has been defiled in sleep, if the monastic house is abundantly supplied with beer and flesh, shall make a standing vigil of an hour for three nights if he is in health and strength.

---

[24] Inserting "secundi psalmi," after "ad consummationem," as do Haddan and Stubbs, I, 115, and Williams, *op. cit.*, p. 282 (who gives an illuminating note), from a parallel passage in the *Penitential of Thirty-five Chapters*, can. 31. Cf. Wasserschleben, *Bussordnungen*, p. 524. The *Penitential of Cummean*, IX, 6, not known to these authors, has "ad secundi psalmi consummationem." See above, p. 111.

[25] Or "the reading"; "missa" is at times employed in the sense of "lectio," Williams, *op. cit.*, p. 283.

[26] "ad secundam." Perhaps "lectionem," or "missam" in the sense of "lectionem" (lesson or reading), is the word omitted.   [27] "errans."

[28] "commotaverit" (has disturbed).

[29] "periculum." On the "oratio periculosa," see above, p. 112, n. 75. Williams notes here (quoting the *Stowe Missal*): "The Liturgic books of Wales, Ireland, and certain Celtic churches on the continent, had the word "periculum" inserted (on the margin probably) in order to enjoin special care in the reading of the prayer of consecration."

[30] "sacrum" instead of the usual "sacrificium." Williams has "the consecrated element."

But if it has poor fare, standing as a suppliant he shall sing twenty-eight or thirty psalms or make satisfaction with an extra work.

23. For good rulers we ought to offer the sacred rites;[31] for bad, never.

24. Presbyters are indeed not forbidden to offer for their bishops.

25. One who is accused of any fault and is checked as an inconsiderate person shall go without supper.

26. One who has broken a hoe[32] which was not broken before, shall either make amends by an extraordinary work or perform a special fast.

27. One who sees any of his brethren violate the commands of the abbot ought not to conceal the fact from the abbot, but he ought first to admonish the offender to confess alone to the abbot the evil he has done, that he be found not so much an informer[33] as one who practices the rule of truth.

Thus far Gildas.

[31] "sacra."

[32] "sarculum." The implement took various shapes. See C. Daremberg et E. Saglio, *Dictionnaire des antiquités grecques et romaines, s.v.*

[33] Manuscript has "dilator," Wasserschleben prints "delator." Cf. p. 171, n. 14, above

CHAPTER III

Penitentials of the Anglo-Saxon Church

1. THE PENITENTIAL OF THEODORE

(668–690, *with later elements*)

[THE IMPORTANCE of this work, emanating from Theodore of Tarsus (archbishop of Canterbury, 668–90) is generally recognized. Perhaps the most original and valuable part of Wasserschleben's essay on the history of the penitentials is that in which he determines the true penitential of Theodore.[1] The tradition of Theodore's authorship of a penitential is attested by numerous references in authors of the eighth, ninth, and tenth centuries. The *Liber pontificalis*, compiled in the late eighth century, has usually been cited in this connection. In one manuscript of this work it is stated that Theodore "with wonderful consideration set forth the sentences of sinners or the number of years one ought to do penance for every sin."[2] This passage, however, appears to be a late addition to the book.[3] Yet it can hardly be later in origin than the *Liber pontificalis*, since it is also found in Paul the Deacon's *History of the Lombards*, written about 790.[4] Half a century later Raban Maur at least twice cited the penitential canons of Theodore, calling them "constitutions" and "capitula."[5] Regino of Prüm prescribes the *Penitential of Theodore* as one of the two from which choice may be made.[6] In Irish penitential writings about the end of the seventh century Theodore was named and quoted.[7] The penitential published by Albers as probably Bede's or of Bede's period, though regarded by others as somewhat later,

---

[1] *Bussordnungen*, pp. 14–37.   [2] L. Duchesne, *Le Liber pontificalis*, II, xxv.

[3] Cf. W. Levison's review of Finsterwalder's work cited below, p. 181, n. 21, in *Zeitschrift der Savigny-Stiftung für Rechtsgeschichte, kan. Abt.*, XIX (1930), 706.

[4] *History of the Lombards*, V, 30. Paul wrote this work after his retirement in 786; he died in 795.

[5] Migne, *P.L.*, CX, 491; 1085. Cf. Schmitz II, p. 511. Although Raban quotes passages found in both books of the present *Penitential of Theodore* Schmitz thinks it unlikely that he knew the book as one work. The reference to "the penitential which Theodore, archbishop of Britain, with the other bishops established," in the work "On the Penance of Laymen," ascribed to Raban Maur and published in the Cologne (1626) edition of his works, VI, 114 (cf. Wasserschleben, *Bussordnungen*, p. 15) may not be from his pen.

[6] See below, pp. 217, 314.

[7] *Coll. can. Hib.*, I, 22; LIV, 12, 13, 14. Theodore is named in the last three of these quotations, all of which are from Book II of the penitential.

and the related *Penitential of Egbert*, refer to Theodore as an authority.[8] But Bede's *History* and the writings of near-contemporaries of Theodore offer no corroboration of his connection with a penitential. The work published by Spelman in 1639 from a Cambridge manuscript as the *Poenitentiale Theodori Archiepiscopi* showed late elements. J. Morin, in his classical history of penitential discipline, rejected the portions of this work authorizing composition but regarded the remainder as the genuine work of Theodore.[9] The whole document was uncritically accepted by Thorpe and appears in full in his *Ancient Laws and Institutes of England*.[10] Meanwhile, in 1677, Jacques Petit published fourteen capitula of a *Poenitentiale Theodori* from a manuscript taken from the library of de Thou, together with a collection of pseudo-Theodorean canons.[11] Wasserschleben, however, discovered manuscripts which led him to adopt as the *Penitential of Theodore* a work in two books, of about equal length, of which the first contains fifteen sections, and the second is the fourteen capitula of Petit.[12] Haddan and Stubbs working independently of Wasserschleben and using a ninth-century Cambridge manuscript superior to any used by him (Codex CCCC 320), reached the same conclusion and later published the newly-discovered *Poenitentiale Theodori*, ascribing it to Theodore "with the utmost confidence."[13]

The *Poenitentiale Theodori* is not, and does not profess to be, a direct work of Theodore of Tarsus. It professes to be made up mainly of answers given by the archbishop to a certain presbyter, Eoda, and edited, after a period of circulation in a confused state, by a scribe who hides behind the vague pseudonym "Discipulus Umbrensium." This mysterious intermediary, the original editor of the penitential, is thought by Haddan and Stubbs to have been "either a native of Northumbria who had been a disciple of Theodore, or, more probably, an Englishman of southern birth who had studied under the northern scholars."[14] Watkins supports the view that he was a southerner who studied in the north, where the Celtic private penance had been adopted.[15] That he had studied under the northern scholars seems to be implied in the language by which he describes himself; but that he was a southerner appears to the present writer much less certain.

F. Liebermann has advanced the view that "Discipulus Umbrensium" was not an Englishman but an Irish disciple of Theodore.[16] A fresh approach to the subject has been made by P. W. Finsterwalder in an

---

[8] See below, p. 223, and Haddan and Stubbs, III, 418.

[9] Joh. Morinus, *Commentarius historicus de disciplina in administratione sacramenti penitentiae* (Paris, 1651; 2d ed., Antwerp, 1682), lib. x, chap. 17.   [10] II, 1–62.

[11] Petit's material will be found reprinted in Migne, *P.L.*, XCIX, 959.

[12] For details of the manuscripts used see Wasserschleben, *Bussordnungen*, pp. 19 ff., 182. Most important is the early ninth-century Vienna codex 2195.

[13] Haddan and Stubbs, III, 173. For a full statement of the manuscripts and editions see pp. 173–76.   [14] Haddan and Stubbs, III, 173.

[15] Watkins, II, 649–50.

[16] "Die Canones Theodori," *Zeitschrift der Savigny-Stiftung für Rechtsgeschichte, kan. Abt.*, XII (1922), 387–410; see p. 401.

elaborate study of the *Canons of Theodore*.[17] Finsterwalder not very convincingly argues that in dedicating his work "to all the Catholics of the English" the compiler indicates that he is not one of these, and supposes that he was one of the eleven disciples whom Willibrord took with him from Ireland to Friesland[18] and hence probably an Irishman. His work, however, was too late to make it possible to regard him as a direct pupil of Theodore.[19] In an additional section of the epilogue which Finsterwalder discovered in the Codex Vat. Pal. Lat. 554, he claims to find references to the heresies of Adalbert and Clement, combated by St. Boniface about 745. In the circle of Boniface, then, the work took its final shape.[20]

Finsterwalder points to the multiplication of copies of the document on the Continent and not in England. His statement that a penitential ascribed to Theodore is first mentioned on the Continent in the ninth century is to be balanced by the references to Theodore's authority in the determination of penance in the possibly authentic works of Bede and Egbert referred to above. Further, the *Irish Collection of Canons*, apparently written in Ireland about 700–725, though believed by Finsterwalder to be the work of St. Boniface, as we have seen, four times quotes the *Penitential of Theodore*.

Finsterwalder's main conclusions as well as his critical methods have been unfavorably examined by W. Levison in an acute review.[21] G. Le Bras has also declared against Finsterwalder's construction of the data and still holds that both parts of the penitential were compiled in England.[22]

The work has evidently been prepared by a person or persons familiar with Welsh and Irish penitential documents. The ungrammatical text of the prologue seems best understood as saying that Theodore had been made acquainted with a certain booklet of the Irish ("libellus scottorum") which Eoda had made the basis of questions asked him to obtain materials for the penitential. The materials in common in Theodore and the *Irish Canons* have led to the belief that this work or part of it, or a collection containing part of it, was the "libellus" referred to.[23] Finsterwalder has shown numerous parallels with the true *Cummean* published by Zettinger, a work written before Theodore's time. His argument renders it highly probable that the "libellus" was Cummean's *Penitential*, either in the form known to us or in a slightly different text.[24]

---

[17] *Die Canones Theodori Cantuariensis und ihre Ueberlieferungsformen*, Weimar, 1929. The work contains, pp. 285–334, a new text of the penitential, in which the author relies largely on the Codex Vat. Pal. Lat. 485, discovered by him.

[18] Bede, *Ecclesiastical History*, V, 10.   [19] Finsterwalder, *op. cit.*, pp. 170 ff.

[20] *Ibid.*, pp. 177 ff.

[21] *Zeitschrift der Savigny-Stiftung für Rechtsgeschichte, kan. Abt.*, XIX (1930), 699–707.

[22] "Notes pour servir à l'histoire des collections canoniques. 1. Judicia Theodori," *Revue historique de droit français et étranger*, 4 ser., 10 an. (1931), pp. 95–131.

[23] Oakley, pp. 105–13. McNeill, p. 61 (*Rev. celt.*, XXXIX, 295).

[24] Finsterwalder, *op. cit.*, pp. 201 ff. Cf. J. T. McNeill, "Note on Cummean the Long and His Penitential," *Rev. celt.*, L (1933), 289 ff.

Possibly Eoda, who is otherwise unknown, may have become acquainted in Northumbria with the Irish and British penitential materials which are repeated in this penitential; or he may have been one of those Englishmen who, as Aldhelm says, in Theodore's time crossed the sea "in fleets" to study in Ireland,[25] some of whom doubtless returned to their native country. He may have given Theodore his first acquaintance with the Celtic documents, though the Celtic practice of private penance had doubtless been made familiar to the primate during his visitations. Eoda was evidently dead, and his materials were in an unorganized state when "Discipulus Umbrensium" undertook the preparation of a sound edition.

Critical editions are given by Wasserschleben,[26] by Haddan and Stubbs,[27] and by Schmitz.[28] Schmitz has given the variants of the Continental manuscripts known to him but has ignored the superior manuscript of the Corpus Christi College Library, used by Haddan and Stubbs. The translation is based upon the edition of Finsterwalder[29] amended at many points from the manuscripts. The document shows evidence of a few later comments and indicates that the scribe consulted various copies in which he found differences and did a little critical editing of his own.[30]]

PREFACE

In the name of Christ. Here begins the preface of the booklet which Father Theodore, having been inquired of by different persons, prepared for the remedy of penance. A pupil of the [North]umbrians, to all Catholics of the English, especially to the physicians of souls, as a suppliant [sends] blessing and greeting[31] in the Lord Christ.

First, then, beloved, from love of your blessedness, I thought it fitting, to set forth whence I have collected the penitential remedies which follow,[32] in order that the law may not, on account of the age or negligence of copyists, be perpetuated in a confused and corrupted state, as is usual—that law which[33] of old time God gave figuratively by its first promulgator and then later committed to the Fathers,

---

[25] S. Aldhelmi, Ep. iii, Migne, *P.L.* LXXXIX, 94. Cf. Bede, *Ecclesiastical History*, III, 27.   [26] *Bussordnungen*, pp. 182–219.   [27] *Op. cit.*, III, 173–204.

[28] *Op. cit.*, II, 545–80.

[29] *Op. cit.*, pp. 285–334. For a discussion of Finsterwalder's treatment of the manuscripts see Introduction, pp. 54 f., 57 ff., 63, n. 36.

[30] See V, 6; IX, 12; XIV, 29. A translation of the greater part of the *Penitential of Theodore* is presented by Sir Henry H. Howorth in *The Golden Days of the English Church*, III, 238 ff. The work is marred, however, by unindicated omissions and numerous incredibly false renderings.   [31] "sanabilem salutem."

[32] Literally, "the treatments of this medicine which follows." The text appears to be in some disorder.

[33] Reading "quam" for "quoniam" with Codex Vindob. 2195.

that they should make it known to their sons that another generation should be acquainted with it; to wit, the [law of] penance, which[33] the Lord Jesus, when he was baptized[34] before us all, proclaimed as the instrument of his teaching for those who had no means of healing; saying: "Do penance,"[35] etc. For the increase of your felicity, He deigned to send from the blessed see of him to whom it is said, "Whatsoever thou shalt loose on earth shall be loosed also in heaven,"[36] one by whom this most wholesome treatment of wounds is to be controlled; "for I," says the Apostle, "have received of the Lord,"[37] and I, beloved, have received from you, by God's favor, that which, in turn, I have handed over to you. For the greater part of these [decisions] the presbyter Eoda, of blessed memory, whose surname was "Christian," is said, by true report, to have received in answer to his questions from the venerable prelate Theodore. Supplementing these also is that element which the divine grace has in like manner provided to our unworthy hands, the things which that man is likewise[38] reported to have searched out, from a booklet of the Irish. Concerning this book, the aged [Theodore] is said to have expressed the opinion that the author was an ecclesiastic.

Further, not only many men but also women, enkindled by him through these [decisions] with inextinguishable fervor, burning with desire to quench this thirst, made haste in crowds to visit a man undoubtedly of extraordinary knowledge for our age. Hence there has been found in divers quarters that conflicting and confused digest[39] of those rules of the second book compiled with the cases adjudged. For which reason I implore, brethren, the most kind indulgence of your favor, through Him who was crucified and [who] by the shedding of His blood in life mightily confirmed what He had preached, that, if for the interests of the practical service I have committed any sin of rashness or ignorance, you will defend me before Him with the support of your intercession. For I call to witness the Maker of all things, that so far as I know my own heart, I have done

---

[34] "initiatus."

[35] Codex Würzburg Mp th q 32 gives the whole sentence: "Poenitentiam agite ad propinquavit enim regnum coelorum." This (with "appro-" for "ad pro-") is the Vulgate rendering of the passage, Μετανοεῖτε·ἤγγικεν γὰρ ἡ βασιλεία τῶν οὐρανῶν (Matt. 4:17), which is rendered in the Authorized Version, "Repent: for the kingdom of heaven is at hand." The Douay version, following the Vulgate has: "Do penance", and so forth.

[36] Matt. 18:18.   [37] Acts 20:24.

[38] Reading "quoque" for "quod," with Ms. Vat. Pal. Lat. 485.

[39] See above, p. 180, and below, p. 215.

these things for the sake of that kingdom of which He preached; and if, as I fear, I undertake something beyond my talents, then, you thus assisting me, let your good will toward a work so necessary implore the pardon of my sin before Him. For in all these things equally and without invidious discrimination, according as I am able, I carefully select out of the whole the more useful things I have been able to find, and I have collected them, prefixing headings to them one by one. For I believe that men of good spirit give attention to these things, of whom it is said: "On earth peace to men of good will."[40]

BOOK ONE

I. Of Excess and Drunkenness

1. If any bishop or deacon or any ordained person has had by custom the vice of drunkenness, he shall either desist or be deposed.

2. If a monk vomits on account of drunkenness, he shall do penance for thirty days.

3. If a presbyter or a deacon [does this] on account of drunkenness, he shall do penance for forty days.

4. If [the offense is] due to weakness or because he has been a long time abstinent and is not accustomed to drink or eat much; or if it is for gladness at Christmas or Easter or for any festival of a saint, and he then has imbibed no more than is commanded by his seniors, no offense is committed. If a bishop commands it no offense is committed, unless he himself does likewise.

5. If a lay Christian[41] vomits because of drunkenness, he shall do penance for fifteen days.

6. Whoever is drunk against the Lord's command,[42] if he has taken a vow of sanctity, shall do penance for seven days on bread and water, or twenty days without fat;[43] laymen, without beer.

7. Whoever in wickedness makes another drunk, shall do penance for forty days.

8. Whoever vomits from excess shall do penance for three days.

9. If with the sacrifice of communion, he shall do penance for seven days; if on account of weakness, he is without guilt.

II. Of Fornication

1. If anyone commits fornication with a virgin he shall do penance

[40] Luke 2:14.　　[41] "fidelis."　　[42] Luke 21:34.
[43] "pinguedine" (fat or butter).

for one year. If with a married woman, he shall do penance for four years, two of these entire, and in the other two during the three forty-day periods[44] and three days a week.

2. He judged that he who often commits fornication with a man or with a beast should do penance for ten years.

3. Another judgment is that he who is joined to beasts shall do penance for fifteen years.

4. He who after his twentieth year defiles himself with a male shall do penance for fifteen years.

5. A male who commits fornication with a male shall do penance for ten years.

6. Sodomites shall do penance for seven years, and the effeminate man as an adulteress.[45]

7. Likewise he who commits this sexual offense once shall do penance for four years. If he has been in the habit of it, as Basil says, fifteen years;[46] but if not, one year less[?][47] as a woman. If he is a boy, two years for the first offense; if he repeats it, four years.

8. If he does this "in femoribus," one year, or the three forty-day periods.

9. If he defiles himself, forty days.

10. He who desires to commit fornication, but is not able, shall do penance for forty or twenty days.

11. As for boys who mutually engage in vice, he judged that they should be whipped.

12. If a woman practices vice with a woman, she shall do penance for three years.

13. If she practices solitary vice, she shall do penance for the same period.

[44] Probably by the "three forty-day periods"; frequently assigned in this penitential, those mentioned in Book II, xiv, 1, p. 212, below, are to be understood. Some modern writers habitually call these "the three lents."

[45] Cf. XIV, 14, below.

[46] Basil, *Epistola canonica ad Amphilochium*, III, canons lviii, lxii (Migne, *P. G.* XXXII, 798 f.), sets a penance of fifteen years for what is apparently here taken to be the same offense. This apparently justifies Wasserschleben's reconstruction of the sentence, which is here followed. Theodore's use of the three "canonical" epistles of Basil, addressed *ca.* 374–75 to his friend Amphilochius, bishop of Iconium—an important source for the study of penance in the fourth century—is mainly confined to the repetition of the periods assigned for the offenses named. Basil has constant reference to the public graded penitential discipline which developed in the early church, while Theodore, though an Eastern, had resigned himself to the private penance which prevailed in England through the influence of the Celtic Church of Ireland. Cf. Introd., p. 26, above, and XIII, 4, below.

[47] "sustinens unum annum"—possibly "taking away one year." Cf. can. 12, below. The passage is obscure.

14. The penance of a widow and of a girl is the same. She who has a husband deserves a greater penalty if she commits fornication.

15. "Qui semen in os miserit" shall do penance for seven years: this is the worst of evils. Elsewhere it was his judgment that both [participants in this offense] shall do penance to the end of life; or twelve[48] years; or as above seven.

16. If one commits fornication with his mother, he shall do penance for fifteen years and never change except on Sundays. But this so impious incest is likewise spoken of by him in another way—that he shall do penance for seven years, with perpetual pilgrimage.

17. He who commits fornication with his sister shall do penance for fifteen years in the way in which it is stated above of his mother. But this [penalty] he also elsewhere established in a canon as twelve years. Whence it is not unreasonable that the fifteen years that are written apply to the mother.

18. The first canon determined that he who often commits fornication should do penance for ten years; a second canon, seven; but on account of the weakness of man, on deliberation they said he should do penance for three years.[49]

19. If a brother commits fornication with a natural brother, he shall abstain from all kinds of flesh for fifteen years.

20. If a mother imitates acts of fornication with her little son, she shall abstain from flesh for three years and fast one day in the week, that is until vespers.

21. He who amuses himself with libidinous imagination shall do penance until the imagination is overcome.

22. He who loves a woman in his mind shall seek pardon from God; but[50] if he has spoken [to her], that is, of love and friendship, but is not received by her, he shall do penance for seven days.

III. Of Thieving Avarice

1. If any layman carries off a monk from the monastery by stealth, he shall either[51] enter a monastery to serve God or subject himself to human servitude.

2. Money stolen or robbed from churches is to be restored fourfold; from secular persons, twofold.

---

[48] Manuscript evidence favors "xii." Other readings are "xv" and "xxii."
[49] Cf. p. 304, n. 42, below.
[50] Reading "autem" for "haec" with the manuscripts.
[51] The manuscripts and context favor "aut" for "ut."

3. Whoever has often committed theft, seven years is his penance, or such a sentence as his priest shall determine, that is, according to what can be arranged with those whom he has wronged. And he who used to steal, when he becomes penitent, ought always to be reconciled to him against whom he has offended and to make restitution according to the wrong he has done to him; and [in such case] he shall greatly shorten his penance. But if he refuses, or is unable, let him do penance scrupulously[52] for the prescribed time.

4. And he who gives notice of stolen goods shall give a third part to the poor; and whoever treasures up goods in excess through ignorance, shall give a third part to the poor.

5. Whoever has stolen consecrated things shall do penance for three years without fat and then [be allowed to] communicate.

IV. Of Manslaughter

1. If one slays a man in revenge for a relative, he shall do penance as a murderer for seven or ten years. However, if he will render to the relatives the legal price,[53] the penance shall be lighter, that is, [it shall be shortened] by half the time.

2. If one slays a man in revenge for a brother, he shall do penance for three years. In another place it is said that he should do penance for ten years.

3. But a murderer, ten or seven years.

4. If a layman slays another with malice aforethought,[54] if he will not lay aside his arms, he shall do penance for seven years; without flesh and wine, three years.

5. If one slays a monk or a cleric, he shall lay aside his arms and serve God, or he shall do penance for seven years. He is in the judgment of his bishop. But as for one who slays a bishop or a presbyter, it is for the king to give judgment in his case.

6. One who slays a man by command of his lord shall keep away from the church for forty days; and one who slays a man in public war shall do penance for forty days.

7. If through anger, he shall do penance for three years; if by accident, for one year; if by a potion or any trick, seven years or more; if as a result of a quarrel, ten years.

[52] "per omnia."
[53] "pecuniam aestimationis," i.e., the "wergeld" or value in law of the slain man.
[54] "odii meditatione."

V. Of Those Who Are Deceived by Heresy

1. If one has been ordained by heretics, if he was without blame [in the matter] he ought to be reordained; but if not, he ought to be deposed.

2. If one goes over from the Catholic Church to heresy and afterward returns, he cannot be ordained except after a long probation[55] and in great necessity. Pope Innocent claimed that such a person is not permitted by the authority of the canons to become a cleric [even] after penance. Therefore if[56] Theodore says this: "only in great necessity," as has been said, he permitted the procedure, who often used to say that he wished that the decrees of the Romans should never be changed by him.

3. If one flouts the Council of Nicaea and keeps Easter with the Jews on the fourteenth of the moon, he shall be driven out of every church unless he does penance before his death.

4. If one prays with such a person as if he were a Catholic cleric, he shall do penance for a week; if indeed he neglects this, he shall the first time do penance for forty days.

5. If one seeks to encourage the heresy of these people and does not do penance, he shall be likewise driven out; as the Lord[57] saith: "He that is not with me is against me."[58]

6. If one is baptized by a heretic who does not rightly believe in the Trinity, he shall be rebaptized. This[59] we do not believe Theodore to have said [since it is] in opposition to the Nicene council and the decrees of the synod; as is confirmed in connection with the Arian converts who did not rightly believe in the Trinity.[60]

7. If one gives the communion to a heretic or receives it from his hand, and does not know that the Catholic Church[61] disapproves it, when he afterward becomes aware [of this] he shall do penance for an entire year. But if he knows and [yet] neglects [the rule] and afterwards does penance, he shall do penance for ten years. Others judge that he should do penance for seven years and, more leniently, for five.

---

[55] "abstinentiam."   [56] Inserting "si," with manuscript support.
[57] Reading with the manuscripts "domino" for "deo."   [58] Matt. 12:30.
[59] "Hoc," apparently inadvertently omitted by Finsterwalder.
[60] The writer has mistaken the canons of Constantinople (381) for those of Nicaea. The council of Constantinople admitted Arians without rebaptism (can. vii, Mansi, III, 563). See also the 8th canon of the synod of Arles (314), Mansi, II, 472.
[61] Reading "catholica ecclesia" for "catholicam ecclesiam."

8. If one, without knowing it, permits a heretic to celebrate the Mass in a Catholic church, he shall do penance for forty days. If [he does this] out of veneration for him [i.e., for the heretic], he shall do penance for an entire year.

9. If [he does this] in condemnation of the Catholic Church and the customs of the Romans, he shall be cast out of the Church as a heretic, unless he is penitent; if he is, he shall do penance for ten years.

10. If he departs from the Catholic Church to the congregation of the heretics and persuades others and afterward performs penance, he shall do penance for twelve years; four years outside the church, and six among the "hearers,"[62] and two more out of communion. Of these it is said in a synod: They shall receive the communion or oblation in the tenth year.[63]

11. If a bishop or an abbot commands a monk to sing a mass for dead heretics, it is not proper or expedient to obey him.

12. If a presbyter is present where he has sung a mass, and another recites the names of dead persons and names heretics together with Catholics, and after the mass he is aware of it, he shall do penance for a week. If he has done it frequently, he shall do penance for an entire year.

13. But if anyone orders a mass for a dead heretic and preserves his relics on account of his piety, because he fasted much, and he does not know the difference between the Catholic faith and that of the Quartodecimans,[64] and [if he] afterward understands and performs penance, he ought to burn the relics with fire, and he shall do penance for a year. If one knows, however, and is indifferent, when he is moved to penance he shall do penance for ten years.

14. If anyone departs from God's faith without any necessity and afterwards receives penance with his whole heart, he shall do penance among the "hearers"; according to the Nicene council, three years without the church and seven years in the church among the penitents, and two years in addition out of communion.[65]

---

[62] See above, p. 8.

[63] Modeled on synod of Ancyra, can. ix.

[64] Inserting "et quartadecimanorum" from Codex Vindob. 2195. Finsterwalder lists only "et quartam decimam" from Vat. Pal. 485 in his critical apparatus. Cf. *Pseudo-Cummean* X, 31, Schmitz I, p. 639, and can. 3 of this section.

[65] Closely modeled on the council of Nicaea, can. xi.

VI. Of Perjury

1. He who commits perjury in a church shall do penance for eleven years.

2. He who [commits perjury] however [because] forced by necessity, for the three forty-day periods.

3. But he who swears on the hand of a man[66]—this is nothing among the Greeks.

4. If, however, he swears on the hand of a bishop or of a presbyter or of a deacon or on an altar or on a consecrated cross and lies, he shall do penance for three years. But if on a cross that is not consecrated, he shall do penance for one year.

5. The penance for perjury is three years.

VII. Of Many and Diverse Evils, and What Necessary Things Are Harmless

1. He who has committed many evil deeds, that is, murder, adultery with a woman and with a beast, and theft, shall go into a monastery and do penance until his death.

2. Of money which has been seized in a foreign province from a conquered enemy, that is, from an alien king who has been conquered, the third part shall be given to the church or to the poor, and penance shall be done for forty days because it was the king's command.[67]

3. He who drinks blood or semen shall do penance for three years.

4. There is pardon for evil imaginations if they are not carried out in action, nor yet by intention.[68]

5. Further, Theodore approved reckoning the twelve three-day periods as the equivalent of a year.[69] Also in the case of sick persons, the value of a man or of a female slave for a year, or to give the half of all his possessions, and if he have defrauded anyone, to restore fourfold, as Christ judged.[70] These are the proofs of what we said in the preface about the booklet of the Irish;[71] in which, as in other matters, sometimes he [the author of the Irish booklet] determined these things therein[72] more strictly in the case of those who are very bad, but sometimes more leniently, as seemed best to him;[73] it set the measure [of penance] for the weak.

---

[66] Meaning a layman, as indicated by the next canon.
[67] The last clause gives the reason for the lightness of the penalty.
[68] "nec consensu." Perhaps the reference is to an agreement to do evil.
[69] See above p. 123, can. 6.   [70] Luke 19:8.   [71] See above, p. 183.
[72] Redundant after "in quo" (in which).
[73] Reading "sibi" for "ibi" with Codex CCCC 320.

6. He who eats unclean flesh or a carcass that has been torn by beasts shall do penance for forty days. But if the necessity of hunger requires it, there is no offense, since a permissible act is one thing and what necessity requires is another.

7. If anyone accidentally touches food with unwashed hands, or [if] a dog, a cat,[74] a mouse, or an unclean animal that has eaten blood [touches it] there is no offense; and if one from necessity eats an animal that seems unclean, whether a bird or a beast, there is no offense.

8. If a mouse[75] falls into a liquid it shall be removed and sprinkled with holy water, and if it is alive it[76] may be taken [for food]; but if it is dead, all the liquid shall be poured out and not given to man, and the vessel shall be cleansed.

9. Again, if that liquid in which a mouse or a weasel is submerged and dies contains much food, it shall be purged and sprinkled with holy water and taken if there is need.

10. If birds drop dung into any liquid, the dung shall be removed from it, and it shall be sanctified with [holy] water, and it shall be clean food.

11. Unwittingly to absorb blood with the saliva is not a sin.

12. If without knowing it, one eats what is polluted by blood or any unclean thing, it is nothing; but if he knows, he shall do penance according to the degree of the pollution.

VIII. Of Various Failings of the Servants of God

1. If a priest is polluted in touching or in kissing a woman he shall do penance for forty days.

2. If a presbyter kisses a woman from desire, he shall do penance for forty days.

3. Likewise if a presbyter is polluted through imagination, he shall fast for a week.

4. For masturbation, he shall fast for three weeks.

5. If any presbyter denies penance to the dying, he is answerable for their souls, since the Lord saith, "On whatever day the sinner is converted, he shall live and not die."[77] For true conversion is possible

---

[74] "pilax."

[75] "surrex," properly "sorex." Sometimes rendered "fieldmouse," but possibly like "mus" any kind of mouse or other small rodent.

[76] That is, apparently, the liquid, though grammatically the mouse.

[77] Cf. Ezek. 33:15, 19.

in the last hour, since the Lord sees not only the time but the heart; for the thief in his last hour, by a confession of one moment, merited to be in paradise.[78]

6. A monk or a holy virgin who commits fornication shall do penance for seven years.

7. He who often pollutes himself through the violence of his imagination shall do penance for twenty days.

8. He who when asleep in a church pollutes himself shall do penance for three days.

9. For masturbation, the first time he shall do penance for twenty days, on repetition, forty days; for further offenses fasts shall be added.

10. If "in femoribus," one year or the three forty-day periods.

11. He who defiles himself shall do penance for forty days; if he is a boy, for twenty days or be flogged. If he is in orders, for the three forty-day periods or a year if he has done it frequently.

12. If anyone renounces the world and afterward resumes a secular habit, if he was a monk and after these things performs penance, he shall do penance for ten years and after the first three years, if he has been approved in all his penance in tears and prayers, the bishop can deal more leniently with him.

13. If he was not a monk when he departed from the Church, he shall do penance for seven years.

14. Basil gave judgment that a boy should be permitted to marry before the age of sixteen if he could not abstain; but that if he is already a monk, [and marries], he is both [classed] among bigamists and shall do penance for one year.

IX. Of Those Who Are Degraded or Cannot Be Ordained

1. A bishop, presbyter, or deacon guilty of fornication ought to be degraded and to do penance at the decision of a bishop; yet they shall take communion. With loss of rank, penance dies, the soul lives.

2. If anyone after he has vowed himself to God takes a secular habit, he assuredly ought not to proceed a second time to any rank.

3. Nor ought a woman [in such a case] to take the veil; it is far better that she should not come to prominence in the Church.

4. If any presbyter or deacon marries a strange woman, he shall be deposed before the people.

[78] Luke 23:43.

5. If he commits adultery with her and it comes to the knowledge of the people, he shall be cast out of the Church and shall do penance among the laymen as long as he lives.

6. If anyone has a concubine, he ought not to be ordained.

7. If any presbyter in his own province or in another or wherever he may be found refuses to baptize a sick person who has been committed to him or on account of the exertion of the journey [declines the duty] so that he dies without baptism, he shall be deposed.

8. Likewise he who slays a man or commits fornication, shall be deposed.

9. It is not permitted to ordain a boy brought up in a monastery[79] before the age of twenty-five.

10. If anyone, before or after baptism, marries a twice married woman,[80] as in the case of twice married men, he cannot be ordained.

11. If anyone who is not ordained performs baptism through temerity, he is cut off from the Church and shall never be ordained.

12. If through ignorance anyone has been ordained before he is baptized, those who have been baptized by that pagan[81] ought to be [re]baptized, and he himself shall not be ordained [again].

This, again, is said to have been differently determined by the Roman Pontiff of the Apostolic See, to the effect that not he who baptizes, even if he is a pagan,[82] but the Spirit of God, ministers the grace of baptism: but also this matter was differently decided in the case of a "pagan" presbyter—he who thinks himself baptized, holding the Catholic faith in his works[83]—these cases are differently decided[84]—that is, that he should be baptized and ordained.

X. Of Those Who Have Been Baptized Twice; How They Shall Do Penance

1. Those who in ignorance have been twice baptized are not required to do penance for this, except that according to the canons they cannot be ordained unless some great necessity compels it.

2. However, those who have been baptized a second time, not ignorantly, [which is] as if they crucified Christ a second time, shall do penance for seven years on Wednesdays and Fridays and during

---

[79] "puerum monasterii."
[80] Reading "bigamam" for Finsterwalder's "viduam" (widow). See above, p. 59.
[81] "gentilis" because unbaptized.   [82] "paganus."   [83] James 2:18.
[84] This clause, "alias haec iudicia habent," looks like a gloss.

the three forty-day periods, if it was on account of some fault. But if they determined [to be baptized] for the sake of cleanness, they shall do penance in this way for three years.

XI. Of Those Who Despise the Lord's Day, and Neglect the Appointed Fasts of the Church of God

1. Those who labor on the Lord's day, the Greeks reprove the first time; the second, they take something from them; the third time, [they take] the third part of their possessions, or flog them; or they shall do penance for seven days.

2. But if on account of negligence anyone fasts on the Lord's day, he ought to abstain for a whole week. If [he does this] a second time, he shall fast for twenty days; if afterwards forty days.

3. If he fasts out of contempt for the day, he shall be abhorred as a Jew[85] by all the Catholic churches.

4. But if he despises a fast appointed in the church and acts contrary to the decrees of the elders, not in Lent, he shall do penance for forty days. But if it is in Lent, he shall do penance for a year.

5. If he does it frequently and it has become habitual to him, he shall be cast out of the Church, as saith the Lord: "He that shall scandalize one of these little ones," etc.[86]

XII. Of the Communion of the Eucharist, or the Sacrifice

1. The Greeks, clergy and laymen, communicate every Lord's day, and those who do not communicate for three Lord's days are to be excommunicated, as the canons state.

2. Likewise the Romans who so wish, communicate; however those who do not so wish are not excommunicated.

3. The Greeks and Romans abstain from women for three days before the [feast of the] loaves of proposition,[87] as it is written in the law.

4. Penitents according to the canons ought not to communicate before the conclusion of the penance; we, however, out of pity give permission after a year or six months.

5. He who receives the sacrament after food shall do penance for

---

[85] Reading "Iudeus" for "fudens," with the manuscripts.   [86] Matt. 18:6.
[87] This is the Douay rendering of "panes propositionis," I Kings 21:6. The A.V. in this passage (I Sam. 21:6) has "shewbread."

seven days. (It is in the judgment of his bishop. This point, that it is in the judgment of the bishop, is not added in some texts.)[88]

6. If the host has become corrupted with dirt accumulated by time it is always to be burned with fire.

7. Moreover, it shall be permitted if necessary that confession be made to God alone. And this [word] "necessary" is not in some codices.

8. He who mislays the host, [leaving it] for beasts and birds to devour, if by accident, he shall fast for three weeks; if through neglect, for the three forty-day periods.

XIII. Of Reconciliation

1. The Romans reconcile a man within the apse; but the Greeks will not do this.

2. The reconciliation of the penitents in the Lord's Supper is by the bishops only—and the penance is ended.

3. If it is difficult for the bishop, he can, for the sake of necessity, confer authority on a presbyter, to perform this.

4. Reconciliation is not publicly established in this province,[89] for the reason that there is no public penance either.

XIV. Of the Penance for Special Irregularities in Marriage

1. In a first marriage the presbyter ought to perform Mass and bless them both, and afterward they shall absent themselves from church for thirty days. Having done this, they shall do penance for forty days, and absent themselves from the prayer; and afterwards they shall communicate with the oblation.[90]

2. One who is twice married shall do penance for a year; on Wednesdays and Fridays and during the three forty-day periods he shall abstain from flesh; however, he shall not put away his wife.

3. He that is married three times, or more, that is in a fourth or fifth marriage, or beyond that number, for seven years on Wednes-

---

[88] "locis." On the manuscript readings see Introduction, p. 60. The first sentence is evidently the original form of this canon; the second appears to be a later addition, and the third a still later comment on this addition.

[89] For the view that "in hac provincia" here means "in Northumberland," see Finsterwalder, *op. cit.*, pp. 158–63. It should be remembered, however, that the work is addressed "to all Catholics of the English."

[90] Perhaps, "with an offering." This word "oblatio" is often used of gifts to the Church, as well as of the sacrament.

days and Fridays and during the three forty-day periods they shall abstain from flesh; yet they shall not be separated. Basil so determined, but in the canon four years [are indicated].

4. If anyone finds his wife to be an adulteress and does not wish to put her away but has had her in the matrimonial relation to that time, he shall do penance for two years on two days in the week and [shall perform] the fasts of religion; or as long as she herself does penance he shall avoid the matrimonial relation with her, because she has committed adultery.

5. If any man or woman who has taken the vow of virginity is joined in marriage, he shall not set aside the marriage but shall do penance for three years.

6. Foolish vows and those incapable of being performed are to be set aside.[91]

7. A woman may not take a vow without the consent of her husband; but if she does take a vow she can be released, and she shall do penance according to the decision of a priest.

8. He who puts away his wife and marries another shall do penance with tribulation for seven years or a lighter penance for fifteen years.

9. He who defiles his neighbor's wife, deprived of his own wife, shall fast for three years two days a week and in the three forty-day periods.

10. If [the woman] is a virgin, he shall do penance for one year without meat and wine and mead.

11. If he defiles a vowed virgin,[92] he shall do penance for three years, as we said above, whether a child is born of her or not.

12. If she is his slave, he shall set her free and fast for six months.

13. If the wife of anyone deserts him and returns to him undishonored, she shall do penance for one year; otherwise for three years. If he takes another wife he shall do penance for one year.

14. An adulterous woman shall do penance for seven years. And this matter is stated in the same way in the canon.

15. A woman who commits adultery[93] shall do penance for three years as a fornicator. So also shall she do penance who makes an unclean mixture of food for the increase of love.[94]

---

[91] Literally, "broken."   [92] "puellam Dei."
[93] Or, according to Wasserschleben's reading of "ad alteram" for "adulterio," "commits an offense with another woman." Several manuscripts have "adulteram."
[94] "quae semen viri sui in cibo miscens ut inde plus amoris accipiat."

16. A wife who tastes her husband's blood as a remedy shall fast for forty days, more or less.

17. Moreover, women shall not in the time of impurity enter into a church, or communicate—neither nuns nor laywomen; if they presume [to do this] they shall fast for three weeks.

18. In the same way shall they do penance who enter a church before purification after childbirth, that is, forty days.

19. But he who has intercourse[95] at these seasons shall do penance for twenty days.

20. He who has intercourse on the Lord's day shall seek pardon from God and do penance for one or two or three days.

21. In case of unnatural intercourse with his wife,[96] he shall do penance for forty days the first time.

22. For a graver offense of this kind[97] he ought to do penance as one who offends with animals.

23. For intercourse at the improper season he shall fast for forty days.

24. Women who commit abortion before [the foetus] has life, shall do penance for one year or for the three forty-day periods or for forty days, according to the nature of the offense; and if later, that is, more than forty days after conception, they shall do penance as murderesses, that is for three years on Wednesdays and Fridays and in the three forty-day periods. This according to the canons is judged [punishable by] ten years.

25. If a mother slays her child, if she commits homicide, she shall do penance for fifteen years, and never change except on Sunday.

26. If a poor woman slays her child, she shall do penance for seven years. In the canon it is said that if it is a case of homicide, she shall do penance for ten years.

27. A woman who conceives and slays her child in the womb within forty days shall do penance for one year; but if later than forty days, she shall do penance as a murderess.

28. If an infant that is weak and is a pagan has been recommended to a presbyter [for baptism] and dies [unbaptized], the presbyter shall be deposed.

29. If the neglect is on the part of the parents, they shall do penance for one year; and if a child of three years dies without baptism,

[95] For this use of "nubere" see Du Cange, s.v.
[96] "Si vir cum uxore sua retro nupserit."   [97] "Si in tergo nupserit."

the father and the mother shall do penance for three years. He gave this decision at a certain time because[98] it happened to be referred to him.

30. In the canon, he who slays his child without baptism [is required to do penance for] ten years, but under advisement[99] he shall do penance for seven years.

XV. Of the Worship of Idols

1. He who sacrifices to demons in trivial matters shall do penance for one year; but he who [does so] in serious matters shall do penance for ten years.

2. If any woman puts her daughter upon a roof or into an oven for the cure of a fever, she shall do penance for seven years.

3. He who causes grains to be burned where a man has died, for the health of the living and of the house, shall do penance for five years.

4. If a woman performs diabolical incantations or divinations, she shall do penance for one year or the three forty-day periods, or forty days, according to the nature of the offense. Of this matter it is said in the canon: He who celebrates auguries, omens from birds,[100] or dreams,[101] or any divinations according to the custom of the heathen, or introduces such people into his houses, in seeking out any trick of the magicians—when these become penitents, if they belong to the clergy they shall be cast out; but if they are secular persons they shall do penance for five years.[102]

5. In the case of one who eats food that has been sacrificed and later confesses, the priest ought to consider the person, of what age he was and in what way he had been brought up or how it came about. So also the sacerdotal authority shall be modified in the case of a sick person. And this matter is to be observed with all diligence in all penance always and rigorously in confession, in so far as God condescends to aid.

---

[98] Reading "quia" for "quo," with manuscript support.
[99] "per consilium."
[100] "auspicia."
[101] "somnia."
[102] Cf. can. 24 of the synod of Ancyra. The language here bears a close resemblance to the Latin version of the Canons of Ancyra by Isidorus Mercator, in which this canon is number 23. See Mansi, II, 534.

BOOK TWO

I. Of the Ministry of a Church, or of Its Rebuilding

1. A church may be placed in another place if it is necessary, and it ought not to be sanctified, except that the priest ought to sprinkle it with [holy] water, and in the place of the altar[103] a cross ought to be set.

2. It is acknowledged that two masses may be celebrated in one day on every altar; and he who does not communicate shall not approach the bread[104] nor the kiss [of peace][105] in the Mass; and he who eats beforehand is not admitted to this kiss.

3. The lumber[106] of a church ought not to be applied to any other work except for another church or for burning with fire or for the benefit of the brethren in a monastery or to bake bread for them; and such things ought not to pass into lay operations.

4. In a church in which the bodies of dead unbelievers are buried, an altar may not be sanctified; but if it seems suitable for consecration, when the bodies have been removed and the woodwork of it has been scraped or washed, it[107] shall be reërected.

5. But if it was previously consecrated, masses may be celebrated in it if religious men are buried there; but if there is a pagan [buried there], it is better to cleanse it and cast [the corpse] out.

6. We ought not to make steps in front of the altar.

7. The relics of saints are to be venerated.

8. If it can be done, a candle should burn near them[108] every night; but if the poverty of the place prevents this, it does them no harm.[109]

_ 9. The incense of the Lord is to be burned on the natal days of saints out of reverence for the day, since they, as lilies, shed an odor of sweetness and asperge the Church of God as a church is asperged with incense, beginning at the altar.

10. A layman ought not to read a lection in a church nor sing the Alleluia, but only the psalms and responses without the Alleluia.

11. As often as they wish, those who dwell in houses may sprinkle

---

[103] Meaning, of course: "in the place where the altar formerly stood."
[104] Reading "panem" for "pacem," with manuscript support.
[105] See above, pp. 81, 152.   [106] "ligna," wood, boards.
[107] Apparently, the altar.   [108] "ibi" (there).
[109] "non nocet eis." The reference may be either to the saints or to the relics.

them with holy water; and when thou dost consecrate water thou shalt first offer a prayer.

II. Of the Three Principal Orders of the Church

1. A bishop may confirm in a field it it is necessary.

2. Likewise a presbyter may celebrate masses in a field if a deacon or the presbyter himself holds in his hands the chalice and the oblation.

3. A bishop ought not to compel an abbot to go to a synod unless there is also some sound reason.

4. A bishop determines cases of poor men up to fifty solidi; but the king, if [the amount in litigation] is above that sum.

5. A bishop or an abbot may keep a criminal as a slave if he [the criminal] has not the means of redeeming himself.

6. A bishop may absolve from a vow if he will.

7. Only a presbyter may celebrate masses and bless the people on Good Friday and sanctify a cross.

8. A presbyter is not obliged to give tithes.

9. A presbyter must not reveal the sin of a bishop, since he is set over him.

10. The host is not to be received from the hand of a priest who cannot recite the prayers or the lections according to the ritual.

11. If a presbyter sings the responses in the Mass, or anything [else], he shall not remove his cope; moreover, he lays it on his shoulders even when he is reading the Gospel.

12. In the case of a presbyter who is a fornicator, if before he was found out he baptized, those whom he baptized shall be baptized a second time.

13. If any ordained presbyter perceives that he was not baptized, he shall be baptized and ordained again, and all whom he baptized previously shall be baptized.

14. Among the Greeks, deacons do not break the holy bread; neither do they say the collect or the "Dominus vobiscum"[110] or the compline.[111]

---

[110] "The Lord be with you." Said before the prayer following the Gospel, in the *Ordo Romanus primus*, 8th century. See E.G.C.F. Atchley, *Ordo Romanus primus*, p. 133.

[111] "completas." The "completa" was usually called the "completorium." Cf. the Rule of St. Benedict, chaps. xvi, xvii, xviii, xlii, and the article "Complies," in Cabrol, *Dictionnaire*.

15. A deacon may not give penance to a layman, but a bishop or a presbyter ought to give it.

16. Deacons can baptize, and they can bless food and drink; they cannot give the bread. Likewise monks or clerics can bless food.

III. Of the Ordination of Various Persons

1. In the ordination of a bishop the mass ought to be sung by the ordaining bishop himself.

2. In the ordination of a presbyter or of a deacon, the bishop ought to celebrate masses as the Greeks are accustomed to do at the election of an abbot or an abbess.

3. In the ordination of a monk, indeed, the abbot ought to perform the mass and complete three prayers over his head; and for seven days he shall veil his head with his cowl, and on the seventh day the abbot shall remove the veil as in baptism the presbyter is accustomed to take away the veil of the infants; so also ought the abbot to do to the monk, since according to the judgment of the fathers it is a second baptism in which, as in baptism, all sins are taken away.

4. A presbyter may consecrate an abbess with the celebration of the mass.

5. In the ordination of an abbot, indeed, the bishop ought to perform the mass and bless him as he bows his head,[112] with two or three witnesses from among his brethren, and give him the staff and shoes.

6. Nuns, moreover, and churches ought always to be consecrated with a mass.

7. The Greeks bless[113] a widow and a virgin together[114] and choose either[115] as an abbess. The Romans, however, do not veil a widow with a virgin.

8. According to the Greeks a presbyter may consecrate a virgin with the sacred veil, reconcile a penitent, and make the oil for exorcism and the chrism of the sick if it is necessary. But according to the Romans these functions appertain to bishops alone.

IV. Of Baptism and Confirmation

1. In baptism sins are remitted; [but] not loose behavior with women,[116] since the children who were born before the baptism of

---

[112] Or "with bowed head" ("inclinato capite"). [113] That is, "consecrate."
[114] "simul." [115] Literally, "both" ("utramque").
[116] "conjunctiones mulierum."

the parents are in such cases in the same status as those born after their baptism.[117]

2. If indeed she who was married before [her] baptism is not regarded as a wife, it follows that the children who were previously begotten can neither be held to be [true] children nor be called brothers among themselves or sharers of the inheritance.

3. If any pagan gives alms and keeps abstinence and [does] other good works which we cannot enumerate, does he not lose these in baptism? No, for he shall not lose any good, but he shall wash away the evil. This Pope Innocent asserted, taking for example what was done concerning the catechumen Cornelius.[118]

4. Gregory Nazianzen declares that the second baptism is that of tears.

5. We believe no one is complete in baptism without the confirmation of a bishop; yet we do not despair.

6. Chrism was established in the Nicene synod.

7. It is not a breach of order[119] if the chrismal napkin[120] is laid again upon another who is baptized.

8. One person may, if it is necessary, be [god]father to a cathechumen both in baptism and in confirmation; however, it is not customary, but [usually] separate persons act as godparents[121] in each [office].

9. No one may act as a godparent who is not baptized or confirmed.

10. However, a man may act as godparent for a woman in baptism, likewise also a woman may act as godparent for a man.

11. Baptized persons may not eat[122] with catechumens, nor give them the kiss;[123] how much more [must this regulation be observed] in the case of pagans.

V. Of the Mass for the Dead

1. According to the Roman Church the custom is to carry dead

---

[117] This is a necessarily somewhat arbitrary expansion of a clause too elliptical to be rendered with certainty: "quia filii, qui ante baptismum, sic et post eorum fiunt." The following canon indicates that ordinarily children born to baptized parents enjoyed advantages over those whose parents were unbaptized. The point in this canon seems to be that children born out of wedlock suffer equal disabilities whether the parents are baptized or not when the children are born.   [118] Acts 10:1, 47.   [119] "absurdum."

[120] "pannus crismatis."   [121] "suscipiunt," undertake the obligations.

[122] "manducare." Possibly this means "to partake of communion," for which catechumens were ineligible.

[123] That is, "the kiss of peace." Cf. p. 199, n. 105, and p. 81, n. 46, above.

monks or religious men to the church, to anoint their breasts with the chrism, there to celebrate masses for them and then with chanting to carry them to their graves. When they have been placed in the tomb a prayer is offered for them; then they are covered with earth or stone.

2. On the first, the third, the ninth, and also on the thirtieth day a mass is celebrated for them, and, if they wished it, [a mass] is observed a year later.

3. A mass is celebrated for a dead monk on the day of his burial and on the third day; afterward as often as the abbot decides.

4. It is the custom also for masses to be celebrated for monks each week, and for their names to be recited.

5. Three masses in a year [are sung] for dead seculars, on the third, the ninth, and the thirtieth day, since the Lord rose from the dead on the third day and in the ninth hour "he yielded up the ghost,"[124] and the children of Israel bewailed Moses for thirty days.[125]

6. For a good layman there is to be a mass on the third day; for a penitent on the thirtieth day, or on the seventh, after the fast; since his neighbors ought to fast seven days and to make an offering at the altar, as in Jesus Ben Sirach we read: "And the children of Israel fasted for Saul";[126] afterward, as often as the priest decides.

7. Many say that it is not permissible to celebrate masses for infants of less than seven years; but it is permitted, nevertheless.

8. Dionysius the Areopagite[127] says that he who offers masses for a bad man commits blasphemy against God.

9. Augustine says that masses are to be performed for all Christians, since it either profits them or consoles those who offer or those who seek [to have it done].

10. A presbyter or a deacon who is not permitted to, or who will not, take communion, may not celebrate masses.

VI. Of Abbots and Monks, or of the Monastery

1. Out of humility and with the permission of the bishop an abbot may relinquish his office. But the brethren shall elect an abbot for

---

[124] Matt. 27:50.   [125] Deut. 34:8.   [126] II Kings 1:12.
[127] The unknown fifth-century writer pseudonymously so-called. It is unlikely that he was, as argued by J. Stiglmayr, Severus of Antioch. Bardy, G., "Autour de Denys l'Aréopagite," *Recherches de science religieuse*, XXI (1931), 201–4.

themselves from among their own number, if they have [a suitable man]; if not, from among outsiders.

2. And the bishop shall not keep an abbot in his office by violence.

3. The congregation ought to elect an abbot after the abbot's death, or while he is alive if he has gone away or sinned.

4. He himself cannot appoint anyone from among his own monks,[128] nor from those without, nor can he give [the office] to another abbot without the decision of the brethren.

5. If, indeed, the abbot has sinned, the bishop cannot take away the property of the monastery, albeit the abbot has sinned; but he shall send him to another monastery, into the power of another abbot.

6. Neither an abbot nor a bishop may transfer the land of a church to another [church] although both are under his authority. If he wishes to change the land of a church, he shall do it with the consent of both [parties].

7. If anyone wishes to set his monastery in another place, he shall do it on the advice of the bishop and of his brethren, and he shall release a presbyter for the ministry of the church in the former place.

8. It is not permissible[129] for men to have monastic women, nor women, men; nevertheless, we shall not overthrow that which is the custom in this region.[130]

9. A monk may not take a vow without the consent of his abbot; if he lacks this, the vow is to be annulled.[131]

10. If an abbot has a monk worthy of the episcopate, he ought to grant this, if it is necessary.

11. A boy may not marry when he has already set before him the vow of a monk.

12. Any monk whom a congregation has chosen to be ordained to the rank of presbyter for them, ought not to give up his former habit of life.

---

[128] "propinquis," possibly "relatives."

[129] Vindob. 2223 has "Among the Greeks it is not customary."

[130] Vindob. 2223 has "custom of this province." The reference appears to be to the numerous double monasteries, such as the famous houses of St. Hilda, Hartlepool, and Whitby, which existed in England. Theodore does not approve but does not propose to suppress them. On this subject see Mary Bateson, "The Origin and Early History of the Double Monasteries," *Royal Historical Society, Transactions*, New Series XIII (1899), 137 ff.; L. Gougaud, *Christianity in Celtic Lands*, pp. 84 ff.

[131] Literally, "broken."

13. But if he is afterwards found to be either proud or disobedient or vicious, and [if] in a better rank [he] seeks a worse life, he shall be deposed and put in the lowest place, or [he shall] make amends with satisfaction.

14. The reception of infirm persons into a monastery is within the authority and liberty of the monastery.

15. Washing the feet of laymen[132] is also within the liberty of a monastery. Except on the Lord's day, it is not obligatory.

16. It is also a liberty[133] of the monastery to adjudge penance to laymen for this is properly a function of the clergy.

VII. Of the Rite of the Women, or Their Ministry in the Church

1. It is permissible for the women, that is, the handmaidens of Christ, to read the lections and to perform the ministries which appertain to the confession of the sacred altar, except those which are the special functions of priests and deacons.
[In a minority of manuscripts this canon reads]:
Woman shall not cover the altar with the corporal[134] nor place on the altar the offerings, nor the cup, nor stand among ordained men in the church, nor sit at a feast among priests.

2. According to the canons it is the function of the bishops and priests to prescribe penance.[135]
[For this canon a number of manuscripts have the following:]
No woman may adjudge penance for anyone, since in the canon no one may [do this] except the priests alone.

3. Women may receive the host under a black veil, as Basil decided.

4. According to the Greeks a woman can make offerings,[136] but not according to the Romans.

---

[132] The "pedilavium," or ceremonial foot washing, usually accompanied baptism in the Celtic Church. The Stowe Missal contains the rubric: "Tunc lavantur pedes eius accepto linteo," *Bradshaw Society Publications*, XXXII (1915), 32. It was also a Gallican, but not a Roman custom. Cf. F. E. Warren, *The Liturgy and Ritual of the Celtic Church*, p. 217. On the development of the rite in England, see H. G. Feasy, *The Ancient English Holy Week Ceremonial*, pp. 107 ff.

[133] "libertas," in the sense that it is not an obligation.

[134] An altar-cloth. See Cabrol, *Dictionnaire*, s.v. "corporal."

[135] The words "ipsum licitum est" are here omitted as not pertinent.

[136] "facere oblationes."

VIII. Of the Customs of the Greeks and of the Romans

1. On the Lord's day the Greeks and the Romans sail and ride; they do not make bread, nor proceed in a carriage, except only to church, nor bathe themselves.

2. The Greeks do not write publicly on the Lord's Day; in the case of special necessity, nevertheless, they write at home.

3. The Greeks and the Romans give clothing to their slaves, and they work, except on the Lord's Day.[137]

4. Greek monks do not have slaves; Roman monks have them.[138]

5. On the day before the Lord's nativity, at the ninth hour, when mass is ended, that is, the vigil of the Lord, the Romans eat; but the Greeks take supper [only] when vespers and mass have been said.

6. In case of plague,[139] both the Greeks and the Romans say that the sick ought to be visited, as [are] other sick persons, as the Lord commands.[140]

7. The Greeks do not give carrion flesh to swine but allow the skins and leather [of carrion] to be taken for shoes, and the wool and horns may be taken [but] not for any sacred [use].

8. The washing of the head is permitted on the Lord's Day, and it is permitted to wash the feet in a solution of lye;[141] but this washing of the feet is not a custom of the Romans.

IX. Of the Communion of the Irish and Britons Who Are Not Catholic in Respect to Easter and the Tonsure[142]

1. Those who have been ordained by Irish or British bishops who are not Catholic with respect to Easter and the tonsure are not united to the Church, but [they] shall be confirmed again by a Catholic bishop with imposition of hands.

2. Likewise also the churches that have been consecrated by these

---

[137] "sine dominico die"; perhaps "without a Sunday rest."

[138] The ownership of slaves by the monks of St. Benedict in the early period has been indicated by John Chapman, *St. Benedict and the Sixth Century*, chap. IX.

[139] "de peste mortalitatis."   [140] Matt. 25:36, 43.

[141] "lexiva," properly "lixivia," with the variant "liusiva" (French "lessive"), water in which ashes were boiled to form a cleansing mixture. See these forms in Du Cange and Forcellini. The *Statuta* of Boniface, 23 (p. 398, below) repeats this canon with "liusiva."

[142] On the controversy between the Roman and the Celtic churches over the Easter and tonsure questions see especially L. Gougaud, *Christianity in Celtic Lands*, pp. 185 ff.; W. Bright, *Chapters in Early English Church History*, pp. 26 ff., 224 ff.; A. Plummer, *Churches in Britain before A.D. 1000*, I, 114 ff.; Bede, *Historia ecclesiastica*, III, 25, 26; and documents given in Haddan and Stubbs, vol. III.

bishops are to be sprinkled with holy[143] water and confirmed by some collect.

3. Further, we have not the liberty to give them, when they request it, the chrism or the eucharist, unless they have previously confessed their willingness to be with us in the unity of the Church. And likewise a person from among these nations,[144] or anyone who doubts his own baptism, shall be baptized.

X. Of Those Who Are Vexed by the Devil

1. If a man is vexed by the devil and can do nothing but run about everywhere, and [if he] slays himself, there may be some reason to pray for him if he was formerly religious.

2. If it was on account of despair, or of some fear, or for unknown reasons, we ought to leave to God the decision of this matter, and we dare not pray for him.

3. In the case of one who of his own will slays himself, masses may not be said for him; but we may only pray and dispense alms.

4. If any Christian goes insane[145] through a sudden seizure, or as a result of insanity slays himself—there are some who celebrate masses for such an one.

5. One who is possessed of a demon[146] may have stones[147] and herbs, without [the use of] incantation.

XI. Of the Use or Rejection of Animals

1. Animals which are torn by wolves or dogs are not to be eaten, nor a stag nor a goat if found dead, unless perchance they were previously killed[148] by a man, but they are to be given to swine and dogs.

2. Birds and other animals that are strangled in nets are not to be eaten by men; nor if they are found dead after being attacked by a hawk, since it is commanded in the fourth [sic] chapter of the Acts of the Apostles to abstain from fornication, from blood, from that which is strangled, and from idolatry.[149]

---

[143] Literally, "exorcized."   [144] Literally, "of the nation of these."
[145] "mente sua exciderit."   [146] "Demonium sustinenti."
[147] The "gagates," or jet, was used as a charm in cases of insanity. See L. Thorndike, *A History of Magic and Experimental Science*, I, 495, 724, 779. J. Evans, *Magical Jewels of the Middle Ages and the Renaissance*, pp. 146, 153, refers to the use of the diamond and the topaz for this purpose.   [148] Literally, "previously killed when alive" ("viva").
[149] Acts 15:29.

3. Fish, however, may be eaten, since they are of another nature.

4. They do not forbid horse [flesh], nevertheless it is not the custom to eat it.

5. The hare may be eaten, and it is good for dysentery; and its gall is to be mixed with pepper for [the relief of] pain.[150]

6. If bees kill a man, they ought also to be killed quickly, but the honey may be eaten.

7. If by chance swine eat carrion flesh or the blood of a man, we hold that they are not to be thrown away; nor are hens; hence swine that [only] taste the blood of a man are to be eaten.

8. But as for those which tear and eat the corpses of the dead, their flesh may not be eaten until they become feeble and until a year has elapsed.

9. Animals that are polluted by intercourse with men shall be killed, and their flesh thrown to dogs, but their offspring shall be for use, and their hides shall be taken. However, when there is uncertainty, they shall not be killed.

XII. Of Matters Relating to Marriage

1. Those who are married shall abstain from intercourse for three nights before they communicate.

2. A man shall abstain from his wife for forty days before Easter, until the week of Easter. On this account the Apostle says: "That ye may give yourselves to prayer."[151]

3. When she has conceived a woman ought to obstain from her husband for three months before the birth, and afterward in the time of purgation, that is, for forty days and nights, whether she has borne a male or a female child.

4. It is also fully[152] permitted to a woman to communicate before she is to bear a child.

5. If the wife of anyone commits fornication, he may put her away and take another; that is, if a man puts away his wife on account of fornication, if she was his first, he is permitted to take another; but if she wishes to do penance for her sins, she may take another husband after five years.

6. A woman may not put away her husband, even if he is a forni-

[150] For the use in medieval medicine of various parts of the hare see O. Cockayne, *Leechdom, Wortcunning and Starcraft of Early England*, I, 343 ff.

[151] I Cor. 7:5.   [152] "per omnia."

cator, unless, perchance, for [the purpose of his entering] a monastery.
Basil so decided.

7. A legal marriage may not be broken without the consent of
both parties.

8. But either, according to the Greeks, may give the other permission to join a monastery for the service of God, and [as it were]
marry it, if he [or she] was in a first marriage; yet this is not canonical.
But if such is not the case, [but they are] in a second marriage,
this is not permitted while the husband or wife is alive.

9. If a husband makes himself a slave through theft or fornication
or any sin, the wife, if she has not been married before, has the right
to take another husband after a year. This is not permitted to one
who has been twice married.[153]

10. When his wife is dead, a man may take another wife after a
month. If her husband is dead, the woman may take another husband
after a year.

11. If a woman is an adulteress and her husband does not wish to
live with her, if she decides to enter a monastery she shall retain the
fourth part of her inheritance. If she decides otherwise, she shall have
nothing.

12. Any woman who commits adultery is in the power of her husband if he wishes to be reconciled to an adulterous woman. If he
makes a reconciliation, her punishment does not concern the clergy,[154]
it belongs to her own husband.

13. In the case of a man and a woman who are married, if he
wishes to serve God[155] and she does not, or if she wishes to do so and
he does not, or if either of them is broken in health, they may still be
completely separated with the consent of both.

14. A woman who vows not to take another husband after her
husband's death and when he is dead, false to her word,[156] takes
another and is married a second time, when she is moved by penitence
and wishes to fulfill her vow, it is in the power of her husband [to
determine] whether she shall fulfill it or not.

15. Therefore, to one woman who after eleven years confessed
[such] a vow, Theodore gave permission to cohabit with the man.[157]

[153] "digamo." We should expect the feminine form "digamae."
[154] "in clero non proficit."   [155] That is, to enter a monastery.
[156] "prevaricatrix."
[157] "nubere cum illo viro." Especially in view of the connection with the previous
canon, this can hardly mean "to marry . . . "

16. And if anyone in a secular habit takes a vow without the consent of the bishop, the bishop himself has power to change the decision if he wishes.

17. A legal marriage may take place equally in the day and in the night, as it is written, "Thine is the day and thine is the night."[158]

18. If a pagan puts away his pagan wife, after baptism it shall be in his power to have her or not to have her.

19. In the same way, if one of them is baptized, the other a pagan, as saith the Apostle, "If the unbeliever depart, let him depart";[159] therefore, if the wife of any man is an unbeliever and a pagan and cannot be converted, she shall be put away.

20. If a woman leaves her husband, despising him, and is unwilling to return and be reconciled to her husband, after five years, with the bishop's consent, he shall be permitted to take another wife.

21. If she has been taken into captivity by force and cannot be redeemed, [he may] take another after a year.

22. Again, if she has been taken into captivity her husband shall wait five years; so also shall the woman do if such things have happened to the man.

23. If, therefore, a man has taken another wife, he shall receive the former wife when she returns from captivity and put away the later one; so also shall she do, as we have said above, if such things have happened to her husband.

24. If an enemy carries away any man's wife, and he cannot get her again, he may take another. To do this is better than acts of fornication.

25. If after this the former wife comes again to him, she ought not to be received by him, if he has another, but she may take to herself another husband, if she has had [only] one before. The same ruling stands in the case of slaves from over sea.

26. According to the Greeks it is permitted to marry in the third degree of consanguinity, as it is written in the Law; according to the Romans, in the fifth degree; however, in the fourth[160] degree they do not dissolve [a marriage] after it has taken place. Hence they are to be united in the fifth degree; in the fourth, if they are found [already married] they are not to be separated; in the third, they are to be separated.

[158] Ps. 73:16.   [159] I Cor. 7:15.
[160] Reading "quarta" for "tertia" with manuscript support, and in accord with the context.

27. Nevertheless, it is not permitted to take the wife of another after his death [if he was related] in the third degree.

28. On the same conditions a man is joined in matrimony to those who are related to him, and to his wife's relatives after her death.

29. Two brothers may also have two sisters in marriage, and a father and a son [respectively] a mother and her daughter.

30. A husband who sleeps with his wife shall wash himself before he goes into a church.

31. A husband ought not to see his wife nude.

32. If anyone has illicit connection or illicit marriage, it is nevertheless permissible to eat the food which they have, for the prophet has said: "The earth is the Lord's and the fullness thereof."[161]

33. If a man and a woman have united in marriage, and afterward the woman says of the man that he is impotent, if anyone can prove that this is true, she may take another [husband].

34. Parents may not give a betrothed girl to another man unless she flatly refuses [to marry the original suitor]; but she may go to a monastery if she wishes.

35. But if she who is betrothed refuses to live with the man to whom she is betrothed, the money which he gave for her shall be paid back to him, and a third part shall be added; if, however, it is he that refuses, he shall lose the money which he gave for her.

36. But a girl of seventeen[162] years has the power of her own body.

37. Until he is fifteen years old a boy shall be in the power of his father, then he can make himself a monk; but a girl of sixteen or seventeen years who was before in the power of her parents [can become a nun]. After that age a father may not bestow his daughter in marriage against her will.

XIII. Of Male and Female Slaves

1. If he is compelled by necessity, a father has the power to sell[163] his son of seven years of age into slavery; after that, he has not the right to sell him without his consent.

2. A person of fourteen [years] can make himself a slave.

3. A man may not take away from his slave money which he has acquired by his labor.

4. If the master of a male and a female slave joins them in marriage

---

[161] Ps. 23:1.
[162] Manuscripts have also "xvi," "xiv," and "tredecim." Finsterwalder reads "xiv."
[163] "tradere."

and the male slave or the female slave is afterward set free, and if the one who is in slavery cannot be redeemed, the one who has been set free may marry a free born person.

5. If any freeman takes a female slave in marriage, he has not the right to put her away if they were formerly united with the consent of both.

6. If anyone acquires [as a slave] a free woman who is pregnant, the child that is born of her is free.

7. If anyone sets free a pregnant slave woman, the child which she brings forth shall be [in a state] of slavery.

XIV. Of Various Matters

1. There are three legitimate fasts in a year for the people; the forty [days] before Easter, when we pay the tithes of the year, and the forty [days] before the Lord's nativity and the forty days and nights after Pentecost.[164]

2. He who fasts for a dead person aids himself. But to God alone belongs knowledge of the dead person.

3. Laymen ought not to be dilatory with respect to their promises, since death does not delay.

4. On no account may the servant of God fight. Let [the matter] be for consultation by many servants of God.

5. One infant may be given to God at a monastery instead of another, even if [the father] has vowed the other; nevertheless it is better to fulfill the vow.

6. Similarly, cattle of equal value may be substituted if it is necessary.

7. If a king holds the territory of another king, he may give it for [the good of] his soul.

8.[165] If anyone converted from the world to the service of God has any royal specie received from a king, that [specie] is in the power of that king; but if it is from a former king, [now] dead, that which he received shall be as his other goods; it is permissible to give it to God with himself.

9. That which is found on a road may be taken away. If the owner is found, it shall be restored to him.

---

[164] These are the "three forty-day periods" ("quadragesimae") so frequently referred to in this and some other penitentials. See above, pp. 96, 103, 160.

[165] Can. 8 is found only in Codex Vindob. 2223.

10. Let the tribute of the church be according to the custom of the province; that is, so that the poor may not so greatly(?)[166] suffer violence on this account in tithes or in any matters.

11. It is not lawful to give tithes except to the poor and to pilgrims, or for laymen [to give] to their own churches.

12. Out of reverence for the new birth,[167] prayer is to be made in white [garments] at Pentecost as prayer is made in the fifty days.[168]

13. Prayer may be [made] under a veil if necessity requires it.

14. The sick may take food and drink at all hours when they desire it or when they are able [to take it] if they cannot [do so] at the proper times.

EPILOGUE[169]

Our [authors], as we said, have written these [canons] in consultation with the venerable Theodore, archbishop of the English. If some[170] suppose they have in their possession in more satisfactory or better form these two rules,[171] we hope they will well use[172] their own [versions] and not neglect[173] ours, in which the parts which seem corrupted[174] are attributed by all to the fault of both scribes and interpreters—pretty barbarous men[175]—so that by some, even [by] those instructed by him, the defective and incorrect passages are rightly said not to be his decisions. Of these, although they are retained by many here and there and in a confused state, in succeeding books we have been able with the aid of Christ the Lord to set in order impartially according to our ability not a few of the chief things out of them. But being still in doubt about this work, we connect with

[166] "tantum."   [167] "regenerationis"—the visitation of the Holy Spirit at Pentecost.
[168] The period between Easter and Pentecost. See above, p. 175.
[169] The epilogue has come down in only two manuscripts, and neither one includes both the beginning and the end. The text is unusually obscure. Finsterwalder, who has brought to light the second of these manuscripts, Vat. Pal. Lat. 554, attempts a translation of most of the section, *op. cit.*, pp. 148 f.; this has been criticized with useful suggestions by W. Levison, *Zeitschr. der Savigny-Stiftung, kan. Abt.*, XIX (1930), 702 f. The suggested reconstruction and interpretation of that part of the epilogue known to them by Haddan and Stubbs (III, 204, n. a. Cf. p. 214, n. 179, below) have also been utilized for the present translation.   [170] Reading "qui" for "quis" with Levison, *op. cit.*, p. 702.
[171] Probably, as Levison suggests, the two books of the penitential.
[172] Finsterwalder emends "uti in deum" to "utendum," Levison to "utantur."
[173] Reading "careant." The manuscript has "carpeant" which may perhaps be taken either in the sense of "select" or "make excerpts from." Possibly "carpeant" has arisen from (1) the change of "r" to the very similar "p," (2) the insertion above "p" of an "r," as a correction for "p," and (3) the incorporation of this "r" in the text with the retention of the erroneous "p."   [174] Reading "corrupta" for "incorrupta."
[175] "vitio utique scriptorum interpretumque viri nimirum barbarum." We should probably read "virorum" and understand "barbarum" as genitive plural.

it passages in certain minor works that are necessary to it, especially in the booklet[176] on penance, which I think can be easily perceived by a discerning person.

It therefore remains further in vindication of our father Theodore to make satisfaction as best we can to you, beloved,[177] who,[178] not finding a full exposition in the utterances of other Catholics, have therefore had recourse to him. In all these matters I, not undeservedly, entreat you, beloved, who have been judging the difficulties of these [inquirers] that on this account you defend me by your merits on the right hand and on the left, while I strive on your behalf in the welter of these [difficulties], Christ being the judge of the contest, against the threatening[179] blows of calumniators. It is easier for these [calumniators] to defame the laborers than to sweat in the zeal of labor; for some of our people have given themselves[180] to abuse the wisest men of the Church of God by the volubility of their tongues. I refer to St. Jerome whom they call an evil speaker to men, to Augustine whom they call loquacious, and to Isidore whom they call an arranger of glosses. I say nothing of the others, when they say that Gregory, our Apostle, easily uttered what others had earlier expounded, a follower in the beaten[181] paths of other men. From this source I have recently heard (what I shudder to tell) that a certain gross[182] follower of heathen fables is abusing[183] the promulgator of the Law of God and chronicler of the whole history of creation,[184] saying, "What could Moses himself, the magician,[185] either know or say to him?"

What, then, can my defense be, since I, in comparison with those whom I have mentioned, am nothing. Yet, "by the grace of God, I am what I am;"[186] may it not have been void in me through him who is able to create all things of nothing and to bring to pass great things from little. On this account, if any Catholic author finds any-

[176] "libellus." Cf. "libellus scottorum" in the Preface.
[177] Literally, "to your love."
[178] Emending "quorum" to "qui" with Haddan and Stubbs.
[179] From this point the text is supplied only by Codex Vat. Pal. Lat. 554, published by Finsterwalder.
[180] Emending "dedicerunt" to "se dederunt."
[181] Reading with Levison "tritis" for "tristis."   [182] "ventricosum."
[183] Changing "sugilla" to "sugillare," with Levison.
[184] Literally, "Writer of the whole work (creation?) of the world."
[185] Reading at Levison's suggestion "magicus" for "maritus." Levison cites Pliny and Apuleius on Moses as a magician. Finsterwalder does not attempt a rendering of this obscure clause.   [186] I Cor. 15:10.

thing anywhere in these canons that he is able to amend, he shall have permission from us to do this reasonably, in view of the fact that[187] unless the parts that are not to be followed are suppressed, when they are held of equal validity they occasion contention to those to whom it is said: "not in contention and envy; But put ye on the Lord Jesus Christ."[188]

2. CANONS ATTRIBUTED TO THEODORE (*ca.* 668–690)

[THE FOLLOWING fifteen canons are culled by Haddan and Stubbs[1] from early documents in which they are found with a mass of other material attributed to Theodore. The principle of selection is that of avoiding materials which duplicate canons of the genuine penitential.[2] On the question of the ascription of these canons to Theodore the editors assert a "presumption against their genuineness." "If they are older than the genuine Penitential, they must have been rejected by the compiler of it; if they are of later date, they are wanting in the authority which alone could compel their reception."[3]

On the manuscripts and editions the reader may see Wasserschleben, *Bussordnungen*, pp. 13–28, Schmitz II, pp. 510–23, and Finsterwalder, *op. cit.*, pp. 11–21. Wasserschleben and Schmitz favor the view that the *Capitula Dacheriana*, from which the majority of these canons are taken, are earlier than the penitential itself, and they apply in this connection the statement of "Discipulus Umbrensium" about the existence of "a conflicting and confused digest" of Theodore's rules.[4] Finsterwalder, too, regards the *Dacheriana* as one of the sources used by "Discipulus Umbrensium" but holds that the collection took shape in the northwestern part of the Frankish Empire, in the region of Corbie, in the early ninth century. The somewhat later *Canones Gregorii*, from which Canon 15 of this selection is derived, he would ascribe to approximately the same area. Two additional canons selected by Haddan and Stubbs from *Pseudo-Cummean* and *Valicellanum* II, respectively, are here omitted. The numbers in brackets with canons 1–14 are those of Finsterwalder's edition of the *Iudicia Theodori*, *op. cit.*, pp. 239 ff.]

1[35]. A free man ought to marry a free woman.

2[55]. According to the Greeks it is acknowledged that two masses may be offered on one altar; according to the Romans, five, on account of the five crosses which the bishop sets up when they are

---

[187] "quasi."   [188] Rom. 13:13–14.   [1] III, 209–12.
[2] "The following are all which are wanting in the genuine work, not being known to belong to other authors, or which vary from it in any material point not already noticed among the various readings of the Penitential, or to be referred, as in some cases of variation in numerical figures, to the mistakes of copyists." *Ibid.*, p. 210.   [3] *Ibid.*
[4] See p. 182, above, and Wasserschleben, *op. cit.*, p. 21, and cf. Schmitz I, p. 516.

consecrated. And he who is proved to have eaten[5] before is not admitted to the kiss.[6]

3[56]. A husband shall keep himself from his wife for forty days before Easter and in the first week after Easter and after Pentecost, for one week.

4[57]. Children brought up in a monastery shall eat flesh for fourteen years.[7]

5[59]. Dead pagans shall be cast out from the places of saints.

6[71]. The abbot is not permitted to give his monastery into the power of another, neither after his death nor while he is alive, neither to an associate nor to a stranger, without the will of the monks; but they themselves shall elect an abbot for themselves. If a prior dies or goes away, the same regulation applies.

7[88]. He who commits murder or theft and fails to make composition with those whom he has injured, when he has confessed his sins to a bishop or a presbyter, ought either to render to them his property or to make composition; if indeed he has not the substance with which to make composition or does not know whom he has injured, his penance is to be the more increased.

8[98]. No[8] dead persons shall be buried in a sanctified church. If indeed the dead have been buried in one that has not yet been sanctified, it shall not be sanctified.[9]

9[99]. If it has been moved from there to another place, even the boards shall be washed;[10] for any church that has been removed to another place shall be sanctified again. [100] However, if it was restored in[11] the same place, it shall be sprinkled with holy water,[12]

10. [The canon given as No. 10 by Haddan and Stubbs stands in the midst of a disconnected passage supplied by Finsterwalder, *op. cit.*, p. 247, note r, the original of which is difficult to reconstruct. Substantially the phrases are found in the *Penitential of Theodore*, II, xiii, 4 and II, xii, 20-23.]

11[132]. A man shall not take communion with an adulterous

---

[5] "to have eaten" omitted in Finsterwalder.

[6] The "kiss of peace." See above, pp. 81, 152, 199.

[7] That is, until they reach the age of fourteen.

[8] Reading with Wasserschleben "nulli" where Finsterwalder has "alii."

[9] Cf. *Poenit. Theod.* II, i, 4, where the "dead" are "unbelievers" and it is the altar that is sanctified (p. 199).

[10] Reading with Wasserschleben "laventur." Finsterwalder has "labentur."

[11] Reading with Codex Paris. Bibl. Nat. Lat. 12021 "in" for "non."

[12] This is contrary to *Poenit. Theod.* II, i, 1. cf. p. 199.

woman; so also a wife shall not enter into the peace of com
with an adulterous husband.

12[144]. He who eats unclean meats and vegetables which are
cooked with [these] meats ought to desist from his ministry.

13[149]. A bishop, a presbyter, or a deacon ought to confess his sin.

14[161]. One ought to pray standing, out of reverence for God.

15[*Canones Gregorii*, 30]. If any cleric comes to a sick pagan, it is
best that he be baptized in the name of the Trinity with water that
has been signed with the cross.

3. SELECTIONS FROM THE PENITENTIAL TENTA-
TIVELY ASCRIBED BY ALBERS TO BEDE

(*Possibly early 8th century, with later additions*)

[THE existence of a tradition that the Venerable Bede was the author
of a penitential finds evidence in the work of Regino of Prüm (d. 915),
who, at the close of a long list of inquiries which he admonishes bishops
to make with regard to the religious conditions in the parishes, places
this requirement: "If he [the priest] have a Roman penitential, either
the one put forth by Bishop Theodore or that by the Venerable Bede,
so that according to what is there written he may either question the
confessant or when he has confessed lay upon him the measure of penance."[1] A number of closely related penitential documents bear the name
of Bede, and Wasserschleben has held that one of them is probably
genuine.[2] C. Plummer states a number of reasons for rejecting Bede's
authorship of this document.[3] Egbert's Penitential, he points out, does
not mention Bede's; nor does Bede anywhere refer to Theodore's Penitential—an indication that he was not interested in such literature.
Plummer, who thinks the penitential literature base and debasing to its
readers, therein utterly failing to appreciate its social function, regards
Bede as too high-minded a saint to be the author of a work parts of
which deal with indecent matters. With all admiration for Bede, it seems
gratuitous to assume that he was of other clay than the saintly authors
of the earlier penitentials. Schmitz, too, is strongly opposed to the theory
of Bede's authorship of any penitential. In his first volume he calls the
work given by Wasserschleben "a confused and worthless compilation,"
and regards it as unworthy of Bede's mind.[4] Writing on the work ascribed to Egbert, he explains the ascription of penitentials to Theodore,

[1] *De synodalibus causis et disciplinis ecclesiasticis*, II, 1, 96. F. G. A. Wasserschleben's
edition, p. 26.

[2] *Bussordnungen*, pp. 37 ff. Text, pp. 220–30. This is the document printed by Martène
and Durand, *Amplissima collectio*, VII, 37 f., from the now lost Andage codex from the
monastery of St. Hubert at Andage in the Ardennes.

[3] *Venerabilis Bedae opera*, I, clvi ff.   [4] Schmitz I, p. 555.

Bede, and Egbert on the ground that they made certain utterances on the administration of penance, which were afterward collected under their names.[5] In his later volume he rejects Bede's, as well as Egbert's, authorship of the penitential which is ascribed to them jointly, the work called by Wasserschleben *Pseudo-Beda* and by Schmitz the *Double Penitential of Bede-Egbert*.[6] Schmitz regards these materials as the work of an Iro-Scottish monk of the late ninth century.

In 1901 Dom Bruno Albers published from a codex which he discovered in the library of the Barberini, Rome (Codex Vat. Barb. Lat. XI, 120, now 477), a penitential text bearing the name of Bede,[7] in which "Gregory the Younger" is referred to as the contemporary pope. Certain decisions somewhat abbreviated from the canons of the Lateran council held in 721[8] are quoted at the close of the document and are introduced with the words: "from a decretal of Gregory the Younger who now[9] rules the Roman Catholic Mother Church." Gregory the Younger is thus identified with Gregory II, whose pontificate was from 715 to 731. Bede died in 735. The penitential is immediately followed in the codex by Bede's *De natura temporum*. Albers combats Schmitz's view that Bede can have written no penitential, but his ascription of this one to Bede is tentative only. He insists, however, that the date of the original of the Bede-Egbert penitential materials is pushed back by this discovery from Schmitz's date, the late ninth century, one hundred and fifty years to the time of Bede's productivity and of Egbert's early activity. He further defends the integrity of the document, despite its apparent disarrangement, and discounts the argument that it is unworthy of so great a man as Bede.

As research proceeds, the Albers document is likely to prove a valuable link in the chain of the penitential literature. At present, however, its significance is not clear. The argument of Albers is weakened by the following considerations:

1. The paragraph invoked to indicate an early date is preceded by a paragraph ascribed to "Saint Boniface the Archbishop." Even if "sanctus" is not technical, we have to remember that Boniface of Crediton did not become archbishop until 732 or receive the See of Mainz until 742. This passage must, therefore, be later than the time of Gregory II. Its contents are so unlike what we should expect from the rigid disci-

---

[5] "Theodor, Beda und Egbert haben keine Bussbücher geschrieben. Dagegen hat Theodor und wahrscheinlich auch Beda und Egbert Weisthümer über die Verwaltung des Busswesens gegeben. Diese Weisthümer sind in späterer Zeit zusammengestellt und als Bussbücher unter den Namen dieser hervorragenden Männer verbreitet worden in England und im fränkischen Reiche." *Op. cit.*, p. 572.

[6] Schmitz II, pp. 644 ff., 675 ff. Text, Wasserschleben, pp. 248–57; Schmitz II, pp. 679–701.

[7] "Wann sind die Beda-Egbertschen Bussbücher verfasst worden, und wer ist ihr Verfasser?" *A.K.K.R.*, LXXXI (1901), 393–420. Text, pp. 399–418.

[8] Compare this series in Mansi, *Concilia*, XII, 263 f.

[9] "nuc" for "nunc," but without the abbreviation stroke.

plinarian to whom it is attributed, that it is probably of considerably later origin. We may rightly hesitate, therefore, to take the statement about Gregory, which follows an excerpt from Isidore, as of a piece with the original document.

2. Albers has failed to observe the fact that the document published by Martène and Durand[10] from a Fleury codex and reprinted by Wasserschleben with the title *Poenitentiale Martenianum*[11] contains (C. xxx) the passage on Gregory the Younger. The same eight canons are there given with the same introductory sentence. Only slight variations of text occur. For "papae Gregorii iunioris qui nuc romanam catholicam regit matrem ecclesiam," the *Martenianum* has "papae Gregorii minoris qui nunc Romanam catholicam gerit matrem ecclesiam." The *Martenianum* is not a true penitential but an assemblage of quoted opinions and decisions on the principles of penance which form a sort of general instruction on the subject. Wasserschleben, not knowing the present document, regarded the passage in the *Martenianum* as quoted from another collection and noted its author's utilization of the work of Egbert.[12] Its compiler may have derived the passage from our document or from another collection not identifiable. The appearance of this passage in two documents not precisely dated raises the question whether we have yet discovered its first use.[13] It assuredly does not date the *Martenianum*;[14] does it then determine the date of the Albers *Bede*, or has the compiler of the latter also derived it from another collection?

If we are forced to abandon Albers's argument concerning the date of this work, there still appears no reason to deny the possibility of its early date or even of Bede's authorship of the major part of it. Its close resemblance to the work reputed to be Egbert's and to the *Double Penitential*, may in fact be probably best accounted for by assuming it to be Bede's. If we consider the close personal relations between Bede and Egbert we need not be averse to the supposition that after Bede's death Egbert utilized penitential materials left by him and gave circulation to them, making such alterations as he chose, in a document which came to be regarded as his own. Bede visited Egbert in 733, about the time of the inception of the latter's work as archbishop. It is not absurd to conjecture that they conferred over the practical aspects of penance with some such roughly-drawn document before them as our present penitential.

---

[10] *Thesaurus novus anecdotorum*, IV, 31.   [11] *Bussordnungen*, pp. 282–300.

[12] *Bussordnungen*, p. 48.

[13] For a full treatment of the objections to Albers's view see W. von Hörmann, "Bussbücherstudien," in *Zeitschrift der Savigny-Stiftung für Rechtsgeschichte, kan. Abt.*, II, 145 ff. This is one of a series of four studies in this journal, comprising I (1911), 195–250; II (1912), 111–81; III (1913), 413–92; IV (1914), 358–485, the last of which gives a fully annotated edition of the *Martenianum*.

[14] Hörmann, *op. cit.*, I, 198; II, 158 ff., assigns to the *Martenianum* a date in the early ninth century, earlier than that of the *Pseudo-Roman Penitential* (*ca.* 830). Fournier et Le Bras (I, 90) date it 802–13.

Oakley calls this document *Pseudo-Bede* I and contrasts it with *Pseudo-Bede* II (that is, the *Pseudo-Beda* of Wasserschleben and Schmitz's *Double Penitential*). He argues that the two works are of separate authorship;[15] but after examining their differences he seems to modify this judgment when he states the probability "that Penitential I formed the model of Penitential II either directly or through an intermediary."[16] The *Double Penitential* contains in fact, most of the text of the Albers document, though with some omissions, extensive additions, and differences in the order of treatment.

The fact that no penitential is included by Bede among the works he lists at the end of his *Ecclesiastical History* (731) as of the years 702–31 can hardly be admitted as a conclusive argument against his having written one, in view of the omission from this list of a number of his other known works. The strongest objection to his authorship of this book is the lack of distinction and originality in the work itself. But the author may have intended a revision, which he did not live to make. Probably too, we should not expect to find the marks of genius in a penitential. The nature of these handbooks excludes sublimity. The most that can be said on this point is that we should hardly have expected the greatest writer of his age to write one of the inferior books of the penitential series.

It has not previously been pointed out that the list of manuals mentioned in this penitential as necessary "arma" for every priest may have a bearing on the question of authorship. These are: psalter, lectionary, antiphonary, missal, baptismal, martyrology, and "computus," to which list the author would add a penitential.[17] It may be noted that Bede himself tells us that he was the author of "Chapters of Readings" (*Capitula lectionum*) on the New Testament, which may be the "lectionary," of a martyrology and of a larger and a smaller work on chronology (*De temporibus*).[18] The first chapter of the larger of these chronological works (*De temporum ratione*) in the Giles edition is entitled *De computo vel loquela digitorum*.[19] But a work which seems to be more in the class of a "computus" is given by Migne as a genuine work of Bede under the title "De ratione computi."[20] It is a dialogue on astronomical calculation. However, even if we are to suppose that the penitential contains intentional references to Bede's works, the additional probability of his authorship from this consideration would be slight. The fact would probably point, however, to a Northumbrian origin.

According to Albers the Codex Barberinianus 477 (formerly XI, 120) has been written by sections at three periods, in the early tenth, the eleventh, and the ninth centuries, and the penitential is in the tenth-century hand. The text is corrupt, but the variants indicated by Albers from the Codex Vat. Pal. Lat. 294 text of the *Double Penitential* supply

[15] *English Penitential Discipline*, p. 127.   [16] *Op. cit.*, p. 129.

[17] Albers, *op. cit.*, p. 400. Cf. the presumably later lists referred to below, pp. 390 f.

[18] *Hist. Eccl.* V, xxiv. Plummer, *op. cit.*, I, 358. See also J. A. Giles, *Miscellaneous Works of Venerable Bede*, VI, vii.   [19] Giles, *op. cit.*, VI, 141–44.   [20] *P.L.*, XC, 579–600.

most of the needed emendations. These are mentioned in the footnotes only when they are widely divergent from the Codex Barberinianus. For further clarification reference has in some cases been made to the Schmitz text of that document and to the Haddan and Stubbs edition of the *Penitential of Egbert*.[21] Many of the decisions contained in this penitential are derived from documents translated above, and much of this unoriginal material has been omitted in the translation. The introductory paragraphs and extensive selections comprising the major part of the body of the work are included. The sections omitted are briefly described in the notes in square brackets. For convenience the titles of sections are here numbered.]

A Work of the Venerable Bede, Presbyter

These few things which follow concerning the remedies of sins we have extracted from[22] the works[23] of our predecessors, in which we used[24] not the authority of a censor but rather the counsel of a fellow sufferer; seriously urging every learned priest of Christ that in everything which he finds here he shall carefully distinguish the sex, the age, the condition, the status, even the very heart of the penitent and shall judge accordingly each [offense] one by one as seems best to him. For [proper penance consists], for some people, in abstaining from foods; for others, in giving alms; for some, in frequent bending of the knees in prayer or in standing in cross-vigil[25] or in doing something else of this sort which belongs to the purgation of sins. By many, all of these things are to be done. It is necessary to correct the faults, all of which must be weighed in the examination of a discriminating judge.

That holy ordinance[26] which was made in the days of our fathers never departed from right ways; they established the remedies of salvation for those who repent of and bewail their passions and vices, since a diversity of offenses occasions a diversity of remedies for penitents, just as [27] the physicians of bodies pursue diverse remedies or are accustomed to make potions against the diversity of sicknesses, or [as do] the judges of secular cases. Therefore, those who are good and just weigh and set forth diverse decisions, even as they judge rightly between the poor and the rich, between one case and another.

[21] III, 413–31.
[22] Reading "ex" for "LXX" as in Vat. Pal. Lat. 294, Schmitz II, p. 654.
[23] "monumentis."   [24] Reading "usi" for "visi," as in Schmitz II, p. 654.
[25] "in cruce"—with arms extended in form of a cross. See above, pp. 32 f., 144.
[26] "institutio."   [27] Emending "vel adsecuntur" to "velut secuntur."

How much more, therefore, O priests of God, is it proper to weigh and set forth for men the diverse remedies of their invisible souls lest through a foolish physician the wounds of souls grow worse, as saith the prophet: "My sores are putrified and corrupted because of my foolishness."[28] O foolish physician, do not deceive thine own soul and his lest thou receive a double, nay a sevenfold or a thousandfold, penalty. Hear Christ when he saith: "If the blind lead the blind, both fall into the pit."[29] If thou dost not consider my judgment, another man neither hears nor sees, who will judge me.[30] O, dost thou not understand that God, the just and powerful Judge, sees and hears, and He both brings into the open the hidden things and requites according to works. And moreover there are indeed some who come to the priesthood like blind dogs running or ravens flying to the carcasses of the dead, not for the sake of the Lord, but rather for the sake of men, panting for earthly honor,[31] blind to divine wisdom. Of such Gregory Nazianzen says: "This I fear,[32] that dogs should give themselves to the pastoral office, especially when they have made no preparation of pastoral discipline in themselves." For Ezekiel saith: "Woe to the shepherds of Israel who fed themselves and not the flock, drank their milk and clothed themselves with their wool, ate that which was fat, and bound not up that which was broken," and so forth.[33] Moreover, Ezekiel saith: "Woe to the priests who eat the sins of my people,"[34] that is, taking their sacrifices to themselves and not praying for them, eating their offerings and not correcting them; who when they hear of men who are about to die, rejoice therein and make themselves ready for the prey as ravens for the carcasses of the dead.

Now, therefore, O brethren, he who would receive the priestly authority shall first consider it on God's behalf and provide his equipment[35] before the hand of the bishop touches his head; that is, a psalter, a lectionary, an antiphonary, a missal, a baptismal,[36] a martyrology for the cycle of the year for preaching with good works,

---

[28] Ps. 37:6.   [29] Matt. 15:14.

[30] A reference to the blind man who is led by a blind man, in the previous quotation.

[31] Reading "propter homines et honorem terrenum" for "propter hominibus et honorem terre, nam," with Schmitz II, p. 662.

[32] Reading "timeo" for "times" with Schmitz II, p. 662.

[33] Based on Ezek. 34:2-4.   [34] Cf. Ezek. 44:29.   [35] "arma."

[36] "baptisterium." See Du Cange, and article "Baptismale" in Cabrol, *Dictionnaire*.

and [a book of] computation with the cycle.[37] This is the law of priests; but afterwards he who is ordained in this order according to the authority of the canons [shall provide] his own penitential, so that thou mayest, first of all examine the distinctions of all cases, without which just judgment cannot stand; for it is written: "In nothing shalt thou appear inconsiderate; but distinguish what thou oughtest to do and where, for how long, when, and how to do it."

For not all are to be weighed[38] in one and the same balance, although they be associated in one fault, but there shall be discrimination for each of these, that is: between rich and poor; freeman, slave; little child, boy, youth, young man, old man; stupid,[39] intelligent;[40] layman, cleric, monk; bishop, presbyter, deacon, subdeacon, reader, ordained or unordained; married or unmarried; pilgrim, virgin, canoness, or nuns; the weak, the sick, the well. He shall make a distinction for the character of the sins or of the men: a continent person or one who is incontinent willfully or by accident; [whether the sin is committed] in public or in secret; with what degree of compunction he [the culprit] makes amends by necessity or by intention; the places and times [of offenses]. The holy Apostles established this ordinance of the Conference; then the holy fathers and St. Pinufius;[41] then the canons of the holy fathers; then [authorities] one after another, for example, Jerome, Augustine, Gregory, and Theodore, from all of whose sayings and judgments we have truthfully arranged these, in order that men may be whole and not weaklings, since "the strong strongly endure torments."[42] Further in Jesus Ben Sirach: "In judging be merciful to the fatherless as a father, and as a husband to their mother."[43] Moreover, St. James saith: "Judgment without mercy

---

[37] "compotum (accurately: computum) cum ciclo." The "computus" or "computum" was a method, here, as frequently, a manual, of computation, by which the fasts and feasts of the year were determined. See *Catholic Encyclopedia*, article "Dominical Letter," V, 109, and p. 220, above.

[38] Reading "non omnibus . . . pensandum" for "non omnibus . . . pensanda," with Schmitz II, p. 662.

[39] Reading "hebes" for "ebitis," as in the Andage manuscript, Haddan and Stubbs, III, 417.

[40] Reading "gnarus" for "ignarus" as in Haddan and Stubbs, III, 417.

[41] Cassian, *Collationes*, XX (Conference of Abbot Pinufius).

[42] Wisd. 6:7. Douay Version has "the mighty are mightily tormented." But the context would suggest that "quia potentes potenter tormenta patiuntur" is quoted in the literal sense given above, rather than in the traditional later interpretation represented by the Douay Version. Cf. p. 151, above.   [43] Ecclus. 4:10.

shall be to him that doeth not mercy. Mercy exalteth itself above judgment";[44] that he himself follow after the same thing even as St. Benedict; that is, they who do penance truly in fasting, in weeping, in alms, in prayers, also do not again the deeds they have committed, and if they do them, they nevertheless do not persevere in these things. For[45] God hath said: "Thou hast thought evil, I have forgiven it; thou hast spoken evil, I have forgiven it; thou hast done evil, I have forgiven it; persistence in evil I forgive not." Therefore, forgive not those who persist in evil, but apply a strict judgment according to the canons that others may be afraid.

I. Of Fornications and Penances for Them

[The section which follows here is made up largely of extracts from Theodore, Finnian, Gildas, and the British synods. Only canons 37–39 on baptism, with which the section closes, are here translated.]

37. A parent whose child dies unbaptized because of negligence, one year, and never without some penance.

38. If a priest whose duty it is [to baptize], has been called and [if he] neglects to come, he shall himself be punished for the damnation of a soul according to the judgment of his bishop.

39. But also it is permitted to all the faithful when they chance to find unbaptized persons about to die, nay it is commanded, that they snatch souls from the devil by baptism, that is, [that they shall] with water simply blessed in the name of the Lord baptize these persons in the name of the Father and of the Son and of the Holy Spirit, plunging them in the water or pouring it over them. Hence the faithful who can do it, especially monks, ought both to have a knowledge of baptizing and, if they are going anywhere at a distance, always to have the eucharist with them.

II. Of Slaughter[46]

1. He who slays a monk or a cleric shall lay aside his weapons and serve God or do penance for seven years.

2. He who slays[47] a layman with malice aforethought or for the possession of his inheritance, four years.

---

[44] James 2:13.
[45] Reading "quia" for "qui" as in Haddan and Stubbs, III, 418.
[46] "De occisione." The heading is supplied from Schmitz II, p. 657.
[47] This word is omitted but to be understood in canons 2 to 7.

3. He who slays to avenge a brother, one year and in the two following years the three forty-day periods and the appointed days.[48]

4. He who slays through sudden anger and a quarrel, three years.

5. He who slays by accident, one year.

6. He who slays in public warfare, forty days.

7. He who slays at the command of his master, if he is a slave, forty days: he who, being a freeman, at the command of his superior slays an innocent person, one year and for the two [years] following, the three forty-day periods and the appointed days.

8. He who by a wound in a quarrel renders a man weak or maimed shall pay for the physician and the fine for the scar,[49] and make compensation for his work while he is recovering, and do penance for half a year. If indeed he has not the means, he shall make good these things in an entire year [of penance].

9. He who rises up to strike a man, intending to kill him, shall do penance for three weeks; if he is a cleric, three months.

10.[50] But if he has wounded him, forty days; if he is a cleric, a whole year; but he shall also pay to the person injured, according to the severity of the wound; even if the law does not require it, he shall pay him whom he has injured, lest the injured cause scandal.

11. A mother who kills her child before the fortieth day[51] shall do penance for one year. If it is after the child has become alive, [she shall do penance] as a murderess. But it makes a great difference whether a poor woman[52] does it on account of the difficulty of supporting [the child] or a harlot for the sake of concealing her wickedness.

III. Of Taking Oaths[53]

1. He who knowingly commits perjury, because compelled by his master, the three forty-day periods and the appointed days.

2. He who, knowing the nature of an oath and of perjury, swears falsely on the hand of a bishop or of a presbyter, or on an altar, or on

---

[48] "legitimas ferias." That is, Wednesdays and Fridays, days of fasting in the Celtic and Anglo-Saxon churches. F. E. Warren, *Liturgy and Ritual of the Celtic Church*, pp. 55, 146; J. Bingham, *Antiquities of the Christian Church*, Bk. XXI, chap. iii (ed. of 1870), II 1193 ff.; K. Holl, *Gesammelte Aufsätze*, II; *Der Osten*, pp. 192 ff.

[49] "macule precium." Cf. p. 107, n. 56, above.

[50] The number is omitted in the Albers text.

[51] Cod. Vat. Pal. Lat. 294 inserts here "in utero" (in the womb).

[52] "pauper": Cod. Vat. Pal. Lat. 294 has "paupercula." Schmitz II, p. 657.

[53] "de iuramento," supplied from Schmitz II, p. 657. Cf. Albers, p. 409.

a consecrated cross shall do penance for three years. If on a cross that has not been consecrated, one year. But if on the hand of a layman, among the Greeks there is no offense.

3.[54] He who without knowing it[55] is induced to commit perjury on behalf of a criminal and who afterward finds out his perjury, one year.

[The next Section (IV) containing six canons is without heading. It deals with unclean foods and corresponds closely to Chapter V of the *Pseudo-Bede* in Schmitz II, pp. 658–59, and to Chapter XXII of the *Double Penitential, ibid.*, p. 693, and consists largely of materials from the *Penitential of Theodore*, I, vii, 7–12. See above, pp. 190 f. Then the compiler seems to make a new beginning by a paragraph on the capital sins.]

V. Of the Capital Sins[56]

1. Now therefore I shall explain the capital offenses according to the canons. First pride, envy, fornication, vainglory, anger of long standing, worldly sadness,[57] avarice, gluttony; and Augustine adds sacrilege, that is, the theft of sacred things (and this is a very great theft) or else a serving of things offered to idols, that is, for auspices and so forth; then adultery, false witness, theft, robbery, continual drunkenness, idolatry, effeminacy, sodomy, evil speaking, perjury. These are capital offenses as St. Paul and Augustine and other saints have reckoned them. For these, liberal alms are to be given and protracted fasting is to be kept; that is, as some judge for the capital [offenses], namely, adulteries, murders, perjuries, acts of fornication, and the like: laymen, three years; clerics, five years; subdeacons, six years; deacons, seven years; presbyters, ten years; bishops, twelve years. If it was habitual: bishops, fourteen years; presbyters, twelve years; deacons, ten years; subdeacons, nine years; clerics, seven years; laymen, five.

[No number 2 is given.]

3. If a monk commits fornication with a handmaiden of God, he shall do penance for seven [years].

[54] Number omitted.

[55] Reading "seductus est nesciens ut periuraret" for "sedutit nescium periurare," with Schmitz II, p. 658.

[56] The text has: "Capitula I. De Capitalia" (!) The Bodleian manuscript of Egbert has "Quae sint capitalia crimina." Haddan and Stubbs III, 418.

[57] II Cor. 7:10. Douay Version has "sorrow of the world."

4. If with a [secular] girl, three years.

5. Of parricides and fratricides some [say] seven [years]; some, fourteen and seven added to these.

VI. Of Greed and Other Vices

1. Moreover, he that is greedy, or covetous, or drunken, or proud, or envious, or grasping, or is long angry,[58] or abusive, or has like faults,[59] which it would be tedious to enumerate shall do penance for three years.

[2–11 are short canons reiterating commonplaces on fornication, adultery, and homicide].

12. Those who sacrifice to demons in great matters, if it is habitual, shall do penance for ten years; in small matters, one year.

13. Auguries and divinations, five years.

14. Those who conjure up storms[60] shall do penance for seven years.

15. Let penance always be observed in this wise, from one year, and thereafter (whatever the nature of the sin), three days each week without wine and mead and without flesh; and he shall fast until vespers and eat of dry food; and always in the three forty-day periods he shall eat of dry food; and he shall fast three days until nones and three days until vespers. And on Sundays, on four days at the Lord's Nativity, in Epiphany, from Easter until Whitsunday, at the Lord's Ascension, at Pentecost, at the festivals of St. Michael and of St. Mary and of St. John the Baptist, and of the Twelve Apostles and of a saint who is [celebrated] in that province—on the aforesaid days he shall partake of the feast[61] as do his companions.

[The one remaining canon of this section, numbered 17 in the Albers text, is a warning against intemperance.]

---

[58] Literally, "or long anger."   [59] Literally, "or things like these."

[60] "emissores tempestatum." Schmitz has an illuminating note on this expression in his text of *Poenit. Valicellanum* I, can. 85. Weather makers, especially those who claimed to produce hail and storms, are condemned in numerous church councils from the Trullan council, 692, to the synod of Paris, 829, Schmitz I, p. 308. Cf. also G. Jecker, *Die Heimat des hl. Pirmin, des Apostels der Alamannen*, pp. 54–56, 139 ff. That crusader against superstition, Agobard of Lyons (d. 840), wrote a tract against belief in this weather magic. Migne, *P.L.*, CIV, 147 ff. Cf. J. A. MacCulloch, *Medieval Faith and Fable*, p. 20. Grimm, *Teutonic Mythology*, IV, 1769, quotes Hartlieb's *Book of All Forbidden Arts*, 1455: "To make hail and sudden shower is one of these arts, for he that will meddle therewith must not only give himself to the devil, but deny God . . . "

[61] "faciat caritatem." See Du Cange, *s.v.* "caritas."

VII

[The following canon is the first of a section without title containing twenty-two canons, chiefly on the sex offenses of monks and clergy.]

1. In the canon of the Apostles the judgment is given that a bishop, a presbyter, [or] a deacon who is taken in fornication or perjury or theft shall be deposed, yet not deprived of communion, for God does not punish twice at the same time.

VIII. Of Taking Oaths

1. Whoever makes oath falsely in a church or on the Gospel or on relics of the saints, seven years; some judge ten years.

2. If on the hand of a bishop or of a presbyter or of a deacon, or if on a consecrated cross, he shall do penance for one year; others judge three years or seven; and on a cross that has not been consecrated, one year, or as some say, four months.[62]

3. But he who is unwittingly led to it and afterward recognizes it,[63] shall do penance for one year or for four forty-day periods or for forty days.

4. If anyone is compelled [to perjure himself] by any reason of necessity, the three forty-day periods; some [say] three years—one of these on bread and water as others judge.

5. Perjurers shall do penance for three years.

6. He who suspects that he is being led into false swearing and nevertheless swears[64] by agreement shall do penance for two years. If anyone swears on the hand of a layman, among the Greeks there is no offense.

[A section (IX), entitled "De machina mulierum" (of the devices of women), on offenses in marriage and magical arts practiced by women is here omitted.]

X. Of Auguries or Divinations[65]

1. He who observes auguries or the oracles which are falsely called

---

[62] Cf. III, 2, p. 226, above.
[63] Supplying "cognoscit" from Cod. Vat. Pal. Lat. 294.
[64] Reading "iurat" for "iuvat."
[65] "Divinationes" supplied from the Penitential of Egbert, VIII, Haddan and Stubbs, III, 424. The text has "Of Auguries or . . . "

"sortes sanctorum,"[66] or divinations, or utters things to come by looking at some sort of writings, or takes a vow on a tree or on anything, except at a church, if clerics or laymen do this they shall be excommunicated from the Church; or else, a cleric shall do penance for three years, laymen two, or one and one-half.[67]

2. If a woman places her child upon a roof or in an oven in order to cure a fever, she shall do penance for five years.

3 and 4.[68] Do not employ adroit jugglers[69] and chanting diviners when the moon is eclipsed, since by sacrilegious custom they trust they can protect themselves by their outcries and magical arts, even [by] the attaching of diabolical amulets whether of grass or of amber to their people or to themselves; nor celebrate Thursday in honor of Jupiter or the Kalends of January according to pagan tradition.[70] Offenders, if clerics, shall do penance for five years; laymen, for three or five years.

[Sections XI and XII, entitled "De minutis peccatis" (Of Minor Sins) and "De furtu" (of Theft), are here omitted.]

XIII. Of Drunkenness

[Canons 1–9 resemble *Poenit. Theod.* I. i.]

[66] The *Sortes sanctorum* were collections of Scripture passages used for divination after the manner of the *Sortes Virgilianae*—that is, the book was opened and the first passage on which the eye alighted was taken as a divine oracle. Augustine in his answer to the questions of Januarius (Ep. LV, cap. xx., Migne, *P.L.*, XXXIII, 222) condemns those "qui de paginis evangelicis sortes legunt." A capitulary of Charlemagne (789) prohibits the practice with reference to the Psalter and the Gospels. A collection entitled *Sortes apostolorum*, used for this purpose, contained nonscriptural material. It closes with the words: "These are the *Sortes sanctorum* which never err nor deceive; that is, ask God and thou shalt obtain what thou desirest. Give thanks to Him." Citation of many pronouncements of the Church against this and other forms of divination will be found in Vacant et Mangenot, *Dict. de théol. cath.* IV, 1441 f., art. "Divination." See also Jecker, *op. cit.*, pp. 54 ff.; 131–54; W. Smith and S. Cheetham, *Dict. of Christian Antiquities*, II (1920), art. "Sortilegium," and the articles on "Divination" in the *Dictionary of Religion and Ethics*, IV, 788 ff., and in the *Catholic Encyclopedia*, V, 48 ff.

[67] The text of this canon is corrupt. The translation has been aided by reference to Codex Vat. Pal. Lat. 294 and Schmitz II, pp. 694 f.

[68] The syntax of these two canons, which in Albers's transcription grammatically belong together, is somewhat obscure. It may be that the attaching of amulets, and so forth, is not intended to be ascribed to the jugglers and diviners, but to the credulous people.

[69] Reading "caragios curiosos" for "caraios cocriocos." "Caraios" is properly "caragios"or "caragos." In Cod. Vat. Pal. Lat. 294 the word is given in Greek characters, "καραγος," and the *Thesaurus linguae Latinae*, *s.v.* "caragius" regards it as probably of Greek origin. Cf. *Coll. can. Hib.* lxiv, 1, "karagios," and 2, "caragiis"; Wasserschleben, *Die irische Kanonensammlung*, pp. 230 f. Cf. also above p. 69. The form "karagios" is used in the *Scarapsus* of St. Pirmin, chap. 22. Jecker, *op. cit.*, p. 54. A "caragius" is a prestidigitator or worker of illusions, a juggler. For the reading "curiosos" see Du Cange, *s.v.* "caragus." On behavior during eclipses see p. 420, n. 17, below.   [70] "causam."

10. Those who are drunk against the command of the Lord,[71] if they have the vow of holiness—this is drunkenness, when it changes the state of the mind, and [when] the tongue babbles and the eyes are wild and there is dizziness and distention of the stomach and pain follows—shall do penance [as follows:] a cleric for seven days; a monk, fourteen; a deacon, three weeks; a presbyter, four [weeks]; a bishop, five [weeks]; laymen, three days, without wine and flesh.

XIV. Of the Eucharist

1. If anyone loses the Eucharist on account of negligence, he shall do penance for one year or the three forty-day periods or forty days.

2. If on account of negligence the host falls on the ground, [the offender] shall sing fifty psalms.

3. He who neglects the host so that there are worms in it or it has not its color and taste shall do penance for twenty or thirty or forty days, and it shall be burned in the fire [and] the ashes of it hidden beneath the altar. If it falls to the ground, he shall do penance for one day.

4. If a drop [from the chalice] falls upon the altar, he shall do penance for three days. If on account of carelessness a mouse eats [the host], thirty or forty [days].

5. He who has lost a small portion of it in the church and [who] does not find it shall do penance for twenty days or sing seventy psalms every day.

6. But he who loses his chrismal[72] in the parish and does not find it shall do penance for forty days; or he shall do penance for the three forty-day periods.

7. He who spills the chalice at the end of the service[73] shall do penance for thirty days.

XV. Of Various Cases

1. He who loses a consecrated object,[74] that is, incense, thuribles, tablets, or a sheet for writing, or salt that has been blessed, bread newly consecrated, or anything of this sort shall do penance for seven days.

---

[71] Luke 21:34.   [72] Cf. p. 114, n. 83.
[73] "solempnitatis," the celebration of the Mass.
[74] "creaturam." Cf. p. 97, n. 48.

[2–8 treat of various offenses connected with the use of unclean foods, and of theft.]

9. If anyone stains his hand with any liquid food with his hand not clean[75] he shall be corrected by one hundred palm thumpings.[76]

11.[77] Moreover, it is well for him who is able to fulfill that which is written in the penitential, but he who is not able, let us give [him] counsel according to the mercy of God. First, for one day on bread and water he shall sing fifty psalms kneeling, or without kneeling, seventy; he shall sing them within the church or in a single place in sequence; and two hundred genuflexions are the equivalent of a day, or one denarius is the equivalent of one day,[78] and three gifts of alms to three poor men are the equivalent of a day. Some say that fifty strokes or fifty psalms are the equivalent of a day, that is, in winter; in autumn and spring, one hundred strokes or a hundred psalms; in summer, one hundred and fifty psalms or strokes. Moreover, for one month he who ought to do penance on water and bread [shall sing] one thousand two hundred psalms kneeling, or without kneeling, one thousand six hundred and eighty, and every day thereafter he shall dine at sext, except that he shall fast until nones on Wednesday and Friday; he shall abstain from flesh and wine [but] take other food after singing.

In the second year the remission of sins will be from the day of the Lord's Nativity until Epiphany and [on] those days aforesaid, which have been noted above,[79] which are not occupied with penance.

He who is not able to do penance in the way we have stated above shall expend for one year twenty-six solidi for alms and shall fast one day each week until nones, and another until vespers, and the three forty-day periods. In the second year, twenty solidi; for the third year, eighteen; this comes to sixty-four solidi.

For criminal offenses powerful men shall do as saith Zacchaeus: "Lord, the half of all my goods I give to the poor; if I have taken anything unjustly, I restore him fourfold";[80] and he shall set free [some] of his slaves and redeem freemen and captives, and from the

---

[75] "et non idonea manu."

[76] "palmatis." In an interesting discussion of "palmata" Du Cange concludes that it probably refers to the beating of the palms of the hands on a hard floor. See above, p. 33.

[77] This canon closely resembles passages found in the *Penitential of Egbert*, in the *Pseudo-Cummean*, and in Regino. See below, pp. 238, 268, 319 f. The Vatican codex Regin. 567, IX–X century, contains an elaborate version of the same provisions.

[78] Following the punctuation in Schmitz II, p. 699.

[79] See above, VI, can. 15.   [80] Based on Luke 19:8.

day in which he ceases to sin he shall be restored to communion.[81] As saith the Apostle: "He who sins through the body shall make amends through the body,"[82] that is, in fastings and vigils and prayers to the Lord. He who is converted after having done all manner of evil, such as bloodshed, theft, fornication, lying, [false] swearing, and all wickedness and who afterward purposes to serve God unto the end, shall do penance for three or for two years or as the priest shall determine. However, he[83] shall himself take thought concerning the medicine of souls, how he may be able to save his own soul and those of others, by instructing, by teaching sound doctrine,[84] since "he that ministers well purchases for himself a good degree"[85] in the presence of Him "who is over all things, God blessed forever."[86] Amen.

XVI. Saint Boniface, the Archbishop, Published This:[87]

How we are able[88] to perform a penance of seven years in one year: A three-day period for thirty days and nights; the singing of the psalms, one hundred and twenty psalters for twelve months, [and] for one day, fifty psalms and five paternosters. One psalter and fifteen paternosters for three days. For one day the *Beati immaculati*[89] four times and seven times "Have mercy on me, O God"[90] and five paternosters, and prostrating himself on the ground seventy times with sighing[91] he shall say the paternoster; and thus shall he do for one day.[92] If he prefers not to sing psalms yet is willing to do penance,[93] he shall frequently prostrate himself in the oratory and say

[81] Literally "shall not cease to communicate."

[82] Not in the New Testament. Cf. Mansi's remark that this is "not in the letters of St. Paul, nor yet that common saying: Through that by which one sins shall he also be punished."—*Concilia*, XII, 498.   [83] That is, the priest.

[84] "sermonem."   [85] I Tim. 3:13.   [86] Rom. 9:5.

[87] The following passage appears in various manuscripts erroneously ascribed to Boniface of Crediton, the Apostle of Germany, d. 755. Labbé published it in his Concilia (1671), VII, 1478, and the text is copied in Migne, *P.L.*, LXXXIX, 887 f. It is substantially contained in the *Penitential of Egbert*, where it forms chapter xvi and is entitled "De dictis sancti Bonifacii archiepiscopi." It occurs again in *Pseudo-Bede*, XVI, and with slight alterations in Regino's *De synodalibus causis et de disciplinis ecclesiasticis*, Book II, chap. ccccxlvi, as "Ex dictis sancti Bonifacii episcopi."

[88] Reading, "possumus" for "possum," with the *Penitential of Egbert*, Haddan and Stubbs, III, 431.   [89] Ps. 118; that is, Ps. 119 in the A.V.   [90] Ps. 50:3.

[91] "in ieccione," properly "iniectione" as in the *Penitential of Egbert*, Haddan and Stubbs, III, 431. Du Cange gives the equivalents "suspirium," "gemitus" (sighing or groaning).

[92] Reading "pro uno die" as in Schmitz II, p. 699, for "pro diebus unum."

[93] Reading "tamen vult penitere" for "et non vult patire" with the Bodleian manuscript (718) of Egbert. Haddan and Stubbs, III, 431.

one hundred times "Have mercy on me, O God"[94] and "Forgive my sins";[95] this shall he do for one day. He who is willing to confess his sins ought to confess[96] with tears, since tears do not ask pardon but deserve it; he shall ask a presbyter to sing mass for him—unless his offenses are capital; [such offenses] he ought previously to wash away with tears. The singing of one mass is enough to make redemption for twelve days; ten masses, for four months; twenty masses, for eight months; thirty masses, for twelve months—if the confessors so determine,[97] with tears. Thanks be to God. Amen.

For a week, three hundred psalms in sequence while kneeling in a church or in one place. Whoever really does not know one psalm and is not able to fast shall reckon the amount [of food] he takes and give a moiety of it in alms.

[The remaining paragraphs consist of certain *Dicta Isidori*, or sayings of St. Isidore of Seville, on consanguinity in marriage, (*Etymologiae*, IX, 28, 29. *Migne*, *P.L.* LXXXII, 560–67) and eight of the seventeen canons of the synod of the Lateran, 721, as indicated in the introduction to this document, p. 218, above. These anathematize those who violate the rule of clerical celibacy. The document closes with a note by the author on the separation of those married within the prohibited degrees.]

4. SELECTIONS FROM ANOTHER PENITENTIAL ASCRIBED TO BEDE

[THE FOLLOWING extracts from the *Penitential of Bede*, given by Wasserschleben,[1] are the principal sections of that document not contained in the Albers text together with some passages resembling the latter though showing considerable variation. Wasserschleben used an eighth-ninth century Vienna manuscript, Nationalbibl. 2223 (olim jur. can. 116), with variants from the Andage manuscript printed in part by Martène and Durand.[2] This text is reprinted with an introductory note by Haddan and Stubbs.[3] The document has a weaker claim to Bede's authorship than the one published by Albers.[4]]

---

[94] Ps. 50:3.   [95] Ps. 24:18.

[96] "ought to confess" supplied from the Bodleian manuscript (718) of Egbert. Haddan and Stubbs, III, 431.

[97] Or, reading with the Bodleian manuscript "confiteri" for "confessores," "if they are willing to confess with tears."

[1] *Bussordnungen*, pp. 220–30.   [2] *Thesaurus novus anecdotorum*, VII, 37 ff.

[3] *Op. cit.*, III, 326–34. Schmitz has edited it from Codex Vat. Pal. Lat. 294, but the text ends with the section on Unclean Flesh—Chap. v, according to his number. Schmitz II, pp. 654–59.   [4] See Oakley's discussion, *English Penitential Discipline*, pp. 117 ff.

V. Of Taking Oaths[5]

5. He who has spoken evil of his brother with anger shall be reconciled to the brother of whom he has spoken evil and do penance for seven days.

6. He who traduces on account of envy or abets a traducer shall do penance for four days. But if [it is done] to his superior, he shall do penance for seven days.

7. He who has hushed up a misdeed of his brother which is a mortal sin and does not rebuke him according to the Gospel rule, first between thee and him alone, then referring his offense to others, then to the Church if it is necessary,[6] shall do penance according to the time [of his silence].

8. He who makes a quarrel among clerics or monks shall be reconciled to those whom he has injured and do penance for a week.

VI. Of Drunkenness

[Of the six canons under this head only nos. 5 and 6 are here given. The rest of the section follows closely *Poenit. Theod.* I, i.]

5. If this[7] happens to anyone after abstinence, and if he is not accustomed to drinking much, when in the joy of some celebration he indulges with unusual freedom at the feast and yet does not take more than is determined by his seniors, his penance is to be much reduced.

6. He who is drunk against the Lord's prohibition[8] and does not vomit shall do penance for seven days.

[Section VII, "Of Unclean Flesh," consists mainly of excerpts from *Poenit. Theod.* I, vii–xii. Two of the manuscripts end at the close of this section.]

VIII. Of the Eucharist[9]

1. If on the day of the mass anyone vomits and dogs eat the vomit, he shall do penance, if he knows of it, for one hundred days; but if not, forty, as we have said above.[10]

---

[5] Canons 1–4 only are on perjury.   [6] Based on Matt. 18:15–17.
[7] That is, vomiting, can. 4.   [8] Luke 21:34.
[9] Schmitz prints this section without numerals. Obviously there ought to be a new title before can. 4.—*viz.*, "De furto" (of theft).
[10] Wasserschleben points out that there is no antecedent to which these words can be referred. Haddan and Stubbs suggest that it is a loose reference to canons 1 and 4 of the previous section; but this seems unjustified.

2. He who loses a small part of the host in a church and does not find it shall do penance for twenty or forty days or for three forty-day periods.

3. He who spills the chalice at the hour of celebration, thirty days.

4. But if anyone commits a theft of capital goods, that is, [steals] a quadruped or breaks open a house, if they are laymen they shall do penance for one year and pay back the value [of the things stolen], or if they cannot pay it back, [they shall] do penance for two years.

5. If they commit any greater theft, three years or such period as the priest determines.

6. If clerics commit such a theft, they shall do penance for five years or such period as the bishop determines.

7. If [anyone] leads or sends a slave or any man into captivity, he shall do penance for three years.

8. He who commits many evil deeds, that is, the shedding of blood, theft, fornication, perjury, and the other evils in which humankind are accustomed to be implicated and afterwards wishes to serve God unto the end of his life shall do penance for two or three years or such period as the priest determines: for this is the best penance, to desist from the accustomed evil deeds and study to please God.

IX. Of the Condition[11] of Men

These things we have compiled, as we said above,[12] concerning the condition of men, [showing] how they ought to do penance or to adjudge it: whether poor or rich, free or a slave; whether a boy or a youth; whether lacking in wisdom or learned; whether a cleric or a monk, whether in orders or without orders. Discretion is becoming to the priest in all decisions and measures of the penances, to exercise foresight and consideration with regard to the remedies of souls, [considering] how they may be able to save their own souls and the souls of others by wholesome speech, in instructing, in teaching, in persuading, in reproving, since he who ministers well "purchases to himself a good degree"[13] before Him "who is over all things, God blessed forever. Amen."[14]

[11] "Qualitate."

[12] The reference is to section I, here omitted. Cf. p. 233, above.

[13] I Tim. 3:13.

[14] Rom. 9:5. Wasserschleben would end the original penitential here. Whatever the authorship of I–IX it seems probable that what follows is by a different writer.

X. *Of the Twelve Three-Day Periods*

1. Twelve three-day periods with three complete psalters and three hundred palm thumpings[15] release from[16] a year's penance.

2. Twenty-four two-day periods with three psalters release from the second year.

3. Seventy-six psalms with bowing[17] at night with three hundred palm thumpings release from a two-day penance.

4. One hundred psalms with bowing at night with three hundred palm thumpings release from a three-day penance.

5. One hundred and twenty special offices with three complete psalters and three hundred palm thumpings release from one hundred solidi of ring gold[18] in alms.

6. Some say, for one year on bread and water, twelve two-day periods; for the second year they shall sing twelve times fifty psalms, kneeling; for the third year at a venerable feast such as he chooses, he shall keep a two-day penance;[19] he shall sing the psalter, standing motionless; for the fourth year he shall receive three hundred strokes with rods [on his] naked [body]; for the fifth year he shall estimate how much his food is worth and give as much in alms; for the sixth year he shall redeem himself according to what he is worth, and at the same price he shall make restitution to him to whom he has done evil, and if he is no longer alive he shall seek out the legal heirs; for the seventh year he shall lay aside every evil and do good.

7. And he who either will not or cannot perform this and the other requirements [shall do penance] as it is written in the penitential.

8. And he who cannot perform that which we have indicated above concerning the psalms shall choose a righteous man who shall perform it for him and shall redeem this [vicarious penance] by his own value[20] or labor.

XI. *Of Giving Counsel*

We read in the penitential [that] for criminal offenses [one is] to do

---

[15] "palmatis." See above, pp. 33, 231, and below, p. 344.

[16] "excus(s)ant" (excuse).

[17] "venia," that is, an inclination or genuflexion. It is the same word as that commonly used for "pardon." The gesture of humiliation was performed in seeking pardon.

[18] "de auro cocto," properly "coctano."

[19] Reading "quale elegit biduana faciat" (*Pseudo-Cummean.* Wasserschleben, *Bussordnungen*, p. 463) instead of "quae legit biduanas biduana facta."

[20] "de suo precio." Probably in the sense of the price of his person obtained by selling his freedom.

penance for one or two or three years on bread and water, or for other, minor offenses, one month or a week. In like manner also with some this provision[21] is hard and difficult. Therefore [to him] who cannot do these things we give the advice that there should be instead of this, psalms and prayer and alms with some days in penance; that is, psalms for one day when he is due to fast on bread and water. These [requirements] are: Kneeling he shall sing in sequence fifty psalms, and without kneeling, seventy, in a church or in one place. For a week on bread and water he shall sing in sequence three hundred psalms, kneeling in a church or in one place; without kneeling, four hundred and twenty. And for one month on bread and water one thousand five hundred psalms, kneeling, and without kneeling, one thousand eight hundred and twenty, and afterward through all the days he shall sup at sext and abstain from flesh and wine; other food, whatever God gives him, he may take after he has sung. And he who does not know the psalms ought to do penance and fast and dispense to the poor every day money of the value of a denarius and fast one day until nones and another until vespers and [then] eat whatever he has.

5. SELECTIONS FROM THE PENITENTIAL OF EGBERT
(ca. 750)

[THE "FOUR distinct works which have been assumed at various times to be the genuine *Penitential of Egbert*" are described by Haddan and Stubbs,[1] who give reasons for the selection of the one here translated as probably an original work of the archbishop.[2] In this view they follow Wasserschleben who noted Raban Maur's early citation of it as Egbert's.[3] They offer, however, additional evidence especially from a Bodleian manuscript not used by Wasserschleben. Critical editions are given by Wasserschleben,[4] Haddan and Stubbs,[5] and Schmitz.[6] In his first volume, ignoring the work of Haddan and Stubbs and not consulting the Bodleian codex used by them, Schmitz concludes against Egbert's authorship of this or any penitential. In his later volume he again rejects the connection of Egbert with this work.[7] Oakley considers the

---

[21] "causa."   [1] *Councils*, III, 415–16.

[2] Egbert was archbishop of York 732–66. He was a disciple and friend of Bede.

[3] *Bussordnungen*, pp. 41 f. Raban Maur used a quotation from the Penitential, chap. vi, in chap. xviii of his *Liber poenitentialis* addressed to Bishop Heribald. Text in Canisius, *Thesaurus monumentorum*, II, ii, 306. Egbert is here called "Egbertus Anglorum episcopus."   [4] *Bussordnungen*, pp. 231–47.

[5] *Op. cit.*, III, 416–31.   [6] Schmitz I, pp. 573–87.   [7] Schmitz II, pp. 648 ff.

argument of Schmitz "very weak," and holds that "the present weight of probability favors the authenticity of the Penitential of Egbert."[8] If Egbert is the author of this penitential in any sense of authorship beyond that of compilation, he must also be regarded as the author of the major part of the document edited by Albers and ascribed to Bede, for the *Penitential of Egbert* contains the greater part of the materials of that document and little else.

The so-called *Penitential of Egbert* consists of a somewhat extended Prologue and sixteen chapters. The chapter titles are: I. Of capital crimes; II. Of minor sins; III. Of parricides or fratricides; IV. Of greed and other vices; V. Of the penance of clerics; VI. Of perjury; VII. Of the devices of women; VIII. Of augury or divination; IX. Of detailed sins; X. Of theft; XI. Of drunkenness; XII. Of the Eucharist; XIII. Of diverse cases; XIV. "As saith the Apostle"; XV. Of the equivalent of a year or of a day; XVI. Of the sayings of St. Boniface the Archbishop. Of these, No. XIV is identical with a passage in the Albers *Bede*, p. 230, above; No. XV is evidently based on the *Irish Canons* II;[9] and No. XVI is the section ascribed to St. Boniface, translated above from the Albers text, and is probably of Frankish origin. Only section XV is here given. The translation follows the text of Haddan and Stubbs, employing some of the variants these editors supply from the Bodleian manuscript 718.]

XV. Of the Equivalent[10] of a Year or of a Day

For the first year some propose four three-day periods with one night intervening. Others say twelve three-day periods, that is, one[11] in one month. Some say the three-day periods [shall be] with whippings or with vigils; and, holding to the three days, some say this and some that.[12] But the equivalent of a day is this: alms[13] to two or three poor men. Others [say] a whole psalter, that is, in summer; in winter, however, and in spring or in autumn, fifty psalms; one [says] twelve blows or strokes,[14] more [or] less; the times are to be discerned;[15] one indicates[16] [an alternative penance?] in the work of another man, or in kneeling twice fifty times; also he indicates three times sixty; and he indicates six times one hundred and twenty, and in the first [year] ten are added; in the second, twenty; thereafter[17] (?), thirty if there is no work.

---

[8] *English Penitential Discipline*, p. 123.   [9] See above, pp. 122 ff.
[10] "pretio."   [11] Literally, "once."
[12] "alii sic, alii vero sic."   [13] "agapem." See Du Cange, s.v. "agape."
[14] "plagas vel percussiones."   [15] From this point the meaning is obscure.
[16] Emending "desinat" to "designat."   [17] "superior."

6. SELECTIONS FROM THE DIALOGUE OF EGBERT
(*ca.* 750)

[HADDAN and Stubbs (III, 403), Oakley (p. 79), and Watkins (II, 654) regard the *Dialogue of Egbert* as a genuine work of the archbishop. It was first printed by Sir James Ware in 1664 from a manuscript of the Cotton Library (Brit. Mus. Cotton Vitellius A XII) and has been republished in the works of Wilkins,[1] Thorpe,[2] Mansi,[3] and Haddan and Stubbs.[4] Mansi conjecturally assigns the date 748; Watkins suggests, *ca.* 750. Egbert became archbishop of York about 732 and retained this post until his death in 766.

The Dialogue is a series of sixteen questions and answers, suitable for the instruction of priests by a bishop, on matters of church discipline. Only Nos. XV and XVI are here given. The others are of slight importance for the history of penance.]

QUESTION XV

What are the crimes which prevent any man from becoming a priest, or for what [offenses] is one deposed who has already been ordained?

ANSWER

The ordination of a bishop, a presbyter, or a deacon is said to be valid when the following conditions obtain: if he is shown to be stained by no serious offense; if he has not a second wife nor one left by a [former] husband; if he has not undergone public penance, and if he does not seem defective[5] in any part of his body; if he is not of servile rank or of objectionable condition by origin; if he is proved free from connections with the court;[6] if he has acquired learning;[7] such a man we elect to be elevated to the priesthood. For the following crimes, indeed, we say that no one may be ordained, but that some who have been elevated are to be deposed: namely, those who worship idols; those who through soothsayers and diviners and enchanters give themselves over as captives to the devil; those who destroy their faith with false witness; those defiled with murders or acts of fornication; perpetrators of thefts; violators of the sacred name of truth by the insolence of perjury. These, moreover, except through public penance must not be admitted to obtain the grace of communion nor to recover the honor of their former dignity; for

---

[1] *Concilia Magnae Britanniae*, I, 82–86.
[2] *Ancient Laws and Institutes of England*, II, 87–96.
[3] *Concilia*, XII, 482–88.   [4] *Councils*, III, 403–13.
[5] "vitiatus."   [6] "curiae."   [7] "litteras" (letters).

it is alien to the Church that penitents should minister the sacred things, who were lately vessels of wickedness.[8]

QUESTION XVI

Of the Four Seasons of Fasting[9]

Whether the appointed fasts of the first, the fourth, the seventh, and the tenth months are to be celebrated at the beginning of these months or otherwise. And explain by an orderly statement on whose authority, or in what manner, or for what reasons they have been instituted, so that they may be celebrated by all uniformly through all Your Worship's sees and [all] the churches of the English.

ANSWER

Since the world is embraced by the four zones of east, west, south, and north, and since man consists of the four elements, that is, fire, air, water, and earth, and the interior sense is maintained by the four virtues, prudence, temperance, fortitude, and justice; and the four rivers of paradise, as a type of the four gospels, flow forth to water the whole earth, and the year revolves in the four seasons,

---

[8] Oakley, *loc. cit.*, calls attention to this passage as evidence for the practice of public penance in England, and points out Watkins's failure to consider it in his denial of this. The qualifications and disqualifications here stated seem to be based upon regulations found in the *Apostolic Canons*, a collection completed about the middle of the fourth century. Cf. cans. 22, 23, 25, 30, 48, 61, 78, 82 of that document. Can. 9 of Nicaea (325) forbids the admission of those who have been ordained notwithstanding their confession of crime. Numerous canons of the fifth and sixth century enjoin penance for delinquent clergy. See for instance the synod of Agde, 506, can. 2, which concedes to such the "communion of strangers" ("communio peregrina"), i.e. the means of subsistence, while they are being corrected by penance. Mansi, VIII, 324. Bingham has remarked on the difficulty created by the apparent inconsistency of provisions that made the undergoing of public penance an impediment to the priesthood and yet required public penance as the means of restoration for clerical offenders, *Antiquities*, XVII, iii, 9 (ed. 1870), p. 1037. His remarks would apply to the present canon. The passage probably should be taken as recording the compiler's vote for public penance in the cases indicated. On the other hand, some elements of this canon can hardly have been in approved eighth century use. For example, we are probably to regard the assumption that one marriage is permitted to a priest as no more than a repetition of antiquated canonical materials. On the demand for the celibacy of priests at this period in England, see H. C. Lea, *History of Sacerdotal Celibacy*, 3d ed., I, 108.

[9] Literally, "Of the fast of the four times." Cf. the alleged instruction of Gregory the Great on this subject, Haddan and Stubbs, III, 52 f., and the council of Cloveshoe (747), can. 18, *ibid.*, p. 368. For further study of the evolution of the four seasons of fasting, see J. Bingham, *Antiquities of the Christian Church*, XXI, ii (1870 ed.), pp. 1190 ff.; Cabrol, *Dictionnaire*, art.: "Jeune"; K. Holl, *Gesammelte Aufsätze*, II, *Der Osten*, "Die Entstehung der vier Fastenzeiten in der griechischen Kirche," pp. 155–203. Cf. also the *Penitential of Theodore*, II, 14, 1, p. 212, above.

spring, summer, autumn, and winter, and everywhere four is distinguished as a perfect number, for these reasons the ancient fathers instituted these[10] four fasts of the seasons according to the law of God and now[11] holy men and apostolic teachers in the New Testament [prescribe them].

Of the first fast.—Concerning the first month the Lord saith unto Moses: "This month shall be to you the beginning of months: it shall be the first in the months of the year."[12] And again the Lord saith to Moses: "Observe the month of the new corn when you came out of the Land of Egypt. It shall be an ordinance unto your generations."[13] This fast the holy fathers appointed in the first week of the first month, Wednesday, Friday, and Saturday,[14] except during the days of Lent. But we, in the Church of the English, keep the same fast of the first month in the first week of Lent as our instructor the Blessed Gregory, in his Antiphonary and Missal, transmitted it, authorized and decreed, through our teacher, the Blessed Augustine, without regarding the reckoning of the first week.

Of the second fast.—The second fast of the fourth month took its rise from the old Law, when the Law was given to Moses on Mount Sinai, and it was commanded by the Lord that the people should be prepared to hear his voice on the third day and that they should not come near their wives.[15] And again, the Lord saith to Moses: "Take the first fruits of all your corn and offer them to the Lord thy God,"[16] which is also established in the New Testament according to that which the Lord saith: "The children of the bridegroom fast[17] while the bridegroom is with them,"[18] and so forth. And[19] according to the convenience of the seasons, after the ascension of the Lord to the skies, his bodily presence being withdrawn, this was then announced as the fast of the fourth month on the second Saturday. However, through the aforesaid legate, the Blessed Gregory, in his Antiphonary and Missal, ordained this same fast, to be celebrated in the Church of the English during the whole week after Pentecost. This is not

---

[10] Emending "autem" to "haec": the abbreviation may have been confused.
[11] "et nunc." Perhaps we should read "etiam."　　　　[12] Exod. 12:2.
[13] For the phraseology, see Exod. 16:32; Deut. 16:1; Lev. 6:18; 23:21, 41.
[14] "sabbato," the Jewish Sabbath.　　　　[15] Exod. 19:11, 15.
[16] Based on Exod. 23:19.
[17] For "ieiunare" the Vulgate has "lugere" (mourn).　　　　[18] Matt. 9:15
[19] "quod," probably referring to the continuation of the quotation, on fasting after the bridegroom is taken away, represented by "et reliqua" (and so forth) in the previous sentence.

only attested by our antiphonaries, but also by those very things which we have seen, with his missals, at the thresholds[20] of the Apostles Peter and Paul.

Of the third fast.—The third fast of the seventh month is prescribed by the Lord through Moses, saying: "Speak unto the children of Israel, and thou shalt say unto them: The tenth day of the seventh month shall be called holy; ye shall humble your souls in a fast. Every soul that is not afflicted in that day shall perish from among his people."[21] On this account, then, this fast is celebrated in the Church according to ancient custom; or else, because the day shortens and the night is lengthened, for at the decline of the sun and the increase of the night our life is shown to decline at the approach of death; which death in God's judgment and in the Resurrection shall be restored to life. And if the end of our life is expressed in the shortening of the days, and the coming of death in the increase of the night, we take it to be necessary to humble our souls every year in memory and remembrance of so great a mystery as, we read, the children of Israel did at this time in fasting and affliction, [in abstinence] not only from food but from all contacts with wickedness, hearkening to the word of the Gospel: "Walk whilst you have the light, that the darkness overtake you not," "for the night cometh when no man can work."[22] The Church of the English is accustomed to celebrate this during the whole week before the equinox, regardless of the reckoning of the third week.

Of the fourth fast.—The fourth fast was observed by men of old in the month of November, according to the command of the Lord when he spake unto Jeremiah: "Take thee a roll of a book, and thou shalt write in it all the words that I have spoken against Israel and Juda." "And it came to pass in the ninth month that they proclaimed a fast before the Lord and all the people in Jerusalem."[23] By this authority of the Divine Scriptures, then, the Catholic Church maintains the custom and celebrates the fast and the observance in the tenth month on the fourth Saturday on account of the coming of the venerable solemn feast of Our Lord Jesus Christ; when for some days earlier continence of the flesh and fasting are to be practiced so that every believer may prepare himself to take the communion of the

---

[20] "limina." The "limina apostolorum" were the churches in Rome dedicated to Peter and Paul.   [21] Lev. 23:10, 27, 29.

[22] John 12:35; 9:4.   [23] Jer. 36:2, 9.

body and blood of Christ devoutly. And the English people have by custom celebrated it always during the whole week before the Nativity of the Lord, not only on the Wednesday and Friday and Saturday; but also, twelve continuous days in fasts and vigils and prayers and distribution of alms, both in the monasteries and in the parishes, before the Nativity, are considered as if keeping the appointed fast. For, since the times of Pope Vitalian and Theodore, archbishop of Canterbury, this custom, thank God, has grown up in the Church of the English and has been coming to recognition[24] as lawful, that not only the clerics in the monasteries but also laymen with their wives and families should come to their confessors and cleanse themselves during these twelve days by tears with the distribution of alms from the fellowship of fleshly concupiscence[25] that they may be the purer when they partake of the Lord's communion on the Lord's Nativity.[26] For, in addition to these, many have fasted on Wednesday and Friday on account of the Passion of Christ and on Saturday on account of the fact that on that day He lay in the tomb.

7. SELECTIONS FROM THE SO-CALLED CONFESSIONAL OF EGBERT (*ca.* 950–1000)

[THE *Confessional of Egbert* was published by Wilkins[1] from the eleventh century Codex Corpus Christi College, Cambridge, 190, which contains both Anglo-Saxon and Latin versions. Thorpe presented an improved Anglo-Saxon text with a Latin translation of his own. In addition to the Corpus Christi codex Thorpe made use of two Bodleian manuscripts which he dated in the tenth and eleventh centuries, respectively, and a Burgundian (Brussels) manuscript of about 1000.[2] Thorpe's Latin is the text printed by Wasserschleben.[3] Wilkins's edition of the early Latin version reappears in the Mansi collection and has been again reprinted by Migne.[4] On linguistic grounds Wilkins asserted the priority of the Anglo-Saxon over this Latin text, and Mansi was of the same opinion.

---

[24] "tenebatur."   [25] Cf. I John 2:16.

[26] Watkins quotes and translates this sentence, and comments on it at some length. He regards it as probably "the earliest example of habitual confession generally practiced in a Christian community," and thinks the adoption of the period before Christmas instead of before Easter "resembles the Eastern usage and may be due to Theodore."—Watkins, II, 636, 654.

[1] *Concilia Magnae Britanniae*, I, 113–33.

[2] *Ancient Laws of England*, I *Secular*, pp. xxv f.; II *Ecclesiastical*, pp. 128–69.

[3] *Bussordnungen*, pp. 300–318.

[4] Mansi, *Concilia*, XII, 431–41; *P.L.*, LXXXIX, 402–12.

On the question of the origin of the Latin version of the *Confessional*, J. Raith notes that he has "puzzled in vain."[5]

R. Spindler has based his recent scholarly edition of the Anglo-Saxon[6] primarily upon the excellent Codex Bodl. Junius 121, placed by Thorpe in the tenth century but by Raith and Spindler, in the eleventh. For the introductory sections Spindler has employed, in addition to the manuscripts used by Thorpe, the eleventh century Cotton Tib. A 3 of the British Museum. Thorpe listed this codex but did not cite readings from it in his edition of the *Confessional*. The Corpus Christi College manuscript begins by stating that "Egbert, archbishop of York, translated these capitula from Latin into English, that the uneducated might be able the more easily to understand them." Wasserschleben, however, thinks Egbert's connection with the work as translator problematical.[7] Haddan and Stubbs hold that Egbert may possibly have written the Anglo-Saxon version, and point out that it is mainly "a translation of parts of Theodore and the so-called *Cummeanus*."[8] Spindler argues that the work originated in a West Mercian cloister, conceivably Ramsay, in the latter half of the tenth century, and regards its introduction as having been inserted from the nearly contemporary Anglo-Saxon version of Halitgar's work—Raith's edition of which has been referred to above.[9]

Whatever its origin the *Confessional* is doubtless one of the earliest fragments of penitential material in the language of the English. It appears to be closely related to the "scrift boc" or penitential in English bequeathed by Bishop Leofric of Exeter on his death in 1072 to the Library of Exeter Cathedral.[10]

The portions here given were translated from Thorpe's Anglo-Saxon edition before the appearance of Spindler's work. Both Thorpe's Latin and the rather disorderly medieval Latin text given by Wilkins have been consulted. The arrangement of Spindler's text differs considerably from that of Thorpe's, but the passages given are substantially identical in both. I have not thought it necessary to adopt Spindler's arrangement or to insert his somewhat involved paragraph numerals; the bracketed numbers are those of the lines of his text.]

When anyone goes to his confessor, he shall prostrate himself before him with the utmost fear of God and [with] humility and in a doleful voice beg him to prescribe for him penance for all those faults which he has committed against God's will; and he shall confess to

---

[5] *Die altenglische Version des Halitgar'schen Bussbuches* (sog. *Poenitentiale Pseudo-Ecgberti*), Hamburg, 1933, p. xxv.
[6] *Das altenglische Bussbuch* (sog. *Confessionale Pseudo-Egberti*), Leipzig, 1934, Text pp. 170–94.
[7] *Bussordnungen*, p. 42.
[8] *Councils*, III, 415. Cf. Oakley, pp. 131 ff.
[9] Spindler, *op. cit.*, pp. 1 ff.; 123 ff.; 165 ff.
[10] Cf. below, p. 428.

him his misdeeds, so that the priest may know what kind of penance he should prescribe for him.

[The remainder of the introduction presents a brief form of general questions and injunctions to be followed by the confessor.]

1. [32–38] It is proper for any priest, when he imposes fasting on men, that he know [in each case] what kind of man he is, strong or weak, rich or poor; how young he is, or how old; whether he is ordained or a layman; what kind of repentance he has; and whether he is a bachelor or a married man. Discrimination among all men is needful, even though they commit similar offenses. Great men are to be more severely judged than lowly according to the decisions of the canons.

[Canon 2 attributes to Theodore a series of prescriptions for the commutation of penance, similar to the provisions of the *Double Penitential*, p. 236, above, and gives a short version of the "twelve remissions" of Cassian. Cf. pp. 99 f., above. Canons 3, 4, and 5 deal with various offenses of the clergy.]

6. [176–79] If any priest makes a journey in his own territory[11] or in any other, and in his journey anyone requests baptism of him and he refuses in order to hasten his journey, ånd [if] the man dies unbaptized,[12] [the priest] shall be deprived of his rank.[13]

7. [180–84] If any mass-priest knows that he is unbaptized, he and all those whom he previously baptized shall be baptized. A Roman pope declared that though a priest be sinful or a heathen, nevertheless the ministry of the Holy Ghost, not that of the man, is in the grace of baptism.

8. [113–15] If anyone loses his rank, a priest or a bishop, he shall do penance until death that his soul may live. If a priest slays a man or secretly[14] commits fornication, he shall be degraded from his rank. If he wounds a man, he shall fast one hundred days.

9. [396–98] When he sings mass a priest shall not wear a cloak or a hood,[15] but he shall lay them[16] over his shoulders if he reads the Gospel.

---

11 "scyre"; one manuscript has "scrift-scyre" (confessor's district).

12 "haeþen" (heathen).   13 "unhadod."

14 "dearnunga." Thorpe omits this word in his Latin rendering.

15 "ne . . . heden ne caeppan." The Old Latin text has "caracalam cassiatam" (a long hooded cloak). Thorpe translates "cucullum nec cappam." See *Cath. Encycl.*, art. "cope," for the late specialization of these terms: "What in Gaul was styled cuculla (cowl) was known to the Casinese monks as cappa."   16 One manuscript has "lay the cloak."

[Canons 10 to 16 deal with ritual offenses, theft by priests, and sex offenses of deacons, monks, and laymen.]

17. [160–70] If any heathen man puts away a heathen woman who is in his power, after they are baptized it matters not whether he has her or not. If one of them is a heathen, the other baptized, the heathen may leave the baptized, as saith the Apostle: "If the unbeliever depart, let him depart."[17] Those who were twice baptized, but without knowing it, are not obliged to fast, but according to the decision of the canons they may not be ordained unless[18] it becomes necessary. If anyone is baptized by a fornicating priest, he shall be promptly rebaptized. If anyone is with his own knowledge twice baptized, that is as if Christ were again crucified; he shall fast for seven years on the two fast days of the week and throughout the three stated fasts.

[Canons 18 to 21 deal with offenses in marriage; 22 to 24, with various cases of homicide. Regulations on marriage and the laws of kinship occupy canons 25 to 28.]

29. [273–76] If a woman works witchcraft[19] and enchantment[20] and [uses] magical philters,[21] she shall fast for twelve months or the three stated fasts or forty days, the extent of her wickedness being considered. If she kills anyone by her philters, she shall fast for seven years . . .

[The remainder of canon 29 and canons 30 and 31 penalize a variety of offenses of women.]

32. [299–307] If anyone sacrifices anything of a minor sort to devils, he shall fast for one year; if something of a major sort, he shall fast for ten years. Anyone who takes food that has been offered to fiends and afterwards confesses to a priest, the priest shall see of what rank the man is, or of what age, or how he is instructed, and then shall he give judgment as it shall seem to him wisest. Anyone who burns corn in the place where a dead man lay, for the health of living men and of his house, shall fast for five years.

33. [300–302; 308–19] If a woman places her daughter on the

---

[17] I Cor. 7:15.

[18] Reading, with two manuscripts, "butan" for "þeah" (although).

[19] "dry-craeft" (druid-craft).   [20] "galdor."

[21] "unlibban." "Unlybba" is "poison used for purposes of witchcraft." Bosworth and Toller, *Anglo-Saxon Dictionary*, *s.v.* Cf. "lib," which is defined as "something medicinal and potent, a harmful or powerful drug."—O. Cockayne, *Leechdoms, Wortcunning and Starcraft in Early England*, II, 397. Thorpe renders the word "maleficia;" the old Latin text has "veneficium."

house top or in the oven, wishing to cure her of fever sickness, she shall fast for seven years. If a woman commits adultery and her husband does not wish to live with her, let her, if she chooses, go into a monastery; if not, let her receive the fourth part of the property.[22] If any woman commits adultery, her punishment is in the hands of her husband. If while her husband lives a woman vows to God that after her husband's death she will have no other and [she] takes another, then rues her failure to fulfill her vow and at the eleventh year after they were united wishes to make it good—she is in the power of her husband, as to whether she shall fulfill it or not: nevertheless, under necessity her husband may live so that she may be with him. If without the bishop's consent anyone takes a vow, it is in the power of the bishop whether he change it or not.

[Canon 34 deals with perjury in its various forms.]

35.[357–70] Those who work on Sunday: these men the Greeks first admonish with words; if they do it again, then some of their property is taken from them; on the third offense they either scourge them or bid them fast for seven days. The Greeks will go to the Eucharist[23] on any Sunday, both laymen and priests; and he who goes not to the Eucharist for three Sundays is excommunicated, according to the judgment of the canons. The Romans likewise go to the Eucharist, but they do not excommunicate those who cannot do this. Among the Greeks, deacons may not break the holy loaf,[24] nor read a collect, nor say the "Dominus vobiscum." On any one altar thou mayest sing two masses daily. He who is not present at the earlier mass, may not come to the kiss before the Eucharist. He who will not go to the Eucharist shall not afterward come to the hand of the mass-priest for the loaf, nor to the Eucharist, nor to the kiss. One may not go to the Eucharist at the hand of a mass-priest who is not able to complete the consecration or the lection according to usage.

36. [371–82] For a departed monk mass may be sung by the third day and afterward as the abbot decides. For a good layman mass may be sung on the third day or after seven days. For a penitent mass may be celebrated after thirty[25] days or after seven days if his relatives

---

[22] "yrfes," literally, "cattle."   [23] "husle" (housel).

[24] Cf. note on "eulogias," p. 260, below.

[25] For "xxx" Thorpe would read "iii." If we adopt "three" we should probably insert a comma after "seven days."

and his friends fast for him and make some gift to the altar for his soul. Among the Romans the custom is that the bodies of deceased men and of religious men are carried into the church and their breasts anointed with the chrism, and mass is sung over them, and then they are borne to the grave with singing; then when they are laid in the grave, earth is cast over them; then mass is sung for them on the first, the third, the ninth, and the thirtieth days, and thereafter as is determined.

37. [382–89] Women may go to the Eucharist under a dark veil, as Basil taught. Among the Greeks women may offer the sacrifice, but not according to the Romans. There are three lawful fasts in the year; one for all the people, namely, the one in the forty days before Easter, when we pay the yearly tithe, and the one in the forty days before the nativity,[26] when all the people pray for themselves and read prayers, and the one in the forty days after Pentecost.[27]

38. [459–67] Fish, though they are found dead, may be eaten, since they are of another nature.[28] Horse flesh is not forbidden, though many nations refuse to eat it. Birds and other animals which are strangled in nets are not to be eaten; not even if a hawk has eaten of them are they afterward to be eaten, if they are found dead, since it is commanded in the Acts of the Apostles: "Ye shall keep yourselves from fornication and from things strangled, and from blood, and from idolatry."[29] The hare may be eaten, and when boiled in water it is good against dysentery and diarrhea; and its gall may be mixed with pepper for sore mouth.[30]

[26] Other readings are "midwinter," and "our Lord's birth time."
[27] Cf. p. 212, above.   [28] "gecynde."   [29] Based on Acts 15:20.
[30] For the medicinal use of various parts of the hare, see O. Cockayne, Leechdoms, Wortcunning and Starcraft in Early England, I, 343 ff.

CHAPTER IV

Penitentials by Irish Authors Which Were. Apparently Compiled on the Continent

1. THE PENITENTIAL OF COLUMBAN (ca. 600)

[THE TEXT of the *Poenitentiale Columbani*, or *S. Columbani abbatis de poenitentiarum mensura taxanda liber*, was published in 1667 by Th. Sirinus from the till then unpublished collection of Columban's works made by Patrick Fleming in 1626. This collection—*Patricii Flemingi collectanea sacra seu S. Columbani acta et opuscula*—was republished by Migne.[1] The text may also be found in Wasserschleben[2] and in Schmitz.[3] The best edition is by O. Seebass.[4] The document is extant in two Bobbio manuscripts now in the National Library of Turin, G V 38, and G VII 16, respectively, the former of the tenth, the latter of the tenth or eleventh century. The text of Fleming is apparently taken from a third manuscript, now lost.

The penitential is in two parts, A and B. The offenses in A are apparently those of monks alone. In an introduction to the document,[5] Seebass combats the view of Schmitz that Columban is not the author of the book and cannot be credited with any penitential. The references in Jonas's *Life of Columban*[6] to the exercise of penance among the people of the district around Luxeuil, while somewhat general,[7] show that a generation later there was an awareness of the penance aspect of Columban's work. Schmitz thought the absence here of specific reference to a penitential book was evidence against such a compilation. But the fact of penitential discipline in an age when Irish abbots were writing penitential books may rather be taken as presumptive evidence that Columban prepared such a book. The close resemblances of the work to the *Penitential of Finnian*, Columban's Irish predecessor, also accord per-

---

[1] *P.L.*, LXXX, 209 ff.; the Penitential begins with col. 223.

[2] *Bussordnungen*, pp. 353–60.   [3] Schmitz I, pp. 588–602.

[4] "Das Poenitentiale Columbani," in *Zeitschr. f. Kirchengesch.*, XIV (1894), 430 ff.; text, pp. 441–48.   [5] *Ibid.*, pp. 430 ff.

[6] The *Vita Columbani* written by Jonas of Bobbio has been edited by Bruno Krusch in *M. G. H.*, *Scriptores rerum Merovingicarum*, IV, 64 ff. An English translation by Munro is contained in the *Pennsylvania Translations and Reprints*, II, 7.

[7] "The people," says Jonas, "flocked together from all sides for the medicine of penance."—*Vita*, 17.

fectly with Columban's authorship. While in all essentials a Celtic book, this penitential shows adaptation to a Frankish environment. Hauck and Seebass have shown that the references to heathen feasts (B. 24) and to the Bonosiac heretics (B. 25) are in accord with the facts of life in the neighborhood of Luxeuil.[8]]

A. [OFFENSES OF MONKS]

1. True penance is to refrain from committing deeds for which penance is to be done but when such are committed, to bewail them. However, since weakness on the part of many, not to say of all, violates this principle [of true penance], the scales of penance ought to be known, of which the ordinance is handed down from the holy fathers in such manner that the duration of penances is determined according to the magnitude of the offenses.

2. If, therefore, anyone sins by planning to sin, that is, [if he] desires to kill a man, or to commit fornication, or to steal, or secretly to feast and become drunk, or indeed to beat anyone, or to desert [from monastic life], or to do anything else of the kind, and [if he] is prepared with his whole heart to do these things, in the case of the greater crimes he shall do penance on bread and water for half a year; in the case of the lesser, for forty days.

3. But if anyone, his sins getting the better of him, actually commits sin, if he commits homicide or the sin of sodomy, he shall do penance for ten years; if he commits fornication only once, a monk shall do penance for three years; if more often, seven years. If he deserts and violates his vows and then promptly returns to penance, he shall do penance for the three forty-day periods, but if he returns after some years, for three years.

4. If anyone commits theft, he shall do penance for a year.

5. If anyone strikes his brother as the result of a quarrel and causes bloodshed, he shall do penance for three years.

6. But if anyone gets himself drunk and vomits, or having imbibed too much vomits the host, he shall do penance for forty days. If through weakness anyone is led to vomit the host, he shall do penance for seven days. If anyone loses the host itself, he shall do penance for a year.

7. If anyone defiles himself, he shall do penance for a year if he is a junior.

[8] McNeill, pp. 43 ff. (*Rev. celt.*, XXXIX, 277 ff.); Watkins, II, 612 ff., and Poschmann II, pp. 63 ff. may also be consulted. See below, p. 256, n. 19.

8. If anyone has knowingly made a false testimony, he shall do penance for two years with the loss of the property [for which he made the statement] or its restitution.

The above rules deal with occasional cases; the following with the details of disorderly morals.

9. One who without asking advice, does by himself anything, or one who objects and says, "I am not going to do it," or one who murmurs, if [his offense] is grave he shall do penance with three special fasts, if slight, with one. A word uttered in simple contradiction is to be punished by fifty stripes; but if with emphasis, with a special penalty of silence; now, if in strife, he shall do penance for a week.

10. But if one traduces another or willingly listens to a traducer, he shall do penance with three special fasts; if the offense is against his superior, he shall do penance for a week.

11. One who, moreover, through pride despises his superior or blasphemes against the rule is to be cast out, unless he immediately says, "I repent of what I said." But if he does not fully humiliate himself he shall do penance for forty days, since he is held back by the disease of pride.

12. The talkative person is to be sentenced to silence, the disturber to gentleness, the gluttonous to fasting, the sleepy fellow to watchfulness, the proud to imprisonment, the deserter to expulsion;[9] everyone shall suffer suitable penalties according to what he deserves, that the righteous may live righteously.

B. [OFFENSES OF CLERICS AND LAYMEN]

Diversity of guilt occasions diversity of penalty; for even the physicians of bodies prepare their medicines in various sorts. For they treat wounds in one way, fevers in another, swellings in another, bruises in another, festering sores in another, defective sight in another, fractures in another, burns in another. So therefore the spiritual physicians ought also to heal with various sorts of treatment the wounds, fevers, transgressions, sorrows, sicknesses, and infirmities of souls. Since these [skills] are the property of only a few, namely, to know how to treat all things unto cleanness,[10] to

[9] "repulsione."
[10] "ad purum." Cf. "sicut mundari solet fimus usque ad purum," III Kings (i.e., I Kings in A.V. and R.V.) 14:10.

restore the feeble[11] to the full state of health—let us set forth even a few things according to the tradition of the elders and in part according to our own understanding; for we prophecy in part, we know in part.[12]

OF THE CAPITAL OFFENSES

We are about to make regulations concerning the offenses which are also punished under the penalty of the law.

1. If a cleric commits homicide and slays his neighbor, he shall do penance for ten years in exile. Thereafter he shall be admitted to his own country if he has well performed his penance on bread and water and is approved by the testimony of the bishop or priest with whom he has done his penance and to whom he was committed, that he may make satisfaction to the parents of him whom he slew, offering himself in place of their son and saying, "Whatever you wish I will do unto you." But if he does not make satisfaction to the man's parents he shall never be admitted into his own country, but shall be like Cain a vagabond and a fugitive upon the earth.[13]

2. If anyone falls most miserably[14] and begets a child, he shall do penance as a pilgrim for seven years on bread and water; then for the first time, at the judgment of the priest, he shall be joined to the altar.

3. But if one commits fornication as the Sodomites did, he shall do penance for ten years, the first three on bread and water; but in the other seven years he shall abstain from wine and meat, and [he shall] not be housed with another person forever.

4. If one commits fornication with women but does not beget a child and it does not come to the notice of men, if he is a cleric [he shall do penance for] three years; if a monk or deacon, five years; if a priest, seven; if a bishop, twelve years.

5. If one commits perjury, he shall do penance for seven years and never afterward take an oath.

6. If one destroys another by his magic, he shall do penance for three years with an allowance of bread and water, and for three years more he shall abstain from wine and meats, and then at last in the seventh year he shall be admitted to communion. But if anyone is a magician for the sake of love and destroys nobody, that

---

[11] Literally, "feeble things" ("debilia").
[12] I Cor. 13:9.
[13] Gen. 4:12.
[14] "ruina maxima." Cf. above, pp. 89, n. 13, 92.

person, if a cleric, shall do penance for an entire year on bread and water; a layman, half that time; a deacon, two years; a priest, three. Especially if by this means anyone deceives a woman with respect to the birth of a child; for this each [of the above] shall add besides six periods of forty days, lest he be chargeable with homicide.

7. If any cleric commits theft, that is, steals his neighbor's ox or horse or sheep or any animal, if he does it once or twice, he shall first make restitution to his neighbor, and he shall do penance for an entire year on bread and water. If he has made a habit of this and is not able to make restitution, he shall do penance for three years on bread and water.

8. But if after his conversion a cleric (either a deacon or one of another rank) who was a layman in the world with sons and daughters, again has relations with his concubine[15] and again begets a child by her, let him know that he has committed adultery and sinned not less than if from his youth he had been a cleric and had sinned with a strange girl; since he has sinned after his vow, after he has consecrated himself to the Lord, and has made void his vow; therefore he shall likewise do penance for seven years on bread and water.

9. If any cleric strikes his neighbor as a result of a quarrel and causes bloodshed, he shall do penance for an entire year; if [the offender is] a layman, for forty days.

10. If anyone practices masturbation or sins with a beast, he shall do penance for two years if he is not in [clerical] orders; but if he is in orders or has a [monastic] vow, he shall do penance for three years unless his [tender] age protects him.

11. If one lusts after a woman and is unable to satisfy his lust, that is, the woman will not comply, he shall do penance for half a year on bread and water, and for a whole year he shall abstain from wine and meats and from the communion of the altar.

12. If one loses the sacrament, he shall do penance for a year; if through drunkenness and greediness he vomits it and negligently forsakes it, he shall do penance for the three forty-day periods on bread and water. But if [he does this] through weakness, he shall do penance for seven days.

But these provisions have been stated concerning clerics and monks together; the remainder concern laymen.

[15] That is, his former wife.

13. Whoever commits homicide, that is, slays his neighbor, shall do penance on bread and water for three years unarmed, in exile, and after the three years he shall come back to his own,[16] rendering to the parents of the dead man filial piety and service in his stead, and so the satisfaction being completed, he shall, at the judgment of the priest, be joined to the altar.

14. If any layman begets a child of another's wife, that is, commits adultery, violating his neighbor's bed, he shall do penance for three years, abstaining from juicy foods and from his own wife, giving in addition to the husband the price of the violated honor of his wife,[17] and so shall his guilt be wiped off by the priest.

15. If any layman, indeed, commits fornication according to the sodomic rite, that is, commits an act of homosexuality, he shall do penance for seven years, in the first three on bread and water and salt and dry fruit of the garden; in the four remaining years he shall abstain from wine and meats; and thus his guilt shall be canceled and the priest shall pray for him, and so he shall be joined to the altar.

16. But if one of the laymen commits fornication with women who are free from the bonds of matrimony, that is, with widows or girls— if with a widow, he shall do penance for one year; if with a girl, for two years, rendering, moreover, the price of her humiliation[18] to her parents. If, however, he has not a wife, but as a virgin is joined to a virgin, if her parents wish it, she shall be his wife, yet on condition that they both previously do penance for a year; and thus they shall be united in marriage.

17. But if any layman commits fornication with a beast, he shall do penance for a year if he has a wife; but if he has not, for half a year. So also shall he do penance who, having a wife, practices masturbation.

18. If any layman or woman overlays his or her child, [such offenders] shall do penance for an entire year on bread and water and for two years more shall abstain from wine and flesh, and thus they shall first be joined to the altar at the judgment of the priest, and the husband shall then be free to return to his bed. For be it known to laymen that in the time when penance is imposed on them by the

---

[16] "in sua."
[17] "pretium pudicitiae . . . uxoris violatae."
[18] "humiliationis eius pretio."

priests they are not permitted to have relations with their wives until after the completion of the penance, for it ought not to be [only] half penance.

19. If any layman commits theft, that is, steals his neighbor's ox or horse or sheep or any animal, if he does it once or twice he shall first make restitution to his neighbor for the damage which he has done, and he shall do penance for the three forty-day periods on bread and water. But if he has been accustomed to commit theft often and is not able to make restitution, he shall do penance for a year and the three forty-day periods and shall promise in no circumstances to do it thenceforth; and so he shall take communion in the Easter of the following year, that is, after two years, having moreover previously given alms to the poor from [the product of] his labor and a feast to the priest who administers his penance; and thus he shall be absolved from the guilt of his evil course.

20. If any layman commits perjury, if it is through cupidity he shall do this: he shall sell all his goods and give them to the poor and be converted anew to the Lord and be tonsured, giving up everything of the world, and shall serve God in a monastery until death. But if it is not through cupidity but through fear of death that he did this thing, he shall do penance for three years unarmed in exile on bread and water, and for two years more he shall abstain from wine and flesh; and so, rendering a life for himself, that is, emancipating a man or woman slave from the yoke of servitude, and giving liberal alms through two years—in all of which period it is permitted to him to use foods freely with the exception of flesh—after the seventh year he shall take communion.

21. If one of the laymen sheds blood in a quarrel or wounds or incapacitates his neighbor, he shall be compelled to make restitution to the extent of the injury. But if he has not the wherewithal to make a settlement, he shall do his neighbor's work as long as the latter is sick, and he shall provide a physician, and after the injured man is well he shall do penance for forty days on bread and water.

22. If any layman gets drunk or eats or drinks to the point of vomiting, he shall do penance for a week on bread and water.

23. If any layman plans to commit adultery or to commit fornication with the betrothed [of his neighbor?] and lusts after the wife of his neighbor and does not accomplish his design, that is, is unable because the woman does not comply, yet he was prepared to commit

fornication, he shall confess his guilt to the priest, and thus he shall do penance for forty days on bread and water.

24. But if any layman eats or drinks beside [pagan] sacred places, if he does it through ignorance he shall promise thenceforth that he will never repeat it and do penance for forty days on bread and water. But if he does this through contempt, that is, after a priest has warned him that this was sacrilege, and has afterward communicated at the table of demons, if he repeats this as well through the vice of gluttony, he shall do penance for three forty-day periods on bread and water. If, indeed, he has done this for the sake of the worship of demons or in honor of their idols, he shall do penance for three years.

25. If any layman through ignorance communicates with the Bonosiacs[19] or other heretics, he shall remain among the catechumens, that is, separated from other Christians, for forty days, and for two other forty-day periods he shall wash away the guilt of the mad communion in the outermost rank of the Christians, that is, among the penitents. But if he has done this from contempt, that is, after he had been warned by the priest and forbidden from defiling himself by the communion of the perverse faction, he shall do penance for an entire year and the three forty-day periods, and for two years more he shall abstain from wine and flesh and thus be joined to the altar after the imposition of hands by a Catholic bishop.

Finally are to be discussed[20] the detailed provisions respecting monks.

26. If anyone leaves a wall unprotected in the night, he shall do penance with a special fast; but if in the daytime, with twenty-four strokes, if it is not when others come up [as enemies?] that he leaves it unprotected. If anyone completely [?] goes out from the wall mentioned,[21] he shall do penance by a special fast.

27. If anyone sitting in the bath,[22] bathes himself completely,[23] he

[19] Adoptionist heretics, flourishing in Burgundy in Columban's time. A. Hauck, *Kirchengeschichte Deutschlands*, I, 277, 367 ff.; H. von Schubert, *Geschichte der christlichen Kirche im Frühmittelalter*, pp. 182, 289.

[20] Reading "agendum" for "angendum" with Fleming.

[21] Seebass reads: "Si quis hunc ipsum absolute processerit." The translation given strictly requires "hoc" for "hunc." The sense is not quite clear. Perhaps we should omit "absolute" (completely), as being anticipated from the following canon. Fleming has "praecesserit" for "processerit."

[22] Reading with Seebass "in lumento sedens," for "iumentum petens," with the explanation offered by him. *Op. cit.*, p. 447, nn. *a, b*.

[23] "absolute." Fleming proposed "absque luto" (without being muddy).

shall do penance with a special fast. If one does this washing as permitted, standing in the presence of his brethren, if without necessity of an extensive removal of mud he shall be corrected with twenty-four stripes.

28. If anyone, indeed, in sitting in the bath, exposes his knees or arms without necessity of washing off mud, he shall not wash for six days, that is, until the second Sunday that disgraceful bather shall not wash his feet. A monk alone may wash his feet while standing in private; a senior, indeed, in public; but in the case of the latter[24] when he washes his feet, he may be washed standing.

29. Before preaching on Sunday, all, except for definite necessities, are to be assembled at the same time, that none be absent from the number of those hearing the precept except the cook and the door-keeper, and let even these see to it if they can that they be present when the sound[25] of the Gospel is heard.

30. But it is commanded to make confessions very diligently, chiefy regarding the motions of the mind, before one goes to mass, lest perchance one approach the altar unworthily, that is, if he has not a pure heart. For it is better to wait until the heart is whole and a stranger to vexation and envy than boldly to come to the judgment of the tribunal; for the altar of Christ is the tribunal, and his body thereon judges with blood those who approach it unworthily. Therefore, just as one must avoid the capital sins before taking communion, so also must one abstain from and wash away the indeterminate vices and fevers of the sick mind before the conjunction of true peace and the covenant of eternal salvation.

Here endeth.

2. SELECTIONS FROM THE REGULA COENOBIALIS OF COLUMBAN (*ca.* 600)

[THE Monastic Rule of Columban has been edited by O. Seebass.[1] In one text of the late eighth century *Concordia regularum* of Benedict of Aniane, in which it is embodied, there is attached to it a document

---

[24] Literally, "the second person mentioned."

[25] "tonitruum" (thunder, perhaps intonation).

[1] "Regula monachorum sancti Columbani abbatis," *Z.K.G.*, XV (1895), 366–86. Cf. his articles, "Fragmente einer Nonnenregel des 7. Jahrhunderts" and "Ein Beitrag zur Reconstruktion der Regel Columbas des Jüngeren," in the same periodical, XVI (1896), 465–70, and XL (1922), 132–37, respectively.

under the title "De diversitate culparum,"[2] otherwise separately extant as *S. Columbani regula coenobialis fratrum* (or *patrum*). This document bears the typical characteristics of the penitentials, though its terms apply to monks only. It appears in a longer and a shorter recension. Seebass would connect only the first nine sections of the shorter recension with the original *Rule* of Columban; while he would attach the remainder to his Penitential.[3] In both recensions the later sections contain some terms not elsewhere found in the writings of Columban, and they have probably received additions by later hands. Seebass has edited the *Regula coenobialis*,[4] printing in small type the material found only in the longer recension. The manuscripts are relatively late, one of the earliest being a St. Gall codex of the tenth or eleventh century in the Stiftsbibliothek, St. Gall, Codex Sangall. 915, which contains the document in its shorter form.[5]

Since the sections regarded by Seebass as belonging to a penitential contain little that is not paralleled in works already given, most of the material here selected is taken from the earlier sections which he thinks were written as part of a monastic rule. The document is remarkable for the frequency and severity with which it employs the discipline of the rod and is of more than usual interest for other features.]

I. [Diverse faults ought to be healed by the medicine of a diverse penance. Therefore beloved brethren],[6] it has been appointed by the holy fathers, beloved brethren, that we should make confession before eating or before going to bed or whenever it shall be convenient, [of all offenses, not only capital offenses, but also minor negligences] since confession and penance deliver [us] from death. Therefore, those little sins are not to be omitted from confession, since, as it is written, he that neglecteth small things shall perish by little and little,[7] [let confession be made before eating, before going to bed, or whenever it shall be convenient to make it.] Therefore he who is not careful with regard to the blessing at table and does not respond, "Amen," is commanded to make amends with six strokes.[8] Likewise he who talks while eating, not because of another brother's need, is commanded to make amends with six strokes; he who says that any-

---

[2] Printed as chap. x of the *Regula* in Migne, *P.L.*, LXXX, 216–24.

[3] *Über Columba von Luxeuils Klosterregel und Bussbuch* (Dresden, 1883), pp. 49–55.

[4] *Z.K.G.*, XVII (1897), 215–34.

[5] For the other manuscripts the reader is referred to the studies of Seebass just cited and to Kenney, pp. 198 f. See also appendix V.

[6] The parts found only in the longer recension are here enclosed in double brackets.

[7] Based on Ecclus, 19:1.

[8] "percussionibus" is omitted in all but two manuscripts, and these two omit the preceding words after "amen."

thing is his own, six strokes; he who does not sign with the cross the spoon which he licks, six strokes; and he who speaks in a loud tone,[9] that is, makes a louder sound than usual, six strokes.

II. If he does not sign with the cross the lamp, that is, when it has been lighted by a junior brother, and does not present it to a senior to be signed, six strokes. If he says that anything is his own, six strokes. [If he does any vain task, six strokes.] He who gouges the table with his knife shall be corrected with ten strokes.

Whoever of the brethren, having been entrusted with the charge of cooking or serving, wastes anything however little, is commanded to make amends by prayer in the church after the completion of the sequence[10] so that the brothers may pray for him. He who forgets to bow in the service,[11] that is, in the sequence (this is the bowing in the church after the close of each psalm) shall do penance in the same way. Likewise he who drops crumbs shall be corrected by a prayer; but so that this slight penance shall be assigned to him if what he has spilled is small.

III. But if out of negligence or from forgetfulness or in the transgression of self-assurance he drops more than usual both of liquids and of solids, he shall do penance by a protracted bowing[12] in the church while they sing twelve psalms at the twelfth [hour], prostrate, moving no member [of his body]. Or indeed, if it is a great amount that he has spilled, reckoning the number of measures[13] of beer or measures of any sort of thing he has spilled and lost by reason of negligence[14] let him know that he has lost that which in so many days he was accustomed normally to receive for his own use, that is, he shall drink water instead of beer [for that time]. Of what is spilled on the table and falls from it, we say that it is enough to seek pardon at the table.

[9] "plausu." Du Cange: "pro strepitu."

[10] "cursus," the "cursus psalmorum et orationum" or sequence of psalms and prayers. See Seebass, *Ueber Columba von Luxeuils Klosterregel und Bussbuch*, pp. 17–29. According to Seebass the "cursus" in the monasteries of Columban contained twenty-four psalms in summer and thirty-six in winter.

[11] "synaxi," usually the celebration of mass, here, as frequently in monastic documents, the cursus. Seebass quotes Donatus (*ca.* 650) "De synaxi, id est de cursu psalmorum et orationum," *op. cit.*, p. 29.

[12] "longa venia." "Venia," literally, "pardon," may mean any penitential act that procures pardon, but it is often specialized to refer to an "inclination" or "genuflexion." See Du Cange, *s.v.*

[13] "quantos metranos"—perhaps "metretas." Some manuscripts have "quadranos."

[14] "intercidente negligentia."

He who when leaving the cloister to engage in prayer does not bow and after receiving the benediction does not make the sign of the cross and does not approach the cross is commanded to make amends with twelve strokes. Likewise he who forgets the prayer before work or after work, twelve strokes. And he who eats without a blessing, twelve strokes. And he who when reëntering the cloister to engage in prayer does not bow within the cloister shall be corrected with twelve strokes. A brother who confesses all these and other things, up to [offenses involving?] a special fast, shall be disciplined[15] by semi-penance, that is, half-penance—and similar provisions concerning these matters.[16]

IV. He who because of coughing in the beginning of the psalm does not sing out well is commanded to make amends by six strokes. Likewise also he who indents with his teeth the cup[17] of salvation. He who fails to keep the rule regarding the offering of the host, six strokes. [An officiating priest who has not pared his nails and a deacon whose beard has not been shaved from his face who are receiving the host [or] approaching the chalice, six strokes.] And he who smiles in the service, that is, in the sequence of prayers,[18] six strokes; if he breaks out into the noise of laughter, a special fast unless it has happened pardonably. [The officiating priest and the deacon in charge of the host ought to take care not to make a mistake through wandering glances; if they neglect this [warning], they shall be corrected by six strokes. He who has forgotten the chrismal,[19] having gone far away for some task, twenty-five strokes; if he leaves it on the ground in a field and finds it at once, fifty strokes; if he sets it up on a tree,[20] thirty; if it remains there during the night, a special fast.] He who unwashed receives the Holy Bread,[21] twelve strokes.

---

[15] Emending "sic temperare interim" to "sit temperandus."

[16] This is a highly conjectural rendering of an obscure passage.

[17] "pertunderit dentibus calicem." At this period chalices were sometimes made of gold, but it is likely that in most monasteries they were of silver or silver alloy. The beautiful Ardach chalice of about 900 is of silver alloyed with copper. Irish influence is noted by students of the development of the chalice and its ornamentation on the Continent. See Cabrol, *Dictionnaire*, art. "Chalice," and *Catholic Encyclopedia*, art. "Chalice."

[18] "in cursu orationum."

[19] See n. 83, p. 114, above.   [20] "in ligno."

[21] "Eulogias." The Holy Loaf, or Eulogia, was an ordinary loaf of household bread which was cut into small slices and distributed to the people immediately after mass. It was "meant to be an emblem of the brotherly love and union which ought always to bind Christians together," D. Rock, *Church of Our Fathers*, I, 110 f. See also art. "Eulogie" in Cabrol, *Dictionnaire;* and Migne, *P.L.*, CIII, 1223, n. *c*.

He who forgets about making the oblation until the time of the office, one hundred strokes.

He who tells idle tales to another and immediately reproaches himself, a bowing[22] only; but if he does not reproach himself [but makes light of[23] the fact that he ought to apologize for these things], a special penalty of silence[24] or fifty strokes. He who when he is refuted[25] in anything merely offers an excuse and does not, seeking pardon, say forthwith "I am at fault; I repent," fifty strokes. He who simply opposes counsel with counsel, fifty strokes. He who disturbs[26] the altar, fifty strokes.

V. He who utters a loud word without restraint, except where there is need, a special penalty of silence or fifty strokes. He who makes excuse for the sake of pardon[27] shall do penance in the same way. He who replies to a brother who is making any statement: "It is not as you say"—apart from the case where seniors say it to juniors only[28]—a special penalty of silence or fifty strokes; except that this only is permissible: that he should reply to his brother of equal status, if there is something more accurately true[29] than [what] the speaker says and he remembers it: "If you well recollect, brother;" and the other, hearing these words, shall not affirm his own statement, but shall humbly say: "I suppose that you remember better; I have exceeded in word through forgetfulness; I repent of what I have said amiss." These are the words of children of God if nothing [is done] through contention, as saith the Apostle, neither by vainglory, but in humility of spirit each esteeming others better than himself.[30] Moreover, he who excuses himself shall be judged not a child of God but a child of the fleshly Adam.

VI. Whoever does not promptly fly to the door of peace of the Lord's humility, opening to others the opportunity for too much contradiction, persisting in his word of pride, shall be cut off from the liberty of holy Church to do penance in his cell until his good intention is recognized and through humility he is again incorporated in the holy congregation.

He who utters a loud speech in condemnation of the work of the

---

[22] "venia." See p. 259, n. 12, above.
[23] "detractaverit." Perhaps "refuses to acknowledge."
[24] "superpositione silentii." Cf. p. 176, above.   [25] "discutitur."
[26] "concusserit," shakes violently, putting it into disorder.
[27] "ad veniam."   [28] "simpliciter."
[29] "veratius."   [30] Based on Phil. 2:3.

doorkeeper, that the doorkeeper does not keep his hours well, a special penalty of silence or fifty strokes. And he who seeing some crime in his brother conceals it until he is corrected for another fault or for this one and then utters this against his brother, three special fasts.[31] He who finds fault with the work of the other brothers or maligns them shall do penance with three special fasts. He who utters accusation against accusation, that is, reproves the one who is reproving him, shall likewise do penance with three special fasts.

VII. He who defames any brother, or listens to a defamer without [immediately] correcting him, three special fasts. He who utters any word of scorn with sadness shall likewise do penance with three special fasts. He who finding fault with something does not wish to make it known to his praepositus until he makes it known to a senior father,[32] three special fasts—unless all this, by confession, arises[33] from modesty. If any brother is said, [if it can be done he shall receive consolation]; if he is able to bear it, he shall meanwhile refrain from confessing it so that he may modestly tell it when his depression has passed off. [The brethren shall pray for him.]

If anyone says urgently to his relative who is dwelling in a very good place:[34] "It is better that you dwell with us, or[35] with some [other] persons," three special fasts. And he who censures the custom of paying respect to a brother shall do penance in the same way.

VIII. He who teaches to a relative who is a learner any trick,[36] or anything imposed by the seniors, so that he may learn his lesson better, three special fasts.

He who dares to say to his praepositus: "You shall not judge my case, but our senior [abbot] or the other brothers," or "We shall all go to the father of the monastery," ought to be corrected for forty days in penance [on bread and water] unless he says [prostrate before the brethren] "I repent of what I said." [Any brother who is kept at any task, however weary he may be, shall nevertheless thus speak to the steward on his own behalf: "If you please I shall tell

---

[31] Possibly we ought to supply "silentii" as in various passages above, and render "special penalties of silence." But see p. 120, n. 29, above.

[32] "patri seniori." For "patri" one manuscript has "patrum." We should expect "fratri" or "fratrum" (a senior brother, a senior of the brethren).

[33] "nisi haec omnia a confessione uerecundiae fiant".

[34] Two manuscripts have "dwelling in another place."

[35] One manuscript has "than."

[36] "consanguineum docet aliquam discentem artem."

the abbot, but if not, I shall not tell him." On behalf of another: "If you repeat [it], it shall not seem hard to you if perchance I tell it to the abbot"—that obedience be guarded.

He who does not report what should be reported[37] until the day following, if he [then] remembers and reports it himself, six strokes; if he forgets until he is questioned, twelve. If anyone forgets until the following day to ask about the penance that is due, six strokes. He who murmurs, who says: "I shall not do it unless the abbot, or a second person, says so," three special fasts. The sequence is not necessary or the leap with twelve strokes. It is forbidden for anyone to hold another's hand.

The steward shall kindly provide the things to be supplied to those who come, both pilgrims and other brothers, and all the brothers shall be prepared to minister [to them] with all service for God's sake. Even if the steward is not aware or is not present, the others shall diligently do what is necessary and take care of their belongings[38] when they give these over ready to be safeguarded; but if they are neglectful, a penance [shall be required] for these things such as in the judgment of the priest it shall seem best to employ].

He who when brought to account does not ask pardon shall do penance with a special fast. He who without asking visits other brothers in their cells shall do penance in the same way, or [he who] goes into the kitchen after nones [without order or command], a special fast; or [he who] without asking goes beyond the wall, that is, beyond the fence of the monastery, a special fast. Youths to whom a bound has been set that they may not speak to one another on both sides, if they go beyond it, three special fasts. [They shall only say this: "Know that we may not speak with you."] And if anyone commands them [to do] what is not permitted, they shall say: "Know that we may not," and if he still commands it, he shall be condemned to three special fasts; but they shall say, "We will do what you say," that the boon of obedience be conserved. This however is to be very specially guarded against, that just as they do not speak to one another directly, so neither shall they converse by the mouth of another brother. But if they knowingly transgress they shall do penance in the same way as if they had spoken together.

He who lets the chrismal fall and breaks nothing shall be corrected with twelve strokes.

[37] "quod commodat" (what [it] is customary [to report]).   [38] "utensilia."

He who utters a vain word ought to be sentenced to silence for two hours thereafter or to twelve strokes.

IX. Penitent brothers, however difficult or dirty the tasks they do, shall not wash their heads except on Sunday, that is, the eighth day; but if this rule is not followed, for fifteen days; or, at least,[39] on account of the increase of their flowing hair each shall follow the judgment of a senior in washing. [Going off the road without asking or blessing, six strokes.] The praepositus of the table, if he knows how, shall impose small penances at the table; and more than twenty-five strokes shall not be given [at one time.]

Penitent brothers and poor men, a penance of psalms; that is, for those who are required to sing psalms on account of a vision in the night, since for an illusion of the devil or because of the nature of the vision some ought to sing thirty, some twenty-four, psalms in order, others fifteen, [and] other poor men, twelve of the psalms in penance; although on Sunday night and in the time of the fifty days[40] penitents shall kneel.[41]

[The remainder of Section IX is omitted. Most of it is in the longer recension only. It deals with small monastic restrictions and directions of which sufficient illustration has already been given. Of Sections X–XV only No. XI and a few sentences from No. XV are here included.]

XI. If anyone holds a conversation with a secular person without an order, twenty-four psalms. If anyone when he has completed his task both fails to ask for another and does something without an order, he shall sing twenty-four psalms. If anyone is double-tongued and disturbs the hearts of his brethren, one day on dry bread[42] and water. If anyone eats in a strange monastery[43] without command and [then] comes to his own monastery, one day on dry bread. Or he

---

[39] "aut certe." From this point the text shows the influence of a seventh century *Rule* for nuns published by Seebass in *Z.KG.*, XVI (1896), 465–70. The meaning of the latter part of the sentence is not very clear.

[40] That is, from Easter to Pentecost. Cf. pp. 175, 213, above.

[41] In view of the custom referred to on p. 308, n. 56, we should expect "shall not kneel." The language here is identical with that of the Nun's Rule referred to in n. 39. It is questionable whether "non" has been dropped by the scribe or whether the regulation as it stands is original; if the latter, the writer was probably consciously attempting to institute a change in the direction of greater austerity. The period of post-Easter rejoicing was already interrupted by the Rogation Days, introduced in the fifth century.

[42] "paxmatio" as usual in X–XV for "paximatio." See p. 102, n. 34, above.

[43] "domo." Perhaps a secular house is meant; but the monastery is evidently referred to as "suae domui" later in the sentence.

who has walked in the world and talks of worldly sin, one day on bread and water. And he who indifferently listens to one who is murmuring and defaming or consents to one who does anything against the rule,[44] by confession, one day on dry bread.

XV. . . . [He who censures otherwise than gently shall be put under observation[45] until he seeks pardon from the brother he has accused and [shall do penance] with thirty blows[46] or fifteen psalms. . . . He who talks familiarly with a woman alone without [the presence of] assured persons shall remain without food or [do penance] for two days on bread and water, or [receive] two hundred strokes . . .

He who speaks while eating, six blows. And he whose voice sounds from table to table, six blows. If it sounds outside from [within] the building, or from without sounds within, twelve strokes. . . .

For saying "mine" or "yours," six strokes. . . .

If he presumes to speak in the stated time of silence, without necessity, seventeen blows. . . .

If he falters[47] in singing a psalm, if he makes a response out of place or too harshly or contumaciously, a special fast. . . .

If he presumes to converse at some length with one who is not a coresident of his own cell, a special fast. If he holds another's hand, a special fast. If he prays with one who is suspended from prayer, a special fast.

If he sees one of his relatives or secular friends or talks to him, without orders, if he receives a letter from anyone, if he presumes to give away [something] without [permission of] his abbot, a special fast. If he hinders anyone from the completion of a necessary act, a special fast. If through ardor of mind he exceeds the lawful measure of religion, a special fast. If on account of his indifference he presumes to hold back another who is eager from a lawful act, a special fast.

. . . The talkative person is to be sentenced to silence, the disturber to gentleness, the gluttonous to fasting, the sleepy fellow to watchfulness, the proud to imprisonment, the deserter to expulsion. Each shall suffer things corresponding to what he deserves, that the righteous may live righteously. Amen.]

[44] Literally, "or one doing anything against the rule, and he consents."   [45] "notetur."
[46] "plagis." "Plaga est percussio dura" (a "plaga" is a severe "percussio") says Raban Maur. Migne, *P.L.*, CXII, 1019. "Percussio" is the word translated "stroke" in this document.
[47] "titubaverit," perhaps: "makes his voice waver mockingly." Cf. p. 279, n. 7, below.

3. FROM THE PENITENTIAL FORMERLY THOUGHT TO BE CUMMEAN'S (*8th century*)

[THE PENITENTIAL known as the *Excarpsus Cummeani* is called by Oakley the *Pseudo-Cummean*.[1] The edition of Fleming in his *Collectanea sacra* (1667) is given in Migne, *P.L.*, LXXXVII, 977–98. Wasserschleben has edited it from six manuscripts,[2] and Schmitz includes it in both his volumes.[3] In his second volume the text is preceded (pp. 560–96) by an extended discussion of the manuscripts, of which he has used ten. While the *Pseudo-Cummean* contains much of the material of the genuine *Cummean*, its compiler has also borrowed freely from the works of Gildas, Columban, and Theodore, and from the *Bigotian Penitential*. It bears a close resemblance to the penitential called by Schmitz *Parisiense* and published in his *Bussbücher* I, pp. 677–97, from a thirteenth-century codex. Schmitz thought the *Parisiense* and the *Excarpsus Cummeani* had their common source in a document now lost. In the earlier of his two volumes he suggested that "possibly this common source is the hitherto undiscovered *Penitential of Cummean*."[4] This was written, of course, before Zettinger's identification of the genuine *Cummean*. The passages which he cited in this connection as common and peculiar to the two documents are not found in Zettinger's text. In his second volume Schmitz, indeed, came to regard the existence of a genuine penitential of Cummean as improbable.[5]

The *Excarpsus*, or *Pseudo-Cummean*, almost certainly belongs to the eighth century and is thus probably earlier than the *Parisiense*. The argument of Schmitz that it cannot be earlier than the first half of the ninth century on account of the resemblance of section III, can. 43 to can. 11 of the synod of Friuli (796) cannot be admitted in view of paleographical evidence, the fact that the passages are not closely parallel, and the possibility that the penitential inspired the Friuli canon. The number of manuscripts would indicate a wide circulation. It is an ample document, furnishing guidance to the confessor on many points and embodying a mass of decisions taken from the venerable codes of two centuries of tradition. Kenney remarks: "The *Pseudo-Cummean* was the form in which the Irish penitentials obtained their greatest popularity in Europe."[6] The possibility that it had some connection with Cummean

---

[1] *English Penitential Discipline*, p. 30.

[2] *Bussordnungen*, pp. 460–93. On the manuscripts, some of which are of the eighth century, see above, p. 63.   [3] Schmitz I, pp. 602–53; Schmitz II, pp. 597–644.

[4] *Op. cit.*, I, 681.   [5] *Op. cit.*, II, 590.

[6] Kenney, p. 243. Cf. Fournier and Le Bras, I, 86, and Le Bras's article "Pénitentiels," in *Dict. de théol. catholique*, XII. G. Jecker in *Die Heimat des hl. Pirmin des Apostels der Alamannen*, pp. 134 ff. (*Beiträge zur Gesch. des alten Mönchtums*, XIII, 1927), has shown a striking parallel with the language of a section of St. Pirmin's *Scarapsus*, which he dates about 724. The word "scarapsus" is equivalent to "excarpsus" as used in the usual title of *Pseudo-Cummean*. *Ibid.*, pp. 82 f. The *Scarapsus* of St. Pirmin, of which Jecker furnishes an edition, is in no sense a penitential.

of Bobbio, who died at a great age in the reign of Liutprand (711–44), can hardly be excluded.

As the body of the document is entirely unoriginal, it is not necessary to give a translation of it here. The introductory sections, however, divided in the Schmitz text into Chapters I and II, contain materials of interest for the development of penitential practice. The first part of Chapter I is a copy of the Prologue of the genuine Cummean. A transition is marked by the words: "In alio loco" (In another place), and the Introduction continues in the paragraphs given below. The reader will note the resemblance to a section of the Introduction to the *Bigotian Penitential* in the first paragraph quoted. The text used is that given in Schmitz II; the passage beginning on page 600. Schmitz follows a ninth-century Darmstadt codex (probably now Cologne 91) and gives variants of the manuscripts and the Fleming edition.]

[LATTER PART OF] CHAPTER I [PRINCIPLES OF PENITENTIAL DISCIPLINE]

But this is to be carefully observed in every penance: how long one continues in his misdeeds, with what learning he is instructed, with what kind of passion he is assailed, with what degree of courage he stands, with what sorrow[7] he seems to be afflicted, and with how great force[8] he has been driven to sin. For almighty God who knows the heart of every man and has bestowed diverse natures will not compute the weights of sins with an exact scale[9] of penance; as the prophecy is: "For the gith shall not be threshed with saws, neither shall the cart wheel turn about upon cummin, but gith and cummin shall be beaten out with a rod. But with a staff shall bread corn be broken small";[10] as this [passage] says: "The mighty shall be mightily tormented."[11] Whence a certain wise man says, "to whom more is intrusted from him shall more be exacted."[12] Therefore let the priests of the Lord learn who preside over the churches, that a part is given to them together with those for whose misdeeds they make satisfaction. But what is it to make satisfaction for a misdeed unless you

---

[7] Literally, "what kind of tearfulness."

[8] Literally, "what kind of weight."

[9] "aequali lancea." The "lancea" was a spear. The idea seems to be that of a steelyard used in weighing.

[10] Isa. 28:27–28. (For "gith" the A.V. has "fitches," modern "vetches.") According to the punctuation in Vulgate and Douay, the words "with a staff" go with "cummin" in the previous sentence. The above passage is substantially quoted in the eighth book of the *Collectio canonica* of Anselm of Lucca (1036–86), who ascribes it to an Irish synod of the time of Charlemagne (Carolus) at which were present Leo, bishop of Rome, and Theodoric, archbishop of England and Ireland! See Wasserschleben, *Bussordnungen*, p. 441. Cf. p. 151, n. 27, above.   [11] Wisd. 6:7.   [12] Based on Luke 12:48.

take the sinner and by warning, exhortation, and teaching, lead him to penance and bring it about that you may be said to have made satisfaction for his misdeed, so that God may be satisfied as a result of such a conversion? When therefore you are such a priest and such is your teaching and your word, there is given to you a part of those whom you have corrected, that their merit may be your reward and their salvation your glory. Lord have mercy.

Of the Measures of Penance

We read in the penitential or the canons that for criminal offenses some ought to do penance for seven years, some for ten or up to twelve or fifteen years, and that for one or two or three of these penance ought to be done on bread and water. Now it is to be understood that for as long as one remains in his sins, for so long is the penance to be extended. But with some this case seems grievous and difficult. Therefore some state, twelve three-day periods for one year in which he ought to do penance on bread and water, and this Theodore approves;[13] others, one hundred days with an allowance of half a loaf of dry bread[14] with salt and water and fifty psalms every night; others, fifty special fasts on alternate days.[15] Moreover, some wise men say that one year on bread and water [is equivalent to] twelve two-day periods; for the second year he shall sing twelve times fifty psalms, kneeling; for the third year he shall make a two-day penance in such a venerable festival as he chooses; he shall sing the Psalter, standing motionless; for the fourth year he shall receive, naked, three hundred strokes with rods; for the fifth year he shall estimate how much his food is worth and give that amount in alms; for the sixth year he shall redeem himself according to what he is worth,[16] and from this amount he shall make restitution to him to whom he did evil; if the latter is not alive, he shall seek out the legal heirs; for the seventh year he shall relinquish all evil and do good. And for small offenses we read that one ought to do penance for a month or a week on bread and water. But whoever is able to fulfill what is written in the penitential—it is good. Yet to those who are too feeble in body or in mind we give the advice that if what we have said above seems grievous to them, [each] when he is due to fast on

[13] Cf. *Poenit. Theod.* I, vii, 5, p. 190, above.
[14] "panis paximatus." Cf. p. 102, n. 34, above.
[15] Literally, "with one night intervening."   [16] That is, his "éric," or wergeld.

bread and water shall [rather] sing for every day fifty psalms, kneeling, and seventy psalms without kneeling, and for one week he shall chant three hundred psalms in sequence, kneeling, or if he is not able to kneel he shall sing four hundred and twenty psalms and fulfill this within a church or in a secret place. Moreover, this same penitent shall make preparation for this, and for whatever time he ought to fast he shall complete it in that order of psalms which we have determined; and afterwards through all his days he shall dine at sext—however, he shall abstain from flesh and wine; he shall receive in sobriety other food which the Lord hath given him after he has chanted the psalms. And he who does not know the psalms and is not able to fast shall choose a righteous man who will fulfill this in his stead, and he shall redeem this with his own payment or labor; this he shall disburse among the poor at the rate of a denarius for every day.

Chapter II. Of the Rich or Powerful Man, How He Redeems Himself for Criminal Offenses

He shall return to the Gospel and imitate Zaccheus who said: "Lord, the half of my goods I give to the poor"; and he adds further, "And if I have unjustly taken anything of another's, I restore him fourfold."[17] And he merited to hear from the Lord: "For this day is salvation come to this house": that is, he receives the remission of all his sins. But according to the traditions of the fathers we determine thus: if perchance they from whom he has unjustly taken something are not in the present world, or if his spirit be not able to do as the Gospel says, he shall give the half. For we are taking this into account, that to the value of his own life he shall disburse so much in silver for alms, and again as much as he is worth in silver he shall bestow of his land on the churches of God for alms, and as much again as he is worth in money he shall use either to set men free from slavery or to redeem captives, and all the things which he has done amiss from that day he shall not repeat, and from the time when he ceases to sin he shall not cease to take the communion of the body and blood and Christ. Let him know that he participates in that sentence, since Zaccheus merited it. But if one of inferior rank, that is, if a slave or a freedman is seeking penance and such faults are

[17] Based on Luke 19:8.

found in him[18] that according to the aforesaid number of years he ought to do penance, and in his case, as usual, it befalls because of weakness or other necessity that he is not able to observe in its entirety what is written in the penitential, then when he ought to do penance for one year on bread and water, he shall [instead] give for alms twenty-six solidi and fast for one day until nones, on another day constantly until vespers, and afterward [he shall] eat what he has; and through the three forty-day periods he shall estimate the amount which he takes and contribute the half in alms. In the second year he shall give twenty solidi, and in this same second year there is remission of penance from Christmas to Epiphany and from Easter until Pentecost. In the third year he shall give nineteen solidi. These make sixty-four solidi from the first until the third year. And that is not to be let slip which the Apostle says, "He who sins through the body shall make amends through the body,"[19] that is, fasting, vigils, supplications, and prayers to God,[20] for it is written, "Giving no offense to any man, that the ministry of God be not blamed, but in all things let us exhibit ourselves as ministers of God."[21] We read that Christ fasted though he committed no sin; likewise also the apostles after the gift of the Holy Spirit. Therefore we ought to be imitators of them with whom we wish to participate in the heavenly kingdom. On this account it is needful to add something by way of payment beyond these things, that is, in fasting on Wednesdays and Fridays from wine or boiled foods, that is, from flesh. Likewise with respect to continence, he shall abstain from his wife on the other days according to what the saints have determined in the canons; these are: the Lord's day and the solemn feasts, whether in two appointed forty-day periods or on Wednesdays and Fridays, knowing that it is written, "He that laboreth more shall receive a greater reward."[22] These are the days which are not reckoned as days of penance: the Lord's day, Nativity, Epiphany,[23] Easter, the Lord's ascension, Pentecost, the day of St. John Baptist, the day of St. Mary ever Virgin, and the days of the Twelve Apostles or of St. Martin, or the venerable festival of that saint who seems to rest in the body in the special province.

[18] "such . . . him" is ungrammatical in the text, but this is the probable meaning.

[19] See above, p. 232, n. 82.

[20] Text is "a Deo"; the preposition is evidently a mistake and we read "Deo" as a dative.

[21] II Cor. 6:3–4. For "ministry of God" ("ministerium Dei") Vulgate has "our ministry" ("ministerium nostrum").   [22] Cf. Luke 10:7; I Tim. 5:18.   [23] "theofania."

CHAPTER V

Anonymous and Pseudonymous Frankish and Visigothic Penitentials of the Eighth and Ninth Centuries

1. THE JUDGMENT OF CLEMENT (*ca.* 700–750)

[HADDAN and Stubbs[1] reprint from Kunstmann the short penitential under the title *Iudicium Clementis*, which is translated below. Kunstmann first published this document[2] from a Munich manuscript, and it was reprinted by Wasserschleben, who collated with this text a manuscript of Heiligenkreuz.[3] Kunstmann's identification of the author with Willibrord (658–739), the Irish-trained English missionary who became bishop of Utrecht in 695, has no support except the fact that at his consecration Willibrord took the name Clemens. This name, however, occurs so frequently among monks and ecclesiastics of the early Middle Ages that any identification of the author without further evidence is perilous. Nothing in the content of the document would definitely exclude the possibility of its authorship by Willibrord Clement; but canon 3 seems to imply a stage of commercialization which is more evident in the generation after his death.][4]

Here begins the Judgment of Clement.

1. If anyone by force or by any device in evil manner breaks into another's property, he shall do penance for three years, one of these on bread and water, and give liberal alms.

2. If anyone belonging to the ministry of holy Church commits any kind of fraud, he shall do penance for seven years, three of these on bread and water.

3. If anyone fasts for a reward and takes upon himself the sins of another, he is not worthy to be called a Christian. He shall fast for himself as much as he promised to fast for the other and give to the poor what he has received.

---

[1] *Councils*, III, 226 f.
[2] *Die lateinischen Poenitentialbücher der Angelsachsen*, pp. 176 f.
[3] *Bussordnungen*, p. 433 f.   [4] See above, pp. 48 ff.

4. If anyone who has a betrothed defiles her[5] and marries her sister, and if[6] she who has suffered defilement kills herself, all who have consented to this deed shall do penance for ten years.

5. If any priest or cleric gets himself or another drunk, if it is for good fellowship[7] he shall do penance for forty days; a layman, seven days; and if he does this from spite,[8] he shall be judged as a murderer.

6. If anyone unwittingly gives to another drink or food in which there was a dead mouse or household beast,[9] he shall perform three special fasts.

7. If through negligence anyone does work on Sunday, either bathes himself, or shaves, or washes his head, he shall do penance for seven days; if he does it again, he shall do penance for forty days; and if he does it through contempt of the day and will not amend, he shall be cast out of the Catholic Church, as a Judas.

8. If through gluttony anyone dines before the appointed hour, without weariness or necessity, he shall do penance for two days on bread and water.

9. If anyone eats and afterward takes communion, he shall do penance for seven days on bread and water. Boys shall be beaten[10] for this.

10. If anyone denies God without necessity and recants, he shall do penance for ten years, three of these on bread and water.

11. According to the canons penitents ought not to take communion before the completion of the penance; however, out of mercy we give permission [for them to do so] after one year or after seven months.

12. If anyone is troubled by a devil and kills himself, it is permitted to pray for him.

13. A woman may not place the unconsecrated host[11] or the linen or the chalice upon the altar, moreover she may not go into the chancel beside the altar.

14. If anyone puts away his legal wife and marries another, he shall be excommunicated by Christians, even if the former wife consents.

---

[5] "vitium ei intulerit."   [6] The Heiligenkreuz codex inserts "perchance."
[7] "pro humanitate."   [8] "per odium."
[9] Probably a cat, as in the *Merseburg Penitential*, can. 86: "a familiare bestia, quod est muriceps."—Wasserschleben, *Bussordnungen*, p. 400.
[10] Emending "vapulent" to "vapulentur."   [11] "oblatam."

15. Legal marriage may not be dissolved unless there is an agreement of both [parties] that they shall remain unmarried.

16. A layman may not read a lection in the church nor sing the alleluia but only[12] the psalms and responses without the alleluia.

17. No spoil shall be received in the church before he who took the spoil does penance.

18. If anyone is troubled by a devil, he may not touch the sacred mysteries. If by the mercy of God and by fasting he is cleansed, he shall after[13] ten years be received in the office of the clerics, not of the priests.

19. If an enemy seizes the wife of anyone, and if he is not able to recover her, after an entire year he may marry another; and if she afterward comes back, she may marry another man.

20. If during any festival anyone coming to the church sings[14] outside it or dances[15] or sings amatory songs,[16] he shall be excommunicated by the bishop or presbyter or cleric and shall remain excommunicate so long as he does not do penance.

2. THE BURGUNDIAN PENITENTIAL (*ca.* 700–725)

[THE *Poenitentiale Burgundense* may be regarded as one of the earliest of a series of anonymous penitentials, very similar in content, which originated in the Frankish lands and circulated in the eighth and ninth centuries.[1] Schmitz has published it from the late eighth-century manuscript in pre-Carolingian minuscule, of the Royal Library of Brussels, Codex Burgund. 8780–8793, now Brussels 2493.[2] It closely resembles the *Bobbio Penitential*, and there is no certainty as to which is the earlier document. In view of the discussions concerning the Bobbio manuscript, possibly both should be ascribed to the first quarter of the eighth century. The introductory paragraph and canon 1 are here omitted. These parts are copied from the *Penitential of Columban*, B, Introduction and canon 1 (p. 251, above), with a few words omitted and numerous corruptions of the text.]

---

[12] "nisi."

[13] Reading "post" for "per," with the Heiligenkreuz codex.

[14] Emending "pallat" to "psallat." Cf. Ps. 68:13. The Heiligenkreuz codex has "spallit." Perhaps, however, we should read "ballat." "Ballare" and "saltare," though sometimes synonymous, are coupled in the Penitential of Silos, xi, where de Berganza notes: "Ballare, id est cantare." See below, p. 289.   [15] "saltat."

[16] Reading "cantationes" for "orationes," with the Heiligenkreuz codex.

[1] Cf. P. Fournier, "Études sur les pénitentiels," IV, in *Revue d'histoire et de littérature religieuses*, VIII (1903), 532–34.

[2] Schmitz II, pp. 319–22. On the manuscript see some remarks contained on pp. 359 f. of Lowe's article cited below, p. 278.

2. If anyone commits homicide by accident, that is, not intentionally, he shall do penance for five years, three of these on bread and water.

3. If anyone consents to the commission of homicide, and [if] it is committed, he shall do penance for seven years, three of these on bread and water. But if he intends it and cannot do it, three[3] . . . of these on bread and water.

4. If anyone commits fornication as the Sodomites did, he shall do penance for ten years, three of these on bread and water, and never sleep with another.

5. If anyone commits perjury, he shall do penance for seven years, three on bread and water, and never afterward take an oath.

6. If anyone commits perjury under compulsion, on account of some necessity, or unaware, he shall do penance for three years, one of these on bread and water.

7. If anyone commits a capital theft, that is, [steals] animals or breaks into houses or robs a well-protected place,[4] he shall do penance for seven years, three of these on bread and water. He who commits a theft of small articles shall do penance for three years.

8. If anyone commits adultery, that is, with another's wife or betrothed, or violates her virginity, if a cleric, he shall do penance for three years, one of these on bread and water; if a presbyter, seven years, three of these on bread and water.

9. If by his magic[5] anyone destroys anybody, he shall do penance for seven years, three of these on bread and water.

10. If anyone is a magician for love and destroys nobody, if he is a cleric, he shall do penance for an entire year on bread and water; if a deacon, three [years], one of these on bread and water; if a priest, five, two of these on bread and water. Especially if by this anyone deceives a woman with respect to her child, each one shall increase [the penance] by five forty-day periods on bread and water, lest he be charged with homicide.

11. If anyone commits fornication with women, if a cleric, he shall do penance for three years; if a monk or a deacon, five years; if a priest, five [years].

---

[3] Something is evidently omitted between "three" and "of these." The *Bobbio Penitential*, can. 4, has: "he shall do penance for three years, two on bread and water."
[4] "meliorem praesidium furaverit." But cf. *Pseudo-Romanum*, 26, p. 304, n. 43, below.
[5] "veneficium."

12. If any cleric [in lower orders] or one of any higher rank, who has had a wife, after his conversion or elevation has intercourse with her again, let him know that he has committed adultery. For this, if he is a deacon, he shall do penance for five years, two of these on bread and water; if a priest, seven, three of these on bread and water.

13. If anyone commits fornication with a nun or a woman vowed to God, as in the above decision each shall do penance according to his order.

14. If anyone through concupiscence or lust commits fornication by himself, he shall do penance for an entire year.

15. If anyone is the violator of a tomb, he shall do penance for five years, three of these on bread and water.

16. If anyone lusts after a woman and is not able to sin with her or [if] the woman refuses him, he shall do penance for an entire year.

17. If anyone neglects the Eucharist, that is, the communion of the body or of the blood of the Lord, and[6] thereby loses it, he shall do penance for an entire year on bread and water.

18. If he vomits it through drunkenness or gluttony, he shall do penance for the three forty-day periods on bread and water. If indeed [it is] through infirmity, he shall do penance for one week.

19. If any cleric or his wife overlays a baby, he [or she] shall do penance for three years, one of these on bread and water.

20. If, indeed, anyone is a wizard, that is, a conjurer-up of storms, he shall do penance for seven years, three of these on bread and water.

21. If anyone intentionally cuts off any member [of his body], he shall do penance for three years, one of these on bread and water.

22. If anyone, moreover, exacts usury from anyone, he shall do penance for three years, one of these on bread and water.

23. If anyone by force or by any device in evil fashion attacks or carries off another's property, he shall likewise do penance according to the above sentence and give liberal alms.

24. If anyone commits sacrilege (that is, they call augurs those who pay respect to omens) whether he takes auguries by birds or by whatever evil device [he does it], he shall do penance for three years on bread and water.

25. If any soothsayer (those whom they call diviners) makes any

6 Literally, "or."

divinations, since this is also of the demons, he shall do penance for five years, three of these on bread and water.

26. If anyone strikes another and sheds blood, he shall do penance for forty days on bread and water.

27. If anyone is greedy or covetous or proud or envious or drunken or [if he] holds his brother in hatred or [is guilty of] other such offenses, which it is tedious to enumerate, he shall do penance for three years on bread and water.

28. If anyone has what is called without reason the *Sortes sanctorum*,[7] or other oracles,[8] or draws lots by any evil device or regards such practices with awe, he shall do penance for three years.

29. If anyone takes a vow or absolves from one by trees or springs or lattices or anywhere except in a church, he shall do penance for three years on bread and water; for this also is sacrilege or of the demons. He who eats or drinks in these places shall do penance for a year on bread and water.

30. If after he has vowed himself to God any cleric reverts once more to the secular habit as a dog to his vomit or takes a wife, he shall do penance for ten years, three of these on bread and water, and [he shall] never afterward be joined in marriage. But if he refuses, a holy synod or the Apostolic See shall separate them from the communion and fellowship of all Catholics. Likewise also a woman, if[9] after she has vowed herself to God she gives way to such a crime, shall undergo an equal sentence.

31. If anyone commits a falsification, he shall do penance for seven years, three of these on bread and water. He who consents, moreover, shall do penance for five years.

32. If anyone practices any kind of hunting, a cleric shall do penance for a year, a deacon, for two years, and a priest, for three.

33. If anyone commits fornication with beasts, if he is a cleric, he shall do penance for two years on bread and water; if a priest, five years, three of these on bread and water.

34. If anyone [does] what many do on the Kalends of January as was done hitherto among the pagans, seats himself on a stag, as it is

[7] See above, p. 229, n. 66.
[8] "sortes" (lots), here probably formulae for divining like the "Sortes sanctorum."
[9] Emending "setale" to "si tale."

called, or goes about in [the guise of] a calf,[10] he shall do penance for three years, for this is demoniacal.

35. If any woman intentionally brings about abortion, she shall do penance for three years on bread and water.

36. If anyone is a wizard,[11] that is, takes away the minds of men by the invocation of demons or renders them mad,[12] he shall do penance for five years, three of these on bread and water.

37. If he violates any virgin or widow, he shall do penance for three years on bread and water.

38. If anyone is an informer,[13] which is abominable, he shall receive the sentence of the above canon.[14]

39. If anyone by any device[15] leads a slave or a man of any sort into captivity or conveys him away, he shall do penance for three years.

40. If anyone intentionally burns with fire[16] anybody's house or premises, he shall undergo the above sentence.

41. If anyone is in any way guilty of deception or neglect with respect to anything concerning the ministry of Holy Church or any other kind of work, he shall do penance for seven years, three of these on bread and water, and then be reconciled.

[10] Emending "vecola" to "vetula" (classical "vitula"). The pagan celebration of the Kalends of January persisted despite continual condemnation in the Church. Numerous fifth- and sixth-century descriptions of the celebration are preserved in the denunciations of prelates. "What rational person could believe" exclaims Caesarius of Arles (d. 543), "that he would find some, of sound mind, who, making a stag ("cervulum facientes") would wish to change themselves into a wild beast? Some are arrayed in skins of cattle ("pecudum"), others put on the heads of beasts."—Migne, *P.L.*, XXXIX, 2001. Schmitz I (pp. 311 f.) points to the condemnation of the celebration by Pope Zachary in 743 and thinks the custom even more prevalent at Rome than in Germany at this period. The *Scarapsus* of St. Pirmin, *ca.* 724, condemns this and numerous other superstitious practices referred to in the penitentials. G. Jecker, *Die Heimat des hl. Pirmin*, pp. 54 ff.; 131 ff.

[11] "mathematicus."

[12] Emending "debacantes fuerit" to "debacantes (debacchantes) fecerit." Cf. *Poenit. Valicellanum*, 80, Schmitz I, p. 303.

[13] "delaturas fecerit." Some of the penitentials of this period in a parallel canon read "ligaturas" for "delaturas" here. "Ligaturas" (amulets), is probably the original of the regulation, "delaturas" having been introduced under the influence of the 73d canon of the synod of Elvira (305), which is entitled "De delatoribus" (Of informers), that is, those who betray Christians to their persecutors. The monks may have understood "dilatura" in the sense of "slander" or "backbiting." See Schmitz II, pp. 306 ff. Fournier, "Études sur les pénitentiels," I, in *Revue d'histoire et de littérature religieuses*, VI (1901), 312 ff.

[14] Literally, "line."

[15] Emending "igneo" to "ingenio," in accord with *Pseudo-Romanum*, 49, and *Valicellanum*, 62.

[16] Reading "igne cremaverit" for "igneo semaverit," as in *Poenit. Bobbiense*, can. 36.

3. SELECTIONS FROM THE BOBBIO PENITENTIAL
(ca. 700–725)

[THIS PENITENTIAL, first published by Mabillon[1] from a partly uncial codex of Bobbio, now Paris B.N. Lat. 13246, was regarded by Wasserschleben as of the seventh or early eighth century.[2] Schmitz has dated it about the middle of the eighth century.[3] A scholarly transcription is furnished by E. A. Lowe, in the Henry Bradshaw Society Publications.[4] Lowe supposes that the codex was written "a little over twelve hundred years ago" by a busy priest in a French area.[5] Both script and contents, however, show a strong Irish influence, while Visigothic elements are also discernible.

The penitential contains forty-seven canons, of which Nos. 1–38 resemble those of the Burgundian so closely that no translation of them is here required. Canons 39–44 are variants of the common class of regulations on sexual and ritual offenses, which are sufficiently illustrated elsewhere in this volume. Of some liturgical interest, however, are canons 46–47 and the two prayers[6] appended to the document, which are given below.]

46. A priest who, when he is offering, lets fall the Eucharist from his hands to the earth, if it is not found shall sweep [the place] with a clean broom and burn [the sweepings] with fire and conceal the ashes of them on the ground under the altar and do penance for a half a year. But if he finds the place, he shall do likewise and do penance for forty days. If, however, it falls [only] to the altar, he shall do penance for one day. If it glances to the ground, he shall lick it up with his tongue. If there was a board [where it fell], he shall scrape it. If there was not, he shall set a board there, that the blood of Christ be not trodden upon, [and shall do penance] for forty days. But if a drop falls upon the altar, he shall suck it up and do penance for three days. If it passes through one linen cloth to another, he shall do penance for six days on bread [and water]; and if to the third [altar-cloth], he shall do penance for seven days; and he shall put the chalice under

---

[1] *Museum Italicum* (1724), I, ii, 392 ff. Mabillon supplies a few footnotes on readings and in interpretation of locutions used and gives (pp. 275 ff.) a description of the codex.

[2] *Bussordnungen*, p. 57; text, pp. 407–12.

[3] Schmitz II, pp. 322 f.; text, pp. 323–26.

[4] Vol. LVIII, *The Bobbio Missal, a Gallican Mass-Book* (1920), 173–76. Cf. Vol. LIII, a facsimile of the codex (1917), and Vol. LXI, *The Bobbio Missal, Notes and Studies*, containing elaborate essays by A. Wilmart, E. A. Lowe, and H. A. Wilson (1924). The last-mentioned volume is of the highest value for those interested in the paleography, date, and provenance of the codex.

[5] *Henry Bradshaw Society Publications*, LXI, 105.

[6] On these see Wilmart, *op. cit.*, "Notice du missel de Bobbio," pp. 12 f.

the linens, pour water [upon them] three times and drink it. If when he raises the chalice he also pours it out on the ground, he shall do penance for ten days on bread and water.

47. If a priest falters[7] on the Lord's Prayer, one day on bread and water. Moreover, he who communicates unwittingly shall do penance for seven days. He who communicates through ignorance shall do penance for six days.

A Prayer over a Penitent

Dearly beloved brethren, let us beseech the almighty and merciful God, Who desires not the death of sinners, but that they be converted and live, that this Thy servant, making amends unto true pardon, be accorded[8] the pardon of mercy; if there are any wounds which he has received from all his offenses after the wave of the sacred bath,[9] in this public confession of his misdeeds may they be so healed that no signs of the scars remain. Through our Lord Jesus Christ.

Another Prayer

Our Savior and Redeemer Who, gracious and pitiful, dost grant pardon not only to penitents but even to all those who do not previously desire to come, as suppliants we seek that the pardon bestowed of the communion of Thy body and blood may win for this Thy servant the celestial benediction. Through [our Lord Jesus Christ].

4. SELECTIONS FROM THE PARIS PENITENTIAL
(*ca.* 750)

[THIS DOCUMENT, called by Wasserschleben *Poenitentiale Parisiense* and by Schmitz *Poenitientiale Parisiense* II,[1] is preserved in an eighth-century uncial codex with Insular symptoms, Paris Bibl. Nat. Lat. 7193, originally part of Codex Vat. Regin. 316.[2] In canons 1–33 it repeats, in improved Latin, most of the canons of the *Burgundian Penitential*. The remainder of the document (canons 34–61) is made up chiefly of canons taken from British and Irish documents. Only the last three canons are here included. For the text see Wasserschleben, *Bussordnungen*, pp. 412–18; Schmitz II, pp. 327–30, and the scholarly transcription by E. A. Lowe, "The Vatican Manuscript of the Gelasian Sacramentary," *Journal*

---

[7] "tutoaverit," "id est si cantando titubaverit," says Mabillon, quoted in Schmitz II, p. 326, n. 1. Cf. p. 265, n. 47, above.

[8] Emending "indulgeat" to "indulgeatur."

[9] That is, if the penitent after his penance or "second baptism" still suffers remorse for his sins.

[1] In view of his discovery of another penitential which he calls *Parisiense*, a work closely resembling the *Excerpt of Cummean*, and probably of the ninth century. See Schmitz I, 677–97.   [2] Cf. Lowe's article cited above, pp. 54, 62.

of Theol. Studies, XXVII (1926), 357–73 (text of *Penitential,* pp. 365–68), who points out the resemblance of the manuscript to that of the *Burgundian,* mentioned above, p. 278.]

59. If anyone keeps in his breast anger with another, he shall be judged a murderer; if he will not be reconciled to his brother whom he holds in hatred, he shall do penance on bread and water until such time as he is reconciled to him.

60. Moreover, concerning the capital sins, that is, homicide adultery, perjury, fornication, impurity, laymen shall do penance for three years; clerics, five; subdeacons, six; deacons, seven; presbyters, ten; bishops, twelve.

61. But concerning the minor sins, that is, theft, false witness, and other such sins: laymen, one; clerics, two; subdeacons, three; deacons, four; presbyters, five; bishops, six [years].

5. SELECTIONS FROM THE FLEURY PENITENTIAL
(*ca.* 775–800)

[THE *Poenitentiale Floriacense* given by Martène in his *De antiquis ecclesiae ritibus,* edition of 1700, from an unnumbered Fleury codex, was reprinted by Wasserschleben.[1] Schmitz republished it from Martène's work, 1788 edition,[2] with an introduction.[3] It is closely related to the *St. Hubert* and *Burgundian* penitentials. In the opinion of Schmitz it belongs to the close of the eighth century. He shows that its contents cannot be earlier than about the middle of the century and points out that it has no trace of Merovingian barbarisms. It opens with an order for administering penance. This passage is substantially identical with that contained in the *St. Gall Penitential,* which follows it both in the work of Wasserschleben and in that of Schmitz. The latter document is called by Schmitz *Poenitentiale Sangallense simplex,* to distinguish it from the *Tripartite St. Gall Penitential,*[4] which is from the same codex, namely, Codex Sangall. 150. The view of Schmitz that the *St. Gall* was written "in course of the ninth century" cannot be accepted, since the codex must be dated about 800.[5] It is therefore of about the same period as the present document. As an illustration of the theology and the psychology of the confessional at this period a translation of the order for penance is here presented.]

In the name of Christ here begin: An order for giving penance

---

[1] *Bussordnungen,* pp. 422–25.   [2] Martène, *op. cit.,* I, 281–83.
[3] Schmitz II, pp. 339–45. The edition of Martène's work dated Antwerp 1763 contains the document at the same page: this edition is the one consulted by me.
[4] See below, pp. 282 ff.   [5] Schmitz II, p. 345. Cf. above, p. 63, n. 34.

according to the tradition of the elder Fathers; [and] how a priest ought to receive the confessions of everyone.

He is required to hold forth[6] the word of salvation and to give the penitent an explanation: how the devil through his pride fell from the angelic dignity and afterward[7] drove the man out of paradise, and [how] Christ accordingly for human salvation came into the world through the virgin's womb and after his resurrection both conquered the devil and redeemed the world from sin and afterward gave the Apostles the grace of baptism by which he should deliver man from his sin; and that he who has sinned, if he does not do penance, shall be sent to hell to be tormented forever; and he who gives his confession to the priests after the commission of an offense shall obtain eternal rewards; or how in the end of the age "He shall come to judge the living and the dead"[8] and to "render to every man according to his work."[9] Let him be questioned as to his belief in the resurrection, or all those things that he is told, or whether he has faith of confession, by which to obtain pardon before God through the judgment of the priest. But if he confesses everything and does not doubt that there is a blessed life for the righteous in Paradise after death and that the gehenna of fire is prepared for sinners, let him be questioned as to what he has done that causes him fear. And when the man has given his entire confession, the priest himself shall prostrate himself before the altar with him, and confessing they shall repeat the psalms with groaning and if possible with weeping, and both, alike prostrate, shall say the passages: "Turn me, O Lord,"[10] and "Our help is in the name of the Lord."[11] And afterward he shall begin, "O Lord, not in thy wrath," I and II,[12] and, "Have mercy upon me, O God," as far as "blot out my iniquity,"[13] and "Bless the Lord, O my soul," I, as far as "thy youth shall be renewed like the eagle,"[14] and the passage, "Remember not our iniquities."[15] And afterward let them together rise up and [let him be questioned][16] once more[17]

---

[6] "exhortari"; a Vulgate and medieval meaning.
[7] The St. Gall Penitential has here "through envy."
[8] II Tim. 4:1; I Pet. 4:5.   [9] Matt. 16:27.   [10] Ps. 6:5.   [11] Ps. 123:8.
[12] The references are apparently to Ps. 6:1 and Ps. 37:1.   [13] Ps. 50:3.
[14] Ps. 102:1–5. The Roman numeral I is probably due to the fact that this is the first of two psalms beginning with these words. Cf. n. 12.   [15] Ps. 78:8.
[16] These words, which occur twice above, are inserted as possibly supplying the lost connection of the passage, in which Martène indicates a lacuna here.
[17] Sangall. 150 has "atque denuo" as here rendered. Martène, ed. 1763, has "atque de uno."

whether he believes that through his confession itself he obtains pardon; if he will do penance; and if he is willing to promise in words that in this matter he will observe as far as he is able whatever is meanwhile determined; or how he ought afterwards to abstain; if he is weak or not; and if he has given an answer on all matters.

If later he offends criminally,[18] either a presbyter or a deacon shall say the collects over his head, and afterward, prostrate[19] on the ground, he shall be commended to the Lord God of heaven, and they shall say the passage, "Confirm this, O God."[20] And so thereafter he shall be treated according to his guilt and his devotion; or it shall be as far as possible indicated to him what definite time [of penance] he has or ought to observe; and the passage: "The Lord keep[21] thee from all evil,"[22] shall be said to him—and thou shalt leave him.

6. SELECTIONS FROM THE TRIPARTITE ST. GALL PENITENTIAL (ca. 800)

[IN AN important section[1] of his work Schmitz has called attention to the tripartite character of such penitentials as the St. Gall document, from which the following extracts are taken, and the work called by him *Capitula iudiciorum poenitentiae* and by Wasserschleben *The Penitential of Thirty-five Chapters*.[2] These documents are composed of materials derived from (1) canons of general authority in the Church, (2) decisions attributed to Theodore, and (3) decisions attributed to Cummean. In the two penitentials named these sections are so clearly marked that the word "tripartite"[3] well describes the documents. But Fournier has pointed out that a number of other penitentials, such as the *Poenitentiale Valicellanum* I, and the "Roman" Penitential of Halitgar are equally indebted to the first two of these sources and in some measure to the third, although in these documents the materials employed have been intermingled and rearranged.[4] The *Tripartite St. Gall Penitential* shows in the Instruction to confessors, with which it is prefaced, affinity with the *Ordo Romanus antiquus* as it appears in the Codex Vallicell. D 5. Schmitz used this parallel[5] to enforce his now discredited view that Roman influence was determinative in the history of the penitentials.

---

[18] Literally, "has criminal cases."
[19] "prostrati": the plural form because the priest is also prostrate, and in agreement with the subject of "shall say," below.   [20] Ps. 67:29.
[21] Vulgate has "custodit"; Douay, "keepeth," for "custodiat" here.
[22] Ps. 120:7.   [1] Schmitz II, pp. 175–251.
[2] "Poenitentiale XXXV capitulorum," *Bussordnungen*, pp. 505–26. Cf. *ibid.*, p. 69.
[3] "dreigegliederte Bussbücher," Schmitz II, p. 175.
[4] "Études sur les pénitentiels," IV, *Revue d'histoire et de littérature religieuses*, VIII (1903), 531 ff.   [5] Schmitz II, pp. 177, 179.

Later studies, however, point to a mid-tenth century date for the *Ordo Romanus antiquus*,[6] thus annulling the force of Schmitz's argument. The penitential is almost certainly earlier than the *Ordo Romanus*, and its Instruction may be one of the sources of the latter. Schmitz edits the *Tripartite St. Gall Penitential* from the eighth-ninth century codex, Sangall. 150, to which, following Wasserschleben, he gives a ninth century date.[7]

The Instruction occurs, with considerable variations, in a number of penitential documents of the late eighth and early ninth century; Schmitz gives a text of the Instruction showing the variants for eight of these.[8] The *Pseudo-Roman Penitential* of Halitgar is a member of this group of documents: the text of its introductory section will be seen to resemble closely the Instruction here quoted. In it and in a number of the other documents the prayers are much more extended than in the present document.]

HOW PENITENTS OUGHT TO BE RECEIVED

As often as we assign fasts to Christians who come to penance, we ourselves ought also to unite with them in fasting for one or two weeks, or as long as we are able; that there be not said to us that which was said to the priests of the Jews by our Lord and Savior: "Woe unto you scribes, who oppress men and lay upon their shoulders heavy loads, but ye yourselves do not touch these burdens with one of your fingers."[9] For no one can raise up one who is falling beneath a weight unless he bends himself that he may reach out to him his hand; and no physician can treat the wounds of the sick unless he comes in contact with[10] their foulness.

So also no priest or pontiff can treat the wounds of sinners or take away the sins from their souls unless in view of the pressing necessity he brings solicitude and prayers and tears. Therefore it is needful for us to be solicitous on behalf of sinners, since we are "members one of another"[11] and "if one member suffers anything all the members suffer with it."[12] And, therefore, if we see anyone fallen in sin, let us also make haste to call him to penance by our teaching. And as often as

---

[6] M. Andrieu, "L'Ordo romanus antiquus et le liber de divinis officiis de Pseudo-Alcuin," *Revue des sciences religieuses*, V (1925), 642–50, argues for this view mainly from its dependence on the work of Pseudo-Alcuin here named.

[7] Schmitz II, pp. 175–79; 345. Wasserschleben, *Bussordnungen*, pp. 108, 425. Cf. pp. 63, 280, above.

[8] Schmitz II, pp. 199–203. Schmitz, without sufficient justification, uses the *Merseburg Penitential* as a basis for his reconstructed text, and the value of the latter is doubtful. [9] Based on Luke 11:46.

[10] Literally, "becomes a participant in." [11] Rom. 12:5. [12] I Cor. 12:26.

thou givest advice to a sinner, give him likewise a penance and tell him at once to what extent he ought to fast and expiate his sins; lest perchance thou forget how much it behooves him to fast for his sins and it become necessary to thee to inquire of him regarding his sins a second time. But the man perhaps hesitates[13] to confess his sins a second time, lest he be judged by thee yet more severely. For not all clerics who come upon this document ought to appropriate it to themselves or read it; but only those to whom it is needful, that is, the presbyters. For just as they who are not bishops and presbyters, ought not to offer the sacrifice, those on whom even the power of the keys of the kingdom of heaven has been bestowed, so also others ought not to take to themselves these decisions. But if the need arises and there is no presbyter at hand, a deacon may undertake [the administration of] penance.

Therefore, as we said above, the bishop or presbyter ought to humble himself and pray with sadness and moaning and tears, not only for his own fault, but also for those of all Christians, so that he may be able to say with the Apostle Paul: "Who is weak and I am not weak; who is scandalized and I am not on fire."[14]

When, therefore, anyone comes to a priest to confess his sins, the priest ought first to pray by himself in the secrets of his own heart:

A Prayer

Lord God almighty, be Thou propitious unto me a sinner, to make me, on behalf of sinners and those who confess their sins, a worthy mediator between Thee and them. And Thou who desirest not the death of sinners, but that they should be converted and live,[15] accept the prayer of Thy servant which I pour forth before the face of Thy Glory, for Thy menservants and maidservants who desire to do penance; that Thou mayest both release them from their sins for the future and keep them unharmed from every offense.

But when he has come to thee, say over him this prayer:

O God, who purifiest the hearts of all who make confession to Thee and dost set free from the chain of the iniquity of all men those who accuse their own conscience, give grace to the captives and grant healing[16] to the wounded, that, the domination of sin having been over-

---

[13] "erubescit" (blushes, is embarrassed).   [14] II Cor. 11:29.
[15] Ezek. 18:23–32; 33:11.   [16] "medicinam."

thrown, they may serve Thee with free minds through [Our Lord Jesus Christ].[17]

And another prayer:

Grant us, O Lord, that as Thou wast moved to favor by the prayers and confession of the Publican[18] so also, O Lord, Thou mayest be favorable to this Thy servant, that, abiding in faithful confession and continuous expiation he may quickly win Thy mercy and that Thou mayest restore him to the holy altars and sacraments, [and that] he be made a partaker[19] in the celestial glory above.[20]

7. SELECTIONS FROM THE PENITENTIAL OF SILOS
(ca. 800)

[A PENITENTIAL from the monastery of Silos (situated in the eastern part of the diocese of Burgos, Spain) was published by F. de Berganza in his *Antiguedades de España* (1721), Appendix III, pp. 666–73, as part of a collection of liturgical books of the monastery made in the eleventh century (1052). Cf. *ibid.*, p. 624, and the *Catholic Encyclopedia*, X, 614, 622. Professor F. Romero-Otazo has edited the penitential from the British Museum Codex Add. 30853, but his study was privately printed, and, as I am informed after oft-repeated attempts to secure a copy, the edition was suppressed on account of printer's errors and only distributed to the members of the author's seminar. It has, however, received an extensive critical review from G. Le Bras in *Nouvelle revue historique de droit français et étranger*, 4 serie, 10 année (1931), pp. 115–31. I have used a photostat of the manuscript employed by Professor Romero-Otazo. It closely resembles the text given by de Berganza, but it includes a section (X, "De incestis conjunctionibus"), which is not in the latter, and two or three short qualifying phrases elsewhere, as well as a few additional, and for the most part illegible, words at the end. Except for the characteristically Spanish use of "b" for both "p" and "v," it has fewer defects than the text of de Berganza; but both are relatively free from grammatical errors. Codex Add. 30853, which was acquired by the British Museum in 1878, is probably of the late eleventh century.[1] The selections given amount to about half of the document. The translation is in general in accord with the manuscript where the latter differs from

---

[17] Part of this phrase is usually left unwritten in the texts of Latin prayers. Here the text has "per" only.   [18] Luke 18:10–14.

[19] "mancipetur." The word suggests a commercial transaction of which the penitent is the object, and by which he recovers his spiritual status.

[20] "sursum." Some parallel texts have "rursum" or "rursus" (once more). Cf. p. 301, below.

[1] Such is the opinion of Professors C. H. Beeson and A. Souter, who have kindly examined the photostat copy. Since de Berganza does not indicate the manuscript used by him, the possibility that he used this codex can hardly be said to be excluded.

de Berganza's text. The Roman numerals are those of the manuscript, while the bracketed numbers are those of the paragraphs of the whole appendix in which it is contained in de Berganza's work.

The subject matter of the *Silos Penitential* is largely contained also in the *Poenitentiale Vigilanum*—a new edition of which also forms a part of Professor Romero-Otazo's unavailable work. The relation of the two documents is not determined. Their common material is largely Insular; much of it is identical with sections of Cummean, of Theodore, and of Pseudo-Cummean. The *Silense* contains in addition material from the Spanish collection of canons known as the *Hispana*. Romero-Otazo regards the *Vigilanum* as the parent document, but Le Bras holds that the two penitentials belong to about the same date, *ca.* 800, and "have a common source which contained almost nothing Spanish."[2] The date, however, is not clearly indicated and may be somewhat later than 800. Professor Romero-Otazo was reported to have in preparation a general work on the Spanish penitentials; but apparently it has not appeared.]

I (98). *Of drunkenness or vomiting.*—If any bishop or any ordained person have the vice of drunkenness, he shall either desist or be deposed. [If] a priest or any cleric gets himself drunk, he shall do penance for twenty days. If he vomits through drunkenness, he shall do penance for forty days. If with the Eucharist, he shall do penance for sixty days. But if a conversus gets himself drunk, he shall do penance for thirty days. If he vomits through drunkenness, he shall do penance for fifty days. If with the Eucharist, he shall do penance for seventy days. If it is a layman, on account of drunkenness he shall do penance for ten days; on account of vomiting he shall do penance for twenty days. If with the Eucharist, he shall do penance for forty days. He who compels a man to get drunk shall do [the same] penance as one who is drunk.

[Penalties are further assigned for drunken offenses at different hours of the day.]

II (99). *Of the host or of its reception.*—[Numerous penalties for the offenses of priests and of people connected with the Eucharist are here omitted.]

Religious women shall abstain from all flesh except fish when they receive the body of the Lord. Likewise a man who is suspended from [the communion of] the body of Christ: in Easter itself he shall partake of the blessed Lamb. If anyone unintentionally swallows a drop of water while he is washing his face and his mouth to take communion, he shall sing a hundred psalms; nevertheless, he shall take the sacred elements. Every Catholic who for a crime[3] is suspended from [the communion of] the body of Christ shall be given communion at the approach of death. The infirm and feeble may take food at any hour.

III (100). *Of baptism and Sunday work.*—He who wishes to be baptized a second time shall do penance for three years. If he is unaware that he was baptized, he shall be baptized. If no priest or layman is present with a catechumen in the hour of death, he shall be promptly baptized by a woman . . . Those who work on the Lord's day—something shall be taken from them; those who walk shall do penance for seven days.

IV (101). *Of perjury and falsification.*—If anyone commits perjury, he shall do penance for seven years. If he perjures himself unwittingly, he shall do penance for three years. He who leads another who is ignorant of it into perjury, shall do penance for seven[4] years. But he who through cupidity willfully perjures himself shall serve God in a monastery until death, his goods being given to the poor. If an innocent man commits perjury under compulsion, he shall do penance for twenty days. If anyone is guilty of falsification, he shall do penance for seven years. But he who consents shall do penance for four years. Otherwise he shall be condemned by such a sentence as corresponds to what he inflicted on his brother.

V (102). *Of theft, incendiarism, or violation [of a tomb].*—If anyone commits theft, he shall restore to his master what was stolen and shall then do penance according to the theft. But if he does not restore, he shall do double penance. If he stole from a monastery of the Church and [the goods] were not restored, he shall do quadruple penance. If he restored those goods to the Church, he shall do double penance. A like plan is to be followed in all cases of damage. And he who puts to the flames anyone's house or courtyard[5] shall do penance according to the damage of the fire. He who violates a tomb shall do penance for five years. If anyone despoils relics,[6] one year on bread and water, and he shall abstain for three years from wine and flesh and restore everything that he removed. . . . If anyone defames his

---

[3] "pro scelere," not in de Berganza's text.   [4] De Berganza has "VIII."
[5] "aream." Cf. *Pseudo-Romanum*, can. 50, p. 307, below.
[6] "martyria." De Berganza in the margin has: "martyria id est reliquias."

father or his mother, he shall do penance after making satisfaction for as long a time as he was in the impiety; but if [he does] not [make satisfaction] he shall do penance for one year.

VI (103). *Of various forms of homicide.*—If anyone willfully commits homicide he shall be excommunicated from the fellowship of Christ's body for two years, and after forty days he shall enter the church and shall do penance for ten years. [Severe penalties are listed for homicide in numerous forms. Abortion is treated as homicide.] If anyone in charge of a sick man goes to sleep and the sick man grows worse and dies without a watcher, the watcher shall do penance for ten days. If he was negligent, he shall do penance for thirty days. But if he was drunk, he shall do penance for one year. Those who are punished for their crimes are not to be laid, with [the customary] psalms and salt, within the tombs of the faithful. If homicides, adulterers, and thieves flee to a church they shall be safe from death, to which they were liable. If anyone denies penance to those who are dying, he is guilty of their souls. If any priest gives a penance to a sick man without his consent or without witnesses, he shall do penance for one year. But if the penitent survives he shall observe the penance.

VII (104). *Of sacrilegious rites.*—If any Christian pays respect to diviners, enchanters, or fortune tellers to observe auguries, omens, or elements, or if they busy themselves with and seek after consultations of writings,[7] dreams, woolen work, or magical practices, he shall do penance for five years. It is not permitted to observe [the customs connected with] wool at the Kalends,[8] or the collections of herbs, [or] to give heed to incantations except to perform everything with the creed and the Lord's prayer.

[Section VIII (105), deals with those guilty of greed and like offenders. Section IX (106), penalizes numerous acts of fornication and enforces clerical celibacy. Section X "De incestis conjunctionibus," not in de Berganza, deals with questions of consanguinity in marriage.]

XI (107). *Of various cases of penitents.*—If anyone abandons his

---

[7] "inspectiones scripturarum." Cf. p. 41, above, and the note on "sortes sanctorum," p. 229, above. The change of number ("they") in this clause is typical and is therefore reproduced in the translation.

[8] Wool was connected with magic in various ways, and was used as an offering to local spirits, *e.g.*, by girls desiring husbands, at the opening of the year. Cf. P. Sébillot, *Le Folklore de France*, IV, 63, referring to practices of more recent times.

own children and does not support them, or if children desert their parents in the season of worship[?][9] judging this to be right, they shall be anathema. . . . If anyone engages in strife in the entrance of a church, he shall receive one hundred and fifty lashes, and if he draws a sword he shall receive two hundred lashes. . . . Christians must not sing or dance[10] when going to marriages. . . . He who by means of some incantation, for whatever reason, bathes himself in reverse position, shall do penance for one year; but without the incantation, he shall do penance for forty days. If on account of illness he bathes below a mill with an incantation, he shall do penance for a year; but without it, he shall do penance for forty days. Those who in the dance wear women's clothes and strangely devise them and employ jaw-bones[?] and a bow and a spade[11] and things like these shall do penance for one year. If any bishop engages in hunting with hounds or hawks, he shall do penance for five years; a cleric, for three years. In case of necessity the washing of the head may be done on the Lord's day. He who imitates[12] or consults demons shall do penance for eight years. If for the health of the living, a woman burns grains where a man has died, she shall do penance for one year. He who in a rage speaks evil to a brother shall make satisfaction and thereafter do penance for seven days. . . . If anyone says that the Lord Jesus was not before he was born,[13] let him be anathema. . . . If anyone believes that by his own power the devil makes thunder or lightning or storms or drouth, let him be anathema. If anyone is known to be absent from church on solemn festival days, he shall be excommunicated. A layman shall not dare to teach where clerics are present. A woman, however learned and holy, shall not presume to teach men in a meeting.[14] . . . If a cleric is vexed by a demon the host must not be offered by him. . . . It was determined that those who, having received penance, slip back to secular things should be suspended from the communion of the faithful or from the body of Christ.

[9] "in occasione cultus."   [10] "ballare vel saltare." Cf. p. 273, n. 14.

[11] "malas et arcum et palam." "Malas" may be "cheeks" or "teeth." In the manuscript "malas" is glossed "magatias" in margin. The *Vigilanum* in a parallel passage (84) has "majas et orcum et pelam": Wasserschleben regards these as Spanish words meaning, respectively: elegantly and ostentatiously dressed rustics; an ogre; and a richly clad child, perhaps prepared for the part of a "Christchild" or a Christophorus. *Bussordnungen*, pp. 71, 533. Wasserschleben had not seen the *Silense*. Since both documents are in Latin, the Latin forms probably stood in the original source as in the present text.

[12] "emulat." Marginal gloss: "figurat." Perhaps "makes images of."

[13] Apparently a survival of Visigothic Arianism.

[14] *Statuta Antiqua*, can. 99. Mansi III, 959.

[Section XII (108) deals with offenses connected with the use of unclean meats. Section XIII (109) lists the fasting seasons.]

XIV (110). *Of the fast of a day, or of forty days.*—Now, whoever is quite unable to keep the above-mentioned fasts properly, if he is a reader, for example, for one day he shall sing fifty psalms, kneeling, and another fifty, standing. But if he is a priest he shall offer two votive [masses] to the Lord. Now, he who is willing to bear whipping shall receive thirty blows with a whip of ten thongs. But he who consents to do "metaniae"[15] shall make satisfaction by a hundred "metaniae,"[16] stretched toward the ground, knees doubled back,[17] head bent, fervently repeating the Kyrie Eleison. If he is supreme commander, he shall pay one solidus; a prince, five argentei; a count, four; an emir,[18] three; a knight, two. A rural worker of any kind, [shall pay] one argenteus; a hired worker, half an argenteus. A poor man, an obolus, which is commonly called a quarta; a very poor man, one siliqua,[19] that is, a harroba. He who has not the strength to do all these things stated above shall do penance otherwise, with groans and tears, unceasingly.

XV (111). *Of a forty-day fast.*—When any priest is under obligation to do penance for a forty-day period on bread and water, let him offer eighty votive masses. A reader shall sing thirty psalters, which make ninety masses. He who ought to bear[20] floggings, twelve hundred[21] blows of the whips; one who is to make satisfaction, shall make satisfaction with four thousand[22] "metaniae." But a supreme commander shall pay forty solidi or redeem a captive; a prince, twenty-five solidi; a count, twenty[23] solidi; an emir, fifteen solidi; a knight, ten solidi; a worker, five solidi; a hired worker, two solidi and four argentei; a poor man, one solidus and two argentei; a very poor man, three argentei and a quarta.

[15] "preces pro venia"—marginal note, de Berganza. "Metania" is from "μετάνοια," and is best explained by the phrases following.
[16] "centies metanias" not in de Berganza's text.
[17] "terratenus fixis manibus, volutis genibus."   [18] "Amirates."
[19] The siliqua was the twenty-fourth part of a solidus.
[20] "Lator id est qui debet sustinere."—Margin, de Berganza.
[21] De Berganza has "TCC." Codex Add. 30853 reads Ṭcc, the Ṭ being shaped ₼. It is evidently a conventionalized symbol, since it differs from both T and M as they elsewhere appear in the manuscript and has a line above it. On T as a symbol for one thousand in Aragon and Navarre, see Du Cange's article on the letter T.
[22] De Berganza has "IIIIT"; the manuscript is probably to be read iiiiT. Multiplication is obviously intended. Cf. iiiiXL and iiiXL in a part of Section VI (103) not here given, undoubtedly with the meaning "four times forty," "three times forty [days]."
[23] De Berganza reads "XXV."

8. SELECTIONS FROM THE PENITENTIAL OF
VIGILA OF ALVELDA (*ca.* 800)

[THE *Poenitentiale Vigilanum*, though written about the beginning of
the ninth century, receives its name from the distinguished tenth century
monk, priest, and scribe, Vigila, abbot of the monastery of St. Martin
of Alvelda, or Albelda, in the diocese of Calahorra, Spain. From the name
of the monastery the penitential is sometimes called *Alveldense*. Vigila
is known for his contribution to the Chronicle of Alvelda which he
brought to the year 976. Cf. Migne, *P.L.*, CXXIX, 1123 f. In this year
also he completed, with the assistance of two skilled illuminators, the
celebrated Codex Vigilanus, a treasure of the Library of the Escurial,
which contains the *Poenitentiale Vigilanum* along with other important
documents. Cf. Ambrosio de Morales (d. 1591), *Opusculos Castelanos*
(1793), III, 67 ff.; the articles on Vigila in the *Encyclopedia universal
illustrada*, LXVIII, 1119 f., and J. W. Bradley, *Dictionary of Minia-
turists*, III, 386. The similarity of this document to the *Penitential of
Silos* has already been noted. Whichever is the earlier, the *Vigilanum*
is much the less independent of Celtic and Frankish sources. Wasserschleben's edition, from the Escurial manuscript,[1] is the basis of the
following extracts. Romero-Otazo's [suppressed] edition from the same
codex appears in 102 canons, whereas Wasserschleben has only ninety-
three.[2]]

37. He who intends to kill himself by hanging or some such plan
(if God does not abandon him to be killed), for this thing shall do
penance for five years.

45. A woman, also, who takes a potion shall consider herself to be
guilty of as many acts of homicide as the number of those she was
due to conceive or bear.

76. If anyone violates the fast of Lent or of the litanies[3] without
any necessity, for one day he shall do penance for ten days.

77. Likewise on those days he who takes flesh ignorantly or
through the necessity of lack of food shall abstain from flesh for one
year. But if without necessity, he shall do penance for four years.

78. If any monk eats of a quadruped without cogent necessity, he
shall do penance for six months.

79. He who drinks a potion for the sake of chastity shall do penance for two years.

80. He who does this in order not to have children shall do penance
for twelve years.

---

[1] *Bussordnungen*, pp. 527–34. Cf. p. 71.
[2] Cf. p. 285, above.   [3] That is, the Rogation Days.

9. SELECTIONS FROM THE ST. HUBERT
PENITENTIAL (*ca.* 850)

[THIS PENITENTIAL was first published by Martène[1] from a manuscript of the Andage monastery of St. Hubert in the Ardennes and is called by Wasserschleben *Poenitentiale Hubertense*. It contains sixty-two canons, of which 1–43 are substantially identical with the Burgundian. But even within this section, and especially in the remaining canons, there are elements derived from Frankish synods of 803 and 814, and a Roman synod of 827. For this reason Schmitz advances the date from the seventh or early eighth century suggested by Wasserschleben to about the middle of the ninth century.[2] Schmitz holds that the compiler was a monk rather than a member of the clergy. The canons here selected either have no parallels in the *Burgundian Penitential* or show considerable variation from the corresponding passages in it.]

14. *Of nuns.*—If any maiden vows herself to the service of God and changes to a secular habit and takes a husband, she shall be deprived of communion and separated from her husband; she shall do penance and not be joined to her husband thereafter. Likewise if she was a consecrated [nun], since it is written: "Vow ye, and pay to the Lord your God."[3] He who commits fornication with these persons shall do the same penance as he who commits fornication with the betrothed or the wife of another.

22. *Of usury.*—If anyone exacts usury from anybody he shall do penance for three years. If he is a cleric, he shall not proceed to holy orders; if a deacon or a presbyter, he shall be deprived of his own rank.

25. *Of soothsayers.*—If anyone pays respect to soothsayers, that is, fortune tellers, criers or quacks, or follows them, he shall do penance for three years and give alms.

28. *Of drunkards.*—If anyone is continually drunken, he shall be suspended from [the use of] wine; only on the Lord's day he shall take wine, lest his stomach be weakened. But if he is not satisfied [with this], he shall do penance for three years and give alms every day.

33. *Of falsification.*—If anyone commits any kind of falsification, either in writings or in measurements or in weights, he shall do penance for seven years. Moreover, he who even consents [to such falsification] shall do penance for five years.

---

[1] *Veterum scriptorum et monumentorum amplissima collectio*, VII, 28–30.

[2] Wasserschleben, *Bussordnungen*, p. 57, text, pp. 377–86; Schmitz II, pp. 331–33, text, pp. 333–39.   [3] Ps. 75:12.

39. *If any dishonor their parents.*—If anyone dishonors his father or mother, he shall do penance for three years. But if he lifts his hand [against them] or strikes blows, he shall do penance as an exile for seven years. But if he returns through the pardon of his parents, or if they are well disposed toward him he shall be received to communion.[4]

42. *Of dancing.*—Anyone who performs dances in front of the churches of saints or anyone who disguises his appearance in the guise of a woman or of beasts, or a woman [who appears] in the garb of a man—on promise of amendment he [or she] shall do penance for three years.

46. *Of a divorced woman.*[5]—If anyone marries a divorced woman, she shall be cast forth from her husband's bed and shall do penance for one year. The Lord Himself said: "He that shall marry her that is put away, committeth adultery."[6]

47. *If any man washes in a bath with a woman.*—If anyone presumes to wash himself in a bath with women, on promise of amendment he shall do penance for one year and not presume to do it again.

48. *Of the funds*[7] *or tithes.*—They who administer the funds of the poor, take tithes of the people, and filch therefrom for themselves something coveted for their worldly gain, shall each make restitution[8] as guilty violators of the Lord's property; they shall be corrected under canonical [penalty] and shall do penance for three years. For it is written, "Such a dispenser the Lord requireth, who receives thence nothing for himself."[9]

50. *If anyone overlays an unbaptized*[10] *baby.*—If anyone overlays an unbaptized baby, she shall do penance for three years. If unintentionally, two years.

51. *Of a god-daughter or god-sister.*[11]—If anyone takes in marriage one who is his daughter or sister from the sacred font or the anointing, they shall be separated and shall do penance for five years. If he commits fornication [with such a person], each shall do penance

---

[4] Omitting the words "aut ibidem ederit," which, as Schmitz points out, are here meaningless and should probably be attached to can. 30, corresponding to *Poenit. Burgund.*, 29, where they occur. Cf. Wasserschleben's footnote.   [5] "de repudiata."
[6] Matt. 5:32.   [7] "synodochia." See Du Cange, *s.v.* "sinodochia."
[8] "restituatur," literally "be restored," possibly in the sense of "readmitted to communion." With this verb the construction changes to singular.
[9] Apparently based on I Cor. 4:2.   [10] "gentilem."
[11] "de filia vel sorore ex sacro fonte vel chrismate suscepta."

for seven years. They shall go forth in exile, and alms shall be given for them.

52. *Of converts and penitents.*—They who are doing penance and have already been converts from secular business and strife, shall abstain from cohabitation with women, and women [shall also abstain] from men, [that they] do not commit their former misdeeds and that they guard themselves from future ones.

53. *Of mourning for the dead.*—If anyone lacerates himself over his dead with a sword or his nails, or pulls his hair, or rends his garments, he shall do penance for forty days.

54. *Of enchantments.*—If anyone sings enchantments for infatuation[12] or any sort of chantings except the holy symbol[13] or the Lord's prayer, he who sings and he to whom he sings shall do penance for the three forty-day periods on bread and water.

55. *Of second marriages.*—It is lawful for anyone, men or women, to contract a second or a third marriage, since the apostolic authority permits this. But each shall fast for three weeks: indeed, he who contracts a fourth [marriage] shall fast for thirty-three weeks.

62. *Of the case of priests.*—If any deacon or priest commits capital crimes, whether he is exposed or [incriminated] by his own confession, whether openly or in secret, he shall be deprived of his rank and be among the "hearers."[14] For the Church requires a blameless priest; therefore, not only those who have given place to mortal [offenses] after their ordination, but also those who have given place to mortal offenses before their ordination are to be rejected; since according to the word of Paul, "no fornicator or unclean or covetous person (which is a serving of idols) hath inheritance in the kingdom of Christ and of God."[15] Therefore, he shall do penance as a suppliant and in submission. Here endeth.

---

[12] "praecantaverit ad fascinum."   [13] The creed.
[14] See above, p. 8.   [15] Eph. 5:5.

CHAPTER VI

Penitentials Written or Authorized by Frankish Ecclesiastics

1. THE SO-CALLED ROMAN PENITENTIAL OF
HALITGAR (ca. 830)

[ABOUT the year 830, Ebbo, archbishop of Reims, wrote to Halitgar, bishop of Cambrai, a letter lamenting the confusion in penitential practice due to the discrepancies and unauthoritative character of the current penitentials and urging Halitgar to undertake a new work that would enable the priests to adjudge penance properly.[1] In his reply Halitgar records his amusement at the request; mindful of his own infirmity and burdened with his tasks, he cannot undertake a literary work at present; but with the difficulty of the task enjoined he recognizes the authority of him who has enjoined it; he does not wish, nor ought he, to give a total refusal.[2]

A year later Halitgar died. His literary works include five books on penance based upon the patristic writers. No section of this work is of the character of a penitential. But there is added to it as Book VI a work called *Poenitentiale Romanum*, which Halitgar claims to have taken "from a book repository of the Roman Church." Wasserschleben denies the truth of Halitgar's statement;[3] Schmitz defends the statement and regards the book as Roman in origin and use.[4] Watkins suggests an origin which shields Halitgar from the charge of misstatement. According to him the book was produced about A.D. 650 in the Frankish lands, but under Celtic influence. Halitgar used the phrase "ex scrinio Romanae ecclesiae" in a loose sense, believing that the penitential was of Roman origin. Halitgar may, he thinks, have availed himself here of a phrase of Boniface in a letter to Nothelm of Canterbury (A.D. 736), in which Boniface asks for certain materials which are not to be found "in scrinio Romanae ecclesiae."[5] Fournier indicates in detail the "tripartite" character of the penitential and regards Halitgar's careful selection of those Insular materials which appeared to him to be in accord with the general

[1] Migne, *P.L.*, CV, 651. [2] *Ibid.*, 654. [3] *Bussordnungen*, pp. 58 ff.
[4] Schmitz I, pp. 466 ff. [5] *History of Penance*, II, 630, 709 f.

discipline, as constituting the document's only claim to be called "Roman."[6]

The view of Schmitz is not sustained by the character of the book itself. Much of it is derived from Celtic and Theodorean sources, and, except for the liturgical additions, it is a typical member of the penitential series. On the other hand, Watkins's defense of the ingenuousness of Halitgar is not convincing. What Halitgar says is: "poenitentiale romanum quem de scrinio romane ecclesie adsumpsimus" (a Roman penitential which we have taken from a book repository of the Roman Church). This seems to involve the claim that the promulgator had been personally responsible for bringing the original from Rome. It is, of course, possible, if we hesitate to charge a distinguished bishop with untruthfulness, to suppose that the work had found its way to a Roman book shelf and had been copied there or simply removed and brought to Cambrai. But the claim is evidently designed to suggest Roman authority, origin, and use. In view of the freedom with which church reformers in that age set up claims of authority for documents of their own creation,[7] it would be idle to contend that Halitgar would certainly not have made the statement if it had not been true. On the whole the most natural conclusion is that Halitgar compiled the penitential, and that, seeking to give it such authority as would secure its general use and end the confusion of which Ebbo had complained, he published it with a specific claim of Roman origin.

The text will be found in Wasserschleben,[8] in Migne,[9] and in Schmitz. Schmitz in his first work edits the document from the tenth century Codex Monac. 3909. In his second study he presents an edition of the entire six books of Halitgar.[10] This edition is the one here principally followed. Wasserschleben's text, from Codex Sangall. 676, differs from it considerably, but is probably equally defensible, as Schmitz, though acquainted with about a score of manuscripts, failed to establish a satisfactory text. The Schmitz text of the Prologue is based on the late ninth or tenth century Codex Paris. 8508; variants are supplied from the Codices Sangall. 570 and 277, both of the ninth century, and Sangall. 679 of the tenth. The canons which form the body of the penitential are given from Codex Paris. 12315 of the twelfth century. Although a part of the Prologue parallels closely[11] the Order of Penance of the *Tri-*

---

[6] "Études sur les pénitentiels," *Revue d'histoire et de littérature religieuses*, VIII (1903), pp. 533 ff., 552 f. Fournier and Le Bras, I, 110.

[7] Schmitz would set aside Wasserschleben's reference to the *Pseudo-Isidorean Decretals* with which Halitgar's literary inspirer Ebbo has been often associated. Fournier and Le Bras have argued for an Armorican origin for this great historic forgery.—*Op. cit.*, I, 196 f.

[8] *Bussordnungen*, pp. 360–77. For earlier editions see *ibid.*, p. 360, n. 1, and Schmitz I, p. 470.   [9] *P.L.*, CV, 695 ff.

[10] Schmitz I, pp. 471–89; II, pp. 252–300.

[11] Cf. the Instruction of the *Tripartite St. Gall Penitential*, above, pp. 282 ff. Schmitz's readings from MSS in his text and notes are not reliable. A few errors have been corrected in our notes. Cf. nn. 45, 47, 60, 62, below.

partite St. Gall, it is included here for the sake of giving this important document in its entirety.]

[HALITGAR'S PREFACE]

Here begins the sixth [book].[12] We have also added to this work of our selection another, a Roman penitential, which we have taken from a book repository of the Roman Church, although we do not know by whom it was produced. We have determined that it should be joined to the foregoing decisions of the canons for this reason, that if perchance those decisions presented seem to anyone superfluous, or if he is entirely unable to find there what he requires respecting the offenses of individuals, he may perhaps find explained, in this final summary, at least the misdeeds of all.

PROLOGUE

How Bishops or Presbyters Ought to Receive Penitents

As often as Christians come to penance, we assign fasts; and we ourselves ought to unite with them in fasting for one or two weeks, or as long as we are able; that there be not said to us that which was said to the priests of the Jews by our Lord and Savior: "Woe unto you scribes, who oppress men, and lay upon their shoulders heavy loads, but ye yourselves do not touch these burdens with one of your fingers."[13] For no one can raise up one who is falling beneath a weight unless he bends himself that he may reach out to him his hand; and no physician can treat the wounds of the sick, unless he comes in contact with their foulness. So also no priest or pontiff can treat the wounds of sinners or take away the sins from their souls, except by intense solicitude and the prayer of tears. Therefore it is needful for us, beloved brethren, to be solicitous on behalf of sinners, since we are "members one of another"[14] and "if one member suffers anything, all the members suffer with it."[15] And therefore, if we see anyone fallen in sin, let us also make haste to call him to penance by our teaching. And as often as thou givest advice to a sinner, give him likewise at once a penance and tell him[15a] to what extent he ought to fast and expiate his sins; lest perchance thou forget how much it behooves him to fast for his sins and it become necessary to thee to inquire of him regarding his sins a second time. But the man will perhaps hesi-

---

[12] That is, of Halitgar's collection.
[13] Based on Luke 11:46.   [14] Rom. 12:5.   [15] I Cor. 12:26.
[15a] Supplying "et dic ei," as in parallels. See above, p. 284.

tate[16] to confess his sins a second time, and be judged yet more severely. For not all clerics who come upon this document ought to appropriate it to themselves or to read it; only those to whom it is needful, that is, the presbyters. For just as they who are not bishops and presbyters (those on whom the keys of the kingdom of heaven have been bestowed) ought not to offer the sacrifice so also others ought not to take to themselves these decisions. But if the need arises, and there is no presbyter at hand, a deacon may admit the penitent to holy communion. Therefore as we said above, the bishops or presbyters ought to humble themselves and pray with moaning and tears of sadness, not only for their own faults, but also for those of all Christians, so that they may be able to say with the Blessed Paul: "Who is weak and I am not weak; who is scandalized and I am not on fire."[17] When therefore, anyone comes to a priest to confess his sins, the priest shall advise him to wait a little, while he enters into his chamber[18] to pray. But if he has not a chamber, still the priest shall say in his heart this prayer:

Let Us Pray

Lord God Almighty, be Thou propitious unto me a sinner, that I may be able worthily to give thanks unto Thee, who through Thy mercy hast made me, though unworthy, a minister, by the sacerdotal office, and appointed me, though slight and lowly, an intermediary to pray and intercede before our Lord Jesus Christ for sinners and for those returning to penance. And therefore our Governor and Lord, who will have all men to be saved and to come to the knowledge of the truth,[19] who desirest not the death of the sinner but that he should be converted and live,[20] accept my prayer, which I pour forth before the face of Thy Clemency, for Thy menservants and maidservants who have come to penance. Through our Lord Jesus Christ.

Moreover, he who on coming to penance sees the priest sad and weeping for his evil deeds, being himself the more moved by the fear of God, will be the more grieved and abhor his sins. And any man who is approaching for penance, if thou seest him in a state of ardent and constant penitence, receive him forthwith. Him who is able to keep a fast which is imposed upon him, do not forbid, but allow him to do it. For they are rather to be praised who make haste quickly to dis-

---

[16] "erubescet" (will blush, be embarrassed).
[17] II Cor. 11:29.   [18] "cubiculum." Cf. Matt. 6:6.
[19] I Tim. 2:4.   [20] Ezek. 18:23-32; 33:11.

charge the obligation due, since fasting is an obligation. And so give commandment to those who do penance, since if one fasts and completes what is commanded him by the priest, he will be cleansed from his sins. But if he turns back a second time to his former habit or sin, he is like a dog that returns to his own vomit.[21] Therefore, every penitent ought not only to perform the fast that is commanded him by the priest but also, after he has completed those things that were commanded him, he ought, as long as he is commanded, to fast either on Wednesdays or on Fridays. If he does those things which the priest has enjoined upon him, his sins shall be remitted; if, however, he afterward fasts of his own volition, he shall obtain to himself mercy and the kingdom of heaven. Therefore, he who fasts a whole week for his sins shall eat on Saturday and on the Lord's day and drink whatever is agreeable to him. Nevertheless, let him guard himself against excess and drunkenness, since luxury is born of drunkenness. Therefore the Blessed Paul forbids it, saying: "Be not drunk with wine, wherein is luxury";[22] not that there is luxury in wine, but in drunkenness.

Here ends the Prologue.

[DIRECTIONS TO CONFESSORS]

If anyone perchance is not able to fast and has the means to redeem himself, if he is rich, for seven weeks [penance] he shall give twenty solidi. But if he has not sufficient means, he shall give ten solidi. But if he is very poor, he shall give three solidi. Now let no one be startled because we have commanded to give twenty solidi or a smaller amount; since if he is rich it is easier for him to give twenty solidi than for a poor man to give three solidi. But let everyone give attention to the cause to which he is under obligation to give, whether it is to be spent for the redemption of captives, or upon the sacred altar, or for poor Christians. And know this, my brethren, that when men or women slaves come to you seeking penance, you are not to be hard on them nor to compel them to fast as much as the rich, since men or women slaves are not in their own power; therefore lay upon them a moderate penance.

Here begins the form for the administration of Penance.
In the first place the priest says, Psalm XXXVII, "Rebuke me

---

[21] Prov. 26:11.   [22] Eph. 5:18.

not O Lord in thy indignation." And after this he says, "Let us pray," and Psalm CII, "Bless the Lord O my soul" as far as "shall be renewed."[23] And again he says: "Let us pray," and Psalm L, "Have mercy," as far as "Blot out my iniquities,"[24] After these he says, Psalm LXIII, "O God, by thy name," and he says, "Let us pray," and says, Psalm LI, "Why dost thou glory," as far as "the just shall see and fear."[25] And he says, "Let us pray:"

O God of whose favor none is without need, remember, O Lord, this Thy servant who is laid bare in the weakness of a transient and earthly body.[26] We seek that Thou give pardon to the confessant, spare the suppliant, and that we who according to our own merit are to blame may be saved by thy compassion through our Lord Jesus Christ.

Another Prayer[27]

O God, beneath Whose eyes every heart trembles and all consciences are afraid, be favorable to the complaints of all and heal the wounds of everyone, that[28] just as none of us is free from guilt, so none may be a stranger to pardon, through our Lord Jesus Christ.

A Prayer

O God of infinite mercy and immeasurable truth, deal graciously with our iniquities and heal all the languors of our souls, that laying hold of the remission which springs from Thy compassion, we may ever rejoice in Thy blessing. Through our Lord Jesus Christ.

A Prayer[29]

I beseech, O Lord, the majesty of Thy kindness and mercy that Thou wilt deign to accord pardon to this Thy servant as he confesses his sins and evil deeds, and remit the guilt of his past offenses—Thou who did'st carry back the lost sheep upon Thy shoulders and did'st hearken with approval to the prayers of the publican when he confessed. Wilt Thou also, O Lord, deal graciously with this Thy servant; be Thou favorable

---

[23] Ps. 102:5.   [24] Ps. 50:3–11.   [25] Ps. 51:3–8.

[26] The text is apparently corrupt.

[27] This prayer in substance appears in the Gelasian Sacramentary. See H. A. Wilson, *The Gelasian Sacramentary*, p. 252. C. Silva-Tarouca, S.J., as cited by Poschmann (II, 116) holds that the Gelasian Sacramentary developed in England from the work of Johannes Archicantor (*ca.* 680) referred to by Bede, *Eccl. Hist.*, IV, 18, and that its formulation is not earlier than 850. The study "Archicantor de S. Pietro a Roma e l'ordo Romanus da lui composto (anno 680)," appeared in *Atti della pontificia accademia Romana di archeologia* (série III) *Memorie*, I, Pt. I (Rome, 1923), 159–219.

[28] Reading "ut" for "et," as in the Gelasian Sacramentary and in Wasserschleben's text.

[29] Found in Gelasian Sacramentary, Wilson, *op. cit.*, p. 14.

to[30] his prayers, that he may abide in the grace of confession,[31] that his weeping and supplication may quickly obtain Thy enduring mercy, and, readmitted to the holy altars and sacraments, may he again be made a partaker[32] in the hope of eternal life and heavenly glory. Through our Lord Jesus Christ.

Prayer of the Imposition of Hands

Holy Lord, Father Omnipotent, Eternal God, Who through Thy son Jesus Christ our Lord hast deigned to heal our wounds, Thee we Thy lowly priests as suppliants ask and entreat that Thou wilt deign to incline the ear of Thy mercy and remit every offense and forgive all the sins of this Thy servant and give unto him pardon in exchange for his afflictions, joy for sorrow, life for death. He has fallen from the celestial height, and trusting in Thy mercy, may he be found worthy to persevere by Thy[33] rewards unto good peace[34] and unto the heavenly places unto life eternal. Through our Lord Jesus Christ.[35]

Here begins the Reconciliation of the Penitent on Holy Thursday. First he says Psalm L with the antiphon "Cor mundum."[36]

A Prayer

Most gracious God, the Author of the human race and its most merciful Corrector, Who even in the reconciliation of the fallen willest that I, who first of all need Thy mercy, should serve in the workings of Thy grace through the priestly ministry, as the merit of the suppliant vanisheth may the mercy of the Redeemer become the more marvelous. Through our Lord Jesus Christ.

Another Prayer

Almighty, everlasting God, in Thy compassion relieve this Thy confessing servant of his sins, that the accusation of conscience may hurt him no more unto punishment than the grace of Thy love [may admit him] to pardon. Through our Lord Jesus Christ.

Another Prayer

Almighty and merciful God, Who hast set the pardon of sins in prompt confession, succor the fallen, have mercy upon those who have confessed,

[30] The Gelasian Sacramentary has "assiste" for "aspira" here.

[31] "in confessione placabilis permaneat." The Gelasian Sacramentary has "flebile" for "placabilis" (in tearful confession).

[32] "mancipetur." Cf. p. 285, n. 19, above. The Gelasian Sacramentary has "reformetur" (may he be renewed).

[33] Reading "tuis" for "tui" with Codex Paris. 12315. This codex omits "peace."

[34] Cf. II Macc. 1:1.

[35] "Per Dominum."

[36] These words ("a clean heart") are from Ps. 50:12

that what is bound by the chain of things accursed, the greatness of Thy love may release.

A Prayer over the Sick

O God, Who gavest to Thy servant Hezekiah[37] an extension of life of fifteen years,[38] so also may Thy greatness raise up Thy servant from the bed of sickness unto health. Through our Lord Jesus Christ.

[PRESCRIPTIONS OF PENANCE]

Of Homicide

1. If any bishop or other ordained person commits homicide. If any cleric commits homicide, he shall do penance for ten years, three of these on bread and water.

2. If [the offender is] a layman, he shall do penance for three years, one of these on bread and water; a subdeacon, six years; a deacon, seven; a presbyter, ten; a bishop, twelve.

3. If anyone consents to an act of homicide that is to be committed, he shall do penance for seven years, three of these on bread and water.

4. If any layman intentionally commits homicide he shall do penance for seven years, three of these on bread and water.

5. If anyone overlays an infant, he shall do penance for three years, one of these on bread and water. A cleric also shall observe the same rule.

Of Fornication

6. If anyone commits fornication as [did] the Sodomites, he shall do penance for ten years, three of these on bread and water.

7. If any cleric commits adultery, that is, if he begets a child with the wife or the betrothed of another, he shall do penance for seven years; however, if he does not beget a child and the act does not come to the notice of men, if he is a cleric he shall do penance for three years, one of these on bread and water; if a deacon or a monk, he shall do penance for seven years, three of these on bread and water; a bishop, twelve years, five on bread and water.

8. If after his conversion or advancement any cleric of superior rank who has a wife has relations with her again, let him know that he has committed adultery; therefore, that he shall do penance as stated above.

---

[37] "ezechiae." Douay Version: "Ezechias."   [38] Isa. 38:5.

9. If anyone commits fornication with a nun or one who is vowed to God, let him be aware that he has committed adultery. He shall do penance in accordance with the foregoing decision, each according to his order.

10. If anyone commits fornication by himself or with a beast of burden or with any quadruped, he shall do penance for three years; if [he has] clerical rank or a monastic vow, he shall do penance for seven years.

11. If any cleric lusts after a woman and is not able to commit the act because the woman will not comply, he shall do penance for half a year on bread and water and for a whole year abstain from wine and meat.

12. If after he has vowed himself to God any cleric returns to a secular habit, as a dog to his vomit, or takes a wife, he shall do penance for six[39] years, three of these on bread and water, and thereafter not be joined in marriage. But if he refuses, a holy synod or the Apostolic See shall separate them from the communion of the Catholics. Likewise also, if a woman commits a like crime after she has vowed herself to God, she shall be subject to an equal penalty.

13. If any layman commits fornication as the Sodomites did, he shall do penance for seven years.

14. If anyone begets a child of the wife of another, that is, commits adultery and violates his neighbor's bed, he shall do penance for three years and abstain from juicy foods and from his own wife, giving in addition to the husband the price of his wife's violated honor.[40]

15. If anyone wishes to commit adultery and cannot, that is, is not accepted, he shall do penance for forty days.

16. If anyone commits fornication with women, that is, with widows and girls, if with a widow, he shall do penance for a year; if with a girl, he shall do penance for two years.

17. If any unstained youth is joined to a virgin, if the parents are willing, she shall become his wife; nevertheless they shall do penance for one year and [then] become man and wife.

18. If anyone commits fornication with a beast he shall do penance for one year. If he has not a wife, he shall do penance for half a year.

19. If anyone violates a virgin or a widow, he shall do penance for three years.

[39] Codex Sangall. 679 has "ten".   [40] "pudicitiae."

20. If any man who is betrothed defiles the sister of his betrothed, and clings to her as if she were his own, yet marries the former, that is, his betrothed, but she who has suffered defilement commits suicide —all who have consented to the deed shall be sentenced to ten years on bread and water, according to the provisions of the canons.[41]

21. If anyone of the women who have committed fornication slays those who are born or attempts to commit abortion, the original regulation forbids communion to the end of life. What is actually laid down they may mitigate somewhat in practice. We determine that they shall do penance for a period of ten years, according to rank, as the regulations state.[42]

Of Perjury

22. If any cleric commits perjury, he shall do penance for seven years, three of these on bread and water.

23. A layman, three years; a subdeacon, six; a deacon, seven; a presbyter, ten; a bishop, twelve.

24. If compelled by any necessity, anyone unknowingly commits perjury, he shall do penance for three years, one year on bread and water, and shall render a life for himself, that is, he shall release a man or woman slave from servitude and give alms liberally.

25. If anyone commits perjury through cupidity, he shall sell all his goods and give to the poor and be shaven and enter a monastery, and there he shall serve faithfully until death.

Of Theft

26. If any cleric is guilty of a capital theft, that is, if he steals an animal or breaks into a house, or robs a somewhat well-protected place,[43] he shall do penance for seven years.

27. A layman shall do penance for five years; a subdeacon, for six; a deacon, for seven; a presbyter, for ten; a bishop, for twelve.

28. If anyone in minor orders commits theft once or twice, he shall make restitution to his neighbor and do penance for a year on bread and water; and if he is not able to make restitution he shall do penance for three years.

---

[41] Cf. council of Ancyra, 314, can. 25. Mansi, II, 521.

[42] Cf. council of Ancyra, 314, can. 21. Mansi II, 520.

[43] The text of Migne (CV, 699) has "majus pretium" (or steals anything of considerable value) for "meliorem praesidium."

29. If anyone violates a tomb, he shall do penance for seven years, three years on bread and water.

30. If any layman commits theft he shall restore to his neighbor what he has stolen [and] do penance for the three forty-day periods on bread and water; if he is not able to make restitution, he shall do penance for one year, and the three forty-day periods on bread and water, and [he shall give] alms to the poor from the product of his labor, and at the decision of the priest he shall be joined to the altar.

Of Magic

31. If one by his magic causes the death of anyone, he shall do penance for seven years, three years on bread and water.

32. If anyone acts as a magician for the sake of love but does not cause anybody's death, if he is a layman he shall do penance for half a year; if a cleric, he shall do penance for a year on bread and water; if a deacon, for three years, one year on bread and water; if a priest, for five years, two years on bread and water. But if by this means anyone deceives a woman with respect to the birth of a child, each one shall add to the above six forty-day periods, lest he be accused of homicide.

33. If anyone is a conjurer-up of storms he shall do penance for seven years, three years on bread and water.

Of Sacrilege

34. If anyone commits sacrilege—(that is, those who are called augurs, who pay respect to omens), if he has taken auguries or [does it] by any evil device, he shall do penance for three years on bread and water.

35. If anyone is a soothsayer (those whom they call diviners) and makes divinations of any kind, since this is a demonic thing he shall do penance for five years, three years on bread and water.

36. If on the Kalends of January, anyone does as many do, calling it "in a stag," or goes about in [the guise of] a calf,[44] he shall do penance for three years.

37. If anyone has the oracles[45] which against reason they call "Sortes Sanctorum,"[46] or any other "sortes,"[45] or with evil device

---

[44] See Introduction. p. 41, and p. 277, n. 10, above. The text is very awkward. Schmitz does not help by reading "ducunt" for "dicunt;" this would require some such rendering as: "and they lead a figure about on a stag."

[45] Reading "sortes" for "fortes," which Schmitz wrongly attributes to Paris. 12315.

[46] See above p. 229, n. 66.

draws lots[47] from anything else, or practices divination he shall do penance for three years, one year on bread and water.

38. If anyone makes, or releases from, a vow beside trees or springs or by a lattice, or anywhere except in a church, he shall do penance for three years on bread and water, since this is sacrilege or a demonic thing. Whoever eats or drinks in such a place, shall do penance for one year on bread and water.

39. If anyone is a wizard,[48] that is, if he takes away the mind of a man by the invocation of demons, he shall do penance for five years, one year on bread and water.

40. If anyone makes amulets, which is a detestable thing, he shall do penance for three years, one year on bread and water.

41. It is ordered that persons who both eat of a feast in the abominable places of the pagans and carry food back [to their homes] and eat it subject themselves to a penance of two years, and so undertake what they must carry out; and [it is ordered] to try the spirit after each oblation and to examine the life of everyone.

42. If anyone eats or drinks beside a [pagan] sacred place, if it is through ignorance, he shall thereupon promise that he will never repeat it, and he shall do penance for forty days on bread and water. But if he does this through contempt, that is, after the priest has warned him that it is sacrilege, he has communicated at the table of demons;[49] if he did this only through the vice of gluttony,[50] he shall do penance for the three forty-day periods on bread and water. If he did this really for the worship of demons and in honor of an image, he shall do penance for three years.

43. If anyone has sacrificed under compulsion [in demon worship] a second or third time, he shall be in subjection for three years, and for two years he shall partake of the communion without the oblation;[51] in the third year he shall be received to full [communion].

44. If anyone eats blood or a dead body or what has been offered

---

[47] Reading "sortitus" for "fortitus," which Schmitz wrongly attributes to Paris. 12315.
[48] "mathematicus."
[49] Cf. I Cor. 10:21.
[50] Reading with Codex Sangall. 679, "sin gulae" for "singuli."
[51] This is evidently derived ultimately from the canons of the council of Ancyra (314), canons 3 to 9. Mansi II, 516. A number of these canons distinguish, in the case of those who have sacrificed to idols, between communion without the oblation (χωρὶς προσφορᾶς) or communion of prayers, and full communion. Penitents who communicate without oblation are the συνιστάμενοι, or co-standers, See Introduction, p. 8.

to idols[52] and was not under necessity of doing this, he shall fast for twelve weeks.

Of Various Topics

45. If anyone intentionally cuts off any of his own members, he shall do penance for three years, one year on bread and water.

46. If anyone intentionally brings about abortion, he shall do penance for three years, one year on bread and water.

47. If anyone exacts usury from anybody, he shall do penance for three years, one year on bread and water.

48. If by power or by any device anyone in evil fashion breaks into or carries off another's goods, he shall do penance as in the above[53] provision and give liberal alms.

49. If by any device anyone brings a slave or any man into captivity or conveys him away, he shall do penance as stated above.

50. If anyone intentionally burns the courtyard or house of anybody, he shall do penance as stated above.

51. If anyone strikes another through anger and sheds blood or incapacitates him, he shall first pay him compensation and secure a physician. If he is a layman [he shall do penance] for forty days; a cleric, two forty-day periods; a deacon, six months; a presbyter, one year.

52. If anyone engages in hunting, if he is a cleric he shall do penance for one year; a deacon shall do penance for two years; a presbyter, for three years.

53. If anyone belonging to the ministry of holy Church is dishonest in respect to any task or neglects it, he shall do penance for seven years, three years on bread and water.

54. If anyone sins with animals after he is thirty years of age, he shall undergo [a penance of] fifteen years and shall [then] deserve the communion. But let the nature of his life be inquired into, whether it deserves somewhat more lenient treatment. If he continually persists in sinning,[54] he shall have a longer penance. But if those who are of the above-mentioned age and have wives commit this offense, they shall undergo [a penance of] twenty-five years in such a way that after five years they shall deserve the communion with the

[52] Cf. I Cor. 8:4; 10:19–20, 28.
[53] Reading "superiore" for "super iure," with Codex Sangall. 679.
[54] The application of this phrase is not altogether clear.

oblation. But if some who have wives and are more than fifty years old commit this sin, they shall deserve the viaticum [only] at the end of life.

Of Drunkenness

55. One who is drunk then with wine or beer violates the contrary command of the Savior and his Apostles;[55] but if he has a vow of holiness, he shall expiate his guilt for forty days on bread and water; a layman, indeed, shall do penance for seven days.

56. A bishop who commits fornication shall be degraded and do penance for sixteen years.

57. A presbyter or a deacon who commits natural fornication, if he has been elevated before taking the monastic vow, shall do penance for three years, shall ask pardon every hour, and shall perform a special fast every week except during the days between Easter and Pentecost.[56]

Of Petty Cases

58. If by accident anyone in neglect lets the host drop and leaves it for wild beasts[57] and it is devoured by some animal, he shall do penance for forty days. But if not [by accident],[58] he shall do penance for one year.

59. If he communicates it in ignorance to those excommunicated from the Church, he shall do penance for forty days.

60. If through negligence the host falls to the ground, there shall be a special fast.

[55] Luke 21:34.

[56] "exceptis quinquagesimis diebus." The term "quinquagesima" was applied to two periods of fifty days, the one before, the other after, Easter. The context suggests the latter signification here. This period was called "quinquagesima paschalis" or "q. laetitiae," and was marked by rejoicing. Tertullian remarks on the fact that in this period, as on Sundays, fasting or kneeling in prayer were excluded. Tert., *De corona*, 3. F. E. Warren, *Liturgy of the Ante-Nicene Church*, pp. 116, 142; *Catholic Encyclopedia*, art. "Quinquagesima," and *Kirchenlexikon*, art. "Quinquagesima." Literally the word means the fiftieth [day], and in this sense it often appears as identical with Pentecost. Cf. the *Peregrinatio Aetheriae* (sixth century): "a Pascha autem usque ad Quinquagesimen, id est Pentecosten, hic penitus nemo ieiunat" (but from Easter unto Quinquagesima, that is, Pentecost, nobody fasts here). Quoted by Duchesne, *Christian Worship*, Appendix, p. 515. The word Pentecost is sometimes used of the period of fifty days as in the *Apostolic Constitutions*, xxxvii., "τῇ τετάρτῃ ἑβδομάδι τῆς πεντηκοστῆς" ("in the fourth week of Pentecost"). The council of Nicaea (can. 20) forbids kneeling in prayer "on the Lord's day and in the days of Pentecost" ("ἐν τῇ κυριακῇ γόνυ κλίνοντες, καὶ ἐν ταῖς τῆς πεντηκοστῆς ἡμέραις").

[57] Reading "feris" for "foris" with Wasserschleben. Cf. Schmitz I, p. 483, and *Prefatio Gildae*, 9. 　　　　　　　　　　[58] Cf. Galland's note in Migne, *P.L.*, CV, 701.

61. We ought to offer [the sacrament] for good rulers;[59] on no account for evil rulers.

62. Presbyters are, indeed, not forbidden to offer for their bishops.

63. He who provides guidance to the barbarians shall do penance for three years.

64. They who despoil monasteries, falsely saying that they are redeeming captives, shall do penance for three years and shall give to the poor all the things which they have taken off.

65. He who eats the flesh of animals whose [manner of] death he does not know, shall do penance for the third part of a year.

66. We set forth the statutes of our fathers before us: boys conversing by themselves and violating the regulations of the seniors shall be corrected with three special fasts.

67. Those who kiss simply, seven special fasts. Lascivious kissing without pollution, eight special fasts. But with pollution or embrace, they shall be corrected with fifteen special fasts.

Of Disorders Connected with[60] the Sacrifice

68. If anyone does not well guard the host, and if a mouse eats it, he shall do penance for forty days. But he who loses his chrismal[61] or the host alone in any place whatever so that it cannot be found, shall do penance for the three forty-day periods or for a year.

69. Anyone who spills the chalice upon the altar when the linens are being removed, shall do penance for seven days.

70. If the host falls into the straw,[62] [the person responsible] shall do penance for seven days.

71. He who vomits the host after loading his stomach to excess shall do penance for forty days; if he casts it into the fire, twenty days.[63]

72. A deacon who forgets to offer the oblation, and fails to provide linen until they offer it,[64] shall do penance in like manner.[65]

[59] Emending "rebus" to "regibus." Cf. *Preface of Gildas*, 23.
[60] Reading with the Codex Paris. 12315, "de discordantibus circa." Other readings are "de dissensibus," "de dissensionibus," and "de dispensationibus."
[61] Cf. p. 114, n. 83, above.
[62] Reading with Wasserschleben and Codex Paris. 12315 "in stramen" for "intra mensam." The reference is to the litter strewn on the floor. Rock explains: "Throughout the whole church, but more especially about the altars and where the shrine stood, the ground was strewed with rushes or sweet smelling herbs."—Rock, *op. cit.*, IV, 52. "intra mensam" is possible in the sense of "not over the edge of the table."
[63] Wasserschleben's version of this canon is used; that of Schmitz is defective.
[64] Reading with Codex Sangall. 679 "offerunt" for "offeruntur."
[65] The passage is obscure and this rendering is doubtful. Cf. *Penitential of Cummean*, XI, 11, p. 115, above.

73. If those little animals[66] are found in flour or in any dry food or in honey or in milk, that which is about their bodies is to be thrown out.

74. He who treats the host with carelessness so that it is consumed by worms and comes to nothing shall do penance for the three forty-day periods. If it was found entire with a worm in it, it shall be burnt, and then its ashes [shall be] concealed under the altar, and he who has been neglectful shall do penance for forty days.

75. If the host falls to the ground from the hand of the officiant, and if any of it is found, every bit of what is found shall be burnt in the place in which it fell, and its ashes [shall be] concealed beneath the altar, and the priest shall do penance for half a year. And if it is found, it shall be purified as above, and he shall do penance for forty days. If it only slipped to the altar, he shall perform a special fast.

76. If through negligence anything drips from the chalice to the ground, it shall be licked up with the tongue, the board shall be scraped, and [the scrapings] shall be burnt with fire; and he shall do penance for forty days. If the chalice drips on the altar, the minister shall suck it up, and the linen which came in contact with the drop shall be washed [three?] times, and he shall do penance for three days.

77. If the priest stammers over the Sunday prayer which is called 'the perilous,'[67] once, forty psalms; a second time, one hundred strokes.

78. If one has taken his father's or brother's widow, such a person cannot be judged unless they have previously been separated from each other.

Of Homicide

79. If anyone slays a man in a public expedition without cause, he shall do penance for twenty-one weeks; but if he slays anyone accidentally in defense of himself or his parents or his household, he shall not be under accusation. If he wishes to fast, it is for him to decide, since he did the thing under compulsion.

80. If he commits homicide in time of peace and not in a tumult, by force, or because of enmity in order to take [the victim's] property, he shall do penance for twenty-eight weeks and restore to his wife or children the property of him whom he has slain.

[66] Perhaps the rodents referred to in can. 68, above.
[67] See p. 112, n. 75; p. 177, n. 29.

Of Sick Penitents

81. But if anyone comes to penance, and if sickness ensues, and if he is not able to fulfill that which has been commanded him by the priest, he shall be received to holy communion, and if it is God's will to restore him to health, he shall fast afterwards.

82. If anyone fails to do penance and perchance falls into sickness and seeks to take communion, he shall not be forbidden; but give him the holy communion and command him that if it please God in his mercy and if he escapes from this sickness, he shall thereafter confess everything and then do penance.

Of Those Who Die Excommunicate

83. But if anyone who had already confessed has died excommunicate and death seized him without warning, whether in the road or in his house, if there is a relative of his let the relative offer something on his behalf at the holy altar, or for the redemption of captives, or for the commemoration of his soul.

Of Incestuous Persons

84. If anyone takes in marriage his wife's daughter, he cannot be judged[68] unless they have first been separated. After they are separated, thou shalt sentence each of them for fourteen weeks, and they shall never come together again. But if they want to marry, either the man or the woman, they are free to do so, but he shall not marry her whom he sent away.

85. In the case of one who takes in marriage a close relative or his step-mother or the widow of his uncle, and of one who takes his father's wife or his wife's sister—the decision is grave: [such an offender] shall be canonically condemned.

Of Things Offered to Idols

86. If while he is an infant anyone through ignorance tastes of those things which were offered to idols or of a dead body or of anything abominable, let that person fast for three weeks.

87. On account of fornication, moreover, many men do not know the number of the women with whom they have committed fornication: these shall fast for fifty weeks.

---

[68] Reading "hic non potest iudicari" for "hic non potestis iudicare," with Sangall. 679

88. But if he ate without knowing it[69] what was offered to idols or a dead thing, pardon shall be given him, since he did this unaware; nevertheless, he shall fast three weeks.

Of Theft Committed through Necessity

89. If through necessity anyone steals articles of food or a garment or a beast on account of hunger or nakedness, pardon shall be given him. He shall fast for four weeks. If he makes restitution, thou shalt not compel him to fast.

90. If anyone steals a horse or an ox or an ass[70] or a cow or supplies of food or sheep which feed his whole household, he shall fast as stated above.

Of Adultery

91. If any woman misleads her mother's husband, she cannot be judged until she gives him up. When they are separated she shall fast fourteen weeks.

92. If anyone who has a lawful wife puts her away and marries another, she whom he marries is not his. He shall not eat or drink, nor shall he be at all in conversation with her whom he has wrongly taken or with her parents. Moreover, if the parents consent to it, they shall be excommunicated.

If a woman seduces the husband of another woman, she shall be excommunicated from the Christians.

93. If anyone of the Christians sees a Christian walking about, or one of his own relatives wandering, and sells him, he is not worthy to have a resting place among Christians, until he redeems him. But if he is not able to find the place where he is, he shall give the price which he received for him and shall redeem another from servitude and fast for twenty-eight weeks.

Of the Penance for Those Thrice Married

94. If any man's wife is dead, he has the right to take another; likewise, also, in the case of a woman. If he takes a third wife, he shall fast for three weeks; if he takes a fourth or a fifth, he shall fast for twenty-one weeks.

[69] "per ignorantiam" in can. 86 is to be taken in a different sense from "nesciens" here. The former phrase apparently has reference to the offender's ignorance of the nature and gravity of the offense; the latter to the fact that he was unaware that what he was eating was forbidden.
[70] "iumentum."

Of Him Who Lacerates Himself

95. If anyone cuts off his hair or lacerates his face with a sword or with his nails[71] after the death of a parent, he shall fast for four weeks, and after he has fasted he shall then take communion.

96. If any pregnant woman wishes to fast, she has the right to do so.

97. A quack,[72] man or woman, slayers of children, when they come to the end of life, if they seek penance with mourning and the shedding of tears,—if he desists, receive him: he shall fast for thirty weeks.

Of Things Strangled

98. If any dog or fox or hawk dies for any cause, whether he is killed by a cudgel or by a stone or by an arrow which has no iron, these are all "things strangled." They are not to be eaten, and he who eats of them shall fast for six weeks.

99. If anyone strikes with an arrow a stag or another animal, and if it is found after three days, and if perchance a wolf, a bear, a dog, or a fox has tasted of it, no one shall eat it; and he who does eat of it shall fast for four weeks.

100. If a hen dies in a well, the well is to be emptied. If one drinks knowingly of it, he shall fast for a week.

101. If any mouse or hen or anything falls into wine or water, no one shall drink of this. If it falls into oil or honey, the oil shall be used in a lamp; the honey, in medicine or in something else needful.

102. If a fish has died in the fishpond, it shall not be eaten; he who eats of it shall fast for four days.

103. If a pig or a hen has eaten of the body of a man, it shall not be eaten nor be used for breeding purposes, but it shall be killed and given to the dogs. If a wolf tears an animal, and if it dies, no one shall eat it. And if it lives and a man afterward kills it, it may be eaten.

Of Polluted Animals

104. If a man has sinned with a goat[73] or with a sheep or with any animal, no one shall eat its flesh or milk, but it shall be killed and given to the dogs.

[71] Reading "ungulis" for "ungulas" with Wasserschleben.
[72] "Herbarius." The characteristic confusion of singular and plural is retained in the translation.
[73] Reading "capra" for "capta" with Codex Sangall. 679 and Paris. 12315.

105. If anyone wishes to give alms for his soul of wealth which was the product of booty, if he has already[74] done penance, he has the right to give it. Here endeth.

2. PENITENTIAL CANONS FROM REGINO'S ECCLESIASTICAL DISCIPLINE (*ca.* 906)

[THE LEARNED MONK Regino became abbot of Prüm in Lorraine in 892, was expelled from the office in 899, and thereafter employed his talents in the service of Rathbod, archbishop of Trier. About 906, at the bidding of Rathbod, he compiled his notable work *Of Synodical Cases and Ecclesiastical Discipline.*[1] This is an extensive collection of varied canonical regulations and includes a considerable number of penitential clauses. While the latter are mainly extracted from the greater penitential books, in some instances they exhibit fresh material or diverge freely from their sources. The canons here selected for translation show Regino's use of the method of the penitentials. His authorization of certain of these books is quoted on page 217, above. The text followed is in Wasserschleben's edition, *Reginonis abbatis Prumiensis, libri duo de synodalibus causis et disciplinis ecclesiasticis,* Leipzig, 1840.[2]]

BOOK I

ccxcii. *Of confession and penance.*—Presbyters ought to admonish the parishioners[3] committed to them that everyone who knows himself to be stricken with the mortal wound of sin should, on the fourth day before Lent,[4] return with all haste to the life-giving mother, the Church; where, confessing with all humility and contrition of heart the evil that he has committed, he shall receive the remedies of penance according to the scale prescribed by the canonical authorities, and he shall be "delivered unto Satan for the destruction of the flesh that the spirit may be saved in the day of the Lord."[5] But not only he who has committed some mortal sin but also every person who recognizes that he has soiled with the stain of sin the immaculate robe of Christ which he received in baptism, shall hasten to come to his own priest and with purity of mind humbly confess all the transgressions, all the sins by which he remembers that he has

---

[74] Reading "si iam" for "suam" with Codex Sangall. 679.

[1] *De synodalibus causis et disciplinis ecclesiasticis.*

[2] For a valuable discussion of Regino's treatise, see Fournier and Le Bras, I, 244–68. The Migne text of the work is entitled: *De ecclesiasticis disciplinis et religione christiana,* P.L., CXXXII, 187–400.   [3] "plebem" (the parish).

[4] That is, Ash Wednesday.   [5] I Cor. 5:5.

offended God; and he shall give attention to whatever is enjoined him by the priest as diligently as if it were uttered by the very mouth of Almighty God and shall very carefully observe it.

ccxcv. *Of penitents.*[6]—At the beginning of Lent all penitents who are undertaking or have undertaken public penance shall present themselves to the bishop of the city before the doors of the church, clad in sackcloth, with bare feet, with their faces downcast toward the earth, by their very garb and countenance proclaiming themselves guilty. Here the deans ought to be present, that is the archpriests of the parishes, with witnesses, that is the presbyters of the penitents, who ought carefully to examine their conversation. And he shall enjoin penance, according to the measure of guilt, through the appointed grades. Thereafter he shall lead them into the church and, prostrate upon the floor, he shall chant with tears, together with all the clergy, the seven penitential psalms, for their absolution. Then rising from prayer, as the canons declare, he shall lay hands upon them; he shall sprinkle them with holy water. He shall first set ashes on their heads, then cover them with sackcloth, and with groaning and frequent sighs he shall intimate to them that, just as Adam was cast out of paradise, so they also for their sins are cast out from the Church. This done, he shall command the attendants to thrust them outside the doors of the church, and the clergy to follow with the responsory: "In the sweat of thy face shalt thou eat bread,"[7] *etc.*, so that when they see Holy Church trembling with perturbation over their misdeeds, they shall not lightly esteem penance. But in the sacred Supper of the Lord they shall again be presented at the threshold of the church.

ccci.[8] *On hearing confession.*—When bishops or presbyters receive the confessions of the faithful they ought to humble themselves and pray with groans of sorrow and with tears not only for their own faults but also for their brother's fall. For the Apostle saith: "Who is weak and I am not weak?"[9]

ccciv. *An order for giving penance.*—After this, question him softly and gently:

[6] This canon is attributed by Regino to "the synod of Agde" ("ex concilio Agathensi") and the ascription is repeated by Burchard, *Corrector*, chap. xxvi, where the passage is quoted. But no such provision appears in the canons of any church council. See Wasserschleben's note, *Regino*, p. 136, and Watkins, *History of Penance*, II, 530, 581, where the canon is translated.   [7] Gen. 3:19.

[8] Attributed by Regino to "The Penitential of Archbishop Theodore or that of the presbyter Bede."   [9] II Cor. 11:29.

Believest thou in the Father and in the Son and in the Holy Ghost? Answer: I believe.

Believest thou that these three Persons are one God? Answer: I believe.

Believest thou that thou shalt arise in the day of judgment in this same flesh in which thou art now, and receive according to what thou hast done, whether it be good or evil?[10] Answer: I believe.

Wilt thou forgive the sins of those who have sinned against thee, as saith the Lord: "If ye will not forgive men their sins, neither will your Father forgive your sins?"[11] Answer: I will.

And inquire diligently of him if he is incestuous or unfaithful to his superior; and if he will not abandon his incest, thou canst not give him penance; but if he will, thou canst. When these matters have been dealt with, the priest ought affectionately to address the penitent in these words:

Brother, do not blush to confess thy sins, for I also am a sinner, and perchance I have done worse deeds than thou hast. Wherefore I warn thee in these things, since it is a habitual fault of the human race as saith the blessed Gregory,[12] both in falling to commit[13] sin, and not to bring out by confessing, what has been committed, but to defend in denying and to multiply the proof in defending. And we who fear not at the devil's instigation to perpetrate base crimes, these very things which indeed we have enacted without any shame, through his persuasion we blush even to confess in words, and, in the presence of a man who is like to ourselves and perchance subject to the same passions, we hesitate to tell what, despicable though the action be, we did not fear to commit without any blush of the mind in the presence of God who seeth all things. Let us then freely confess what we have committed under no one's compulsion. But if we hide our sins they shall be brought to light by him who is both the accuser and the instigator of sin. For he is the same who inciteth us to sin and accuseth us when we have sinned; if therefore we are to forestall him in this life and be ourselves the accusers of our own wickedness, let us flee the iniquities of the devil, our enemy and accuser, as Paul beareth witness saying: "If we would judge ourselves, certainly we should not be judged."[14]

---

[10] Based on II Cor. 5:10.   [11] Based on Matt. 6:15.

[12] Gregory the Great, *Moralia*, Book XXII, chap. xv; Migne, *P.L.*, LXXIX., 230.

[13] Emending "dimittere" to "committere," with Gregory, *loc. cit.*   [14] I Cor. 11:31.

But if the priest sees that he is bashful, let him again proceed:

Perchance, beloved, not all things that thou hast done quite come to memory. I will question thee: take care lest at the persuasion of the devil thou presume to conceal anything.

And then he shall question him in order thus:

Hast thou committed murder either accidentally or willfully, or in the avenging of relatives, or at the command of thy lord, or in public war? If thou hast done it willfully, thou shouldst do penance for seven years; if unintentionally or by accident, five years. If for the avenging of a relative, one year, and in the two years thereafter, the three forty-day periods and the appointed days. If in war, forty days. If thou art a freeman, and at the command of thy lord thou hast slain a slave who is innocent, one year and during two other years, three forty-day periods and the appointed days. If the slave is worthy of death, thou shalt do penance for forty days.

Question: Hast thou cut off the hands or feet of a man, or gouged out his eyes, or wounded a man? For mutilation thou shouldst do penance for one year; for wounding he shall [sic] do penance for forty days.

Question: Hast thou committed perjury, whether for greed of the world, or under compulsion and of necessity, or for thy life or that of thy relatives, or unwittingly; or hast thou knowingly led others into perjury? If thou hast committed perjury knowingly and led others into perjury, thou oughtest to do penance for seven years. If unwittingly, for one year and three forty-day periods. If for life or limb, three forty-day periods.

Question: Hast thou committed theft, or sacrilege, or acts of destruction, or robbery, taking what was not thine? If thou hast broken into buildings by night and taken off animals, or [committed] a graver offense—to the value of forty solidi, thou shouldst do penance for one year and repay the value. If thou dost not repay it, thou shalt do penance for two years. If thou hast committed a greater theft, thou shouldst do penance for three years. And if thou hast often done it, seven years. For a small theft, twenty days; boys, ten days. If thou hast taken anything from a church, which is sacrilege, thou shalt do penance for seven years.

Question: Hast thou committed adultery with the wife or the

betrothed of another, or defiled a virgin, whether a nun dedicated to God or an unattached[15] woman, that is, one without a husband, or thine own maidservant? If thou hast had intercourse with another's wife or with a nun, thou shalt do penance for seven years; if with a virgin, two years; if with a widow, one year. If thou hast put away thy wife and attached thyself to another, thou shalt do penance for seven years; if it is with an unattached[16] woman, three forty-day periods and the appointed fasts; if with thine own maidservant, thou shall do penance for forty days.

. . .

Question: Hast thou done anything that the pagans do at the Kalends of January, in [the guise of] a stag or a cow?[17] Thou shalt do penance for three years.

Question: Hast thou done or said anything in any task, or hast thou begun it, with fortune telling or a magical trick? Thou shouldst do penance for one year.

Question: Hast thou placed thy child on a roof or on an oven for some healing, or hast thou burnt grains where there was a dead man? Thou shouldst do penance for five years.

Question: Hast thou sung diabolical songs[18] over the dead? Thou shalt do penance for twenty days.

. . .

cccxl. *Of Lent.*—He who has intercourse with his wife during the forty days before Easter and refuses to abstain from her shall do penance for one year, or he shall pay to the church his own value, namely, twenty-six solidi, or distribute it to the poor. If it happened through drunkenness, not habitually, he shall do penance for forty days.

cccxcviii. *That diabolical songs be not sung at night hours over the bodies of the dead.*—Laymen who keep watch at funerals shall do so with fear and trembling, and with reverence. Let no one there presume to sing diabolical songs nor make jests and perform dances which pagans have invented by the devil's teaching. For who does not know that it is diabolical, and not only alien from the Christian religion, but even contrary to human nature, that there should be

---

[15] "absoluta."   [16] "vacante."
[17] "in cervulo vel in vegula." Cf. pp. 41, 277, above.
[18] Or "formulae" ("carmina").

singing, rejoicing, drunkenness, and that the mouth be loosed with laughter, and that all piety and feeling of charity be set aside, as if to exult in a brother's death, in the place where mourning and sobbing with doleful voices for the loss of a dear brother ought to resound? If indeed we read that the fathers of the Old and of the New Testament in many places deplored with weeping the death of holy men, yet nowhere do we read that they rejoiced because they departed from the world. For all Egypt wept for the Patriarch Jacob seventy days. And Joseph and his brethren, when they took away their father into the land of Canaan for burial, "at the threshing floor of Atad which is situated beyond Jordan, celebrating the exequies with a great and vehement lamentation, spent seven full days."[19] Moreover, so great was the mourning that from this the place received its name. And of the blessed Stephen we read that "devout men buried him or took order for his funeral and made great mourning over him."[20] And therefore such unsuitable rejoicing and pestiferous songs are on God's authority to be wholly forbidden. But if anyone wishes to sing, let him sing the *Kyrie eleison*. But if he does otherwise,[21] let him be quite silent. If, however, he will not be silent, he shall be forthwith denounced by all, or adjured that he no longer has God's permission to stay there, but is to withdraw and go to his own house. On the morrow, moreover, he shall be so punished that others may fear.

BOOK II [COMMUTATIONS AUTHORIZED BY REGINO]

ccccxlvii. *What is to be done for one month.*—For one month which a person ought to spend doing penance on bread and water, he shall sing twelve hundred psalms, kneeling; and if [it is done] without kneeling, sixteen hundred and eighty. And if he wishes and is unable to refrain, he shall dine every day at sext, except that on Wednesday and Friday he shall fast until none. He shall not partake of meat and wine; he may take other things.

ccccxlviii. *What for one week.*—For one week he shall sing three hundred psalms with genuflexions or chant them in order in a single place.

ccccxlix. *What for one year.*—One who really does not know the

---

[19] Gen. 50:10.

[20] Acts 8:2. Douay version omits the words "buried him or," and renders "curaverunt," as here, "took order for his funeral."

[21] "Sin aliter," that is, if he will not sing the "Kyrie."

psalms and cannot fast, for a year during which he ought to fast on
bread and water shall give in alms twenty-six solidi and fast until
nones one day each week (that is, Wednesday), and another day
(that is, Friday) until vespers. And he shall estimate how much he
consumes in three forty-day periods and contribute a moiety of it in
alms.

ccccl. *Of the equivalent of one year.*—In the first year some allow
four three-day periods, others twelve three-day periods, that is, one
in each month. Some say they perform a three-day period by persisting in scourgings and vigils for three days.

ccccli. *Of the equivalent of one day.*—But the equivalent of one day
is a supper[22] for two or three poor men, or one denarius. Some prescribe
a whole psalter in summer; however, in winter, spring, or autumn,
fifty psalms. Some prescribe twelve stripes or strokes.[23]

cccclii. *Again, of the commutation of one day.*—Therefore, he who
can fulfill what is written in the penitential shall give thanks to God.
But to him who cannot complete it, we give advice through the mercy
of God. First, for one day on bread and water let him sing fifty psalms
kneeling, or seventy, standing in a single place, or give one denarius,
or feed three poor men. Some say fifty strokes, or fifty psalms, for
one day in fall, winter or spring, or in spring a hundred strokes or
fifty psalms; in summer one psalter or a hundred strokes.

ccccliii. *Of the commutation of three years.*—He who is not able to
do penance as we have said above in the first year shall expend in
alms twenty-six solidi, in the second year, twenty, in the third,
eighteen; this comes to sixty-four solidi. Powerful men shall do for
their sins as Zacchaeus did. For he said to the Lord: "Lord, the half
of all my goods I give to the poor, and if I have wrongfully taken
anything I restore it fourfold."[24] And he shall set free some of his
slaves and redeem captives, and from the heart forgive those who sin
against him. And he who commits forbidden things shall abstain even
from things permissible and afflict the body with fasts, vigils, and
frequent prayers. For the flesh when gladsome drew us into guilt;
afflicted, it leads us back to pardon.

ccccliv. [Conclusion.][25]— . . . Behold, we have set in order the

---

[22] "agapen."   [23] "plagas vel percussiones."   [24] Based on Luke 19:8.
[25] The major part of this chapter consists of the version of the paragraph ascribed to
St. Boniface which is given on p. 232, above. The following words are, however, Regino's
own conclusion to the book.

variant opinions of various fathers concerning the remedies of sins or
the lightening of penance, leaving to the judgment of the wise priest
what he may decide to be beneficial and useful to the penitent soul.

3. SELECTIONS FROM THE CORRECTOR AND PHYSICIAN OF BURCHARD OF WORMS
(ca. 1008-12)

[BURCHARD was a distinguished ecclesiastic who was elevated from the
diaconate to the see of Worms in the year 1000 and died in 1025. He was
active in church reforms and on terms of close acquaintance with the
three emperors of his period, Otto III, Henry II, and Conrad II. His
literary labors were also considerable. His most important work is the
Decretum, written about 1008-12. This is an extensive collection of documents on church government and discipline, selected and edited in accordance with the author's ecclesiastical interests. The work is divided
into twenty books, comprising in the text used by Migne 1785 chapters.[1]
Designed to meet the needs of his own clergy, the *Decretum* soon obtained
general circulation, and it was constantly employed by canonists of
the subsequent period.

Throughout the work, Burchard made large use of Regino of Prüm's
Ecclesiastical Discipline and of a late ninth century anonymous Italian
collection known as the *Anselmo dedicata;* but he treated his sources
with extreme freedom.[2] He shows a reaction against the high papal tendency of the latter of these works, and he strongly asserts the authority
of the bishops and of the provincial assemblies of bishops.

Burchard's work, following the Frankish penitentials, combines Irish
and Anglo-Saxon penitential canons with Roman. There is much penitential material wrought into various parts of the *Decretum*. Book XIX
of the collection, called in Burchard's introduction *Corrector et medicus*,
represents the author's systematization of the authoritative materials on
penance. Its method is that of an interrogatory, in which the confessant
is specifically questioned on his sins, and terms of penance are indicated.
The numerous manuscripts of the *Corrector* differ considerably with
respect to readings.[3] The manuscript used by Wasserschleben[4] contains

---

[1] The *Decretum* occupies columns 537 to 1058 of Migne, *P.L.*, CXL. For an illuminating
historical treatment of the work see Fournier and Le Bras, I, 364-421. This study follows
Fournier's fundamental investigation in "Le Décret de Burchard de Worms," *Revue
d'histoire ecclésiastique*, XII (1911), 451-73; 670-701. The problems of Burchard's sources
and his use of them are treated by the same author in: "Études critiques sur le Décret de
Burchard de Worms," *Nouvelle revue historique de droit français et étranger*, XXXIV
(1910), 41-112; 213-21; 289-331; 564-84. In these studies Fournier supplies ample reference to the other literature of the subject.

[2] "En réalité Burchard a traité les textes avec une liberté extrême," Fournier, "Le
Décret . . . " p. 453.

[3] For a description of the manuscripts, Schmitz II, pp. 392 ff. should be consulted.
M. Manitius, *Geschichte der lateinischen Literatur des Mittelalters*, II, 60, lists manuscripts
and editions.   [4] Codex Vallicell. F8. *Bussordnungen*, pp. 624-82.

263 canons. The text used by Migne, from the edition published at Cologne in 1548 and at Paris in 1549, contains 159 chapters which vary in length from a few lines to twenty-five of Migne's ample columns. Chapter V alone of this text corresponds to the first 180 of Wasserschleben's canons. Schmitz has edited what he regards as the original form of the book under the title: *Poenitentiale ecclesiae Germaniae*, a title invented by the Ballerini.[5] The manuscript employed, Codex Vat. Lat. 4772, is held by Schmitz to be the earliest extant, belonging to the early eleventh century. Though written at Arezzo this manuscript displays its Frankish source by the introduction of a number of Germanic words. It contains only the material of the first thirty-three chapters of the Migne text. The first four chapters of the latter constitute an introductory section on the procedure in administering penance. In the Schmitz text this is preceded by an elaborate *ordo*, with numerous prayers. Another eleventh century manuscript known to Wasserschleben and Schmitz, Vat. Lat. 3830, omits both these introductions, as does the fourteenth century manuscript which Wasserschleben makes the basis of his text, Codex Vallicell. F8. Schmitz follows the Ballerini, though not without some misgivings, in the opinion that the *Corrector* was substantially in circulation before Burchard, and was not compiled but appropriated by him.[6] This view has been rejected by Fournier on arguments that seem incontestable.[7] In his monograph on Burchard[8] A. M. Koeniger earlier combated the view of Schmitz. Fournier's elaborate studies have indicated in great detail the sources used by Burchard. In a table of the sources of each book which he furnishes[9] it is indicated that Book XIX has thirty-five fragments from Regino, ten from the collection known as *Dionysio-Hadriana*, eight from the Forged Decretals, one from Merovingian, and twelve from Carolingian councils, seven from the *Collectio canonum Hibernensis*, three from the capitularies of bishops, fifty from various penitentials, ten from ecclesiastical writers, and twenty-three from undetermined sources or composed by Burchard himself.

Attention has been called in the Introduction[10] to the element of superstition and folklore in the Decretum and particularly in the *Cor-*

---

[5] In *De antiquis collectionibus et collectoribus canonum* (1753–57). In this acute examination of the documentary history of canon law the brothers Peter and Jerome Ballerini refuted the errors of Quesnel. The work is contained in Migne, *P.L.*, LVI, 11–354. The section on Burchard is repeated in CXL, 497 ff.

[6] Schmitz II, pp. 385 ff., 402. Text, pp. 403–67.

[7] "Études critiques," pp. 213–21. Fournier indicates the numerous parallels with other parts of the *Decretum,* and points out that the manuscript upon which Schmitz relies itself numbers the book as nineteenth in the collection: "Incipit liber nonus decimus qui Corrector vocatur." These words follow the Order for Penance for which this manuscript is remarkable. Burchard calls his twentieth book (on theological questions) "Speculator," as he designates this one "Corrector."

[8] *Burchard I von Worms und die deutsche Kirche seiner Zeit* (Munich, 1905), pp. 132 f.

[9] "Études," facing p. 112.   [10] Pp. 41 ff., above.

rector; and the use of the work by J. Grimm in his *Deutsche Mythologie* has been referred to. In a footnote at the beginning of a section of extracts, Grimm remarks:

Whence did Burchard draw this large chapter, 19, 5? . . . . The German words in it, "holda," "werwolf," "belisa," lead me to think that, here more than anywhere, he puts together what he himself knew of German superstitions, with additions from other collections.[11]

Following Koeniger, Fournier, and other scholars, the translator has used Migne's text as a basis. For convenience the sections of the long Chapter V have been numbered in accordance with the text of Schmitz; these numbers agree with those of Wasserschleben as far as Section 24. Schmitz has also been consulted for the manuscript variants.]

ARGUMENT OF THE BOOK

This book is called "the Corrector" and "the Physician," since it contains ample corrections for bodies and medicines for souls and teaches every priest, even the uneducated, how he shall be able to bring help to each person, ordained or unordained; poor or rich; boy, youth, or mature man; decrepit, healthy, or infirm; of every age; and of both sexes.

Chapter I. At What Time the Priests of the Parishes Ought, by Canonical Authority, to Require the Contentious to Come to Peace and Delinquents to Penance

In the week preceding the beginning of Lent the priests of the parishes shall assemble the people to themselves and reconcile the contentious by canonical authority and settle all quarrels and then first give the penance to those who confess; so that before the beginning of the fast comes about, all shall have confessed and received their penance, that they may be able freely to say: "And forgive us our debts as we also forgive our debtors."[12]

[Chapter II, is made up of sections from Regino, I, ccxcii and ccci (see above, p. 314), who in turn has partly depended on Halitgar.]

Chapter III. Prayer to Be Said by the Priest for Those Who Come to Penance

Lord God Almighty, be Thou propitious unto me a sinner, that I may be able worthily to give thanks unto Thee, who through Thy mercy

[11] English edition (*Teutonic Mythology*), 1888, IV, 1743.
[12] Matt. 6:12.

hast made me, though unworthy, a minister in the sacerdotal office, and appointed me, though slight and lowly, an intermediary to pray and intercede before our Lord Jesus Christ, Thy Son, for sins,[13] and for those returning to penance. And therefore, our Governor and Lord, who will have all men to be saved and to come to the knowledge of the truth,[14] who desirest not the death of the sinner but that he should be converted and live, accept my prayer, which I pour forth before the face of Thy Clemency, for Thy menservants and maidservants who had come to penance,[15] that Thou mayest give to them the spirit of compunction, that they may escape from the snares of the devil by which they are held bound and by a worthy satisfaction return to Thee. Through the same our Lord Jesus Christ Thy Son.

Chapter IV. Of Confession and Penance and Reconciliation, and of the Questioning of Those Who Wish to Confess Their Sins, and the Order for Administering Penance to Them

Then the priest shall softly and gently question him first on the faith, as he holds it, and shall say:

Believest thou in the Father and in the Son and in the Holy Ghost? Answer: I believe.

Believest thou that these three Persons are one God? Answer: I believe.

Believest thou that thou shalt arise in the day of judgment in this same flesh in which thou art now, and receive according to what thou hast done, whether it be good or evil?[16] Answer: I believe.

Wilt thou forgive the sins of those who have sinned against thee, as saith the Lord: "If ye will not forgive men their sins, neither will your Father forgive your sins"?[17] Answer: I will.

And thou shalt inquire diligently of him if he is incestuous, or unfaithful to his superior; and if he will not abandon his incest thou canst not give him penance; but if he will, thou canst. When these matters have been dealt with, the priest ought affectionately to address the penitent in these words:

Brother, do not blush to confess thy sins, for I also am a sinner, and perchance I have done worse deeds than thou hast. Wherefore I warn thee in these things, since it is a habitual fault of the human race, as saith the blessed Gregory, both in falling to commit sin and

---

[13] "pro peccatis" should probably read "pro peccantibus" (for sinners), as in *Pseudo-Romanum*, p. 298, above.   [14] I Tim. 2:4.

[15] To this point the prayer is a repetition of that in the *Pseudo-Romanum*, p. 298, above.   [16] Based on II Cor. 5:10.   [17] Based on Matt. 6:15.

not to bring out by confessing what has been committed, but to defend in denying and in defending to multiply that which had been disproved. And we who fear not at the devil's instigation to perpetrate base crimes, these very things which by his work we have enacted without any shame, through his persuasion we blush to confess at least in words, and in the presence of a man who is like to ourselves and perchance subject to the same passions, with a reprehensible refusal we hesitate to tell what we did not fear to commit without any blush of the mind in the presence of God who seeth all things. Let us then freely confess what we have committed under no one's compulsion. If we indeed hide our sins, they shall be brought to light by him who is both the accuser and the instigator of sin. For he is the same who inciteth us to sin and accuseth us when we have sinned; if therefore we are to forestall him in this life and be ourselves the accusers of our own wickedness, let us flee the iniquities of the devil, our enemy and accuser, as Paul beareth witness saying: "If we would judge ourselves, certainly we should not be judged."[18]

Chapter V. [Confession and Penance, continued]

But if the priest sees that he is bashful, let him again proceed. And then he shall question him in order thus:

Perchance, beloved, not all things that thou hast done quite come to memory. I will question thee: take care lest at the persuasion of the devil we conceal anything.

1. Hast thou committed murder willfully, without necessity, not in warfare, but because of the desire to take his goods for thyself, and so hast slain him? If thou hast, thou shouldst fast, as is customary, on bread and water, for the forty continuous days which the common people call a "carina";[19] and thou shalt observe this for seven succeeding years.

2. In the first year, after these forty days thou shouldst entirely abstain from wine, mead, fat, cheese, and from all fat fish; except on those feast days which are celebrated by all the people in that diocese. And if thou art on a great journey, in the king's army, or prevented by any infirmity, then thou mayest make composition for Tuesday, Thursday, and Saturday with one denarius, or the value of one

---

[18] I Cor. 11:31.
[19] Usually "carena," from Lat. "quarentena" or "quadragena"—a period of forty days.

denarius, or by feeding three poor men, but on condition that thou use only one of those three things stated above, that is, thou shalt drink either wine or mead or honeyed beer. After thou hast come home or been restored to health thou shalt have no permission to make composition. After the completion of a full year thou shalt be led to the church, and the kiss of peace shall be conceded to thee.

3. In the second year and the third thou shalt fast in the same way, except that on Tuesdays, Thursdays, and Saturdays thou shalt have the right to make composition at the above-named price, wherever thou art. Everything else thou shalt diligently observe as in the first year.

4. Through the four several years that remain, thou shouldst fast for the three forty-day periods, through the legal days. The first is before Easter, with the other Christians; the second, before the feast of St. John the Baptist, and if any time is left over, thou shalt complete it afterward; the third is before the Lord's Nativity: thou shalt abstain from wine, from mead, from honeyed beer, from flesh, from fat, from cheese, and from fat fishes.

5. And in the four years referred to above on Tuesday, Thursday, and Saturday, thou shalt take whatever thou wilt. For Monday and Wednesday thou canst make composition at the price already stated. Thou shalt always keep Friday on bread and water. And having completed these requirements thou shalt receive the holy communion, on this condition, that thou be never without penance as long as thou livest, but that during thy whole life thou shalt do penance on bread and water every Friday; and if thou wilt thou shalt have the right to make composition with one denarius or the value of one denarius, or thou shalt feed three poor men.

6. We concede these things to thee from mercy, not according to the severity of the canons, for the canons prescribe thus: If anyone on purpose and through cupidity commits murder, he shall renounce the world and go into a monastery of monks and there serve God always.

[Sections 7 to 14 deal with less grave cases of homicide, e.g., in the avenging of relatives, on sudden anger, in war, by command of a superior, where the guilt is shared by others.]

15. Hast thou committed parricide, that is, slain a father, mother, brother, sister, father's brother, mother's brother, mother's sister, father's sister, or done any such thing? If by accident, not inten-

tionally, and if thou didst not in thine anger intend to strike but it happened accidentally, thou shouldst do penance as if [ordinary] homicide had been intentionally committed. But if by design, and if thou didst it in thine anger, thou shouldst observe this, that for the period of one year thou shalt remain in front of the doors of the church praying for the mercy of the Lord. The full year completed, thou shalt be led into the church. Then thou shalt stand in one corner of the church until the period of one year is ended. When these provisions are fulfilled, if the fruit of penitence is perceived in thee, thou shalt become a sharer in the body and blood of Christ, that thou be not hardened by despair. Thou shalt not eat flesh all the days of thy life. Moreover, thou shalt fast until nones daily except on feast days and Sundays. Further, three days a week, thou shalt abstain from wine, mead, and honeyed beer. Thou shalt not dare to bear arms except against the pagans. And wherever thou goest, thou shalt not be conveyed in a carriage but shalt proceed on thine own feet. If thou hast a wife thou shalt not be separated from her; but if thou hast not, thou shalt not take one. But as to the time of this penance, it shall be for thy bishop to decide, that he may be able to extend or diminish it according to thy conduct.

[Sections 16 to 22 deal with cases of accidental homicide through unguarded use of arrows, clubs, stones, axes, etc.]

23. Hast thou slain thy superior or been in a conspiracy to bring about his death or [that of] thy wife, part of thy body? We propose to thee two plans; take that which is more agreeable to thee. The first is this: Renounce this passing world and enter a monastery and humble thyself under the hand of the abbot and observe with simple mind all things which shall be commanded thee by him.

24. But the second plan is this: Lay down thine arms and give up all secular business; thou shalt not eat flesh or fat all the days of thy life except the day of the Lord's Resurrection, and the day of Pentecost, and the day of the Lord's Nativity. At other times thou shalt do penance on bread and water, sometimes with beans and vegetables. Continue at all times in fasts, in vigils, in prayers. Thou shalt never drink wine or mead or honeyed beer except on those three days aforesaid. Thou shalt not take a wife; thou shalt not have a concubine; thou shalt not commit adultery; but thou shalt remain perpetually without the hope of marriage. Thou shalt never wash thyself in a bath; thou shalt not mount a horse; thou shalt not bring the

cause of thyself and another into the assembly of the faithful. Thou shalt never sit in the feasts of those who make merry. In the church thou shalt stand humbly behind the door, separated from other Christians. Thou shalt commend thyself as a suppliant to those who come in and go out. Thou shalt consider thyself unworthy of the communion of the body and blood of the Lord all the days of thy life. But at the very end of thy life, if thou hast observed the plan, we grant that thou mayest receive it as a viaticum.

25. Hast thou slain, or been in a plot to slay, a penitent who was doing public penance and was in that vesture or garment in which they who are fasting for a "carina" are accustomed to be? If thou hast done this, thou shouldst keep that fast which he began and observe all that which is prescribed above concerning those who have committed murders intentionally and through cupidity.

[Nos. 26 and 27 deal, respectively, with wounds that result in mutilation and with the slaying of a robber. In the latter case a period of penance is prescribed on the ground that the slain man was "created in the image of God and baptized in His name." Nos. 28 and 29 have reference to giving information that results in murder and placing a man where others slay him.]

30. Hast thou thyself or someone through thy plotting slain one of the men of the Church, dedicated to God, either a psalm singer or a doorkeeper or a reader or an exorcist or an acolyte or a subdeacon or a deacon or a presbyter? If thou hast, thou shouldst do penance for each of these several orders according to their respective ranks. So shalt thou do: thou shalt do penance for a psalm singer the forty days on bread and water which are called in German[19] a "carina," with the seven following years. Likewise for a doorkeeper, for a reader, for an exorcist, for an acolyte, for a subdeacon, for a deacon, for a presbyter; for every presbyter has eight orders. Wherefore, everyone who willfully kills a presbyter ought so to do penance as if eight murders had been intentionally committed and never be without penance. Moreover, according to the council of Worms[20] thou shalt do penance in this way: If thou hast willfully slain a priest, thou shalt not eat flesh, and thou shalt not drink wine all the days of thy life. Thou shalt fast daily until vespers except on feast days and Sundays; thou shalt not bear arms; thou shalt not mount a horse.

[19] "Teutonice."
[20] Council of Worms, 868, can. 26. Mansi, XV, 874.

Thou shalt not enter the church for five years, but shalt stand in front of the church doors. After the five years, enter the church; but thou shalt not take communion, but stand or sit in a corner of the church. However, when a period of twelve[21] years is ended, permission is granted to thee to communicate, and riding is allowed. But thou shalt continue to keep the other provisions three days a week, that thou mayest deserve to be more completely purified.

[Nos. 31–37 deal with perjury and unnecessary and blasphemous swearing.]

35. If thou hast sworn by God's hair or by His head or made use of any other blasphemous expression against God, if thou hast done so but once unwittingly, thou shalt do penance for seven days on bread and water. If after having been upbraided for it thou hast done it a second or a third time, thou shalt do penance for fifteen days on bread and water. If [thou hast sworn] by heaven or by the earth or by the sun or by the moon or by any other creature, thou shalt do penance for fifteen days on bread and water.

[Nos. 38–40 are on theft and robbery.]

40. If thou hast committed robbery, thou shouldst have a heavier penance; for it is more distressing that thou hast seized something by force in the owner's sight than that thou hast stolen from him in his sleep or absence. If thou hast committed theft because of necessity so great, I say, that thou hadst no means of life and on account of the pinch of hunger and hast stolen only food outside the church, and if thou hast not had the habit of doing it, restore what thou hast carried off and do penance for three Fridays on bread and water. But if thou art unable to restore it, thou shalt do penance for ten days on bread and water.

[Nos. 41–57 deal with acts of adultery and fornication and violations of church rules regarding the marriage relation. Secret marriage and the failure to observe continence on Sundays, during Lent, and in other periods of fasting are among the offenses penalized. No. 58, on false witness, places this offense on a par with adultery and intentional murder. Nos. 59–70 comprise a section entitled "Of the magic art" in the Migne edition. These provisions testify to the prevalence of pagan magical practices in Burchard's age.]

60. Hast thou consulted magicians and led them into thy house

[21] Council of Worms has "ten."

in order to seek out any magical trick, or to avert it; or hast thou invited to thee according to pagan custom diviners who would divine for thee, to demand of them the things to come as from a prophet, and those who practice lots[22] or expect by lots to foreknow the future, or those who are devoted to auguries or incantations? If thou hast, thou shalt do penance for two years in the appointed fast days.

61. Hast thou observed the traditions of the pagans, which, as if by hereditary right, with the assistance of the devil, fathers have ever left to their sons even to these days, that is, that thou shouldst worship the elements, the moon or the sun or the course of the stars, the new moon or the eclipse of the moon; that thou shouldst be able by thy shouts or by thy aid to restore her splendor, or these elements [be able] to succour thee, or that thou shouldest have power with them—or hast thou observed the new moon for building a house or making marriages? If thou hast, thou shalt do penance for two years in the appointed fast days; for it is written "All, whatsoever ye do in word and in work, do all in the name of our Lord Jesus Christ."[23]

63. Hast thou made knots,[24] and incantations, and those various enchantments which evil men, swineherds, ploughmen, and some-times hunters make, while they say diabolical formulae[25] over bread or grass and over certain nefarious bandages, and either hide these in a tree or throw them where two roads, or three roads, meet, that they may set free their animals or dogs from pestilence or destruction and destroy those of another? If thou hast, thou shalt do penance for two years on the appointed days.

64. Hast thou been present at or consented to the vanities which women practice in their woolen work, in their webs, who when they begin their webs hope to be able to bring it about that with incanta-tions and with the beginning of these the threads of the warp and of the woof become so mingled together that unless they supplement these in turn by other counter-incantations of the devil, the whole will perish? If thou hast been present or consented, thou shalt do penance for thirty days on bread and water.

65. Hast thou collected medicinal herbs with evil incantations, not with the creed and the Lord's prayer, that is, with the singing of the "credo in Deum" and the paternoster? If thou hast done it otherwise

---

[22] "Sortes exercent." Cf. p. 276, above.
[23] Col. 3:17.　　　　　[24] "Ligaturas."　　　　　[25] "carmina."

[than with the Christian formulae mentioned] thou shalt do penance for ten days on bread and water.

66. Hast thou come to any place to pray other than a church or other religious place which thy bishop or thy priest showed thee, that is, either to springs or to stones or to trees or to crossroads, and there in reverence for the place lighted a candle or a torch or carried thither bread or any offering or eaten there or sought there any healing of body or mind? If thou hast done or consented to such things, thou shalt do penance for three years on the appointed fast days.

67. Hast thou sought out oracles[26] in codices or in tablets, as many are accustomed to do who presume to obtain oracles from psalters or from the Gospels or from anything else of the kind? If thou hast, thou shalt do penance for ten days on bread and water.

68. Hast thou ever believed or participated in this perfidy, that enchanters and those who say that they can let loose tempests should be able through incantation of demons to arouse tempests or to change the minds of men? If thou hast believed or participated in this, thou shalt do penance for one year on the appointed fast days.

69. Hast thou believed or participated in this infidelity,[27] that there is any woman who through certain spells and incantations can turn about the minds of men, either from hatred to love or from love to hatred, or by her bewitchments can snatch away men's goods? If thou hast believed or participated in such acts, thou shalt do penance for one year in the appointed fast days.

70. Hast thou believed that there is any woman who can do that which some, deceived by the devil, affirm that they must do of necessity or at his command, that is, with a throng of demons transformed into the likeness of women, (she whom common folly calls the witch Huida),[28] must ride on certain beasts in special nights and be numbered with their company? If thou hast participated in this infidelity, thou shouldst do penance for one year on the appointed fast days.

[Nos. 71–74 are concerned, respectively, with abuse of parents, theft from a church, selling a person into captivity, and arson. No. 75 introduces a series of offenses due both to gluttony and to excessive

---

[26] "sortes."   [27] "illius incredulitatis."
[28] "strigam holdam." "Strigam" not in Migne, is found only in Cod. Vat. 4772, according to Schmitz.

austerity, in connection with the fasts and feasts of the Christian year.]

78. Hast thou fasted on the Lord's day on account of abstinence and religion? Thou shalt do penance for twenty days on bread and water.

80. Hast thou compelled one who is doing penance publicly to eat and drink more than that which was commanded him and not forthwith given on his behalf a denarius in alms? If thou hast, thou shalt do penance for ten (five?) days on bread and water.

81. Hast thou despised anyone who when thou wast fasting could not fast and was eating? If thou hast, thou shalt do penance for five days on bread and water.

83. Hast thou habitually eaten and drunk more than was needful to thee? If thou has thou shalt do penance for ten days on bread and water; for the Lord says in the Gospel: "Take heed that your hearts do not become heavy with surfeiting and drunkenness."[29]

85. Hast thou ever been drunk through vainglory, in such wise, I say, that thou didst boast thyself in this, that thou wast able to surpass others in drinking and so through thy vanity and through thy urging hast led thyself and others to drunkenness? If thou hast, thou shalt do penance for thirty days on bread and water.

[No. 88 deals with attendance at Mass and continence in Lent.]

89. Hast thou despised the Mass or the prayer or the offering of a married presbyter so, I say, that thou wouldst not confess thy sins to him or receive from him the body and blood of the Lord for the reason that he seemed to thee to be a sinner? If thou hast, thou shalt do penance for one year in the appointed fast days.

[Here begins a long section on pagan superstitions, Nos. 90–104.]

90. Hast thou believed or participated in this infidelity, that some wicked women, turned back after Satan, seduced by illusions and phantoms of demons, believe and affirm: that with Diana, a goddess of the pagans, and an unnumbered multitude of women, they ride on certain beasts and traverse many areas of the earth in the stillness of the quiet night, obey her commands as if she were their mistress, and are called on special nights to her service? But would that these only should perish in their perfidy and not drag many with them into the ruin of their aberration.[30] For an unnumbered multi-

---

[29] Based on Luke 21:34.   [30] "infirmitatis."

tude, deceived by this false opinion, believe these things to be true, and in believing this they turn aside from sound faith and are involved in the error of the pagans when they think there is any divinity or heavenly authority except the one God. But the devil transforms himself into the form and likeness of many persons, deluding in sleep the mind which he holds captive, now with joy, now with sadness, now showing unknown persons, he leads it through some strange ways, and while only the spirit suffers this, the unfaithful mind thinks that these things happen not in the spirit but in the body. For who is not in night visions led out of himself, and who while sleeping does not see many things which he never saw while awake? Who then is so foolish and stupid that he supposes that those things which take place in the spirit only, happen also in the body? When the prophet Ezekiel saw and heard visions in the spirit, not in the body, he himself spoke thus: "Immediately," saith he, "I was in the spirit."[31] And Paul does not venture to say that he was "caught up" in the body.[32] Therefore it is to be openly announced to all that he who believes such things loses the faith; and he who has not sound faith in God is not His, but [belongs to him] in whom he believes, that is, the devil. For it is written of our Lord: "All things were made by him, and without him was made nothing."[33] If thou hast believed these vanities, thou shalt do penance for two years on the appointed fast days.[34]

91. Hast thou observed funeral wakes, that is, been present at the watch over the corpses of the dead when the bodies of Christians are guarded by a ritual of the pagans; and hast thou sung diabolical songs there and performed dances which the pagans have invented by the teaching of the devil; and hast thou drunk there and relaxed thy countenance with laughter, and, setting aside all compassion and emotion of charity, hast thou appeared as if rejoicing over a brother's death? If thou hast, thou shalt do penance for thirty days on bread and water.

[31] Based on Ezek. 2:2 and similar passages.
[32] II Cor. 12:2.   [33] John 1:3.
[34] This passage is abbreviated from Regino, *De synodalibus causis et de disciplinis ecclesiasticis*, II, ccclxxi, where it is erroneously ascribed to the council of Ancyra. It is virtually identical with a passage in Pseudo-Augustine, *De spiritu et anima* (cap. 28), given in Migne, *P.L.*, XL, 799. See Wasserschleben, *Regino*, pp. 354 ff. Burchard has given his extract the penitential form by affixing a statement of the penalty. Readers of Latin may refer to the note by Baluze. Migne, *P.L.*, CXXXII, 451–52.

92. Hast thou made diabolical phylacteries or diabolical characters, which some are accustomed to make at the persuasion of the devil, of grass or of amber; or hast thou observed Thursday in honor of Jupiter? If thou hast done or consented to such [deeds], thou shalt do penance for forty days on bread and water.

93. Hast thou plotted with other conspirators against thy bishop or against his associates so, I say, as to ridicule or mock at either the teaching or commands of thy bishop or priest? If thou hast, thou shalt do penance for forty days on bread and water.

94. Hast thou eaten anything offered to idols, that is, the offerings that are made in some places at the tombs of the dead or at springs or at trees or at stones or at cross roads, or [hast thou] carried stones to a cairn, or wreaths[35] for the crosses which are placed at cross roads?[36] If thou hast, or hast given thy consent to any such things, thou shalt do penance for thirty days on bread and water.

96. Hast thou done or consented to those vanities which foolish women are accustomed to enact, [who] while the corpse of a dead person still lies in the house, run to the water and silently bring a jar of water, and when the dead body is raised up, pour this water under the bier, and as the body is being carried from the house watch that it be not raised higher than to the knees, and do this as a kind of means of healing? If thou hast done or consented to this, thou shalt do penance for ten days on bread and water.

97. Hast thou done or consented to what some people do to a slain man when he is buried? They give a certain ointment into his hand, as if by that ointment his wound can be healed after death, and so they bury him with the ointment. If thou hast, thou shalt do penance for twenty days on bread and water.

98. Hast thou done or said anything by way of sorcery or magic in beginning any task and hast not invoked the name of God? If thou hast, thou shouldst do penance for ten days on bread and water.

99. Hast thou done anything like what the pagans did, and still do, on the first of January in [the guise of] a stag or a calf?[37] If thou

[35] "ligatura," literally, "knots" or "bandages."

[36] It has been shown that the crosses set up at cross roads in Germany in the late Middle Ages were often erected in expiation of a murder. They were often the scenes of strange worship. Possibly we have here an early reference to the expiatory crosses. On this subject, see E. Mogk, "Der Ursprung der mittelalterlichen Sühnekreuze," *Berichte und Verhandlungen der sächischen Akademie der Wissenschaft*. Philol. Hist. Cl., LXXXI (1929), 1–28.

[37] See above, pp. 277, n. 10, 305.

hast, thou shalt do penance for thirty days on bread and water.

100. Hast thou defamed or spoken evil of anybody by reason of envy? If thou hast, thou shouldst do penance for seven days on bread and water.

101. Hast thou done what many do? They scrape the place where they are accustomed to make the fire in their house and put grains of barley there in the warm spot; and if the grains jump [they believe] there will be danger, but if they remain, things will go well. If thou hast, thou shalt do penance for ten days on bread and water.

102. Hast thou done what some do when they are visiting any sick person? When they approach the house where the sick person lies, if they find a stone lying nearby, they turn the stone over and look in the place where the stone was lying [to see] if there is anything living under it, and if they find there a worm or a fly or an ant or anything that moves, then they aver that the sick person will recover. But if they find there nothing that moves, they say he will die. If thou hast done or believed in this, thou shalt do penance for twenty days on bread and water.

103. Hast thou made little, boys' size bows and boys' shoes,[38] and cast them into thy storeroom or thy barn so that satyrs or goblins[39] might sport with them, in order that they might bring to thee the goods of others so that thou shouldst become richer? If thou hast, thou shalt do penance for ten days on bread and water.

104. Hast thou done what some do on the first of January (that is on the eighth day after the Lord's Nativity)—who on that holy night wind magic skeins,[40] spin, sew: all at the prompting of the devil beginning whatever task they can begin on account of the new year? If thou hast, thou shalt do penance for forty days on bread and water.

[Nos. 105–26 deal with fornication, adultery, incest, homosexual practices, and other sex offenses. The penalties for these offenses are in general much lighter than in the early Celtic codes, and the psalm singing which is so generally prescribed in the latter is here omitted. Nos. 127–31 deal with the eating of unclean foods.]

[38] "suturalia." See Du Cange, s.vv. "sotilaria," "subtalaria." Cf. also p. 69, above.
[39] "pilosi" (the hairy ones).
[40] "filant." Du Cange makes "filare"="filia rhombo circumvolvere" (to wind yarn in a magic circle).

132. Hast thou committed any falsification or fraud in measures or in weights, in such wise, I say, as to sell thy goods to other Christians by a false measure or with unfair weights? If thou hast done or consented to this, thou shouldst do penance for twenty days on bread and water.

133. If thou, being a married man, hast shamed the nakedness of any woman, as, I say, her breasts and her shameful parts—if thou hast, thou shalt do penance for five days on bread and water. But if thou art not married, two days on bread and water.

134. Hast thou washed thyself in the bath with thy wife and other women and seen them nude, and they thee? If thou hast, thou shouldst fast for three days on bread and water.

135. Have strangers come to thee in time of need, and hast thou not received them into thy house, and hast thou not had mercy on them as the Lord commanded? If so, thou shalt do penance for five days on bread and water.

136. Hast thou set fire to a church or consented thereto? If thou hast, rebuild the church and distribute to the poor the value of thyself, that is, thy wergeld;[41] and thou shalt do penance for fifteen years on the appointed fast days.

[Nos. 137–48 are taken up mainly with offenses connected with irregularity or irreverence in worship, but the section contains also penalties for the misappropriation of church offerings, nonpayment of tithes, and oppression of the poor.]

139. Hast thou had any communion with an excommunicated person in such wise, I say, that thou didst pray together with him in a church or anywhere, or hast thou greeted him, as [for instance] to say "Hail!"[42] Or didst thou receive him into thy house or show him any kindness[43] secretly or openly, except when he wanted to go at the same time with thee, on the same road, to make satisfaction, and then for one or two nights or as far as the journey's end, setting him apart from others, thou hast given him necessary provisions? If thou hast done otherwise, then thou also art likewise excommunicate just as he is, and thou shouldst do penance for the forty days on bread and water which they call a "carina," repeating this for seven successive years.

142. Hast thou oppressed the poor who were thy neighbors, who

[41] "wiregeldum."   [42] "Ave."   [43] "humanitatem."

were not able to defend themselves, or taken away their goods against their will? If thou hast, thou shalt render to them their own and do penance for thirty days on bread and water.

145. Hast thou done what some are accustomed to do? When they come to church at the beginning they move their lips a little as if they were praying, on account of the others standing or sitting about them, and presently they hasten to [give attention to] stories and gossip; and when the priest addresses them and exhorts them to pray, they nevertheless turn again to their stories, not to the responses nor to the prayer. If thou hast, thou shouldst do penance for ten days on bread and water.

146. Hast thou kept secret thy brother's sin which was unto death and hast thou not corrected him that he should return to his right mind, nor come to the aid of thy brother laid under a burden? If thou hast so done, thou shalt do penance for as long a time as thou hast been silent.

147. Hast thou defended the guilty on account of mercy or friendship, and in this hast thou been unmerciful to the innocent? If thou hast, thou shalt do penance for thirty days on bread and water.

148. Hast thou caused Mass to be sung for thee and those holy things offered while thou wast in a house, whether thine own house or some other place, not in the church? If thou hast, thou shouldst do penance for ten days on bread and water.

[Sections 149–81 constitute another long series of provisions with regard to pagan superstitions, magical practices, and revolting offenses chiefly accompanied by some element of magic.]

149. Hast thou believed what some are wont to believe? When they make any journey, if a crow croaks from their left side to their right, they hope on this account to have a prosperous journey. And when they are worried about a lodging place, if then that bird which is called the mouse-catcher,[44] for the reason that it catches mice and is named from what it feeds on, flies in front of them, across the road on which they go, they trust more to this augury and omen than to God. If thou hast done or believed these things, thou shouldst do penance for five days on bread and water.

150. Hast thou believed what some are wont to believe: when they have occasion to go out somewhere before daylight, they dare not go,

[44] "muriceps." Cf. p. 120, n. 28, above. Evidently here a kind of owl.

saying that it is the morrow and it is not permitted to go out before cock crow and that it is dangerous because the unclean spirits have more power to harm before cock crow than after and that the cock by his crowing is more potent to banish and allay them than that divine mind that is in a man by his faith and the sign of the cross. If thou hast done or believed this, thou shouldst do penance for ten days on bread and water.

151. Hast thou believed what some are wont to believe, either that those who are commonly called the Fates exist, or that they can do that which they are believed to do? That is, that while any person is being born, they are able even then to determine his life to what they wish, so that no matter what the person wants, he can be transformed into a wolf, that which vulgar folly calls a werewolf,[45] or into any other shape. If thou believest what never took place or could take place, that the divine image can be changed into any form or appearance by anyone except almighty God, thou shouldst do penance for ten days on bread and water.

152. Hast thou believed what some are wont to believe, that there are women of the wilds, called "the sylvan ones" who they say are in bodily form, and when they wish show themselves to their lovers and, they say, have taken delight with these, and then when they wish they depart and vanish? If thou so believest, thou shalt do penance for ten days on bread and water.[46]

153. Has thou done as some women are wont to do at certain times of the year? That is, hast thou prepared the table in thy house and set on the table thy food and drink, with three knives, that if those three sisters whom past generations and old-time foolishness called the Fates should come they may take refreshment there; and hast thou taken away the power and name of the Divine Piety and handed it over to the devil, so, I say, as to believe that those whom thou callest "the sisters" can do or avail aught for thee either now or in

[45] Some manuscripts have: "what is called in German a werewolf (Werwulff)." On this passage and on the general subject of the werewolf legends see J. A. MacCulloch, *Medieval Faith and Fable*, pp. 81–88; 312 f.; and the edition of Petronius, *Cena Trimalchionis*, by W. E. Waters, note on section 62.

[46] In one manuscript there is inserted here the following: In all these things foregoing priests ought to have great discretion, that they make a distinction between him who has publicly sinned and done penance publicly, and him who has sinned in private and voluntarily made confession. While the above interrogations are common to women and men those following pertain specially to women.

the future? If thou hast done or consented to this, thou shalt do penance for one year on the appointed days.

167. Hast thou drunk the holy oil[47] in order to annul a judgment of God or made or taken counsel with others in making anything in grass or in words or in wood or in stone or in anything foolishly believed in, or held them in thy mouth, or had them sewn in thy clothing or tied about thee, or performed any kind of trick that thou didst believe could annul the divine judgment? If thou hast, thou shouldst do penance for seven years on the appointed days.

170. Hast thou believed what many women, turning back to Satan, believe and affirm to be true, as thou believest in the silence of the quiet night when thou hast gone to bed and thy husband lies in thy bosom, that while thou art in bodily form thou canst go out by closed doors and art able to cross the spaces of the world with others deceived by the like error and without visible weapons slay persons who have been baptized and redeemed by the blood of Christ, and cook and eat their flesh and in place of their hearts put straw or wood or anything of the sort and when they are eaten make them alive again and give an interval of life? If thou hast believed this, thou shalt do penance for forty days, that is, a "carina," on bread and water, and in the seven succeeding years [perform a similar penance].

175. Hast thou done what some women filled with the discipline of Satan are wont to do, who watch the footprints and traces of Christians and remove a turf from their footprint and watch it and hope thereby to take away their health or life? If thou hast done or consented to this, thou shouldest do penance for five years on the appointed days.

180. Hast thou done what some women do at the instigation of the devil? When any child has died without baptism, they take the corpse of the little one and place it in some secret place and transfix its little body with a stake, saying that if they did not do so the little child would arise and would injure many? If thou has done, or consented to, or believed this, thou shouldst do penance for two years on the appointed days.

181. Hast thou done what some women, filled with the boldness of the devil are wont to do? When some woman is to bear a child

[47] "chrisma."

and is not able, if when she cannot bear it she dies in her pangs, they transfix the mother and the child in the same grave with a stake [driven] into the earth. If thou hast done or consented to this, thou shouldst do penance for two years on the appointed days.

[Besides those given below the remaining sections (182–94) of Chapter V contain penalties for overlaying of infants, prostitution, failing to bring children to baptism at the proper times, neglect of the sick, eating meat in Lent, and working on Sunday.]

185. Hast thou done what some women are wont to do? When a child is newly born and immediately baptized and then dies, when they bury him they put in his right hand a paten of wax with the host and in his left hand put a chalice also of wax, with wine, and so they bury him. If thou hast, thou shouldst do penance for ten days on bread and water.

186. Hast thou done what some adulteresses are wont to do? When first they learn that their lovers wish to take legitimate wives, they thereupon by some trick of magic extinguish the male desire, so that they are impotent and cannot consummate their union with their legitimate wives. If thou hast done or taught others to do this, thou shouldst do penance for forty days on bread and water.

191. Hast thou done what some are wont to do? When they come to church, on the very road, they display their vanities and speak idle things, and on that same road think of nothing that pertains to the welfare of the soul, and when they come into the atrium of the church, where the bodies of the faithful are buried, and while they tread upon the graves of their neighbors, they do not ponder what may be their condition, nor utter any mention [of them] or any prayers for them to the Lord, as they ought to do. If thou hast neglected this, thou shalt do penance for ten days on bread and water and see that it does not happen to thee again; but whenever thou enterest into the atrium of the church, pray for them and ask those sainted souls whose bodies rest there to intercede with the Lord for thy sins as far as they are able.

193. Hast thou done what some women are wont to do? They take off their clothes and anoint their whole naked body with honey, and laying down their honey-smeared body upon wheat on some linen on the earth, roll to and fro often, then carefully gather all the grains of wheat which stick to the moist body, place it in a mill, and make the mill go round backwards against the sun and so grind it

to flour; and they make bread from that flour and then give it to their husbands to eat, that on eating the bread they may become feeble and pine away. If thou hast [done this], thou shalt do penance for forty days on bread and water.

194. Hast thou done what some women are wont to do? When they have no rain and need it, then they assemble a number of girls, and they put forward one little maiden as a leader, and strip her, and bring her thus stripped outside the village, where they find the herb henbane which is called in German "belisa";[48] and they make this nude maiden dig up the plant with the little finger of her right hand, and when it is dug up they make her tie it with a string to the little toe of her right foot. Then while each girl holds a twig in her hands, they bring the aforesaid maiden, dragging the plant behind her, to a nearby river and with these twigs sprinkle her with the water and thus they hope that by their charms they shall have rain. Afterwards they bring back the nude maiden from the river to the village between their hands, her footsteps being turned about[49] and changed into the manner of a crab.[50] If thou hast done or consented to this, thou shouldst do penance for twenty days on bread and water.

[In Chapter VI of the Migne text the confessor proceeds with a recital of the eight principal sins ("octo principalia vitia"), with their brood of derived sins. The passage is here attributed to the *Penitential of Theodore*. It is apparently indebted to the Sections VII ff. of the penitential called *Pseudo-Theodore* by Wasserschleben, who copies the text of this document[51] from F. Kunstmann, *Die lateinischen Poenitentialbücher der Angelsachsen*, pp. 43–105. Kunstmann in turn follows the text of B. Thorpe's *Ancient Laws of England*, II, 1–62, which is based upon a Cambridge manuscript. Wasserschleben and subsequent writers have regarded the *Pseudo-Theodore* as a ninth century work. See especially Oakley, *op. cit.*, pp. 31 f. The order in which the deadly sins are listed corresponds to the order in *Pseudo-Theodore* and is also identical with that tabulated by T. H. Dudden from a study of the works of Gregory the Great.[52] In the latter, "superbia" (pride) is set apart from the other seven as the "queen of the vices." It is described in this text as "the be-

---

[48] Modern German "Bilsen."
[49] "transpositis." Perhaps this means "reversed," that is, she walks backward.
[50] "cancri" probably with some reference to the sign of the Zodiac "cancer."
[51] *Bussordnungen*, pp. 566–622.
[52] *Gregory the Great, His Place in History and Thought*, II, 388.

ginning of every sin and the queen of all evils." The lists of derived sins also bear a close resemblance to those supplied by Gregory. An entirely different order is followed in Columban's *Instructiones*, XVII, "De octo vitiis principalibus," which corresponds closely to Cassian, *Collationes*, V, 2ff. As already indicated, pp. 101, 148, 156, the Cassian-Columbanus order is followed in the *Penitential of Cummean*, the *Old Irish Penitential* edited by Gwynn, and the *Bigotian Penitential*.

The confessor now indicates (Chapter VII) *seriatim* the proper treatment for the deadly sins, and the instruction illustrates the principle: "Contraries are cured by their contraries."[53]]

Chapter VII. Of the Virtues by Which These Vices Can Be Overcome, and of the Conclusion of Penance

Therefore, if thou has been proud hitherto, humble thyself in the sight of God. If thou hast loved vainglory, take thought lest on account of transitory praise thou lose an eternal reward. If the rust of envy hath hitherto consumed thee—which is a very great sin and above all things detestable, since an envious man is compared to the devil, who first envied man the gift which he himself had lost through his own fault—do penance and prune thy advantage over others. If dejection overcometh thee, practice patience and longsuffering. If the fever of avarice oppresses thee, consider that it is the root of all evils and is compared to idolatry and that hence it behooveth thee to be liberal. If anger (which findeth lodgment in the breasts of fools), vexeth thee thou oughtst to be controlled in thy spirit, and thou shalt put it to flight from thee by tranquillity of mind. If gluttony hath enticed thee in order to devour thee, follow after temperance; if lust,[54] promise chastity.

Then shall the penitent prostrate himself on the ground and say with tears: Both in these and in all vices, in whatsoever ways human frailty can sin against God its creator—either in thought or speech or deed or love or lust—I confess that in all I have sinned and acknowledge myself guilty above all men in the sight of God. Humbly, then, I plead with thee, a priest of God, that thou intercede for me and for my sins to the Lord our Creator, so that I may deserve to obtain pardon and grace for these and all my transgressions.

Then shall the priest prostrate himself with the penitent on the ground and chant the following psalms:

[53] See above, pp. 44, 92, 101.   [54] "luxuria."

[Psalms and prayers follow.]

[Chapter VIII, "The healthful antidote for souls," quotes the Prophetic Scriptures, Gregory Nazianzen, Jerome, Augustine, and refers to the penitentials of Bishop Theodore, "the Roman Pontiffs," and Bede. Burchard critically remarks that "in the penitential of Bede many valuable things are found, but also many things that have been inserted by others, which are in accord neither with the canons nor with the other penitentials." The chapter closes with an exhortation to mercy except toward those stubbornly persevering in evil.]

Chapter IX. The Penance for a Year That Is to Be Spent in Fasting on Bread and Water Ought to Be Performed According to This Plan

From the *Roman Penitential*.[55] The penance for one year, which is to be spent in fasting on bread and water, ought to be as follows: He shall fast three days in each week, namely, Monday, Wednesday, and Friday, on bread and water. And on three days, namely, Tuesday, Thursday, and Saturday, he shall abstain from wine, mead, honeyed beer, meat, fat, cheese, and eggs, and from every kind of fat fish. He may, however, eat little fishes if he is able to obtain them. If he cannot obtain them, he may, if he wishes, eat one kind of fish only and beans and vegetables and apples, and drink beer. And on Sundays, and at Nativity, those four days; and at Epiphany, one day; and at the feast of Ascension and at Pentecost, four days; and at the feast[56] of St. John Baptist, and that of Holy Mary, and that of the Twelve Apostles, and that of St. Michael, and that of St. Remigius, and that of All Saints, and that of St. Martin, and in the festival of the saint who is celebrated in the diocese—in the aforesaid days he shall fraternize[57] with other Christians, that is, he shall use the same food and drink as they. But he must nevertheless in all things beware of drunkenness and surfeiting.

[Chapter X treats similarly the second year. Chapters XI to XXV are short paragraphs prescribing a variety of "redemptions" or commutations of penance. Burchard ascribes all but four of these to "the Roman Penitential," but Fournier has traced them to other sources. A few of them are given. They may be compared with those found on pages 268, 319 f., above.]

[55] Cf. p. 295, above, and p. 411, below.
[56] "missa."   [57] "faciat charitatem."

Chapter XI. Of Those Who Are Not Able to Fast and to Fulfill What Is Written in the Penitential

If one is able to fast and to fulfill what is written in the penitential, it is good, and let him render thanks to God. But to him who is not able we, through God's mercy, give the following advice, that it be not necessary either for him or for anyone else either to despair or to perish.

Chapter XII. Of the Redemption of the Day[58] of Fasting on Bread and Water

For one day on which he is to fast on bread and water he shall sing fifty psalms, kneeling, if possible, in a church; but if he cannot he shall do this in a convenient place and shall feed one poor man; and on that day, he shall eat what he chooses except wine, meat, and fat.

[Chapter XIII prescribes seventy psalms "standing rigid" (stando intente), for those unable to hold a kneeling posture for so long a time.]

Chapter XV. Another Method

He who does not know the psalms shall redeem one day on which he is to do penance on bread and water, if he is rich, with three denarii, and if he is poor, with one denarius; and on that day he shall take what he chooses except wine, meat, and fat.

Chapter XVII. Another Method

Some say that twenty palm thumpings[59] suffice for one day.

Chapter XIX. Of This Redemption of One Month of Fasting on Bread and Water

For one month in which he is to fast on bread and water, he shall sing 1200 psalms, kneeling. But if he cannot do this, he shall sing 1680 psalms, sitting or standing, without kneeling; if possible, in a church; but if not, in one place. And, if he wishes, and if he cannot refrain, he shall dine at sext every day except Wednesday and Friday, when he shall fast until nones. And he shall abstain the whole

[58] Text has "illius anni," where "anni" should obviously be "diei."
[59] See above, pp. 33, 231.

month from meat and fat and wine. But he shall take other food after he has sung the before-mentioned psalms. By this plan the whole year is to be redeemed.

[Chapter XXVI repeats substantially the text of Regino, *De synodalibus causis*, I, ccxcv, a passage apparently derived from a seventh century source. See above p. 315, n. 6. Various extracts follow in Chapters XXVII to XXXIII. Here Schmitz would end the original contents of the book. The remaining chapters (XXXIV to CLIX) are, however, of similar character to those just preceding this supposed conclusion. Many of the provisions come from the ancient church discipline. Those which are of the type represented by the penitentials are without originality. For an attempt to indicate the sources and correct Burchard's often erroneous ascriptions, Fournier's "Études,"[60] and the literature cited by him, should be consulted.]

[60] See above, pp. 295 ff.

CHAPTER VII

Selections from Later Penitential Documents

1. FROM THE PENITENTIAL OF BARTHOLOMEW ISCANUS, BISHOP OF EXETER, 1161–84

[BARTHOLOMEW ISCANUS, a native of Brittany, was a zealous and distinguished prelate of the Anglo-Norman Church. During his tenure of the see of Exeter he became celebrated through his connection with the controversy between Becket and Henry II. His writings include an extensive penitential, portions of which are here given from the twelfth century British Museum Codex Cotton Faust. A VIII. A short extract with the penalties omitted, published from this manuscript in Thomas Wright's *Reliquiae antiquae*, I, 285 f., has been translated from this source under the heading "A Batch of Superstitions" by G. G. Coulton in *Life in the Middle Ages*, I, 33 ff. Cf. pp. 60 f. and 349 f. Other manuscripts containing this penitential include the following: British Museum, Royal Collection 5 E VII, art. 3; 7 E I; 8 C XIV, art. 1; 8 D III, art. 2; Cotton Vitell. A XII; Paris, Bibl. Nat. Lat. 2600; Oxford, St. John's College, manuscripts 163 and 165. The work is largely a compilation of patristic opinions, conciliar decisions, and materials from the older penitentials, all set down with free variation from the sources, much in the manner, and probably somewhat under the influence, of Burchard. In Cotton Faust. A VIII the document contains 134 capitula with many subheads which indicate the alleged sources by title. A scholarly edition of this penitential would probably shed considerable light on the use of various canonical collections in England. A few selections only are here presented.

Added in proof: Adrian Morey in *Bartholomew of Exeter, Bishop and Canonist* (Cambridge, 1937) lists (pp. 164 ff.) eighteen manuscripts of the penitential, including all those mentioned above, and publishes the text of the document (pp. 175–300) from the Cotton Vitell. A XII. He denies, without explanation, Bartholomew's authorship of the section (folios 8–39) of Cotton Faust. A VIII, from which the following selections are made. Nevertheless, with the exception of the passage on magic these selections are all contained in Morey's text (pp. 177 f., 208 f., 210, 241 f.) His footnotes cite numerous parallels in the collections of Burchard, Ivo of Chartres, Gratian, and Peter Lombard.]

[CONDITIONS OF PENANCE]

(fol. 8v, col. 1) The things that properly appertain to penitents so that they cannot be remitted or relaxed by priests:

There are, however, some things that properly appertain to penitents so that no authority is conceded to priests or bishops to omit or relax them; such are true penitence, a pure confession making satisfaction to those against whom they who say that they are penitent have offended and from the heart forgiving those who have offended against them.

Things which for various reasons ought to be either relaxed or fully remitted:

Some things indeed [are] such that, for a variety of considerations they ought to be relaxed or omitted. Such are alms, prayers, fasts, groans, tears, silence, and useful manual labor, watchings, genuflexions, corporal blows, which someone calls disciplines, or cudgelings, or inflictions(?),[1] poorness and roughness of clothing, pilgrimages and such works of charity and castigation. . . .

(fol. 15v, col. 1) A pure confession is to be sought by the priests from sick persons who are placed in peril of death.[2]

(fol. 15v, col. 2) We have spoken of the penance of the infirm and of grave but hidden sins. But now let us come down to the penances of persons in health for mortal and public sins, which are determined by the holy fathers. . . . Since, therefore, as the Apostle testifies, "there is no respect of persons with God,"[3] and it is to be avoided in all judgments, much more ought it to be shunned in the judgment of penance, that no priest ever either in favoritism or in hatred of any person shall judge otherwise than [by] what he finds in the sacred canons or what seems to him just according to the authority of the holy Scriptures and ecclesiastical usage. If, therefore, physicians who try to apply medicine to bodies in no wise spare on account of respect for the person of anyone, in the use of cautery or knife or other severe measures, those whom they desire to heal, much more is this principle to be observed by those who are physicians not of bodies but of souls. For penance is to be reckoned not according to the duration of the time but according to the zeal of the mind and

---

[1] "suppositiones." So also Royal Collection 8 D III. Cotton Vitell. A XII and Royal Collection 5 E VII have "superpositiones"; Royal Collection 7 E I has "superstitiones"(!)
[2] This is attributed in the text to the *Penitential of Theodore*, but is apparently based on the council of Mainz, 847, can. 26. Mansi, XIV, 910.   [3] Rom. 2:11.

the mortification of the body. But "a contrite and humble heart God doth not despise."[4] . . .

Of Homicide Commited of One's Own Accord. From the Decretals of Pope Melchiades[5] and of the Council of Tribur (fol. 16v, col. 1)

If anyone commits homicide, of his own accord and through cupidity, thus shall he do penance. First let him not have permission to enter a church in those first forty days; he shall go barefoot and use no carriage; he shall be in woolen garments, excepting drawers; he shall not bear arms; and he shall take no food in those forty days except only bread and salt, and drink pure water, and he shall have no fellowship with other Christians nor with another penitent, either in food or in drink, until the forty days are fulfilled. No one else shall eat of the food which he takes. But in consideration of the nature or weakness of the person, he may by all means be allowed some apples or vegetables or beans, as seems good. And he is in every way forbidden on canonical authority to associate with any woman in these days; nor shall he come to his own wife, or sleep with any man. He shall be near a church and shall bewail his sins before its doors; and he shall [not?] go from place to place but be in one place those forty days. And if perchance there are those who lie in wait for him in his way, his penance shall meanwhile be deferred until he is granted peace from his enemies by the bishop. And if he is detained by illness so that he cannot do penance properly, his penance shall be deferred until he is restored to health. If, however, he is detained by a long illness it shall pertain to the judgment of the bishop how he ought to treat the guilty man who is ill. Thus, the forty days being completed, he shall wash in water, receive his clothing and shoes, and cut his hair.[6] [In the year following he is to abstain from mead, honeyed beer, flesh, cheese, and fat fishes, except in festivals or on a long journey or in military service or in illness, when these requirements may be partially redeemed by payments or alms. Further provisions are added for the remainder of the five-year period of penance.]

---

[4] Ps. 50:19. The paragraph contains materials from the council of Chalon, 813, can. 34, and the council of Mainz, 847, can. 31. Mansi, XIV, 100, 911.

[5] The Forged Decretals contain a section entitled *Decreta Melchiadis papae*, no part of which, however, seems related to this paragraph, Migne, *P.L.*, CXXX, 237 ff.; Melchiades was Pope, 311–14.

[6] Cf. council of Tribur, 895, can. 55. Mansi, XVIII, 156.

Of Perjury (fol. 24v, col. 1)

Perjury is a very grave sin. For who appears to despise God more than he who in the very sin which he commits against God, invokes God as judge and avenger upon his own soul, saying: So help me God and these holy things? He who knowingly commits perjury also either disbelieves or neglects the sanctity of the whole Christian profession, since an oath constitutes the end of every controversy in ecclesiastical affairs, and in secular matters many controversies are terminated by an oath. Indeed the judgments which are publicly called laws are never completed without an oath. Diverse heavy penances are therefore laid down by the holy fathers against perjurers for a variety of perjuries. [Judgments of Chrysostom, Augustine, and various popes are recited.]

Of Magic (fol. 32r, col. 1)

If anyone pays respect to soothsayers, augurs, enchanters, or makes use of philters, let him be anathema. Whoever by any magic turns aside a judgment of God, shall do penance for two years. He who is a magician for the sake of love and does not bring it to success shall do penance for two years. If he does, five years. If adultery results, ten years. . . . He who strives to take away another's supply of milk or honey or of other things by any incantation, or [tries] by magic to gain it for himself, shall do penance for three years. . . . They who by any incantation disturb the calm of the atmosphere or who by invocation of demons confuse the minds of men shall do penance for five years. They who, deceived by the illusion of a demon, believe and profess that they go or ride in the service of her whom the stupid crowd call Herodias or Diana with a countless multitude and obey her commands shall do penance for one year. She who lays a table with three knives for the service of the Fates[?],[7] that they may predestinate good things to those who are born there, shall do penance for two years. A woman who by a magical trick [prevents the consummation of a legal marriage] shall do penance for five years. [Those who make vows beside trees or water, those who keep the New Year with pagan rites, and those who make magical knots or charms and hide them in the grass or in a tree or at a cross roads to free their animals from pestilence must each do penance for

[7] Emending "personarum" to "parcarum." Cf. Burchard, *Corrector*, V, 153, p. 338, above.

two years.] He who places his child upon a roof or in an oven in order to restore his health, or who for this purpose uses charms or characters or things fashioned for sorcery or any trick, and not godly prayers or the liberal art of medicine, shall do penance for forty days. . . . He who practices divinations from the funeral of any dead person or from his body or from his clothing, lest the dead take vengeance, or in order that another not in the same house shall die, or to gain by this something toward his advantage or health shall do penance for forty days. He who at the feast of St. John Baptist does any work of sorcery to seek out the future shall do penance for fifteen days. He who believes that anything comes out favorably or unfavorably because of the croaking of a young crow, or a raven, or meeting a priest or any animal shall do penance for seven days. He who casts into a granary or storehouse a bow or any such thing for the devils which they call fauns to play with, that they may bring more [grain], shall do penance for fifteen days. He who in visiting a sick man draws any inference of good or evil from the moving of a stone in going or returning shall do penance for ten days. He who believes that the masculine or feminine shape of any animal can be transformed into that of a wolf[8] shall do penance for ten days. He who watches the footsteps of Christians and believes that by taking away a turf from the spot he can take away[9] anyone's voice . . .

2. FROM ALAIN DE LILLE'S PENITENTIAL BOOK
(ca. 1175–1200)

[ALANUS DE INSULIS, or Alain de Lille, ca. 1114–1203, was a pupil of Abailard and was distinguished both for his mystical and for his scholastic writings. Among his works there was said to be a treatise entitled *Libri quattuor de poenitentia*. But when Carolus de Visch looked for this, he could not find the work, as he states in Migne, *P.L.*, CCX, 279 ff. Instead, he published a *Liber poenitentialis* of which he found three manuscripts.

Within more recent times, however, C. Bäumcker (*Philosophisches Jahrbuch der Görres-Gesellschaft*, VI, 1893, pp. 422–59) claims to have discovered the original work of Alain de Lille, in four books, dedicated to the archbishop of Bourges and called *Poenitentiarius*, in the codex

---

[8] Wright reads: "Qui masculam vel feminam in lupinam effigiem alicuius animalis" . . . The manuscript has "masclm." Perhaps "vel" has been omitted before "alicuius," and we should translate: "He who believes that a male or female [child] can be transformed into the shape of a wolf or that of any animal." Cf. Burchard, *Corrector*, V, 151, p. 338, above.

[9] An infinitive verb is required. Wright supplies "nocere" (hurt or harm); but evidently "tollere," following "tollendo" in the previous phrase, is to be understood.

Lilienfeld 144, s. XII/XIII, f. 124–141ᵛ. His evidence seems quite convincing. According to Bäumcker, the Lilienfeld manuscript contains all the material which is in the edition of de Visch and in that of an early print of Augsburg (1515)to which Kunstmann (*Gelehrte Anzeigen*, Munich, 1852, pp. 605 f.) and later F. Vering (*A.K.K.R.*, XXX, 1873, p. 228) call attention. Both these shorter texts consist of materials extracted from the Lilienfeld version. The latter is, moreover, richer in material of a canonical, cultural-historical nature, and it contains indications of its sources (Greg., Jerome, Theod., Bede, Rom. Penit., etc.). Very recently Miss Gamer (who has furnished me with the principal facts here stated) has found other references to manuscripts dedicated to Henry, archbishop of Bourges (see Appendix, p. 441).

Bäumcker considers the possibility that two writers bore the name of Alain de Lille, and thinks that the *Poenitentiarius* may not have been written by the celebrated author of this name.

The *Liber poenitentialis* is not a code of penances like the older penitentials, but a more general guide to the confessor. Since a full examination of the manuscripts is neither possible in the present circumstances nor important in the case of so late and unoriginal a document, the following extract is taken from the only available edition, that of Migne, *P.L.*, CX, 282 ff. The passage offers an interesting comparison with the first selection from Robert of Flamesbury, p. 353, below.]

Col. 295. *Penances Civil, Solemn, Private, Ecclesiastical*

Some penances are civil, some ecclesiastical. The civil are those which are laid upon men according to the determinations of the civil laws; of these, some are solemn, some private. The solemn are those which are publicly inflicted for the major crimes; the private are those which are secretly inflicted. But these civil penalties are either mitigated or rendered more severe for various causes and are rather to be called penalties than penances. Ecclesiastical satisfactions are properly called penances since they usually proceed from inward penitence. But some of the ecclesiastical penances are solemn, others private. Solemn penance is that which is inflicted for major or notorious crimes, or for those crimes which one has confessed or of which one has been convicted; this is usually called a "carena." And as it is for major crimes, so it pertains to the higher prelates of the Church to inflict it. [Common priests bind or loose in minor sins; the major sins are reserved. The clergy are not subject to solemn penance, but to a certain public penance which consists of suspension from the choir and the table of their brethren.] That solemn penance which is inflicted on laymen ought not to be repeated on account of the solemnity of that penance, lest from repetition it be lowly esteemed.

3. FROM THE LAURENTIAN PENITENTIAL
(ca. 1200; based on materials of 538 and 789)

[SCHMITZ published a penitential of fifty-seven canons from a thirteenth century manuscript in the Laurentian Library, Florence.[1] Like many others of late date it shows dependence on Burchard. The canon translated below, however, in the main goes back to the legislation of Charlemagne, and is ultimately dependent on the council of Orléans of 538. It furnishes an interesting example of the provisions made in the penitentials for observance of Sunday. The legislation in canon and civil law on this subject in the early Middle Ages has been investigated by W. Thomas.[2] Besides the parallels shown in the footnotes, similar injunctions appear in a sermon of Raban Maur.[3]]

47. We decree the observance with all reverence of all Lord's days from evening until evening,[4] and abstinence from illicit work; [that] is, that there be no gainful trade, nor a tribunal in which anyone is adjudged to death or punishment, unless for the sake of making peace. We also determine according to what the Lord hath commanded in the Law,[5] that servile work be not done on the Lord's days, as my father[6] commanded in his synodal edicts, that men shall neither carry 'on rural labors—the cultivation of vineyards, or the planting of hedges, or the setting out of groves or the felling of trees—nor assemble to the tribunals; nor shall trading take place, nor hunting be engaged in. There are three tasks requiring carts[7] that may be done on the Lord's day: Provisioning a hostelry with bread,[8] the care of work animals(?),[9] and, if it is specially needful, the carrying of someone's corpse to the burial place. Women shall not make woven work on the Lord's day; they shall not wash the head; they shall not sew garments together, nor pluck wool. It is not permissible to

[1] Schmitz I, 786–91.   [2] *Der Sonntag im frühen Mittelalter*, Göttingen, 1929.
[3] Migne, *P.L.*, CX, 76 ff.; quoted by Thomas, pp. 113 ff.
[4] Lev. 23:32.   [5] Exod. 20:8–10; Lev. 23:7, 8, 21, 28.
[6] "genitor." Charlemagne in his General Admonition of 789, in the passage on which the present canon is based, has "my 'genitor' of good memory," a reference to the council of Verno held under Pippin in 755, can. 14, which in turn is based upon the council of Orléans, 538, can. 28. For these passages see Mansi, IX, 19; *M.G.H., Leges*, II.i.36, 61.
[7] "carraria opera."
[8] Reading "hostilia caria victualia": the text has "hostialia." The parallel passages in the *Leges* have "ostilia carra vel victualia."
[9] "angaria," a word used in many senses and generally in the *Leges* to denote enforced personal service. Originally "angarius" was "a mounted messenger" (Gr. "ἄγγαρος") and "angaria" meant "the service of a messenger." W. H. Maigne d'Arnis in his *Lexicon manuale* glosses "angaria" as "corvée des transports." It meant, among other things, especially a shed to accommodate animals and carts used in hauling. Our word "hangar" is a derivative. Cf. Du Cange, *s.vv.* "angaria," "parangaria," and "perangaria."

scutch flax or to wash a garment or to shave the crown—in order that honor and repose may in every way be accorded to the Lord's day. But they shall come together from all sides to the celebration of masses and shall praise God for all the benefits which he has deigned to bestow upon us in that day.[10] On the Lord's day it is not permissible to sail and ride for business in connection with any tasks, nor to make bread, nor to bathe, nor to write; for if anyone projects or carries on work, he shall do penance for seven days. The washing of the head may be done in case of sickness. If any offerings are permitted on the Lord's day, they ought to be made on Saturday by people who are fasting. If anyone fasts on the Lord's day he shall fast for a whole week. Before the giving of the dismissal[11] and the benediction,[12] no Christian shall leave the church.

4. FROM THE PENITENTIAL OF ROBERT OF FLAMESBURY (*ca.* 1207–15)

[A DISCUSSION of the *Penitential of Robert of Flamesbury* is furnished by J. Dietterle in "Die Summae confessorum," *Z.K.G.*, XXIV (1903), 363–74. On the manuscripts, see this article, p. 365. The author is not certainly known, but he may have been at one time dean of Salisbury. The first of the selections following is taken from J. Morinus, *Commentarius de disciplina in administratione penitentiae* (ed. of 1681), p. 320. Cf. Poschmann II, p. 162. The others are from Dietterle's article, pp. 369 and 371.]

(1) Penance is either public, or solemn, or private. Solemn penance is that which takes place at the beginning of the [lenten] fast since the penitents are expelled from the church with solemnity, in ashes and sackcloth. This is also public because it takes place publicly. Public penance which is not solemn is that which takes place before the church without the above-mentioned solemnity, such as a pilgrimage. Private penance is that which is done privately every day in the presence of a priest. No one but a bishop or one authorized by him may enjoin solemn penance, except under necessity: in that case even a layman shall have power to reconcile the penitent. An ordinary priest enjoins public, just as [he enjoins] private, penance, and at any time.

[10] Reading with *Leges*, II.i, 61, "in illa die" for "millia dies."
[11] "missam," here probably referring to the use of the phrase "ite, missa est" with which the service ended.
[12] Schmitz punctuates so as to attach this clause to the previous sentence.

(2) [The priest is warned against any negligence, favoritism, or irregularity in penance. If he cannot induce the confessant to undertake canonical penance he is to say to him]: Brother, it is necessary for thee to be punished in this life or in purgatory: but incomparably more severe will be the penalty of purgatory than any in this life. Behold, thy soul is in thy hands. Choose therefore for thyself whether to be sufficiently punished in this life according to canonical or authentic penances or to await purgatory. [The penance may be cautiously mitigated by the priest however.]

(3) Concerning remissions which consist in the building of churches or of bridges or in other matters, different men have different opinions as to how much value they have and for whom. But we, whatever is said, commend such remissions to all, especially to those who are burdened and weighed down with sins and penances.

5. FROM ICELANDIC PENITENTIALS OF THE TWELFTH AND FOURTEENTH CENTURIES

FROM THE PENITENTIAL OF THORLAC THORHALLSON (1178–93)

[THORLAC THORHALLSON, born 1133, was Bishop of Skalholt in Iceland from 1178–1193.[1] Under the authority of Archbishop Eystein, or Augustine, of Drontheim (1161–88), he was instrumental in the establishment of ecclesiastical law, which had been introduced into Iceland by his predecessor, Thorlac Runolfson, about 1123. The later Thorlac furnished his clergy with a penitential in Icelandic, which is preserved in two Copenhagen manuscripts, Codices Arn. Magn. 624 and 625. The Icelandic church historian, Finnus Johannaeus (Jonsson), presents the Icelandic text together with a Latin version.[2] His Latin is copied by Schmitz together with a superior Latin rendering prepared for Schmitz by J. Frederiksen with notes on the difficult expressions in the original from the edition in *Diplomatarium Islandicum*, I, 240–44. To the document proper Schmitz adds some later Icelandic penitential materials taken by Johannaeus from Codex Arn. Magn. 624.[3]

The *Penitential of Thorlac* penalizes the offenses of bestiality, adultery, incest, theft, sacrilege, magic, and negligence in the celebration of the Eucharist. Homicide strangely receives no notice; but in general the document shows the influence of the penitentials attributed to Bede and

---

[1] An early thirteenth-century life of Thorlac is given by G. Vígfusson and F. Y. Powell, *Origines Islandicae*, I, 458–502. The Icelandic text is accompanied by an English translation. His authorship of a penitential ("skrifta-boð") is affirmed, p. 480.

[2] *Historia ecclesiastica Islandiae*, IV (1778), 150–60.

[3] Schmitz II, pp. 707–15.

Egbert. While the original penalties are severe, commutations are offered in a lax spirit.]

These penances Bishop Thorlac commanded for the gravest capital sins.

[For homosexuality and bestiality Thorlac prescribed:] a nine-year or a ten-year penance: the three thorough fasts[4] yearly: the first before the feast of John the Baptist, the second before the feast of Michael, the third before the feast of Advent; however, fasts are to be kept on alternate days and on two nights of each week. He commanded that one hundred genuflexions be made each day of the fasts of Advent when nine lections are not held; and as many paternosters are to be said. Every Friday in Lent the "discipline" is to be used, at least five blows of the rod or strap so as to wound. Downy clothing, except cushions, and also linen clothing, are to be put aside during the lenten period and the fast of Advent; but on Friday or on a day of vigils he shall make some genuflexions, and for three years he shall not receive the Lord's body.

[Similar provisions for various grave offenses follow.]

Night fasts may never be commuted; but the other fasts may be commuted if he is willing to make a hundred genuflexions for a day, or to say the paternoster fifty times.

If he wishes, let him give an offering, as much as suffices for one dinner or victuals for two days.

With these penances he shall receive all the indulgences that have been appointed.

Men who are in good health shall so bend their knees that both the knees and the elbows touch the ground.

For violation of a woman . . . he shall perform the above-mentioned penance;[5] he shall [also] sing the paternoster fifty times on the festival days or make one hundred genuflexions on work days, [repeating this penance] as many times as he offended.

---

[4] "gagnfaustur" (pl.). Johannaeus renders this "jejunia solida" (thorough, genuine, or uninterrupted fasts). The word has been rendered as the equivalent of "gangfasta" (the Rogation fast). Cf. Old English "gang days," so-called from the perambulation of the parishes which accompanied the fast days before Ascension. See Cleasy-Vígfusson, *Icelandic-English Dictionary*, s.v. "gang-fasta," and p. 359, n. 4, below. For a full historical discussion of the variant applications of "gagnfasta" see Maurer, "Ueber die norwegisch-islandischen gagnföstur," *Sitzungsber. der königl. bayer. Akademie der Wissenschaften*, philos.-philol. Classe, 1881, pp. 225–58. The term seems not applicable, in all its uses, to any recognized fasting period.

[5] Six to nine years, according to circumstances.

If anyone receives the Lord's body unworthily, he shall refrain from it as many times, and he shall add twelve blows.

For theft he shall be punished by the restitution of what was stolen if it can be made, and he shall perform a minor penance; but for a serious theft, a major penance, if he cannot make restitution, and if the theft was committed rather from malice than on account of need. He shall be punished for the theft with fasts and flagellations and prayers and genuflexions, and he shall perform other penance until what he stole is restored.

A rich man shall always be more severely punished than a poor man for the same sin; the hale, than the sick; the learned, than the unlearned; a man of superior, than a man of inferior rank; a fortunate man, than an unfortunate; and adult, than one of minor age. . . .

Bishop Thorlac commanded that the priest, if after the singing on the previous day he let the chalice fall upon the altar and spilled it, shall give twelve cubits of altar cloth, or that he shall provide for a poor man for half a month and wash the board where it fell; but he himself shall drink it after communion; if, however, it fell elsewhere,[6] he shall burn it.[7]

. . . or if anyone in a rage sheds the blood of a Christian man, or if anyone in any way injures a priest, or if anyone violently attacks his father, or if anyone embraces a woman who is quite unwilling, or if anyone going about by night seeks illicit knowledge or practices a magical trick or anything pertaining to magic, or if anyone does what the heathen do, the bishop shall indicate the penalty, provided it is confessed to the priest before being confessed to the bishop.

If a priest has sung mass without being equipped with all these requisites, namely, the amice and the alb, the stole and the chasuble, the maniple, the corporal, the chalice, the paten, wine and water, the host, the consecrated altar stone, attached or unattached,[8] also the necessary books, and the wax tapers, and two fasting men besides himself; or if the priest previously breaks his fast on the day on which he sings mass, or if he sings more than two masses on the same day; or if the priest pretends to sing mass, yet does not sing it;

---

[6] Elsewhere than on the altar.

[7] Cf. the provisions in *Cummean*, XI, 23, 26, and *Theod.* I, XII, 6, pp. 115 f., 195, above.

[8] The altar stone or slab was the slab of stone which formed the upper surface of the altar. Moveable consecrated altar stones were used where the altar itself was not consecrated or where it was made of wood. See D. Rock, *The Church of Our Fathers*, I, 192 ff.

or if he openly neglects the commands of God or of the bishop; then let the bishop determine his punishment. Moreover, the priest, when he is notified of it, shall perform [the service]. Mass may be sung even though the slab[9] and the linens have not been consecrated, or where there are no wax tapers, unless this takes place because of contumacy, on which account a small penalty is indicated.

If any priest forgets nones or another of the hours, he shall sing it, if he can, when it first enters his mind; and he shall add the entire *Beati immaculati*.[10]

[The following provisions are from a later addition to Thorlac's work.]

The rules which the blessed bishop Thorlac authorized have already been repeated; these we observe with difficulty, though he transmitted them to us in mild form. . . . We do not grant the sacraments in those cases in which he forbade them; we also command that penance be imposed for the same length of time as formerly, as he commanded. The thorough fasts and the genuflexions are henceforth to be lightened; in minor penances there shall be the same abstinence from linen and downy clothing as he enjoined and the same scourging and prayers. We do not exclude from receiving the Lord's body those who are bound by the chain of marriage even though they once or twice offend with another if the offense is not done openly and alienation of the married pair does not result from it, and if abandonment of the sin and amendment are promised. We permit each party to the marriage to undergo penance for the other for all those matters that come between them and require expiation. We allow the sacred offices to be performed on a feast day, even if there are fasts to be redeemed. An example of all the thorough fasts: for a sin of the flesh with one woman or for incest that has been committed, we command that [the fast] be performed in fifty days of fasting on alternate days, and [that] on the intervening days [there shall be performed] thirty genuflexions and recitations of the paternoster. We do not forbid the sacraments to those who do not keep the working days of the week of Easter or[11] holy week, not including the ember days in the beginning of Lent,[12] besides the

---

[9] "tabula," probably the altar stone.　　　[10] Ps. 118.

[11] "edur." Johannaeus loosely renders this "et."

[12] That is, the Wednesday, Friday, and Saturday of the week beginning the first Sunday in Lent.

Ash Wednesdays;[13] but their guilt shall be pointed out at once and the remaining penance rightly performed. . . .

The form of oath for the principal person himself shall be as follows: I swear that I have [not] done that for which I am defamed either in my own person or by a subordinate acting on my orders: I have not given counsel or authority [for the act]. The compurgators, moreover, shall swear thus: "We believe that he has sworn the truth," or, "that what he has sworn is true."

The penance of fourteen years for the graver offenses of those who commit incest with relatives of the second degree or of first degree of affinity and similar offenses [is to be performed as follows].

First, fast a "carena"[14] for forty days on water and bread; go barefoot and do not enter a church; do not ride a horse; abstain from linen clothing; do not bear arms; avoid intercourse with all men as regards sleep, food, or drink until the "carena" imposed by the will of a confessor is discharged, and according to emergencies and circumstances thou shalt be deprived of part of thy food; abstain utterly from association with a woman; live in one place and do not walk about much for amusement or curiosity. Every twenty-four hours while the "carena" lasts spend a period reciting the psalter; eat dry foods twice on the Lord's day. After the forty days are discharged, thou shalt wash, resume thy shoes, and shave thy hair. Through an entire year thou shalt stand without the church, except in the time from Maundy Thursday[15] to the end of the week of Easter, through the time of the Lord's Nativity until after the feast of Circumcision, in the feast of Epiphany, of Ascension, of Pentecost, in the feast of Mary in early summer. In the second year likewise, except on feast days. Thereafter for three years stand without the church through the time of Advent and Lent and the thorough fasts. Do not partake of the holy supper within three years, unless placed in peril of life. Keep the thorough fasts through fourteen years; in this period fast on Monday and Wednesday on dry foods, but in the nights, on water. During the lenten period fast for the stated time on dry foods, but on Friday, on water, and recite two psalters each week.

[Descriptions of the penance for seven years or more, perpetual penance, and the penance for adultery follow. The substitution of alms for certain penalties of fasting is provided for.]

---

[13] "dies capitales." Ash Wednesday was called "caput ieiunii" (the beginning of the fast).   [14] See above, p. 325.
[15] "Skirdegi." Johannaeus, "dies viridium"; Schmitz, erroneously, "viridum."

FROM THE PRECEPTS OF THE BISHOPS OF HORLAR: JÖRUNDUS,
LAURENTIUS, AND EGILLUS (*ca.* 1267–1341)

[SCHMITZ[1] takes from Johannaeus[2] a document from Codex Arn. Magn.
175, which claims to contain "precepts" authorized by Jörundus,
Laurentius, and Egillus, bishops of Horlar. Jörundus Thorsteini occupied
this see, 1267–1313; Laurentius Kalfi, 1323–31; and Egillus Ejulfson,
1331–41.[3] We may hardly exclude the possibility that these regulations
were prepared through the collaboration of the three leaders while
Jörundus was bishop. It seems more probable, however, that Jörundus
was the promulgator of the code and that its authority was reaffirmed
by the later bishops named.

Schmitz points out that, as compared with Thorlac's Penitential, this
document shows a marked mitigation of the penalties. Penance is in a
large degree public. The penitent is, however, permitted to participate
in certain festivals of the Church and in the third year to attend the
regular Sunday services. Fines are demanded, not as redemptions of
penance, but as compensation for the offense itself.]

In the name of God, Amen. These precepts have been authorized
by the Lords Jörundus and Laurentius and Egillus, bishops of Horlar,
and enjoined upon the praepositi, that they may command suitable
penalties for those who are to discharge them.

In the special case of those who are at fault in the fourth degree
of consanguinity or of affinity, or in similar cases; a fast of water
during twenty nights on water and bread or other fruits of the
earth, or if these are lacking, on half a pound of dried fish; and every
fasting night let them recite the paternoster and the psalter, falling
on their knees at every paternoster. They shall stand without the
church during the time of Lent, in Advent, and in the thorough fasts;
but on festival days they shall have access to the church. They shall
observe the minor thorough fasts[4] through the next year, that is,
they shall eat milk foods once a day on Mondays and Wednesdays
and recite the paternoster seven times, falling on their knees each
time, and the Ave Maria nine times. In the year following this, they
shall keep the thorough fasts, taking food only once on Wednesdays,

---

[1] Schmitz II, pp. 715 ff.; text, pp. 717–19.

[2] *Historia ecclesiastica Islandiae*, II, 188–90.

[3] P. B. Gams, *Series episcoporum*, 2d ed., pp. 334 f.

[4] Possibly the reference here may be to the Rogation fasts, though in general the term
"gagnfaustum" evidently has a more extended significance. Maurer (*op. cit.*, p. 236) finds
the references to this fast in this document "peculiar." The major Rogation fast was normally April 25. The minor Rogation fast days, ordinarily called simply Rogation days, were
the Monday, Tuesday, and Wednesday preceding the Feast of Ascension. Cf. *Catholic
Encyclopedia*, XIII, 110, and p. 355, n. 4, above.

and at the same time reciting the paternoster, falling on their knees, five times. In the third year they shall observe the thorough fasts by recitation of prayers and by reciting the paternoster five times, with one Ave Maria. A fine of twelve ounces of silver[5] . . .

[Penances are indicated for various other offenses of consanguinity, including the "spiritual consanguinity" contracted in baptism or confirmation. There are references to the "new ecclesiastical law" ("ius ecclesiasticum recentius"), as the basis of some of the prescriptions.]

For intentional homicide a penalty of three forty-day periods is inflicted, the first of which is this: that one should fast, with the exception of the Lord's day only, on water and bread or on a morsel of dried fish weighing half a pound. He shall observe the second forty-day period in this way: he shall fast on Wednesdays and Fridays on water, the nights also included; he shall recite the psalter and the paternoster; and genuflexions shall be made every night. In the third forty-day period the nights are also to be counted. For three years thereafter he shall be forbidden the use of the means of grace; he shall pay a fine of nine marks for his offense.

For accidental homicide the same fitting penalty is inflicted as that for simple adultery, namely, a forty-day period and a fine of three marks.

If monks or canons regular are discovered in the notorious crime of incontinence, the same fitting penalty as for voluntary homicide shall be inflicted upon them; the women with whom they have been intimate, shall also undergo the same penalty.

If a sacred object is stolen from a place that is not sacred, or an object not sacred from a sacred place, the same fitting penalty as for simple adultery shall be inflicted. But if a sacred object is stolen from a sacred place, let the fitting penalty for double adultery be inflicted.

[Violators of churches or cemeteries do penance as for double adultery and pay fifteen marks to the church or the bishop.]

6. FROM THE PENITENTIAL OF CIUDAD (*ca.* 1410–14)

[THIS PENITENTIAL is ascribed by various early authorities to Andreas Hispanus, bishop of Ciudad-Roderigo, and later penitentiary of the

---

[5] Icel. "aurar," pl. of "eyrir," an ounce of silver.

Roman Church. See Wasserschleben, *Bussordnungen*, p. 97. Although Chevalier (*Bio-bibliographie*, I, 221) distinguishes between "André d'Espagne" and "André d'Escobar" it is probable that Andreas the Spaniard, author of the penitential, is really the ecclesiastic cited by C. Eubel (*Hierarchia catholica medii aevi*, I, 69) as "Andreas Didaci (d'Escobar)." Cf. *ibid.*, pp. 196, 348, 496. He became bishop of Ciudad in 1410. There is a probability that he is the Andreas who in 1414 received from the anti-pope Benedict XIII the titular see of Tabor in Palestine; but if so, he returned to the Roman obedience, for he was appointed to Ajaccio in Italy in 1422, and in 1428 to Megara in Greece. About 1432 he became penitentiary at Rome. Chevalier doubtfully places his death in 1455.

The *Poenitentiale Civitatense* was popular at the end of the Middle Ages and was frequently printed. Wasserschleben has taken his text (*Bussordnungen*, pp. 688–705) from an early undated incunabulum in the Vienna Library. He cites numerous parallels with the canons of Astesanus.[1] The more original sections are here translated.]

53. If anyone beats or arrests a bishop or drives one out from his own see, he is excommunicate, and his property shall be handed over to that church whose bishop has been persecuted. And if he was a simple cleric, the attacker is to be deposed and is to do penance for seven years.

54. If a patron or advocate of the church, or other official, slays or mutilates a cleric or a presbyter, he shall lose the right of patronage or of advocacy and his infeudated fief and shall never be admitted to the society of clerics nor to liberty.

79. If anyone knowingly commits simony, before he is absolved some penance is enjoined upon him. He is obliged to renounce the benefice simoniacally acquired and to give money to that church and restore all the fruits he has seized and which could be seized; and understand this for a layman as well as for a cleric, for anyone by whom money has been received or simony committed; this sin is so grave in the Church of God that all [other] sins are counted as nothing in comparison with it, since by simony, cupidity, and avarice, the whole Church of God is confounded, defamed, despoiled, and committed to the rule of robbers, spoilers, obscure nobodies, ruffians, and fornicators. And this simony has subverted faith, honesty, and the other good qualities of the virtues, in the Church of God, and on account of the fruits rendered and the ecclesi-

---

[1] See below, p. 427, and F. H. Vering, "Zur Geschichte der Pönitentialbücher," *A.K.K.R.*, XXX (1873), 221 f.

astical honors to be had, teaches neglect of God and of faith in Him, and corrupts with every venality ecclesiastical benefices and the sacraments, and it impels many ecclesiastics, especially our superiors who seemed to rule the people, to become false and unjust; to have one thing secreted in their breast, another held under the tongue; to honor God only with the lips and the ecclesiastical ornaments, but in the heart to sell our Lord God Jesus Christ and his sacraments and his spouse publicly and to the scandal of all Christendom; not once but several times; not as Judas for thirty pence, but often for three thousand florins. "But woe to that man through whom scandal of this kind cometh."[2] "It were good for him, if that man had not been born."[3] And since this sin of simony is so grave, the very heaviest penance is to be imposed for it, as compared with other sins; also, since the simoniac in orders does not receive the function of his order but is suspended as respects himself and as respects others, neither bishop nor cardinal nor any other priest can absolve him from this sin of simony, excepting only the vicar of Christ, namely, the pope, and then all that he is to restore [shall] first [be restored], since he entered not by the door, but in another way, as a thief and a robber,[4] and his sin shall not be forgiven until he restores what was taken.

80. And since usury is a species of theft, verily if anyone is a usurer he shall be admitted neither to the communion of the body of Christ, nor to the church, unless he first restores the usuries he has taken, if he is able to pay them; afterwards also an arbitrary penance is imposed for this sin through confession, after he pays to him, or when he gives a bond for the payment.

98. Anyone who kills a Jew or a pagan shall do penance for forty days.

111. A falsifier of money or of measures or of instruments or of agreements, as long as he lives shall abstain on bread and water.

112. If a thief confesses or earnestly seeks confession, he shall be buried in the cemetery and prayer shall be made for him and the body of Christ shall be given to him.

122. A priest who by sign or word or in any other way reveals the confession of another shall be thrust into a monastery to do perpetual penance.

[2] Cf. Matt. 18:7; Mark 9:41; Luke 17:1.
[3] Mark 14:21.
[4] Based on John 10:1.

124. A priest who slays a robber in self-defense shall do penance for two years.

127. If anyone falsifies a measure or money, he shall make restitution and do penance for thirty days on bread and water.

135. He who cannot pay the expenses of litigation[5] shall be punished according to the will of the judge.

139. He who persecutes with enmity a cardinal of the Holy Roman Church shall be punished with a very severe penalty; also those who know of it and consent to it.

149. And if the confessant is ill, then let the confessor be cautious, for he is not to give him a penance but to make it clear to him . . . saying to him in effect: If thou wert well thou shouldst do such and such a penance for thy sins, but since thou art ill I do not enjoin it upon thee; but when thou shalt recover thou shalt do it, or thou shalt come to me or to another priest and receive penance afresh; but if thou shalt die of this illness, make thy will and give so much or cause so much alms to be given for thy soul.

7. FROM THE MILAN PENITENTIAL AND ITS ABRIDGMENT

From the Milan Penitential of Cardinal Borromeo
(ca. 1565–82)

[The work called by editors "the Milan Penitential" (*Poenitentiale Mediolanense*) emanates from Cardinal St. Charles Borromeo, 1538–84, a distinguished leader of the Counter-Reformation. As archbishop of Milan 1564–84, Borromeo labored for church reform and the establishment of discipline. The present document appeared as an "Instruction on Confession," issued under his authority, in *Acta ecclesiae Mediolanensis* (1582), and was later published by J. Besombes in *Moralia Christiana* (1711). The text was republished by Wasserschleben[1] from the latter work and copied by Schmitz.[2]

The *Milan Penitential* is largely dependent upon Burchard's *Corrector;* it is also indebted to the Canons of Astesanus. The main body of the document, however, is arranged in the order of the commandments of the Decalog. After the treatment of the Tenth Commandment occurs a short section on the Seven Deadly Sins, one on Gluttony and Drunkenness, another on Various Sins, and in conclusion the Declarations given below. The opening and concluding passages alone are here presented.]

---

[5] "litis."
[1] *Bussordnungen*, pp. 705–27.
[2] Schmitz I, pp. 809–32.

Penitential Canons, Knowledge of Which Is Necessary for Parish Priests and Confessors, Set Forth according to the Plan and Order of the Decalog

The fathers taught how very necessary for priests who are engaged in hearing the confessions of penitents is a knowledge of the penitential canons. And indeed if all things that pertain to the method of penance are to be administered not only with prudence and piety but also with justice, assuredly the pattern of this ought to be taken from the penitential canons. For there are, so to speak, two rules by which priests and confessors are so directed as both to discern the gravity of an offense committed and in relation to this to impose a true penance: that they severally accurately investigate both the things that pertain to the greatness of the sin and those that pertain to the status, condition, and age of the penitent and the inmost sorrow of the contrite heart—and then, that they temper the penance with their own justice and prudence. And indeed the method explained by the fathers so disposed these things and everything else that is complicated of this necessary knowledge, that, as was said above in its proper place, the penitential canons set forth according to the plan of the Decalog are held over to the last part of the book, whence some knowledge of them can be drawn by the confessor-priests themselves. . . .

Declarations

The confessor, while he understands from those things that are set down herewith that the penances are varied with regard both to the times and to the persons, and that a certain calculation of things to be commuted is applied, yet acts on his own will in all those matters which require mitigation or moderation, as was indicated at the outset.

Concerning the penance which is determined for the appointed days,[3] the confessor shall take care that by this expression is understood Monday, Wednesday, and Friday, days ordered for the fast of penance in the canon law.

The fast of the "carina," which is sometimes provided for in the penitential canon, is so called because it used to last through forty days on bread and water, as Burchard ofttimes explains. Some call

[3] "per legitimas ferias."

it "carina," some "carena," others "carentena," others "quadra-gena."

A penance appointed for three forty-day periods is to be understood in this way: that he on whom it is imposed shall fast on bread and water for three forty-day periods, the first of which is before the day of the Lord's Nativity; the second, before Easter of the Resurrection; the third evidently that which was held in the thirteen days before the day of the Feast of St. John Baptist, as can be seen from the decree of the council of Seligenstadt.[4]

FROM THE ABRIDGMENT OF THE MILAN PENITENTIAL (*ca.* 1700)

[SCHMITZ found an eighteenth century Brussels manuscript, Codex Burgund. 5835–36, containing a set of canons selected and abbreviated from the Milan Penitential, and published these at the end of his second volume,[1] as the latest fragment of the genuine penitential literature. The Abridgment follows the arrangement of the original document, with the difference that the sixth and seventh Commandments are inter-changed, the additional sections noted above are omitted, and two difficult sentences are added. With slight omissions the Abridgment is translated below. The original penitential has been referred to for the correction of a few readings.]

The chief penitential canons collected according to the order of the Decalog from various councils and penitentiary books in the In-struction of St. Charles B[orromeo]

On the First Commandment of the Decalog

1. He who falls away from the faith shall do penance for ten years.

2. He who observes auguries and divinations [and] he who makes diabolical incantations, seven years. One who beholds things to come[2] in an astrolabe,[3] two years.

3. If anyone makes knots or enchantments, two years.

4. He who consults magicians,[4] five years.

On the Second Commandment

1. Whoever knowingly commits perjury, shall do penance for forty days on bread and water, and seven succeeding years; and he

---

[4] "Saligustadiensis"—properly "Salegunstadiensis." The council of Seligenstadt (1022) declares (can. 1): "That in the fourteen days before the festival of St. John Baptist all Christians be in abstinence from flesh and blood . . . " Mansi, XIX, 396.

[1] Schmitz II, pp. 729–32.

[2] Reading with the original *Milan Penitential* "futura" for "furta."

[3] Cf. p. 43, above.   [4] Reading with the *Milan Penitential* "magos" for "maios."

shall never be without penance. And he shall never be accepted as a witness; and after these things he shall take communion.

2. He who commits perjury in a church, ten years.

3. If anyone publicly blasphemes God or the Blessed Virgin or any saint, he shall stand in the open in front of the doors of the church on seven Sundays, while the solemnities of the masses are performed, and on the last of these days, without robe and shoes, with a cord tied about his neck; and on the seven preceding Fridays he shall fast on bread and water; and he shall then by no means enter the church. Moreover, on each of these seven Sundays he shall feed three or two or one,[5] if he is able. Otherwise he shall do another penance; if he refuses, he shall be forbidden to enter the church; in [case of] his death he shall be denied ecclesiastical burial.

4. He who violates a simple vow shall do penance for three years.

On the Third Commandment

1. He who does any servile work on the Lord's day or on a feast day shall do penance for seven days on bread and water.

2. If anyone violates fasts set by Holy Church, he shall do penance for forty days on bread and water.

3. He who violates the fast in Lent shall do a seven-day penance for one day.

4. He who without unavoidable necessity eats flesh in Lent shall not take communion at Easter and shall thereafter abstain from flesh.

On the Fourth Commandment

1. He who reviles his parents shall be a penitent for forty days on bread and water.

2. He who does an injury to his parents, three years.

3. He who beats [them], seven years.

4. If anyone rises up against his bishop, his pastor and father, he shall do penance in a monastery all the days of his life.

5. If anyone despises or derides the command of his bishop, or of the bishop's servants, or of his parish priest, he shall do penance for forty days on bread and water.

On the Fifth Commandment

1. He who kills a presbyter shall do penance for twelve years.

[5] The *Milan Penitential* adds "pauperem" (poor man).

2. If anyone kills his mother, father, or sister, he shall not take the Lord's body throughout his whole life, except at his departure; he shall abstain from flesh and wine, while he lives; he shall fast on Monday, Wednesday, and Friday.[6]

3. If anyone kills a man he shall always be at the door of the church, and at death he shall receive communion.

[Sections 4–10 omitted.]

On the Sixth Commandment

[Sections 1–6 omitted.]

7. If any woman paints herself with ceruse[7] or other pigment in order to please men, she shall do penance for three years.

8. If a priest is intimate with his own spiritual daughter, that is, one whom he has baptized or who has confessed to him, he ought to do penance for twelve years; and if the offense is publicly known, he ought to be deposed and do penance for twelve years on pilgrimage, and thereafter enter a monastery to remain there throughout his life. For adultery penances of seven, and of ten, years, are imposed; for unchaste kissing or embracing a penance of thirty days is commanded.

On the Seventh Commandment

1. If anyone commits a theft of a thing of small value he shall do penance for a year.

2. He who steals anything from the furniture of a church or from the treasury, or ecclesiastical property, or offerings made to the church shall be a penitent for seven years.

3. He who retains to himself his tithe or neglects to pay it, shall restore fourfold and do penance for twenty days on bread and water.

4. He who takes usury commits robbery; he shall do penance for three years on bread and water.

On the Eighth Commandment

1. He who conspires in falsification of evidence shall be a penitent for five years.

2. A forger[8] shall do penance on bread and water as long as he lives.

---

[6] Reading with the *Milan Penitential* "sexta feria" for "IV feria."

[7] "cerusa," properly "cerussa," white-lead used in mixing paint.

[8] "falsarius."

3. If anyone slanders his neighbor, he shall be a penitent for seven days on bread and water.

On the Ninth and Tenth Commandments

1. He who basely covets another's goods and is avaricious shall be a penitent for three years.

2. If anyone desires to commit fornication, if a bishop, he shall be a penitent for seven[9] years; if a presbyter, five; if a deacon or monk, three; if a cleric or layman, two years.

He who sees no reason for the refusal or delay of his absolution, the hater, the withholder, he who occasions scandals, he who denies or declines to leave off his sin, he who refuses to flee from the occasion of sin, or he who has given no signs of sorrow . . . [10]

[Note Subjoined by Compiler or Copyist]

Saint Mary Magdalene de Pazzi, as is related in her Latin *Life*, Chapter XXX,[11] affirmed that Christ had revealed to her that he would require the expiation in purgatory of a penance of seven years or longer of those who neglect the canons of penance.

[9] Reading with the *Milan Penitential* "septem" for "III."

[10] The untranslated words are: "monitum sterili cum cruce remittos." If we read "remittas," the phrase begins to make sense: "After warning him thou shalt send him back [to his penance] with [wearing?] a sterile (?) cross." Perhaps "monitum" is to be taken to mean not "warned" but "made conspicuous." Under the Inquisition offenders were sometimes sentenced to wear two yellow crosses on the breast, and something similar may be intended here. This suggestion would be more attractive if "cruce" were a plural. But why "sterili"? I have failed to find "crux sterilis" as a technical term. If not a corruption, "sterili" may have had for the author the sense of barren because, alas, a mere badge of delinquency.

[11] St. Mary Magdalene de Pazzi (1556–1607) was an ecstatic Carmelite nun of Florence, remarkable for her sorrow over the tortures of those in purgatory and for her excited visions in which she witnessed their agonies. Various accounts of her life and miracles are given in *Acta sanctorum*, XIX, 175–348. For her effectual intercession for her brother and other sufferers in purgatory, see pp. 235 ff. Probably the reference to her was not contained in the original.

CHAPTER VIII

Penitential Elements in Medieval Public Law

---

1. SELECTIONS FROM EARLY IRISH LAW

[THE Irish code known as the *Senchus Mór* was compiled at a period shortly after the introduction of Christianity. According to the statement with which it is prefaced, the compilation was made under the High King Loeghaire mac Neill (428–58). It is further alleged in this document that St. Patrick and two other bishops collaborated in the preparation of the code with Dubhthach, the poet, and other representatives of the pre-Christian learning and legal customs of Ireland. The *Senchus* was designed, we learn, to combine "the judgments of true nature which the Holy Ghost had spoken through the mouths of the Brehons" (Irish judges) whose disciples "exhibited from memory what their predecessors had sung," with the "Word of God in the written law and the New Testament." History must take from Patrick in this incident the two companion bishops mentioned, and leave doubtful his participation in the framing of the *Senchus Mór*. But we have at least good reason to suppose that Patrick visited Tara, the capital of King Loeghaire, and consulted with the King and with his poet and adviser, Dubhthach Moccu Lugir.[1]

The only law tract here quoted, except the *Senchus Mór*, is the strongly clerical document known as the *Sequel to the Crith Gabhlach*, which betrays its late date by references to the emperor and is thought to belong either to the period 800–840 or to the late tenth century.

The *Senchus Mór*, and the other medieval collections of Irish law decisions, have been edited and translated by W. N. Hancock and others in *Ancient Laws of Ireland* (6 vols., 1865–1901), from which work the present illustrations are taken. Many incidental references to penance and allied matters occur in these laws which are in themselves too slight for quotation here. Only a few of the more revealing passages are given. Although the reader will observe that the obscurities of the texts have partially baffled the translators, he will be able for the most part to discern the significance of the references to penance. The footnotes are my own.]

[1] E. MacNeill, *Saint Patrick, Apostle of Ireland* (London, 1934), pp. 100 ff.

a. EXTRACT FROM THE *Senchus Mór. ca.* 445(?).

[*Ancient Laws of Ireland*, I, 59 ff.].—If wounding or theft or lying or adultery be committed by a bishop, or by a Herenach[2] to whom marriage is not allowed, they shall not resume the same dignities, even though they do penance and pay 'eric'-fine;[3] or, (as some say), it is the virgin bishop only that does not resume it; the bishop of one wife resumes it if he does penance within three days. If he has been guilty of false witness, or false testimony, or false judgment, or violation of a contract, or false arbitration, or of giving a false character, he resumes the same dignity, but so as he does penance, and pays 'eric'-fine in proportion to the crime; and if they move from their dignity, they should attain to a higher one.

And this is the change, the lector shall be installed in the bishopric, and the bishop shall become a hermit or a pilgrim; and if they [i.e. the bishops, while in either condition of these] commit trespass, they shall never have honor price, even though they should do penance, and pay 'eric'-fine.

What this is derived from is this: "if [anyone] stumble under noble rank, no 'dire'-fine can be had except a 'cumhal'[4] for the grades of wisdom, and there is nothing for the grades of the church, for it was in that grade they violated their dignity, in right of which they hitherto had honor-price."

All men whose office did not compel them to frequent the church before, have a 'cumhal' for frequenting the church. If a person of six grades of the church has done these deeds, he shall move to a higher grade, so as he does penance in proportion to the dignity of the grade, however insignificant the crime. And the crime is also to be paid for, if it be persons of the grades of wisdom, or professors of learning, or [the grades] of the church, or kings, or Ollambhs[5] or Brewys[6] [that have committed these deeds].When they [the Brewys] have not increase of property [to entitle them to recover their rank], they must do penance at their own church, to recover as much of their honor-price as they have lost, and penance for the person whom they have quarrelled with, if penance is due to him; and adultery is not more lawful for him than any other illegality.

If it be [any of] the seven degrees of chieftains that have done

---

[2] An Irishman.   [3] Composition.
[4] [The value of] a female slave. Cf. p. 119 above, n. 19.
[5] Learned men of the highest rank.   [6] Farmers.

these deeds, i.e. violation of security, or guaranty, or pledge, or unlawful wounding, or burning, it is increase of property they must have
to recover their grade, or they must do penance and pay 'eric'-fine;
or, it is 'eric'-fine alone, i.e. a 'cumhal' to the person whom they have
injured, if he be of a grade to which penance is not due.

[*Op. cit.* III, 31].—The enslaved shall be freed, [and] plebeians shall
be exalted by [receiving] church grades, and by performing penitential service to God.

Gloss on the above: By penitential service, i.e. by doing service
to God in penitence, i.e. in pilgrimage.

[*Op. cit.*, III, 73].—If it be pilgrimage that his soul's friend[7] has enjoined upon him.

Gloss on the above: If his soul's friend has enjoined upon him to
go on a pilgrimage after [his having committed] the murder of a
tribesman or murder with concealment of the body.

[*Op. cit.*, III, 107].—My son, that thou mayest know [when] the
head of a king is upon a plebian, [and] the head of a plebeian upon
a king.

Gloss on the above: That is, the case in which the head of a king
is upon a plebeian, is when the son of [a man of] the plebeian grade
has learned until he becomes one of the septenary grade, i.e. till be
becomes a bishop, or a chief professor,[8] so that he is entitled to a fine
of seven 'cumhals' of penance, and seven 'cumhals' of 'eric'-fine.

b. From the Tract Known as the Sequel to the Crith Gabhlach (*ca.* 800–840)

Ancient Laws of Ireland, IV, 363 ff.—What is the penalty of wounding a virgin bishop?

Answer: Three victims to be hanged from every hand that
wounded him; half the debt of wounding is paid for insulting him.
. . . [As to] shedding his blood; if it reaches to the ground, as blood
that requires a tent, the guilty person is to be hanged for it; or it is
seven 'cumhals' [that are to be paid] for his sick maintenance and his
'eric'-fine.

If it [the wound] be in his face, the breadth of his face of silver
is to be paid, and of the crown of his head of gold, and he sues him

---

[7] "anmchara" (confessor).
[8] "fer leigind" (man of learning, or, of reading), often the chief teacher of a monastery.
Cf. p. 122, n. 33, above.

[for every time] that he is reproached with the blemish in a crowd, to the end of three years; from that out it is a 'cumhal' in public [that is due], unless he forgives him. . . .

If any of his hair is pulled out, there is a 'sed' due for every hair of it to twenty hairs.[9]

[Provisions follow for the "virgin priest," and for the "bishop of one wife."]

As to the penitent bishop now; to the extent of two-thirds he reaches to a bishop of one wife: nine 'cumhals' and two cows [are the penalty] for wounding him. . . . It is the same with the penitent priest; it is a 'cumhal' that is between him and the penitent bishop.

It is the same with every grade that grows above another unto the end, it is a 'cumhal' that is between them, so that it is three 'cumhals' that are paid for wounding a penitent cleric (or clerical student) and half thereof for insulting him. . . .

[Various provisions, some of them involved and scarcely intelligible, are given with regard to lay recluses and clerical students, both of which groups are treated as of two classes, "virgin" and "of one wife."]

[As to] a lay recluse of whom a soul-friend and a priest gave a character; his 'sed' is of equal 'dire'-fine with that of the virgin clerical student, i.e. a 'cumhal' for them.

2. SELECTIONS FROM EARLY WELSH LAW
a. The "Welsh Canons" (ca. 550–650)

[THE ORIGIN and early use of these canons is veiled in complete obscurity. Wasserschleben and Haddan and Stubbs observed the close parallels between them and certain provisions of the later Welsh codes and regarded them as of Welsh origin. The cautious view of Haddan and Stubbs is: "On the whole they may be pronounced probably Welsh; and if so, belong to that period (ca. A.D. 500×650) during which both the Welsh church and the Welsh principalities appear to have become organized." This is perhaps intended to suggest coöperation between ecclesiastics and statesmen in framing these canons. H. Williams, however, dismisses them from treatment in connection with the sixth century penitential writings on the ground that they are not ecclesiastical but "an interesting collection belonging to Welsh national law."[10] F. Seebohm seriously questions the Welsh origin of the canons and thinks them to have been made up of "excerpta" from various sources and, as a

---

[9] Cf. p. 124, above.   [10] *Cymmrodorion Record Series*, III, 286.

collection, possibly of Irish or of continental origin; though he supposes that "some of them may have been used, amongst others, by the Church in South Wales."[11]

Canons 2–13, 36 and 51 are found closely paralleled and in some cases virtually repeated in the Latin version of the Laws of Hywel (Howel) the Good (d. *ca.* 950), Book II, App. xlix–lvii, as given in A. Owen, *Ancient Laws and Institutes of Wales*, II, 875–79. The later document evidently embodies a version of these canons, which were probably at the time of Howel's legislation at least three centuries old, and of which one extant manuscript goes back to the late eighth or early ninth century. This fact seems to show that the canons had been preserved through the intervening period in Wales and that they were in the tenth century regarded as Welsh.

Without attempting to solve the problem of the origin of these canons we place the collection in this chapter because, while it helps to illuminate the penitentials, it is clearly not a penitential document. Not only does it omit scales of penance, it also ignores the Church concept of sin, and it appeals to no supernatural sanctions. It may have been framed or compiled by ecclesiastics; but the ecclesiastical elements in it are unobtrusive. It deals with a series of common offenses and secular issues, such as would arise between neighbors in a comparatively primitive agricultural community. But the evidence which the document offers of the legal customs of the time, especially of compurgation and composition, is useful as illustrating something of the environment in which the penitentials developed and from which they absorbed many elements.[12]

The *Canones Wallici* have been published by Martène and Durand,[13] by Wasserschleben[14] and by Haddan and Stubbs.[15] The manuscripts used by the editors are the ninth century Codex Paris. 12021, and the Paris. 3182 of the tenth or eleventh century. The first mentioned forms the text of the editions, while footnotes supply variants from the other manuscript and from the Welsh Laws. Codex Hatton 42 has also been consulted for the translation. Wasserschleben, p. 124, and Haddan and Stubbs, I, 127, refer also to a ninth century codex, Lyons 203. Seebohm has given a free translation of canons 1–6 and 12 (*op. cit.*, pp. 108 f.).]

[11] *Tribal Custom in Anglo-Saxon Law*, pp. 105 ff.

[12] The numerous scholars who have explored the field of Welsh legal history have treated these canons with strange neglect. They are not included in A. Owen's edition of the *Ancient Laws and Institutes of Wales*, published by the Record Office in 1841. T. P. Ellis in his extensive work on *Welsh Tribal Law and Custom in the Middle Ages* writes as if no such document existed ("It is unsafe to say there was no attempt at codifying before the time of Hywel Dda," I, 5). None of the contributors to the *Hywel Dda Millenary Volume* (1928, *Aberystwith Studies* X) refers to the collection, though it finds mention in the Bibliography.

[13] *Thesaurus novus anecdotorum*, IV, 13 ff.

[14] *Bussordnungen*, pp. 124 ff. and cf. p. 8.

[15] *Councils*, I, 127 ff.

1. If anyone commits homicide by intention,[16] he shall pay three female slaves and three male slaves and shall receive security.

2. If anyone is sued at law and determines to be rigorous in stating the truth[17] and is slain for this intention, we command that two[18] female slaves and two male slaves ought to be paid. But if he has lost a hand or a foot or any other member, he shall in like manner be prepared to accept[19] two-thirds of the price.

3. If anyone has been suspected on account of a murder, and if evidence to prove it[20] is lacking, forty-eight men shall be named, twenty-four of whom shall swear[21] in a church that he is truthful; so shall he depart without needing to stand suit.[22]

4. If a slave kills a freeman, and this was through the freeman's fault,[23] and if he was slain with a cudgel or an axe or a hoe[24] or with a knife, that murderer shall be given over to the parents, and they shall have power to do [with him] what they will.

5. If any master permits his slave to bear arms and he slays a freeman, the master shall be prepared to hand over the slave and another with him.

6. If any freeman kills the slave of another without blame[25] [he

[16] Paris. 3182 and Hatton 42 have "contentione" (as a result of strife).

[17] This seems a possible rendering of "et praestando verum durus esse voluerit." The variations from Paris. 3182 are given by Haddan and Stubbs but this manuscript does not lend itself to translation. The Hatton manuscript reads: "et praestandi ratione diras esse voluerit et inficiatus fuerit." The passage may, however, receive some light from the Welsh Laws, II, xlix, 3: "Siquis fuerit in judicio compulsus et dandi rationes durus esse voluerit, et invitus fuerit . . . ," which apparently means that he is a stubborn and unwilling witness, "hard in giving reasons" and "unwilling," after he has been arrested and brought to court. Seebohm has for the whole clause: "tries to resist arrest," but does not attempt to justify this.   [18] Paris. 3182 and Hatton 42 have "five."

[19] Literally, "know himself about to accept."   [20] "titulus comprobandi."

[21] Later Welsh law exhibits constant use of this method of compurgation in proof. See especially Ellis, op. cit., II, 304 ff. T. A. Levi, "The Laws of Hywel Dda in the Light of Roman and Early English Law" (Aberystwith Studies X), p. 54, remarks that the compurgators were not a jury, but were still (in the tenth century) chosen by the accused— a result of the fact that "the whole process was a survival of kindred solidarity."

[22] "sine causa," as in can. 16. But cf. cans. 22, 39, 55. This seems preferable to the reading "sine culpa" (without blame) in Paris. 3182 and Hatton 42.

[23] "et culpa ingenui fuerit hoc." But perhaps we should insert "sine" (without), before "culpa," as in can. 6. However the Paris manuscript reads "plaga ingenuus aut" for "culpa . . . hoc" (the freeman was slain by a blow from . . .).

[24] "aut dextrali aut dubio." The Paris manuscript reads: "aut de securi bidubioque." "Bidubium" is rendered by Du Cange "falcastrum," a sickle-shaped instrument, possibly a bill-hook. But in Goetze-Loewe, Corpus glossariorum Latinorum, the equivalent given is "δίκελλα" (hoe or mattock).

[25] "sine culpa." Paris. 3182 and Hatton 42 have "sine causa." But the use of "culpa" in the next sentence seems intentionally parallel to its use here. Perhaps we should render the words with Seebohm "without fault (of the slave)."

shall give] two male slaves to the master. But if the slave of the other was to blame, another slave shall be restored to his master.

7. If anyone murders a man in a quarrel or cuts off his hand or his foot or [destroys] his eye, he shall be prepared to pay a female slave or a male slave. But if he cuts off the thumb of his hand, the half of a female slave, that is the half of the value [of one], or the half of a male slave.

8. If anyone strikes a man with a spear or a sword so that [one] may see the interior parts, he shall be prepared to pay three silver pounds.

9. If anyone strikes the head of another so that [one] may see the membrane of his brain, he shall be compelled to pay six[26] silver pounds.

10. If anyone strikes another with a lance and pierces his arm or his foot so that he does not disable[27] the member, he shall be prepared to give three[28] silver pounds.

11. If anyone discovers in his villa[29] a horse or an ox or any animal that has been stolen or bound or slain, we command that he provide proper compurgators[30] and then he shall have no damages [to pay]; but if they do not swear, he shall pay.

12. If anyone commits murder and attempts flight, his relatives shall have a period of fifteen days in which they may make partial restitution and remain secure or themselves leave the country; after this if the slayer himself wants to come, he shall pay the half that remains and live secure. But if meanwhile he has been killed by relatives of the slain,[31] the female or male slaves whom the debtors had accepted shall be restored to the relatives of the slain man.[32]

[26] The other manuscripts have "three."

[27] Interpreting the reading "non noceat" of the text in the light of Welsh Laws, II, xlix, 17, "non debilitaverit." [28] The other manuscripts have "two."

[29] On the village community in medieval Wales, see J. E. Lloyd, *A History of Wales*, I, 295 ff.; T. P. Ellis, *Welsh Tribal Law and Custom in the Middle Ages*, I, 212 ff.; T. G. Jones, "Social Life as reflected in the Laws of Hywel Dda," in *Aberystwith Studies*, X, 107; A. Owen, *Ancient Laws and Institutes of Wales*, I, Index, s. vv. "trev," "cantrev," "erw." The "tref" or village area consisted of 256 "erws" of 4320 sq. yds. each. A "trefgorrd" was a cluster of homesteads. Lloyd regards village communities as populated by descendants of the ancient inhabitants who had been reduced to servitude by the invading Celts. He thinks the "free trefs" were not hamlets, but areas of open country inhabited by cultivators of higher status, and under a landowner who was called "uchelwr" (high-man). The "uchelwrs" were "the nearest approach to nobility to be found in Welsh society" (p. 297).

[30] "iuratores." [31] "by . . . slain" in Paris. 3182 only.

[32] Following Paris. 3182 and in part Hatton 42. The slaves pledged by the slayer's relatives in payment for the first homicide are to be returned because vengeance has been taken. By the second homicide the former creditors have made themselves debtors.

13. If anyone casts a spear at another and the man is uninjured, he shall be compelled to pay one silver pound; if there was a wound, he shall make amends according to the laws.[33]

14. If he tramples another's grain field, whatever quantity of grain the owner with another fit person swears to have been the amount of the damage that he suffered shall without question be restored.

15. If hogs stay on another man's grain field through the greater part of a night their owner shall pay four pints;[34] but if through the lesser part of a night, he shall pay one pint.[35]

16. If anyone is under suspicion on account of [an act of] fornication, and the evidence to prove it is lacking, he shall swear in three churches[36] with his kinsmen from the least to the greatest,[37] and he shall have no trial.[38] But if they do not swear, he shall pay a female slave.

17. If anyone loses a mare[39] or a cow or any beast and finds it with someone, and if it is proved to have been in the person's possession for three months,[40] we command that he be paid threefold.[41]

18. If any boy up to the age of fifteen years commits any offense, he is not to be held to be "sub iudice" except to receive discipline;[42] after this age, however, he shall also restore what has been stolen.

19. If a man's hogs have trespassed [for] acorns and are caught, let him be prepared to give a young pig. But if he on his own account drove them, he shall not hesitate to give a full grown hog.

20. If any slave commits a theft or a fault, he shall be beaten with whips[43] and shall restore what has been stolen.

21. If any freeborn man commits a theft and dies in the act of committing it, none of his relatives shall be subject to inquisition.[44]

22. If any freeborn man or slave commits a theft by night and in

[33] The last clause is found only in Paris. 3182 and in Hatton 42.
[34] "quadrisextarium." Perhaps this is the amount of grain to be restored for each hog.
[35] "but . . . pint" from Paris. 3182 and Hatton 42.   [36] "bassilicis."
[37] "a minoribus usque ad majorem." Cf. Heb. 8:11, "a minore usque ad majorem."
[38] "causam."
[39] Reading "equam" for "aetiam." But perhaps "aetia" is connected with the Greek "ἔτειος" (yearling).
[40] Literally, "with whom he shall have been able to find it, and it shall have been proved with that person for three months."
[41] Paris. 3182 reads: "If someone takes away from a man a horse or a cow or any beast the debtor shall restore whatever he asks back together with its food."
[42] "disciplinam," probably corporal punishment.
[43] Reading "flagellis" for "fragillis."
[44] "nullus a suis habeat quaestionem."

the act of committing it is struck with a spear and killed, he who slays him shall have no need to make restitution.[45]

23. If anyone is under suspicion on account of a theft, and if the evidence to prove it against him is lacking, his case shall be postponed[46] for some[47] days until either his falsehood or his truthfulness shall come to light.

24. If anyone is sued at law and will not come [to trial], this shall be established[48] by witnesses, [and] he shall be compelled to pay one silver pound, and whatever is demanded of him he shall make good without delay.

25. If anyone buys a field, if he does no wrong, the heir shall relinquish the inheritance to his heir.

26. If anyone voluntarily relinquishes [a property], he has no power to demand it back.[49] A wounded man shall be compensated[?] according to the blow.[50]

27. If anyone for the sake of fornication corrupts another's wife, when they are taken they shall be put to death; and he who kills them, let him not fear that he will have any lawsuit.[51]

28. If anyone buys a male slave or a female slave or any beast or anything, and if a contract has been made with him, unless he presents the deed or has guarantors, he shall be prepared to compound for the theft.[52]

29. If anyone buys a Gallic[53] or a Saxon horse or one of any [other] breed, this shall be established by witnesses, if, however, a contract is made[54] they shall mutually equalize their witnesses; thus let them make the deal[55] on equal terms.[56]

30. But if anyone demands witnesses and has none, but is attempting to devise deception,[57] he shall be prepared to restore threefold.

[45] "nullam habeat causam reddendi."   [46] Literally, "sealed."
[47] Paris. 3182 and Hatton 42 read "twenty."
[48] "adprobatur." Paris. 3182 and Hatton 42 have "probetur." Cf. "comprobetur et" in canon 29.   [49] Reading "repetendi" for "repetenti."
[50] "Iesus secundum plagam se noverit rediturum." The passage is probably corrupt.
[51] "nullam se timeat habere causam." Cf. can. 3 and can. 22.
[52] Literally, "he shall know himself as a thief about to make composition."
[53] Reading "Gallicum" for "calfaicum." Paris. 3182 has "de Gallis vel de Saxonibus vel de qualibet gente."
[54] Reading "si autem consignatum fuerit" with Paris. 3182 for "et cum ipso consignatum fuerit."   [55] "dividant" in the sense of "sell one by one."
[56] Reading "sic ita aequale" with Paris. 3182 for "si ita equales."
[57] Literally, "to seek out a lie."

31. If anybody's animals stay on his neighbor's grass unharmed, he shall pay eight pounds of silver alloy.[58] But if they have been taken in the pasture, he shall pay four pounds of silver alloy.[58]

32. If anyone loses his female or male slave, and if he suspects someone, twenty-four men shall be named and twelve of these shall swear that he is truthful; but if they do not swear, he shall pay without an oath.

33. If anyone loses a horse, six men shall be summoned of whom three shall swear, and no damages shall be awarded.

34. But if he loses a cow or an ox, four out of all shall be summoned of whom two shall swear, and no damages shall be awarded.

35. If anyone strikes another so that he fractures his skull,[59] he shall pay three cows.

36. If anyone strikes another with a slap in the face so that blood or a bruise[60] appears, he shall pay one silver pound.

37. If anyone is struck when interposing in a conflict, we command that he receive half the [ordinary] compensation according to the blow.

38. If any slave kills another's slave, he shall remain alive as the joint property[61] of the masters.

39. If anybody's animal, whether ox or cow, kills another with its horn, the live one and the dead one shall be the joint property of the owners.[62] But if a bull kills a cow or an ox, his owner shall have no need to make restitution.

40. If a layman wishes to sue a cleric in any cause, they shall come to a bishop for decision [of the case].

41. If a cleric wishes to sue a layman, they ought to come to a judge for decision.[63]

42. If anyone disposes of an inheritance at his death, we command that whatever he has conveyed before witnesses, shall all remain and not be taken away.

[58] "stagni." "Stagnum" is identical with "stannum," which in the Vulgate, where it appears five times, is understood as "tin" by translators. Here, however, it is apparently an alloy of silver and lead. See Du Cange; A. Sleumer, *Kirchenlateinisches Wörterbuch;* and Harper's *Latin Dictionary, s.v.* "stannum."   [59] "os suum superius."
[60] "livido."   [61] "commonis."
[62] The text "commones ejus erunt," if it means anything, makes both the property of the owner of the animal which does the damage. This cannot be intended. The rendering follows Paris. 3182: "in commone dominorum existant."
[63] Literally, "to the decision of a judge"; reading with Hatton 42 "(a) iudicis ad sententiam" (the "a" has been inserted before "iudicis" by a corrector) for "ad judicis poenitentiam," which seems improbable in the context. Paris. 3182 has "ad iudicis astantiam."

43. If any contention has arisen over the boundary of a piece of land, witnesses shall be procured and the boundary which existed before shall remain the same.

44. If a cleric has been sued in a case and nothing is known against his reputation,[64] the case shall be determined on his own oath.[65]

45. But if he previously bore an ill reputation, compurgators shall be summoned and the case shall be determined as if he were a layman.[66]

46. If anyone having committed a fault comes to a priest for confession of his own will,[67] we command that he be not condemned by anybody.

47. But if he is resolved to deny it and it is proved by another,[68] even if he is known to have done this in time of rebellion,[69] he shall pay his own price in court and be prepared to give thrice [that amount later].

48. If anyone calls God to witness[70] and despises Him, he shall be condemned from the position of judgment(?).[71]

49. If anyone buys a field or a villa, and if he commits a capital theft, he shall be put to death and the land which he has bought shall be confiscated.[72]

50. But if his son or daughter or brother commits the theft and attempts flight, he shall pay a female slave or a male slave and possess the field. But if they remain innocent, the heir shall relinquish it to his heirs.

51. If anyone gives a slap to another[73] so that neither blood nor bruise appears, he shall pay five solidi.

[64] "nulla in eum fama fuit cognita." "Fama" is used in this and the following canon in the frequent ecclesiastical sense of a rumor of some evil or scandalous deed. Paris. 3182 has "infamiam" (ill repute) in a different construction.

[65] Reading with Paris. 3182 "in ipsius iuramento" for "ipsius jure."

[66] Literally, "in lay fashion."

[67] Following Wasserschleben, Haddan and Stubbs would read "ex spontanea voluntate" for "exportare voluntate"; but "ad" is perhaps also required before "confessionem" as in Paris. 3182 which reads simply "sponte ad confessionem." Probably "uoluntate" was originally a gloss on "sponte sua."

[68] Paris. 3182 has "si quod aliis abstulerit" (if he has taken anything from others), instead of "quodsi negare voluerit" (But . . . deny it). Hatton 42 agrees with Paris. 3182 except that it omits "aliis." Cf. Wasserschleben's note, p. 132.

[69] "in rebelli tempore."   [70] "in fidejussorem," as surety or guarantor.

[71] "a judici condictione." The exact sense of the penalty is not clear. Possibly the protection of the law is withdrawn.   [72] Literally, "revert to the fisc."

[73] The text has "Si quis alapa alium occiderit" (. . . kills with a slap). The reading adopted is from Hatton 42 and Paris. 3182: "si quis alapam alteri impigerit." The Welsh laws have "si quis alicui dederit alapam."

52. If anyone makes strife in front of a church he is compelled to pay one silver pound, and this shall be given[74] as alms to the needy.

53. If anyone strikes another with a whip, he shall pay one silver pound; if in front of a church, it shall be reckoned to the church as alms.

54. If anyone buys a female slave or a male slave, and if a fault appears in him before the completion of a year, we command that he be returned to his former master.

55. But if a year has elapsed, whatever fault there is in the slave, the vendor shall have no need to make restitution.[75]

56. If anyone buys a horse,[76] if no fault appears in him during one month he shall by no means be returned.

57. He who protects a horse from a robber,[77] if [it is] in the same country, he shall receive six scruples; if in another country, a river having been crossed, he shall receive the third part of its value.

58. If anyone strikes another with a cudgel and draws blood, he shall pay a cow; but if he inflicts a greater injury,[78] we commend that composition be made according to the judgment.[79]

59. If he arrests[80] a female slave or a male slave in flight in a place where they could escape for two miles,[81] he shall receive in reward the third part of their value. In other words, if it was a female slave, he who captures her shall receive as a reward two pounds, if a male slave, three pounds, of silver alloy.

60. If anyone finds[82] a horse and is able to catch it, he shall receive as a reward the third part of its value, or one uncia.[83]

[74] Literally, "loaned."

[75] "nullam habeat causam," "reddendi" being understood, as in canon 3. Cf. can. 22, and can. 39. Paris. 3182 has "reiciendi," and Hatton 42 "reieciendi"; but they omit "venditor," and thus make the word apply to the buyer: "he shall have no reason to reject [the slave]."

[76] In the Laws of Hywel (ca. A.D. 940) the vendor was required to guarantee animals sold, with great detail. According to the Gwentian recension of this code a horse was to be guaranteed for three mornings for the staggers, three months for the glanders, and one year for the farcy. Owen, Ancient Laws, I, 707. Cf. p. 265. See also Ellis, op. cit., I, 376.

[77] Literally, "drives a horse before a robber." Cf. Owen, Ancient Laws, I, 709: "Whoever shall protect a horse against thieves in the same country with its owner, has four legal pence."   [78] "plagam," inserted from the Paris. 3182.

[79] Reading with Paris. 3182: "secundum iudicium componi praecipimus." The text has "secundum componendi praecipimus aliam."

[80] Reading "presserit" for "preserit." Perhaps we should read "prehenderit."

[81] Omitting "sive in." Possibly this read originally "sive iii," "or three [miles]."

[82] "indicaverit" (shall have pointed out, or detected).

[83] Originally "uncia" meant the twelfth part of anything; here it refers to a coin. Seebohm takes it to be the twelfth part of a libra (pound) and equal to twenty-four "scripula"

61. No man shall hold the woodland of another's capital villa,[84] whether [it is] wet or dry, nor his seaweed, unless he gives it for oxen as fodder.

62. If anyone does otherwise, he shall be censured.

63. If anyone takes to pasture the horse of another and [finds that] he is pasturing his own horse, if [the horse] recognizes the pasture, he shall certainly not hesitate to go into it with his horse; and we determine that the horse is his own.[85]

64. If any man of rank[86] threatens his neighbor,[87] [or] even if he voluntarily decides to go away, he has power to sell either his house and his garden except the hedge that surrounds the crops and grass.

65. If a layman strikes a cleric, he shall both redeem his hand according to the stated laws[88] and come to penance.

66. If any cleric strikes a layman, he shall without question pay according to the blow as if he were a layman.

67. If anyone intercedes in a dispute and is struck by the one who is lying, he[89] shall be prepared to make composition by the laws according to the blow. But if he was struck by the one who is speaking the truth, we command that he receive composition half from the one who is speaking the truth and half from the liar. In like manner also we say this [is to be done] in case of [his] death.

[The remaining four canons are found only in Codex Paris. 3182, and are numbered 59 to 62 by editors of that manuscript.]

(68) If anyone in regular law has with the consent of the fathers joined his daughter to a bridegroom,"[90] and [the latter] intends to have in addition a slave woman as a concubine, he shall be excluded from the Church of God and from the table of every Christian unless he is called back to penance.

---

or twenty-seven and a quarter grammes. The "scripulum" was the weight of twenty-four grains of wheat. *Tribal Custom and Anglo-Saxon Law*, p. 6.

[84] Cf. Seebohm, *op. cit.*, pp. 33 ff., on "villatae" or "grazing districts." It is uncertain what unit is meant.

[85] "Si quis caballum alterius inpastoriaverit et suum pastoriaverit, si pastoriam agnoverit, sine dubio cum caballo non dubitet invadere et suum proprium eum esse praecipimus." The rendering given is conjectural. Cf. p. 71, above.

[86] "capitalis." Apparently the master of a "capital villa." Perhaps the "uchelwr." See n. 20, above. Paris. 3182 and Hatton 42 have: "villam vendere capitalem"(if anyone wishes to sell a capital villa).

[87] "vicinum." Here perhaps a tenant. Apparently we should understand after "neighbor", "and the latter on that account decides to go away."

[88] "dictis legibus," "legibus" being supplied from Paris. 3182.

[89] That is presumably the striker.

[90] "nupto filiam;" Wasserschleben has "nuptam filio".

(69) If anyone who has power in his own affairs is resolved to have his slave woman in marriage,[91] if he afterwards wants to sell her, it shall not be allowed. But if he is resolved to sell her, we command that he shall be condemned, and we place that slave woman at the disposal of a priest.

(70) If any Catholic lets his hair grow in the fashion of the barbarians, he shall be held an alien from the Church of God and from the table of every Christian until he mends his fault.

(71) If a dog eats anything [belonging to one who is not his owner], nothing is paid for his first offense, unless [he does it] when alone. But if he offends[92] a second time, the master of the dog shall pay for what the dog ate.[93]

b. FROM THE LAWS OF HOWEL THE GOOD

[THE *Ancient Laws of Wales* were edited in two volumes by Aneurin Owen in 1841. The Laws of Hywel Dda, or Howel the Good, were collected mainly from traditional usages, before the middle of the tenth century. Their compilation has been traditionally connected with a visit of King Howel to Rome about 926, and Haddan and Stubbs (I, 211) tentatively date their promulgation in the year 928, though with an explanation that leaves a wide range of uncertainty. J. E. Lloyd holds the view that the journey to Rome is authenticated, but that it was not connected with the promulgation of the Laws, which could only have taken place after Howel extended his power over all Wales, that is, not earlier than 942. Howel died in 950, hence "the great legislative achievement attributed to him must be dated between 942 and 950."[94]

The Laws appear in Owen's work in the three considerably divergent redactions in which they are extant, the *Venedotian Code*, of the province of Gwynedd, the *Dimetian Code*, of Dyved, and the *Gwentian Code*, of Gwent or Monmouth. According to the best authorities these codes all reached their present form about two and a half centuries after the time of Howel.[95] Haddan and Stubbs have given the Welsh texts of the three codes in parallel columns, with translation.[96] The passages selected are quoted from their translation of the *Dimetian Code*.]

---

[91] "et de rebus suis habet potestatem." Perhaps the meaning is: "has power [to take her] by virtue of his property rights."

[92] Literally, "he shall have sinned."

[93] This canon is based on *Can. Hib.*, V, 2. See above, p. 128.

[94] "Hywel Dda: the Historical Setting," in *Aberystwith Studies* X: *Hywel Dda Millenary Volume*, p. 4.

[95] Cf. Lloyd, *op. cit.*, p. 6; A. W. Wade-Evans, *Welsh Medieval Law*, p. vii. Wade-Evans censures Owen's application to the codes of the names given above. For the *Dimetian Code* he proposes, *The Book of Blegywryð*, from the name of its supposed original editor. *Op. cit.*, pp. ix ff.   [96] Haddan and Stubbs, I, 211–83.

Dimetian Code I, xii. 1 (Haddan and Stubbs, I, 227).—The priest of the household is to have the garment in which the king shall do penance during Lent, against Easter; and in like manner the priest to the queen is also to have her garment.

Dimetian Code II, xviii. 1 (p. 247).—If a man take a wife by gift of kindred, and he desert her before the end of the seven years; let him pay her three pounds, as her agweddi,[97] if she be the daughter of a breyr;[98] and one pound and a half, as her cowyll;[99] and six score pence, as her gobyr;[100] if she be the daughter of a taeog,[101] one pound and a half, as her agweddi; six score pence as her cowyll; and twenty-four pence, as her gobyr.

Dimetian Code II, iii. 16 (p. 253).—If a thief come to a priest to confess, and to name his confederates in theft, and swear thereto, at the door of the churchyard, and at the door of the church, and at the door of the chancel, without desiring concealment; whatever may happen to him afterwards, the priest is to be believed in respect to what has been told him by the thief: and it is similar in regard to a person who shall inform of a thief and of theft; if he swear in like manner to his information in the presence of the priest.

Dimetian Code II, i. 32 (p. 263).—If there be a relative of the murderer, or of the murdered, who is an ecclesiastic in holy orders, or in an ecclesiastical community, or leprous, or dumb, or an idiot, such neither pays nor receives any part of galanas.[102] No vengeance is to be exercised against any one of those for galanas; neither are they to avenge a relative that is killed: and they cannot in any way be compelled to pay, or receive, anything on account of galanas.

3. SELECTIONS FROM EARLY ENGLISH LAW

[THE LAWS of the early English kings have been carefully edited by F. Liebermann with a German translation.[103] More recent volumes by F. L. Attenborough[104] and A. J. Robertson[105] present the texts of these laws with English translation and notes. The codes of the various kings

---

[97] Marriage dower. For exposition of the Welsh terms in this extract see especially the glossary appended to A. W. Wade-Evans, *Welsh Medieval Law.*

[98] A class of freeman.

[99] The gift of the bridegroom to the bride.

[100] Dues paid to the lord on marriage.   [101] villain.

[102] Body-price, corresponding to the Anglo-Saxon wergeld.

[103] *Gesetze der Angelsachsen,* 3 vols., 1898–1916.

[104] *Laws of the Earliest English Kings,* 1922.

[105] *The Laws of the Kings of England from Edmund to Henry I,* 1925.

were generally framed under ecclesiastical influence, frequently with the advice of bishops and clergy assembled in council. With few exceptions the texts are in Anglo-Saxon.

In the selections given below the references to Attenborough and Robertson are supplied, and, except in the case of a Latin original, their translations are adopted. These extracts are reprinted by kind permission of Macmillan and Company, American representatives of the Cambridge University Press.]

From the Laws of Kent: Ethelbert, ca. 600 (Attenborough, pp. 4–9)

[The following decisions were, according to the statement of an early copyist, established by King Ethelbert "in the lifetime of Augustine," i.e., 597–(?)604. No. I of the series accords to the bishop greater protection from theft than to the king himself.]

1. [Theft of] God's property and the Church's shall be compensated twelve fold; a bishop's property eleven fold; a priest's property nine fold; a deacon's property six fold; a clerk's property three fold. Breach of the peace shall be compensated doubly when it affects a church or a meeting place.

4. If a freeman robs the king, he shall pay back a nine fold amount.

21. If one man slays another, the ordinary wergeld to be paid as compensation shall be 100 shillings.

23. If a homicide departs from the country, his relatives shall pay half the wergeld.

33. For seizing a man by the hair, 50 sceattas shall be paid as compensation.

[Fines for numerous injuries to parts of the body are listed.]

From the Laws of Wihtred, ca. 695 (Attenborough, pp. 25–27.)

1. The Church shall enjoy immunity from taxation.

3. Men living in illicit unions shall turn to a righteous life repenting of their sins, or they shall be excluded from the communion of the Church.

9. If a servant, contrary to his lord's command, does servile work between sunset on Saturday evening and sunset on Sunday evening, he shall pay 80 sceattas to his lord.

12. If a husband, without his wife's knowledge, makes offerings to devils, he shall forfeit all his goods or his *healsfang*.[106] If both [of

---

[106] Apparently the amount which constituted a first installment on the wergeld.

them] make offerings to devils they shall forfeit their *healsfangs* or all their goods.

From the Laws of Wessex: Ine, ca. 688–94 (Attenborough, pp. 37–41)

[Bishops Hedde and Erconweald and a convention of clergy aided King Ine and his council in the framing of these laws. A number of them are designed to protect the Church.]

2. A child shall be baptized within 30 days. If this is not done, [the guardian] shall pay 30 shillings compensation.

3. If a slave works on Sunday by his lord's command, he shall become free, and the lord shall pay a fine of 30 shillings.

11. If anyone sells one of his own countrymen, bond or free, over the sea, even though he be guilty, he shall pay for him with his wergeld and make full atonement with God[107] [for his crime].

From the Laws of Alfred the Great, ca. 890 (Attenborough, p. 67)

[The date of these laws is thought by Attenborough[108] to be some years earlier than that adopted by Liebermann, viz., 892–93. Alfred's laws were set down after a study of those of Ethelbert, Ine, and other English kings.]

5. §4. The privilege of sanctuary belonging to a church includes also the following: if anyone takes refuge in a church, because of any offense which up to that time had been kept secret, and there confesses his sin in God's name, half the punishment shall be remitted him.

5. §5. We decree that he who steals on Sunday, or during Christmas or Easter, or on Holy Thursday, or at Rogation Days, shall pay in each case double compensation, just as he must [if he steals] during Lent.

From the So-Called Laws of Edward and Guthrum, ca. 925 (Attenborough, p. 105)

4. And in the case of incestuous unions, the councillors have decided that the king shall take possession of the male offender, and the bishop the female offender, unless they make compensation before God and the world as the bishop shall prescribe, in accordance with the gravity of the offence.

---

[107] "& wið Godd deoplice bete."　　　[108] *Op. cit.*, p. 35.

From the Laws of Athelstan, 925(?)–39(?) (Attenborough pp. 141 f.)

I. 26. And if anyone swears a false oath and it becomes manifest he has done so, he shall never again have the right to swear an oath; and he shall not be buried in any consecrated burial ground when he dies, unless he has the testimony of the bishop, in whose diocese he is, that he has made such amends as his confessor has prescribed to him.

§1. And his confessor shall make known to the bishop within thirty days whether he has been willing to make amends. If he [the confessor] does not do so, he shall pay such compensation as the bishop is willing to allow him [to pay].

III. 3 (Latin: Liebermann I, 170). Thirdly, all[109] feelingly thank thee, their most beloved lord, for the favor thou hast granted to men who have forfeited,[110] that is, that the forfeiture shall be pardoned to all for every theft whatsoever, which was committed before the council of Faversham, on the condition that they ever after cease from every evil deed, and confess all their robbery and make amends between now and August.

From the Laws of Edmund, ca. 942–46 (Robertson, p. 7)

I. 3. If anyone sheds the blood of a Christian man, he shall not come anywhere near the king until he proceeds to do penance, as the bishop appoints for him or his confessor directs him.

6. Those who commit perjury and practice sorcery shall be cast out forever from the fellowship of God, unless they proceed with special zeal to undertake the prescribed penance.

From the Laws of Ethelred, ca. 1008 (Robertson, pp. 85, 87, 108, 115)

V. 22. And every Christian man . . . shall frequently go to confession, and freely confess his sins, and readily make amends as is prescribed for him.

29. And if any excommunicated man, unless it be one who is a suppliant for protection, remains anywhere near the king, before he has readily submitted to the amends required by the church, it shall be at the risk of [losing] his life or his possessions.

[109] That is, the bishops and councillors in Kent.

[110] Or "men who are forfeit." Athelstan's Laws, II, 1, 3, 7, have severe provisions including the capital penalty for theft. On the test of the ordeal men were put in prison for theft to be liberated only when compensation was fully made. Probably "forisfactis hominibus" and "forisfactura" here have reference to delinquency in these payments which presumably created a problem through the protracted imprisonment of many.

VII. 2. §1. [Latin: Liebermann I, 260.] [During the Monday, Tuesday and Wednesday before Michaelmas] every person shall go to confession, and barefooted, to the church, and in amendment and desistence [from them] shall renounce all his sins.

VII. 1. [Anglo-Saxon parallel to above: Robertson, p. 115.] It is our desire that the whole people, as a national penalty, [fast] on bread and herbs and water for three days, namely, on the Monday, Tuesday and Wednesday before Michaelmas.

2. And everyone shall come barefoot to church without gold or ornaments and shall go to confession.

From the Laws of Canute, ca. 1030 (Robertson, pp. 169, 195 ff.)

I. 18*b*. §1. *Concerning confession.*—But let us very zealously turn from sins, and let us all readily confess our misdeeds to our confessors and altogether cease [from evil] and zealously make amends.

II. 38. §1. And in all cases the greater a man is and the higher his rank, the more stringent shall be the amends which he shall be required to make to God and to men for lawless behavior.

§2. And ecclesiastical amends shall always be diligently exacted in accordance with the directions contained in the canon law, and secular amends in accordance with secular law.

39. [The slayer of a minister of the altar is to do penance and pay wergeld.]

§1. And he shall begin to make amends both to God and men within 30 days, under pain of forfeiting all that he possesses.

41. *Concerning men in holy orders.*—If a minister of the altar commits homicide or perpetrates any other great crime, he shall be deprived of his ecclesiastical office and banished, and shall travel as a pilgrim as far as the pope appoints for him, and zealously make amends. . . .

§2. And unless he begins to make amends both to God and men within 30 days, he shall be outlawed.

44. If a condemned man desires confession, it shall never be refused him.

4. SELECTIONS FROM FRANKISH AND VISIGOTHIC LAW

[IN THE Frankish territories Church and State were so closely associated that civil legislation cannot always be clearly distinguished from ecclesiastical. The following extracts from the laws of Frankish kings and emperors will indicate how the civil power, as a matter of course, supported and reinforced the ecclesiastical discipline of penance. It is of interest to observe, for example, how, at the demand of an imperial capitulary, the ecclesiastical authorities prepared (*ca.* 803) lists of topics for the examination of ordinands. In each of the extant schedules of this class a penitential is included (p. 390). It is not specified which of the numerous available penitentials is to be used; and about 813 the question "Which penitential?" is raised, only to be left to subsequent inquiry, in an uncompleted draft of a capitulary of Charlemagne (p. 391). In that year, however, the council of Chalon, as has already been noted, in vigorous epithets denounced all penitentials and demanded their complete abandonment.[111] The position of the government seems to have been definitely favorable to the use of penitentials, though no one document was selected as authoritative. The government alliance with the Church in the assertion of the claims of excommunication is well illustrated by King Arnulf's response to the clergy at Tivoli, 895 (p. 391).]

Capitulary of Carloman, Following a Synod Held under Boniface, 742.
M.G.H., Leges, II, i, 25; *Concilia,* II, i, 3. Mansi, XII, 366

1. . . . We ordain that [Boniface and his clergy] assemble a synod each year, so that in our presence the decrees of the canons and the laws of the Church may be reëstablished and the Christian religion reformed. And church property fraudulently taken we restore and return to the churches. We remove from church emoluments and degrade false priests and adulterous or licentious deacons and clerics and compel them to penance.

2. We prohibit all the servants of God without exception from carrying armor or fighting or going at all into the army or against the enemy, except only those who are chosen for this purpose on account of the divine ministry, namely, to perform the solemn rites of masses and to bring the patronage[112] of the saints. That is: the commander in chief shall have with him one or two bishops, with chaplain priests, and each general one priest, who shall be able to adjudge and state the penance for men confessing their sins. And we also forbid to all the priests of God those huntings and wanderings with dogs in the woods; likewise let them not have hawks[113] and falcons.

6. We ordain likewise, that after this synod (which took place on

---

[111] See above, p. 27.
[112] "patrocinia"—protection (plural).
[113] "acceptores" for "accipitres," as sometimes in late classical Latin.

the twenty-first of April),[114] when any one of the servants of God or handmaidens of Christ has fallen into the crime of fornication, he [or she] shall do penance in prison on bread and water. And if [the offender] is an ordained presbyter he shall remain two years in prison, and beforehand he shall appear whipped and scourged, and afterward the bishop shall add [to this penalty]. But if a cleric or a monk falls into this sin, after three whippings he shall be put in prison and shall do penance there during the course of a year. Likewise veiled nuns shall be restrained with the same penance, and all the hair of their heads shall be shorn.

The First Capitulary of Charlemagne, ca. 769. M.G.H., Leges, II, i, 45.

1. [All participation of priests in war is forbidden, but] the commander shall have with him one or two bishops with their chaplain priests and each prefect one priest who can judge persons who confess their sins and indicate the penance.

7. We determine that every bishop carefully visit his diocese each year and that he take pains to confirm the people and to teach and examine the parishioners and to prohibit pagan celebrations and diviners or soothsayers or auguries, amulets, incantations, and all kinds of pagan filth.

10. We decree that priests take great care for the incestuous and criminals, lest they perish in their wickedness and their souls be required of them [the priests] by Christ, the severe judge. Likewise of the infirm and penitents, that when they die they may not pass away without the anointing with consecrated oil and reconciliation and the viaticum.

Capitulary for the Saxon Territories, 775–90. M.G.H., Leges, II, i, 68 f.

4. If anyone out of disrespect for Christianity despises the holy lenten fast, and eats flesh, he shall be put to death; but yet it shall be taken under consideration by a priest whether perchance it happens to anyone that he has eaten flesh by reason of necessity.

6. If anyone, deceived by the devil, believes after the manner of the pagans that any man or woman is a witch and eats men, and if on this account he burns [the alleged witch] or gives her flesh to be eaten or eats it, he shall be punished by capital sentence.

---

[114] The editors suppose that this clause, "quae fuit XI Kalendas Maias," was added later when the capitula were combined with the canons of the council of Lestines (745).

14. If, however, on account of these mortal crimes which he has secretly committed anyone voluntarily flees to a priest, and making his confession, is willing to do penance, on the priest's testimony he shall be exempted from death.

21. If anyone makes a vow at springs or trees or groves, or makes any offering according to the custom of the pagans and partakes of a meal in honor of the demons, if he is a noble he shall pay sixty solidi, if a freeman, thirty, if a villain,[115] fifteen. If indeed they have not the wherewithal to pay at once, they shall be given over to the service of the church until these solidi are paid.

From a Capitulary of Charlemagne, 803. M.G.H., Leges, II, i, 113 (repeated p. 428)

1. Of the murderers of clerics. If anyone slays a subdeacon he shall make composition with three hundred solidi; he who slays a deacon, four hundred; he who slays a presbyter, six hundred; he who slays a bishop, nine hundred solidi. He who slays a monk shall be judged guilty to the extent of four hundred solidi.

Examination Questions for Ordinands. M.G.H., Leges, II, i, 234 f., 237

[The Capitulary of the Missi, 803, cap. 2, required that priests should be examined before ordination. On these pages are given two lists of questions or topics of examination, probably prepared shortly afterward. (Cf. the lists of Ghaerbald of Liége and of Heito of Basel, *ibid.*, pp. 243, 363.) The former of the two lists calls for examination on the Creed, the Lord's Prayer, the Canons, the Penitential, the Missal, the Gospel, Homilies, the Divine Office, and the Baptistry. No. 3 of these questions is:]

How you know or understand the penitential?

[The second list differs considerably from the first, and contains references to the Sacramentary, the Computus, or manual for computing the movable feasts, and the *Pastoral Care* of Gregory the Great. No. 7 mentions:]

The penitential.

[From a list of requirements for the priesthood framed in some diocesan synod.]

That he be instructed in the canons and know his penitential well.

---

[115] "litus," elsewhere "letus," "latus," "lazzus." Cf. A. S. "laet," member of an agricultural class below freemen and superior to slaves.

*From a Capitulary of Bishop Ghaerbald of Liége, 802–10, cap. 9.
M.G.H., Leges, II, i, 243*

That everyone, so far as he is able, make sure of the equipment of his church, namely, in respect to the paten and the chalice, the chasuble and the alb, the Missal, Lectionary, Martyrology, Penitential, Psalter, or other books that he can [obtain], the cross, the reliquary;[116] as we have said: so far as he is able.

*From an Uncompleted Draft of a Capitulary of Charlemagne, ca. 813.
M.G.H., Leges, II, i, 179*

15. That every presbyter shall have a schedule[117] of the major and the minor vices, by means of which he shall be able to recognize [them] or to preach [about them] to those under him, that they may avoid the snares of the devil.

20. Concerning the determination of penance: we leave for inquiry by what penitential or in what manner penitents shall be judged. And concerning incestuous persons [we leave for inquiry] who are permitted to form unions, who are not.

*From a Capitulary of the Missi, Attigni, 854, no. 8. M.G.H., Leges,
II, ii, 278*

Of men who have been put under the ban and under penance, and who always behave worse; assuredly they are to be taken by the Missi and put in confinement.

A Law of Ludwig II, 845–50. M.G.H., Leges, II, ii, 83

Through the several parishes the people shall be diligent to observe those festivals which their own bishop proclaims to be celebrated, so that they shall neither neglect those things which their priests admonish them to cultivate nor in vain superstition presume to celebrate those which are by no means to be observed. If, indeed, any are found who refuse compliance to their priests they shall be detained by the officers of the state and compelled to undergo the satisfaction of penance which the priests may impose.

Council of Tivoli, 895, cap. 3. M.G.H., Leges, II, ii, 214 f.

The King's[118] answer, and general statement on excommunicated persons. We, therefore, to whom have been committed the care of

---

[116] "capsa."   [117] "capitula," a list by chapters. Perhaps a penitential is meant.
[118] Arnulf's.

the realm and the responsibility for the churches of Christ, are not otherwise able to rule and govern the kingdom and empire in ecclesiastical justice, unless with the zeal of faith we hunt down those who throw into disorder Christ's "church not having spot or wrinkle," as the Apostle saith"[119] . . . Therefore, not displaying power, but showing forth justice, we command and by our authority enjoin upon all counts of our realm, that after they are stricken with the anathema of excommunication and yet are not inclined to do penance they shall be arrested by these [officers] and brought before us, so that they who revere not the divine judgments shall be smitten with human sentences, as[120] it is said by a certain wise man: "The king that sitteth upon the throne of judgment scattereth away all evil with his look."[121] For if they so rise up as rebels that they attempt to resist those who arrest them and are killed in this foolhardiness, no penance shall be inflicted on their slayers by judgment of the bishops, and by our command no composition of wergeld shall be exacted from them; and their neighbors and relatives shall be bound with an oath not to take vengeance for them on the slayers, but to observe peace and concord toward them.

Laws of Receswinth, ca. 666. Lex Visigothorum, VI, 5, 13. M.G.H., Leges, I, 278 f.

We decree that any master or mistress who without the investigation of a judge and evidence of a crime cuts off a manservant's or maidservant's hand, nose, lip, tongue, even ear, or foot, or gouges out an eye, or cuts off any part of the body, or commands that such be cut off or pulled out, shall be bound under penance in an exile of three years with the bishop in whose diocese[122] he appears to reside, or with him in whose diocese the deed appears to have been committed.

5. NOTE ON PENITENTIAL PROVISIONS IN NORSE LAW

[A CONSIDERABLE number of references to penance occur in the Gulathing Law and the Frostathing Law of eleventh and twelfth century Norway. These collections have been translated by L. M. Larson.[123] In

---

[119] Eph. 5:27.   [120] "unde," literally, "whence."
[121] Prov. 20:8.   [122] "territorio."
[123] *The Earliest Norwegian Laws, being the Gulathing Law and the Frostathing Law.* Translated from the Old Norwegian. Columbia University Press, New York, 1935. (Records of Civilization: Sources and Studies, XX.)

the Gulathing code penance is demanded for labor on Sunday; for refusing to fast on Friday; for eating horse-flesh; for leaving a corpse un-
buried; for marriage within the prohibited degrees; for sorcery and
witchcraft; for heathen sacrifices; and for eating the flesh of animals
that have died of themselves.[124] The Church Law of Archbishop Eystein,[125] which forms a part of the Law of the Frostathing, and is to be
dated not later than 1080, the year of the bishop's exile, requires penance
for eating flesh on Friday, and for cohabitation on days in which it is
prohibited by the Church.[126] The references to penance in these documents are, however, relatively few. Many offenses which under Frankish
law would subject the doer to penance along with non-ecclesiastical
satisfactions have here assigned to them penalties only of the latter sort.
Even in those instances in which the Norse laws require penance they
fail to indicate its duration and nature.]

[124] *Op. cit.*, pp. 45–58.   [125] See above, p. 354.   [126] *Op. cit.*, pp. 241, 249.

CHAPTER IX

Synodical Decisions and Ecclesiastical Opinions relating to the Penitentials

1. FROM THE CANONS OF THE COUNCIL OF CLOVESHOE (747)

[THE FOLLOWING extract from canon 27 of the council of Cloveshoe illustrates the rise of vicarious penance, an abuse connected with certain relaxations permitted in some of the penitentials. The council was held under Cuthbert, archbishop of Canterbury, in 747. The text of this paragraph is found in Wilkins, *Concilia*, I, 99; Mansi, XII, 406; and Haddan and Stubbs, III, 373 f. The canon is entitled: "Of the profitableness of the sacred psalmody."]

[Sinners are to fast and sing psalms in person, not vicariously, though they are to invite the intercession of as many of the servants of God as possible.]

We must discuss this matter the more at length for the reason that recently a certain man rich according to this world, seeking to have reconciliation speedily accorded him for some grave sin he had committed, asserted in writing that this same misdeed, as he had been assured by many persons, was so fully expiated that if he should be able to live yet three hundred years the [requirement regarding] fasting would have been fully met by these means of satisfaction; namely, the psalmody, fasting, and alms of others, without fasting on his own part, and no matter how little he should fast. Therefore, if the divine justice can be appeased by others in this way, why, ye foolish boasters, are rich men—who are able with bribes to purchase the limitless fastings of others for their own offenses—said by the voice of Truth to enter the Kingdom of Heaven with more difficulty than a camel goes through a needle's eye?[1]

[1] Matt. 19:24.

2. FROM THE CAPITULARIES OF THEODULF
OF ORLEANS (*ca.* 798)

[THE LEARNED ecclesiastic Theodulf, *ca.* 760–821, was a Spanish Visigoth who distinguished himself at the court of Charlemagne, and, at an uncertain date before 798, became bishop of Orléans. In an effort to reform the clergy of this diocese, he issued two capitularies in sections of which instruction is given for the administration of the penitential discipline. Theodulf favors the principles of the ancient canons, which demanded public penance for capital sins. Watkins regards him as definitely opposed to the penitentials, and "the originator and guide of the anti-penitential party which in a few years will find a voice in the council of Chalon."[2] He may have imparted an impulse in this direction, but the antithesis is not so sharply drawn in his mind as this judgment would indicate. On the same page Dr. Watkins states that Theodulf "nowhere makes any direct mention of the penitentials." In his second capitulary, however, the bishop authorizes a judicious and guarded use of some unidentified "penitentiale"[3] as an aid to the priest in obtaining a full confession.

Capitulary I was translated into Anglo-Saxon in the late tenth century. The Anglo-Saxon version is given by B. Thorpe, with an English translation, in *Ancient Laws of England*, II, 394–443, under the title "Ecclesiastical Institutes." A. S. Napier has edited it from the Bodleian Codex 865 (early eleventh century) partly Latin and partly Anglo-Saxon text in *Early English Text Society, Original Series* 150 (1916). This Anglo-Saxon version is quite independent of that of Thorpe. In the following extracts from Capitulary I, the paragraph numbers are followed by the column references in Migne, *P.L.*, CV. In Capitulary II, paragraph numbering is lacking, and the column reference alone appears.]

I. xxvi. [col. 199.] Priests should warn against the grave sin of perjury for we hear that certain persons lightly estimate this crime and impose a relatively slight measure of penance upon perjurers. They ought to know that the penance to be imposed for perjury is such as is imposed for adultery, for fornication, for homicide, and for the other criminal faults. If, then, anyone who has committed perjury or any criminal sin, fearing the protracted hardship of penance refuses to come to confession, he is to be cast out of the Church, or from the communion and society of the faithful, so that no one shall either eat or drink or pray with him, or receive him into his house.

I. xxx. [col. 200.] [We ought to confess our sins frequently every day to God with tears, using the fiftieth or the twenty-fourth or the

<hr/>

[2]Watkins, II, 695.   [3] See below, p. 397.

thirty-first or another penitential psalm.] For the confession which we make to priests also brings to us this advantage that receiving from them salutary counsel, the most health-giving observances of penance, or mutual prayers, we wash away the stains of sins. But the confession which we make to God alone helps in this way, that in so far as we are mindful of our sins, God is forgetful of them, and on the other hand in so far as we are forgetful of them, God remembers.

I. xxxi. [col. 201.] Confessions are to be given for all the sins that are committed either in act or in thought. [The eight principal vices are enumerated.] When, therefore, anyone comes to confession [the priest] ought diligently to inquire how and on what occasion he committed the sin which he confesses that he has done, and he ought to indicate the penance according to the measure of the deed.

I. xxxvi. [col. 203.] One week before the beginning of Lent confessions are to be given to the priests, the penance is to be received, persons disagreeing are to be reconciled, and all contentions composed; and they ought to forgive one another their debts . . . And so, entering the season of the blessed Lent, they shall approach holy Eastertide with their minds clean and purified and renew themselves by penance, which is the second baptism. For as baptism purges sins, so does penance. And since after baptism the sinner cannot be baptized again, this remedy of penance is given by the Lord that by it instead of a second baptism post-baptismal sins may be washed away. [Here follow the seven remissions of sin. See above p. 99, n. 5.]

II. [col. 211.] But as the medicine of sin is to be applied, it ought to be according to the canons of authentic holy fathers, not according to the pleasure of a man, nor according to his will. And in this concern the will or favor of man is not to be striven for, but the will of God is to be sought out in all the Holy Scriptures. . . . Capital and mortal offenses are to be publicly bewailed, according to the institution of the canons and of the holy fathers. But we do not deny that mortal offenses may be pardoned also by secret satisfaction—the intent of the mind having first been changed, however . . . The measure of penance, to be sure, depends on the decision of the priest. The priest, most diligently examining and comprehending the determinations of the holy fathers, ought to state the penance according to their authority for those making confession. Truly the authority of the canons and of the holy fathers is a very firm foundation.

[Penalties for a variety of offenses are here laid down on the principle of public penance for public sins and secret penance for secret sins.]

[col. 219.] But he who makes confession shall bend his knees with the priest before God and then confess whatever he is able to recall from his youth—his behavior in all particulars. And if he cannot recall all his misdeeds, or if perchance he hesitates, the priest ought to ask him whatever is set down in the penitential—whether he has fallen into this offense or another. But, nevertheless, not all the offenses ought to be made known to him, since many faults are read in the penitential which it is not becoming for the man to know. Therefore the priest ought not to question him about them all, lest perchance, when he has gone away from him, at the devil's persuasion he fall into some one of those offenses of which he previously did not know.

3. FROM THE LETTERS OF ALCUIN OF YORK

[ALCUIN (ca. 735–804), the scholar of York and leader of the educational and ecclesiastical reform under Charlemagne, does not refer specifically to the penitentials. His interest in promoting confession of sins to priests is apparent especially in his letters "to the dear brethren and fathers in the Gothic province" (Septimania) and "to the most noble sons of Holy Church in Ireland." The extracts given below from these documents are in *M.G.H., Epistolae Karol. aevi.*, II, 216–18, 438; they are also found in Migne, *P.L.*, C, 338–39, 502.]

From Alcuin's Letter to the Goths of Septimania, ca. 798

[Alcuin urges confession to priests, which he has learned is neglected in the Gothic province.]

If thou sayest: "It is good to confess to the Lord":[4] yet it is good to have a witness of this confession. . . . Greatly hast thou offended thy Lord, and wilt thou not have another reconciler except thyself? . . . . Ought we not in sacred baptism to give to the priests of Christ confession of our faith and renunciation of Satan and so be washed from all sins through the priestly ministry, by the operation of divine grace? Why then in the second baptism of penance also ought we not to be absolved likewise with priestly help, the same divine grace being pitiful, from all the sins committed after the first baptism.

---

[4] Ps. 91:2. Douay version has "give praise" for "confiteri."

If sins are not exposed to the priests, why are the prayers of reconciliation written in the sacramentary? How shall the priest reconcile one whom he does not know to be a sinner?

From Alcuin's Letter to the Irish, ca. 792–804

And no one, senior or junior, secular or monastic, man or woman, shall hesitate to confess his sins and to make amends by penance for whatever he has done against God's will. It is better to have one man a witness of his sins unto the salvation of his soul than to look for the accusation of devilish deceit before the Judge of all the ages and before the choirs of angels and the multitude of the whole human race. Indeed, while a man lives in this world confession and penance are fruitful; in the judgment that is to come there will forsooth be penance, but one that is not fruitful, since everyone shall be judged according to his works.[5]

4. FROM THE SO-CALLED CONSTITUTIONS OF BONIFACE (*ca.* 813–40)

[THE SO-CALLED *Statuta Bonifacii* has been with some probability ascribed by Seckel[6] to a Bavarian synod of the period 800–40. Seckel shows that in its complete form it cannot be earlier than 813. The following extracts indicate a departure from the ancient or "canonical" discipline in reconciliation and an approximation to the procedure of the penitentials. On the ascription of other penitential writings to Boniface see pp. 218, 232. The document is in Mansi, XII, 386.]

xxxi. And since we are prevented by a variety of circumstances[7] from observing in full the canonical regulations regarding the reconciliation of penitents, it is not for this reason to be entirely set aside. Every priest will take care, immediately after receiving the confession of penitents, that they be severally reconciled, with the prayer appointed. Indeed, to those who are dying the communion and reconciliation are to be offered without delay.

xxxii. He who during illness asks for penance, if it happens that while the priest who has been invited is coming [he is] overcome with weakness and becomes speechless or passes into delirium, those who

---

[5] Cf. Prov. 24:12.
[6] "Benedictus Levita und die sogenannte Statuta quaedam S. Bonifacii," in *Neues Archiv f. ältere deutsche Geschichtskunde*, XXIX (1904), 308–24, and XXXV (1910), 119. Cf. Poschmann II, p. 112 f.; Fournier et Le Bras, I, 113.
[7] Literally, "a various necessity."

hear him shall bear witness, and he shall receive penance. And if he is continually believed to be about to die, he shall be reconciled by imposition of hands and the Eucharist shall be thrust into his mouth. If he survives he shall be notified by the above-mentioned witnesses of the fulfillment of his request, and he shall be subjected to the rules of penance for such time as the priest who administers the penance shall approve.

xxxiii. If any presbyter or cleric observes auguries or divinations or dreams or lots or phylacteries, that is [magical] writings, let him be prepared to undergo the penalties of the canons.

5. FROM FRANKISH COUNCILS OF THE EARLY NINTH CENTURY

[IN MAY AND JUNE, 813, Charlemagne assembled councils at Arles, Reims, Mainz, Chalon-sur-Saône, and Tours; and their findings were, it would appear, presented to a general convention of bishops for the Frankish territories held shortly afterward at Aachen, as our selection from the canons of Tours indicates. We have no canons which are indubitably the findings of the Aachen synod. Watkins would ascribe to it the canons quoted from an uncompleted draft of a capitulary of about 813, cited above, p. 391. The decisions of these provincial councils on penance, especially those referring specifically to the penitentials, reveal the conflict between the advocates of the ancient penance and the priests who were following the penitential manuals. For a discussion of this controversy see especially Watkins, II, 700 ff.[8] The unsuccessful but persistent activity of the campaign against the penitentials launched at Chalon in 813, is indicated by the decision of the council of Paris, 829, to put all these soul-destroying booklets to the flames. The stated objections to them are mainly their lack of authority and their laxity as compared with the ancient canons.]

The Council of Arles, 813, Can. 26. *M.G.H.*, *Concilia*, II, i, 253; Mansi, XIV, 62

That those who have been convicted of public crime shall be publicly sentenced for it and shall do public penance according to the canons.

The Council of Reims, 813. *M.G.H.*, *Concilia*, II, i, 255 f.; Mansi, XIV, 78, 80

12. In all these proceedings the method of penance was discussed,

---

[8] Selections from the canons are given by Watkins pp. 674 ff.; some of these are translated, pp. 702 ff.

so that the priests should more fully understand how they ought to receive confessions and indicate penance to the penitents according to the canonical institution.

13. The scheme of the eight principal sins was discussed, that everyone might know the variations of these and know how with God's help to guard himself from them and to preach to others [on the subject].

16. That bishops and presbyters examine how they may estimate the sins of confessants and set the time of their penance.

31. That discrimination between penitents be observed—who should do penance publicly and who secretly.

The Council of Mainz, 813. *M.G.H., Concilia*, II, i, 272; Mansi, XIV, 75

46. That the evil of drunkenness by all means be avoided. We command to beware in every way of the great evil of drunkenness, from which all the vices crop out; but as for him who refuses to shun it, we decree that he be excommunicated until [he shall make] suitable amendment.

53. Of incestuous persons. We command that bishops by all means take pains in like manner to examine incestuous persons. And if they refuse to do penance they shall be expelled from the church until they come back for penance.

The Council of Chalon, 813. *M.G.H., Concilia*, II, i, 278 ff.; Mansi, XIV, 98 ff.

24. In the case of bishops, presbyters, deacons, and monks who have been slain, it is for the lord emperor to inquire to whom the murder-price is to be paid.

25. In many places the doing of penance according to the ancient institution of the canons has lapsed from use, and neither is the order of the ancient custom of reconciliation observed: let help be sought from the lord emperor, that if anyone sins publicly he may be punished by public penance and be excommunicated and reconciled in accordance with his deserts according to the order of the canons.

32. But we have also found that this is in need of amendment, that some when they confess their sins to the priests do not confess them in full. Since therefore it is the case that man is of two substances, namely, soul and body, and since sometimes sin arises from

a motion of the mind, sometimes by the feebleness of the flesh, those sins ought to be searched out with careful inquiry, that there may be a full confession from both, that is to say, that they confess both these things which are done through the body and those in which the fault is in thought alone. The confessor of his sins is therefore to be instructed to make confession concerning the eight principal sins, without which one may hardly live in this life, since prompted by these, he has sinned either in thought, or in deed (which is more serious). Truly, the more subtly hatred, envy, pride, or other such pests of the soul creep about, the more dangerously they hurt.

33. Some say that sins ought to be confessed to God alone; others, however, hold that they should be confessed to priests; both of which are practiced within Holy Church, not without much fruit. [Ps. 31:5, 6, and James 5:16 are cited in support of each, respectively.] The confession, then, which is made to God purges away sins; that which is made to a priest teaches how these same sins may be purged away. For God the author and dispenser of salvation and health and of many things, supplies this by the invisible ministration of his power and by the work of many physicians.

34. Since, therefore, on the testimony of the Apostle, "there is no respect of persons with God,"[9] and it is to be avoided in all judgments, much more ought it to be shunned in this judgment of penance, that no priest should ever, through either favor or hatred of anyone's person, judge otherwise than what he finds in the sacred canons or what seems to him just according to the authority of the Holy Scriptures and the custom of the Church. If, therefore, physicians who try to apply medicine to bodies never, through respect of anyone's person, spare, to those whom they desire to cure, cautery or knife or any other severities, much more is [this principle] to be observed by those who are physicians not of bodies but of souls. For the penance is not to be calculated by the duration of time, but by the ardor of the mind and the mortification of the body. But a contrite and a humble heart God will not despise.[10]

38. Moreover, the measure of penance to those who confess their sins ought to be imposed, as was said above, either by the institution of the ancient canons, or by the authority of the Holy Scriptures, or by ecclesiastical custom, the booklets which they call ";peniten-

[9] Cf. Rom. 2:11.   [10] Ps. 50:19.

tials" being repudiated and utterly cast out, of which the errors are obvious, the authors undetermined;[11] of which it might be fitly said: They slew souls which should not have died and saved souls alive which should not have lived;[12] which, while they inflict certain light and strange sentences of penance for grave sins, according to the prophetic word, "sew cushions under every elbow and make pillows for the heads of persons of every age, to catch souls."[13]

The Council of Tours, 813, Can. 22. *M.G.H., Concilia*, II, i, 289; Mansi, XIV, 86

The bishops and presbyters are to discuss with careful forethought how they shall assign the time of abstinence to those who confess to them their faults, so that the abstinence may be determined according to the degree of the sin, since these decisions are presented with variation by different priests, and undiscerningly. Hence, it seems to us necessary, that when all the bishops shall have assembled to the sacred palace[14] they should give instruction concerning whose penitential book, of those written by the men of old, is preferably to be followed.

The Council of Paris, 829, Can. 32. *M.G.H., Concilia*, II, ii, 633; Mansi, XIV, 559

That the booklets which they call "penitentials" be wholly abolished, since they are opposed to the authority of the canons.

Since many priests, partly by carelessness, partly by ignorance, impose the measure of penance upon those who confess their state of sin at variance with what the canonical laws decree, making use, forsooth, of certain booklets written in opposition to canonical authority, which they call "penitentials," and on this account they do not cure the wounds of sinners but rather bathe and stroke them, illustrating[15] this prophecy: "Woe to them that sew cushions under every elbow and make pillows to catch souls,"[16] to all of us in common it seemed salutary that each one of the bishops in his diocese diligently seek out these erroneous booklets and when they are found give them to the flames, that through them unskilled priests may no longer deceive men. Moreover, priests who either by reason of reward

---

[11] "certi errores, incerti auctores."   [12] Cf. Ezek. 13:19.   [13] Ezek. 13:18.
[14] That is, at Aachen, where a general meeting was to be held shortly after this and the other provincial councils (May–June). Cf. Watkins, II, 706 ff.
[15] Literally, "falling into."   [16] Ezek. 13:18.

or of affection or of fear or, indeed, of partiality, fix the times and the measure of the penance according to the will of the penitents, shall hearken to what the Lord terribly saith by the prophet Ezekiel [Ezek. 13:8–10, 18–19, quoted]. Unskilled priests, also, are to be informed with careful attention by their bishops, how they may know both how to inquire the sins of confessants discreetly, and how to impose on them a suitable measure of penance according to canonical authority; since hitherto, through their carelessness and ignorance the wickedness of many remains unpunished, and there is no doubt that this is conducive to the ruin of souls.

The Council of Mainz, 852, Can. 11. *M.G.H., Leges,* II, ii, 189

Of homicide.—If four or five or even more make a quarrel against one man, and if he is wounded by them and dies, according to the determinations of the canons,[17] if each of them inflicted a blow, [each] shall be judged as a homicide and shall undergo a penance of seven years, that is, he shall immediately do penance for forty days on bread and water and beans and vegetables; he shall abstain from his wife and from entering the church; then, for three years he shall abstain from flesh, wine, mead, and honeyed beer, except on feast days and in serious weakness; further, for the remaining four [years], in the appointed fast days of each week and in the three forty-day periods of each year, he shall abstain from flesh only. [Albgis, who has run away to Moravia with the wife of Patrichus, is assigned a seven-year penance with certain disabilities lasting throughout life. Batto, charged with five murders, is to abstain from marriage and continue in penance throughout life.]

6. FROM THE PENITENTIAL WRITINGS OF RABAN MAUR

[RABAN MAUR (784–856), pupil of Alcuin and teacher in the monastery of Fulda where he was abbot, 822–42, became archbishop of Mainz in 847. His extensive but largely dependent writings include a work entitled *The Training of Clerics*[18] (*ca.* 819) and two treatises on penance: a *Penitential*[19] (*ca.* 841) addressed to Heribald, bishop of Auxerre; and the

---

[17] Council of Elvira (305), can. 5. Mansi, II, 6.
[18] *De clericorum institutione.* Migne, *P.L.*, CVII, 293–419; *De institutione clericorum libri tres,* ed. A. Knoepfler, Munich, 1901.
[19] *Poenitentiale,* Migne, *P.L.*, CX, 467–94.

Book of Penitents[20] (*ca.* 842) addressed to Otgar, his predecessor in the see of Mainz.

In the *Training of Clerics* Raban advocates public penance for public sins and secret penance for secret sins which are revealed only to the bishop or priest, "lest the weak in the Church be scandalized, seeing the penalties of those of whose cases they are entirely ignorant."[21] This work contains an elaborate exposition of the cure of sins by their contrary penalties, a principle employed in the penitentials, as we have seen, and derived from Cassian.[22]

The penitential is largely composed of extracts from the councils and Fathers. Raban resorts, however, to the *Penitential of Theodore* to resolve a question regarding a magical potion: "For concerning those who practice the magical art and give attention to auguries, we have the constitutions of Theodore, archbishop of the race of the English, in which it is written . . . " and he quotes Theodore, I, xv, 1–4.[23]

The *Book of Penitents* is of similar content to the previous work and represents an attempt to restore as far as possible the ancient usages.

In a letter to Humbert, bishop of Würzburg, written in 842, Raban, in treating of the question of the prohibited degrees of consanguinity in a marriage, says:

> Likewise also in the capitula of Theodore, archbishop of the race of the English, we find what things he wrote regarding the matters necessary: that according to the Greeks it is permitted to marry in the third degree of consanguinity, but in the fifth according to the Romans; who, however, do not dissolve marriages made in the third degree if they have been previously contracted by parties who were unaware [of the rule]. Of the same conditions [people] are joined in marriage to those related to them as [one is joined] to relatives of his wife after his wife's death.[24] But this Theodore, a native of Tarsus in Cilicia, Pope Vitalian ordained a bishop at Rome and sent to Britain: hence, he was also fully grounded in the customs of the Eastern churches and there could not be concealed from him any of the things which the Greeks and Romans of that time had in authorized observance—especially since he was perfectly instructed in both languages.][25]

7. FROM A NINTH-CENTURY TRACT ON COMPOSITION

[SCHMITZ published from a Munich codex, Monac. Codex Lat. 3909, which he assigned to the twelfth century, a set of regulations for composition. The document is associated in the manuscript with the two works of Raban Maur on penance referred to above, p. 403 f. The con-

---

[20] *Liber poenitentium*, Migne, *P.L.*, CXII, 1397–1424.
[21] *De. cl. inst.*, II, 30. Migne, *P.L.*, CVII, 342.
[22] *De. cl. inst.*, II, 38, Migne, *P.L.*, CVII, 415 ff. Cf. p. 179 and n. 5, above.
[23] *Poenitentiale* II, xxx. Migne, *P.L.*, CX, 491.
[24] "according . . . death" is a close paraphrase of the *Penitential of Theodore*, II, xii, 26–28.   [25] Migne, *P.L.*, CX, 1085 f.

tents suggest a ninth century date, and Schmitz regards the fragment as belonging to that period.[26] It offers a remarkable explanation of the development of protective composition for the clergy, with illustrations from what purports to be Frankish law.][27]

Of the Composition of Sacrilegious Persons

Composition is, properly speaking, any satisfaction by which each culprit settles for any misdeed. For whether this satisfaction is affliction of body or mind, or a sum of money, whatever is rendered by the culprit for the misdeed committed is rightly called composition; since over against the deed committed, one, as it were, of equal weight is set. In this it appears that just as the bond of concord is dissolved when the damage is incurred, so it is forged anew when the satisfaction is undertaken. At the time when the emperor Charles instituted composition for the murder of clerics, he who killed a presbyter was not compelled to pay anything for the grade of the diaconate or the subdiaconate, since nothing was commanded concerning a presbyter but only this: He who kills a presbyter shall pay in composition six hundred solidi.[28] But on this account composition was then ordered by the emperor Charles to be paid only for the grade of the presbyter—the composition of a presbyter for his diaconate and subdiaconate being passed over in silence—because the hot rage of wicked men did not yet so fiercely strive to rend the sacred order. But after that rage so burned everywhere that it was regarded as a trifle and esteemed a small matter to destroy anyone in sacred orders, princes not unreasonably saw fit to command by their edicts that if a presbyter was killed or suffered under any false accusation, they would exact compositions for each several antecedent grade, so, you see, in one and the same person, separate compositions for every grade are paid, as is shown in the capitulary of King Charles, chapter 29.

For it is ordered in this document:

If anyone inflicts any injury or dishonor upon a bishop he shall make composition for a life, and everything that he possessed shall be bestowed upon the church of which [the bishop] is the recognized head;

[26] Schmitz I, p. 736. Text, pp. 737–74.

[27] For the other manuscripts, and the spurious character of the documents, see M.G.H., Concilia, II, ii, 834–35, and the literature there cited.

[28] M.G.H., Leges, II, i, 113 (ca. 803). Repeated in a collection of ca. 827, ibid., p. 428. Cf. ibid., pp. 361 f., and Mansi, XIV, 273.

and to us thrice the ban, that is, sixty[29] solidi, shall be paid; or he shall be attached in service to our fisc to serve continually until he is able to redeem himself according to his wergeld thrice over. Holy Church consists in her priests; wherefore they who do injury to, or bring contumely upon, bishops or other priests, are heavily punished. For the maligning of priests touches Christ, since they function in the Church in his stead and at his delegation. If anyone distresses [?] or despoils or cudgels a presbyter, he shall make composition in this way: He shall be compelled to pay the several compositions for the several grades. For the grade of an acolyte he shall pay two hundred solidi; for that of an exorcist, the same. As also for that of a janitor and that of a reader, together with the ban and the guilt incurred[30] from [injury to] these grades. Next, the composition for a subdeacon is three hundred solidi, together with the ban and the guilt incurred. For a deacon, it is four hundred solidi with the ban and the offense incurred. For a presbyter, however, it is six hundred solidi with the ban and the guilt incurred. It ought not, then, to be ambiguous to us now, that if a presbyter is killed or dishonored, the several compositions ought lawfully to be paid for all the grades that are comprised in his.[31] Therefore the composition of a presbyter shall be one hundred and five librae. The six hundred solidi for the presbyterate and four hundred for the diaconate taken together make one thousand solidi, that is, fifty librae. But the three hundred solidi for the subdiaconate and eight hundred for the other four grades make one thousand one hundred solidi. It shall be, therefore, as was said above, one hundred and five librae[32] besides[33] the ban. Moreover, the ban[34] is multiplied by seven for the seven grades and makes twenty-one librae; and so the total composition for a presbyter is one hundred and twenty-six[35] librae. Now the forty-day periods[36] which are ordered to be multiplied as many times make twenty-one; for the six for a presbyter, four for a deacon, three for a subdeacon make thirteen;[37] then two computed for each grade amount to eight; therefore the forty-day periods multiplied in this manner make twenty-one.[38]

[29] Reading "III id est LX" for "III. I. LX."

[30] "bannum et facinus . . . illatum."

[31] "qui sunt in eo" (that are in him).

[32] Here the words "as was said above" are repeated.

[33] Reading "praeter" for "propter."

[34] The "bannus" was redeemed by a payment of sixty solidi or three librae. This is provided in numerous documents of the Carolingians. The reference is of course to the "bannus imperialis": the missi were also authorized to employ the "bannus"; and, in some documents, to put their own value on its redemption. Cf. *M.G.H.*, *Leges*, II, ii, 300.

[35] Reading "et VI" for "et CI."

[36] "karrinae". The forms "carena", "carina" are more common. See above, p. 325, n. 19.

[37] The text has "XIIII."

[38] The council of Thionville (821?) provides—with compositions similar to those here stated—five forty-day periods of penance ("quadragesimae") for the murder of a subdeacon, six for that of a deacon, and seven for that of a presbyter. *M.G.H.*, *Leges*, II, i, 361. Cf. above p. 36, n. 50.

[The remainder of the document contains alleged conciliar decisions of similar import.]

8. FROM POPE NICHOLAS I'S ANSWERS
TO THE BULGARIANS (866)

[IN 866 Pope Nicholas I, endeavoring to establish the Bulgarian Church under papal authority, received from his new spiritual subjects in Bulgaria a series of questions on ritual and polity. Their *Consulta* included a request for a manual of penance—"judicium penitentiae." There is no evidence to show how they had been led to make this request. In course of his detailed *Responsa* Nicholas promises to send the "judicium," but cautions against its coming into the possession of laymen, who may not perform a "ministry of judgment."[39] The book referred to in the brief and inexplicit language of Nicholas, was in all probability a penitential; though it does not appear whether he had as yet any particular one of these manuals in mind. The text is in Migne, *P.L.*, CXIX, 1008.]

lxxv. The "Judgment of Penance" for which you ask, our bishops whom we have sent into your country will indeed bring with them among the documents; or assuredly the bishop who will be ordained among you will exhibit it at a suitable time; for it is not proper for secular persons to have any such thing, for in fact no ministry of judgment by this means is accorded to them.

9. FROM HINKMAR OF REIMS

[HINKMAR, 806–82, the most distinguished ecclesiastic of the ninth century, was archbishop of Reims for thirty-seven years (845–82). Like most of the prelates of his time he was interested in reviving the ancient canons in the administration of penance. His capitulary of 857 shows a vigorous attempt to bring public criminals to public penance. In a work on predestination of 859, written during the controversy on that subject, Hinkmar refers to the presentation of a written confession ("libellus penitentiae") by Ebbo after his deposition from the see of Reims, 830. In his book on the *Divorce of Lothar* (860), however, he stoutly defends the secrecy of the confessional. A treatise entitled *De excommunicatis vitandis, de reconciliatione et de fontibus juris ecclesiastici*, formerly ascribed to Bernald of Constance (d. *ca.* 1100), is held by Saltet to be a plagiarized edition of an otherwise lost work of Hinkmar, originally entitled *De concordantia canonum.*[40] This document reverts to the ancient

[39] Cf. the language of Theodulf of Orleans, p. 397, above.
[40] L. Saltet, *Les Réordinations, une étude sur le sacrement de l'ordre*, pp. 395 ff. (Appendice I).

doctrine that penance can be accorded only once but admits the fact of the modern neglect of this rule.[41]]

From a Capitulary of Hinkmar, 857. Mansi, XV, 491 f.

1. That every priest shall take the greatest care, if it chance that a public murder or adultery or perjury or any criminal offense has been openly committed in his parish, that he forthwith, if the author of the deed or one who consents to it can come, exhort him to come to penance before the dean and his fellow-presbyters; and whatever these find out, or whatever action they take, he shall report to our fellow ministers, his rulers,[42] who are established in the State:[43] so that within fifteen days the public sinner shall come to our presence, if we are within our own diocese, and according to the canonical tradition receive public penance with imposition of hands. And if we are at a distance from our diocese, the year and day of the month[44] shall be carefully noted, when each one committed a public crime, and when he came to penance in presence of the ministers, or when he came for the imposition of our hands. [Priests are to confer on these cases from month to month and report to the bishop, that he may be able to judge when each penitent is to be reconciled. Any who refuse to come to penance are to be cut off from the Church until they repent. Clergy who are tardy in taking action in the matter will be suspended.]

From Hinkmar's *Second Dissertation on Predestination*, Chap. xxxvi. Migne, *P.L.*, CXXV, 391

And after all these things, the same former bishop Ebbo gave out a book of penance in which he set forth in writing the offenses that he had previously confessed to his judges and witnesses; and this book of satisfaction he read publicly in the church of Reims, and to this day the diligence of the Reims record room[45] preserves it among [the records of] other deeds.

From Hinkmar's *Treatise on the Divorce of Lothar and Thietberga.* Migne, *P.L.*, CXXV, 634, 641

[A bishop who refuses communion to one who has made secret confession to him is to be denied communion by other bishops.]

---

[41] Migne, *P.L.*, CXLVIII, 1184. *M.G.H.*, *Libelli de lite*, II, 115.   [42] "magistris."
[43] "civitate." If this means "city" the "magistri" referred to may be ecclesiastical.
[44] "kalendarum" (of the Kalends).   [45] "scrinii."

For what else is it to refuse communion to one who has confessed an offense but to publish the confession of the offense? . . . And it stands as something known to every person for himself that there is nobody who would not hesitate to utter his sins to his prelate if he feared that he would be shamed or exposed.[46]

[In condemning the reading to a synod of Thietberga's confession, first given in secret to Bishop Gunther of Cologne, Hinkmar cites Leo I's prohibition of this procedure,[47] and argues that there is a fundamental difference between this case and that of Ebbo who wrote his own confession and presented it to the synod after his trial and deposition.]

10. FROM THE SPURIOUS CANONS
OF KING EDGAR (*tenth century*)

[THE CANONS printed by Thorpe as enacted under King Edgar (961–75) have long been regarded as of doubtful authenticity. The view of Jeremy Collier, who discussed and paraphrased the document in his *Ecclesiastical History of Great Britain*, ed. 1852, I, 438–43, was that except for the penitential section they appear to issue from some synod, but that this section, since it is written in the singular number, "seems to be the orders of some single prelate." Modern comment on the document may be found in H. Böhmer, *Kirche und Staat in England und in der Normandie im XI. und XII. Jahrhundert*, pp. 45, 76; F. Liebermann, *Die Gesetze der Angelsachsen*, II, ii, 357; Oakley, p. 135; Fournier et Le Bras, I, 354. These writers, like Collier, and in disagreement with Thorpe and Wasserschleben, deny the authenticity of the canons but regard them as of about the same period, the work of an independent canonist. W. Stubbs, *Memorials of St. Dunstan*, p. cvii, connects them with St. Dunstan, who controlled the religious policy of Edgar; but some reasons against this view were earlier stated by J. Johnson, *A Collection of The Laws and Canons of the Church of England* (1720), new edition by J. Barow (1850), I, 408.

The document is remarkable for an extreme laxity in respect to commutations and vicarious penance. In the section "Of Penitents," many redemptions of penance by gifts are indicated (can. 14). These include the building of churches, the gift of land to a church, improvement of highways, and the building of bridges.

The Anglo-Saxon text is given by Thorpe, with translation, *Ancient Laws of England*, II, 244–89. The passage below is from the section "Of Powerful Men," Thorpe, p. 287]

---

[46] "denudari vel publicari."
[47] See above, pp. 12 ff.

Thus may a powerful man and rich in friends with the support of his friends greatly lighten his penance:

[After confession let him undertake penance with much sighing, lay aside his weapons and wear woolen or hair cloth garments] and so do, that in three days the series of vii years be dispensed with thus: let him proceed with aid; and first let him take with him xii men, and let them fast iii days on bread, and on green herbs, and on water; and get, in addition thereto, in whatever manner he can, seven times cxx men, who shall also fast for him iii days; then will be fasted as many fasts as there are days in vii years.

11. FROM THE HOMILIES OF AELFRIC
(ca. 955–1020)

[THE AUTHOR of the *Homilies* from which the following extract is taken was probably the abbot of Eynsham and not, as has sometimes been thought, either of the two nearly contemporary Aelfrics who became archbishops, the one of York and the other of Canterbury. His dates are about 955–1020. The selections are from B. Thorpe's translation in *Homilies of the Anglo-Saxon Church*, 2 vols., London, 1844.]

[Thorpe, I, 165.] Now is the pure and holy time drawing nigh, in which we should atone for our remissness: let, therefore, every Christian man come to his confessor ("scrifte") and confess his secret sins and amend by the teaching of his instructor; and let everyone stimulate another to good by good example, that all people may say of us, as was said of the blind man when his eyes were enlightened; that is, all people who saw that miracle praised God, who liveth and reigneth ever without end. Amen.

[Thorpe, II, 603.] No sin is so deep that a man may not expiate it, if he cease from evil and with all true repentance by the instruction of teachers repent of his offenses. . . . No man shall delay to atone for his sins, because God promises to every penitent forgiveness of his sins but he promises not to any procrastinator certain life till the morrow. Let no man be ashamed to make known his sins to one teacher, for he who will not in this world confess his sins with true repentance shall be put to shame before God Almighty, and before his hosts of angels, and before all men, and before all devils, at the great doom, when we shall all be gathered . . . For no man obtains forgiveness of his sins from God unless he confess them to some

man of God and by his doom expiates them. The man who desires
to confess and expiate his sins shall grant forgiveness to all those
men that have before offended him, as it stands in the Pater Noster
and as Christ said in the Gospel: he said, "Unless with inward heart
ye forgive those men that sin against you, the Heavenly Father will
not forgive you your sins."[48]

12. FROM PETER DAMIAN'S *LIBER GOMORRHIANUS* (1051)

[At a time when the penitentials were in general use and no longer opposed north of the Alps, the Italian ascetic and reformer St. Peter
Damian (1007–72) in his *Liber Gomorrhianus*, addressed to Pope Leo IX,
flays the laxity of the clergy in the administration of penance and sar-
castically exposes the confusion of authority in the penitentials. The
passage is translated from the text in Migne, *P.L.*, CXLV, 172.]

But who then put together these canons? Who in the purple grove
of the Church presumed to sow such spiny, stinging plants of thorn?
It is surely established that all authentic canons were either arrived
at in the venerable synodical councils or promulgated by holy fathers,
pontiffs of the apostolic see. Neither may any man by himself issue
canons, but this privilege appertains only to him who is observed to
sit in the chair of the Blessed Peter. But these spurious upstarts[48a] of
canons of which we are speaking, are both known to be excluded by
the sacred councils and proved to be utterly foreign to the decrees
of the fathers. It therefore follows that rules which are seen to proceed neither from the decretal pronouncements of the fathers nor
from the sacred councils are in no wise to be held to be among the
canons. For whatever is not reckoned as within the species is without
doubt recognized to be alien to the genus. But if the name of the
author is sought, certainly it cannot be told, for it cannot be uniformly found in the various codices. For in one place is written:
"Theodore says," in another: "The Roman Penitential says," in
another: "The Canons of the Apostles." The titles read in one way
here, in another there; and since they do not deserve to have a single
author, without doubt they lose all authority. For rules which waver
under so many unascertained authors, confirm none in clear authority. [They must yield to canons of unquestionable authority.]

[48] Matt. 6:15; Mk. 11:25.   [48a] "vitulamina" (sprouts or shoots).

13. FROM THE SYNODICAL CONSTITUTIONS OF ODO, BISHOP OF PARIS (*ca.* 1197). Mansi, XXII, 678 f.

vi. 1. Priests shall apply the greatest care and caution with regard to confession, namely, that they diligently search out sins, the habitual ones severally, the occasional ones only indirectly, by means of some circumstance,[49] still in such a way that the matter of confession is supplied from the sins.

2. Priests shall select for themselves a place easy of access in the church, so that they can be seen by all generally; and no one shall hear confessions in secret places or without the church, except in great need or sickness.

3. The priest shall have a lowly countenance in confession, and he shall not look at the face of the confessant, especially of a woman, on account of the obligation of honor; and he shall patiently hear what she says in a spirit of mildness and to the best of his ability persuade her by various methods to make an integral confession, for otherwise he shall say that it is of no value to her.

8. Having heard the confession the confessor shall always ask the confessant if he is willing to refrain from every mortal sin; otherwise, indeed, he shall not absolve him nor impose a penance upon him, lest he confide in that, but he shall warn him to do once more whatever good he can, that God may enlighten his heart unto penance.

9. In imposing slight penances priests shall take heed to themselves, for the nature of the penance ought to be according to the nature of the guilt and the capacity of the confessant.

14. In confession confessors shall take heed to themselves not to inquire the names of persons with whom confessants have sinned, but only the circumstances and nature [of the sins], and if the confessant tells [the names] the confessor shall rebuke him and shall hold this as secret as the sin of the confessant.

15. He shall not dare to reveal anybody's confession to any persons, from anger or hatred, or even from fear of death, by sign or word, generally or specially, as in saying, "I know what kind of persons you are." And if he reveals it, he ought to be degraded without mercy.

---

[49] "a longe per aliquam circumstanciam." The Vulgate expression "a longe" is regularly rendered "afar off" in the Douay Version. Detachment as opposed to scrupulous thoroughness is apparently implied.

14. FROM THE COUNCIL OF WESTMINSTER, HELD UNDER HUBERT WALTER, ARCHBISHOP OF CANTERBURY (*ca.* 1200). Mansi, XXII, 715

IV. *Of Penance*

Since the more carefulness is to be applied to penance, which is the second plank after shipwreck, as reparation is the more necessary after fall, we, following the provisions of the sacred canons, command that priests diligently give heed in penance to the circumstances, the condition[50] of the person, the magnitude of the fault, the time, the place, the cause, the delay made in [a state of] sin, the devotion of mind of the penitent. And let penance be so enjoined on the wife that she may [not] be placed under her husband's suspicion for any secret and heinous sin: the same is to be observed in the case of the husband. And let no priest after a lapse and before he confesses presume to approach the altar in order to celebrate. This we add to cure the covetousness of priests: that in penance masses be not enjoined on those who are not [themselves] priests. Saving in all things [the honor and privilege of the most Holy Roman Church].[51]

15. FROM THE CANONS OF THE FOURTH LATERAN COUNCIL (1215). Mansi, XXII, 1007–10

xxi. Every Christian of either sex, after attaining years of discretion, shall faithfully confess all his sins to his own priest at least once a year, and shall endeavor according to his ability to fulfill the penance enjoined him, reverently receiving the sacrament of the Eucharist at least at Easter, unless perchance, on the advice of his own priest, for some reasonable cause, he determines to abstain for a time from receiving it. Otherwise he shall both be withheld from entrance to the church while he lives and be deprived of Christian burial when he dies. Wherefore this salutary enactment shall be frequently published in the churches lest anyone assume a veil of excuse in the blindness of ignorance.

But if anyone for a right reason wishes to confess his sins to a priest who is not his own, he shall first ask and obtain permission from his own priest, since otherwise the other priest cannot loose or bind him.

[50] Emending with Mansi "quantitatem" to "qualitatem."
[51] The words bracketed are represented by "etc." in the text. The full phrase is given in canon 1 (col. 713).

The priest, moreover, shall be discreet and cautious, so that in the manner of the skillful physician he may pour wine and oil upon the wounds of the injured, diligently searching out the circumstances both of the sinner and of the sin, that from these he may prudently understand what manner of advice he ought to offer him and what sort of remedy he ought to apply, employing various measures in order to heal the sick. Further, he is to give earnest heed that he does not in any wise betray the sinner by word or sign or in any other way; but if he needs more prudent advice he shall seek this cautiously without any divulging of the person, since we decree that he who shall presume to reveal a sin made known to him in the adjudication of penance, is not only to be deposed from the priestly office but also to be thrust into a strict monastery to do perpetual penance.

16. NOTE ON THE DECREES OF THE COUNCIL OF TRENT

[THE FOURTEENTH SESSION of the Council of Trent, 1551, adopted a Declaration on the Sacrament of Penance in nine chapters which are too extensive and too easily accessible to be included here.[52] It is taught in this pronouncement that sacramental penance and confession are of divine institution, and that priests alone have authority to remit confessed sins, while the pope may reserve this authority in the case of "more atrocious and serious offenses." On secret confession the teaching is that public confession is not divinely forbidden nor yet commanded.]

17. LUTHER AND CALVIN ON CONFESSION AND PENANCE

[THE DEVELOPMENT of Luther's teaching on confession and penance is admirably outlined by H. E. Jacobs in the introduction to his translation of the Reformer's Confitendi ratio[53] of 1520. In this treatise as elsewhere Luther stresses the religious condition and experience of the sinner and repudiates the practice of scrupulously detailed analyses of sins in the confessional. He refers to "the hateful and wearisome catalogues of distinctions," calling this method useless and harmful.[54] An earnest confession to God should precede confession to a priest. Luther's Short Catechism of 1529 contains a section (No. V) entitled "A Short Method of Confessing to the Priest, for the Use of Simple Folk," which accords

[52] Latin text, with English translation from J. Waterworth, Canons and Decrees of the Council of Trent, in P. Schaff, Creeds of Christendom, II, 139-58.
[53] Works of Martin Luther, I (Philadelphia, 1915), 75 ff.
[54] Op. cit., p. 91.

with these principles.[55] The *Augsburg Confession* (1530), Article 4, "Of Confession," while declaring against "the enumeration of offenses," retains the use of the confessional and of absolution.

Calvin's teaching on confession to God is similar to that of Luther. The secret confession to God is to be followed, where such is desirable, by a voluntary confession to men. But Christians are under no compulsion to "enumerate their sins." Besides the general confession of the worshipping congregation two kinds of private confession are, according to Calvin, authorized in Scripture. Quoting James 5:16 he advocates a mutual private confession between Christians. A second kind of private confession is made to him who, among the members of the church, seems best fitted to receive it. This person will ordinarily be the pastor. Moreover, ministers are by their calling appointed "to subdue and correct our sins." They are said in Matt. 16:19 and 18:18 "to remit sins and to loose souls." No special method of confession is of divine appointment. A soul in distress should seek relief and consolation by "private confession with his pastor." But pastors should "lay no yoke upon conscience" in this matter. "Confession of this sort ought to be free, so that it be not required of all, but recommended to those alone who feel that they need it."[56] The discipline established by Calvin in Geneva, however, involved penalties graded according to the gravity of the offenses with some resemblance to the principles of the penitentials. A memory of early church penance is also discernible in the marked element of public humiliation with which these medieval features were combined. The Ordinances of the Council of Geneva for 1551, for example, required that blasphemers should for a first offense spend a day and a night in confinement on bread and water, and thereafter kneel on both knees, kiss the ground, and ask pardon of God. To this was added a fine of ten sous. The penalties mounted with each succeeding offense. For the fourth, in addition to imprisonment, fasting, and a fine, the offender must go into exile for six months.][57]

18. FROM THE CONSTITUTIONS AND CANONS ECCLE-SIASTICAL OF THE CHURCH OF ENGLAND
(1604). E. Cardwell, *Synodalia*, I, 310

cxiii. [Ministers and parish officials are to "present" offenders to ecclesiastical superiors for discipline.]

[55] *Works of Martin Luther*, VI (Philadelphia, 1932), 215 f.; B. J. Kidd, *Documents of the Continental Reformation*, pp. 216 f.

[56] *Institutio Christianae religionis* (*Institutes of the Christian Religion*), III, iv, 4–12. Text in *J. Calvini opera selecta* (ed. P. Barth and G. Niesel, Munich, 1931), IV, 89–99. Translations of the *Institutes* by J. Allen and by H. Beveridge may be consulted.

[57] *Corpus reformatorum*, XXXVIII a (=*Calvini opera*, X a), 59 ff. A section of these regulations ("On frivolous oaths") is translated by G. Harkness, *John Calvin, the Man and His Ethics* (New York, 1931), p. 103.

Provided always, that if any man confess his secret and hidden sins to the minister for the unburdening of his conscience, and to receive spiritual consolation and ease of mind from him; we do not any way bind the said minister by this our Constitution, but do straitly charge and admonish him, that he do not at any time reveal and make known to any person whatsoever any crime or offense so committed to his trust and secrecy, (except they be such crimes as by the laws of this realm his own life may be called in question for concealing the same,) under pain of irregularity.

Appendices

APPENDIX I

An Eighth-Century List of Superstitions

[THE *Indiculus superstitionum et paganiarum* is a list of thirty superstitious and pagan practices belonging to the eighth century. It is preserved in Codex Vat. Pal. Lat. 577, where it follows the canons of the council held under Carloman and Boniface, 742. It has been attributed to Boniface, but is regarded by its editors in the *Monumenta* as a memorandum made by some private person. Possibly it is a synopsis of a document in which these practices were condemned under penalties as in the treatment of similar practices in the penitentials. It has been pronounced by Kurth "a true syllabus of the religious errors of eighth century Christians." For a valuable analysis of the *Indiculus*, see Hefele-Leclercq, III, ii, 836–43. A German rendering is given by F. Sehetbauer, *Das Kirchenrecht bei Bonifatius*, pp. 112 ff. The translation is from the text in *M.G.H.*, *Leges*, II, i, 222 f.]

1. Of sacrilege at the graves of the dead.
2. Of sacrilege over the departed, that is, "dadsisas."[1]
3. Of the swinish feasts[2] in February.
4. Of the little houses,[3] that is, sanctuaries.[4]
5. Of sacrilegious acts in connection with churches.[5]
6. Of the sacred rites of the woods which they call "nimidas."[6]
7. Of those things which they do[7] upon stones.

[1] Du Cange takes "dadsisas" in the sense of "dapes" "feasts," such as were sometimes celebrated in honor of the dead. Grimm interprets the word etymologically as the equivalent of a dirge ("dod"=dead; "sissas" in Old Saxon=Lat. "neniae"), *Deutsche Mythologie*, II, 1027 (Eng. ed., III, 1228). For variations of this view, see Hoffmann-Krayer and Bächtold-Stäubli, *Handwörterbuch des deutschen Aberglaubens*, II, s.v. "dadsisas". If, as seems probable, the practice was similar to the Irish keening-dirge (see above p. 40) it took place before the burial, and we should read the previous phrase "super defunctos" (over the departed) in that light, rather than, as understood by Hefele-Leclercq, "over the graves of the dead."

[2] "spurcalibus." A festival kept in honor of the advancing sun. It was attended by the sacrifice of swine. The word "sporkelmonat" is retained in some parts of Lower Germany for February.   [3] "casulis."

[4] "fanis." These structures were booths or huts for pagan worship, made of branches of trees.

[5] Editors refer to *Statuta Bonifacii*, 21, which prohibits choruses of secular persons and the singing of girls, and banquets, in a church.

[6] Grimm calls "nimidas" a plural masculine form, of which the nominative singular is "nimid," and thinks it related to Latin "nemus"—a (sacred) grove. *Op. cit.*, II, 540 (Eng. ed., II, 648).   [7] Pagan rites were often connected with certain stones.

8. Of the sacred rites of Mercury and of Jupiter.[8]

9. Of the sacrifice which is offered to any of the saints.[9]

10. Of amulets and knots.

11. Of the fountains of sacrifices.[10]

12. Of incantations.

13. Of auguries, the dung or sneezing of birds or of horses or of cattle.

14. Of diviners or sorcerers.

15. Of fire made by friction from wood, that is, the "nodfyr."[11]

16. Of the brains of animals.[12]

17. Of the observance of the pagans on the hearth or in the inception of any business.

18. Of undetermined[13] places which they celebrate as holy.

19. Of the bed-straw[14] which good folk[15] call Holy Mary's.

20. Of the days which they make for Jupiter and Mercury.[16]

21. Of the eclipse of the moon—what they call, "Triumph, Moon!"[17]

22. Of storms, and horns, and snail shells.

23. Of furrows around villas.

24. Of the pagan course which they call "yrias,"[18] with torn garments or footwear.

25. Of this, that they feign for themselves that dead persons of whatever sort are saints.

26. Of an idol made of dough.[19]

27. Of idols made of rags.

[8] To the Germans these deities would be Wodan and Thor.

[9] Cf. The Capitulary of Carloman, 742 (cited above p. 388), which refers (can. 5) to pagan rites performed by foolish men beside churches, "under the names of saints, martyrs or confessors."

[10] That is, fountains where sacrifices are celebrated.

[11] The editors cite the prohibition in the Capitulary of Carloman, 742, can. 5. of "those sacrilegious fires which they called "nied-fyr." The "nodfyr" or "need-fire" was also called "reibfeuer" because it was lighted by rubbing together sticks regarded as male and female. Grimm, op. cit., I, 174. For late instances of the need-fire in Britain see Eleanor Hull, Folklore of the British Isles, pp. 160 ff.

[12] Heads of animals were sometimes sacrificed. The brains may have been examined by diviners.

[13] "incertis." Hefele-Leclercq cite the case of a place, hitherto unknown to be sacred, where a person is suddenly stricken with apoplexy.

[14] Accepting Eckhardt's emendation of "petendo" to "petenstro" (Bettstroh), as in the modern "Muttergottesbettstroh" (Our Lady's bedstraw), a plant.

[15] "boni" seems to be used in derision.

[16] Days consecrated to Thor and Wodan, whether merely called by their names (cf. Thursday, Wednesday), or marked by ceremonies in worship of these deities.

[17] "Vince luna." Probably the words were shouted by the celebrants, fearful of the moon's destruction. Raban Maur has a vivid description of a demonstration with shouts, horns, and gruntings like those of swine during an eclipse to scare away the monster that threatens to devour the moon. Migne, P.L., CX, 78 f. For a condensed rendering of part of this passage see Hull, op. cit., pp. 62 f. Cf. pp. 41, 229, 330, above.

[18] Or reading with Massmann, "frias" from Frea, goddess of fruitfulness. The celebration apparently resembled the Roman Lupercalia.

[19] Literally, "moistened flour."

28. Of an idol which they carry through the fields.

29. Of wooden feet or hands in a pagan rite.

30. Of this: that they believe that women command the moon[20] that they may be able to take away the hearts of men, according to the pagans.

[20] The manuscript reads "femine luna comedet." The editor prints "lunam comendet." The translation is based on the emendation "commendant." If we read "comedant" we should render: "swallow up the moon." See Hefele-Leclercq, *loc. cit.*

APPENDIX II

Selections from the Customs of Tallaght

(*ca.* 831–40)

[TALLAGHT, anciently Tamlachta, near Dublin, had a monastic community founded by Maelruain, who, according to the *Annals of Ulster*, died in 792. He is regarded as the principal founder of the reform movement whose followers were called Culdees. The "Customs of Tallaght" are described in an anonymous document of about 831–40 by an admiring disciple of the founder's successor Maeldithruib. The document has been edited by E. J. Gwynn and W. J. Purton: "The Monastery of Tallaght," in the *Proceedings of the Royal Irish Academy*, XXIX, C (1911), 115–79; text, pp. 127 ff. The following extracts from the translation supplied by the editors are of interest to students of the penitentials. Dr. Gwynn and his publishers have kindly given their consent to the republication of these paragraphs. I have supplied a few notes. The document is closely related to the probably later "Rule of the Culdees," edited by W. Reeves, *The Culdees of the British Isles*, pp. 84–97, and to "The Rule of Tallaght," edited by E. J. Gwynn from a late manuscript, *Hermathena*, XLIV (1927), Second Supplemental Volume. On the Culdees see J. A. Duke, *The Columban Church* (1932), pp. 165–70, and Kenney, pp. 468 ff.]

18. There is nothing that a man does on behalf of one that dies that does not help him, whether it be vigil or abstinence, or reciting intercessory prayers or almsgiving, or frequent benediction. Moedoc and all his monks were a full year on bread and water to obtain the release of the soul of Brandub mac Echach. Sons ought to do penance for the souls of their departed parents *et coetera*.

20. He[1] considers that priests who go astray, however fervent their penitence may be, should not be allowed to enter episcopal orders. For they consider that to enter episcopal orders is a purification for one who transgresses the priestly orders.

23. Concerning the matter of spiritual direction, some think it sufficient if they have merely made their confession, though they do no penance afterwards. He does not approve of this. He thinks it well, however, that one should show them what is profitable to them, even though he does not ask for confessions. This is what Helair did in the matter: at first he had received many, but he ended by sending them all

---

[1] That is, apparently, Maeldithruib, abbot of Tallaght, whose death is supposed to have occurred in 840. Gwynn and Purton, *op. cit.*, pp. 120 ff. Cf. Kenney, p. 471.

away, because he saw that their penance was not zealously performed, and also that they concealed their sins when making confession. After that he finally refused to receive anyone at all to spiritual direction. However, he would sometimes allow holy persons to consult him.

24. As for Maelruain he was not stiff in refusing to receive them finally. He had no great desire even to receive Maeldithruib. This is what he said: "Didst thou ask permission of those whom thou didst leave before coming hither?" "Yea," said Maeldithruib. "Even artisans," said Maelruain, "the smiths, the wrights, etc., none of them likes a man of his household to go to anyone else." "What thou sayest has been looked to," said Maeldithruib; "I obtained authorization and permission." Then he made submission to the authority of Maelruain. Then said Maelruain: "A year of repurification shalt thou have among us," said he. "Thrice forty nights shalt thou be on bread and water, save for a cup of milk on Sundays only," and he had permission to mix a cup of whey in the water in the summer-Lent only. Now till that time he had been under the spiritual direction of Echtguide.

43. This is their practice, to wash the hands after plying the scourge, whether it be to read aloud the Gospels that a man goes after doing penance, or whether it be to the kitchen or any other matter—he washes his hands.

52. In the case of penance laid on sickly persons, this is what he thinks right, as to the continual preparing for meals: alternate reviving and mortifying is practiced on them, lest the perpetual confinement should cause their death; and this is done, if it can be managed without their knowledge, by telling his servant privately, "Let a *seland*[2] be brought to them in their pottage or on bread" [but it is more usual to bring it to them in the pottage]. Once it happened that the abbot who was in Iona saw that the recluses had a bad colour. Thereupon he went to the cook and himself made the pottage for that day. He added one-third of water to the daily allowance and boiled the water. When this third had boiled away, he put a lump of butter on each man's allowance, and boiled it on the water, and then put meal over it, and so he did every day. Then they noticed the change in their colour, and knew not what had caused it, since they saw the usual ration unchanged. So when their colour came back and they revived, he continued alternately to mortify and revive them from their dying state after this fashion.

64. . . . Some, however, make false confessions about themselves, in order to increase the penance laid upon them; but this is not right.

69. . . . When, however, there is in the Rules *"superponat"* or *"superpositio,"*[3] this is properly applicable to a half-ration and half-fast; *"cena careat,"*[4] however, is used when a fast is meant—that is, *"cena in nocte."*[5]

73. This is the authority for the habitual use of gruel. There was a

---

[2] See p. 160, n. 4 above.
[4] "he shall go without supper."
[3] Cf. pp. 31, 120, above.
[5] "the supper at night."

great gathering of the saints of Ireland in Mag Lena. This is what brought them together: they were grieved that penitents died on bread and water in the days of the elders who lived before them. Then they fasted against God on account of this. Then an angel came to them and said to them: "Wonder not," said he, "if the bread and the water cannot sustain the penitents to-day. The fruits and plants of the earth have been devastated; so that there is neither strength nor force in them to-day to support anyone. The falsehood and sin and injustice of men have robbed the earth with its fruits of their strength and force. When men were obedient to God's will the plants of the earth retained their proper strength. At that time water was no worse for sustaining anyone than milk is to-day." Then the angel told them to mix some meal with their butter to make gruel, so that the penitents should not perish upon their hands (?), because the water and the bread did not suffice to support them.

74. There were three kinds of gruel after that—gruel upon water, and gruel between two waters [while it does not sink right down to the bottom of the vessel, it does not float above on top of the water], and gruel under water. However, [in this case] it reaches the bottom of the vessel; the grain carries it downwards. Those whose sins are lighter and who deserve a year or two of penance, get gruel upon water. Those, however, whose sins are graver, who deserve four or five years, get gruel between two waters. Those, however, who have committed great sins and deserve seven years or more, as do bishops or priests who fall into mortal sin, or homicides, and so forth, get gruel under water, etc. A cleric by whom a captive is killed should, he considers, do penance like any other homicide.

78. He does not consider it right for anyone not to exact confession about everything from him to whom thou art confessor, without sparing him at meal-time if thou happen to be beside him, and he does not care about the healing effect of that confession; thou shouldst read the Rule and the Penitential aloud in his presence,[6] and [do not] spare such persons, lest thou perish through indulgence to another.

79. Now, he does not consider that it matters if anyone accepts the spiritual direction or receives the confession of a man that is older or more venerable than he is [for example, his tutor or an elder brother], if there be no one else at hand of sufficient authority for him to consult with. He should not, however, lay upon such persons strict injunctions; but let him read the books before them,[6] so that he may gain the more knowledge (?).

[6] Cf. p 3, above.

APPENDIX III

Irish Canons from a Worcester Collection
(*ca.* 1000)

[THE FOLLOWING three canons (in Latin) are printed in an article by Mary Bateson on the codex in which they appear, the Corpus Christi College, Cambridge, Manuscript 265. The manuscript is thought to have been written by Oswald, a nephew of the bishop of Worcester of that name, about the year 1000.[1] Miss Bateson entitles the section: "Three Unknown Irish Canons."]

1. If anyone in any way breaks into the place of keeping of the chrismal of any saint, or a place of keeping for staves or cymbals, or takes away anything by robbery, or in any way injures a man, he shall make sevenfold restitution and remain through five years in hard penance on pilgrimage abroad. And if his penance is commendable, let him afterwards come to his own[2] country; but if not, let him remain in perpetual exile.

2. If anyone breaks into the place of keeping of a Gospel book or removes anything by robbery, he small make sevenfold restitution, on account of the sevenfold grace of Christ and on account of the seven ecclesiastical ranks;[3] but he shall also remain through seven years in hard penance on pilgrimage. But if he does not do penance he is to be excommunicated from the whole Catholic Church and from the communion of all Christians, and burial in holy ground is not to be accorded to him.

3. If any tyrant[4] binds anyone attached to a bishop, he shall release him safe and sound and make restitution, and he shall render to the bishop three other men of equal worth with all their substance, and he himself shall remain in the penance of a hard pilgrimage alone for a period of ten years; and if he touches him so as to wound him, he shall render to the bishop seven men with all their substance, and he himself shall remain alone on pilgrimage for the space of twenty years. But if he kills him, he shall render to God all his inheritance and all his substance with the inheritances and substance of his associates, and he himself

---

[1] "A Worcester Cathedral Book of Ecclesiastical Collections, made *c.* 1000 A.D.," *English Historical Review*, X (1895), 712–31.

[2] Emending "solam" to "suam."

[3] Cf. p. 127, n. 77, 141, n. 13, above.　　　　　[4] "'tirranus," glossed "rex" (king).

shall go on perpetual pilgrimage, or, more mildly, on a pilgrimage of thirty years; he shall live without flesh and wife and horse, on dry bread, and with meagre clothing and not stay for two nights in one house save only in the principal festivals or if sickness lays hold of him. And if his associates are unwilling, they shall divide all their substance between God and man, and so shall they themselves remain in commendable[5] penance for the space of seven years.

[5] "probabili." In can. 1 the word "commendable" is used to translate "laudabilis."

On Documents Omitted

THE PRESENT WORK is necessarily selective. Several times the space occupied would have been required to present all the documents of the series in their entirety. Besides the secondary documents represented here by selections only, a considerable number are entirely omitted on the ground of their relative historical insignificance. Most of the published documents omitted from the text are comprised in the following list. The titles are given in alphabetic order.

1. The Arundel Penitential

This work was carefully edited from the British Museum manuscript in which it is extant, by Schmitz (I, pp. 432–65), in the interest of his theory of the Roman origin of the penitentials. Fournier gives reasons for dating it in the tenth or eleventh century and regarding it as of slight influence. "Études sur les pénitentiels," V, *Revue d'histoire et de littérature religieuses*, IX (1904), 98 f.

2. The Penitential Canons of Astesanus, ca. 1317

These canons, extracted from the fifth book of the *Summa de casibus* of the Franciscan Astesanus (of Asti, d. 1330) were first printed at Venice in 1584, and appear in Schmitz's first volume (I, pp. 800–808). They deal mainly with the offenses of priests. They are largely drawn from a section of the *Confessional* of St. Bonaventura (d. 1274), but employ materials from other thirteenth century writers and are through these sources indebted chiefly to the section on Penance in the *Decretum* of Gratian (*ca.* 1140). E. Friedberg, *Corpus juris canonici*, I, 1159–1247 (Grat. *Decret.*, II, xxxiii, 3). Cf. Wasserschleben, *Bussordnungen*, pp. 96 f. Gratian is in turn directly or indirectly indebted to Burchard.

3. The So-called Penitential of Boniface

A. J. Binterim published in 1822 in an appendix to his edition of the *De diaconis nunquam penitentiae sacramenti ministris* of K. Blascus, a penitential which he, through a misreading, ascribed to Boniface, and in 1829 reprinted it in his *Denkwürdigkeiten der christ-katholischen Kirche*, V, iii, 430–36. Binterim explains Regino's failure to mention it along with the penitentials of Theodore and Bede on the ground that it was regarded as a shortened form of the work of Bede. It is really based on part of the *Pseudo-Bede*, or *Double Penitential*.[1] The references of Boniface to Bede in his extant letters show that about 745 he had slight knowledge of Bede's works;[2] nor is it probable that the *Pseudo-Bede* was

---

[1] See above, p. 218.
[2] Haddan and Stubbs, III, 358 ff. Cf. M. Manitius, *Geschichte der lateinischen Litteratur des Mittelalters*, I (1911), 147.

compiled within the lifetime of Boniface. Like the section of the latter of which it is a condensed transcript, it is cast in questionnaire form. The error of ascribing it to Boniface is revived without argument by G. Kurth, who further gratuitously asserts that it is "the earliest German penitential."[3] It is probably a product of the ninth century.[4]

4. The Capitula Iudiciorum, or Penitential of Thirty-Five Chapters

The text of this document is in Wasserschleben, *Bussordnungen*, pp. 505–26, and in Schmitz I, pp. 653–76, and II, 217–51. It is a member of the series of Frankish composite penitentials of the late eighth or early ninth century and was afterwards employed by the framers of canon law collections. Cf. Fournier et Le Bras, I, 433.

5. The Poenitentiale Pseudo-Egberti

J. Raith in *Die altenglishe Version des Halitgar'schen Bussbuches (sog. Poenitentiale Pseudo-Ecgberti)*, Hamburg, 1933, has edited this extensive Anglo-Saxon penitential. He dates it in the second half of the tenth century, and finds it made up of extracts from Halitgar and Pseudo-Cummean, with elements from Theodore and Egbert. There exists an old Latin version, the origin of which is unknown. Wilkins published both versions (*Concilia*, I, 113–43) from the eleventh century Corpus Christi College, Cambridge codex now numbered 190. The Latin has been reprinted by Thorpe and by Wasserschleben. Haddan and Stubbs regard the Latin as "a close translation of the Anglo-Saxon," and the Anglo-Saxon with the exception of Book II, Chapter 1, as a paraphrase of Halitgar's work. They also suggest that Egbert may actually have put into Anglo-Saxon the sections from Theodore and Pseudo-Cummean, and that the translator of Halitgar "put the whole work together under his [Egbert's] name." In these judgments Raith concurs. Raith conveniently supplies with the text the passages from Halitgar and other sources used by the compiler.

6. Leofric's Scrift boc on englisc

The *Scrift boc on englisc*, or *Anglo-Saxon Penitential*, bequeathed by Bishop Leofric at his death in 1072 to the Library of Exeter Cathedral (F. E. Warren, *The Leofric Missal*, pp. xxii f.) was identified by Humphrey Wanley in G. Hickes, *Antiquae literaturae septentrionalis libri duo*, II (1705), 110, as a document now contained in Codex 190 of the Library of Corpus Christi College, Cambridge. This eleventh century codex is described at length by M. James, *Catalogue of the Manuscripts of Corpus Christi College*, I, 452–63, with extracts from Mary Bateson's article, "A Worcester Cathedral Book of Ecclesiastical Collections," *English Historical Review*, X (1895), 712–31. Cf. p. 425, above. See also Max Förster in *The Exeter Book of Old English Poetry* (1933), p. 27, n. 93. The Scrift boc forms the third main division of the codex, consisting of pages 365–420, and is written partly in Latin and partly in Anglo-Saxon. For a reference to the 1933 edition of the *Exeter Book* previous to its appearance I was indebted to Prebendary H. E. Bishop, Librarian of Exeter Cathedral, and for the reference to the

---

[3] *Saint Boniface* (5th ed.), p. 191.
[4] On manuscripts and origin, see Wasserschleben, *Bussordnungen*, p. 89; Schmitz I, p. 745.

Catalogue of Manuscripts to the Honorary Assistant Librarian, Marjorie Creighton. J. Raith's *Die altenglische Version des Halitgar'schen Bussbuches* (*sog. Poenitentiale Pseudo-Ecgberti*), Hamburg, 1933, and R. Spindler's *Das altenglische Bussbuch* (*sog. Confessionale Pseudo-Egberti*), Leipzig, 1934, companion studies by two Munich professors of English, have made use of the Anglo-Saxon sections of the document. Raith lists the incipits of the codex, *op. cit.*, pp. xii ff. The *Scrift boc* is an unoriginal compilation of materials drawn from earlier documents attributed to Cummean, Theodore, Egbert and Halitgar.

7. *The Penitentiale Casiniense*, or *Penitential of Monte Cassino*, also called *Poenitentiarium summorum pontificum*

This work is largely dependent on the *Capitula iudiciorum* and took shape in Italy in the late ninth or the tenth century. Schmitz erroneously regarded it as Roman and dated it 700–750. See his introduction and text, I, pp. 388–402, and cf. Fournier, "Études . . . ," III, in *Rev. d'hist. et de litt. relig.*, VII (1902), 121 ff., and Fournier et Le Bras, I, 352.

8. *The Penitential of Fulbert of Chartres* (1006–1028)

For this genuine but very short and entirely unoriginal document see Wasserschleben, *Bussordnungen*, pp. 623 f.; Schmitz I, pp. 773 f. It is incorporated in the *Decretum* of Ivo of Chartres, *ca.* 1100.

9. *The Penitential Ascribed to Gregory III* (731–741)

Wasserschleben places the *Pseudo-Gregory III* in the ninth century; Fournier et Le Bras, in the middle of the ninth century. It is probably Italian in origin, but it shows the influence of Spanish councils as well as of Celtic materials current in Francia. See *Bussordnungen*, pp. 84, 535–47; Fournier et Le Bras, I, 351.

10. *The Penitentiale Martenianum*

This work was published by Martène et Durand in *Thesaurus novus anecdotorum*, IV, 31 ff., from a Fleury codex and was called by them simply "Antiqua collectio canonum poenitentialium." See Wasserschleben, *Bussordnungen*, p. 48, and for the text, pp. 282–300. It has since been definitively edited by W. von Hörmann: "Bussbücherstudien," in *Zeitschrift der Savigny-Stiftung für Rechtsgeschichte, kan. Abt.*, IV (1914), 358–485. Cf. p. 219, above. Fournier et Le Bras (I, 90) date the document 802–13. It is a confused compilation of materials from Theodore and other English and Irish sources.

11. *The Merseburg Penitential*

Text in Wasserschleben, *Bussordnungen*, pp. 387–407; Schmitz II, pp. 358–68. This long penitential contains with slight variation the entire *Burgundian Penitential*, and in addition (canons 41–169) much material from Cummean and Theodore. The barbarisms in the text indicate a late eighth century Frankish origin. Fournier shows that the *Merseburg* is the parent of the *Valicellanum I*. See his "Études . . . ," I, *Rev. d'hist. et de litt. relig.*, VI, 313 ff.

12. *The Reims Penitential*

For the text of the *Penitentiale Remense*, see Wasserschleben, *Bussordnungen*, pp. 497–504. Cf. Schmitz I, pp. 645 ff. The document is a variant edition of *Pseudo-Cummean*.

13. *The "Simple" St. Gall Penitential*

On the date and connections of the *Poenitentiale Sangallense simplex* see above, p. 280. The nineteen canons which comprise the provisions of the document are virtually identical with materials in the Burgundian and related penitentials.

14. *The Pseudo-Theodore*

This document, published as the genuine *Penitential of Theodore* by B. Thorpe (*Ancient Laws of England*, II, 1–62), is a compendious and orderly ninth century work dependent on Cummean and Theodore. In Kunstmann's text, copied by Wasserschleben, its fifty canons are divided into two sections of fifteen and thirty-five canons, respectively. The first group of canons is based in part upon an arrangement of the deadly sins (*Bussordnungen*, pp. 566–622).

15. *The First Vallicellian Penitential*

The *Poenitentiale Valicellanum I* was edited by Schmitz (I, pp. 239–342) from a late tenth century codex (E. 15) of the Library of the Vallicelli at Rome. Schmitz (I, pp. 227 ff.) argues for its independence of Celtic and Frankish sources, and regards it as representing Roman usage in the eighth century. His view has been refuted by F. H. P. Hinschius (*System des katholischen Kirchenrechts*, V, 92) and by Fournier ("Études . . . " I, in *Rev. d'hist. et de litt. relig.*, VI, 1901, 289–317). These writers establish the dependence of *Valicellanum I* immediately upon the *Merseburg Penitential* and ultimately upon Celtic and Anglo-Saxon sources. Fournier holds that it took shape in territory conquered by the Franks from the Lombards in Italy about the end of the eighth or the beginning of the ninth century.

16. *The Second Vallicellian Penitential*

This document was called by Wasserschleben *Valicellanum I*, and was published in part by him (*Bussordnungen*, pp. 547–50), and more fully, but not completely, by Schmitz (I, pp. 350–88). The Schmitz text omits introductory sections given by Wasserschleben and contains a body of canons (Nos. 11 to 83) omitted by Wasserschleben. Schmitz has edited it carefully in the development of his Roman theory. Fournier thinks it the work of an Italian canonist of the tenth or early eleventh century, who collected a large number of "judicia" of Frankish origin, modified these according to his own taste and that of his time, adding some canons then in circulation in Italy. "Études . . . " II, in *Rev. d'hist. et de litt. relig.*, VII (1902), 59–70. The manuscript is Codex Vallicell. C. 6.

To be distinguished from the above, and from each other, are Wasserschleben's *Valicellanum II* and *Valicellanum III* and Schmitz's *Valicellanum III*. These are all late documents of no great importance.

17. *The Vienna Penitential*

The *Poenitentiale Vindobonense*, from a tenth century Vienna codex, is found in Wasserschleben, *Bussordnungen*, pp. 418–22, and in Schmitz II, pp. 351–56. It contains the *Burgundian Penitential* without significant variation and (canons 43–94) an additional miscellany of canons, many of which are also found in the *Merseburg* and the *Valicellanum I*. It probably belongs to the late ninth century.

NOTE ON OLD GERMAN "BEICHTEN"

A series of six "Beichten," or formulae for confession, in Old German, dating from the eighth and ninth centuries, were published by K. Müllenhoff and W. Scherer in their *Denkmäler deutscher Poesie und Prosa aus dem VIII–XII Jahrhundert* (1864), sections lxxi–lxxvi, and they appear with additional apparatus in the third edition of this work by G. Steinmeyer, 1892. They are designed for use by the people in the general or public confession of sins on high festival days and sometimes on Sundays. They contain numerous phrases translated from the penitentials and show the influence of the sermons of Caesarius of Arles. Their literary history and practical function have been investigated by F. Hautkappe in *Ueber die altdeutschen Beichten und ihre Beziehungen zu Cäsarius von Arles*, Münster, 1917. An earlier formula of similar character in Latin is that of Othmar, abbot of St. Gall (d. 759), given in Wasserschleben, *Bussordnungen*, p. 437, which is reprinted and partially translated in Watkins, II, 637, 657.

APPENDIX V

The Manuscripts of the Penitentials

THESE LISTS have been compiled for the most part from editions of penitential documents and from catalogues of libraries. Accordingly, such details as the folios and the age of the MSS are sometimes either lacking or doubtful. Relatively few of the MSS, about one-fifth, have been examined by the compiler, for which are used the symbols given below with their meanings.

*Photostatic copies of one or more folios of the MS have been examined.

**The MS has been examined.

†The penitential material in the MS was discovered or identified by the compiler; cf. pp. 67 ff.

As a rule, the older numbers of MSS are included only when the newer ones have not yet appeared in standard works.

For details on the collations of MSS see pp. 56 f., for details on the editions cited in Section A see the separate introductions to the translations of the penitentials in this volume. For a discussion of the treatment of MSS in the editions of the penitentials in general and of some important MSS in particular, see above, pp. 51–61.

Although the compiler of these tables has taken pains to check the MSS in whatever sources were available, accuracy cannot be claimed throughout. But it is hoped the tables will prove to be a valuable hand list of all known and some hitherto unidentified MSS of the penitentials. Only in a few cases, notably the MSS of Alain de Lille's *Penitential Book*, have the modern numbers and locations not been traced satisfactorily. Beyond that, it is quite probable that a systematic study of manuscript centers will bring to light new penitential material and make necessary additions to these lists. Several MSS have never before appeared in published editions of penitentials. As stated in the Introduction, p. 68 above, only the penitentials proper are included here.

A. THE MANUSCRIPTS

Arranged in the order of the documents

CANONS ATTRIBUTED TO ST. PATRICK (edited by Spelman, Wilkins, Haddan and Stubbs)

*Cambridge, Corpus Christi College 279, s. IX/X, pp. 1–10.

Cambridge, Corpus Christi College 298, No. 22, s. XV (imperfect).

PENITENTIAL OF FINNIAN (edited by Wasserschleben; reprinted by Schmitz)

**Paris, Bibl. Nat. Lat. 3182(olim Bigot. 89), s. XI (?), pp. 176-77.

**Paris, Bibl. Nat. Lat. 12021 (olim Sangerm. 121), s. IX, ff. 134^v–35.

**St. Gall, Stiftsbibl. 150, s. IX in., ff. 365–77.

**Vienna, Nationalbibl. 2233 (olim theol. 725), s. IX in., ff. 25^v–58^v.
PENITENTIAL OF CUMMEAN (edited by Zettinger. Cf. also the Penitential
   formerly thought to be Cummean's)
   **Rome, Vat. Pal. Lat. 485, s. IX, ff. 101–7^v.
IRISH CANONS (edited by Martène and Durand, Wasserschleben, Haddan
   and Stubbs; reprinted in part by Moran)
   ?Cambrai, Bibl. Munic. 576 (now 625), s. IX.
   ?Cambridge, Corpus Christi College 279, s. IX/X.
   **Paris, Bibl. Nat. Lat. 3182 (olim Bigot. 89), s. XI(?), pp. 177, 302,
      306–7, 312, 279–80 (in the order of Bks. II–VI).
   **Paris, Bibl. Nat. Lat. 12021 (olim Sangerm. 121), s. IX, f. 139.
CANONS OF ADAMNAN (edited by Martène and Durand, d'Achéry, Migne,
   Wasserschleben, Haddan and Stubbs, Robertson)
   *London, Brit. Mus. Cotton Otho E XIII, s. X in., ff. 141^v–43.
   †Lyon, Bibl. de la Ville 203, s. IX.
   Orléans, Bibl. de la Ville 193 (221), s. VIII/IX, p. 212 (fragmentary
      and worn).
   *Oxford, Bodl. Hatton 42, s. IX, ff. 132^v–33^v.
   **Paris, Bibl. Nat. Lat. 3182 (olim Bigot. 89), s. XI(?), pp. 164–65.
   **Paris, Bibl. Nat. Lat. 12021 (olim Sangerm. 121), s. IX, ff. 132^v–33^v.
LAW OF ADAMNAN (edited by K. Meyer)
   Brussels, Bibl. Roy. Burgund. 2324–40, A.D. 1627, pp. 76–85^v.
   Oxford, Bodl. Rawlinson B. 512, s. XV, ff. 45^{aI}–51^{bI}.
IRISH COLLECTION OF CANONS (edited by Martène and Durand,
   d'Achéry, Migne, Wasserschleben)
   Cambrai, Bibl. Munic. 619 (=679), s. VIII ex. (incomplete).
   Cambridge, Corpus Christi College 279, s. IX/X.
   Chartres, Bibl. de la Ville 124 (=127), s. X, ff. 2–75.
   **Cologne, Dombibl. 210 (olim Darmst. 2178), s. VIII, ff. 1–121
      (incomplete).
   Karlsruhe, Landesbibl. Reichenau XVIII, s. IX in., ff. 75–82.
   London, Brit. Mus. Cotton Otho E XIII, s. X in. (damaged by
      fire).
   Munich, Staatsbibl. Lat. 4592.
   Orléans, Bibl. de la Ville 193 (221), s. VIII/IX, pp. 23–206.
   Oxford, Bodl. Hatton 42, Pt. 1, s. IX.
   **Paris, Bibl. Nat. Lat. 3182 (olim Bigot. 89), s. XI(?), pp. 19–160.
   **Paris, Bibl. Nat. Lat. 12021 (olim Sangerm. 121), s. IX, ff. 33–127.
   Paris, Bibl. Nat. Lat. 12444.
   Rome, Bibl. Vallic. A 18, s. X, ff. 58–136.
   Rome, Vat. Lat. 1339, s. X(?) (excerpts).
   St. Gall, Stiftsbibl. 243, s. IX.
   Tours, Bibl. de la Ville 556, s. XI (incomplete).
   Würzburg, Universitätsbibl. Mp th qu 31, s. VIII/IX.
OLD IRISH TABLE OF COMMUTATIONS (edited by K. Meyer, variant read-
   ings by Gwynn)

Dublin, Roy. Irish Acad. 3 B 23, s. XV, ff. 13–16.

Oxford, Bodl. Rawl. B 512, s. XV, ff. 42^{bI}–44.

BIGOTIAN PENITENTIAL (edited by Wasserschleben, Schmitz)

**Paris, Bibl. Nat. Lat. 3182 (olim Bigot. 89), s. XI(?), pp. 289-99.

OLD IRISH PENITENTIAL (edited by Gwynn)

Cheltenham, an unnumbered codex, s. XV ex., ff. 47–48^v.

Dublin, Roy. Irish Acad. 3 B 23, s. XV ex., ff. 16–28 (imperfect).

Dublin, Roy. Irish Acad. 23 P 3, A.D. 1467, ff. 15– (prefaces).

Dublin, Roy. Irish Acad. 23 P 16, 23 H. IJ ("Leabhar Breac"), s. XIV/XV at p. 186 (a fragment).

Oxford, Bodl. Rawl. B 512, s. XV, ff. 39–40^v (prefaces).

CANONS OF SIXTH CENTURY WELSH SYNODS (*a*. Of North Britain; *b*. Of the Grove of Victory), BOOK OF DAVID, PREFACE OF GILDAS ON PENANCE (edited by Martène and Durand, Migne, Wasserschleben, Haddan and Stubbs, Schmitz, in part by Moran; the Preface of Gildas also by Mommsen, Williams)[1]

**Paris, Bibl. Nat. Lat. 3182 (olim Bigot. 89), s. XI(?), pp. 281–82, 282–83, 280–81.

PENITENTIAL OF THEODORE (edited by Thorpe, Spelman, Petit, Martène and Durand, d'Achéry, Labbé and Cossart, Migne, Wasserschleben, Haddan and Stubbs, Schmitz, Finsterwalder)[2]

*Basle, Universitätsbibl. Fragmentensammlung *Bd. I, No. *3C, s. IX, ff. 1–8^v (fragments of a MS formerly of Fulda, probably to be identified with G. Becker, *Catalogi bibliothecarum antiqui* 13, 12).[3]

**Berlin, Staatsbibl. Ham. 132, s. IX, ff. 243^v–47 (U II).

Brussels, Bibl. Roy. 363 (olim Burgund. 10127–44), s. VIII, ff. 58–65 (U II).

Cambridge, Corpus Christi College 190, see p. 443 below.

**Cambridge, Corpus Christi College 320, s. IX, Pt. 2, pp. 1–44 (U I and II).

**Cologne, Dombibl. 91 (Darmst. 2179), s. VIII, ff. 82–90^v, 112^v (U II).

**Cologne, Dombibl. 210, s. VIII, ff. 122–51.

London, Brit. Mus. Add. 8873, s. XII.[4]

---

[1] These documents, published from but one MS, are also to be found in MS Cambrai 625 (=576), s. IX, ff. 52–, according to *Catalogue général des MSS des bibliothèques de France* (Paris, 1891), XVII.

[2] U I and II, or U II after a MS indicates that the most important transmission of the text of Theodore, that of the "Discipulus Umbrensium," is to be found in the codex.

[3] Cf. the suggestion of W. Levison in his review of Finsterwalder's edition of Theodore, *Savigny-Stiftung für Rechtsgeschichte, kan. Abt.* XIX (1930), 700, and his references to P. Lehmann, *Fuldaer Studien* (1925), 6 f, 50 f, and *Quellen und Untersuchungen zur lateinischen Literatur des Mittelalters, begr. von L. Traube*, IV (1912), 113, n. 8.

[4] Not 8872. Finsterwalder gives both numbers in his edition of Theodore, see *op. cit.*, pp. xix, 5, 31.

London, Brit. Mus. Cotton Vesp. D XV (=38505), s. X/XI at
ff. 84–101ᵛ.

Merseburg, Dombibl. 103, s. IX (fragment).

Munich, Staatsbibl. Lat. 3852 (olim Aug. 152), s. XI at f. 66 (fragment).

Munich, Staatsbibl. Lat. 6241 (olim Fris. 41), s. IX/X, ff. 33ᵛ–35.

Munich, Staatsbibl. Lat. 6245, s. XI.

Munich, Staatsbibl. Lat. 14780 (olim Em. e 2), s. IX, ff. 1–25.

Munich, Staatsbibl. Lat. 22288 (olim Windberg 88), s. XI/XII,
ff. 16ᵛ–35ᵛ (U I and II).

Paris, Bibl. Nat. Lat. 1454, s. IX/X, ff. 216–20ᵛ (U II).

Paris, Bibl. Nat. Lat. 1455, s. X, ff. 80– (U II).

**Paris, Bibl. Nat. Lat. 1603, s. VIII/IX, ff. 92ᵛ–103 (U II).

Paris, Bibl. Nat. Lat. 2123, s. IX, ff. 55ᵛ–65.

**Paris, Bibl. Nat. Lat. 3182 (olim Bigot. 89), s. XI(?), pp. 165–73.

**Paris, Bibl. Nat. Lat. 3846, s. IX at ff. 259–62ᵛ (U II).

Paris, Bibl. Nat. Lat. 3848 B, s. IX, ff. 1–13.

Paris, Bibl. Nat. Lat. 12021 (olim Sangerm. 121), s. IX, ff. 127ᵛ–32ᵛ.

Paris, Bibl. Nat. Lat. 12445 (olim Sangerm. 366), s. IX ex., ff. 153–
56 (U II).

Paris, Bibl. Nat. Lat. 13452 (olim Sangerm. 940), s. XVII/XVIII,
f. 1– (U I and II).

Rome, Vat. Lat. 5751, s. X, ff. 41ᵛ–.

**Rome, Vat. Pal. Lat. 485, s. IX, ff. 107ᵛ–13 (U I and II).

**Rome, Vat. Pal. Lat. 554, s. IX at f. 1 (fragment of U II).

*St. Gall, Stiftsbibl. 150, s. IX in., pp. 355–60 (U II).

Stuttgart, Oeffentl. Bibl. HB VI 109 (C5),⁵ s. IX/X, ff. 120–32
(U II).

Stuttgart, Oeffentl. Bibl. HB VI 112 (C4), s. XI, ff. 81–87 (U II).

**Vienna, Nationalbibl. 2195 (olim Salisb. 324), s. IX in., ff. 1–24ᵛ
(U I and II).

**Vienna, Nationalbibl. 2223 (olim jur. can. 116), s. VIII/IX, ff. 1–17
(U I and II).

**Würzburg, Universitätsbibl. Mp th qu 32, s. VIII, ff. 2–12ᵛ (U I
and II).

Two unnumbered MSS (codices Thuani) which belonged to the de Thou collection
were used by J. Petit for his edition of Theodore in 1677 (*Poenitentiale Theodori
Archiepiscopi Cantuariensis, Lutetiae Parisiorum,* 1677).

PENITENTIAL OF BEDE (edited by Martène and Durand, Wasserschleben,
Kunstmann, Schmitz, Haddan and Stubbs, Albers)⁶

⁵ Not 107 (C5). Finsterwalder, *op. cit.,* gives both; see pp. xix, 5, 124.

⁶ For the sake of convenience the different traditions of Bede are not separated in this
list of MSS. *Albers* following a number will distinguish the MSS which Albers used for
his edition of Bede; *Another,* those used by Wasserschleben for his Bede which appears on
pp. 220–30 of his *Bussordnungen* and in this volume under the name of *Another Penitential
attributed to Bede.* The rest of the MSS contain still other versions of Bede.

Andage, an unnumbered codex now lost (see p. 51 above) which Martène and Durand and Wasserschleben used for their editions (*Another*).

Cheltenham, Library of Sir Th. Phillipps (olim Middlehill 1750: cf. Haenel, Catal. p. 850) (*Another?* See Wasserschleben, *Bussordnungen*, p. 220).

Düsseldorf, Landesbibl. B 113, s. IX.

Freising, No. 3 (mentioned by Wasserschleben, *Bussordnungen*) = Freising 111, now Munich 6311 (q.v.)? (*Another*).

Heiligenkreuz, Stiftsbibl. 217, s. X.

Montpellier, École de Médecine 387, s. IX/X.

**Munich, Staatsbibl. Lat. 3851 (olim Aug. 151), s. IX(?), ff. 38–52.

Munich, Staatsbibl. Lat. 3853 (olim Aug. 153), s. XI.

Munich, Staatsbibl. Lat. 6311 (olim Fris. 111), s. X, f. 107.

Munich, Staatsbibl. Lat. 12673 (olim Ransh. 73), s. X, ff. 2–.

Paris, Bibl. Nat. Lat. 3878, s. XII.

Ranshoven, *see* Munich 12673.

*Rome, Vat. Barb. Lat. 477 (olim XI. 120), s. X in. at ff. 60–74 (*Albers*).

**Rome, Vat. Pal. Lat. 294, s. XI at ff. 87^v–90 (*Albers*).

St. Gall, Stiftsbibl. 682.

Vienna, Nationalbibl. 2223 (olim jur. can. 116), s. VIII/IX, ff. 17–22 (*Another*).

PENITENTIAL OF EGBERT (edited by Martène and Durand, Wilkins, Thorpe, Spelman, Labbé and Cossart, Mansi, Wasserschleben, Schmitz, Haddan and Stubbs)

Andage, an unnumbered codex now lost, mentioned by Martène and Durand.

Freising, No. 3 (mentioned by Wasserschleben, *Bussordnungen*) = Freising 111, now Munich 6311 (*q.v.*)?

Munich, Staatsbibl. Lat. 6311 (olim Fris. 111), s. X, f. 108.

Munich, Staatsbibl. Lat. 12673 (olim Ransh. 73), s. X, f. 6.

Oxford, Bodl. 718, s. X/XI, pp. 209–11.

Ranshoven, see Munich.

Rome, Vat. Lat. 1347, s. IX/X.

**Rome, Vat. Lat. 1352, s. XI, ff. 86^v– .

**Rome, Vat. Pal. Lat. 294, s. XI at ff. 83–87^v.

**Rome, Vat. Pal. Lat. 485, s. IX, ff. 73–79^v.

**Rome, Vat. Pal. Lat. 554, s. VIII at ff. 5–13.

St. Gall. Stiftsbibl. 677, s. X.

**Vienna, 2223 (olim jur. can. 116), s. VIII/IX, ff. 77^v–87.

DIALOGUE OF EGBERT (edited by Ware; reprinted by Wilkins, Thorpe, Mansi, Haddan and Stubbs)

London, Brit. Mus. Cotton Vitell. A XII, s. XII.

CONFESSIONAL OF EGBERT (edited by Wilkins, Thorpe, Mansi, Migne, Wasserschleben, Haddan and Stubbs, Raith)

Brussels, Bibl. Roy. 2498 (olim Burgund. 8558–63), s. XI in., ff. 140^v–45.

Cambridge, Corpus Christi College 190, s. XI, pp. 366–84.

London, Brit. Mus. Cotton Tib. A III, s. XI, ff. 96–7.

Oxford, Bodl. Jun. 121, s. XI ex., ff. 87^v–101.

Oxford, Bodl. Laud. 482 (olim F. 17), s. XI, ff. 30^v–40.

PENITENTIAL OF COLUMBAN (edited by Sirinus from Fleming's unpublished edition, Migne, Bibl. PP. Max., Wasserschleben, Schmitz, Seebass)

Bobbio, an unidentified codex from which Fleming first made his edition, and probably neither of the two Bobbio MSS now in Turin, which are listed below.

Turin, Bibl. Naz. G V 38, s. X, ff. 125–30^v.

Turin, Bibl. Naz. G VII 16, s. X/XI, ff. 62^v–70^v (damaged by fire).

REGULA COENOBIALIS OF COLUMBAN (edited by Goldast, Messingham, Fleming, Holsten, Bibl. PP. Max., Seebass)

Cologne, Stadtarchiv, 231, s. XV, e6^v–f. 1^v.

Milan, Bibl. Ambros. G 58 sup., s. X(?), ff. 40–44.

Munich, Staatsbibl. Lat. 14949, s. XV, ff. 1–8.

Munich, Staatsbibl. Lat. 28118(?),[7] s. VIII ex.

St. Gall, Stiftsbibl. 915, s. X/XI, pp. 170–84.

Vienna, Nationalbibl. 1550, s. XII/XIII, ff. 74^v–79^v.

Vienna, Nationalbibl. 3878, s. XV, ff. 173–75^v.

PENITENTIAL FORMERLY THOUGHT TO BE CUMMEAN'S (edited by Fleming, Migne, Wasserschleben, Schmitz)

Avignon, Bibl. de la Ville 175, s. IX, f. 54^v (fragment).

Basle, Universitätsbibl. O IV 35, s. X (fragment).

**Berlin, Staatsbibl. Lat. 105 (Phillipps 1667), s. IX in., ff. 203^v–20.

Brussels, Bibl. Roy. 363 (olim Burgund. 10134), s. VIII, ff. 65–70.

**Cologne, Dombibl. 91 (olim Darmst. 2179), s. VIII, ff. 90^v–112^v.

*Copenhagen, Roy. Libr. Ny Kgl. S. 58, s. VIII in., ff. 1^v–35.

Einsiedeln, Klosterbibl. 326, s. X(?), ff. 35–66.

Karlsruhe, Landesbibl. Reichenau I C (=99), s. IX and VIII.

Merseburg, Dombibl. 103, s. IX.

**Munich, Staatsbibl. Lat. 6243 (olim Fris. B G 8 and Fris. 43),[8] s. VIII, ff. 217–29 (cf. also above, p. 63, n. 34).

Munich, Staatsbibl. Lat. 22288 (olim Windberg 88), s. XI/XII, ff. 1– .

---

[7] O. Seebass gives number 12118, s. IX in., in enumerating the MSS of the *Regula coenobialis* (*Zeitschr. f. Kirchengesch.*, XL [1922], 137). This number, however, does not exist. In his *Notae Latinae*, W. M. Lindsay mentions 28118, s. VIII ex., as "containing 'Regulae patrum'." Probably this is the codex which Seebass meant, inasmuch as the *Regula coenobialis* is sometimes called *Regula patrum Hibernensium* in the MSS.

[8] These two numbers, so I found, do not designate two separate MSS as Wasserschleben thought (see *Bussordnungen*, p. 460); both are old numbers of the same codex. Fris. B G 8, antedating Fris. 43, is not registered in the catalogue, but can still be seen in the MS itself.

Oxford, Bodl. 311, s. X, ff. 33–62.
Oxford, Bodl. 572, s. IX/X, ff. 51–70.
**Paris, Bibl. Nat. Lat. 1603, s. VIII/IX, ff. 104–38.
**Rome, Vat. Lat. 1339, s. X(?), ff. 171^v–77.
Rome, Vat. Lat. 1349, s. X, f. 193 (prologue).
Rome, Vat. Lat. 5751, s. X.
St. Gall, Stiftsbibl. 150, s. IX in., pp. 285–87. Cf. Tripartite St. Gall.
St. Gall, Stiftsbibl. 550, s. IX, pp. 162–234.
St. Gall, Stiftsbibl. 675, s. IX, pp. 224–67.
Strasbourg, Bibl. de la Ville C V 6, s. IX.[9]
Stuttgart, Oeffentl. Bibl. HB VI 112 (C4), s. XI, ff. 49– .
Stuttgart, Oeffentl. Bibl. HB VI 113, s. VIII, ff. 203–23.
Vienna, Nationalbibl. 2225 (olim theol. 651), s. X, ff. 13^v–23.
Vienna, Nationalbibl. 2233 (olim theol. 725), s. IX in., ff. 1–25^v.
Zürich, Universitäts = u. Kantonsbibl. Rheinau XXX, s. VIII/IX, ff. 28– .

JUDGMENT OF CLEMENT (edited by Kunstmann, Wasserschleben, Haddan and Stubbs)
Heiligenkreuz, Stiftsbibl. 217, s. X.
Munich, Staatsbibl. Lat. 3853 (olim Aug. 153), s. XI.
Paris, Bibl. Nat. Lat. 3878, s. XII.

BURGUNDIAN PENITENTIAL (edited by Schmitz)
*Brussels, Bibl. Roy. 2493 (olim Burgund. 8780–93), s. VIII ex., ff. 1^v–6^v.

BOBBIO PENITENTIAL (edited by Mabillon, Wasserschleben, Schmitz, Lowe)
Paris, Bibl. Nat. Lat. 13246, s. VIII in., ff. 286^v–91.

PARIS PENITENTIAL (edited by Wasserschleben, Schmitz, Lowe)
*Paris, Bibl. Nat. Lat. 7193, s. VIII, ff. 41–54.

FLEURY PENITENTIAL (edited by Martène and Durand, reprinted by Wasserschleben and Schmitz)
Fleury, an unnumbered MS, now lost; it was used by Martène and Durand for their edition. Cf. also the Introduction, p. 51, above.

TRIPARTITE ST. GALL PENITENTIAL (edited by Wasserschleben, Schmitz)
Heiligenkreuz, Stiftsbibl. 217, s. X (extracts).
**St. Gall, Stiftsbibl. 150, s. IX in., pp. 285–318 (cf. Cummean and Theodore).
**Vienna, Nationalbibl. 2223 (olim jur. can. 116), s. VIII/IX, ff. 22–41.

PENITENTIAL OF SILOS (edited by de Berganza, Romero-Otazo. See footnote 1, p. 285, above)
*London, Brit. Mus. Add. 30853, s. XI, ff. 309–24.

---

[9] Doubtless this MS, mentioned by Wasserschleben, was burnt with the rest of the Strasbourg codices in 1870; cf. W. Weinberger, *Catalogus catalogorum*, 1902, p. 40, n. 1.

PENITENTIAL OF VIGILA OF ALVELDA (edited by Ballerini, Wasserschleben, Romero-Otazo. See p. 291, above)

    Escurial, Real Bibl. Ff. 148, A.D. 976.

ST. HUBERT PENITENTIAL (edited by Martène, Wasserschleben, Schmitz) Andage (now Paris?), an unnumbered codex; cf. the Introduction, p. 51, above.

    Merseburg, Dombibl. 103, s. IX, ff. 112-19 (extracts of the former).

SO-CALLED ROMAN PENITENTIAL (edited by Stewart, Morinus, Canisius-Basnage, Bibl. PP.Max., Migne, Wasserschleben, Schmitz)

    **Berlin, Staatsbibl. Ham. 290, s. XI in., f. 36 (Preface of Bk. VI).

    Brussels, Bibl. Roy. Burgund. 10037, s. IX (a reference only to Bk. VI).

    Ghent, Bibl. de l'Univ. 506, s. X/XI in.

    **Munich, Staatsbibl. Lat. 3909, s. XI, ff. 75^v-89 (=Bk. VI).

    Munich, Staatsbibl. Lat. 12673, s. X, ff. 66^v-74 (=Bk. VI).

    Munich, Staatsbibl. Lat. 14532, s. X, ff. 26- (fragments of Bk. VI).

    Munich, Staatsbibl. Lat. 17195, s. XII, ff. 61-78 (fragments of Bk. VI).

    Novara, Bibl. Capitol. LXXI. 134, s. X.

    Paris, Bibl. Nat. Lat. 2341, ff. 231-33^v (fragments of Bk. VI).

    Paris, Bibl. Nat. Lat. 2373, s. XI and XII, ff. 7-26.

    Paris, Bibl. Nat. Lat. 2998, s. X, ff. 1-63^v.

    **Paris, Bibl. Nat. Lat. 8508, s. IX/X, ff. 128-35 (extracts from Bk. VI).

    **Paris, Bibl. Nat. Lat. 12315, s. XII, ff. 94-98^v (=Bk. VI).

    Paris, Bibl. Nat. Lat. 18220, f. 126 (a fragment of Bk. VI).

    †*Rome, Vat. Reg. Lat. 207, s. IX, ff. 85-105.

    St. Gall, Stiftsbibl. 277, s. IX, p. 144 (extracts from Bk. VI).

    St. Gall, Stiftsbibl. 570, p. 135, s. IX (extracts from Bk. VI).

    **St. Gall, Stiftsbibl. 676, s. XI/XII, pp. 26-36 (fragments of Bk. VI).

    **St. Gall, Stiftsbibl. 679, s. X, pp. 5-152 (Bk VI: 123-52).

    Verona, Bibl. Capitol. LXXI, s. X.

REGINO'S ECCLESIASTICAL DISCIPLINE (edited by Migne, Wasserschleben)

    Gotha, Herz. Bibl. 131 (145), s. X, ff. 1-130.[10]

    Luxemburg, Landesbibl. 29, s. XII, ff. 25-283.

    Paris, Bibl. Nat. Lat. 17527 (olim reg., fonds de l'Oratoire, num. 20), s. X.

    Trier, Stadtbibl. 1362, s. X, ff. 207.[11]

    Vienna, Nationalbibl. 694 (olim theol. 79), s. XI, ff. 20-168^v.

    Wolfenbüttel, Herz. Bibl. Helm. 32, s. X/XI, ff. 14-117.

    Wolfenbüttel, Herz. Bibl. August. 83.21, s. X, f. 172.

---

[10] Manitius, M., *Gesch. d. lat. Literatur d. Mittelalters*, Bd. I, 699, lists Gotha 141 for Regino; the same MS?

[11] Manitius, *loc. cit.*, and the catalogue of Trier MSS (by Keuffer) give only 927; the same MS?

Wasserschleben, in his edition of Regino, says that Theiner reported three Vatican MSS of Regino, but further details were lacking. Also that Binterim, *Pragm. Gesch. d. Nationalconcilien* (1835), I, 256, mentions another MS of Regino. This, so Wasserschleben says, is interpolated and not valuable.

CORRECTOR AND PHYSICIAN OF BURCHARD OF WORMS (edited by Quesnel, Migne, Ballerini, Wasserschleben, Schmitz. Besides there is a Cologne edition of 1548 and a Paris edition of 1549)

Bamberg, Staatl. Bibl. P. I. 5.

Brussels, Bibl. Roy. 2500 (olim Burgund. 6110–11), s. XIII, ff. 5ᵛ– 47.

**Cologne, Dombibl. 119 (olim Darmst. 2118), s. XI, ff. 1–204.

**Darmstadt, Hess. Bibl. 913, XI/XII(?), ff. 1–52ᵛ.

Dresden, Sächs. Landesbibl. A 118, s. XII, ff. 1–48 (extracts only).

Escurial, Real Bibl. D I. I, f. 233– , f. 396 (extracts).

Escurial, Real Bibl. Z IV. I, A.D. 1755, ff. 5–165ᵛ.

Frankfurt a. M., Archiv., s. XI (loose leaves).

Freiburg i. B., Univ. Bibl. 311 ff., A.D. 1034–46.

Göttweih, Stiftsbibl. 343 schwarz—305 rot, s. XV.

London, Brit. Mus. Arundel 173, s. XII, ff. 132– .

Munich, Staatsbibl. Lat. 2593, s. XIII, ff. 157–86.

Munich, Staatsbibl. Lat. 3909, s. XI (extracts).

Munich, Staatsbibl. Lat. 4570, A.D. 1108, ff. 1–237.

Munich, Staatsbibl. Lat. 5801 c, s. XII, ff. 1–173.

Munich, Staatsbibl. Lat. 12205, s. XIV at ff. 37–48 (extracts).

Munich, Staatsbibl. Lat. 18094, s. XII, ff. 1–241.

Olmütz, Kapitelarchiv.

†**Paris, Bibl. Nat. Lat. 14869, s. XIII, ff. 112–20.

Rome, Bibl. Vallic. B 58, S. XIII.

Rome, Bibl. Vallic. F 8, s. XIV, ff. 161– .

Rome, Bibl. Vallic. F 92, s. XIV, ff. 1–180.

**Rome, Vat. Lat. 1352, s. XI, ff. 56–84.

Rome, Vat. Lat. 1355, s. XI, ff. 1–34.

Rome, Vat. Lat. 3830, s. XI.

Rome, Vat. Lat. 4227, s. XII.

Rome, Vat. Lat. 4772, s. XI in.

**Rome, Vat. Reg. 224, s. XII, ff. 1–46ᵛ.

St. Gall, Stiftsbibl. 674, s. XII, p. 435.

Turin, Bibl. Naz. I. VI. 22, s. XII.[12]

Vercelli, Bibl. Capitol. 94.

Vienna, Nationalbibl. 354 (olim Salisb. 202), s. XII.

Vienna, Nationalbibl. 926 (olim 843), s. XIII, ff. 1–38ᵛ.

Vienna, Nationalbibl. 2245 (olim univers. 633), s. XII, f. 1.

---

[12] The MS itself was destroyed in the great fire; but see the notes on it by Fournier, in *Mélanges Mandonnet*, II, 39.

PENITENTIAL OF BARTHOLOMEW OF EXETER (unpublished[13]; a small extract is printed in Thomas Wright, *Reliquiae antiquae* I, 285 f., and a translation of that in G. G. Coulton, *Life in the Middle Ages*, I, 33 ff.)

*London, Brit. Mus. Cotton Faust. A VIII, s. XII or XIII, ff. 3–38^v.
*London, Brit. Mus. Cotton Vitell. A XII, s. XII, ff. 137– .
*London, Brit. Mus. Royal Collection 5 E VII art. 3, s. XII, ff. 104–.
*London, Brit. Mus. Royal Collection 7 E I, s. XII, ff. 6–.
*London, Brit. Mus. Royal Collection 8 D III, art. 2, s. XII, ff. 49^v–.
London, Brit. Mus. Royal Collection 8 C XIV, art. 1 (fragment).
Oxford, St. Johns College 163 (according to Cox; olim 3 A 3), s. XII.
Oxford, St. Johns College 165 (according to Cox; olim 3 A 10), s. XIII.
Paris, Bibl. Nat. Lat. 2600, s. XIII.

ALAIN DE LILLE'S PENITENTIAL BOOK (edited at Augsburg in 1515 and again by C. de Visch in Migne)

The MS situation of this document is complex and unsatisfactory. It has been discussed on pp. 350–51, above. Three MSS are reported by Carolus de Visch as follows:

MS Duacensis, in the University of Douai, of the Library George Colvenerius.
MS Dunensis, of the bibliotheca Dunensis.
MS bibliothecae S. Gisleni, ordinis Benedicti, in Hannonia (modern Hainaut?)

An early Augsburg edition is said to contain material similar to that in Migne. Cl. Bäumcker (*Philosophisches Jahrbuch der Görres- Gesellschaft*, VI [1893], 422–59) says that the three MSS and the Augsburg text contain but extracts from a fuller edition which is to be found in:

*Lilienfeld Stiftsb. 144, s. XII/XIII, f. 124–41^v (containing a dedication to Henry, Archbishop of Bourges). Bäumcker claims that this is the original work known as the *Poenitentiarius* and not necessarily by the well-known Alain de Lille.

In attempting to identify the MSS mentioned, I have found several references to A. de Lille's *Penitential Book* in Belgian and French catalogues of which I give the following:[14]

Bruges, Bibl. publ. de la ville 28, s. XIII, ff. 26ra–33ra.
Bruges, Bibl. publ. de la ville 93, s. XIII, ff. 88rb–95ra.

Very probably one of the Bruges codices, both of which formerly were in Dunes, represents the Dunensis of C. de Visch.

Paris, Bibl. de l'Arsenal 400 (containing a dedication to Henry, Archbishop of Bourges).
**Paris, Bibl. Nat. Lat. 5504, s. XIII, ff. 86–109.
Reims, Bibl. Mun. 510, ff. 97–106 (containing a dedication to Henry, Archbishop of Bourges).

[13] Added in proof: an edition has just appeared. See p. 60, n. 24, and p. 346.
[14] Cf. also B. Hauréau, *Notices et extraits de quelques manuscrits latins de la Bibliothèque Nationale* (Paris, 1890–93), I, 242–43.

On examining the MSS Paris 5504 and Lilienfeld 144 I found that the Paris text agrees in substance with the Migne text, as far as a cursory examination could show; but when I collated a few pages of the two MSS from the beginning with the Migne text, I discovered that the readings of the Paris MS are closer to those of the Lilienfeld codex.

LAURENTIAN PENITENTIAL (edited by Schmitz)

Florence, Bibl. Laurenz. Plut. XXIX, cod. XXXIX, misc., s. XIII, ff. 32– .

PENITENTIAL OF ROBERT OF FLAMESBURY (edited by Morinus, in part by Dieterle)[16]

Bamberg, Staatl. Bibl. 64, s. XIII(?), ff. 1–64.

Erlangen, Universitätsbibl. 233 a, s. XII/XIII.

Leipzig, Universitätsbibl. 345/2, s. XIII(?), ff. 38–69^v.

Münster, Bibl. d. Akad. 316 (Bd. XIV).

Paris, Bibl. Nat. Lat. 13454.

Paris, Bibl. Nat. Lat. 16418.

Prague, Univ. Libr. Lobk. 432, s. XIII, ff. 1–68^v.

ICELANDIC PENITENTIALS

a. The Penitential of Thorlac Thorallson (edited by Johannaeus, Schmitz)

Copenhagen, Univ. Libr., cod. Arn. Magn. 624.

Copenhagen, Univ. Libr., cod. Arn. Magn. 625.

b. Precepts of Bishops Horlar, Jörundus, Laurentius, Egillus (edited by Johannaeus, Schmitz)

Copenhagen, Univ. Libr., cod. Arn. Magn. 175.

PENITENTIAL OF CIUDAD (edited by Wasserschleben)

Among the incunabula at Vienna is one consisting of eight folios in 4°, which is the only known source of this penitential. From it Wasserschleben made his edition.

MILAN PENITENTIAL (edited by Besombes, Wasserschleben, Schmitz)

First published by Cardinal Borromeo, its author, in the *Acta ecclesiae Mediolanensis*, 1582, from which it was republished by Besombes, in 1711. It is to be found also, in an abridged form, in the following MS: Brussels, Bibl. Roy. Burgund. 5835-36, s. XVIII.

WELSH CANONS (edited by Martène and Durand, Wasserschleben, Haddan and Stubbs)

London, Brit. Mus. Otho E XIII, s. X in., ff. 156–57^v.

Lyon, Bibl. de la Ville 203, s. IX.

†*Oxford, Bodl. Hatton 42, s. IX, ff. 130–32^v.

**Paris, Bibl. Nat. Lat. 3182 (olim Bigot. 89), s. XI(?), pp. 160–64.

*Paris, Bibl. Nat. Lat. 12021 (olim Sangerm. 121), s. IX, ff. 135–38.

---

[16] For other MSS see Hauréau, *op. cit.*, V (1890), 164. On the Prague MS see P. Lehmann, "Mitteilungen aus HSS," III (1932), 18, in *Sitzungsber. d. bayer. Akad. d. Wissensch., philos.-histor. Abteil.*, 1931/32. Heft 6.

B. THE LIBRARIES

Where the manuscripts are to be found

ANDAGE (present location of MS unknown; cf. p. 51, above)
 A lost MS: *Another Penit. attrib. to Bede, Penit. of Egbert, St. Hubert Penit.*

AVIGNON, *Bibliothèque de la Ville*
 175, s. IX: f. 54ᵛ, *Penit. form. thought to be Cummean's* (fragment).

BASLE, *Universitätsbibliothek*
 O IV 35, s. X: *Penit. form. thought to be Cummean's.*
 Fragmentensammlung Bd. *I, no. *3 C, s. IX: ff. 1–8ᵛ (probably to be identified with Becker 13, 12; see note 3, p. 434 above), *Penit. of Theodore.*

BAMBERG, *Staatliche Bibliothek*
 P I. 5: *Corrector of Burch.*
 64, s. XIII(?): ff. 1–64, *Penit. of Rob. of Flamesbury.*

BERLIN, *Preussische Staatsbibliothek*
 Ham. 132, s. IX: ff. 243ᵛ–47, *Penit. of Theodore* (U II).
 Ham. 290, s. XI in.: f. 36, *So-Called Roman Penit.* (Preface of Bk. VI).
 Lat. 105 (Phillipps 1667), s. IX in.: ff. 203ᵛ–20, *Penit. form. thought to be Cummean's.*

BOBBIO (now Milan?)
 An unidentified codex of *Columban's Penit.*

BRUGES, *see* DUNES *and* p. 441, above, *Alain de Lille's Penit. Bk.*

BRUSSELS, *Bibliothèque Royale*
 Burgund. 2324–40, A.D. 1627: pp. 76–85ᵛ, *Law of Adamnan.*
 Burgund. 5835–36, s. XVIII: *Milan Penit.* (abridgment of A).
 Burgund. 6110–11, now No. 2500, s. XIII: ff. 5ᵛ–47, *Corrector of Burch.*
 Burgund. 8558–63, now No. 2498, s. XI in.: ff. 140ᵛ–45, *Conf. of Egbert.*
 Burgund. 8780–93, now 2493, s. VIII: ff. 1–6, *Burgundian Penit.*
 Burgund. 10037, s. IX: *So-called Roman Penit.* (a reference to Bk. VI).
 Burgund. 10127–44, now No. 363, s. VIII; ff. 58–65, *Penit. of Theodore* (U II); ff. 65–, *Penit. form. thought to be Cummean's.*

CAMBRAI, *Bibliothèque Municipale*
 576 (now 625), s. IX: *Irish Canons* (?) (see also p. 432, n. 1, above).
 619 (=679), s. VIII ex.: *Irish Coll. of Canons.*

CAMBRIDGE, *Corpus Christi College Library*
 190, s. XI: pp. 366–84, *Conf. and Penit. of Egbert* (as M. R. James points out in his catalogue of the MSS of CCCC, there are only extracts of Theodore in this MS).
 279, s. IX/X: pp. 1–10, *Canons attrib. to St. Patrick; Irish Coll. of Canons, Irish Can.* (?).
 298, No. 22, s. XV: *Canons attrib. to St. Patrick* (imperfect).
 320, Pt. 2, s. IX: pp. 1–44, *Penit. of Theodore.*

CHARTRES, *Bibliothèque de la Ville*
  124 (olim 127), s. X: ff. 2–75, *Irish Coll. of Canons.*
CHELTENHAM, *Library of Sir Thomas Phillipps* (?)
  A MS·of the O. Irish Penit., s. XV ex.: ff. 47–48ᵛ.
  A MS (olim Middlehill 1750) of *Another Penit. attrib. to Bede* (? See Wasserschleben, *Bussordnungen*, p. 220).
COLOGNE, *Dom-und Diözesanbibliothek*
  91 (olim Darmst. 2179), s. VIII: ff. 90ᵛ–112ᵛ, *Penit. form. thought to be Cummean's;* ff. 82–90ᵛ, 112ᵛ, *Penit. of Theodore* (U II).
  118, s. X: ff. 135ᵛ–55, *Another Penit. attrib. to Bede.*
  119 (olim Darmst. 2118), s. XI: ff. 1–204, *Corrector of Burch.*
  210 (olim Darmst. 2178), s. VIII: ff. 1–121, *Irish Coll. of Canons;* ff. 122–51, *Penit. of Theodore.*
  ———— *Stadtarchiv*
  231, s. XV: e6ᵛ–f1ᵛ, *Reg. Coen. of Columban.*
COPENHAGEN, *University Library*
  Cod. Arn. Magn. 175: *Icelandic Penit. of Bishops Hol., Jör., Laur., Egall.*
  Cod. Arn. Magn. 624: *Icelandic Penit. of Thor. Thorallson.*
  Cod. Arn. Magn. 625: *Icelandic Penit. of Thor. Thorallson.*
  ———— *Royal Library*
  Ny Kgl. S. 58 8°, s. VIII in.: ff. 1ᵛ–35, *Penit. form. thought to be Cummean's.*
DARMSTADT, *Hessische Bibliothek*
  913, s. XI/XII(?): ff. 1–52ᵛ, *Corrector of Burch.*
DOUAI (?)
  A MS of *Alain de Lille's Penitential Book* from the library Gg. Colvenerius in the University of Douai, as reported by Carol. de Visch in Migne, *P.L.*, CCX, 284 (see above, p. 441).
DRESDEN, *Sächsische Landesbibliothek*
  A 118, s. XII: ff. 1–48, *Corrector of Burch.*
DUBLIN, *Royal Irish Academy Library*
  3 B 23, s. XV ex.: ff. 13–16, *O. Irish Table of Commutations;* pp. 16–28, *O. Irish Penit.*
  23 P 3, A.D. 1467: ff. 15– , *O. Irish Penit.* (prefaces).
  23 P 16, 23 H. IJ., s. XIV/XV: p. 186, *O. Irish Penit.* (fragment).
DUNES (now Bruges?)
  A MS of *Alain de Lille's Penitential Book* from the "Bibl. Dunensis," as reported by Carol. de Visch, Migne, *P.L.*, CCX, 284 (see above, p. 441).
DÜSSELDORF, *Landesbibliothek*
  B 113, s. IX: *Bede.*
EINSIEDELN, *Klosterbibliothek*
  326, s. X(?): ff. 35–66, *Penit. form. thought to be Cummean's.*
ERLANGEN, *Universitätsbibliothek*
  233 a., s. XII/XIII: *Penit. of Rob. of Flamesbury.*

ESCURIAL, *Real Biblioteca*
Ff. 148, A.D. 976: *Penit. of Vigila of Alvelda.*
D I. I (olim I F 1–I H 11): ff. 233– , f. 396, *Corrector of Burch.* (extracts).
Z IV. I, A.D. 1755: ff. 5–165ᵛ, *Corrector of Burch.*

FLEURY (present location unknown; cf. p. 51, above)
A lost MS: *Fleury Penit.*

FLORENCE, *Biblioteca Mediceo-Laurenziana*
Plut. xxix, cod. xxxix misc., s. XIII: ff. 32– , *Laurentian Penit.*

FRANKFURT AM MAIN, *Archiv*
A few loose leaves, s. XI: *Corrector of Burch.*

FREIBURG IM BREISGAU, *Universitätsbibliothek*
311 ff., s. XI: *Corrector of Burch.*

FREISING, *see* MUNICH

GHENT, *Bibliothèque de l'Université*
506, s. X/XI in.: *So-called Roman Penit.*

GOTHA, *Herzogliche Bibliothek*
131 (145), s. X: ff. 1–130, *Regino's Eccl. Disc.*

GÖTTWEIH, *Stiftsbibliothek*
343 schwarz—305 rot, s. XV: *Corrector of Burch.*

HAINAUT (HANNONIA, now Paris?)
A MS of *Alain de Lille's Penitential Book*, from "Bibliotheca S. Gisleni in Hannonia," as reported by Carol. de Visch in Migne, *P.L.*, CCX, 284 (see above, p. 441).

HEILIGENKREUZ, *Stiftsbibliothek*
217, s. X: *Bede; Judg. of Clement; Tripartite St. Gall Penit.*

KARLSRUHE, *Landesbibliothek*
Reichenau IC, s. IX and VIII: *Penit. form. thought to be Cummean's.*
Reichenau XVIII, s. IX in.: ff. 75–82, *Irish Coll. of Canons.*

LEIPZIG, *Universitätsbibliothek*
345/2, s. XIII(?): ff. 38–69ᵛ, *Penit. of Rob. of Flamesbury.*

LILIENFELD, *see Alain de Lille's Penit. Bk.*, p. 441, above.

LONDON, *British Museum*
Additional 8873, s. XII: *Penit. of Theodore.*
Additional 30853, s. XI: ff. 309–24, *Penit. of Silos.*
Arundel 173, s. XII: ff. 132– , *Corrector of Burch.*
Cotton Faustina A VIII, s. XII or XIII: ff. 3–38ᵛ, *Penit. of Bartholomew.*
Cotton Otho E XIII, s. X in.: ff. 141ᵛ–43, *Canons of Adamnan;* ff. 156–57ᵛ, *Welsh Canons; Irish Coll. of Canons.*
Cotton Tib. A III, s. XI: ff. 96–7, *Conf. of Egbert.*
Cotton Vespasian D XV (olim 38505), s. X/XI at ff. 84–101ᵛ, *Penit. of Theodore.*
Cotton Vitellius A XII, s. XII: ff. 137– , *Penit. of Bartholomew; Dial. of Egbert.*

Royal Collection 5 E VII, art. 3, s. XII: ff. 104–, *Penit. of Bartholomew.*
Royal Collection 7 E I, s. XII: ff. 6–, *Penit. of Bartholomew.*
Royal Collection 8 D III, art. 2, s. XIII: ff. 49ᵛ–, *Penit. of Bartholomew.*
Royal Collection 8 C XIV, art. 1 (fragment): *Penit. of Bartholomew.*

LUXEMBURG, *Bibliothèque Nationale*
     29, s. XII: ff. 25–283, *Regino's Eccl. Disc.*

LYON, *Bibliothèque de la Ville*
     203, s. IX: *Canons of Adamnan; Welsh Canons.*

MERSEBURG, *Dombibliothek*
     103, s. IX: ff. 112–19, *Penit. of St. Hubert; Penit. form. thought to be Cummean's; Penit. of Theodore* (a fragment).

MILAN, *Biblioteca Ambrosiana*
     G 58 sup., s. X(?): ff. 40–44, *Reg. Coen. of Columban.*

MONTPELLIER, *École de médecine*
     387, s. IX/X: *Bede.*

MUNICH, *Staatsbibliothek*
Codices Latini Monacenses:
     2593, s. XIII: ff. 157–86, *Corrector of Burch.*
     3851 (olim Aug. 151), s. IX(?): ff. 38–52, *Bede.*
     3852 (olim Aug. 152), x. XI at f. 66: *Penit. of Theodore.*
     3853 (olim Aug. 153), s. XI: *Bede; Judg. of Clement.*
     3909, s. XI: ff. 75ᵛ–89, *So-called Roman Penit.; Corrector of Burch.*
     4570, A.D. 1108: ff. 1–237, *Corrector of Burch.*
     4592: *Irish Coll. of Canons.*
     5801 c, s. XII: ff. 1–173, *Corrector of Burch.*
     6241 (olim Fris. 41), s. IX/X: ff. 33ᵛ–35, *Penit. of Theodore.*
     6243 (olim Fris. 43; olim Fris. B G 8),[16] s. VIII: ff. 217–29, *Penit. form. thought to be Cummean's* (cf. also above, p. 63, n. 34).
     6245, s. XI: *Penit. of Theodore.*
? 6311 (olim Fris. 111), s. X: f. 107, *Bede;* f. 108, *Penit. of Egbert.* Perhaps this is the MS meant by an old number, Fris. 3, said by Wasserschleben to contain Bede and Egbert, the corresponding new number of which does not contain penitential material.
     12118, *see* 28118.
     12205, s. XIV at ff. 37–48, *Corrector of Burch.*
     12673 (olim Ransh. 73), s. X: ff. 2– , *Bede;* f. 6, *Penit. of Egbert;* ff. 66ᵛ–74, *The So-called Roman Penit.*
     14138 s. XV: ff. 195–221, *Corrector of Burch.*
     14532 (olim Em.), s. X: ff. 26– , *So-called Roman Penit.* (four books: extracts from Book VI).
     14780 (olim Em. e 2), s. IX: ff. 1–25, *Penit. of Theodore.*
     14949 (olim Em. w 6), s. XV: ff. 1–8, *Reg. Coen. of Columban.*
     17195, s. XII: ff. 61–78, *So-called Roman Penit.* (Book VI: extracts only).

[16] See footnote 8, above.

18094, s. XII: ff. 1–241, *Corrector of Burch.*

22288 (olim Windberg 88), s. XI/XII: ff. 1– , *Penit. form. thought to be Cummean's;* ff. 16ᵛ–35ᵛ, *Penit. of Theodore* (U I, II).

28118 (?) (see footnote 7, above), s. VIII ex.: *Reg. Coen. of Columban.*

MÜNSTER, *Bibliothek der Akademie*

316 (Bd. XIV): *Penit. of Rob. of Flamesbury.*

NOVARA, *Biblioteca Capitolare*

LXXI 134, s. X: *So-called Roman Penit.*

OLMÜTZ, *Kapitelarchiv*

A MS of the *Corrector of Burch.*

ORLÉANS, *Bibliothèque de la Ville*

193 (olim 221), s. VIII/IX: p. 212, *Canons of Adamnan* (on last folio of MS,ʳbadly ̯worn); p. 23–206, *Irish Coll. of Canons.*

OXFORD, *Bodleian Library*

311, s. X: ff. 33–62, *Penit. form. thought to be Cummean's.*

572, s. IX/X: ff. 51–70, *Penit. form. thought to be Cummean's.*

718, s. X/XI: ff. 209–11, *Penit. of Egbert.*

Hatton 42, s. IX: ff. 130–132ᵛ, *Welsh Canons;* ff. 132ᵛ–33ᵛ, *Canons of Adamnan; Irish Coll. of Canons.*

Jun. 121, s. XI ex.: ff. 87ᵛ–101, *Conf. of Egbert.*

Laud. 482 (olim F. 17), s. XI: ff. 30ᵛ–40, *Conf. of Egbert.*

Rawlinson B 512, s. XV: ff. 39–40ᵛ, *O. Irish Penit.;* ff. 42ᵇᴵ–44, *O. Irish Table of Commutations;* ff. 45ᵃᴵ–51ᵇᴵ, *Law of Adamnan.*

———— *St. Johns College Library*

3 A 3 and 10 (=163 and 165), s. XII and XIII resp.: *Penit. of Bartholomew.*

PARIS, *Bibliothèque Nationale*

Fonds Latin

1454, s. IX/X: ff. 216–20ᵛ, *Penit. of Theodore* (U II).

1455, s. X: ff. 80– , *Penit. of Theodore* (U II).

1603, s. VIII/IX: ff. 92ᵛ–103, *Penit. of Theodore* (U II); ff. 104–38, *Penit. form. thought to be Cummean's.*

2123, s. IX: ff. 55ᵛ–65, *Penit. of Theodore.*

2341: ff. 231–33ᵛ, *So-called Roman Penit.* (fragments).

2373, s. XI-XII: ff. 7–26, *So-called Roman Penit.* (all 6 books).

2600, s. XIII: *Penit. of Bartholomew.*

2998, s. X: ff. 1–63ᵛ, *So-called Roman Penit.* (all 6 books).

3182 (olim Bigot. 89), s. XI(?): pp. 19–160, *Irish Coll. of Canons;* pp. 160–64, *Welsh Canons;* pp. 164–65, *Canons of Adamnan;* pp. 165–73, *Penit. of Theodore;* pp. 176–77, *Penit. of Finnian;* pp. 280–81, *Preface of Gildas;* pp. 281–82, *Canons of Sixth C. Welsh Synods;* pp. 282–83, *Book of David;* pp. 289–99, *Bigotian Penit.;* pp. 177, 302, 306–7, 312, 279–80, *Irish Canons* (Bks. II–VI).

3846, s. IX: ff. 259–62ᵛ, *Penit. of Theodore* (U II).

3848 B, s. IX in.: ff. 1–13, *Penit. of Theodore.*

3878, s. XII: *Bede; Judg. of Clement.*

5504, see p. 441, above, *Alain de Lille's Penit. Bk.*

7193, s. VIII: ff. 41–54, *Paris Penit.*

8508, s. IX/X: ff. 128–35, *So-called Roman Penit.* (of Bk. VI, extracts only).

12021 (olim Sangerm. 121), s. IX: ff. 33–127, *Irish Coll. of Canons;* ff. 127^v–32^v, *Penit. of Theodore;* ff. 132^v–33^v, *Canons of Adamnan;* ff. 134^v–35, *Penit. of Finnian;* ff. 135–38, *Welsh Canons;* ff. 138–39, *Irish Canons.*

12315 (olim Sangerm. 326), s. XII: ff. 94–98^v, *So-called Roman Penit.*

12444: *Irish Coll. of Canons.*

12445 (olim Sangerm. 366), s. IX ex.: ff. 153–56, *Penit. of Theodore* (U II).

13246, s. VIII in.: ff. 286^v–91, *Bobbio Penit.*

13452 (Sangerm. 940), s. XVII/XVIII: ff. 1– , *Penit. of Theodore* (U I, II).

13454: *Penit. of Rob. of Flamesbury.*

14869, s. XIII: ff. 112–20, *Corrector of Burch.*

16418: *Penit. of Rob. of Flamesbury.*

17527 (olim reg., fonds de l'Oratoire, num. 20), s. X: *Regino's Eccl. Disc.*

18220: f. 126, *So-called Roman Penit.* (fragment of Bk. VI).

———— *Bibliothèque de l'Arsenal*

400: *Alain de Lille's Penit. Bk.*, see above p. 441.

Two unnumbered MSS of the de Thou collection (codices Thuani) were used by Petit for his edition of Theodore in 1677 (*Poenitentiale Theodori Archiepiscopi Cantuariensis, Lutetiae Parisiorum,* 1677).

PRAGUE, *University Library*, Collection Lobkowitz

432, s. XIII: ff. 1–68^v, *Penit. of Rob. of Flamesbury.*

RANSHOVEN, *see* MUNICH 12673

REIMS, *Bibliothèque Municipale*

510: ff. 97–106, *Alain de Lille's Penit. Bk.*, see above, p. 441.

ROME, *Biblioteca Vallicelliana*

A 18, s. X: ff. 58–136, *Irish Coll. of Canons.*

B 58, s. XIII: *Corrector of Burch.*

F 8, s. XIV: ff. 161– , *Corrector of Burch.*

F 92, s. XIV: ff. 1–180, *Corrector of Burch.*

———— *Biblioteca Vaticana*

Vat. Lat. 1339, s. X(?): ff. 171^v–77, *Penit. thought to be Cummean's; Irish Coll. of Canons.*

Vat. Lat. 1347, s. IX/X: *Penit. of Egbert.*

Vat. Lat. 1349, s. X: f. 193, *Penit. form. thought to be Cummean's* (prologue).

Vat. Lat. 1352, s. XI: ff. 56–84, *Corrector of Burch.;* ff. 86^v– , *Penit. of Egbert.*

Vat. Lat. 1355, s. XI: ff. 1–34, *Corrector of Burch.*

Vat. Lat. 3830, s. XI: *Corrector of Burch.*

Vat. Lat. 4227, s. XII: *Corrector of Burch.*

Vat. Lat. 4772, s. XI in.: *Corrector of Burch.*

Vat. Lat. 5751, s. X: *Penit. form. thought to be Cummean's;* ff. 41ᵛ–
Penit. of Theodore.

Vat. Barb. Lat. 477 (olim XI. 120), s. X in. at ff. 60–74, *Penit. ascr.
by Albers to Bede.*

Vat. Pal. Lat. 294, s. XI at f. 83–87ᵛ, *Penit. of Egbert* (fragment);
ff. 87ᵛ–90, *Penit. ascr. by Albers to Bede.*

Vat. Pal. Lat. 485, s. IX: ff. 73–79ᵛ, *Penit. of Egbert;* ff. 101–107ᵛ,
Penit. of Cummean; ff. 107ᵛ–13, *Penit. of Theodore* (U I and II).

Vat. Pal. Lat. 554, s. IX at f. 1, *Penit. of Theodore* (U II epilogue):
s. VIII at ff. 5–13, *Penit. of Egbert.*

Vat. Regin. Lat. 207, s. IX: ff. 85–105, *So-Called Roman Penit.*

Vat. Regin. Lat. 224, s. XII: ff. 1–46ᵛ, *Corrector of Burch.*

For 3 Vatican MSS of *Regino's Eccl. Disc.* see p. 440, above.

ST. GALL, *Stiftsbibliothek*

150, s. IX in.: pp. 285–318, *Tripartite St. Gall;* pp. 355–60, *Penit. of
Theodore* (U II); 365–77, *Penit. of Finnian.*

243, s. IX: *Irish Coll. of Canons.*

277, s. IX: p. 144, *So-called Roman Penit.* (of Bk. VI extracts only).

550, s. IX: pp. 162–234, *Penit. form. thought to be Cummean's.*

570, s. IX: p. 135, *So-called Roman Penit.* (of Bk. VI extracts only).

674, s. XII: p. 435, *Corrector of Burch.*

675, s. IX: pp. 224–67, *Penit. form. thought to be Cummean's.*

676, s. XI/XII: pp. 26–36, *So-called Roman Penit.* (of Bk. VI only
fragments).

677, s. X: *Penit. of Egbert.*

679, s. X: pp. 5–152, *So-called Roman Penit.*

682: *Another Penit. attrib. to Bede.*

915, s. X/XI: pp. 170–84, *Reg. Coen. of Columban.*

STRASBOURG, *Bibliothèque de la Ville* (see note 9, p. 438, above)

C V 6, s. IX: *Penit. form. thought to be Cummean's.*

STUTTGART, *Oeffentliche Bibliothek*

HB VI 109 (olim C 5), s. IX/X: ff. 120–32, *Penit. of Theodore* (U II).

HB VI 112 (olim C 4), s. XI: ff. 49– , *Penit. form. thought to be
Cummean's;* ff. 81–87, *Penit. of Theodore* (U II).

HB VI 113, s. VIII: ff. 203–23, *Penit. form. thought to be Cummean's.*

TOURS, *Bibliothèque de la Ville*

556, s. XI: *Irish Coll. of Canons.*

TRIER, *Stadtbibliothek*

1362,[17] s. X: ff. 207, *Regino's Eccl. Disc.*

TURIN, *Biblioteca Nazionale*

G V 38, s. X: ff. 125–30ᵛ, *Penit. of Columban.*

G VII 16, s. X/XI: ff. 62ᵛ–72ᵛ.

[17] The same as MS No. 927? See footnote 11, p. 439 above.

I VI 22, s. XII: *Corrector of Burch.* (see above, p. 440).

VERCELLI, *Biblioteca Capitolare*
94: *Corrector of Burch.*

VERONÀ, *Biblioteca Capitolare*
LXXI, s. X: *So-called Roman Penit.*

VIENNA, *Nationalbibliothek*
354 (Salisb. 202), s. XII: *Corrector of Burch.*
694 (olim. theol. 79), s. XI: ff. 20–168ᵛ, *Regino's Eccl. Disc.*
926 (olim 843), s. XIII: ff. 1–38ᵛ, *Corrector of Burch.*
1550, s. XII/XIII: ff. 74ᵛ–79ᵛ, *Reg. Coen. of Columban.*
2195 (olim Salisb. 324), s. IX in.: ff. 1–24ᵛ, *Penit. of Theodore* (U I and II).
2223 (olim jur. can. 116), s. VIII/IX: ff. 1–17, *Penit. of Theodore* (U I and II); ff. 17–22, *Another Penit. attrib. to Bede;* ff. 22–41, *Tripartite St. Gall Penit.;* ff. 77ᵛ–87, *Penit. of Egbert.*
2225 (olim theol. 651), s. X: ff. 13ᵛ–23, *Penit. form. thought to be Cummean's.*
2233 (olim theol. 725), s. IX in.: ff. 1–25ᵛ, *Penit. form. thought to be Cummean's;* ff. 25ᵛ–58ᵛ, *Penit. of Finnian.*
2245 (olim univers. 633), s. XII: ff. 1–32ᵛ, *Corrector of Burch.*
3878, s. XV: ff. 173–75ᵛ, *Reg. Coen. of Columban.*

Among the *Incunabula* of the Library is one of eight folios, small quarto, from which Wasserschleben published the *Penitential of Ciudad.*

WOLFENBÜTTEL, *Herzogliche Bibliothek*
August. 83.21, s. X: ff. 172, *Regino's Eccl. Disc.*
Helmst. 32, s. X/XI: ff. 14–117, *Regino's Eccl. Disc.*

WÜRZBURG, *Universitätsbibliothek*
Mp th qu 31, s. VIII/IX: *Irish Coll. of Canons.*
Mp th qu 32, s. VIII: ff. 2–12ᵛ, *Penit. of Theodore* (U I and II).

ZÜRICH, *Universitäts- und Kantonsbibliothek*
Rheinau XXX, s. VIII/IX: ff. 28– , *Penit. form. thought to be Cummean's.*

Selected Bibliography

Index

The principal matters omitted from the Index are: (1) citations of documents and editions given in the notes for purposes of textual comparison only; (2) references to Migne and other editors of modern extensive collections frequently referred to; (3) names of editors of penitentials where they occur not in connection with significant opinions or arguments; (4) a few names of authors cited only incidentally; (5) titles of works other than penitentials and related documents.

Words for which explanatory notes have been supplied are included, but not those given in the notes merely to indicate or establish readings. The words "bishop," "priest," and "cleric" are separately indexed, but "presbyter," "deacon," and "subdeacon," which usually occur closely grouped, are included without differentiation under "clergy." Manuscripts referred to by catalogue number are indexed only through Section III of the Introduction: The letter "n" following a page number indicates that the reference is to a footnote. The numbers in italic type after the name of a document indicate the pages on which the document, or part thereof, is discussed and translated.